Academic Learning Series: Network+ Certification, 3/e

A-P@ssword#A/B

Textbook

Craig Zacker

PUBLISHED BY
Microsoft Press
A Division of Microsoft Corporation
One Microsoft Way
Redmond, Washington 98052-6399

Library of Congress Cataloging-in-Publication Data pending.

    ISBN 0-07-295553-8
    (McGraw-Hill)
    ISBN 0-7356-2026-1
    (Microsoft Learning)

Printed and bound in the United States of America.

1 2 3 4 5 6 7 8 9   QWT   9 8 7 6 5 4

Distributed in Canada by H.B. Fenn and Company Ltd.

A CIP catalogue record for this book is available from the British Library.

Microsoft Press books are available through booksellers and distributors worldwide. For further information about international editions, contact your local Microsoft Corporation office or contact Microsoft Press International directly at fax (425) 936-7329. Visit our Web site at www.microsoft.com/learning/. Send comments to *moac@microsoft.com*.

Microsoft, Microsoft Press, Windows, Windows NT, and Windows Server are either registered trademarks or trademarks of Microsoft Corporation in the United States and/or other countries. Other product and company names mentioned herein may be the trademarks of their respective owners.

Acquisitions Editor: Linda Engelman
Project Editor: Maria Gargiulo
Technical Editor: Michelle Truman
Copyeditor: Merianne Marble
Indexers: Gary Frazier and Priscilla Gruenewald
Production Services: IQUAD Productions

SubAssy Part No. X10-52858
Body Part No. X10-23987

CONTENTS AT A GLANCE

CHAPTER 1: Networking Basics 1
CHAPTER 2: Network Cabling. 43
CHAPTER 3: Network Connection Hardware 105
CHAPTER 4: Data-Link Layer Protocols 155
CHAPTER 5: Network Layer Protocols 201
CHAPTER 6: Transport Layer Protocols 251
CHAPTER 7: TCP/IP. 281
CHAPTER 8: Networking Software. 357
CHAPTER 9: Network Security and Availability 435
CHAPTER 10: Remote Network Access 493
CHAPTER 11: Network Troubleshooting Tools. 525
CHAPTER 12: Network Troubleshooting Procedures 577

CONTENTS

About This Book xv
    Target Audience xv
    Prerequisites xv
    The Textbook xv
    The Supplemental Course Materials CD-ROM xvi
        eBook Setup Instructions. xvii
    The Lab Manual xvii
    Notational Conventions xviii
    Keyboard Conventions xix
    Coverage of Exam Objectives. xix
    The Microsoft Certified Professional Program. xxviii
        Certifications xxix
        MCP Requirements. xxix
    About the Authors. xxx
    For Microsoft Official Academic Course Support xxxi
    Evaluation Edition Software Support xxxi

CHAPTER 1: **Networking Basics** 1
    Understanding Network Communications 2
        Network Media 2
        LANs, WANs, and MANs 3
        Signals and Protocols. 5
        Broadband and Baseband Communications 8
    Introducing the OSI Reference Model 10
        Protocol Interaction 12
        Data Encapsulation. 13
        The Physical Layer. 16
        The Data-Link Layer 18
        The Network Layer 22
        The Transport Layer 26
        The Session Layer 30
        The Presentation Layer. 33
        The Application Layer 34
    Summary. 36
    Exercises. 37
        Exercise 1-1: Defining Networking Terms .37
        Exercise 1-2: Identifying OSI Layer Functions. 37
        Exercise 1-3: Associating Protocols with OSI Model Layers 38

Review Questions. 38

Case Scenarios 40

CHAPTER 2:   **Network Cabling**. **43**

Understanding Network Cables. 44

　　Cable Topologies. 44

　　Cabling Standards. 52

　　Cable Types 54

Pulling Cable. 65

　　External Installations. 65

　　Internal Installations. 74

Making Connections 82

　　Two-Computer Networking 82

　　Connecting External Cables 86

　　Connecting Internal Cables. 87

Summary 97

Exercises. 98

　　Exercise 2-1: Identifying Network Cable Types 98

　　Exercise 2-2: Cable Troubleshooting 98

　　Exercise 2-3: Internal and External Cabling 99

　　Exercise 2-4: Identifying Cable Installation Tools. 99

Review Questions. 99

Case Scenarios 102

CHAPTER 3:   **Network Connection Hardware** **105**

Using Network Interface Adapters 106

　　Understanding Network Interface Adapter Functions 107

　　Selecting a Network Interface Adapter. 112

　　Installing a Network Interface Adapter. 114

　　Configuring a Network Interface Adapter 116

　　Installing Network Interface Adapter Drivers. 117

　　Network Adapter Configuration Tools 118

　　Troubleshooting a Network Interface Adapter 122

Using Network Hubs 123

　　Understanding Ethernet Hubs 124

　　Understanding Token Ring MAUs 127

Using Advanced Network Connection Devices. 129

　　Bridging 129

　　Routing. 135

　　Switching 141

　　Using Gateways. 144

Summary 146

Exercises. 147

    Exercise 3-1: Hub Concepts. 147

    Exercise 3-2: Bridging Concepts. 147

    Exercise 3-3: Using Switches 148

Review Questions. 149

Case Scenarios 153

    Scenario 3-1: Segmenting a Network 153

    Scenario 3-2: Boosting Network Performance. 154

CHAPTER 4:   Data-Link Layer Protocols 155

Ethernet. 156

    Ethernet Standards. 156

    The Ethernet Frame 160

    CSMA/CD Mechanism 165

    Physical Layer Specifications. 167

Token Ring. 178

    Physical Layer Specifications. 179

    Token Passing 180

    Token Ring Frames 182

Fiber Distributed Data Interface (FDDI) 185

    Physical Layer Specifications. 185

    The FDDI Frames. 187

Wireless Networking 189

    Wireless Networking Standards 189

    The IEEE 802.11 Physical Layer. 190

    The IEEE 802.11 MAC Layer. 191

Summary. 193

Exercises. 194

    Exercise 4-1: IEEE Standards and Technologies 194

    Exercise 4-2: CSMA/CD Procedures. 194

    Exercise 4-3: Selecting a Data-Link Layer Protocol 194

    Exercise 4-4: FDDI Concepts 195

    Exercise 4-5: IEEE 802.11 Concepts 195

Review Questions. 195

Case Scenarios 199

    Scenario 4-1: Troubleshooting an Ethernet Network 199

    Scenario 4-2: Designing an Ethernet Network. 199

CHAPTER 5:   **Network Layer Protocols**...................201

Internet Protocol (IP)...202

   IP Standards...202

   IP Functions...203

   Understanding IP Addressing...........................216

Internetwork Packet Exchange (IPX)............................227

   IPX Functions...227

NetBIOS Extended User Interface (NetBEUI)...................232

   NetBEUI Standards...233

   NetBIOS Naming..233

   The NetBEUI Frame..234

AppleTalk..238

Summary..242

Exercises..243

   Exercise 5-1: Understanding IP Functions...............243

   Exercise 5-2: Calculating Subnet Masks................244

   Exercise 5-3: Understanding IPX Properties.............244

   Exercise 5-4: NBF Protocols..............................244

Review Questions..245

Case Scenarios..248

   Case Scenario 5-1: Choosing a Network Layer Protocol.......248

   Case Scenario 5-2: Subnetting a Class C Address............249

   Case Scenario 5-3: Calculating a Subnet Mask...............249

CHAPTER 6:   **Transport Layer Protocols**.................251

TCP/IP and the Transport Layer................................252

   Transmission Control Protocol (TCP).....................252

   User Datagram Protocol (UDP)...........................266

   Ports and Sockets..267

Novell NetWare and the Transport Layer......................269

   Sequenced Packet Exchange (SPX).......................269

   NetWare Core Protocol (NCP)............................271

Summary..274

Exercises..275

   Exercise 6-1: TCP Header Fields..........................275

   Exercise 6-2: TCP and UDP Functions.....................275

   Exercise 6-3: Port Numbers...............................276

Review Questions..276

Case Scenarios..278

   Case Scenario 6-1: Troubleshooting TCP..................278

   Case Scenario 6-2: Using Port Numbers...................279

CHAPTER 7: **TCP/IP** **281**

Introducing TCP/IP 282

TCP/IP Development 282

TCP/IP Standards 285

The TCP/IP Protocol Stack 290

TCP/IP Protocols 292

Link Layer Protocols 292

Address Resolution Protocol (ARP) 293

Internet Protocol (IP) 297

Internet Control Message Protocol (ICMP) 297

TCP/IP Transport Layer Protocols 303

Application Layer Protocols 303

IP Routing 306

Understanding Routing 306

Router Products 307

Understanding Routing Tables 308

Building Routing Tables 314

Configuring TCP/IP 325

Configuring TCP/IP in Windows 326

Configuring TCP/IP in UNIX/Linux 338

Configuring TCP/IP in NetWare 343

Summary 346

Exercises 347

Exercise 7-1: TCP/IP Layers and Protocols 347

Exercise 7-2: TCP/IP Protocols 348

Exercise 7-3: Routing Tables 348

Exercise 7-4: Static and Dynamic Routing 349

Exercise 7-5: Windows TCP/IP Configuration Requirements 349

Review Questions 350

Case Scenarios 354

Case Scenario 7-1: Creating Static Routes 354

Case Scenario 7-2: Choosing a Routing Method 355

Case Scenario 7-3: Configuring TCP/IP Clients 356

CHAPTER 8: **Networking Software** **357**

Client/Server and Peer-to-Peer Networking 358

Using Server Operating Systems 359

Microsoft Windows 359

Novell NetWare 371

UNIX and Linux 376

Apple Macintosh 381

Connecting Clients. 382
    Microsoft Windows Client Capabilities 383
    UNIX/Linux Client Capabilities 391
    Macintosh Client Capabilities 392
Understanding Directory Services. 394
    The NetWare Bindery. 394
    Novell eDirectory 395
    Windows NT Domains 397
    Active Directory 399
    Network Information System (NIS) 400
Understanding TCP/IP Services 401
    Using Dynamic Host Configuration Protocol (DHCP). 402
    Host Files 410
    Understanding the Domain Name System (DNS) 412
    Windows Internet Name Service (WINS) 423
Summary 425
Exercises. 426
    Exercise 8-1: Selecting an Operating System 426
    Exercise 8-2: Network Operating System Products 426
    Exercise 8-3: Directory Service Concepts 427
    Exercise 8-4: DHCP Message Types 427
Review Questions 428
Case Scenarios 432
    Case Scenario 8-1: Deploying eDirectory 432
    Case Scenario 8-2: Troubleshooting DHCP. 433
CHAPTER 9:   **Network Security and Availability** **435**
Understanding Firewalls 436
    Packet Filtering Firewalls 437
    Stateful Packet Inspection Firewalls 445
Using Network Address Translation (NAT) 446
    NAT Communications 446
    NAT Types 447
    NAT Security 449
    Port Forwarding 449
    NAT Implementations 450
Using a Proxy Server 451
    Proxy Packet Inspection. 452
    Adaptive Proxy 452
    Proxy Server Implementations 453

Understanding Security Protocols. 454

    IPSec 454

    Layer Two Tunneling Protocol (L2TP) 459

    Secure Sockets Layer (SSL). 460

    Kerberos 461

Providing Fault Tolerance 462

    Data Availability 462

    Server Availability 467

Performing Backups. 469

    Backup Hardware 470

    Backup Software 475

Summary. 485

Exercises. 486

    Exercise 9-1: Identifying Security Protocols 486

    Exercise 9-2: Data Availability Technologies. 486

    Exercise 9-3: Distinguishing Between Incremental and Differential
    Backups 487

Review Questions. 487

Case Scenarios 490

    Case Scenario 9-1: Designing a Network Backup Solution 490

    Case Scenario 9-2: Recovering from a Disaster 490

CHAPTER 10:   **Remote Network Access** **493**

Remote Connection Requirements 494

WAN Connection Types 495

    Public Switched Telephone Network. 495

    Integrated Services Digital Network (ISDN) 497

    Digital Subscriber Line (DSL). 499

    Cable Television (CATV) Networks 501

    Leased Lines. 503

    Frame Relay 505

    SONET/Synchronous Digital Hierarchy 507

    Asynchronous Transfer Mode (ATM) 507

Remote Networking Protocols. 508

    Serial Line Internet Protocol (SLIP) 509

    Point-to-Point Protocol (PPP) 510

    Point-to-Point Protocol over Ethernet. 514

    Virtual Private Networks (VPNs). 515

    Terminal Connections. 516

Summary. 518

Exercises. 519

    Exercise 10-1: Remote Connection Technologies 519

    Exercise 10-2: WAN Concepts. 520

    Exercise 10-3: PPP Connection Establishment 520

Review Questions. 520

Case Scenarios 523

    Case Scenario 10-1: Selecting a WAN Technology 523

CHAPTER 11: Network Troubleshooting Tools. 525

Logs and Indicators 526

    Power and Drive Lights 526

    Link Pulse LEDs 526

    Speed Indicator LEDs 529

    Collision LEDs 530

    Error Displays. 530

    Event Logs 531

    Network Management Products 535

    Performance Monitors. 536

    Protocol Analyzers 542

Network Testing and Monitoring Tools 550

    Crossover Cables. 550

    Hardware Loopback Connectors 551

    Tone Generators and Tone Locators 551

    Wire Map Testers 553

    Multifunction Cable Testers. 554

    Fiber Optic Cable Testing. 556

TCP/IP Utilities 557

    Ping. 557

    Traceroute 559

    Ifconfig, Ipconfig.exe, and Winipcfg.exe. 560

    ARP 562

    Netstat 563

    Nbtstat.exe. 566

    Nslookup 568

Summary. 570

Exercises. 571

    Exercise 11-1: Network Indicators 571

    Exercise 11-2: Network Testing Equipment 571

    Exercise 11-3: TCP/IP Utilities 572

    Exercise 11-4: Identifying TCP/IP Utility Output 572

Review Questions 573

Case Scenarios 576

    Case Scenario 11-1: Troubleshooting a Cable Installation 576

CHAPTER 12: **Network Troubleshooting Procedures** **577**

Troubleshooting a Network 578

    Establishing the Symptoms 578

    Identifying the Affected Area 580

    Establishing What Has Changed 581

    Selecting the Most Probable Cause 582

    Implementing a Solution 582

    Testing the Results 582

    Recognizing the Potential Effects of the Solution 583

    Documenting the Solution 583

Network Troubleshooting Scenario: "I Can't Access a Web Site" 584

    Incident Administration 584

    Gathering Information 585

    Possible Cause: Internet Router Problem 587

    Possible Cause: Internet Communication Problem 590

    Possible Cause: DNS Failure 591

    Possible Cause: LAN Communications Problem 597

    Possible Cause: Computer Configuration Problem 602

    Possible Cause: User Error 608

Summary 610

Exercises 610

    Exercise 12-1: Network Troubleshooting 610

    Exercise 12-2: Network Hardware Problems 611

Review Questions 611

Case Scenarios 614

    Case Scenario 12-1: Identifying the Affected Area 614

    Case Scenario 12-2: Assigning Priorities 614

    Case Scenario 12-3: Locating a Problem's Source 615

Glossary **617**

Bibliography **669**

Index **673**

System Requirements **697**

ABOUT THIS BOOK

Welcome to *Network+ Certification*. Through lectures, discussions, demonstrations, textbook exercises, and classroom labs, this course teaches you the skills and knowledge necessary to work as an entry-level administrator of a computer network. The twelve chapters in this book walk you through key concepts of networking theory and practice, including a study of protocols, operating systems, and troubleshooting.

TARGET AUDIENCE

This textbook was developed for beginning information technology (IT) students who want to learn to support and troubleshoot local area networks (LANs) and wide area networks (WANs) consisting of computers running Microsoft and other operating systems. The target audience will provide direct, front-line user support, either at a help desk or call center, or they will use their knowledge to work in their own network support business.

PREREQUISITES

This textbook requires that students meet the following prerequisites:

■ A working knowledge of the desktop PC running one of the current Microsoft Windows operating systems.

■ Prerequisite knowledge and course work as defined by the learning institution and the instructor.

THE TEXTBOOK

The textbook content has been crafted to provide a meaningful learning experience in an academic classroom setting.

Key features of this textbook include the following:

■ Learning objectives for each chapter that prepare the student for the topic areas covered in that chapter.

■ Chapter introductions that explain why the information is important.

- An inviting design with screen shots, diagrams, tables, bulleted lists, and other graphical formats that makes the book easy to comprehend and supports a number of different learning styles.

- Clear explanations of concepts and principles, and frequent exposition of step-by-step procedures.

- A variety of reader aids that highlight a wealth of additional information, including:

  - Note – Real-world application tips and alternative procedures, and explanations of complex procedures and concepts

  - Caution – Warnings about mistakes that can result in loss of data or are difficult to resolve

  - Important – Explanations of essential setup steps before a procedure and other instructions

  - More Info – cross-references and additional resources for students

- End-of-chapter review questions that assess knowledge and can serve as homework, quizzes, and review activities before or after lectures. (Answers to the textbook questions are available from your instructor.)

- Chapter summaries that distill the main ideas in a chapter and reinforce learning.

- Case scenarios, approximately two per chapter, that provide students with an opportunity to evaluate, analyze, synthesize, and apply information learned during the chapter.

- Comprehensive glossary that defines key terms introduced in the book.

THE SUPPLEMENTAL COURSE MATERIALS CD-ROM

This book comes with a Supplemental Course Materials CD-ROM, which contains a variety of informational aids to complement the book content:

- An electronic version of this textbook (eBook). For information about using the eBook, see the section titled "eBook Setup Instructions" later in this introduction.

- An eBook of the *Microsoft Encyclopedia of Networking, Second Edition*.

- Microsoft PowerPoint slides based on textbook chapters, for note-taking.

■ Microsoft Word Viewer and Microsoft PowerPoint Viewer.

A second CD-ROM contains a 180-day evaluation edition of Microsoft Windows Server 2003.

> **NOTE** The 180-day evaluation edition of Windows Server 2003 provided with this book is not the full retail product; it is provided only for the purposes of training and evaluation. Microsoft Technical Support does not support evaluation editions.

eBook Setup Instructions

The eBook is in Portable Document Format (PDF) and must be viewed using Adobe Acrobat Reader.

▶ **Using the eBooks**

1. Insert the Supplemental Course Materials CD-ROM into your CD-ROM drive.

   > **NOTE** If AutoRun is disabled on your machine, refer to the Readme.txt file on the CD.

2. On the user interface menu, select Textbook eBook and follow the prompts. You also can review any of the other eBooks provided for your use.

   > **NOTE** You must have the Supplemental Course Materials CD in your CD-ROM drive to run the eBook.

THE LAB MANUAL

The Lab Manual is designed for use in either a combined or separate lecture and lab. The exercises in the Lab Manual correspond to textbook chapters and are for use in a classroom setting supervised by an instructor.

The Lab Manual presents a rich, hands-on learning experience that encourages practical solutions and strengthens critical problem-solving skills:

■ Lab Exercises teach procedures by using a step-by-step format. Questions interspersed throughout Lab Exercises encourage reflection and critical thinking about the lab activity.

- Lab Review Questions appear at the end of each lab and ask questions about the lab. They are designed to promote critical reflection.

- Lab Challenges are review activities that ask students to perform a variation on a task they performed in the Lab Exercises, but without detailed instructions.

Students who successfully complete the Lab Exercises, Lab Review Questions, and Lab Challenges in the Lab Manual will have a richer learning experience and deeper understanding of the concepts and methods covered in the course. You will be better able to answer and understand the testbank questions, especially the knowledge application and knowledge synthesis questions. You will also be much better prepared to pass the associated certification exams if you choose to do so.

NOTATIONAL CONVENTIONS

The following conventions are used throughout this textbook and the Lab Manual:

- Characters or commands that you type appear in **bold** type.

- Terms that appear in the glossary also appear in **bold** type.

- *Italic* in syntax statements indicates placeholders for variable information. *Italic* is also used for book titles and terms defined in the text.

- Names of files and folders appear in Title caps, except when you are to type them directly. Unless otherwise indicated, you can use all lowercase letters when you type a filename in a dialog box or at a command prompt.

- Filename extensions appear in all lowercase.

- Acronyms appear in all uppercase.

- `Monospace` type represents code samples, examples of screen text, or entries that you might type at a command prompt or in initialization files.

- Square brackets [ ] are used in syntax statements to enclose optional items. For example, [*filename*] in command syntax indicates that you can type a filename with the command. Type only the information within the brackets, not the brackets themselves.

- Braces { } are used in syntax statements to enclose required items. Type only the information within the braces, not the braces themselves.

KEYBOARD CONVENTIONS

■ A plus sign (+) between two key names means that you must press those keys at the same time. For example, "Press ALT+TAB" means that you hold down ALT while you press TAB.

■ A comma (,) between two or more key names means that you must press the keys consecutively, not at the same time. For example, "Press ALT, F, X" means that you press and release each key in sequence. "Press ALT+W, L" means that you first press ALT and W at the same time, and then you release them and press L.

COVERAGE OF EXAM OBJECTIVES

This book is intended to support a course that is structured around concepts and practical knowledge fundamental to this topic area, as well as the tasks that are covered in the objectives for the CompTIA Network+ exam. The following table correlates the exam objectives with the textbook chapters and Lab Manual lab exercises. You may also find this table useful if you decide to take the certification exam.

> **NOTE**   The Microsoft Learning Web site describes the various MCP certification exams and their corresponding courses. It provides up-to-date certification information and explains the certification process and the course options. See http://www.microsoft.com/learning/ for up-to-date information about MCP exam credentials and about other certification programs offered by Microsoft.

Textbook and Lab Manual Coverage of Exam Objectives for CompTIA Network+

Objective	Textbook Chapter	Lab Manual Content
DOMAIN 1.0: Media and Topologies		
1.1 Recognize the following logical or physical network topologies given a schematic diagram or description:	Chapter 2	
Star/Hierarchical		
Bus		
Mesh		
Ring		
Wireless		

Textbook and Lab Manual Coverage of Exam Objectives for CompTIA Network+ (Continued)

Objective	Textbook Chapter	Lab Manual Content
DOMAIN 1.0: Media and Topologies (Continued)		
1.2 Specify the main features of 802.2 (LLC), 802.3 (Ethernet), 802.5 (Token Ring), 802.11b (wireless) and FDDI networking technologies, including: Speed Access Method Topology Media	Chapter 4	Lab 4
1.3 Specify the characteristics (e.g., speed, length, topology, cable type, etc.) of the following: 802.3 (Ethernet) standards 10Base-T 100Base-TX 10Base2 10Base5 100Base-FX Gigabit Ethernet	Chapter 4	Lab 4
1.4 Recognize the following media connectors and/or describe their uses: RJ-11 RJ-45 AUI BNC ST SC	Chapter 2	Lab 2, Lab 3

Textbook and Lab Manual Coverage of Exam Objectives for CompTIA Network+ (Continued)

Objective		Textbook Chapter	Lab Manual Content
DOMAIN 1.0: Media and Topologies (Continued)			
1.5	Choose the appropriate media type and connectors to add a client to an existing network.	Chapter 2	Lab 2, Lab 3
1.6	Identify the purpose, features, and functions of the following network components:	Chapter 2, Chapter 3, Chapter 10	Lab 2, Lab 3
	Hubs		
	Switches		
	Bridges		
	Routers		
	Gateways		
	CSU/DSU		
	Network Interface Cards/ISDN adapters/system area network cards		
	Wireless access points		
	Modems		
DOMAIN 2.0: Protocols and Standards			
2.1	Give an example/identify a MAC address	Chapter 4	Lab 4
2.2	Identify the seven layers of the OSI model and their functions	Chapter 1	Lab 1
2.3	Differentiate between the following network protocols in terms of routing, addressing schemes, interoperability and naming conventions:	Chapter 5	
	TCP/IP		
	IPX/SPX		
	NetBEUI		
	AppleTalk		

Textbook and Lab Manual Coverage of Exam Objectives for CompTIA Network+ (Continued)

Objective		Textbook Chapter	Lab Manual Content
DOMAIN 2.0: Protocols and Standards (Continued)			
2.4	Identify the OSI layers at which the following network components operate:	Chapter 3	
	Hubs		
	Switches		
	Bridges		
	Routers		
	Network Interface Cards		
2.5	Define the purpose, function and/or use of the following protocols within TCP/IP:	Chapter 7	Lab 5, Lab 7, Lab 11
	IP		
	TCP		
	UDP		
	FTP		
	TFTP		
	SMTP		
	HTTP		
	HTTPS		
	POP3/IMAP4		
	TELNET		
	ICMP		
	ARP		
	NTP		
2.6	Define the function of TCP/UDP ports. Identify well-known ports.	Chapter 6	Lab 6

Textbook and Lab Manual Coverage of Exam Objectives for CompTIA Network+ (Continued)

Objective		Textbook Chapter	Lab Manual Content
DOMAIN 2.0: Protocols and Standards (Continued)			
2.7	Identify the purpose of the following network services: DHCP/BOOTP DNS NAT/ICS WINS SNMP	Chapter 8, Chapter 9	Lab 8, Lab 10
2.8	Identify IP addresses (Ipv4, Ipv6) and their default subnet masks.	Chapter 5	Lab 5, Lab 6, Lab 7
2.9	Identify the purpose of subnetting and default gateways.	Chapter 5, Chapter 7	Lab 7, Lab 8
2.10	Identify the differences between public vs. private networks.	Chapter 5	
2.11	Identify the basic characteristics (e.g.,speed, capacity, media) of the following WAN technologies: Packet switching vs.circuit switching ISDN FDDI ATM Frame Relay SONET/SDH T1/E1 T3/E3 OCx	Chapter 10	

Textbook and Lab Manual Coverage of Exam Objectives for CompTIA Network+ (Continued)

Objective	Textbook Chapter	Lab Manual Content
DOMAIN 2.0: Protocols and Standards (Continued)		
2.12 Define the function of the following remote access protocols and services: RAS PPP PPTP ICA	Chapter 10	Lab 10
2.13 Identify the following security protocols and describe their purpose and function: IPSec L2TP SSL Kerberos	Chapter 9	Lab 9, Lab 10
DOMAIN 3.0: Network Implementation		
3.1 Identify the basic capabilities (i.e., client support, interoperability, authentication, file and print services, application support, and security) of the following server operating systems: UNIX/Linux NetWare Windows Macintosh	Chapter 8	Lab 8
3.2 Identify the basic capabilities of client workstations (i.e., client connectivity, local security mechanisms, and authentication).	Chapter 8	Lab 8
3.3 Identify the main characteristics of VLANs.	Chapter 3	

Textbook and Lab Manual Coverage of Exam Objectives for CompTIA Network+ (Continued)

Objective		Textbook Chapter	Lab Manual Content
DOMAIN 3.0: Network Implementation			
3.4	Identify the main characteristics of network attached storage.	Chapter 9	
3.5	Identify the purpose and characteristics of fault tolerance.	Chapter 9	
3.6	Identify the purpose and characteristics of disaster recovery.	Chapter 9	Lab 9
3.7	Given a remote connectivity scenario (e.g.,IP, IPX, dial-up, PPPoE, authentication, physical connectivity etc.), configure the connection.	Chapter 10	Lab 10
3.8	Identify the purpose, benefits, and characteristics of using a firewall.	Chapter 9	Lab 9, Lab 10
3.9	Identify the purpose, benefits, and characteristics of using a proxy	Chapter 9	Lab 9
3.10	Given a scenario, predict the impact of a particular security implementation on network functionality (e.g., blocking port numbers, encryption, etc.).	Chapter 9	Lab 9
3.11	Given a network configuration, select the appropriate NIC and network configuration settings (DHCP, DNS, WINS, protocols, NETBIOS/host name, etc.).	Chapter 7	Lab 3, Lab 5, Lab 7

Textbook and Lab Manual Coverage of Exam Objectives for CompTIA Network+ (Continued)

Objective	Textbook Chapter	Lab Manual Content
DOMAIN 4.0: Network Support		
4.1 Given a troubleshooting scenario, select the appropriate TCP/IP utility from among the following: Tracert Ping Arp Netstat Nbtstat Ipconfig/Ifconfig Winipcfg Nslookup	Chapter 11	Lab 11
4.2 Given a troubleshooting scenario involving a small office/home office network failure (e.g., xDSL, cable, home satellite, wireless, POTS), identify the cause of the failure.	Chapter 12	Lab 12
4.3 Given a troubleshooting scenario involving a remote connectivity problem (e.g., authentication failure, protocol configuration, physical connectivity) identify the cause of the problem.	Chapter 12	Lab 10
4.4 Given specific parameters, configure a client to connect to the following servers: UNIX/Linux NetWare Windows Macintosh	Chapter 8	Lab 8

Textbook and Lab Manual Coverage of Exam Objectives for CompTIA Network+ (Continued)

Objective	Textbook Chapter	Lab Manual Content
DOMAIN 4.0: Network Support (Continued)		
4.5 Given a wiring task, select the appropriate tool (e.g., wire crimper, media tester/certifier, punch down tool, tone generator, optical tester, etc.).	Chapter 2, Chapter 11	
4.6 Given a network scenario, interpret visual indicators (e.g.,link lights, collision lights, etc.) to determine the nature of the problem.	Chapter 11	
4.7 Given output from a diagnostic utility (e.g., tracert, ping, ipconfig, etc.), identify the utility and interpret the output.	Chapter 11	Lab 11
4.8 Given a scenario, predict the impact of modifying, adding, or removing network services (e.g.,DHCP, DNS, WINS, etc.) on network resources and users.	Chapter 8	Lab 8
4.9 Given a network problem scenario, select an appropriate course of action based on a general troubleshooting strategy. This strategy includes the following steps: Establish the symptoms Identify the affected area Establish what has changed Select the most probable cause Implement a solution Test the result Recognize the potential effects of the solution Document the solution	Chapter 12	Lab 12

Textbook and Lab Manual Coverage of Exam Objectives for CompTIA Network+ (Continued)

Objective	Textbook Chapter	Lab Manual Content
DOMAIN 4.0: Network Support (Continued)		
4.10 Given a troubleshooting scenario involving a network with a particular physical topology (i.e.,bus, star/ hierarchical, mesh, ring, and wireless) and including a network diagram, identify the network area effected and the cause of the problem.	Chapter 12	Lab 12
4.11 Given a network troubleshooting scenario involving a client connectivity problem (e.g., incorrect protocol/client software/authentication configuration, or insufficient rights/permissions), identify the cause of the problem.	Chapter 12	Lab 12
4.12 Given a network troubleshooting scenario involving a wiring/ infrastructure problem, identify the cause of the problem (e.g.,bad media, interference, network hardware).	Chapter 12	

THE MICROSOFT CERTIFIED PROFESSIONAL PROGRAM

The MCP program is one way to prove your proficiency with current Microsoft products and technologies. These exams and corresponding certifications are developed to validate your mastery of critical competencies as you design and develop, or implement and support, solutions using Microsoft products and technologies. Computer professionals who become Microsoft certified are recognized as experts and are sought after industry-wide. Certification brings a variety of benefits to the individual and to employers and organizations.

MORE INFO   For a full list of MCP benefits, go to http://www.microsoft.com/learning/itpro/default.asp.

Certifications

The MCP program offers multiple certifications, based on specific areas of technical expertise:

- **Microsoft Certified Professional (MCP)**   In-depth knowledge of at least one Windows operating system or architecturally significant platform. An MCP is qualified to implement a Microsoft product or technology as part of a business solution for an organization.

- **Microsoft Certified Systems Engineer (MCSE)**   Qualified to effectively analyze the business requirements for business solutions and design and implement the infrastructure based on the Windows and Windows Server 2003 operating systems.

- **Microsoft Certified Systems Administrator (MCSA)**   Qualified to manage and troubleshoot existing network and system environments based on the Windows and Windows Server 2003 operating systems.

- **Microsoft Certified Database Administrator (MCDBA)**   Qualified to design, implement, and administer Microsoft SQL Server databases.

- **Microsoft Certified Desktop Support Technician (MCDST)**   Qualified to support end users and to troubleshoot desktop environments on the Microsoft Windows operating system.

MCP Requirements

Requirements differ for each certification and are specific to the products and job functions addressed by the certification. To become an MCP, you must pass rigorous certification exams that provide a valid and reliable measure of technical proficiency and expertise. These exams are designed to test your expertise and ability to perform a role or task with a product, and they are developed with the input of industry professionals. Exam questions reflect how Microsoft products are used in actual organizations, giving them real-world relevance.

- Microsoft Certified Professional (MCP) candidates are required to pass one current Microsoft certification exam. Candidates can pass additional Microsoft certification exams to validate their skills with other Microsoft products, development tools, or desktop applications.

- Microsoft Certified Systems Engineer (MCSE) candidates are required to pass five core exams and two elective exams.

- Microsoft Certified Systems Administrator (MCSA) candidates are required to pass three core exams and one elective exam.

- Microsoft Certified Database Administrator (MCDBA) candidates are required to pass three core exams and one elective exam.

- Microsoft Certified Desktop Support Technician (MCDST) candidates are required to pass two core exams.

ABOUT THE AUTHORS

The textbook, Lab Manual, pretest, testbank, and PowerPoint slides were written by instructors and developed exclusively for an instructor-led classroom environment.

Craig Zacker is a writer, editor, and networker whose computing experience began in the days of teletypes and paper tape. After making the move from minicomputers to PCs, he worked as an administrator of Novell NetWare networks and as a PC support technician while operating a freelance desktop publishing business. After earning a master's degree in English and American literature from New York University, Craig worked extensively on the integration of Microsoft Windows NT into existing internetworks, supported fleets of Windows workstations, and was employed as a technical writer, content provider, and Webmaster for the online services group of a large software company. Since devoting himself to writing and editing full-time, Craig has authored or contributed to many books on networking topics, operating systems, and PC hardware, including MCSA/MCSE Self-Paced Training Kit: Microsoft Windows 2000 Network Infrastructure Administration, Exam 70-216, Second Edition and MCSA Training Kit: Managing a Microsoft Windows 2000 Network Environment. He has also developed educational texts for college courses and online training courses for the Web and has published articles in top industry publications. For more information on Craig's books and other works, see *http://www.zacker.com*.

Heather Osterloh has earned industry recognition as a Cisco Certified Network and Design Professional (CCNP/CCDP), Network Associate Sniffer Trainer, Certified Network Expert (CNX) for Ethernet and Token Ring, Novell CNI/ECNE, Microsoft Certified Systems Engineer (MCSE), and Microsoft Certified Trainer (MCT). She also has obtained Cisco Certified Internetworking Expert (CCIE) status, for the written portion of the exam, and is currently waiting to take the practical lab exam.

Having spent the last 17 years training and consulting worldwide, Heather is an acknowledged leader in the networking industry. She is the author of three networking books: *CCNA 2.0 Prep Kit 640-507 Routing and Switching (MacMillan*

Press), IP Routing Primer Plus (SAMS Publishing), and TCP/IP Primer Plus (SAMS Publishing). She is also the author of several popular Microsoft, Cisco, and Novell video series geared to the busy professional.

FOR MICROSOFT OFFICIAL ACADEMIC COURSE SUPPORT

Every effort has been made to ensure the accuracy of the material in this book and the contents of the CD-ROM. Microsoft Learning provides corrections for books through the World Wide Web at the following address:

http://www.microsoft.com/learning/support/

If you have comments, questions, or ideas regarding this book or the companion CD-ROM, please send them to Microsoft Learning using either of the following methods:

- Postal Mail:

  Microsoft Learning

  Attn: Network+ Certification, Editor

  One Microsoft Way

  Redmond, WA 98052-6399

- E-mail: moac@microsoft.com

Please note that product support is not offered through the above addresses.

EVALUATION EDITION SOFTWARE SUPPORT

A 180-day software evaluation edition of Microsoft Windows Server 2003 Evaluation Edition is provided with this textbook. This is not the full retail product and is provided only for training and evaluation purposes. Microsoft and Microsoft Technical Support do not support this evaluation edition. It differs from the retail version only in that Microsoft and Microsoft Technical Support do not support it, and it expires after 180 days. For information about issues relating to the use of evaluation editions, go to the Support section of the Microsoft Learning Web site (*http://www.microsoft.com/learning/support/*).

For online support information relating to the full version of Windows Server 2003 that might also apply to the evaluation edition, go to *http://support.microsoft.com.* For information about ordering the full version of any Microsoft software, call Microsoft Sales at (800) 426-9400 or visit *http://www.microsoft.com.*

CHAPTER 1
NETWORKING BASICS

Upon completion of this chapter, you will be able to:

- List the services provided by network protocols.

- Describe how protocols enable networked computers to communicate.

- Identify the layers of the OSI reference model.

- Describe the functions associated with each of the OSI model layers.

This chapter introduces the basic principles and architectural structures of computer network communications. There are many different kinds of data networks—from an enterprise network used by a large corporation to a simple two-node **local area network (LAN)** used in a private home. However, many of the same principles apply to all networks, regardless of size or complexity. The concepts and structures discussed in this chapter are referred to repeatedly in the rest of this textbook as well as in real-life networking situations. Even if you skip other chapters in this book, you should read and fully understand this one. You will need it, both for the rest of the course and on the job.

UNDERSTANDING NETWORK COMMUNICATIONS

When you connect two or more computers together so they can communicate with each other, you create a data network. This is true whether you connect the computers with cables, wireless technologies such as infrared or radio waves, or modems and telephone lines. Therefore, although most people might not be aware of it, connecting to the Internet in any way makes your computer part of a data network.

Computers are generally networked together for two reasons: to share hardware resources and to share data. For example, networking enables multiple computers to share a single printer or to open the same documents. Resource sharing was the original motivation for creating computer networks, and all of the technologies you will learn about in this course are designed to facilitate this end efficiently and securely.

Network Media

The technology connecting networked computers together, no matter what form it takes, is called the *network medium*. Copper-based cables are the most common form of network medium, but a network can also use fiber optic cables (which are nonmetallic) as its medium, or it can use a variety of wireless media. The network medium can be owned by an individual or company, or it can be furnished by a third-party service provider such as a telephone company.

When you purchase the equipment needed to connect multiple computers together in your home, for example, the cables you install are the network medium, and you are completely responsible for them. When you use a dial-up modem to connect your computer to an **Internet service provider (ISP)**, your local telephone company provides the network medium connecting your computer to the ISP's server. These same principles apply to a business network, whether it connects a handful of computers together or connects tens of thousands. The company owns the network medium that connects computers in the same location together, while outside providers usually supply the network media for longer distance connections.

> **NOTE   Compound Media**   The network medium connecting two computers together does not have to consist of one single technology. For example, when you connect to your ISP using a dial-up modem connection, the signals transmitted by your computer might pass through a standard telephone cable connecting your modem to the wall jack, through a copper cable connecting your home to a local telephone company facility, through a fiber optic cable in the telephone company's own network, and then through another copper cable leading to the

ISP's computer. When you are using an outside provider for network connectivity, you often have no way of knowing exactly what types of media are being used.

LANs, WANs, and MANs

A LAN is a group of computers located within relatively close proximity and connected by a common medium, such as a particular type of cable. Each computer and other communicating device on the LAN is called a **node**. A LAN is characterized by three primary attributes: its **topology**, its medium, and its protocols. The topology is the pattern in which the computers are connected. In a bus topology, a network cable connects each computer to the next one, forming a chain. In a star topology, each computer is connected to a central nexus called a **hub** or **switch**. A ring topology is essentially a bus network with the two ends joined together.

> **MORE INFO**   **Understanding Topologies**   You learn more about the various types of network topologies and how they affect network communications in Chapter 2, "Network Cabling."

The network medium, as defined earlier, is the actual physical connection between the networked computers. The topology and the medium used on a particular LAN are specified by the protocol operating at the data-link layer of the International Organization for Standardization (OSI) model, such as **Ethernet** or Token Ring. You will learn more about protocols and the OSI model layers later in this chapter and throughout the course. Ethernet, for example, supports several different topologies and media. When building a new LAN, you typically select one topology and medium, such as unshielded twisted pair (UTP) cable in a star topology, and use the same topology and medium for all of the computers on that LAN. There are, however, hardware products that let you connect computers to the same LAN with different media. You might use these products when you have two existing networks that you want to connect together by using different types of cable, or when you want to combine cabled and wireless systems on the same LAN.

In most cases, a LAN is confined to a room, a floor, or perhaps a building. To expand the network beyond these limits, you can connect multiple LANs together using devices called **routers**. This forms an **internetwork**, which is essentially a network of networks. A computer on one LAN can communicate with the systems on another LAN if the two LANs are connected using a router. By connecting LANs in this way, you can build an internetwork as large as you need. Many sources use the term *network* when describing a LAN, but just as many use the same term when referring to an internetwork.

NOTE **Internetworks and the Internet**   It is important to distinguish between the generic term *internetwork* (with a lowercase "i"), which is any collection of interconnected LANs, and the Internet. The Internet is the ultimate example of an internetwork, but not every internetwork involves the Internet.

In many cases, an internetwork is composed of LANs in distant locations. To connect remote LANs together, you use a different type of network connection: a **wide area network (WAN)** connection. WAN connections can use telephone lines, radio waves, or any one of many other technologies, typically furnished by an outside provider such as a telephone company. WAN links are usually point-to-point connections, meaning that they connect only two systems. This is in direct contrast to a LAN, which can connect many systems together using a shared network medium. An example of a WAN connection would be the case of a company with two offices in distant cities, each with its own LAN and connected by a leased telephone line. This type of WAN connection is illustrated in Figure 1-1.

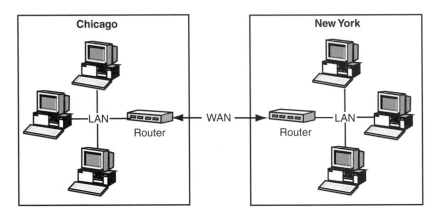

Figure 1-1   WAN connections create internetworks by connecting LANs in distant locations.

Each end of the leased line is connected to a router, and the routers are connected to the individual LAN at each site. Routers are essential when you connect LANs together using a WAN link, because WANs almost invariably use different media than LANs, and you need a router to connect two different network types together. Using the WAN connection, a computer on either LAN can communicate with any computer on the other LAN.

MORE INFO **Exploring WAN Technologies**   You learn about the various types of communications technologies used to create WAN connections in Chapter 10, "Remote Network Access." Routers and other network connection devices are covered in Chapter 3, "Network Connection Hardware."

In addition to LANs and WANs, there is another type of network that deserves mention here, even though it is not critical to this course. A **metropolitan area network (MAN)** is a data network that services an area larger than a LAN does, and smaller than a WAN does. The most common types of MAN implementation seen today are the fiber optic networks run by cable television (CATV) providers. When you access the Internet using your CATV network, you share bandwidth with your neighbors because you are all connected to the same Ethernet network.

Signals and Protocols

Computers can communicate over a network in many ways and for many reasons, but much of the networking process is not directly concerned with the nature of the data transmitted over the network medium. By the time the data generated by the transmitting computer reaches the cable or other medium, it has been reduced to signals that are native to that medium. These signals might be electrical voltages on a copper cable network, pulses of light on a fiber optic cable network, or infrared or radio waves on a wireless network.

These signals form a code that the network interface in a receiving computer converts back into the binary data understood by the software running on that computer. The computer then interprets the binary data, converting it into information it can use in a variety of ways. Of course there is a great deal more to the network communications process than this description indicates, but one of the primary elements of computer networking is the reduction of complex data structures into simple signals that can be transmitted over a network medium and then converted back into the same data structures on the destination system. The software components that perform this reduction on a computer are known collectively as the **protocol stack**, shown in Figure 1-2. At the top of the stack are the applications running on the computer and at the bottom is the connection to the network medium.

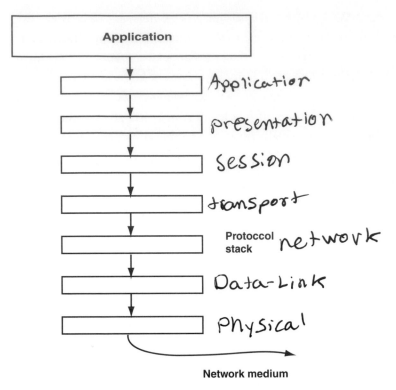

Figure 1-2   A networked computer's protocol stack

In some cases, a network consists of computers that are nearly identical; they run the same version of the same operating system and use all the same applications. Other networks consist of many different computing platforms, all running entirely different software. It might seem that the identical computers would communicate more easily than the different ones would, and in some ways this is true. But no matter what kind of computers the network uses or what software the computers are running, they must have a common language to understand each other. These common languages are called **protocols**, and computers use many of them during even the simplest exchanges of network data. Just as two people must speak a common language to communicate, two computers must have one or more protocols in common. The various protocols running on a computer comprise the stack that connects the applications and the network medium.

A network protocol can be relatively simple or highly complex. The bottom component of the protocol stack defines the sequence of signals transmitted over the network medium. In this case, the protocol is simply a code—such as a pattern of electrical voltages—that defines the binary value of a bit of data: 0 or 1. The concept is the same as that of Morse code, in which a pattern of dots and dashes represents a letter of the alphabet.

More complicated networking protocols can provide a variety of services, including the following:

- **Packet acknowledgment**   The transmission of a return message by the recipient to verify the receipt of a packet or packets. A **packet** is the fundamental unit of data transmitted over a data network.

- **Segmentation**   The division of a lengthy data stream into segments sufficiently small for transmission over the network inside packets.

- **Flow control**   The generation, by a receiving system, of messages that instruct the sending system to speed up or slow down its rate of transmission.

- **Error detection**   The inclusion in a packet of special codes used by the receiving system to verify that the content of the packet wasn't damaged in transit.

- **Error correction**   The retransmission of packets that have been garbled or lost in transit.

- **Data compression**   A mechanism for reducing the amount of data transmitted over a network by eliminating redundant information.

- **Data encryption**   A mechanism for protecting the data transmitted over a network by encoding it using a cryptographic key already known by the receiving system.

In most cases, protocols are based on public standards developed and published by an independent committee rather than a single manufacturer or developer. Public standards ensure the interoperability of different types of systems, because manufacturers can use the protocols without incurring any obligation to a particular company. There are still a few proprietary protocols in use, however, that have been developed by a single company and have never been released into the public domain.

Some of the organizations that are responsible for the protocol standards used today are as follows:

- **Institute of Electrical and Electronics Engineers (IEEE)**
  The U.S.-based society responsible for the publication of the IEEE 802 working group, which includes the standards that define the protocols commonly known as Ethernet and Token Ring, as well as many others.

- **International Organization for Standardization (ISO)**   A worldwide federation of standards bodies from over 100 countries, responsible for the publication of the OSI reference model document.

- **American National Standards Institute (ANSI)**   A private, nonprofit organization that administers and coordinates the U.S. voluntary standardization and conformity assessment system. ANSI is the official U.S. representative to the ISO, as well as to several other international bodies.

- **Internet Engineering Task Force (IETF)**   An ad hoc group of contributors and consultants that collaborates to develop and publish standards for Internet technologies, including the Transmission Control Protocol/Internet Protocol (TCP/IP) protocols.

- **Telecommunications Industry Association/Electronic Industries Alliance (TIA/EIA)**   Two organizations that have joined together to develop and publish the Commercial Building Telecommunications Wiring Standards, which define how the cables for data networks should be installed.

- **Telecommunication Standardization Sector of the International Telecommunication Union (ITU-T)**   An international organization within which governments and the private sector work together to coordinate the operation of telecommunication networks and services, and to advance the development of communications technology. ITU-T was formerly known as the Comité Consultatif International Téléphonique et Télégraphique (**CCITT**).

One of the most important things to remember about computer networking is that all of the computers on a network use many different protocols during the communications process, and all of these protocols work together to form the protocol stack. For example, you might see a reference to an Ethernet network in a book or an article. While Ethernet is certainly a protocol running on the network that the author is discussing, it is not the only protocol running on the network. There are many other protocols running at the same time, and although they might not be as relevant to the author's subject as Ethernet is, they are no less important to the overall networking process.

Broadband and Baseband Communications

In most cases, LANs use a shared network medium. All of the computers on the LAN are connected to a network that can carry only one signal at a time, and the systems take turns using it. This type of network is called a **baseband** network. To make sharing a baseband network among many computers practical, the data transmitted by each system is broken up into discrete *packets*. If you were to tap into the cable of a baseband network and interpret the signals as they flow by, you would see a succession of packets generated by various systems and destined for various systems, as shown in Figure 1-3.

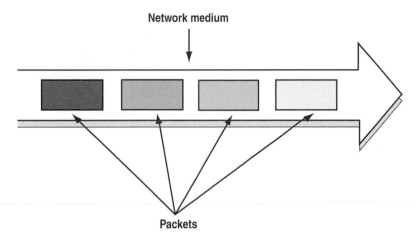

Figure 1-3   In a packet-switching network, the medium carries a seemingly random stream of packets generated by various computers on the network.

When your computer transmits an e-mail message, for example, it is broken into many packets, and the computer transmits each packet separately. If another computer on the network also wants to transmit, it sends one packet at a time, too. When all of the packets constituting a particular transmission reach their destination, the receiving computer reassembles them back into your original e-mail message. This is the basis for a **packet-switching** network.

Packet switching introduces potential problems into the networking process. Because each packet is transmitted separately, it is possible for the packets comprising a single message to take different routes to the same destination. As a result, the packets can arrive at the destination system out of order. It is also possible for some packets to be lost entirely and never arrive at the destination. On a network that uses packet switching, the receiving system must have a means of reassembling the packets in the proper order and a mechanism for detecting missing or corrupted packets. You will learn about the techniques used to provide these services in the discussions of specific protocols found in Chapters 4, 5, and 6, later in this textbook.

NOTE   Cell Switching   Some networks use a technique called **cell switching**, which is similar to packet switching, but instead of using packets, which are variable in size, they use cells, which are a uniform size. Most LAN technologies use packet switching; the only cell-switching LAN in recent use is **Asynchronous Transfer Mode (ATM)**, which uses 53-byte cells.

The alternative to a packet-switching or cell-switching network is a **circuit-switching** network, in which two systems wanting to communicate establish a path (called a *circuit*) through the network, which connects them before they transmit any information. That circuit remains open throughout the life of the exchange and is broken only when the two systems are finished communicating. This is an impractical solution for computers on a baseband network, because two systems connected by a circuit could conceivably monopolize the network medium for long periods of time, preventing other systems from communicating. Circuit switching is more common in environments like the **Public Switched Telephone Network (PSTN)**, in which the connection between your telephone and that of the person you're calling remains open for the entire duration of the call.

Test your knowledge of networking terms and concepts by completing Exercise 1-1, "Networking Definitions," now.

To make circuit switching practical, telephone companies use broadband networks. Because of the growing popularity of CATV and Digital Subscriber Line (DSL) Internet access products, the term *broadband* has become synonymous with being high-speed, but this is actually not the case. A **broadband** network is the opposite of a baseband network, in that it is capable of carrying multiple signals on a single cable simultaneously, using a process called **multiplexing**. CATV networks, for example, are broadband because they carry signals providing dozens of television channels at the same time. A cable TV service runs a single cable into your home, but if you have more than one television set, the fact that you can watch a different program on each TV proves that the one cable is carrying multiple signals simultaneously. When the CATV service also provides Internet access, those signals share the same cable with the television signals. In virtually all cases, broadband networks require relatively large amounts of bandwidth to carry multiple signals efficiently, but it is not solely the speed of the network that defines it as broadband-capable.

INTRODUCING THE OSI REFERENCE MODEL

So far in this chapter, you have learned that computers on a network rely on protocols for their communication, and that the protocols form a stack that runs from the computer's network interface up to the applications running on the computer. To delineate the functions of various protocols and illustrate how the protocols interact, the stack is divided into layers. The industry standard definitions for the layers of the protocol stack are called the **Open Systems Interconnection (OSI) reference model**.

The OSI model divides the networking process into seven layers, which are as follows:

- Application

- Presentation

- Session

- Transport

- Network

- Data-link

- Physical

> **NOTE** **Exam Objective** *Objective 2.2 for the Network+ exam requires students to identify the seven layers of the OSI model and their functions.*

These theoretical divisions make it easier to learn and understand the concepts involved in network communications. At the top of the model is the application that requires access to a resource on the network, and at the bottom is the network medium itself. As data moves down through the model, the protocols operating at the various layers prepare and package it for transmission over the network. Once the data arrives at its destination, it moves up through the layers on the receiving system, where the same protocols perform the same process in reverse.

The OSI model is defined by a document called "The Basic Reference Model for Open Systems Interconnection," which was published in 1983 by the ISO as document ISO 7498, and by the CCITT (now known as the ITU-T) as X.200. Each of these organizations began developing its own networking model specification, but eventually they combined their efforts to produce a single document. This document defines the functions of the seven layers shown in Figure 1-4. Originally, this seven-layer structure was to be the model for a new protocol stack, but this stack never materialized in a commercial form. Instead, the OSI model has come to be used with the existing network protocols as a teaching and reference tool.

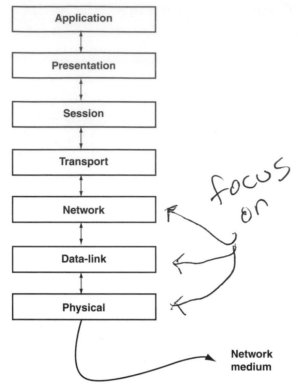

Figure 1-4   The OSI reference model

Most of the networking protocols commonly used today predate the OSI model, so they don't conform exactly to the seven-layer structure. The original plan called for the creation of a stack with protocols exactly analogous to the layers of the OSI model. This would have been a convenient arrangement for networking students and professionals, compared with the untidy situation found today. In the protocol stacks used today, single protocols often perform the functions assigned to two or more of the layers in the OSI model, and the boundaries between protocols often don't exactly conform to the model's layer boundaries. However, the model remains an excellent tool for studying the networking process, and professionals frequently make reference to functions and protocols associated with specific OSI model layers.

Protocol Interaction

The protocols comprising the stack on a networked computer work together to provide all of the services required by a particular application. Generally speaking, the services provided by the protocols are not redundant. If, for example, a protocol at one layer provides a particular service, the protocols at the other layers do not provide exactly the same service. Protocols at adjacent layers in the stack provide services to each other, depending on the direction in which the data is flowing. The data on a transmitting system originates in an application at the top of the protocol stack and works its way down through the layers. Each protocol provides a service to a protocol operating at the layer below it. At the bottom of the protocol stack is the network medium itself, which carries the data to another system on the network.

When the data arrives at its destination, the receiving computer performs the same procedure as the transmitting computer performed, except in reverse. The data is passed up through the layers to the receiving application, with each protocol providing a service to the protocol in the layer above it. For example, if a protocol at layer three on the transmitting computer is responsible for encrypting data, the same protocol at layer three of the receiving system is responsible for decrypting it. Because of these complementary functions, the protocols at the various layers in the transmitting system's stack can be said to communicate with their equivalent protocols operating at the same layers on the receiving system, as illustrated in Figure 1-5.

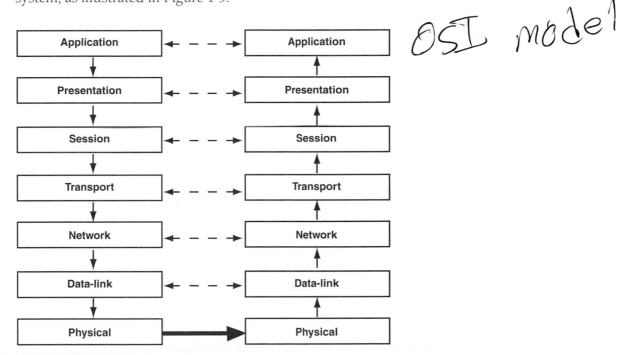

OSI model

Figure 1-5   Protocols operating at the same layer in the stack on different systems can be said to communicate indirectly by providing complementary services.

Data Encapsulation

The primary interaction between the protocols operating at the various layers of the OSI model takes the form of each protocol adding a header (and in one case, a footer) to the information it receives from the layer above it. For example, on a typical LAN, when an application generates a request for a network resource, an application layer protocol packages the request as a **protocol data unit (PDU)** and sends it on its way down through the protocol stack.

Application	Application request
Presentation	
Session	
Transport	
Network	
Data-link	
Physical	

When the PDU reaches the transport layer, a transport layer protocol creates its own PDU by adding a header to the request. This header consists of fields containing information implementing that protocol's functions, and the original application layer request becomes the data field, or payload, for the transport layer PDU.

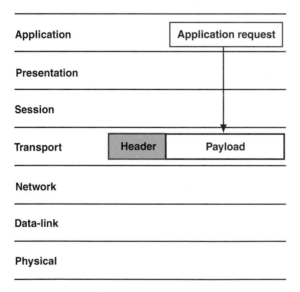

The transport layer protocol, after adding its header, passes the new PDU down to the network layer. The network layer protocol then adds its own header in front of the transport layer protocol's header, forming a network layer PDU. Thus, the transport layer PDU, consisting of the original application layer request and the transport layer protocol header, becomes the payload in the network layer PDU.

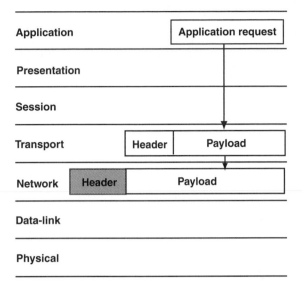

In the same way, the network layer PDU is passed down to the data-link layer, where it becomes the payload of the data-link layer PDU. However, this time the protocol at the data-link layer adds both a header and a footer.

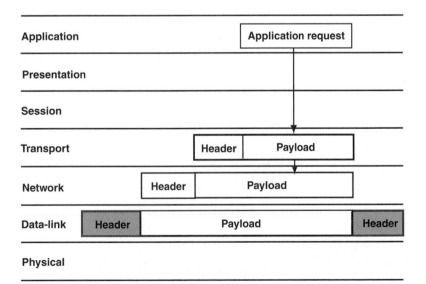

The final product, or packet, is ready for conversion to signals appropriate to the medium and transmission over the network. After the packet reaches its destination, the entire process is repeated in reverse. The protocol at each successive layer of the stack (traveling upward this time) processes and removes the header applied by its equivalent protocol in the transmitting system. When the process is complete, the original request arrives at the application for which it was destined in the same condition as when it was generated.

The process by which protocols add their own information to that received from the layers above them in the OSI model is called **data encapsulation**. This process is functionally similar to the process of preparing a postal letter for mailing. The application request is the letter itself, and the protocol headers represent the process of putting the letter into an envelope, addressing it, stamping it, and mailing it.

> **MORE INFO**   *Demonstration Video*   Run the DataEncapsulation video located in the Demos folder on the CD-ROM accompanying this book for a demonstration of the data encapsulation process.

The functions of the OSI model layers, from the bottom to the top of the protocol stack, are covered in the following sections.

The Physical Layer

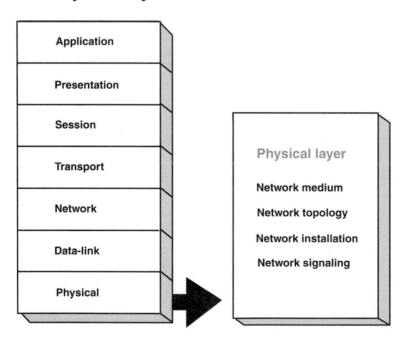

The **physical layer**, at the bottom of the OSI model, is, as the name implies, the layer that defines the nature of the network's hardware elements, such as the following:

- What medium the network uses

- The topology of the network

- How the network is installed

- The nature of the signals used to transmit binary data over the network

LAN Physical Layer Specifications

The physical layer also defines what kind of network interface must be installed in each computer and what other connection hardware to use, such as hubs or switches. Physical layer options include various types of copper or fiber optic cable, as well as many different wireless solutions. In the case of a LAN, the physical layer specifications are directly related to the data-link layer protocol used by the network. When you select a data-link layer protocol, you must use one of the physical layer specifications supported by that protocol.

For example, Ethernet is a data-link layer protocol that supports several different physical layer options. You can use one of two types of coaxial cable with Ethernet: any one of several types of twisted pair cable, or fiber optic cable. The specifications for each of these options include a great deal of detailed physical layer requirements, such as the exact type of cable and connectors to use, how long the cables can be, and how many hubs you can have. Meeting these specifications is required in order for the protocol to function properly.

Some aspects of the physical layer are defined in the data-link layer protocol standard, but others are defined in separate specifications. One of the most commonly used physical layer specifications is the "Commercial Building Telecommunications Cabling Standard," published jointly by ANSI and the TIA/EIA as document 568B. This document includes detailed specifications for installing cables for data networks in a commercial environment, including the required distances from sources of **electromagnetic interference (EMI)** and other general cabling policies. In most cases, large network cabling jobs are outsourced to specialized contractors, and any such contractor you hire for a LAN cabling job should be very familiar with TIA/EIA 568B and other such documents, including your local building codes.

MORE INFO Cable Installation Guidelines   For more information on the standards governing network cable installations, see Chapter 2, "Network Cabling."

WAN Physical Layer Specifications

In the case of WAN technologies, the physical layer specification is independent of the data-link layer. WAN connections are usually point-to-point, meaning that they involve only two systems. Therefore, the data-link layer protocol used on a WAN is simpler and more generic than those used on LANs, because there is no need for many of the mechanisms that LAN protocols require to support a shared network medium. A single data-link layer protocol such as **Point-to-Point Protocol (PPP)** can therefore support a variety of physical layer technologies without modification.

> **MORE INFO**   WAN Physical Layer Specifications   *For more information on the physical layer protocols used on WANs, see Chapter 10, "Remote Network Access."*

Physical Layer Signaling

The other communications element found at the physical layer is the particular type of signaling used to transmit data over the network medium. For copper-based cables, these signals are electrical charges. For fiber optic cables, the signals are pulses of light. Other types of network media can use radio frequencies, infrared pulses, or other types of signals. In addition to determining the nature of the signals, the physical layer dictates the signaling scheme that the computers use. The signaling scheme is the pattern of electrical charges or light pulses used to encode the binary data generated by the protocols at the upper layers of the OSI model. Ethernet systems use a signaling scheme called Manchester encoding, and Token Ring systems use a scheme called Differential Manchester.

The Data-Link Layer

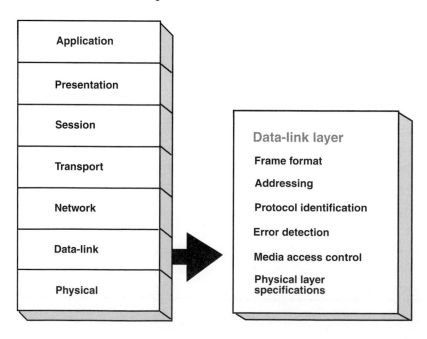

The protocol at the **data-link layer** is the conduit between the computer's networking hardware and its networking software. Network layer protocols pass their outgoing data down to the data-link layer protocol, which packages the data for transmission over the network. When the other systems on the network receive the transmitted data, their data-link layer protocols process it and pass it up to the network layer.

When it comes to designing and building a LAN, the data-link layer protocol you choose is the single most important factor in determining what networking hardware you buy and how you install it. To implement a data-link layer protocol, you need the following hardware and software:

- Network interface adapters
- Network cables (or other media) and connecting hardware
- Network hubs or switches (in some cases)
- Network adapter drivers

Network interface adapters, hubs, and switches are designed for specific data-link layer protocols and are not interchangeable with products for other protocols. Some network cables are protocol-specific, while others can be used with various protocols. The data-link layer protocol itself is implemented by the network interface adapter in combination with the network adapter driver running on the computer. Some data-link layer functions are performed by the adapter independently, before incoming data is passed to the computer and before outgoing data leaves it. Other functions are performed by the driver after the adapter passes incoming data to the computer and before the computer passes outgoing data to the adapter.

By far the most popular data-link layer LAN protocol in use today (and throughout the history of the LAN) is Ethernet. Token Ring is a distant second, followed by other protocols such as Fiber Distributed Data Interface (FDDI) and ATM. The specifications for data-link layer LAN protocols typically include the following three basic elements:

- A format for the frame (that is, the header and footer applied to the network layer data before transmission)
- A mechanism for regulating access to the network medium
- One or more physical layer specifications for use with the protocol

> **NOTE**   **Ethernet and Token Ring**   For more detailed information on the Ethernet, Token Ring, and FDDI protocols, see Chapter 4, "Data-Link Protocols." For more information on ATM, see Chapter 10, "Remote Network Access."

These three components are discussed in the following sections.

Frame Format

The data-link layer protocol encapsulates the data it receives from the network layer protocol by adding a header and footer, forming a **frame** (as shown in Figure 1-6).

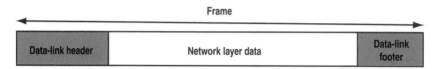

Frame

Data-link header	Network layer data	Data-link footer

Figure 1-6   A typical data-link layer protocol frame

> **NOTE**   **Naming Data Structures**   Protocols operating at different layers of the OSI model have different names for the PDUs they create by adding headers to the data they receive from the layer above. The PDU created by a data-link layer protocol, for example, is called a "frame," while network layer PDUs are called "datagrams." "Packet" is a more generic term used to describe the PDU at any stage of the data encapsulation process.

The functions of the data-link layer frame for a LAN protocol include the following:

■ **Addressing**   To continue the postal analogy mentioned earlier in this chapter, the data-link layer protocol's header and footer are the equivalent of the envelope used to mail a letter. The header contains the address of the system sending the packet and the address of its destination system. For LAN protocols like Ethernet and Token Ring, these addresses are 6-byte hexadecimal strings assigned to network interface adapters by their manufacturers. The addresses are referred to as hardware addresses or Media Access Control (MAC) addresses, to distinguish them from addresses used at other layers of the OSI model.

> **NOTE**   **Data-Link Communications**   It is important to understand that data-link layer protocols are not concerned with the delivery of packets to their final destination, unless the destination is on the same network as the source. Data-link layer protocols are limited to communication with systems on the same LAN. The hardware address in a data-link layer protocol header

always refers to a computer on the same local network, even if the data's ultimate destination is a system on another network. It is the network layer protocol that is responsible for communications with other networks, as you will learn later in this chapter.

- **Network layer protocol identification** A computer can use multiple protocols at the network layer, and the data-link layer protocol frame usually contains a code that specifies which network layer protocol generated the data in the packet, so that the data-link layer protocol on the receiving system can pass the data to the appropriate protocol at its own network layer.

- **Error detection** To ensure that packets arrive at their destinations intact, data-link layer protocols typically include an error detection mechanism, which takes the form of a **cyclical redundancy check (CRC)** computation performed on the payload data by the transmitting system, the results of which are included in the frame's footer. On receiving the packet, the receiving system performs the same computation and compares its results to those in the footer. If the results match, the data has been transmitted successfully. If they do not, the receiving system assumes that the packet is corrupted and discards it.

Media Access Control

The computers on a LAN usually share a common network medium, making it possible for computers on the network to transmit data at the same time. When this happens, a packet **collision** occurs, and the data in both packets is lost. One of the primary functions of the data-link layer protocol in this type of network is to provide a mechanism that regulates access to the network medium. This mechanism, called a **Media Access Control (MAC)** mechanism, provides each computer with an equal opportunity to transmit its data, while minimizing the occurrence of packet collisions. The MAC mechanism is one of the primary defining characteristics of a data-link layer protocol.

> **NOTE MAC Mechanisms** For more detailed information about these MAC mechanisms, see Chapter 4, "Data-Link Layer Protocols."

Physical Layer Specifications

The MAC mechanisms used on LANs can function only on networks that comply with physical layer specifications included in the data-link layer protocol standards. For example, if an Ethernet network exceeds the maximum cable length restrictions in the protocol standard, the computers cannot reliably detect collisions when they occur. MAC is one of the primary reasons that LAN data-link layer protocols such as Ethernet and Token Ring encompass the physical layer as well. Because WAN links are usually point-to-point connections between two systems only, they do not need MAC mechanisms, so the data-link layer protocols that WANs use, such as PPP and **Serial Line Internet Protocol (SLIP)**, are not bound to specific physical layer standards.

The Network Layer

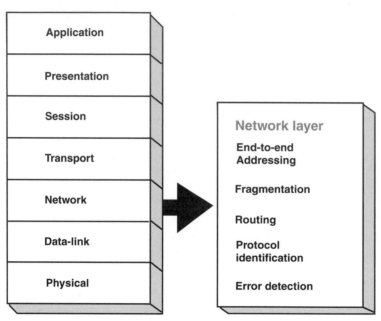

At first glance, the **network layer** seems to duplicate some of the functions of the data-link layer, such as addressing. This is not so, however, because data-link layer protocols function only on the local LAN, while network layer protocols are responsible for end-to-end communications. This means that the protocol is responsible for a packet's complete journey from the system that created it to its final destination. The source and destination computers can be on the same LAN, on different LANs in the same building, or on LANs separated by thousands of miles. When you connect to a server on the Internet, for example, the packets your computer creates might pass through dozens of different networks before reaching their destination. These networks might use different data-link layer protocols, but they all use the same network layer protocol.

Like the data-link layer protocol, the network layer protocol encapsulates the data it receives from the transport layer above it by applying a header, as shown in Figure 1-7. The PDU created by the network layer protocol, which consists of the transport layer data plus the network layer header, is called a **datagram**.

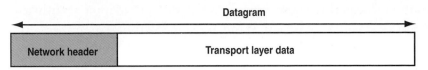

Figure 1-7   The network layer protocol packages transport layer information into a datagram.

There are three network layer protocols used on data networks today. The **Internet Protocol (IP)** is the cornerstone of the **Transmission Control Protocol/Internet Protocol (TCP/IP)** suite and is the most commonly used network layer protocol. Novell NetWare has its own network layer protocol, called **Internetwork Packet Exchange (IPX)**. The **NetBIOS Enhanced User Interface (NetBEUI)** protocol is used on some small Microsoft Windows networks. Most of the functions attributed to the network layer are based on the capabilities of IP.

> **NOTE   Understanding NetBEUI**   NetBEUI is an unusual protocol that does not fit precisely into any one layer of the OSI model. Depending on the resources you consult, you might see NetBEUI referred to as a transport or session layer protocol as well. For the purposes of this course, however, NetBEUI is treated as a network layer counterpart to IP and IPX and is covered in more detail in Chapter 5, "Network Layer Protocols."

The functions associated with the network layer are discussed in the following sections.

Addressing

The network layer protocol header contains source address and destination address fields, just as the data-link layer protocol does. However, in this case, the destination address is the packet's final destination, which might be different from the data-link layer protocol header's destination address. For example, when you type the address of a Web site in your browser, the packet your system generates contains the address of the Web server as its network layer destination, but the data-link layer destination is the address of the router on your LAN that gives you Internet access.

IP has its own addressing system that is completely independent of the computer hardware and separate from the data-link layer addresses. Each computer on an IP network is assigned a 32-bit IP address by an administrator or an automated service. This address identifies both the network on which the computer is located and the computer itself, to uniquely identify any computer on any network. IPX, on the other hand, uses one address to identify the network on which a computer is located, and uses the network interface adapter's hardware address to identify a specific computer on the network. NetBEUI identifies computers using a Network Basic Input/Output System (NetBIOS) name assigned to each system during its installation.

Fragmentation

Network layer datagrams might have to pass through many different networks on the way to their destinations, and the data-link layer protocols used on each network can have different properties and limitations. One limitation is the maximum packet size permitted by the protocol. For example, Token Ring frames can be as large as 4500 bytes, but standard and Fast Ethernet frames are limited to 1500 bytes. When a 4500-byte datagram originating on a Token Ring network routes to an Ethernet network, the network layer protocol must split it into pieces no larger than 1500 bytes each, as shown in Figure 1-8. This process is called *fragmentation*.

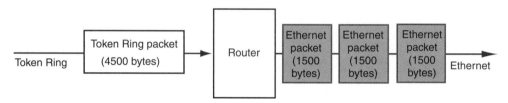

Figure 1-8   The network layer fragmentation process

During the fragmentation process, the network layer protocol splits the datagram into as many pieces as necessary to make each small enough for transmission using the data-link layer protocol. Each fragment becomes a packet that continues the journey to the network layer destination. The fragments are not reassembled until all of the packets comprising the datagram reach the destination system. In some cases, datagrams might be fragmented, and their fragments might have to be fragmented again repeatedly before reaching their destination.

Routing

Routing is the process of directing a datagram from its source, through an internetwork, to its ultimate destination using the most efficient path possible. On complex internetworks such as the Internet or a large corporate network, there are often many possible routes to a given destination. Network designers deliberately create redundant links so that if one of the routers on the network fails, traffic can still find its way to its destination.

Routers connect the individual LANs that make up an internetwork. The function of a router is to receive incoming traffic from one network and transmit it to a particular destination on another network. There are two types of systems involved in internetwork communications: end systems and intermediate systems. **End systems** are the sources or ultimate destinations of individual packets. Routers are **intermediate systems**. End systems use all seven layers of the OSI model; packets arriving at intermediate systems travel only as high as the network layer. The network layer protocol on the router processes the packet and sends it back down through the stack to be transmitted to its next destination, as shown in Figure 1-9.

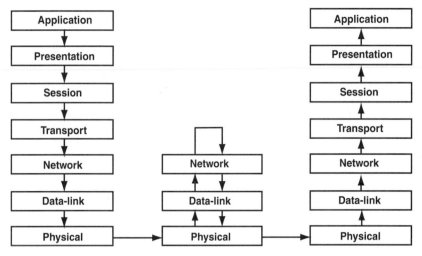

Figure 1-9   The network layer protocol in a router accepts incoming packets and transmits them to the next stop on their journey.

To properly direct packets to their destinations, routers maintain information about the network in tables that they store in memory. The information in the tables can either be entered manually by an administrator or gathered automatically from other routers using specialized routing protocols. A typical routing table entry specifies both the address of another network and the next router that packets should use to get to that network. Routing table entries also contain a metric that rates the comparative efficiency of that particular route. If there are two or more routes to a particular destination, the router selects the more efficient one and passes the datagram down to the data-link layer for transmission to the next **hop** specified in the table entry. On large networks, routing can be an extraordinarily complicated process, but most of it is automated and invisible to the average user.

NOTE   Network Layer Routing   Not all network layer protocols are capable of routing. IP and IPX can both route traffic, but NetBEUI cannot.

Network Layer Error Detection

Earlier in this chapter, you learned that data-link layer protocols include an error detection mechanism, in the form of a CRC value transmitted in the frame's footer. Data-link layer error detection only provides protection for the transmission from one system to another on the same LAN, not for the entire end-to-end transmission. This is why there are error detection mechanisms at the upper layers as well. Comprehensive end-to-end error detection and error correction is more likely to occur at the transport layer, but it is possible for network layer protocols to provide error detection services as well. IP, for example, includes a field in its header that contains a CRC value, but this CRC is calculated on the IP header fields only, not on the payload that the protocol has received from the transport layer.

Transport Layer Protocol Identification

Just as the data-link layer header contains a code identifying the network layer protocol that generated the payload it carries in its frames, the network layer header identifies the transport layer protocol from which it received the payload in its datagrams. With this information, the receiving system can pass the incoming datagrams to the correct transport layer protocol.

The Transport Layer

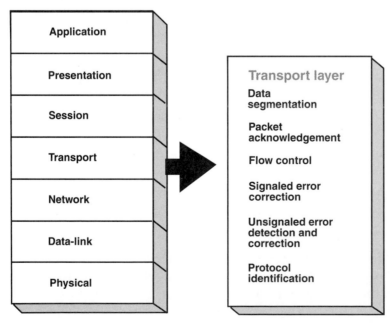

The **transport layer** protocols provide services that complement those provided by the network layer. Together, a network layer protocol and a transport layer protocol must achieve the quality of service required by the application that is using the network. In most cases, the transport and network layer protocols used to transmit data are thought of as a matched pair, as in the case of the TCP/IP combination, from which the TCP/IP protocol suite takes its name. This combination includes IP, running at the network layer, and TCP, which runs at the transport layer. However, most protocol suites provide two or more transport layer protocols that provide different levels of service. The alternative to TCP is the **User Datagram Protocol (UDP)**, which is also used in combination with IP. The IPX protocol suite also provides a choice between transport layer protocols, including the **NetWare Core Protocol (NCP)** and **Sequenced Packet Exchange (SPX)**.

> **NOTE** **Transport Layer Services** For more information on the services provided by the TCP/IP and IPX transport layer protocols, see Chapter 6, "Transport Layer Protocols."

Connection-Oriented and Connectionless Protocols

In most cases, the difference between the protocols within a particular protocol suite provided at the transport layer is that some are connection-oriented and some are connectionless. A **connection-oriented protocol** is one in which the two communicating systems exchange messages to establish a connection before they transmit any application data. When a connection is established, it is assigned a logical channel identifier, which the systems can then use to reference that particular connection. The establishment of the connection ensures that the systems are both active and ready to exchange data. TCP, for example, is a connection-oriented protocol. When you use a Web browser to connect to an Internet server, the browser and the server first perform what is known as a three-way handshake to establish the connection. Only then does the browser transmit the address of the desired Web page to the server. When the data transmission is complete, the systems perform a similar handshake to break down the connection.

Connection-oriented protocols can also provide services such as data segmentation, packet acknowledgment, flow control, and end-to-end error detection and correction. Systems generally use this type of protocol to transmit relatively large amounts of information that can't tolerate even a single bit error, such as data or program files, and these additional services ensure the correct transmission of the data. Because of these services, connection-oriented protocols are often said to be "reliable," a technical term referring to the fact that each packet transmitted using the protocol has been acknowledged by the recipient, and has been verified as having been transmitted without error. The drawback of this type of protocol is that it greatly increases the amount of control data exchanged by the two systems. In addition to the extra messages needed to establish and terminate the connection, the header applied by a connection-oriented protocol is substantially larger than that of a connectionless protocol. For example, in the case of the TCP/IP transport layer protocols, TCP uses a 20-byte header, while UDP, a connectionless protocol, uses only an 8-byte header.

A **connectionless protocol** is one in which there is no preliminary communication between the two systems before the transmission of application data. The sender simply transmits its data to the destination without knowing if the receiving system is ready to receive data, or whether it even exists. Systems generally use connectionless protocols, such as UDP, for brief transactions that consist only of single requests and responses, or for the transmission of data that can tolerate the loss of a few bits, such as an audio or video stream. In the case of a request/response transaction, the response from the recipient functions as a tacit acknowledgment of the transmission.

Transport Layer Functions

Transport layer protocols provide a variety of functions, depending on criteria such as the following:

- Whether it is a connection-oriented or connectionless protocol

- The quality of service required by the application generating the data

- The services provided by the network layer protocol

Some of these services are described in general terms in the following sections. For more detailed descriptions of how specific protocols perform these functions, see Chapter 6, "Transport Layer Protocols."

Data Segmentation

When applications generate data that will be transmitted over a network, they are not concerned with, or even aware of, the nature of the network to which the computer is connected. Therefore, connection-oriented transport layer protocols often have to split the data stream for a particular network transaction into sections suitable for transmission via individual packets. This process is called *segmentation*.

The segmentation process is critical to many of the other functions provided by the connection-oriented transport layer protocols, because it is during segmentation that the individual packets are numbered for future reference. The packet acknowledgment, flow control, and error correction mechanisms in the transport layer protocol use these segment numbers to specify which packets have to be retransmitted. In addition, the protocol uses the segment numbers to reconstitute the original application message when packets arrive at the destination out of sequence.

Packet Acknowledgment

Packet acknowledgment is the mechanism that ensures the proper delivery of each data segment by a connection-oriented protocol. During the data segmentation process, an application layer data stream is divided into segments, and each segment is numbered. The segments are then stored on the transmitting system and are not deleted until the receiving system has acknowledged their receipt.

Packet acknowledgment implementations can take several forms. In some cases, the receiving system generates a separate acknowledgment message for each segment it receives. This method is effective, but it also generates a great deal of additional network traffic. Today, most connection-oriented protocols enable the receiving system to acknowledge multiple packets with a single message.

Flow Control

Flow control is a mechanism that enables a receiving system to regulate the speed at which the transmitting system sends packets. This prevents the receiving system from being overwhelmed by too many packets. The network interface adapter in every computer has a buffer in which it can store incoming packets, where they wait until the system is ready to process them. If too many packets arrive too quickly, the buffer fills up, and some packets must be discarded. To prevent this from happening, the receiving system sends a message to the transmitting system, requesting that it slow down the transmission rate of packets for a particular logical channel identifier. When there is sufficient room in the buffer again, the receiving system can send another message requesting that the transmitting system speed up its transmissions.

Flow control messages can take the form of separate packets dedicated to that purpose, but the TCP protocol integrates the flow control mechanism into its packet acknowledgment messages.

Transport Layer Error Detection and Correction

Transport layer protocols often provide the most comprehensive error detection service of the entire protocol stack and provide error correction as well. Earlier in this chapter, you learned that data-link layer protocols often use a CRC calculation to detect transmission errors, but these protocols cannot correct the errors. Instead, they rely on the transport layer protocol to retransmit packets that have been lost or corrupted. This type of error is called a **signaled error**, because another protocol informs the transport layer protocol which packets must be retransmitted.

An **unsignaled error** is one that has not already been detected by a protocol at another layer; for these types of errors, the transport layer protocol must perform the entire process. To detect errors, transport layer protocols typically use a CRC calculation on the entire packet, including the payload received from the application layer. This is the only end-to-end error connection mechanism that includes the application data. To correct errors, the receiving system generates messages that acknowledge the receipt of all packets except those that have failed the CRC check or never arrived at the destination, and it sends the messages to the transmitting system, which then resends the unacknowledged packets.

Application Layer Protocol Identification

Transport layer protocols typically provide a path through the layers above, just as network and data-link layer protocols do. The headers for both TCP and UDP, for example, include port numbers that identify the applications from which the packet originated and for which it is destined.

The Session Layer

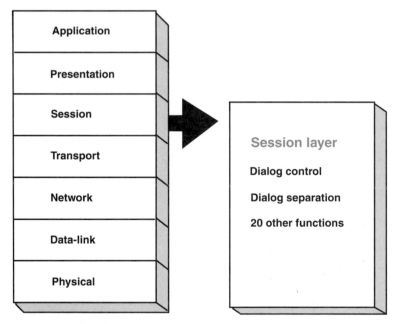

The **session layer** is the point at which the actual protocols used on networks begin to differ substantially from the OSI model. There are no separate protocols at the session layer, as there are at the lower layers. Instead, session layer functions are integrated into protocols that also include functions attributed to other layers, such as presentation, application, and sometimes even transport. Some of the protocols that provide session layer services are as follows:

- **Network Basic Input/Output System (NetBIOS)**   An interface and protocol, developed by IBM, that provides services spanning the transport, session, presentation, and application layers.

- **NetBIOS Enhanced User Interface (NetBEUI)**   An extension of NetBIOS used as a LAN communications protocol by Microsoft products. NetBEUI was the default networking protocol in early versions of Windows, such as Microsoft Windows NT 3.1 and Microsoft Windows for Workgroups.

- **AppleTalk Data Stream Protocol (ADSP)**   A protocol in the AppleTalk suite that is responsible for establishing reliable connections among networked computers.

- **Printer Access Protocol (PAP)**   A protocol that provides computers on AppleTalk networks with access to Postscript printers.

The transport, network, data-link, and physical layers are concerned with the efficient transmission of data across the network, but once you reach the session layer, factors such as addressing, packet acknowledgment, error detection, and flow control are completely transcended. All of the functions in the top three layers of the OSI model work under the assumption that the lower layers are capable of delivering messages in an efficient and timely manner.

Because of its name, the session layer is often mistakenly described as being concerned with the network logon process (which establishes a "session" between a client and a server) and with the security issues related to the client/server connection. In fact, the session layer does not have a single primary function, as the lower layers do. For example, you could say that the primary function of the network and transport layers is to send data from one end system to another with a specific quality of service. The session layer, by contrast, is more of a "toolbox," containing a variety of functions. The OSI model standard defines 22 services for the session layer, many of which are concerned with the ways in which networked systems exchange information. Many of these services are quite obscure to everyone except application developers.

> **NOTE**   *Session Layer Redundancy*   At the time when both the ISO and the CCITT were developing their own standards for what became the OSI model, there were two different sets of functions for the session layer. As a result of the compromise between the bodies, the final OSI model standard includes two tools each for many of the functions the session layer can perform.

Some of the most important session layer functions are concerned with the exchange of data by the two end systems involved in a connection. However, the session layer is not concerned with the nature of the data being exchanged, but rather with the exchange process itself, which is called a *dialog*. Maintaining an efficient dialog between connected computers is more difficult than it might appear at first. Consider, for example, a connection between Computer A and Computer B. Computer A transmits a series of packets to Computer B, which contain segments of an application layer message. Computer A then receives a reply from Computer B stating that it has not received the final segment. How does Computer A know when Computer B sent the reply? Computer B could have generated the reply after Computer A transmitted the final segment, indicating that the segment was lost or corrupted, and that Computer A must retransmit it. However, it is also conceivable that Computer B sent the reply before Computer A transmitted the final segment, and that Computer B has now received the segment and does not require it to be retransmitted.

This is a simple example of what is called a *collision case*. This example, at worst, could result in the needless retransmission of one packet. However, if this type of confusion were to occur repeatedly throughout the dialog, the results could be substantially more severe. The session layer functions include mechanisms that help the systems maintain an efficient dialog. The most important of these services are dialog control and dialog separation.

Dialog Control

The exchange of information between two systems on the network is a dialog, and dialog control is the selection of a mode that the systems will use to exchange messages. When the dialog is begun, the systems can choose one of two modes: two-way alternate (TWA) mode or two-way simultaneous (TWS) mode. In TWA mode, the two systems exchange a data token, and only the computer in possession of the token is permitted to transmit data. This eliminates problems caused by messages that cross in transit. TWS mode is more complex, because there is no token and both systems can transmit at any time, even simultaneously.

> **NOTE** **Session Layer Tokens**   The dialog control tokens used by session layer functions are not related to the token frames used in the token passing MAC mechanism, or to the Token Ring data-link layer protocol.

Dialog Separation

Dialog separation is the process of creating checkpoints in a data stream that enable communicating systems to synchronize their functions. The difficulty of checkpointing depends on whether the dialog is using TWA or TWS mode. Systems involved in a TWA dialog perform minor synchronizations that require only a single exchange of checkpointing messages, but systems using a TWS dialog perform a major synchronization using a major/activity token.

The Presentation Layer

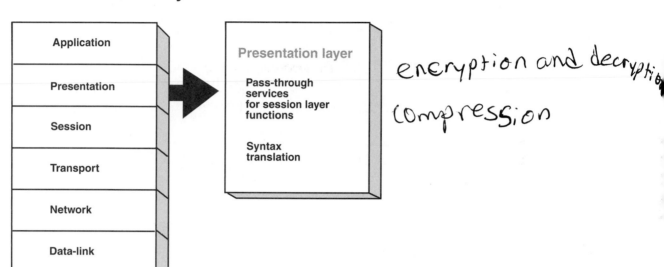

encryption and decryption
compression

Each layer of the OSI reference model can communicate only with the layers directly above and below it. For an application layer protocol to request services from the session layer, it must go through the **presentation layer**. For this reason, the presentation layer provides pass-through services for all 22 session layer functions, so that application layer protocols can issue requests for session layer functions to the presentation layer, which passes the requests down to the session layer.

Although the presentation layer does not change the session layer functions as it relays requests between the layers, it does perform a crucial translation process that is the layer's only native function. When an application generates a message, it uses its own native syntax. However, this syntax might be different from that of the application that will receive the message. The difference between the two could result from the use of compression or encryption on one of the systems, or from a different bit-encoding method.

Test your
knowledge of
OSI model
layers and
their functions
by completing
Exercise 1-2,
"OSI Layer
Functions,"
now.

To resolve this incompatibility, the presentation layer can translate the syntax of a message. The translation occurs in two stages. The presentation layer on the sending system translates the message from its native form, which is called an **abstract syntax**, to a **transfer syntax**, which is a common syntax agreed upon by the two connected end systems. After the message is transmitted, the receiving system translates the message from the transfer syntax to that computer's own abstract syntax.

The Application Layer

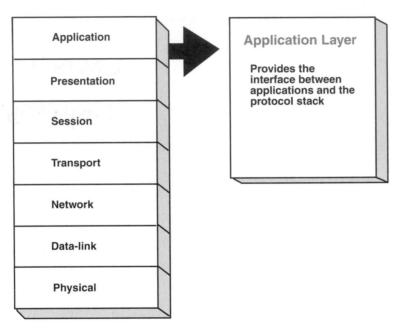

The **application layer**, at the top of the protocol stack, is the entrance point that programs use to access the OSI model and use network resources. All of the processes operating at the other layers are triggered when a program calls for the services of an application layer protocol. For example, an e-mail client application provides users with tools to create a message, but it does not have actual networking capabilities built into it. When the client is ready to send the e-mail message, it calls a function of the **Simple Mail Transfer Protocol (SMTP)**, which is the application layer protocol that most e-mail programs use. SMTP then generates an appropriately formatted message and starts it on its way down through the layers of the protocol stack.

There are many application layer protocols—more than at any other layer of the OSI model. Some of the most commonly used application layer protocols, most of which will be discussed later in this course, are as follows:

- Dynamic Host Configuration Protocol (DHCP)

- Domain Name System (DNS)

- File Transfer Protocol (FTP)

- Hypertext Transfer Protocol (HTTP)

- Internet Mail Access Protocol (IMAP)

- Network File System (NFS)

- Open Shortest Path First (OSPF)

- Post Office Protocol (POP)

- Routing Information Protocol (RIP)

- Simple Network Management Protocol (SNMP)

- Simple Mail Transfer Protocol (SMTP)

Application layer protocols often include session and presentation layer functions, which is why there are virtually no dedicated presentation or session layer protocols. As a result, a typical packet is encapsulated four times before being transmitted over the network, by protocols running at the application, transport, network, and data-link layers.

Test your knowledge of protocols and the OSI model layers at which they operate by completing Exercise 1-3, "Protocols and the OSI Model," now.

Applications and application layer protocols are integrated to varying degrees. In the case of the e-mail client mentioned earlier, the client program is a separate application, and SMTP is implemented as part of the TCP/IP protocol suite. However, in other cases, the application layer protocol is indistinguishable from the application. For example, the FTP and Telnet protocols are applications in themselves.

SUMMARY

- Computer networks use signals to transmit data, and protocols are the languages computers use to communicate.

- Protocols provide a variety of communications services to computers on a network.

- Local area networks (LANs) usually connect computers using a shared, baseband medium, and wide area networks (WANs) link distant networks using point-to-point connections.

- The Open Systems Interconnection (OSI) reference model consists of seven layers: physical, data-link, network, transport, session, presentation, and application.

- The OSI model layers do not correspond exactly to the protocol stacks used on actual networks because the protocols predate the model.

- The physical layer defines the nature of the network medium, how it is installed, and the type of signaling devices used.

- The data-link layer protocols used on LANs include physical layer specifications.

- The network and transport layer protocols work together to provide an end-to-end communication service that achieves the quality of service required by the application requesting network services.

- The functions of the session, presentation, and application layers are often combined into a single application layer protocol.

- Signaling protocols are used to transmit data as 1's and 0's

EXERCISES

Exercise 1-1: Defining Networking Terms

Match the concepts on the left with the definitions on the right.

1. Broadband *B*
2. Circuit switching *D*
3. Baseband *E*
4. Topology *A*
5. Cell switching *C*

The pattern used to install a network medium

A medium that carries multiple signals simultaneously

A network in which messages are split into equal-sized pieces before transmission

A network in which a connection is established before any data is transmitted

A medium that carries only one signal

Exercise 1-2: Identifying OSI Layer Functions

For each of the functions listed below, specify the OSI model layer with which it is associated.

1. Dialog separation - *session*
2. Syntax translation - *presentation*
3. Routing - *network*
4. Segmentation - *transport*
5. Differential Manchester signaling - ~~*network*~~ *physical*

application
presentation
session
transport
network
data-link
physical

Exercise 1-3: Associating Protocols with OSI Model Layers

For each of the protocols listed below, specify the OSI model layer with which it is most closely associated.

1. Ethernet *physical* ✓
2. SMTP *application* ✓
3. SPX *network* ✓
4. IPX *transport* ✗
5. Token Ring *physical* ✓
6. UDP *transport* ✓
7. IP *network* ✓
8. NCP *network* ✓
9. SNMP *application* ✓
10. TCP *presentation/session* ✓

REVIEW QUESTIONS

1. At which of the following OSI model layers do protocols not provide error correction capabilities? Choose all answers that are correct.

   a. Data-link *yes*

   b. Transport *yes*

   c. Session *no*

   d. Presentation *no*

2. Which of the following OSI model layers includes pass-through services for the session layer functions?

   a. Application *n*

   b. Transport *n*

   c. Presentation *yes*

   d. Physical *no*

3. Which layer of the OSI model always provides the address of a packet's final destination?

   a. Network

   b. Transport

   c. Data-link

   d. Physical

4. Which of the following protocols are connectionless? Choose all answers that are correct.

   a. TCP

   b. UDP

   c. IP

   d. IPX

   e. SPX

5. Which of the following terms describes a network running the Ethernet protocol? Choose all answers that are correct.

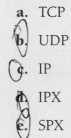

   a. Baseband

   b. Circuit-switching

   c. Token passing

   d. LAN

6. Which of the following organizations is responsible for publishing the TCP/IP protocol standards?

   a. IEEE

   b. IETF

   c. ISO

   d. ITU-T

7. Which of the following protocols do not include physical layer specifications? Choose all answers that are correct.

a. Ethernet

b. PPP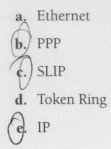

c. SLIP

d. Token Ring

e. IP

CASE SCENARIOS

Scenario 1-1: Diagnosing a Network Layer Problem

You receive a call from one of your clients who says he has a network layer problem on his three-segment internetwork. You ask how he knows it is a network layer problem. The client says that his users can access all of the servers on the company internetwork, but they can't access the Internet. Is the client right or wrong in assuming that there is a network layer problem? Why?

a. The client is wrong, because a network layer problem would prevent the users from accessing servers on other LANs.

b. The client is wrong, because the users should be able to access the Internet, despite a network layer problem.

c. The client is right, because Internet access is provided by a router, which has probably malfunctioned.

d. There is no way to tell if the client is right or wrong from the information given.

Scenario 1-2: Troubleshooting an Internetwork Problem

You are troubleshooting a communications problem on your company's Ethernet internetwork that consists of five TCP/IP LANs, all connected to a sixth LAN, which is used to provide a transit path between all other LANs. This type of LAN is called a backbone by routers. Mark, a user on one of the LANs, can connect to computers on the same LAN but not to computers on any of the other LANs. No other users have reported problems. Which one of the following could be the problem?

   a. A network layer problem on the backbone network

   b. A physical layer problem on Mark's LAN

   c. A network layer problem on Mark's LAN

   d. A physical layer problem on the backbone network

CHAPTER 2
NETWORK CABLING

Upon completion of this chapter, you will be able to:

- List the cabling topologies used to build local area networks (LANs).

- Name the types of cables used to build LANs.

- Understand the grading systems used for the various cable types.

- Describe how to install cables externally, secure them in place, and run them around common obstacles.

- Explain the steps involved in an internal cable installation.

- Describe the wiring of a crossover cable.

- Connect bulk cables to jacks using a punchdown block tool.

- Attach RJ-45 connectors to make patch cables.

This chapter examines the primary hardware component used to build a typical LAN: the cables. Most LANs use cables for the network medium, and there are several different types, including coaxial, twisted pair, and fiber optic. It is essential for you to understand these cable types, their strengths and weaknesses, and how they are installed.

UNDERSTANDING NETWORK CABLES

Most LANs use some form of cable as their network medium. Although wireless media are more capable now than ever before, cables are more reliable and generally provide faster transmission speeds than other media. Selecting a cable type for a LAN is largely based on which data-link layer protocol the LAN will use. Data-link layer protocols, such as Ethernet and Token Ring, provide several cable specifications from which to choose. Each specification identifies which type of cable to use, which grade of cable to use, and the basic guidelines for installing it. Your choice of cable type should be based on the requirements of your installation, the nature of the network site, and, of course, your budget.

Cable Topologies

As explained in Chapter 1, "Networking Basics," the physical topology of a network is the pattern in which the cable or other network medium connects the computers and other devices together. A LAN's topology is directly related to the type of cable it uses. You cannot select a particular type of cable and install it using just any topology. However, you can create individual LANs using a different cable and topology for each LAN and connect them together using devices such as bridges, switches, and routers. When you choose the components with which to build a LAN, the topology should be one of the most important criteria for selecting a cable type. The three primary topologies used to build LANs are as follows:

- Bus

- Star

- Ring

You should also be familiar with the following additional topologies:

- Hierarchical star

- Mesh

- Wireless

> **NOTE   Exam Objectives**   Objective 1.1 for the Network+ exam calls for students to "recognize the following logical or physical network topologies given a schematic diagram or description: star/hierarchical, bus, mesh, ring, and wireless."

The Bus Topology

A network that uses the **bus** topology is one in which the computers are connected in a single line, with each system cabled to the next system, as shown in Figure 2-1. The original Ethernet specification called for the use of a bus topology with coaxial cable, a type of network that is rarely seen today. The cabling of an Ethernet bus network can take two forms: thick or thin. **Thick Ethernet** networks use a single length of coaxial cable, and the computers are connected to the coaxial cable using smaller individual cables called **attachment unit interface (AUI)** cables (sometimes called *transceiver cables*), as shown on the top half of Figure 2-1. **Thin Ethernet** networks use separate lengths of a narrower type of coaxial cable, and each length of cable runs from the network interface adapter in one computer to the adapter in the next, as shown in the bottom half of Figure 2-1.

Thick Ethernet

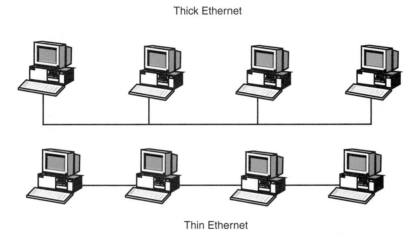

Thin Ethernet

Figure 2-1   Bus topology cabling options

When any one of the computers on a bus network transmits data, the signals travel down the cable in both directions, reaching all of the other systems. A bus network always has two open ends, which must be terminated. **Termination** is the process of installing a resistor pack at each end of the bus to negate the signals that arrive there. Without terminators, the signals reaching the end of the bus would reflect back in the other direction and interfere with the newer signals being transmitted.

The main disadvantage of the bus topology is that a single faulty connector, faulty terminator, or break in the cable affects the functionality of the entire network. Signals that cannot pass beyond a certain point on the cable fail to reach all of the computers beyond that point. In addition, when a component failure splits the network into two segments, each half of the cable also has one unterminated end. On the half of the network that does receive the signals transmitted by each computer, signal reflection garbles the data. This is one of the primary reasons that bus networks are rarely used today.

The Star Topology

While in a bus topology, the computers in a network are connected to each other, the **star** topology uses a central cabling nexus—either a physical layer device called a *hub* or *concentrator*, or a data-link layer device called a *switch*. In a star network, each computer is connected to the hub by a separate cable, as shown in Figure 2-2. Most of the Ethernet LANs today, and many LANs using other protocols as well, use the star topology. Star LANs can use any one of several different cable types, including various grades of twisted-pair and fiber optic cable.

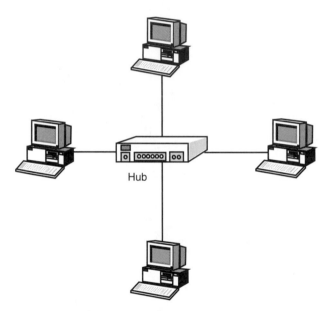

Figure 2-2   The star topology

The **unshielded twisted pair (UTP)** cables used on most Ethernet LANs are usually installed in a star topology. Functionally, a star network uses a shared network medium, just as a bus network does. Despite the fact that each computer connects to the hub with its own cable, the hub propagates all signals entering through its ports out through all of its other ports. Signals transmitted by one computer are therefore received by all other computers on the LAN.

The main advantage of the star topology is that each computer has its own dedicated connection to the hub, providing the network with greater fault tolerance than in a bus network. If a single cable or connector fails, only the computer connected to the hub by that cable is affected. The disadvantage of the star topology is that an additional piece of hardware—the hub—is required to implement it. If the hub fails, the entire network goes down. However, this is a relatively rare occurrence because hubs are simple devices that are usually located in a protected environment, such as a data center or server closet.

The Hierarchical Star Topology

It might seem as though the size of an Ethernet network using the star topology is limited to the number of ports in the hub. However, if your network grows until all of the hub ports are filled, you can still expand it by adding a second hub, and in some cases, a third and a fourth. To add a second hub to a star network, you connect it to the first hub using a standard cable and a special port in one of the hubs called an *uplink port*. This creates what is known as a **hierarchical star** *topology* (sometimes known as a *branching tree* network), as shown in Figure 2-3. A standard 10-Mbps Ethernet network can support up to four hubs connected in this fashion, but **a Fast Ethernet** network can generally support only two.

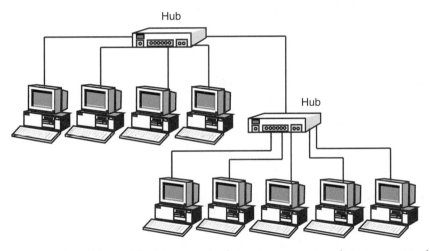

Figure 2-3   A hierarchical star network uses two or more interconnected hubs.

The Ring Topology

In terms of signal transmissions, the **ring** topology is like a bus in that each computer is logically connected to the next. However, in a ring network, the two ends are connected instead of being terminated, thus forming an endless loop. This enables a signal originating on one computer to travel around the ring to all of the other computers and eventually back to its point of origin. Networks using data-link layer protocols such as Token Ring, which use the token passing Media Access Control (MAC) mechanism, are wired using a ring topology. The most important thing to understand about the ring topology is that, in most cases, it is strictly a logical construction, not a physical one. To be more precise, the ring exists in the wiring of the network, but not in the cabling.

NOTE Cabling vs. Wiring   *A cable is a device that contains a number of signal conductors, usually in the form of separate wires. A twisted-pair cable, for example, contains eight individual wires within a single sheath.*

When you look at a network that uses the ring topology, you might be puzzled to see what looks like a star. In fact, the cables for a ring network connect to a hub and physically, they take the form of a star. The ring topology is actually implemented logically, using the wiring inside the cables, as shown in Figure 2-4. Ring networks use a special type of hub, called a **Multistation Access Unit (MAU),** which receives data through one port and transmits it out through each of the others in turn (not simultaneously, as with an Ethernet hub).

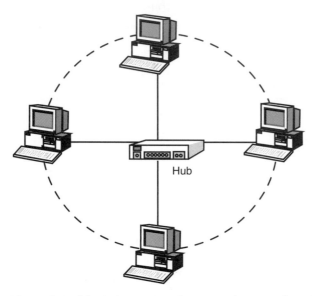

Figure 2-4   Most ring networks use a ring topology in a logical sense only; the cables are actually arranged in the form of a star.

For example, when the computer connected to port number 3 in an eight-port MAU transmits a data packet, the MAU receives the packet and transmits it out through port number 4 only. When the computer connected to port number 4 receives the packet, it immediately returns it to the MAU, which then transmits it out through port number 5, and so on. This process continues until the MAU has transmitted the packet to each computer on the ring. Finally, the computer that generated the packet receives it again and is then responsible for removing it from the ring. If you were to remove the wire pairs from the sheaths of the cables that comprise a ring network, you would have a circuit running from the MAU to each computer and back to the MAU, forming a ring.

The fact that the ring topology's physical design is that of a star makes it possible for the network to function even when a cable or connector fails. The MAU contains circuitry that removes a malfunctioning workstation from the ring, but still preserves the logical topology. By comparison, a network that is literally cabled as a ring would have no MAU, so a cable break or connector failure would cause the network to stop functioning completely. The one commonly used protocol that does include an option for a physical ring topology, **Fiber Distributed Data Interface (FDDI),** exemplifies the use of a double ring, which consists of two separate physical rings with traffic flowing in opposite directions. When computers are connected to both rings, the network can still function despite a cable failure.

The Mesh Topology

The **mesh** topology, in the context of local area networking, is more of a theoretical concept than an actual real-world solution. On a mesh LAN, each computer has a direct, dedicated connection to every other computer, as shown in Figure 2-5. This is also known as a *fully connected topology*. In reality, this topology only exists on a two-node LAN. For a mesh network with three computers or more, it would be necessary to equip each computer with a separate network interface adapter for every other computer on the network. Thus, for a five-node network, each computer would require four network interface adapters, and the LAN would consist of 20 separate connections, which is certainly not practical. A ten-node mesh network would consist of 40 separate connections. A mesh LAN would provide excellent fault tolerance, however, as there is no single point of failure that can affect more than one pair of computers.

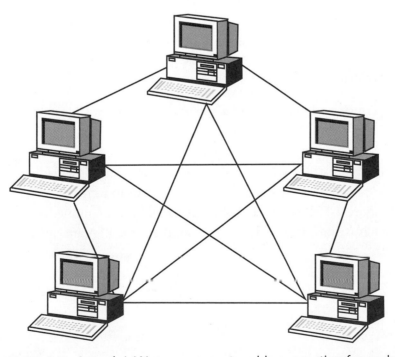

Figure 2-5 A mesh LAN uses a separate cable connection for each pair of computers.

NOTE   Calculating Mesh LAN Connections   To calculate the number
of connections required for a mesh LAN, use the formula $n(n-1)/2$, where n
is the number of computers on the LAN.

In internetworking, you can actually use the mesh topology as a cabling
arrangement. A mesh internetwork has multiple paths between two destinations,
made possible by the use of redundant routers, as shown in Figure 2-6. This
topology is common on large enterprise networks because it enables networks to
tolerate numerous possible malfunctions, including router, hub, and cable
failures. In nearly all cases, when you see a reference to a mesh topology in actual
use, this is the application being cited.

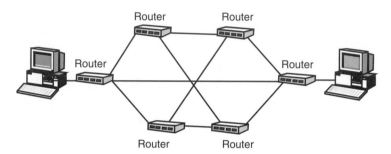

Figure 2-6   Internetworks can use a mesh topology to provide redundant paths
between networks.

Wireless Topologies

The term *topology* usually refers to the arrangement of cables that forms a
network, but it doesn't have to. Although wireless networks use what are called
unbounded media, the computers still use specific patterns to communicate with
each other. Wireless LANs (WLANs) have two basic topologies: the ad hoc
topology and the infrastructure topology.

An **ad hoc** topology consists of two or more wireless devices communicating
directly with each other. The signals generated by WLAN network interface
adapters are omnidirectional out to a range that is governed by environmental
factors, as well as the nature of the equipment involved. This range is called a
basic service area (BSA). When two wireless devices come within range of each
other, as shown in Figure 2-7, they can connect and communicate, immediately
forming a two-node network. Wireless devices within the same BSA are called a
basic service set (BSS).

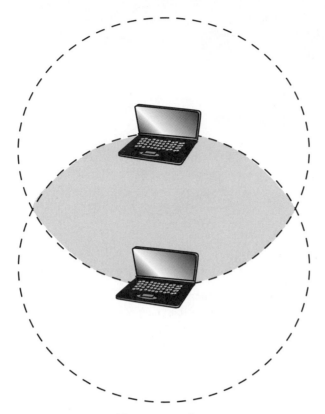

Figure 2-7   An ad hoc network

Other wireless devices coming within the transmission range of the first two can also participate in the network. Ad hoc networking is not transitive, however. A wireless device that comes within range of another device, but still lies outside the range of a third, can only communicate with the device in its range.

> **NOTE   Using Ad Hoc Networks**   The ad hoc topology is most often used on home networks, or for very small businesses that have no cabled network components at all.

An **infrastructure topology** uses a wireless device called an *access point* as a bridge between wireless devices and a standard cabled network. An access point is a device that connects to an Ethernet network (or other cabled network) with a cable, but that also contains a wireless transceiver. Other wireless devices coming within range of the access point can communicate with the cabled network (as well as other wireless devices), just as though they were connected by a cable themselves, as shown in Figure 2-8. The access point functions as a transparent bridge, effectively extending the cabled LAN to include the wireless devices.

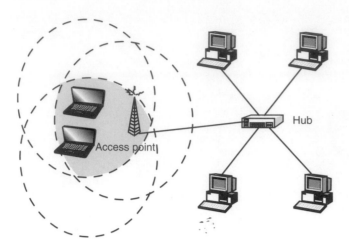

Figure 2-8   An infrastructure network

NOTE   Infrastructure Network Communications   On an infrastructure network, wireless devices communicate only with the access point; they do not communicate with each other directly. Therefore, even if two wireless computers are within range of each other, they must still use the access point to communicate.

Most business networks use the infrastructure topology because it provides complete connectivity between wireless devices and the cabled network.

Cabling Standards

Prior to 1991, there were no standards defining the nature of the cabling used for LANs, other than the physical layer specifications in the data-link layer protocol standards and materials created by manufacturers of specific networking products. This resulted in hardware incompatibilities and in confusion for cable installers. It was eventually recognized that the networking industry needed a standard defining a cabling system that could support a variety of different networking technologies. To address this need, the American National Standards Institute (ANSI), the Electronic Industries Alliance (EIA), and the Telecommunications Industry Association (TIA), along with a consortium of telecommunications companies, developed a document called the ANSI/EIA/TIA-568 Commercial Building Telecommunications Cabling Standard. This document was revised in 1995, and again in 2001, and is now known as ANSI/TIA/EIA-T568-B.

The T568-B standard defines a structured cabling system for voice and data communications in office environments that has a usable life span of at least 10 years, that supports the products of multiple technology vendors, and that can use any of the following cable types:

- Unshielded twisted pair (UTP) (100 ohm, 22 or 24 AWG)

- **Shielded twisted pair (STP)** (150 ohm)

- Multimode optical fiber (62.5/125 mm)

- Singlemode optical fiber (8.3/125 mm)

For each cable type, the standard defines the following elements:

- Cable characteristics and technical criteria determining the cable's performance level

- Topology and cable segment length specifications

- Connector specifications and pinouts

The standard also includes specifications for the installation of the cable within the building space. In doing this, the standard divides the building into the following subsystems:

- **Building entrance**   The location where the building's internal cabling interfaces with outside cabling

- **Telecommunications closet**   The location of localized telecommunications equipment such as the interface between the horizontal cabling and the backbone

- **Equipment room**   The location of equipment providing the same functions as that in a telecommunications closet, but which might be more complex

- **Backbone cabling**   The cabling that connects the building's various equipment rooms, telecommunications closets, and the building entrance, as well as connections between buildings in a campus network environment

- **Horizontal cabling**   The cabling and other hardware used to connect the telecommunications closet to the work area

- **Work area**   The components used to connect the telecommunications outlet to the workstation

Thus, a typical cable installation for a modern building might consist of the following elements:

- Cables for external telephone and other services enter through the building entrance and run to the equipment room, which contains the Private Branch Exchange (PBX) system, network servers, and other equipment.

- A backbone network connects the equipment room to various telecommunications closets throughout the building, which contain network connection devices such as hubs, switches, bridges, or routers.

- Horizontal cabling originates in the telecommunications closets and runs out into the work areas, terminating at wall plates.

- The wall plates in the work area are connected to computers and other equipment using patch cables.

In addition to the T568-B standard, there are other TIA/EIA standards that provide guidelines for specific types of cabling within and between the subsystems listed here. Some of these other standards are as follows:

- TIA/EIA-569-A   Commercial Building Standard for Telecommunications Pathways and Spaces

- TIA/EIA-606   Administration Standard for Commercial Telecommunications Infrastructure

- J-STD-607-A   Commercial Building Grounding (Earthing) and Bonding Requirements for Telecommunications

Any contractor that you hire to perform an office cable installation should be familiar with these standards and should be willing to certify that his work conforms to these standards.

Cable Types

Three primary types of cable are used to build LANs: coaxial, twisted-pair, and fiber optic. Coaxial and twisted-pair cables are copper-based and carry electrical signals; fiber optic cables use glass or plastic fibers to carry light signals.

> **NOTE** **Exam Objectives**   Objective 1.5 for the Network+ exam calls for students to "choose the appropriate media type and connectors to add a client to an existing network."

Coaxial Cable

Coaxial cable is so named because it contains two conductors within the sheath. Unlike other two-conductor cables, however, which are usually side-by-side, coaxial cable has one conductor inside the other, as illustrated in Figure 2-9. At the center of the cable is the copper core that actually carries the electrical signals. The core can be solid copper or braided strands of copper. Surrounding the core is a layer of insulation, and surrounding that is the second conductor, typically made of braided copper mesh. This second conductor functions as the cable's ground, which completes the electrical circuit. Finally, the entire assembly is encased in an insulating sheath made of PVC or Teflon.

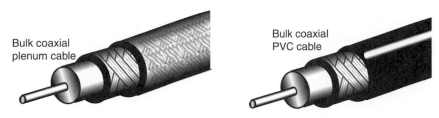

Figure 2-9   Coaxial cable consists of two electrical conductors sharing the same axis, with insulation in between and encased in a protective sheath.

> **CAUTION   Selecting Coaxial Cables**   The outer sheath—also called a casing—of an electrical cable can be made of different types of materials, and the sheath you select for your cables should depend on local building codes and the location of the cables in the network's site. Cables that run through a building's air spaces (called *plenums*) usually must have a sheath made of a material such as Teflon that doesn't generate toxic gases when it burns. Plenum cable costs more than standard PVC-sheathed cable and, because it is less flexible, is somewhat more difficult to install, but it's an important feature that should not be overlooked when you are purchasing cable.

Two types of coaxial cable have been used in local area networking: **RG-8**, also known as thick Ethernet, and **RG-58**, which is known as thin Ethernet. Both of these cable designations can have the suffix /U, indicating that the cable has a solid core, or A/U, indicating that the core is stranded. These two cables are similar in construction but differ in thickness (0.405 inches for RG-8 versus 0.195 inches for RG-58), in the types of connectors they use, and in how they are installed. Both cable types are wired using the bus topology.

Because of their differences in size and flexibility, thick and thin Ethernet cables are installed differently. For a thick Ethernet network, the RG-8 cable usually runs along a floor. On Ethernet networks, the transceiver is an integral component of every network interface, responsible for transmitting and receiving data over the network medium. Thick Ethernet is the only form of Ethernet network that uses a transceiver that is separate from the network interface adapter. The transceiver itself connects to the coaxial cable using a device called a *vampire tap*, named for the metal teeth with which it penetrates the cable sheath to connect to the copper conductor inside. The transceiver is then connected to the network interface adapter in the computer using a separate AUI cable (also called a *transceiver cable*). All of the other Ethernet physical layer standards have their transceivers integrated into the network interface adapter card and do not require separate AUI cables.

In addition to vampire taps, thick Ethernet networks use two other types of connectors. The RG-8 coaxial cable segments are joined using N-connectors, and the AUI cables attach to network interface adapters using a D-shell connector called an AUI connector. These connectors are shown in Figures 2-10 and 2-11.

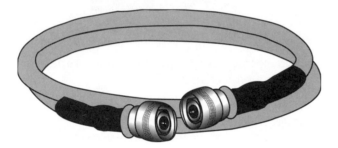

Figure 2-10   The N-connectors used on thick Ethernet networks

Figure 2-11   The AUI connectors used on thick Ethernet networks

The RG-58 cable used for thin Ethernet networks is thinner than RG-8 and much more flexible, so it is possible to run the coaxial cable right up to the computer's network interface, eliminating the need for a separate AUI cable. Thin Ethernet cables use Bayonet-Neill-Concelman (BNC) connectors, as shown in Figure 2-12, which attach to network interface adapters using a T-connector. The T-connector plugs directly into the adapter and has two connectors for attaching cables, as shown in Figure 2-13. This enables each computer to connect to the bus by attaching cables running to its upstream and downstream neighbors.

Figure 2-12   The BNC connectors used on thin Ethernet networks

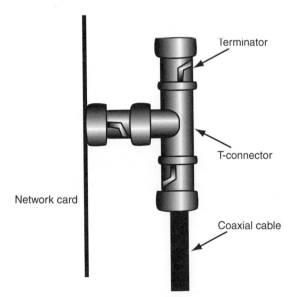

Figure 2-13   The T-connectors used on thin Ethernet networks

NOTE   **BNC Connector Origins**   Various sources cite a number of different meanings for the BNC acronym, including "British Naval Connector" and "Bayonet Nut Connector." In fact, the BNC connector was invented by and named after two engineers—Paul Neill and Carl Concelman, neither of whom was British—who developed the connector in the late 1940s.

Coaxial cable is used today for many applications, most noticeably cable television (CATV) networks. It has fallen out of favor as a LAN medium, however, due to the bus topology's fault-tolerance problems, and to the size and relative inflexibility of the cables, which make them difficult to install and maintain.

Twisted-Pair Cable

Twisted-pair cable installed in a star topology is the most common type of network medium used in LANs today. Most new LANs use UTP cable, but there is also an STP variety for use in environments more prone to electromagnetic interference (EMI). UTP cable contains eight separate copper conductors, as opposed to the two used in coaxial cable. Each conductor is a separate insulated wire, and the eight wires are arranged in four pairs, twisted at different rates. The twists prevent the signals on the different wire pairs from interfering with each other (called **crosstalk**) and also provide resistance to outside interference. The four wire pairs are then encased in a single sheath, as shown in Figure 2-14.

Figure 2-14   A UTP cable has four separate wire pairs, with each pair individually twisted, and all enclosed in a protective sheath.

The connectors used for twisted-pair cables are called **RJ-45** (in which RJ stands for Registered Jack), as shown in Figure 2-15. These connectors are of the same design as the **RJ-11** connectors used on standard telephone cables, except that they have eight electrical contacts instead of four or six.

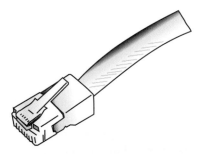

Figure 2-15   An RJ-45 connector used by twisted-pair cables

Twisted-pair cable has replaced coaxial cable in the data networking world
because it has several distinct advantages. First, because it contains eight separate
wires, the cable is more flexible and thus simpler to install than the more
solidly constructed coaxial cable. The second major advantage is that there
are thousands of qualified telephone cable installers who can easily adapt to
installing LAN cables as well. Twisted-pair cable has been used for telephone
installations for decades; its adaptation to LAN use began in the 1980s. In new
construction, the same contractor often installs telephone and LAN cables
simultaneously.

UTP Cable Grades

UTP cable comes in a variety of different grades, called categories by the TIA/EIA.
The categories define the signal frequencies that the various cable types support,
along with other characteristics, such as resistance to certain types of
interference. The higher the category number, the higher the cable quality. These
categories, the cable frequencies, and their applications are listed in Table 2-1.

Table 2-1 **TIA/EIA UTP Cable Categories**

Category	Frequency	Applications
1	Up to 0 MHz	Voice-grade telephone networks only, alarm systems; not for data transmissions
2	Up to 1 MHz	Voice-grade telephone networks, IBM minicomputer and mainframe terminals, ARCnet, LocalTalk
3	Up to 16 MHz	Voice-grade telephone networks, 4-Mbps Token Ring, 10Base-T Ethernet, 100Base-T4 Fast Ethernet, and 100VG-AnyLAN
4	Up to 20 MHz	16-Mbps Token Ring networks
5	Up to 100 MHz	100Base-TX Fast Ethernet, Synchronous Optical Network (SONET), and Optical Carrier (OC3) Asynchronous Transfer Mode (ATM)
5e	Up to 100 MHz	1000Base-T (Gigabit Ethernet) networks
6	Up to 250 MHz	1000Base-T (Gigabit Ethernet) networks

NOTE *Selecting a Cable Grade* When you install a network using a
particular grade of cable, you must be aware of more than just the cable's
rating. You must also be sure that all of the connectors, wall plates, and
patch panels you use for the network are rated for the same category as
the cable. A network connection is only as strong as its weakest link.

Category 3 (CAT3) cable was designed for voice-grade telephone networks and eventually came to be used for Ethernet because a great deal of it was already installed. CAT3 cable is sufficient for 10-Mbps Ethernet networks (where it is called 10Base-T), but it is generally not used for Fast Ethernet (except with special equipment). If you have an existing CAT3 cable installation, you can use it to build a standard Ethernet network, but virtually all new UTP cable installations today use at least Category 5 (CAT5) cable. CAT3 cable is installed today only for telephone networks.

> **NOTE   CAT3 and Fast Ethernet**   There is a seldom-used Fast Ethernet protocol called 100Base-T4 that is designed to use CAT3 UTP cable and run at 100 Mbps. This is possible because 100Base-T4 uses all four wire pairs in the cable, while 100Base-TX uses only two pairs. See Chapter 4, "Data-Link Layer Protocols," for more information.

CAT5 UTP is suitable for 100Base-TX Fast Ethernet networks running at 100 Mbps, as well as for slower protocols. The standard for Category 5e (CAT5e) UTP cable was ratified by the TIA/EIA in 1999 and is intended for use on 1000Base-T networks. 1000Base-T is the Gigabit Ethernet standard designed to run on UTP cable with 100-meter segments, making it a suitable upgrade path from Fast Ethernet. The CAT5e standard does not call for an increase in the frequency supported by the cable over that of CAT5 (both are 100 MHz), but it does elevate the requirements for some of the other CAT5 testing parameters, such as various forms of crosstalk, and adds other new parameters.

> **MORE INFO   Cable Testing**   For more information on cable testing parameters and specifications, see Chapter 11, "Network Troubleshooting Tools."

The Category 6 (CAT6) standard was ratified in 2002 and provides higher performance levels and more stringent specifications for resistance to crosstalk and system noise than CAT5e does. CAT6 cables are rated at a frequency of 250 MHz. A proposed Category 7 standard, which has not yet been ratified, pushes the frequency rating to 600 MHz.

> **NOTE   Using UTP Wire Pairs**   Most Ethernet networks use only two of the four wire pairs in the UTP cable: one for transmitting data and one for receiving it. However, this does not mean that you are free to use the other two pairs for another application, such as voice telephone traffic. The presence of signals on the other two wire pairs is almost certain to increase the amount of crosstalk on the cable, which could lead to signal damage and data loss.

STP Cable Grades

STP cable is similar in construction to UTP but has only two pairs of wires, with additional foil or mesh shielding around each pair. The additional shielding in STP cable makes it preferable to UTP in installations where EMI is a problem, often due to the proximity of electrical equipment.

The properties of the STP cable itself were defined by IBM during the development of the Token Ring protocol. These STP cable types are as follows:

- **Type 1A**   Two pairs of 22 AWG wires, each pair wrapped in foil, with a shield layer (foil or braid) around both pairs, and an outer sheath of either PVC or plenum-rated material

- **Type 2A**   Two pairs of 22 AWG wires, each pair wrapped in foil, with a shield layer (foil or braid) around both pairs, plus four additional pairs of 22 AWG wires for voice communications, within an outer sheath of either PVC or plenum-rated material

- **Type 6A**   Two pairs of 22 AWG wires, with a shield layer (foil or braid) around both pairs, and an outer sheath of either PVC or plenum-rated material

- **Type 9A**   Two pairs of 26 AWG wires, with a shield layer (foil or braid) around both pairs, and an outer sheath of either PVC or plenum-rated material

> **NOTE**   **TIA/EIA STP Standards**   The TIA/EIA-T568-B standard recognizes only two of these STP cable types: Type 1A for use in backbones and horizontal wiring, and Type 6A for patch cables.

Token Ring STP networks also use large, bulky connectors called **IBM data connectors (IDCs)**, shown in Figure 2-16. However, most Token Ring LANs today use UTP cable. All Token Ring networks, both UTP and STP, use a logical ring topology implemented in a MAU, even though the cable is installed in the form of a star.

Figure 2-16   An IBM data connector

Fiber Optic Cable

Fiber optic cable is a completely different type of network medium from twisted-pair or coaxial cable. Instead of carrying signals in the form of electrical voltages over copper conductors, fiber optic cables transmit pulses of light over a glass or plastic filament. Fiber optic cable is completely resistant to the EMI that so easily affects copper-based cables. Fiber optic cables are also much less susceptible than copper cables are to **attenuation**—the tendency of a signal to weaken as it travels over a cable. On copper cables, signals weaken to the point of unreadability after 100 to 500 meters (depending on the type of cable). Some fiber optic cables, by contrast, can span distances up to 120 kilometers without excessive signal degradation. Fiber optic cable is therefore the medium of choice for installations that span long distances or connect buildings on a campus. Fiber optic cable is also inherently more secure than copper cable because it is impossible to tap into a fiber optic link without affecting normal communication over that link.

A fiber optic cable, illustrated in Figure 2-17, consists of a clear glass or clear plastic core that actually carries the light pulses, surrounded by a reflective layer called the cladding. Surrounding the cladding is a plastic spacer layer, a protective layer of woven Kevlar fibers, and an outer sheath. Because the inner surface of the cladding is reflective, the light pulses traveling along the core can bounce off the sides of the cladding. This effect enables the light waves to travel through the cable unobstructed, despite the cable's having been bent around corners.

Figure 2-17   Fiber optic cable has a glass or plastic core surrounded by cladding that reflects the light pulses back and forth along the cable's length.

There are two primary types of fiber optic cable: singlemode and multimode. The thicknesses of the core and of the cladding are the main differences between them. The measurements of these two thicknesses are the primary specifications used to identify each type of cable. **Singlemode fiber** typically has a core diameter of 8.3 microns (millionths of a meter), with the thickness of the core and cladding together being 125 microns. This is generally referred to as 8.3/125 singlemode fiber. Most of the **multimode fiber** used in data networking is rated as 62.5/125.

Singlemode fiber uses a single-wavelength laser as a light source, and as a result, it can carry signals for extremely long distances. For this reason, singlemode fiber is more commonly found in outdoor installations that span long distances, such as telephone and CATV networks. This type of cable is less suited to LAN installations because it is much more expensive than multimode cable and it has a higher bend radius. This means that it cannot be bent around corners as tightly and is therefore more difficult to install.

Multimode fiber, by contrast, uses a light-emitting diode (LED) rather than a laser as a light source and carries multiple wavelengths. Multimode fiber cannot span distances as large as singlemode can, but it bends around corners more easily and is much less expensive.

Fiber optic cables use one of two connectors, the **straight tip (ST)** connector, shown in Figure 2-18, or the **subscriber connector (SC)**, shown in Figure 2-19.

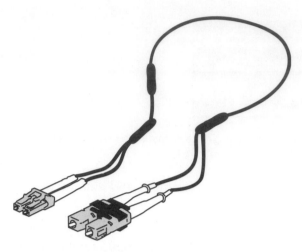

Figure 2-18   The ST connector used with fiber optic cables

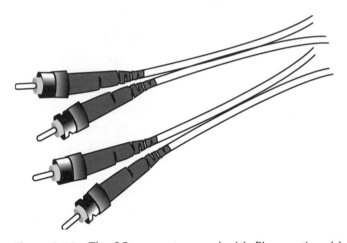

Figure 2-19   The SC connector used with fiber optic cables

Test your knowledge of the cable types used to build networks and their applications by completing Exercise 2-1, "Identifying Network Cable Types," now.

Installing, testing, and maintaining fiber optic cable is completely different from working with copper cables. The tools and testing equipment required for an installation are different, as are the cabling guidelines. Generally speaking, fiber optic cable is more expensive than twisted-pair or coaxial cable, both in materials and labor, although prices have come down in recent years.

Test your knowledge of the limitations imposed on specific cable types by completing Exercise 2-2, "Cable Trouble-shooting," now.

Fiber optic cable has been around for decades, but it has only become practical with the advent of high-speed networking protocols that can take advantage of its capabilities. Virtually all of the data-link layer protocols in use today support the use of fiber optic cable in some form, and many include specifications for multiple fiber types. As with copper, fiber optic cables are usually installed in a star or ring topology. Unlike copper, however, fiber optic cable is sometimes installed using a physical ring topology, instead of a logical ring. The FDDI specifications even define a double ring topology, which consists of two separate rings, each with signals running in opposite directions. Computers connected to both rings then have a measure of fault tolerance that is not provided by a single physical ring.

> **NOTE** **Exam Objectives**   Objective 1.4 for the Network+ exam calls for students to "recognize the following media connectors and/or describe their uses: RJ-11, RJ-45, AUI, BNC, ST, and SC."

PULLING CABLE

Installing network cables is called *pulling cable*, because the process often involves threading one end of a cable through a wall or ceiling and then pulling the rest of the cable through from the other end. Depending on the type of cable involved and the nature of the site, installing cable can be very simple or extraordinarily complex. This discussion concentrates primarily on the installation of UTP cable, which is by far the most popular network medium used today.

External Installations

An external installation is one in which you use prefabricated UTP cables (that is, cables with the connectors already attached) and run them from each computer to a hub near the location of the equipment. You don't have to run cables through walls or ceilings, attach connectors to bulk cable, or buy additional hardware, such as wall plates and patch panels. External installations are also portable; you can coil up the cables and take them with you if you have to move the network. The drawbacks of an external installation are that the cables are often visible, and obstacles between the various pieces of network equipment can make running the cable difficult. However, you can take steps to help minimize these drawbacks.

The fundamentals of an external cable installation are as follows. (Detailed information about the individual steps of the procedure appears later in this lesson.)

▶ **Performing an External Cable Installation**

1. Select the locations for the computers (and other network-connected devices, such as printers) and your hub. The hub should be in a central location relative to the computers, both to keep the cable lengths to a minimum and to avoid having too many cables running along the same route.

2. Plan the exact route for each of the cables, from the computer (or other device) to the hub. Examine all of the obstacles, such as furniture, doorways, and walls, on each route, and plan how you are going to run your cables around or through them.

3. Measure the route from each computer to the hub, taking the entire path of the cable into account. Include vertical runs around doorways, paths through walls, and other obstacles. Leave at least a few extra yards of slack to compensate for unforeseen obstacles and adjustments in the location of the computer or hub.

4. Buy prefabricated cables of the appropriate lengths, and if necessary, colors, for each run. If you're installing UTP cable, make sure that all of the cables you buy are rated at least CAT5. It's a good idea to use cables with molded boots on the connectors to protect them from damage.

5. Lay out the cables loosely for each cable run without connecting them to the equipment or securing them to the walls. Be sure to leave enough slack to reach around doorways or other obstacles, and at each end, so that the connectors can reach the computer and the hub comfortably.

6. Starting at one end of each cable run, secure the cable to the walls, floor, or woodwork, working your way to the other end. Make sure that none of the cables is compressed or kinked anywhere along its length and that all cables are protected from damage caused by foot traffic or furniture.

7. When the cables are secured, plug one end of each cable run into the hub and the other end into the computer or other device. When the hub is connected to a power source and the computer is turned on, the link pulse lights in the hub and the computer's network interface adapter (if one exists) should light up, indicating that a proper connection has been established.

The network most obviously suitable for an external cable installation is one in which all of the computers and other devices are located in the same room. A one-room network eliminates the single biggest problem of external cable installations: running cables between rooms, or worse, between floors. For a small, one-room network, you can generally run the cables along the walls around the room, securing them to the baseboards or running them behind furniture, as shown in Figure 2-20. You can also buy prefabricated UTP cables in a variety of colors to match your décor and keep the installation as discreet as possible.

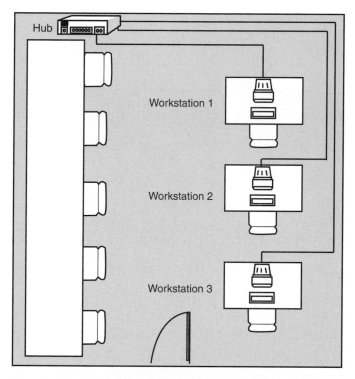

Figure 2-20   A simple external installation runs cables around the perimeter of the room.

CAUTION   *Avoid Loose Cables*   *One thing you want to avoid in any cable installation is a loose cable running across a floor. Not only is this a hazard to foot traffic, but stepping on cables can eventually damage them, possibly causing intermittent network outages that are difficult to troubleshoot.*

Problems arise if you have to run cables to computers or other devices located in the center of the room, rather than next to a wall. There are several solutions, depending on your environment. You can buy rubber cable protectors that run across the floor; a cross-section of two cable protectors is shown in Figure 2-21. These provide a safe conduit for the cable and prevent people from tripping. You can also run prefabricated cables through a drop ceiling and then down through a ceiling tile to the appropriate location on the floor. This can look odd, but you can buy thin floor-to-ceiling service poles that provide a safe cable conduit and a neater appearance. When you begin thinking about running cables through the ceiling, however, you should consider whether an internal installation might be a better idea.

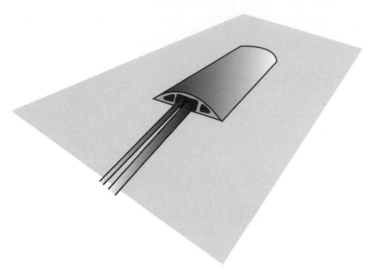

Figure 2-21   Rubber cable protectors might be unsightly, but in situations where you must run cables across the floor, they provide effective protection.

Securing External Cables

Although it's possible to run cables around a room and leave them loose, it's a good idea to secure them in place. Securing cables ensures that they won't move into a high-traffic area where they can be stepped on or otherwise damaged. It also prevents people from accidentally yanking on the cable, which can damage the connectors. There are a number of hardware solutions you can use to secure your cables. However, you should first lay out your cables in the exact route from one connection to the other. Don't fasten the cables as you run them, or you run the risk of falling short of the destination and having to start over.

Stapling cables to walls or baseboards is the simplest—and usually the least expensive—solution. However, do not use the standard square staples used in most staple guns, which can crush the cable and damage the wires within it. Instead, buy individual staples. An individual staple has either a cap at the top that simplifies the task of hammering it into the wall, or a cable holder consisting of a semicircular plastic sleeve with a wire brad through it. Hammering the brad into the wall anchors the sleeve with the open end into the wall, as shown in Figure 2-22.

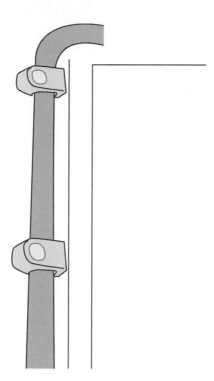

Figure 2-22 Individual staples hold cables securely to a surface without squeezing the sheath.

If you have a significant amount of cable to install, it might be worth the expense to buy a staple gun designed specifically for cable installations, one that shoots round-headed staples and has an adjustable depth setting. The idea is for the staples to be well secured to the wall with the cable still loose enough to be pulled through them freely. If the cable cannot move laterally through the staple, the staple is secured too tightly. If you accidentally pierce the cable sheath with a staple, you should start over with a new cable. This type of stapler might not be available at your local home store, but computer dealers who carry bulk cable and other network cabling supplies often have them. A good stapler of this type can use square as well as round-topped staples, so it's potentially useful for other jobs.

Another option for securing cables in place is to use cable ties, which are loops of plastic or fabric that secure to a surface and can hold one or more cables. Some of these products use a nylon hook-and-ratchet design (much like the flexible handcuffs that police use) and often come with an eyelet for nailing the tie to a wall. Others consist of a wider loop of cloth or plastic, the ends of which are attached using a hook and loop fastener, such as Velcro. Examples of cable ties are shown in Figure 2-23. Cables ties are more visible than staples, and they are more often used to secure bundles of cables in place. An advantage of Velcro ties is that they can be opened so you can add more cables as your network grows.

Figure 2-23   Cable ties

> **NOTE**   **Protecting Cables**   Both staples and cable ties are excellent
> solutions for securing cables to a wall or another surface, but they don't
> provide any protection from objects that might bump into the wall and
> squeeze the cable. If at all possible, you should secure the cables in a way
> that makes it difficult for furniture or other objects to come into contact
> with them.

Another option that provides better protection than staples or cable ties in
securing cables is called a *raceway*. A raceway is a small, enclosed conduit, usually
made of plastic, that holds cables inside and is designed to run along walls. Some
raceways screw to the wall and others have an adhesive backing; the screw-in
models are definitely more secure. Because the raceway completely encloses the
cables within a rigid housing, they are protected from bumps and abrasions.

Raceways are more expensive and more difficult to install than staples or cable
ties. Because raceways are rigid, you have to buy fittings of the right size and
shape, but raceways allow you to run the cables up and down walls or around
corners or doorways while completely enclosing them. The products are usually
modular, meaning that you can buy straight runs, corners, and other components
separately, all of which fit together, as shown in Figure 2-24. Raceways usually
come in a limited range of colors; most are a neutral putty color, which,
depending on your décor, might or might not be very noticeable.

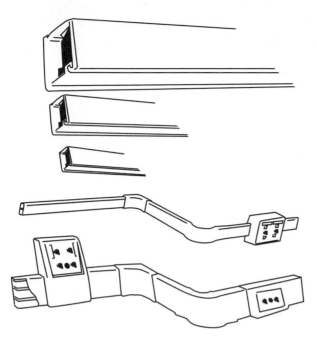

Figure 2-24   Raceways completely enclose cables and protect them from damage.

> **NOTE**   **Bulk Cables and Raceways**   You can also buy surface-mounted connection boxes that attach to the raceway, enabling you to run bulk cable and connect it directly to the jacks in the boxes. This is the functional equivalent of an internal installation without your having to run cables inside walls or ceilings. If you are installing a network in a building with cinderblock walls, for example, this might be your only option for a bulk cable installation.

Running Cables Around Doors

One of the most common obstacles encountered during a one-room external cable installation is a doorway. Generally speaking, if you can avoid doorways by running your cables the long way around the room, you should do so, even if it means using a longer cable. However, sometimes you have no choice but to run the cable past a doorway, and this leaves you two options: you can run the cable up and around the door, or you can run it on the floor along the doorway's threshold.

In most cases, you should avoid the latter option. Even if you secure the cable to the floor well, you expose it to repeated compressions from foot traffic, which can eventually damage the wires inside. Therefore it is better to run the cable underneath the threshold, if possible. If there is a threshold in the doorway that you can remove temporarily, you can route the cable underneath it, as long as there are no sharp edges exposed that might cut the cable sheath.

Most of the time, however, you will have to run your cable up and over the doorway, using staples to hold it in place, as shown in Figure 2-25. This is usually not a difficult task, especially if there is a wooden molding around the doorway, but it can be unsightly because it brings the cables up to eye level. You might want to try to find cabling in a color that closely matches the walls, or even paint over the cable after it's installed.

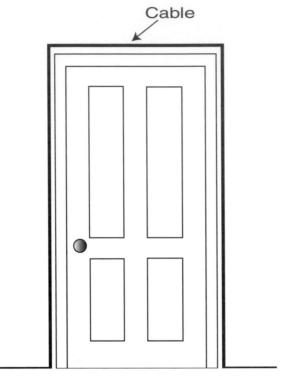

Figure 2-25   Staple cables securely around a doorway rather than routing the cable along the floor across the doorway.

Running multiple cables over a single doorway can be even more problematic. Consider adding an additional hub to your network so that you can get by with only one cable over the doorway, or using a raceway large enough to hold multiple cables.

> **NOTE   Estimating Cable Length**   Running cable around a doorway adds significantly to the cable length, so be sure to factor doorways into your cable length estimations.

Running Cables to Other Rooms

When you have computers in different rooms, even an external installation can become complicated. There are generally two ways to get a cable from one room to another: through the door or through the wall. Running cable along the floor across a doorway causes problems, but running cable through a doorway is often an acceptable solution. To run cable through a doorway, there must be sufficient space for the cable to pass between the bottom of the door and the floor, even when the door is closed.

Running a cable through a wall is also an acceptable solution, even if it isn't strictly an external installation. The best course of action is to select a spot on the wall that's hidden by furniture in both rooms and to drill a hole that is large enough to pass the cable through from one room to the other. When you're running a prefabricated cable through a wall, you must drill holes that are large enough for the connector to pass through. Taping one end of the cable to a length of straightened coat hanger wire makes it easier to thread the cable through the wall to the other side.

> **NOTE**   **Drilling Through Walls**   When drilling through a wall, be sure to avoid any cables or pipes that might be inside the wall. Although it might be tempting to use a very long bit to drill through both sides of the wall at once, it is usually safer to drill a hole in one side, then use a long screwdriver to probe inside the wall and to poke a hole through the far side. Using this method, you won't accidentally drill through a vital service connection. This also ensures that the holes in both sides of the wall line up properly.

Running Cables Between Floors

In many cases, the most difficult external installation is one that spans two or more floors of the same building. It can be difficult to find an appropriate place to run the cables, and the installation might require special tools. In a wooden structure, drilling a hole in the floor is relatively easy, but you must carefully plan the location of the hole from both above and below, so that you don't end up with a cable hanging down through the middle of a ceiling. If both stories of the building have walls in the same places, you can sometimes drill through the floor inside a wall, using wall plate holes for access to the interior of the wall. This might require a special drill with a right-angle chuck and a long bit, or you might be able to drill up through the floor from below. One method of finding the proper location for the hole is to drill a 1/8-inch-diameter hole down through the floor right next to the wall and push a bent coat hanger through to mark the location. From the floor below, find the protruding coat hanger, measure about 2 inches from your first hole in the direction of the wall, and drill a 3/4-inch hole upward, as shown in Figure 2-26. You should then be able to push your cable up through the floor and grab it from above. As always, make sure that you don't disturb any of the building's service connections in the process.

Figure 2-26   Running cables up through a floor into the interior of a wall can be tricky, but it makes for a neater installation.

In an office building, you are more likely to find some sort of conduit between floors through which you can run your cables. If this conduit is an air space that is part of the building's ventilation system, be sure to use the proper cable for the installation. Your local building codes might require a plenum-rated cable, and failure to use the correct cable can result in penalties and a forced reinstallation. If no such conduit exists, however, you might have a difficult time because the floors in commercial office buildings are often made of concrete that is several inches thick. Drilling through it might require heavy tools and a consultation with an engineer and building inspector.

Internal Installations

Most professional cable installations are internal, meaning that all of the cables are run inside walls, ceilings, or floors. Unlike an external installation, which typically uses a single prefabricated cable to run from each computer all the way to the hub, an internal cable installation splits the connection into three parts, as shown in Figure 2-27. The main part of the connection is a length of bulk cable that runs from a wall plate in the vicinity of each computer to a patch panel at the location of the hub. The other two elements are relatively short, prefabricated cables called *patch cables*, which connect the network interface adapter in the computer to the wall plate and the patch panel jack to a hub port.

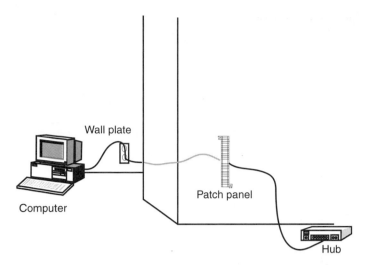

Figure 2-27   Each internal cable connection consists of three parts: a bulk cable connection inside the walls and two patch cables.

Internal installations use bulk cable, which is a long, unbroken length of cable, usually supplied on a large spool, with no connectors attached, as shown in Figure 2-28. The installer pulls off as much cable as she needs for a particular run, cuts it off the spool, and attaches the ends to the wall plate jacks and the patch panel jacks. The patch cables are prefabricated, relatively short in length, and already have RJ-45 connectors attached. You can also purchase modular RJ-45 connectors and attach them to lengths of bulk cable to make your own patch cables. This enables you to use only as much cable as you actually need, which is often considerably less than you need when using prefabricated cables.

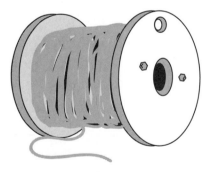

Figure 2-28   Bulk cable on a spool

To use bulk cable, you must have the appropriate tools and fittings to attach connectors to both ends. The advantages of bulk cabling are that it is easier to pull the cable without the connectors attached to it, you have more options in the types of connectors you use, and you save money by buying cable in large quantities.

UTP cable intended for use as a patch cable or an external cable is generally made from stranded wire, which makes the cable more flexible, but also makes it more difficult to use for internal cable installations, which rely on punchdown connections (described later in this chapter). Cable for internal installations generally uses solid wire conductors, which work well with the punchdown connectors. Solid wire cable is less expensive than stranded wire cable, and it is more resistant to attenuation, enabling you to have longer cable runs.

> **NOTE   Cable Lengths**   Although the Ethernet standards state that you can run UTP cable up to 100 meters between a computer and a hub, you rarely, if ever, see a prefabricated cable that long. The stranded wire used in prefabricated cables is one of the reasons for this. For cable runs longer than 30 meters, you should always use a solid wire cable. You can also buy prefabricated solid wire cables from some specialty vendors.

Professionals who specialize in data and telephone cabling perform most internal cabling jobs. As mentioned earlier, in new construction, both data and telephone cable systems are often installed simultaneously. Pulling cable for this type of installation is not especially difficult, but it helps to have the proper tools and a strong sense of organization. When installing a large network, all those cables running through the same ceiling system tend to look alike, so it's important to proceed systematically and label each cable run carefully to avoid retracing your steps later.

The basic steps involved in installing internal cable runs are as follows.

▶ Installing Internal Cables

1. Select the locations for your computers and other network-connected devices and a central, protected location for your hubs and patch panel. One end of each cable run will terminate at the patch panel, so be sure to select a location with sufficient access to the entire site, away from possible sources of EMI, and with room to work easily.

2. Plan the routes for your cables from the patch panel to the location of each wall plate or other connector, taking into account all obstacles, such as barrier walls, light fixtures, and plenums.

3. With your spool of bulk cable located at the patch panel site, label the lead end of the cable with its intended location.

4. Feed the lead end of the bulk cable into the ceiling, wall, or floor into which you will install it and pull the cable to the location of the wall plate. Do not cut the cable off the spool until you have pulled it all the way to

the wall plate. Leave several yards of slack inside the ceiling, wall, or floor to avoid problems making the connections or locating the equipment.

5. Secure the cables in place along their routes so that they can't shift location or be damaged by other people working in the same area.

6. Label the end of the cable with the name of the wall plate location, and cut the cable from the spool. Never cut an unlabeled cable from the spool.

7. Proceed with the cable connection process, as detailed later in this chapter.

Some of the practices you should avoid when pulling cable are as follows:

- **Kinking and tugging on the cable**   The TIA/EIA T-568 standard recommends a maximum tension of 25 pounds when pulling cable.

- **Crushing or pinching the cable**   Any fastener or architectural element that squeezes the cable can eventually damage the wires inside, affecting signal transmissions.

- **Making turns greater than 90 degrees**   Sharp turns can negatively affect the conductivity of the wires within the cables.

- **Exposing cable to heat and moisture**   Locations with high temperatures and humidity can increase the rate at which signals attenuate as they travel along the cable.

To a large extent, the difficulty of an internal cabling job depends on the construction of the site. The typical office building, with plasterboard walls and drop ceilings, is an ideal environment for cable installation. You can usually run the cables freely through the ceiling to any room on the floor, and then drop them down inside the walls to a wall plate at almost any location. Of course, these projects rarely come off without a hitch, and there are a variety of barriers that the cable installer might encounter. These barriers can include sources of EMI that can disturb data signals, fire breaks that prevent you from running cable down from the ceiling, asbestos insulation, service components such as ventilation ducts and light fixtures, and structural components, such as concrete pilings and steel girders. All of these obstructions should be detected during the network planning process, however, when you should establish a proper route around or through them for each cable run.

> **NOTE   Modifying the Structure**   Never cut, drill through, or otherwise disturb a structural member of a building without consulting someone with full knowledge and responsibility for the consequences. Apart from engineering concerns, there are local fire laws and building codes to consider. Violating them means that you, the installer, might be held responsible not only for making the job right later, but for any applicable fines and penalties. If you outsource the cabling job to a contractor, your contract should stipulate that the installer is responsible for the legality of the installation.

In other types of buildings, you might run into conditions that make an internal cable installation difficult, if not impossible. If there is no access to the interiors of ceilings or walls, consider other solutions, such as an under-floor cable installation or the surface-mounted raceways described earlier in this lesson.

Installing a Cable Run

When installing multiple cable runs, you typically start at the location of the patch panel, which is where one end of each cable run will terminate. The other ends can be spread out all over the site, but one end of all these cables comes together at this point. With your spool of bulk cable at the patch panel location, you typically proceed by stripping a few yards of cable off the spool, threading it through the ceiling to the proper location, leaving sufficient extra cable to reach the connectors, labeling the cable, and only then cutting it off the spool. Be sure to label each end with a piece of tape or some other type of tag so that you can tell which cable is which. It is essential that you have a master diagram of the space with all of the cable runs and their names. This is important not only for installation, but for troubleshooting afterward.

Pulling the cable through the ceiling space is the actual work of installing cable. The process goes much more smoothly when there are at least two people working together, so that one person can pass the cable inside the drop ceiling to the other person. The tools involved in this process are simple but essential. Several ladders are a must, of course, but beyond that you might be surprised to see which other tools professional installers use to pull cable.

A simple ball of string is often the cable installer's most valuable tool. If you have multiple cable runs going to destinations that are close together, you can tape one end of a length of string to the leading end of your cable. After you get the cable to its destination, you can tape the other end of the string to another cable and pull it through the ceiling to the same destination. You can also buy prefabricated cable pullers, as shown in Figure 2-29, which might make the job a little bit easier.

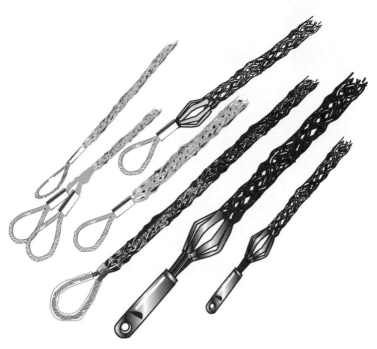

Figure 2-29   A cable puller allows you to attach multiple cables and pull them all through a ceiling, wall, or floor at once.

When moving the cable through the ceiling, you can stick to the basic "coil and throw" technique. A person on one ladder coils up a length of cable and throws it to a person on another ladder some distance away. Throwing the cable inside a small ceiling space can be difficult, however, and installers have come up with other methods, some of which are quite ingenious.

The "official" tool for extending cable through ceiling spaces is called a **telepole**. A telepole is a telescoping pole, rather like a collapsible fishing rod, with a hook at one end to which you connect a cable, as shown in Figure 2-30. You insert the collapsed telepole with the attached cable into the ceiling, then extend the pole and hand off the cable end to the next person down the line. This is a brilliant idea, but the telepole is a specialized piece of equipment that many installers find they don't really need. Many installers use yardsticks or flexible nylon rods that they push through the ceiling. With a little practice, you can make an effective cabling tool out of a tennis ball with one end of a string taped to it. Simply throw the ball through the ceiling, and use the string to pull a cable through along the same route.

Figure 2-30   By connecting one end of a cable to the hook on a telepole, you can easily push it through wall or ceiling spaces.

Securing Cables

It's just as important to secure internally installed cables as it is to secure externally installed ones. The object here is not as much cosmetic as it is preventing the cables from being moved. Remember that you might not be the only person who pokes around inside the drop ceiling. Maintenance people have access to light fixtures, ventilation ducts, and other components, and securing your cables ensures that they won't be moved closer to possible sources of damage or interference. Another advantage of a drop ceiling is that the framework used to suspend the ceiling panels provides many places to secure cables. Nylon cable ties are good for this purpose, as are the plastic ties used with trash bags.

Dropping Cables

After you have pulled the cable to the approximate location of the computer or other device to which it will connect, drop it down inside the wall to which you will affix the wall plate. Most commercial office buildings use metal studs and do not have horizontal cross members inside the walls, which makes it relatively easy to drop cables to wall plate locations down near the floor. In most cases, vertical cable drops are easily accomplished. Cut a hole in the wall where you will install the wall plate, thread the cable down inside the wall from the ceiling, and pull the cable out through the hole. Later, you attach the cable to the connector in the wall plate, push the excess cable back into the wall, and cover the hole by mounting the wall plate over it.

If you encounter a horizontal barrier inside a wall that prevents the cable from dropping down to the location of the wall plate, you have several options. One option is to cut another hole in the wall to drill through the barrier. This is more feasible if the barrier is wood rather than metal, but in any case, you will have to patch the wall afterward. Another option is to move the wall plate to the left or right and hope you find an unblocked passage in the wall. You can also place the wall plate just above the barrier. As a last resort, you can entirely avoid dropping the cable inside the wall by installing a raceway from the ceiling down to a surface-mounted connection box. This is not as neat as a true internal cable run, but it's better than leaving a loose cable hanging from the ceiling.

As with horizontal cable runs, there are special tools that can make the process of dropping a cable easier. A **fish tape** is a flexible band of metal or fiberglass that winds up on a reel and has a hook on the end, much like a plumber's snake. You push the tape up to the ceiling through the hole in the wall, attach the cable to the hook, and pull it down and out through the hole. You can also run the tape down and out through the hole to pull a cable up to the ceiling, or through the ceiling to the floor above, as shown in Figure 2-31. Many professional installers have devised their own tools for catching hold of cables inside walls. You can probably make do with a bent coat hanger most of the time.

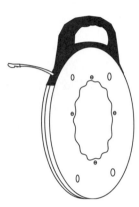

Figure 2-31   You can use a fish tape to pull cables up and down inside walls.

Depending on where and how you will install your patch panel, you might also have to drop the other end of your cable run down through a wall as well. Smaller networks often use patch panels that mount on a wall, and you can drop the cables down to a hole that will eventually be located behind the mounted panel. Larger networks might use rack-mounted equipment, in which case the cables can drop down from an open ceiling into the back of the rack assembly.

Pulling Other Cable Types

UTP cable is easy to install because it is thin and quite flexible. Other types of cable have different properties, however, that can make the process of pulling cable more difficult. The RG-58 coaxial cable used for thin Ethernet networks is roughly the same diameter as UTP, but it is heavier and less flexible. Therefore, it is possible to install this type of cable internally, but it tends not to bend around corners as tightly.

The biggest disadvantage of an internal coaxial installation is the fact that thin Ethernet networks use a bus topology. This means that you must pull one length of cable to each computer, and then pull another length of cable from that computer to the next one. Two cables must protrude from the wall and connect to the T-connector mounted on the computer's network interface adapter to connect it to the network properly.

Thick Ethernet networks use RG-8 coaxial cable, which is nearly half an inch thick and very inflexible. This type of cable is hardly ever used today, but even when it was used, it was rarely installed internally. Thick Ethernet's main advantage for the cable installer is that each computer uses a separate cable that connects the network interface adapter to the main RG-8 trunk. Therefore, only one cable has to protrude through the wall.

To test your understanding of internal and external cable installations, complete Exercise 2-3, "Internal and External Cabling," now.

Pulling fiber optic cable is roughly similar to pulling UTP. The multimode fiber used for most LAN connections is reasonably flexible, but the nature of the medium dictates that the cable's placement, as it turns around corners, must be more precise with respect to the bend radius. One advantage of fiber optic cable is that it is immune to EMI, so many of the obstacles around which you must normally route copper-based cables, such as fluorescent light fixtures, are of no consequence in a fiber optic installation.

MAKING CONNECTIONS

After all your cable runs are in place, you're ready to make the connections so that the computers can communicate with each other through the hubs. Depending on the type of cable installation you've performed—internal or external—the connection process can be extremely simple or quite complex. In some cases, you must be familiar with the function of each wire inside the UTP cable, whereas in others, you never have to see the wires inside the cable at all.

Two-Computer Networking

The simplest possible LAN consists of two computers, with network interface adapters installed, connected by a single cable. If the two computers are located in the same room, the cable installation should be very simple. However, if the computers are far away from each other, and especially if they're located in different rooms or on different floors, the cable installation might require special attention.

Back in the days when an Ethernet network meant coaxial cable, it was possible to connect two computers' network interface adapters with a thin Ethernet cable, thus setting up a simple two-node network. Today, however, the standard for Ethernet networking is UTP cable, and this generally requires a hub.

The hub on an Ethernet network provides a vital service by sending across the signals between the transmit and receive wires. This enables the signals that each computer sends over the transmit wires to arrive at the receive connections at the other computers. When you connect two Ethernet network interface adapters directly using a standard UTP cable, there is no hub, so this crossover is absent. For these two computers to be able to communicate, you must use a special cable called a **crossover cable**, which wires the transmit contacts in each connector to the receive contacts in the other connector.

> **NOTE   Distance Limitations**   One limitation of a UTP Ethernet network without a hub is that the two computers can be no more than 100 meters apart. On a standard UTP network, the Ethernet hub functions as a repeater. This enables each cable connecting a computer to the hub to be 100 meters long, for a total span of 200 meters between computers when they are connected to the same hub.

If you are connecting two computers in the same room, you can buy a prefabricated crossover cable and simply plug the ends into the network interface adapters in the two computers. Be aware, however, that you might have trouble finding a crossover cable in your local computer store. Virtually all computer stores stock basic networking equipment, such as network interface adapter cards, hubs, and prefabricated UTP cables. Larger stores might have crossover cables, but you might find it easier to order one from an online or catalog dealer, particularly if you need a relatively long crossover cable.

If you want to use a crossover cable to connect two computers in different rooms or on different floors, you might have to perform an internal installation by running cable through the building's walls, ceilings, or floors. If this is the case, the cable that you use for a crossover connection is the same as that for a hub-based network, and the procedures for pulling the cable are the same as those detailed earlier in this chapter. A crossover installation differs from standard installation in the attachment of the wires to the connectors at each end of the cable.

As explained earlier, a UTP cable contains eight separate wires, grouped into four twisted pairs. The RJ-45 connector at each end of the cable (whether it is male, as on a patch cable, or female, as part of a wall plate or patch panel) has eight conductive contacts, to which the eight wires must be attached. When you plug a male connector into a female one, the corresponding contacts touch, creating electrical circuits. Figure 2-32 shows the functions of the eight contacts on a standard 10Base-T or 100Base-TX Ethernet network connector.

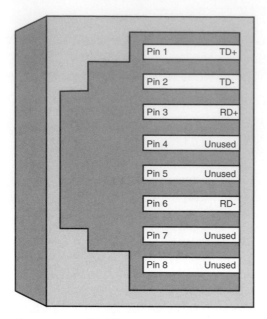

Figure 2-32   RJ-45 connector contact assignments for 10Base-T and 100Base-TX networks

NOTE   Using 100Base-T4   While 10Base-T and 100Base-TX networks use only four of the eight wires in a UTP cable, a 100Base-T4 network uses all eight. The four wires that are designated as unused in the figure can carry signals in either direction on a 100Base-T4 network.

Standard network cable runs and prefabricated cables use **straight-through connections**. In a straight-through connection, each wire is attached to the same contact in both connectors, as shown in Figure 2-33. The transmit contacts at one end are connected to the transmit contacts at the other end, and the receive contacts are connected in the same way. This is possible because the crossover circuit is supplied in the hub, which makes the job much easier for the cable installer.

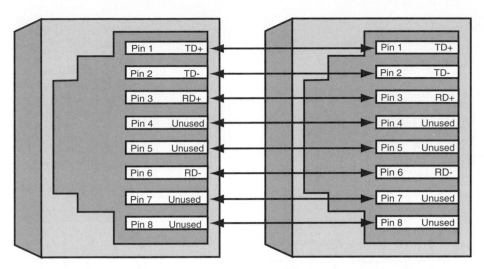

Figure 2-33   Straight-through connections use the eight wires in a UTP cable to connect the corresponding contacts in the connectors at each end.

To create a crossover connection in the cable, you must connect the two transmit contacts to their corresponding receive contacts, as shown in Figure 2-34. The positive transmit data (TD+) contact at each end is connected to the positive receive data (RD+) contact at the other end. Likewise, the two negative transmit data (TD−) contacts are connected to the two negative receive data (RD−) contacts. When you install a cable using a crossover connection like this, you cannot use the cable run with a hub, because the crossover circuit in the hub would cancel out the crossover circuit in the cable. In other words, the TD+ contact that is crossed to the RD+ contact in the cable would be crossed again, back to the TD+ contact, inside the hub. In the event that you had to expand the network, for example, the only way you could use this connection with a hub would be to plug the cable into the hub's uplink port, which does not run through a crossover circuit.

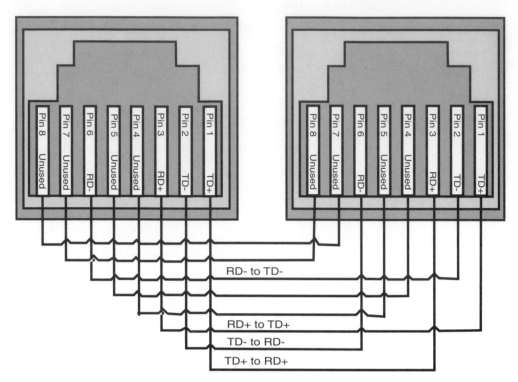

Figure 2-34   A crossover cable connection attaches the TD contacts in one connector to the RD contacts in the other, eliminating the need for a hub.

Connecting External Cables

If you've installed prefabricated cables externally, making your final connections is simply a matter of plugging them into the hub and the network interface adapters in the computers. Set up the hub in a central location, preferably where it is protected from traffic or vibrations that can loosen the cable connections, and connect it to a power source. Plug each cable's connector into one of the hub's ports. Push the connector firmly into the socket until it clicks. Do not use the hub's uplink port for a computer connection unless the port has a switch that enables you to disable the crossover circuit. Most hubs have LEDs that correspond to the ports; these will not light up until you connect the other ends of the cables to the computers and turn them on.

At the other end of each cable, you should have a computer that is set up and ready to go. Shut the computer down and plug the network cable into the jack provided by the computer's network interface adapter. Again, make sure that it clicks into place. If the jack does not fit in the socket, you're probably trying to plug the cable into a modem jack, which won't work.

Most Ethernet network interface adapters have at least one LED next to the RJ-45 connector; adapters integrated into the motherboard might or might not have LEDs. One of the LEDs lights up when the adapter is connected to an operating hub. When you turn on the computer, the adapter generates a signal called a **link pulse** and transmits it over the cable. When the hub receives the signal, it responds with a signal of its own. If either the adapter or the hub is a Fast Ethernet device, the devices use these link pulse signals to negotiate the fastest speed they have in common. For example, when you plug a dual-speed adapter into a Fast Ethernet hub, the link pulse signals enable the two devices to determine that they can both operate at 100 Mbps, and they configure themselves to use that speed.

> **NOTE**   **Network Interface Adapter LEDs**   Many of the network interface adapters manufactured today have two LEDS, one of which is a link pulse LED and the other of which specifies the speed at which the device is operating.

If you connect a dual-speed network interface adapter to a standard Ethernet hub, the adapter determines that it must run at 10 Mbps to use the hub, and it adjusts itself accordingly. When this negotiation is complete, the LEDs on both the hub and the adapter should light up, even if you haven't yet installed the network adapter driver on the computer. If the LEDs do not light up, there might be a problem with your cable connection, or possibly with the adapter or hub. See Chapter 12, "Network Troubleshooting Procedures," for more information about what to do next.

Assuming that the LEDs on both the network interface adapter and the hub do light up, the cable installation is complete. If you haven't done so already, you must install the networking software components on your computers, after which your network should be operational.

Connecting Internal Cables

If you have installed bulk cable internally, the process of making your final connections is more complicated. The essential steps for making each cable connection are as follows:

▶ **Completing Internal Cable Connections**

1. Connect one end of the cable run to a port in a patch panel.

2. Connect the patch panel port to a hub port using a patch cable.

3. Connect the other end of the cable run to a port in a wall plate.

4. Mount the wall plate in the wall.

5. Use a patch cable to connect the port in the wall plate to the network interface adapter in a computer.

Connector Components

When you install bulk cable, you must buy the connectors you need and the tools for attaching the connectors separately. Most internal installations use wall plates for the computer end of each cable run, and one or more patch panels for the hub end. A wall plate is a metal or plastic face plate that screws into a hole in a wall, much like an electrical outlet, except that the wall plate contains female RJ-45 connectors (jacks) instead of electrical outlets. A connector on the back of the wall plate jack contains the contacts to which you attach the wires inside the UTP cable. You must connect the eight wires at each end of a cable run to a jack at each end of the cable. When the cable is connected and the wall plate installed, the cable is hidden in the wall, and the only visible part is the front of the wall plate. Just as you would with a telephone cable, you can then plug a patch cable into the jack.

As shown in Figure 2-35, some wall plates have integrated jacks, while others are modular. You can buy wall plates that hold one, two, four, or more jacks, and you can insert different types of jacks to support various types of cable connections. For example, in new construction, it's possible to install telephone and data network cables simultaneously and to use a single wall plate as the terminus for both networks. If you do this, be sure to label the jacks carefully so that users don't confuse them.

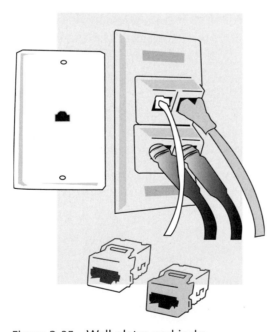

Figure 2-35   Wall plates and jacks

A patch panel, sometimes called a *punchdown block*, is similar in function to a wall plate but contains many more jacks. A patch panel is essentially a face plate or box with a number of RJ-45 jacks mounted in it. It provides a row of ports on its front, as shown in Figure 2-36. A patch panel is not a hub; it is nothing more than a nexus that provides a convenient place to terminate the hub end of all your cable runs. You plug patch cables into the patch panel's ports to connect them to hub ports, thus completing the connection at that end. Patch panels are available in a variety of sizes and configurations and are either mounted on a wall or integrated into a rack-mounted system.

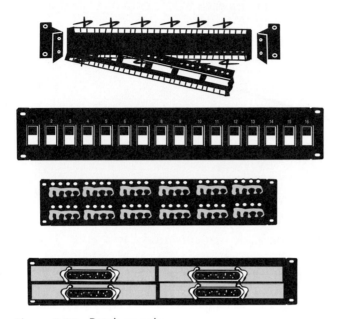

Figure 2-36   Patch panels

▶ Punching Down

The process of connecting the ends of your bulk cable runs to the jacks in your wall plates and patch panels is called *punching down*. Each jack contains eight sets of contacts that correspond to the eight wires in the cable. Punching down a cable consists of the following steps:

1. Strip some of the insulating sheath off the cable end to expose the wires.

2. Separate the twisted wire pairs at the ends.

3. Strip a small amount of insulation off each wire.

4. Insert the wires into the appropriate contacts in the jack.

5. Press the bare wire down between the two metal contacts that hold it in place.

6. Cut off the excess wire that protrudes past the contacts.

Remember that you must repeat this process at both ends for each of your internal cable runs. This can be a lot of work, but fortunately there are tools that simplify the process. A *punchdown block tool*, shown in Figure 2-37, is a handheld device that you use to insert each wire between its set of contacts. The tool strips the insulation off the wire, presses it into place between the contacts, and cuts off the excess wire. This tool is essential for an internal UTP cable installation. Without it, the process of stripping, installing, and cutting each wire is extremely laborious.

Figure 2-37   A punchdown block tool

Your punchdown block tool must be the same type as your jacks. The types usually refer to the configuration of the blade that cuts off the wire ends. The jacks (or blocks) most often used today are called *110-style*. You can purchase a tool designed specifically for this type of block, or a modular one with interchangeable parts to support multiple block types.

The most important part of the punchdown process is matching the wires to the correct contacts. The wires inside the UTP cable are color-coded orange, green, blue, and brown. The positive wire in each pair is solid-colored, and the negative wire has a white stripe. You can buy jacks that have corresponding colors on the contacts, so that you simply have to match the wires to the same-colored contacts when punching down. You should always punch down the wires in a connector in the same order, which traditionally begins with the white-striped wire in a pair first, then the colored wire, in the following color order: blue, orange, green, and then brown.

To punch down a cable, strip about two inches of sheathing off the end, and then untwist each of the four wire pairs. Then lay the cable down in the center of the jack and spread out the wires so that they sit between the appropriate sets of contacts, as shown in Figure 2-38. To protect the wires, the beginning of the cable sheath should be no more than one eighth of an inch from the jack. Take care to untwist each wire pair only as much as necessary for the wire to fit between the contacts. The wire pairs are not twisted simply for organizational purposes; the twists provide an essential function by preventing the signals on the various wire pairs from interfering with each other. Each pair uses a different number of twists per foot, and you want to preserve this configuration as much as possible.

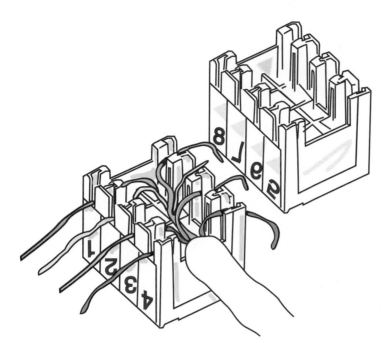

Figure 2-38   Lay out the wires between the appropriate contacts and use the tool to punch them down.

When you have the wires laid out on their respective contacts, take the punchdown tool and place it over the first set of contacts, with the blade on the outside of the jack and the handle of the tool tilted slightly outward. Press down firmly on the tool. This presses the wire into place, stripping off the insulation as it goes, and cutting off the loose wire end. Repeat this process for the remaining seven wires, and be sure to remove the wire ends that have been cut off. This process takes a bit of getting used to, so it's a good idea to buy some extra jacks for practice before you start working with your actual cables. This is another good reason to allow some extra slack in your cable runs. If you make a mistake, you can simply cut off the end of the cable and start again with a new jack.

After you have punched down all eight wires, you can insert the jack into the wall plate or patch panel, if necessary. Then mount the wall plate into the hole that you cut previously, pushing all of the excess cable inside the wall. Mount the patch panel on the wall or rack after you've punched down all of your cables.

> **NOTE** **Exam Objectives**   *Objective 4.5 for the Network+ exam calls for students, "when given a wiring task, [to] be able to select the appropriate*

tool (e.g., such as a wire crimper, media tester/certifier, punch down tool, tone generator, or optical tester, etc.)."

Wiring Standards

When punching down cables or attaching connectors, there are several standards you can use to determine which wires in the cable correspond to which pins in the connector. The most current RJ-45 pinout standard, called 568A and illustrated in Figure 2-39, is published as part of the TIA/EIA-T568 document, but there are two other significant pinouts: 568B and Universal Service Order Codes (USOC).

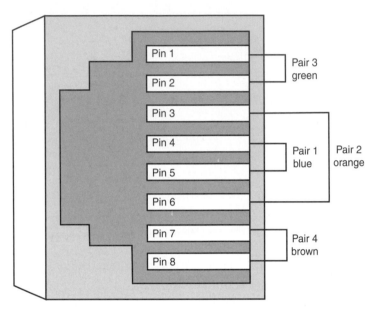

Figure 2-39   The 568A pinout standard for RJ-45 connectors

The original pinout for voice communications in the U.S. was called the USOC standard, as illustrated in Figure 2-40. Of the prominent pinout standards, USOC is the only one that must not be used for data communications, because pins 1 and 2 are connected to wires in separate pairs, which will interfere with network signaling.

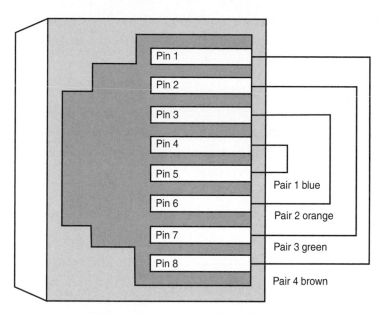

Figure 2-40   The USOC pinout standard for RJ-45 connectors

AT&T noticed this shortcoming in the USOC pinout during its early research into data networking, and developed a new pinout called 258A. The TIA/EIA eventually published this standard as part of the TIA/EIA-T568-A document, calling it the 568B pinout, as shown in Figure 2-41. Thus, while the 568B pinout was published by the TIA/EIA after the 568A standard, 568B is actually older.

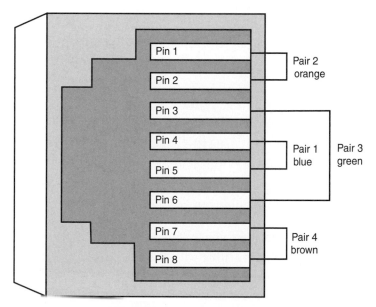

Figure 2-41   The 568B pinout standard for RJ-45 connectors

The 568A and 568B pinouts are nearly identical, but the green and orange wire pairs are transposed. The two standards are functionally identical as well, with neither one providing a performance advantage over the other. The only reason to pay attention to which pinout standard a network uses is to make sure that both ends of all cable runs are punched down using the same standard.

Some vendors have available prefabricated cable products using all three pinouts. Whether you choose 568A or 568B for your patch cables does not matter, because they both are already wired straight through. Just make sure that you do not buy USOC cables. When installing bulk cable, the best practice is to select either 568A or 568B and make sure that everyone participating in the installation uses the pinout you have selected. The only way you can run into problems in this procedure is if people are using different pinouts to punch down opposite ends of the same cable.

Installing Patch Cables

A patch cable is simply a shorter length of cable, both ends of which have standard male RJ-45 connectors that connect a wall plate to a computer's network interface adapter, or to connect a patch panel port to a hub port. You can buy prefabricated cables for this purpose, or you can build them yourself. Making the final connections is no different from the external cable installation process described earlier in this chapter. If you have an unbroken connection between a network interface adapter and a hub, and both devices are switched on, the link pulse LEDs at both ends should light up, indicating that communication is possible. If the LEDs don't light up, the troubleshooting process is a bit more involved than that for an external cable installation because there are more components to check for problems. See Chapter 12, "Network Troubleshooting Procedures," for more information.

Attaching Connectors

Although wall plates and patch panels make for the neatest installation, you don't have to go this route. You can instead attach male RJ-45 connectors to the ends of your cables and plug them directly into your hubs and network interface adapters, just as you would with prefabricated cables. You can also attach these connectors to shorter lengths of cable to build your own patch cables.

Male RJ-45 connectors for UTP come in the three following configurations. Ensure that your RJ-45 connectors are compatible with the selected cable.

- Round cable with stranded wire
- Round cable with solid wire
- Flat cable (commonly referred to as *silver satin*) with stranded wire

> **CAUTION   Avoid Silver Satin Cables**   Silver satin cables are designed
> for telephone network connections and should not be used for data
> networking.

Attaching male RJ-45 connectors to UTP cable requires another special tool,
called a *crimper*, shown in Figure 2-42. A crimper is a jawed device that looks like
a large pair of pliers. The crimper has a set of dies inside that enables you to
squeeze the two halves of an RJ-45 connector together with the wires inside. As
with the punchdown process, you strip some of the sheath off a cable and lay the
wires out in the bottom half of the connector, making sure to use the same wiring
standard at both ends. You then lay the other half of the connector on top of the
wires and squeeze the handles of the crimper to lock the two halves together. This
process is trickier than using a punchdown tool, because you have to get all eight
wires in place at the same time. Some practice is necessary to get the hang of it.
When you consider the price of the crimper and the dies (about $75) plus the
bulk cable and connectors you might ruin while learning how to crimp properly,
not to mention your valuable time, buying prefabricated patch cables might be a
more economical alternative.

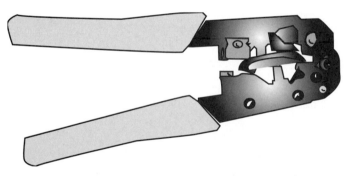

Figure 2-42   A crimper

> **NOTE   Testing Cables**   Testing is an essential part of every cable
> installation. You can test your cable runs by simply connecting up your
> computers and hubs to see if they work. Professional cable installers use
> a special cable-testing device to check for problematic conditions that
> might not be immediately apparent in a real-world test. For more
> information about testing cable runs, see Chapter 11, "Network
> Troubleshooting Tools."

Making Fiber Optic Connections

Fiber optic cables differ from copper cables in almost every way, including the
way their connectors are attached. Unlike the connectors used on copper cables,
which completely contain the end of the cable and provide their own conductors,
ST and SC connectors used on fiber optic cables are really just sleeves that fit

around the end of the cable and let the central core protrude from the end. The connector's only function is to lock the signal-carrying core in place when it's plugged into the jack.

The process of attaching a connector to a multimode fiber optic cable basically consists of stripping the outer sheath off the end of the cable, gluing the connector in place with an epoxy adhesive, allowing the adhesive to cure, and then polishing the protruding core so that the pulses of light carried by the cable reach their terminus in the best possible condition. Singlemode cables are terminated by permanently splicing a *pigtail* to them, which is a short length of cable with a connector already attached to it. This is necessary because the tolerances of singlemode fiber are much tighter than those of multimode.

To test your familiarity with the tools used to install cables, complete Exercise 2-4, "Identifying Cable Installation Tools," now.

Professional fiber optic cable installers typically use a tiny electric oven to cure the epoxy; otherwise, the adhesive must be left to cure overnight. There are several products on the market that are designed to speed up or simplify this process, such as quick-setting adhesives and connectors that crimp on with no adhesive at all. Some professionals swear by these, but others prefer to stick with the traditional method.

SUMMARY

- Three basic topologies are used to cable local area networks (LANs): bus, star, and ring. Other topologies include mesh and hierarchical star, as well as two wireless topologies: ad hoc and infrastructure.

- Coaxial cables have two conductors, use bayonet-Neill-Concelman (BNC) and **attachment unit interface (**AUI) connectors in the bus topology, and are no longer commonly used for LAN installations.

- Unshielded twisted pair (UTP) cable in the star topology is the most common network medium used today. UTP cables use RJ-45 connectors.

- Fiber optic cable uses light pulses instead of electrical voltages for signaling and is resistant to many forms of interference that affect copper cables. Fiber optic cables are installed using a star or ring topology and either subscriber connector (SC) or straight tip (ST) connectors.

- External UTP cable installations use prefabricated cables to connect computers directly to hubs. You typically install external cables along the walls of a room, and you use staples, cable ties, or raceways to secure them in place.

- Internal cable installations use bulk cable, which you pull through walls, ceilings, or floors.

- To connect two computers without a hub, you must use a crossover cable connection, which reverses the transmit and receive signals.

- External cables have the connectors attached, and you simply plug them into your computers and hubs to make the final connections. For internal cables, you must manually attach a jack at each end, which becomes part of the wall plate or patch panel.

- The process of attaching a cable to a jack is called punching down, and it requires a specialized punchdown block tool.

- Patch cables connect wall plates to computers and connect patch panel ports to hub ports. You can build your own patch cables using a crimper for attaching RJ-45 connectors.

EXERCISES

Exercise 2-1: Identifying Network Cable Types

Match the network cable types in the left column with the descriptions in the right column that are most closely associated with them.

1. UTP
2. Singlemode fiber optic
3. STP
4. Coaxial cable
5. CAT5e UTP
6. Multimode fiber optic

a. Used in the bus topology
b. Used for the original Token Ring networks
c. Used for Gigabit Ethernet networks
d. Contains eight wires
e. Used for LANs that span long distances
f. Carries signals generated by a laser

Exercise 2-2: Cable Troubleshooting

For each of the following scenarios, specify whether the network will function properly based on the information given. If not, explain why.

1. Ten computers with 100Base-T4 Fast Ethernet network interface adapters are connected to a hub using 100-meter lengths of CAT3 UTP cable.

2. Networks in two buildings 1000 meters away from each other are connected together using singlemode fiber optic cable with RJ-45 connectors.

3. Fifteen computers are connected to a Token Ring network using a physical ring topology.

4. A Fast Ethernet network is constructed using 100Base-TX equipment and CAT5e UTP cable, with two of the wire pairs in the cable dedicated to data signals and the other two to voice telephone signals.

Exercise 2-3: Internal and External Cabling

For each of the following network scenarios, state whether you would perform an internal or external cable installation, and give a reason why.

1. A 10-node UTP network installed in a temporary office space by a seasonal business

2. A 100-node corporate UTP network being installed in a newly constructed office building

3. A 50-node thick Ethernet network being moved to a new location

Exercise 2-4: Identifying Cable Installation Tools

Match the tools in the left column with the proper functions in the right column.

1. Telepole   **a.** Used to attach male RJ-45 connectors to UTP cables

2. Punchdown block tool   **b.** Pulls cables up through walls

3. Fish tape   **c.** Used to attach UTP cables to jacks

4. Raceway   **d.** Used to pull cable through drop ceilings

5. Crimper   **e.** Secures and protects external cable runs

REVIEW QUESTIONS

1. What is the name of an Ethernet cable that contains two electrical conductors?

    a. An STP cable

    b. A coaxial cable

    c. A dielectric cable

    d. A UTP cable

2. What are the names of two common conditions that degrade the signals on copper-based cables?

3. Which topology requires the use of terminators?

   a. Bus

   b. Star

   c. Ring

   d. Mesh

4. Which of the following topologies is, in most cases, implemented logically, not physically?

   a. Bus

   b. Star

   c. Ring

   d. Mesh

5. How many wire pairs are actually used on a typical UTP Ethernet network?

   a. One

   b. Two

   c. Three

   d. Four

6. Which of the following components is not required for an internal cable installation?

   a. A raceway

   b. A wall plate

   c. A patch panel

   d. A punchdown block tool

7. What components of an internal cable network do patch cables connect? (Choose all correct answers.)

   a. Hubs to computers

   b. Computers to wall plates

   c. Computers to patch panels

   d. Wall plates to patch panels

   e. Patch panels to hubs

8. Which tool do you use to make a patch cable?

   a. A pair of pliers

   b. A punchdown block tool

   c. A fish tape

   d. A crimper

9. What is the primary function of the twists in a twisted pair cable?

   a. They bundle the positive and negative wires together.

   b. They prevent the cables from catching fire.

   c. They protect the signals against crosstalk.

   d. They separate the wire pairs.

10. In a crossover cable, the TD– contact at one end is connected to which contact at the other end?

    a. TD+

    b. TD–

    c. RD+

    d. RD–

11. Which of the following is not a function of the punchdown block tool?

    a. To cut off the wire ends

    b. To strip the sheath off the cable

    c. To strip the insulation off the wires

    d. To push the wires down between the contacts

12. What is the name of the signal that a network interface adapter exchanges with a hub?

    a. Link pulse

    b. Test wave

    c. Crossover circuit

    d. Punchdown block

13. Why should all your cable runs use the same wiring standard?

   a. Because Ethernet can only transmit signals over wires of a certain color

   b. Because the wires in a UTP cable are different gauges and carry signals differently

   c. To ensure that all of the connections are wired straight through

   d. To prevent crosstalk

CASE SCENARIOS

Scenario 2-1: Installing UTP Cable

A network consultant is just starting his own business and has contracted to perform an internal cable installation for a company with 25 computers in a single, newly constructed office building. The network will run 100Base-TX Fast Ethernet on CAT5 UTP cable, with most of the cable runs located inside the walls and the drop ceiling. After examining the site, the consultant has made a list of the components he will need, including bulk cable, wall plates, a patch panel, two hubs, a network interface adapter for each computer, and prefabricated patch cables. Because the consultant is just starting out, he also has to buy the specialized cable installation tools he will need. Which one of the following tools is absolutely essential to perform this installation?

1. A crimper

2. A punchdown block tool

3. A telepole

4. A fish tape

Scenario 2-2: Expanding a Network

Despite not having any formal training in computers or networking, the owner of a small real-estate firm is understandably proud of having designed and installed the 10Base-T Ethernet LAN for her six-person office. In recent months, business has been booming, and the company has hired four new employees. However, all of the ports on the office's eight-port Ethernet hub are now in use, and it is time to enlarge the network by adding another hub. The owner purchases a second hub, identical to the first one. After connecting the uplink ports of the two hubs with a CAT3 UTP cable, she then plugs the computers for the new employees into the new hub's other ports. She soon finds that the users on each hub can see each other's computers on the network, but they cannot see the computers plugged into the other hub. Which of the following is likely to be the problem?

1. The cable connecting the two hubs must be CAT5 or better.

2. The cable connecting the two hubs should only be plugged into the uplink port on one of the hubs.

3. The cable connecting the two hubs must be a crossover cable.

4. A router is needed to connect two Ethernet hubs together.

CHAPTER 3
NETWORK CONNECTION HARDWARE

Upon completion of this chapter, you will be able to:

■ Describe the functions of a network interface adapter.

■ List the various types of network interface adapters on the market.

■ Understand the network interface adapter installation and troubleshooting process.

■ Describe the different types of hubs.

■ Understand the functions of a hub.

■ Add additional hubs to a network.

■ Understand the concept of a collision domain.

■ Describe the function of a bridge.

■ List the types of bridges available.

■ Describe the functions of a switch.

■ Understand how switches can improve network efficiency.

■ Identify the basic types of switches available.

■ Understand the functions of a router.

■ List the various types of routers.

■ Distinguish between a router and a gateway.

In Chapter 2, "Network Cabling," you learned about the types of cables used to construct local area networks (LANs). In this chapter, you will study the devices that the cables connect: the network interface adapters installed in computers and other network devices, and the hubs that connect the computers on a network. You will also learn about more advanced connectivity devices—bridges, switches, routers, and gateways—that are used to construct larger networks. You must understand the functions of these devices if you manage any network larger than a single LAN.

USING NETWORK INTERFACE ADAPTERS

A **network interface adapter** (called a *network interface card*, or *NIC*, when the adapter is a separate card installed in a computer's expansion slot) is the component that provides the link between a computer and the network. On a computer on a LAN, the network interface adapter and its device driver perform most of the functions of the data-link layer protocol and the physical layer.

Every computer must have an adapter that connects to the system's expansion bus and provides an interface to the network medium. On many newer computers, the network interface adapter is integrated into the motherboard. In some cases, the adapter is an expansion card that plugs into the system's Peripheral Component Interconnect (PCI), PC Card, or Industry Standard Architecture (ISA) bus, as shown in Figure 3-1.

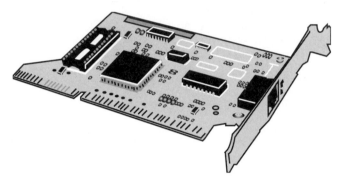

Figure 3-1   Network interface adapters often take the form of expansion cards.

Network interface adapters are not limited to computers. Other devices that connect directly to a network also have them, including printers, network attached storage (NAS) devices, and routers. In addition, not all network interface adapters are intended to connect computers to standard client/server LANs. Certain adapters can connect computers and other devices to a specialized network called a **Storage Area Network (SAN)**. A SAN is a separate network dedicated to communications between servers and external storage devices, such as redundant array of independent disks (RAID) arrays Most SAN adapters use a protocol called Fibre Channel rather than one of the standard LAN protocols, such as Ethernet and Token Ring.

Understanding Network Interface Adapter Functions

Network interface adapters and their drivers perform many functions that are crucial to getting data to and from the computer over the network. The sequence of functions that occurs each time a network interface adapter transmits data over a network is described in the following list.

1. **Data transfer.** Data originating in an application remains in the computer's memory as it is passed down through the protocol stack to the data-link layer. At the data-link layer, the data is transferred from system memory to the network interface adapter using a system technology such as programmed I/O, or in some cases direct memory access (DMA) or shared memory.

2. **Data buffering.** Network interface adapters transmit and receive data one frame at a time, so they have built-in buffers that let them store data arriving from the computer or from the network until a frame is complete and ready for processing. An Ethernet network interface adapter for a desktop computer typically has 4 KB of buffer space—2 KB for its transmit buffer and 2 KB for its receive buffer. Network interface adapters for servers or for other protocols, such as Token Ring, can have more buffer space—often 64 KB or more—that is divided between transmit and receive buffers using one of several configurations.

3. **Data encapsulation.** The network interface adapter and its driver build the data-link layer frame around the data generated by the network layer protocol and passed down to the data-link layer for transmission. For incoming traffic, the adapter verifies that the packets have arrived without errors, using the cyclical redundancy check (CRC) value stored in the frame's footer. The adapter then scans the destination address in the frame's header to determine whether the packet should be passed up to the network layer. If the packet is passed up, the network interface adapter strips off the data-link layer frame and sends the payload data to the network layer protocol specified in the frame header.

4. **Media Access Control (MAC).** The network interface adapter implements the MAC mechanism that the data-link layer protocol uses to regulate access to the network medium.

In networks using the **Carrier Sense Multiple Access with Collision Detection (CSMA/CD)** mechanism, the adapter does the following:

❏ Listens to the network

❏ Transmits when the medium is clear

❏ Detects packet collisions when they occur

❏ Retransmits packets as needed

In **token passing** networks, the adapter does the following:

❏ Captures the token frame

❏ Transmits its data

❏ Removes the data from the ring when it returns to its source

❏ Generates a new token

5. **Parallel/serial conversion.** In parallel communications, systems send multiple bits at one time, using a separate channel for each bit. For example, the communication between a computer and a network interface adapter is nearly always parallel, because the expansion buses that the computer and the adapter use to communicate are 16 or 32 bits wide.

   The only exception to this is an adapter that connects to the computer, using a **universal serial bus (USB)**. In serial communications, the systems send one bit at a time. For a network interface adapter to transmit the data it receives from the computer over the network, it must convert each 16 or 32 bits it receives simultaneously over the bus connection into a stream of 16 or 32 sequential bits that it can send on the network medium. For data arriving from the network, the adapter must perform the same conversion in reverse, by sending a series of incoming serial bits to the computer using parallel communications. Serial communication is used by all baseband LANs.

6. **Signal encoding and decoding.** The network interface adapter implements a physical layer encoding scheme, such as Manchester encoding on Ethernet networks, or Differential Manchester encoding, on Token Ring networks. The physical layer encoding scheme converts the binary data generated by the network layer, now encapsulated in the data-link layer frame, into a pattern of electrical voltages, light pulses, or whatever other signal type the network medium uses. For packets arriving from the network, the adapter converts the signals back into their original binary data.

7. **Data transmission and reception.** Finally, the network interface adapter takes the data it has encoded, amplifies the signals to the appropriate amplitude, and transmits them over the network medium. For incoming data, the adapter detects and reads signals of the appropriate type and amplitude arriving from the network.

When a packet is received, these same steps occur in reverse (with the exception of step 4, Media Access Control, which is not needed for incoming traffic). In addition to these basic functions that are performed by all network interface adapters, specific models have additional features, such as those described in the following sections.

Half-Duplex and Full-Duplex Communications

Most of the network media used on LANs today have separate channels for transmitting and receiving data. For example, computers on unshielded twisted pair (UTP) networks use one wire pair for transmitting data and another pair for receiving it. Despite this fact, however, the systems on these networks nearly always operate in half-duplex mode. In **half-duplex** mode, a system can be either transmitting or receiving data at any one time, but it cannot do both simultaneously. However, some Ethernet network interface adapters can operate in **full-duplex** mode, which means that they can transmit and receive data at the same time, as shown in Figure 3-2. To run a full-duplex LAN, all of the devices connected to the network must have network interfaces capable of full-duplex operation.

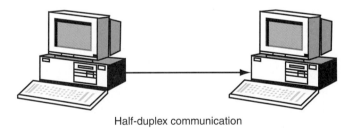

Half-duplex communication

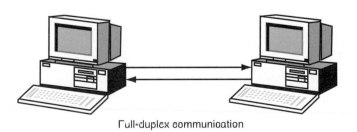

Full-duplex communication

Figure 3-2   Half-duplex and full-duplex communications

Running a LAN in full-duplex mode effectively doubles the bandwidth of the network because the systems can send twice as much data in the same amount of time. Full-duplex communication also eliminates the need for a MAC mechanism because two computers can transmit data at the same time without causing a collision.

Processor Offloading

Many of the tasks in network communications are highly processor intensive, and it has become common for higher-end network interface adapters to take on some of that processing themselves to lessen the burden on the system processor. Various adapter products can include special-purpose processor chips, which enable the adapter to take on some or all of the following tasks:

- **Bus mastering**   Under normal circumstances, when data is transferred from system memory to a network interface adapter using an expansion bus, the system processor functions as an intermediary, reading data from the source and sending it to the destination. In bus mastering, an expansion card arbitrates access to the bus, freeing up the processor clock cycles that were formerly devoted to that process.

- **Checksum processing**   As discussed in Chapter 1, "Networking Basics," error detection can occur at several layers of the Open Systems Interconnection (OSI) reference model. The Internet Protocol (IP), Transmission Control Protocol (TCP), and User Datagram Protocol (UDP) all include error detection functions. This error detection takes the form of a CRC (or *checksum*) calculation that is performed by the transmitting system and then repeated by the destination system. If the results of the two calculations match, then no error has occurred. Some network interface adapters can perform IP, TCP, and UDP checksum calculations themselves, relieving the system process of the need to perform those calculations.

- **TCP segmentation processing**   When a computer on a TCP/IP network transmits a large amount of data in a single TCP transaction, the TCP protocol at the transport layer must split the data into segments of appropriate size and assign a sequence number to each segment. Some network interface adapters can take on these processes themselves, rather than force the system processor to do them.

- **IPSec processing**   IP security (IPSec) is a collection of security standards that enable computers on a TCP/IP network to encrypt and digitally sign their transmissions. This prevents anyone who intercepts the transmissions from deciphering their contents. The encryption and signature calculations can place an extremely heavy burden on the system processor, depending on the amount of data being secured and the length of the encryption keys the system is configured to use. Offloading these processes to the network interface adapter can have a noticeable effect on system performance.

Autonegotiation

Virtually all newer Ethernet network interface adapters can run at multiple speeds. Most adapters support both 10- and 100-megabit per second (Mbps) transmissions, and many also support 1000-Mbps transmissions. These multispeed devices all have a mechanism that enables them to automatically negotiate the speed at which they will operate.

The first version of the Ethernet standard that included a UTP cable specification, called 10Base-T, required network devices to transmit a *normal link pulse (NLP)* signal to verify the integrity of each device's link to the other devices on the network. Most network interface adapters and hubs had a single light-emitting diode (LED) that would illuminate when the device was connected to a network with other functioning devices. If the LED did not light, either the device or the network connection itself was faulty.

The Fast Ethernet standards built on this concept by changing the NLP signal to a *fast link pulse (FLP)*, which includes information about the device's capabilities in the link pulse signal. When a Fast Ethernet or Gigabit Ethernet network interface adapter connects to an Ethernet hub or switch, it transmits its own FLP signals and receives signals back from the other device. The adapter is advertising its maximum speed, while the hub or switch does the same. The two devices then configure themselves to use the maximum speed they have in common.

Network Management

Enterprise networks often use network management systems to track the performance of critical network components. A network management system consists of a central console and a series of programs called *agents*, which are incorporated into hardware and software components scattered around the network. An agent transmits information about the performance of a specific component back to the console on a regular schedule, using a specialized protocol such as the **Simple Network Management Protocol (SNMP)**.

Some network interface adapters have agents built into them, so they can report information about the network performance of the computers into which they are installed. SNMP agents can also generate messages called *traps*, which they can send to the console immediately when a specific situation occurs.

Wake on LAN

Wake on LAN is a feature that lets an administrator power up a computer remotely. One of the most persistent irritants for system administrators who work on computers at remote locations during off hours is when the users turn their systems off, contrary to instructions. In the past, the administrator either had to travel to the computer to turn it on again or work on the system at another time.

Wake on LAN lets a network interface adapter operate in a low power mode, even when the computer is turned off. When the adapter is in this mode, it continues to monitor the traffic arriving over the network, although it takes no action unless it receives a special wake-up packet from the administrator. When it receives a wake-up packet, the adapter sends an instruction to the computer's motherboard, which causes the motherboard to activate the power supply and start the system.

To implement Wake on LAN, both the network interface adapter and the motherboard must support the standard. Wake on LAN is incorporated into many network interface adapters.

Selecting a Network Interface Adapter

In addition to having the features you need, the network interface adapters you choose for your network devices must also accommodate all the requirements of your computers and your network, as follows:

- **Data-link layer protocol**   You must select a network interface adapter for the particular data-link layer protocol your network uses, such as Ethernet or Token Ring; they are not interchangeable. The adapter must also support the specific variant of your data-link layer protocol. In the case of an Ethernet network, for example, there are network interface adapters supporting standard Ethernet, Fast Ethernet, Full-Duplex Fast Ethernet, or Gigabit Ethernet, using a variety of physical layer standards.

- **Transmission speed**   Virtually all newer Ethernet adapters support either Fast Ethernet (100 Mbps) or Gigabit Ethernet (1000 Mbps) speeds. Fast Ethernet adapters can fall back to 10-Mbps standard Ethernet, and Gigabit Ethernet adapters can fall back to 100 or 10 Mbps. To run an Ethernet network at a particular speed, all of its components, adapters, cables, and hubs or switches must support the standard you want to use.

- **Network interface type**   In all network interface adapters, the network interface itself is, in most cases, a cable jack such as an RJ-45 jack for UTP cables, a straight tip (ST) or subscriber connector (SC) jack for fiber optic cables, or a bayonet-Neill-Concelman (BNC) or Attachment Unit Interface (AUI) connector for a coaxial cable connection; however, the interface can also be some type of wireless transceiver. Network interface adapters have different types of network cable connectors, depending on the types of cables they support. Some adapters support a single type of cable and have only one connector, while others have more than one connector. This arrangement allows you to connect the computer to different types of network media. For example, a combination Ethernet adapter might have three cable connectors (RJ-45, BNC, and AUI), but you can only use one of the connectors at a time. Combination adapters can be much more expensive than those with only one connector.

- **System bus type**   Network interface adapters that plug into a PCI bus slot are generally preferable to those that plug into an ISA slot because the slots are self-configuring and the bus is much faster than ISA, but you can use an ISA adapter if the computer has only ISA slots available. For portable systems, network interface adapters use either the PC Card bus or the MiniPCI bus. When you select a PC Card adapter, make sure it supports the CardBus standard if your computer supports it. CardBus is an interface specification that provides the equivalent of PCI performance to PC Card peripherals. There are also network interface adapters that plug into a computer's USB port, but the USB 1.1 interface runs at a maximum of 1.2 Mbps and provides relatively poor performance, even when compared with ISA. Adapters supporting the USB 2.0 standard are also available and provide suitable performance for a 100-Mbps network.

- **Hardware resources required**   A network interface adapter, like most components, requires hardware resources to communicate with the computer it is installed in. Most adapters require an interrupt request (IRQ) line and might also need other resources, such as an I/O port address or a memory address. Because most network interface adapters and computers now support the plug and play (PnP) standard, manually allocating network resources is largely a thing of the past. However, it is still important to consider whether a computer with many other devices installed has the resources a network interface adapter needs.

- **Driver availability**   A network interface adapter requires a driver for the operating system running on the computer. Virtually all newer adapters have drivers available for all of the current Microsoft Windows operating systems, but if you plan to run another operating system, such as Novell NetWare or UNIX/Linux, be sure that the adapter you select has drivers available for the operating system you are using.

Installing a Network Interface Adapter

When you install a network interface adapter card, you perform the following processes:

1. Physically insert the network interface adapter card into the computer.

2. Configure the card to use appropriate hardware resources.

3. Install the card's device driver.

Depending on the age and capabilities of the computer, these processes can be very simple or quite a chore.

> **MORE INFO** **Demonstration Video**   Run the NIC Installation video located in the Demos folder on the CD-ROM accompanying this book for a demonstration of a NIC installation.

▶ **Physically Installing a Network Interface Adapter**

The following procedure describes installing a network interface adapter card into a standard expansion slot on a desktop computer.

> **CAUTION** **Grounding Yourself**   Before touching the internal components of the computer or removing the NIC from its protective bag, be sure to ground yourself by touching the metal frame of the computer's power supply, or use a wrist strap or antistatic mat to protect the equipment from damage done by electrostatic discharge.

1. Turn off the power to the computer and unplug the power cord.

   Inserting an expansion card into a slot while the computer is on can destroy the card and cause serious injuries. Accidentally dropping a screw or slot cover can also cause serious damage if the computer is powered up.

2. Open the computer case.

   In some instances, this is the most difficult part of the installation process. You might have to remove several screws to loosen the case cover and wrestle with the computer a bit to get the cover off. Many newer systems, on the other hand, secure the case cover with thumbscrews and are much easier to open.

3. Locate a free slot.

    You must check to see what type of slots (ISA or PCI) are available in the computer before you select a card. Most adapters now use the PCI bus, but some ISA models are still available. The PCI bus is preferable if you are planning to connect the computer to a Fast Ethernet or other 100-Mbps network. The ISA bus is gradually being phased out in favor of PCI, both in network interface adapters and in computers.

4. Remove the slot cover.

    Empty slots are protected by a metal cover that prevents them from being exposed through the back of the computer. Loosen the screw securing the slot cover in place, and remove both the screw and slot cover.

5. Insert the card into the slot. Line up the edge connector on the card with the slot and press it down until it is fully seated, as shown in Figure 3-3.

6. Secure the card by replacing the screw that held the slot cover on.

    This seats the card firmly in the slot. Some network technicians omit this step, but it is an important one, since a yank on the network cable can pull the card partially out of the slot and cause intermittent problems that are difficult to diagnose.

7. Replace the cover on the computer case and secure it with the fasteners provided.

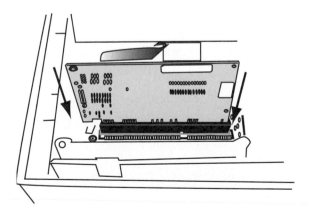

Figure 3-3   Press the adapter down firmly until it is seated all the way into the slot.

NOTE **Testing a Network Interface Adapter** It's usually a good idea to fully test the network interface adapter card by connecting it to the LAN and running it before you close the case and return the computer to its original location. It seems that newly installed components are more likely to malfunction if you put the cover on before testing them.

Configuring a Network Interface Adapter

When you have a computer and a network interface adapter that both support the PnP standard, the resource configuration process is automatic. The computer detects the adapter, identifies it, locates free resources, and configures the adapter to use those resources. However, you must understand more about the configuration process because you might use computers or network interface adapters that don't support PnP, or you might encounter situations in which PnP doesn't quite work as advertised. Improper network interface adapter configuration is one of the main reasons a computer fails to communicate with the network, so knowing how to troubleshoot the configuration is a useful skill.

Configuring a network interface adapter is a matter of configuring it to use certain hardware resources, such as the following:

- **IRQs** Hardware lines that peripheral devices use to send signals to the system processor, requesting its attention

- **I/O port addresses** Locations in memory that are assigned for use by particular devices to exchange information with the rest of the computer

- **Memory addresses** Areas of upper memory that are used by particular devices, usually for installation of a special-purpose basic input/output system (BIOS).

- **DMA channels** Pathways used by devices to transfer information to and from system memory

Network interface adapters do not usually use memory addresses or DMA channels, but they can do so. Every network interface adapter requires an IRQ and an I/O port address to communicate with the computer.

For a network interface adapter (or any type of adapter) to communicate with the computer in which it is installed, the hardware (the adapter) and the software (the adapter driver) must both be configured to use the same resources. Before the creation of the PnP standard, you had to configure the network interface adapter itself to use a particular IRQ and I/O port and then configure the network interface adapter driver to use the same settings. If the settings of the network interface adapter and the driver do not match, it's sort of like dialing the wrong number on a telephone; the devices are both speaking, but they don't intend to speak to the device on the other end of the line. In addition, if the network interface adapter is configured to use the same resources as another device in the computer, both of the conflicting devices will likely malfunction.

On older adapters, you configure the hardware resource settings by installing jumper blocks or setting dual inline package (DIP) switches. If you are working with a card such as this, you must configure the card before you install it in the computer. In fact, you might have to remove the card from the slot to reconfigure it if the settings you've chosen are unavailable. Newer adapters use a software interface to set the resource settings. This makes it easier to reconfigure the settings if there is a conflict. The PnP cards available today include a configuration interface, but you shouldn't need to use it unless your computer doesn't properly support PnP.

When you're working with older equipment, determining the right resource settings for the adapter can be a trial-and-error process. Older adapters often have a relatively limited number of available IRQ and I/O port settings, and you might have to try several before you find a configuration that works. Newer cards have more settings to choose from, making the configuration process easier.

Installing Network Interface Adapter Drivers

The device driver is an integral part of the network interface adapter. The device driver enables the computer to communicate with the adapter and implements many of the required functions. Virtually all network interface adapters come with a disk containing drivers for the major operating systems, but in many cases you won't even need the disk because most operating systems include drivers for the popular network interface adapter models.

In addition to configuring the network interface adapter's hardware resource settings, PnP also installs the appropriate driver, assuming that the operating system includes one. If it doesn't, you must use the driver software included with the adapter. Like any piece of software, network interface adapter drivers are upgraded from time to time, and you can usually obtain the latest driver from the adapter manufacturer's Web site. However, you don't need to install every new driver release that becomes available unless you're experiencing problems and the new driver is designed to address those problems. In other words, network interface adapter drivers are often subject to the "if it's not broken, don't fix it" rule.

Network Adapter Configuration Tools

The various operating systems have different tools for installing and configuring network interface adapters and their drivers. Some of these tools are examined in the following sections.

Microsoft Windows Network Interface Adapter Configuration

In the 32-bit Windows operating systems, including Microsoft Windows Server 2003, Microsoft Windows XP, Microsoft Windows 2000, Microsoft Windows NT, Microsoft Windows Me, Microsoft Windows 98, and Microsoft Windows 95, the primary tool for managing and configuring network interface adapters (as well as all the other hardware components in the system) is the Device Manager utility. You access Device Manager in the System Properties dialog box in Control Panel or from the Computer Management console, as shown in Figure 3-4.

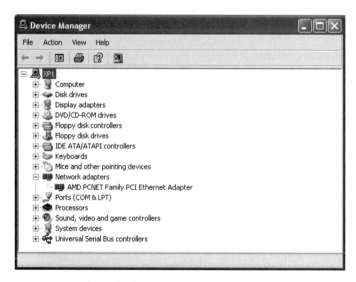

Figure 3-4   The Windows XP Device Manager utility

Device Manager provides a hierarchical display listing all of the hardware components in the computer. For each component, including network interface adapters, you can open a Properties dialog box, shown in Figure 3-5, which lets you perform the following tasks:

- View the current status of the device

- Enable and disable the device

- Install, update, and roll back device drivers

- View and configure hardware resource settings

- Configure advanced device driver parameters

Figure 3-5   A network interface adapter's Properties dialog box

Device Manager can inform you when a newly installed network interface adapter is experiencing a resource conflict with another device. You can use the program to find out which device the adapter is in conflict with and which resource you need to adjust to eliminate the conflict.

Novell NetWare Network Adapter Configuration

Novell NetWare servers load their network interface adapter drivers from the command prompt, but the operating system includes utilities that create script files containing the appropriate commands to load the drivers. The script that loads the network interface adapter drivers is called Autoexec.ncf, and it contains commands like those shown in the following example:

```
LOAD PCNTNW.LAN PCI SLOT=2 FRAME=ETHERNET_II NAME=PCNTNW_1_EII
```

The NetWare configuration utilities are menu-driven programs that let an administrator select configuration parameters for device drivers from a list of settings. Using the menu selections, the program then adds the appropriate commands to the Autoexec.ncf file with the corresponding command line arguments. The utilities for the various versions of NetWare are as follows:

- **Install.nlm**   In NetWare versions earlier than version 5, the Install.nlm utility was used to load and configure the drivers for all of the major system components, including the network adapter drivers.

- **Nwconfig.nlm**   Beginning in NetWare version 5, the functionality of the Install.nlm program was moved to the Nwconfig.nlm utility.

■ **Hdetect.nlm**   Beginning in NetWare version 6.5, the network
interface adapter configuration capabilities of Nwconfig.nlm were
moved to the Hdetect.nlm utility.

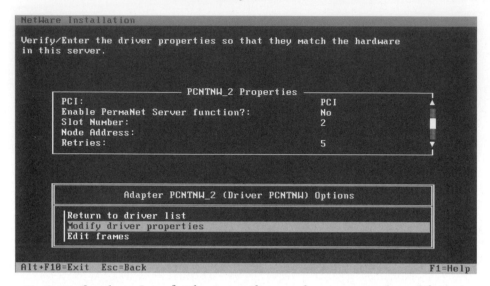

■ **Inetcfg.nlm**   Inetcfg.nlm is a utility used to create and modify a
comprehensive internetworking configuration for a NetWare server,
including the device driver configuration for the network interface
adapters. When you run Inetcfg.nlm for the first time, the program
imports the commands from Autoexec.ncf into its own script files.
From this point on, you use Inetcfg.nlm to configure the network
interface adapter drivers, rather than Nwconfig.nlm or Hdetect.nlm.

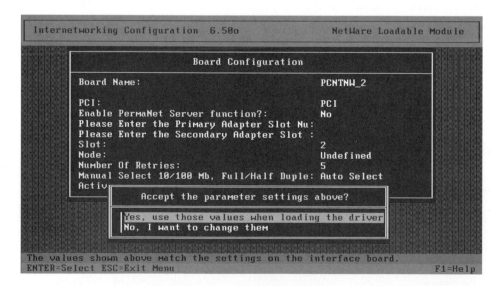

UNIX/Linux Network Adapter Configuration

Many of the distributions of UNIX and Linux have different graphical utilities that let you configure the properties of a network interface adapter, but the one tool they all have in common is the command line program called ifconfig. When you run ifconfig with no arguments, the program displays the status of the currently active network interfaces, as shown in Figure 3-6.

```
[root@localhost /root]#
[root@localhost /root]# ifconfig
eth0      Link encap:Ethernet  HWaddr 00:0C:29:8F:BD:4D
          inet addr:10.1.100.12  Bcast:10.1.100.255  Mask:255.255.255.0
          UP BROADCAST RUNNING MULTICAST  MTU:1500  Metric:1
          RX packets:32 errors:0 dropped:0 overruns:0 frame:0
          TX packets:6 errors:0 dropped:0 overruns:0 carrier:0
          collisions:0 txqueuelen:100
          Interrupt:10 Base address:0x10e0

lo        Link encap:Local Loopback
          inet addr:127.0.0.1  Mask:255.0.0.0
          UP LOOPBACK RUNNING  MTU:16436  Metric:1
          RX packets:6 errors:0 dropped:0 overruns:0 frame:0
          TX packets:6 errors:0 dropped:0 overruns:0 carrier:0
          collisions:0 txqueuelen:0

[root@localhost /root]# _
```

Figure 3-6   The default ifconfig display

To configure specific hardware resource settings, you use the ifconfig program with command line arguments such as the following:

- *interface*   Identifies the network interface adapter that the program should configure, using an abbreviation such as **eth0**

- **irq** *addr*   Specifies the IRQ line that the network interface adapter should use, where *addr* is an integer specifying a valid IRQ line

- **io_addr** *addr*   Specifies the starting I/O address that the network interface adapter should use, where *addr* is a value specifying a valid location in the system's I/O memory space

- **mem_start** *addr*   Specifies the starting address in shared memory that the network interface adapter should use, where *addr* is a value specifying a valid location in the system's shared memory space

■ **media** *type*   Specifies the physical network connector that the
network interface adapter should use, where *type* is a value such as
AUI, 10base2 (for a BNC connector), 10baseT (for an RJ-45 connector),
or auto (to automatically sense the connector the device is using)

Troubleshooting a Network Interface Adapter

When a computer fails to communicate with the network, the network interface
adapter might be at fault, but it's far more likely that some other component is
causing the problem. Before addressing the network interface adapter itself,
check for the following problems:

■ Make sure the network cable is firmly seated into the connector on the
network interface adapter. If you're using a hub, check the cable
connection there as well. Loose connections are a common cause of
communications problems.

■ Try using a different cable that you know is working. If you are using
permanently installed cable runs, plug the computer into another jack
that you know is functioning properly and use a different patch cable.
The cable could be causing the problem, even if there is no visible fault.

■ Make sure the proper device driver is installed. Check the driver
documentation and the Web site of the network interface adapter
manufacturer for information on possible driver problems on your
operating system before you open up the computer.

■ Check to see that all of the other software components required for
network communications, such as clients and protocols, are properly
installed and configured.

If you cannot find a problem with the driver, the cable, or the network
configuration parameters, look at the network interface adapter itself. Before you
open the computer case, check to see if the adapter's manufacturer has provided its
own diagnostic software. In some cases, the manufacturer provides a utility that lets
you manually configure the adapter's hardware resources and that also includes
diagnostic features to test the functions of the card. If you're using PnP, you might
not have even looked at the disk included with the adapter, but you should now.
You should exhaust all other options before you actually open the computer.

If the adapter diagnostics program indicates that the device is functioning
properly, and assuming that the software implementing the upper layer protocols
is correctly installed and configured, the problem is probably caused by the

hardware resource configuration. Either there is a resource conflict between the network interface adapter and another device in the computer, or the network interface adapter is not configured to use the same resources as the network interface adapter driver. Use the configuration utility supplied with the adapter to see what resources the network interface adapter is physically configured to use, and then compare this information with the driver configuration. You might have to adjust the settings of the card or the driver, or even those of another device in the computer, to accommodate the card.

If the diagnostics program finds a problem with the card itself, you need to open up the computer and physically examine the adapter. If the adapter is malfunctioning due to a static discharge or a manufacturer's defect, there is not much you can do except replace it. Before you do this, however, you should check to see that the card is fully seated in the slot, since this is a prime cause of communication problems. If the card is not secured with a screw, press it down firmly into the slot at both ends and secure it.

If the problem persists, remove the card from the slot, clean out the slot with a blast of compressed air, and install the card again. If there is still a problem, use another slot, if one is available. If the adapter still fails to function properly, install a different adapter in the computer. You can use either a new one or one from another computer that you know is working properly. If the replacement adapter functions, then you know that the original adapter itself is to blame, and you should replace it.

USING NETWORK HUBS

A hub, also known as a *concentrator*, is a device used to connect all of the computers on a star or ring network. From the outside, a hub, shown in Figure 3-7, looks like nothing more than a box with a series of cable connectors and LEDs in it. Hubs come in a variety of sizes, from four- and five-port devices designed for home and small business networks to large rack-mounted units with 24 ports or more. Hubs typically have link pulse LEDS, just as network interface adapters do, and sometimes they have additional indicators that signal the activity or speed of each port. Installing a single hub is simply a matter of connecting it to a power source and plugging in the cables that are connected to the network interface adapters in your computers. However, it is important to understand what goes on inside a hub.

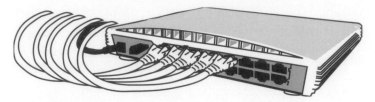

Figure 3-7   Hubs have ports into which you plug the cables connected to your computers' network interface adapters.

Like network interface adapters, hubs are associated with specific data-link layer protocols. Ethernet hubs are the most common because Ethernet is the most popular data-link layer protocol, but Token Ring networks also have hubs, and other protocols, such as Fiber Distributed Data Interface (FDDI), can also use hubs.

Understanding Ethernet Hubs

In technical terms, an Ethernet hub functions as a **multiport repeater**. A repeater is a device that amplifies a signal, to counteract the effects of attenuation. For example, if you have a thin Ethernet network with a cable segment longer than the prescribed maximum of 185 meters, you can install a repeater in the segment to strengthen the signal and extend the maximum segment length. This type of repeater, with only two BNC connectors, is rarely seen now because few networks use thin Ethernet anymore. The hubs used on UTP Ethernet networks are also repeaters, but they have many RJ-45 ports instead of just two BNC connectors.

When signals enter an Ethernet hub through any of its ports, the hub amplifies the signals and immediately transmits them through all of the other ports. This is what enables a star-configured network to have a single shared medium, even though each computer has its own separate cable. The hub relays the packets transmitted by any computer on the network to all of the other computers, while it amplifies the signals.

Selecting a Hub Speed

The Ethernet hubs on your network must conform to the same standards as your other equipment. If you want to run a Fast Ethernet network, you must use Fast Ethernet hubs, as well as Fast Ethernet adapters and Category 5 (CAT5) cables. Although virtually all of the newer Ethernet network interface adapters support multiple transmission speeds, many Ethernet hubs do not. Some hubs autonegotiate between speeds of 10 and 100 Mbps or 10, 100, and 1000 Mbps, but many products support only a single speed.

Generally speaking, multispeed hubs are necessary only when you are planning an upgrade path for a network that has computers running at various speeds. For example, if some computers on your network still have older 10-Mbps standard

Ethernet adapters, while others have 10/100-Mbps dual-speed adapters, a dual-speed hub will enable each computer to operate at its best possible speed. If all of the computers on your network have 10/100-Mbps adapters, you can save money by purchasing a single-speed 100-Mbps hub (unless, of course, you are planning to upgrade all of your computers to Gigabit Ethernet).

Using Smart Hubs

The hubs used on most Ethernet networks are purely physical-layer devices. This means that the hub works with the signals that are native to the network medium, such as electrical voltages, but it does not interpret the signals, read the data inside the packets, or even recognize that there is data there. This type of hub is relatively inexpensive because there is no complex circuitry or programming involved. However, there are Ethernet hubs with more intelligence that can process the data they receive in more elaborate ways.

Some hubs with greater data processing capabilities provide a service called *store and forward*, which means that the hub has buffers that can retain packets to retransmit them through specific ports as needed. This is one step short of a switch, which reads the destination address from each incoming packet and transmits it only to the system for which it is intended.

Intelligent hubs can also include management features that enable them to monitor the operation of each of the hub's ports. In most cases, an intelligent hub uses SNMP to transmit periodic reports to a centralized network management console. This type of management isn't necessary on a small LAN, especially because it significantly increases the price of the hardware, but it can be a boon to the network administrator of a large enterprise network that has dozens of hubs .

Connecting Hubs

You can build a simple Ethernet LAN by plugging a number of computers into a single hub, but what happens when your network outgrows your hub and you have more computers than ports? The solution is to get another hub and connect it to the first one. Large networks can have several interconnected hubs forming large LANs, which are in turn connected by routers. Almost every Ethernet hub on the market has an extra port called an *uplink port*, which is used to connect to another hub instead of to a computer. The uplink port is wired differently from the other ports in the hub.

> **NOTE** **Switched Uplink Ports** On some hubs, the uplink port is switched, meaning that you can choose whether that port uses the crossover circuit or not. This is an important factor to consider when evaluating hubs because the switched port might count toward the total

number of usable ports in the hub. For example, a hub advertised as having eight ports might have one that is switchable, while an eight-port hub with a dedicated uplink port might have eight regular ports and one uplink port, for a total of nine. Be sure you know what you're getting before making a purchase.

As explained in Chapter 2, "Network Cabling," UTP cables are nearly always wired straight through, meaning that each of the contacts at one end of the cable is wired to the same contact at the other end. For network communications to occur, the signals that a computer sends out through its transmit contacts must arrive at the destination computer through its receive contacts. If you were to use a straight-through UTP cable to connect two computers directly, the signals sent by one computer using its transmit contacts would arrive at the other computer's transmit contacts instead of the receive contacts, and no communication would occur.

> **NOTE   Using a Crossover Cable**   As described in Chapter 2, "Network Cabling," you can create a simple two-node Ethernet network without using a hub by connecting the network interface adapters of two computers directly, using a crossover cable. A crossover cable is a UTP cable that has the transmit pins on one end of the cable wired to the receive pins on the other end, thus eliminating the need for the crossover circuit in the hub. However, because you're eliminating the repeater from the network, the crossover cable can be no longer than 100 meters.

Another function of the hub in an Ethernet network is to provide the crossover circuit that connects the transmit pins to the receive pins for each connection between two computers. The uplink port is the only port in the hub that does not have a crossover circuit. When you connect the uplink port in one hub to a regular port in another, you enable the computers plugged into one hub to connect to those plugged into the other hub, with only a single crossover between them. Without the uplink port, connecting one hub to another would cause a connection between computers on different hubs to go through two crossover circuits, resulting in a straight through connection. For the same reason, you should never connect the uplink port in one hub to the uplink port in another, since this would also result in a straight through connection.

> **MORE INFO   Demonstration Video**   Run the HubCrossover video located in the Demos folder on the CD-ROM accompanying this book for a demonstration of an Ethernet hub's crossover circuit.

You can create a larger Ethernet network by connecting hubs together, but there are limits to the number of hubs you can have on a single LAN. The Ethernet standards define the number of hubs you can use, based on the network media you are using and whether you are running standard Ethernet, Fast Ethernet, or Gigabit Ethernet. For more information on the Ethernet cabling guidelines, see Chapter 4, "Data-Link Layer Protocols."

Using Stackable Hubs

Because of the limitations on the number of hubs you can use on a LAN, one logical solution for building large LANs is to simply make hubs with more ports in them. However, manufacturing hubs with hundreds or thousands of ports is economically impractical, so manufacturers have developed stackable hubs instead. Stackable hubs have a proprietary connector that lets you connect multiple hubs together without violating the Ethernet cabling guidelines. Although you might have ten separate 24-port hubs, stacking them (instead of connecting them using their uplink ports) enables them to function like a single 240-port hub.

Understanding Token Ring MAUs

The hubs used on Token Ring networks might look like Ethernet hubs, but they could not be more different. A Token Ring hub is referred to as a **multistation access unit (MAU**, or sometimes MSAU). Unlike Ethernet hubs, Token Ring MAUs are passive devices, meaning that they do not function as repeaters. However, MAUs perform data-link layer functions that are crucial to the operation of the Token Ring network. The primary difference between a Token Ring MAU and an Ethernet hub is that the MAU does not retransmit all incoming traffic out through the other ports simultaneously. Instead, it transmits the packets serially, to each computer in turn.

For example, when a packet arrives at a MAU through port 5, the MAU transmits it out through port 6 and then waits for the computer connected to port 6 to return the packet to the MAU through that same port. Only then does the MAU transmit the packet out through port 7, waiting for it to return before transmitting it out through port 8, as illustrated in Figure 3-8.

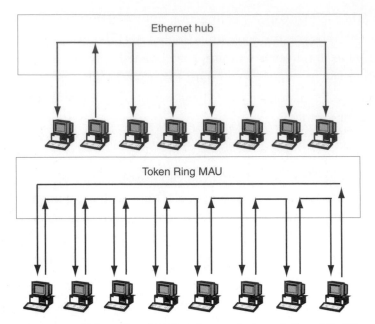

Figure 3-8   Token Ring MAUs relay packets serially, while Ethernet hubs transmit them in parallel.

After the MAU has transmitted the packet to each of the computers on the network and has received it back each time, it sends the packet to the system that originally created it, and that system removes it from the network. This process enables the computers in a physical star topology to communicate as though they are cabled in a ring topology.

On an Ethernet network, if one computer is turned off or disconnected from the hub, it fails to receive the incoming packets, but this does not affect the other computers on the network. On a Token Ring network, the role of each computer is as critical to the packet transmission process as the MAU. If the MAU sends a packet out through a port and the computer on that port fails to return the packet to the MAU, the ring is broken and the packet is lost, which halts communication for the whole network.

Test your knowledge of hubs and their functions by completing Exercise 3-1, "Hub Concepts," now.

To prevent this from occurring, Token Ring MAUs perform an initialization process on each port when the connected computer starts up. The computer informs the MAU of its presence, and the MAU activates the port, adding the system to the logical ring. Ports to which no computer is connected are never added to the ring, and the MAU skips them when forwarding packets. These unused ports are said to be in the loopback state. Token Ring MAUs also do not have an uplink port, but they do have dedicated Ring In and Ring Out ports that connect one MAU to another.

USING ADVANCED NETWORK CONNECTION DEVICES

Using cables, network interface adapters, and a hub, you can build a simple Ethernet LAN. However, there are limits to the maximum size of a single LAN, so large installations need other devices—such as bridges, switches, routers, and gateways—to make it possible for hundreds or thousands of computers to communicate with each other. These devices are associated with different layers of the OSI reference model, as shown in Figure 3-9.

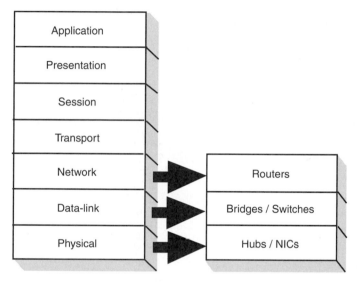

Figure 3-9   Network connection devices and their OSI model layers

These devices are discussed in the following sections.

> **NOTE**   **Network+ Exam Objectives**   *Objective 2.4 for the Network+ exam requires students to "identify the OSI layers at which the following network components operate: hubs, switches, bridges, routers, and network interface cards."*

Bridging

A **bridge** is a device that connects networks at the data-link layer of the OSI model. As explained earlier in this chapter, hubs connect networks at the physical layer and are unaware of the data structures operating at the higher layers. When you expand your network by adding another hub, the result is no different from substituting a hub with more ports for the old one—each packet generated by a computer on the network reaches every other computer. A bridge, on the other hand, provides packet filtering at the data-link layer, meaning that it propagates only the packets that are destined for systems on the other side of the bridge.

If you have a large LAN that is experiencing performance degradations due to excessive collisions or high traffic levels, you can fix the problem by splitting the network in half and connecting the two halves with a bridge.

Connecting LANs with a Bridge

A bridge is a physical unit, typically a box with two ports in it, that you use to connect network segments. You can use a bridge to join two existing LANs (as long as they are using the same data-link layer protocol) or to split one LAN into two segments. Bridges operate in what is called **promiscuous mode**, meaning that they read and process all of the packets transmitted over the network segments. The network interface adapters in computers, by contrast, read the destination address in each packet and process only those that are addressed to that computer; all others are discarded.

Because a bridge functions at the data-link layer, it can interpret the information in the data-link layer protocol header. Data packets enter the bridge through one of its ports. The bridge then reads the destination address in the data-link layer protocol header and decides how to process that packet. This process is called *packet filtering*. If the destination address of a packet arriving from one network segment is that of a computer on the other segment, the bridge transmits it out through the other port. If the destination address is that of a computer on the same network segment as the computer that generated it, the bridge discards the packet.

> **NOTE Bridging and the Network Layer** Although bridges can read the contents of a packet's data-link layer protocol header, they cannot go any higher up the protocol stack than the data-link layer. A bridge cannot read the contents of the data field in a data-link layer frame, which contains the information generated by a network layer protocol. Therefore, bridges are not network layer protocol–specific and can be used on a LAN running TCP/IP, Internetwork Packet Exchange (IPX), or any other protocols at the network layer.

Figure 3-10 shows two LANs connected by a bridge. When a computer on one LAN transmits a packet to a computer on the other, the bridge receives that packet and relays it to the other LAN. In this case, the destination system receives the packet just as if the two computers were on the same LAN. If a computer on one LAN transmits a packet to another computer on the same LAN, the bridge receives the packet and discards it, because there is no reason for the packet to go to the other LAN. Using a bridge (theoretically) cuts the unnecessary traffic passing over each network segment in half because packets not needed on the other network segment don't go there.

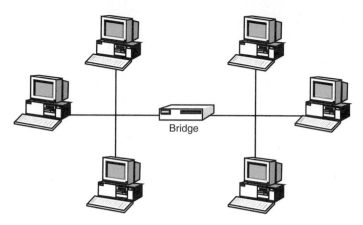

Figure 3-10   A bridge filters the packets passing between two LANs or two LAN segments by reading their data-link layer protocol headers.

Transparent Bridging

For a bridge to filter packets effectively, it has to know which computers are located on each network segment. Bridges maintain an internal address table that lists the hardware (or MAC) addresses of the computers on both segments. When the bridge receives a packet and reads the destination address in the data-link layer protocol header, it checks that address against its lists. If the address is associated with a segment other than that from which the packet arrived, the bridge relays it to that segment.

> **NOTE   Address Table Sizes**   Bridge manufacturers often specify the number of addresses that the device can maintain in its tables. In most cases, bridges can maintain address tables that are far larger than required by any network, but it's still a good idea to check this specification before you make a purchase.

The question still remains, however, of where the bridge gets the information in its address tables. Originally, network administrators had to manually create the lists of hardware addresses for each segment connected to the bridge, which is obviously an onerous chore. Today, bridges use a technique called **transparent bridging** to automatically compile their own address lists. When you activate a transparent bridge for the first time, it begins processing packets. For each incoming packet, the bridge reads the source address in the data-link layer protocol header and adds it to the address list for the network segment over which the packet arrived. At first, the bridge doesn't have the information it needs to decide whether it should relay the packet or discard it, so the bridge errs on the side of caution and relays the packet to the other network segment. When enough packets pass through the bridge to enable the compilation of the address tables, the bridge begins using them to filter the incoming packets.

To provide redundancy in the event of an equipment failure, administrators can install multiple bridges between network segments. However, this practice can cause data loss when multiple bridges process the same packets and determine that the source computer is on two different network segments. In addition, it's possible for multiple bridges to forward broadcast packets around the network endlessly, in what is called a *bridge loop*. To prevent these problems, bridges communicate among themselves using a protocol known as the **spanning tree algorithm (STA)**, which selects one bridge to process the packets. All other bridges on that network segment remain idle until the first one fails.

Source Route Bridging

It is typical for Ethernet networks to use transparent bridging and the STA, but Token Ring networks use a different system. Instead of the bridges themselves selecting a designated bridge between two segments, Token Ring systems select for themselves which bridge they will use. The technique these systems use is called *source route bridging,* and it works when each system transmits All Rings Broadcast (ARB) frames over the network. As each bridge processes these packets (by forwarding them to all connected segments, as with any broadcast), it adds a route designator to them, identifying the bridge and the port through which it received the packet. When ARB packets arrive at the destination, the receiving system sends all of them back to the source. Bridges use the route designators to avoid sending packets to the same bridge twice, and the original source system uses the returned packets to determine which bridge provides the most efficient route through the network to a given destination.

Bridges and Collisions

A **collision domain** is a network (or part of a network) that is constructed so that when two computers transmit packets at precisely the same time, a collision occurs, causing both packets to be lost. All hosts that are affected by a collision belong to the same collision domain. When you add a new hub to an existing network, the computers connected to that hub become part of the same collision domain as the original network because hubs immediately relay the signals that they receive, without filtering packets.

Bridges, on the other hand, do not relay signals to the other network until they have received the entire packet. For this reason, two computers on different sides of a bridge that transmit at the same time do not cause a collision, even though they are both part of the same LAN. The two network segments connected by the bridge are said to form two different collision domains.

On an Ethernet network, collisions are a normal and expected part of network operations, but when there are too many collisions, network efficiency decreases because more packets must be retransmitted. An increase in the number of collisions on a network is the natural result of an increase in the number of computers on that network. The more systems sharing the network medium, the more likely it is that two will transmit simultaneously. When you split the network into two collision domains with a bridge, the reduction in traffic on the two network segments results in fewer collisions, fewer retransmissions, and greater efficiency.

Bridges and Broadcasts

The broadcast domain is another important concept in bridging. A **broadcast** message is a packet with a special destination address that causes it to be read and processed by every computer that receives it. By contrast, a **unicast** message is a packet addressed to a single computer on the network, and a **multicast** message is addressed to a subset of computers on the network that all perform a particular function. A **broadcast domain** is the group of computers that receive a broadcast message transmitted by any one of the computers in the group.

Broadcasts are a crucial part of the networking process. The most common way for computers to locate a particular system on the local network is to transmit a broadcast message that asks, in essence, "Is any computer on this network using this IP address or this Network Basic Input/Output System (NetBIOS) name?" and then wait for that computer to reply, as shown in Figure 3-11. From that reply message, the broadcaster can determine the destination computer's hardware address and send subsequent packets to it as unicasts.

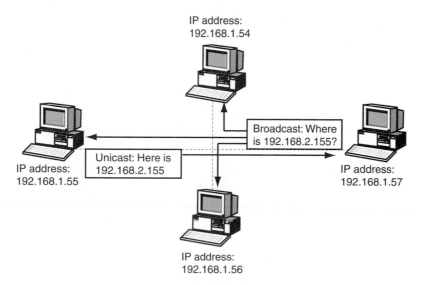

IP address:
192.168.1.54

Broadcast: Where
is 192.168.2.155?

Unicast: Here is
192.168.2.155

IP address:
192.168.1.55

IP address:
192.168.1.57

IP address:
192.168.1.56

Figure 3-11   Computers use broadcast messages to locate specific systems on the LAN.

Adding a bridge separates a network into two different collision domains, but the segments on either side of the bridge remain part of the same broadcast domain because the bridge always relays all broadcast messages from both sides. This behavior mitigates the benefit of the bridge somewhat because some of the broadcast traffic being relayed is not used by the systems on the other side of the network. For example, if a computer generates a series of broadcast messages to locate another computer on the same network segment, the bridge propagates those broadcasts to the other segment, even though they are superfluous. However, the retention of a single broadcast domain is what enables the two network segments to remain part of the same LAN. Using a bridge is not like using a router, which separates the segments into two independent LANs with separate collision and broadcast domains.

Bridge Types

A *local bridge* is the standard type of bridge used to connect network segments that use the same data-link layer protocol and that are at the same location. This is the simplest type of bridge because it doesn't have to modify the data in the packets; it simply reads the addresses in the data-link layer protocol header and passes the packet on or discards it. There are, however, two other types of bridges you can use to handle segments of different types and those that are at different locations: translation bridges and remote bridges.

Translation Bridging

A **translation bridge**, shown in Figure 3-12, is a data-link layer device that connects network segments using different network media or different protocols. This type of bridge is more complicated than a local bridge: in addition to reading the headers in the packet, the translation bridge strips the data-link layer frame off the packets it relays to other network segments and encapsulates the data in a new frame for transmission on the other segment. A translation bridge can therefore connect an Ethernet segment to a Token Ring segment or connect two different types of Ethernet segments (such as 100Base-TX and 100Base-T4) while maintaining a single broadcast domain. Because of the additional packet manipulations, translation bridging is slower than local bridging, and translation bridges are also more expensive. Because there are other types of devices that can connect different network types, such as routers, translation bridges are seldom used.

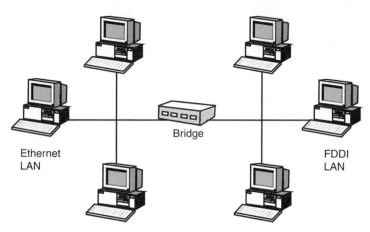

Figure 3-12   Translation bridges let you build a single network using multiple protocols or media types.

Remote Bridging

Test your
knowledge of
bridging
functions by
completing
Exercise 3-2,
"Bridging
Concepts,"
now.

A **remote bridge** connects two network segments at distant locations using some form of wide area network (WAN) link. The link can be a modem connection, leased telephone line, or any other type of WAN technology. The advantage of using a remote bridge is that you reduce the amount of traffic passing over the WAN link, which is usually far slower and more expensive than the local network.

Routing

A router is a device that connects two networks together, forming an internetwork. Unlike bridges and switches, routers function at the network layer of the OSI reference model. This means that a router can connect networks that run on different data-link layer protocols (such as Ethernet and Token Ring), as long as all of the systems are running the same network layer protocol. TCP/IP is the most popular protocol suite in use today, and IP is TCP/IP's network layer protocol, so most of the router information you come across refers to IP routing. However, IPX and AppleTalk are also routable.

When a computer on a LAN wants to transmit data to a computer on another network, the system sends its packets to a router on the local network and the router forwards them to the destination network. In many cases, the destination system is not located on an adjacent network, so the router has to forward the packets to another router. On a large internetwork, such as the Internet, packets might have to pass through a dozen or more routers on the way to their destination. The following sections discuss the routing process in greater detail.

Segments and Backbones

When a small network begins to grow, it is possible to join LANs together with routers in a haphazard manner for a while. However, building a large enterprise network by connecting many LANs is a complex undertaking that requires careful planning. One of the most common designs for a large internetwork is a series of segment LANs connected by a backbone LAN.

The term *segment* is sometimes used synonymously with LAN or network to refer to any collection of networked computers, but in this context, "segment" refers to a LAN composed of user workstations and other end-user devices, such as printers. An enterprise network consists of many such segments. All of these segments are connected to another LAN, called a **backbone network**, by means of routers. The backbone exists primarily as a conduit that enables the computers on different segments to communicate with each other. One common configuration for an office building with multiple floors, as illustrated in Figure 3-13, calls for a horizontal segment connecting all of the workstations on each floor and a backbone running vertically from the top of the building to the bottom, with a router on each floor connecting the horizontal segment to the backbone.

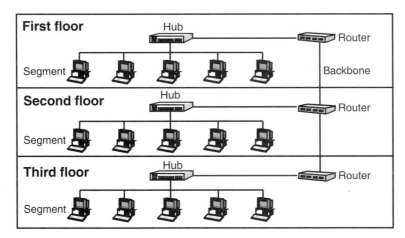

Figure 3-13   An enterprise network consisting of a horizontal segment on each floor and a backbone connecting the segments together

This type of configuration increases network efficiency by using the backbone to carry all of the traffic going from one segment to another. With this model, no packet ever has to traverse more than three LANs. By contrast, if you were to connect the horizontal segments together in sequence, daisy chain fashion, most of the internetwork packets would have to travel through many more segments to reach their destinations, burdening the intermediate segments with through traffic for no good reason.

Packet Routing

Because routers operate at the network layer, they transcend the limitations of the data-link layer protocols. Packets arriving at the router travel up through the protocol stack to the network layer and the router strips the data-link layer frame away. Once the router determines where to send the packet, it passes the data down to a different network interface, which encapsulates it within a new data-link layer frame for transmission. If the data-link layer protocols on the two networks the router connects use different-sized packets, the router might have to fragment the network layer data and create multiple frames that are small enough for transmission over the outgoing network.

Routers are more selective than hubs, bridges, and switches about the packets they forward to other ports. Because they operate at the boundaries of LANs, routers do not forward broadcast messages, except in certain specific cases. A router forwards a packet based on the destination address in the network layer protocol header, not on the hardware address used at the data-link layer. A router has an internal table (called a *routing table*) that contains information about the local and adjacent networks, and it uses this table to determine where to send each packet. If the packet is destined for a system on one of the networks to which the router is connected, the router transmits the packet directly to that system. If the packet is destined for a system on a distant network, the router transmits the packet across one of the adjacent networks to another router.

For example, consider a typical corporate internetwork composed of a backbone and several horizontal segments connected to the backbone by means of routers, as shown in Figure 3-14. The computers on each segment use the router connecting that segment to the backbone as their default gateway. The computers transmit all of the packets they generate either to a specific system on the local network or to the default gateway.

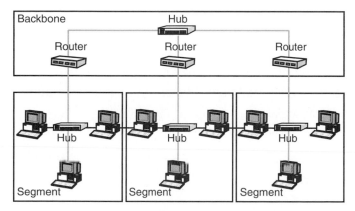

Figure 3-14 In a typical internetwork configuration, the routers are responsible for directing the packets to their next interim destination.

When a computer on one of the segments transmits a packet to a destination on another segment, the following process takes place:

1. The computer generates a packet containing the address of the final destination system in the network layer protocol header and the address of its default gateway router in the data-link layer protocol header and transmits the packet onto the horizontal segment network.

2. The default gateway router receives the packet, strips away its data-link layer frame, and reads the destination address from its network layer protocol header.

3. Using the information in its routing table, the gateway determines which router it must use to access the network on which the destination system is located and which interface it must use to access the router.

4. The gateway constructs a new data-link layer frame for the packet, using the backbone's data-link layer protocol (which can be different from the protocol used on the segment) and specifying the router leading to the destination network as the data-link layer destination address. The gateway then transmits the packet over the backbone network.

5. When the packet reaches the next router, the process repeats itself. The router again strips away the data-link layer frame and reads the destination address from the network layer protocol header. This time, however, the router's routing table indicates that the destination system is on the horizontal segment to which the router is attached. The router can therefore construct a new data-link layer frame that transmits the packet directly to the destination system.

When a packet has to pass through multiple networks on the way to its final destination, each router that processes it is referred to as a hop, as shown in Figure 3-15. Routers often measure the efficiency of a given path through the network by the number of hops required to reach the destination. One of the primary functions of a router is to select the most efficient path to a destination based on the data in its routing tables.

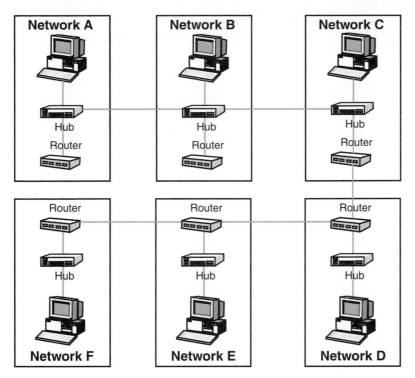

Figure 3-15   A sample internetwork in which the computer on system A is six hops away from the computer on system F

WAN Routing

In addition to connecting networks at a single location, such as a corporate internetwork, routers can also connect distant networks using WAN links. In fact, with the increasing use of switches instead of routers for LAN-to-LAN connections, WAN connections are rapidly becoming the most common application for routers on the enterprise network.

Organizations with multiple branch offices often connect the networks in those offices by installing a router at each location and connecting the routers by means of leased telephone lines or some other WAN technology, such as frame relay. Because each location maintains a separate broadcast domain, the only packets that pass over the WAN links are those destined for systems on the other networks. This arrangement minimizes the amount of traffic passing over those links (even more so than a bridge), which minimizes the cost of the WAN.

A WAN router is most commonly used to connect a network to an Internet service provider (ISP), providing the computers on the network with access to the Internet. The Internet is the ultimate example of a routed internetwork—thousands of networks are connected together using many different kinds of routers. To connect your LAN to the Internet, you install a router that can connect to an ISP, using any type of link, such as a dial-up modem, Integrated Services Digital Network (ISDN) connection, or leased line. You then configure the router to forward all traffic not destined for the local network to the ISP, which relays it to the Internet.

> **MORE INFO** Routing TCP/IP   For more information about routing tables, routing protocols, and specific IP routing practices, see Chapter 7, "TCP/IP."

Router Types

At one time, most routers were large, complex devices costing tens or hundreds of thousands of dollars, and they were used only on large enterprise networks. Today, routers take many different forms and are common equipment, even in homes. It is true that some routers are large, powerful, and very expensive. Generally speaking, routers are more expensive than switches, bridges, or hubs. You can find routers on large corporate networks, where they're mounted in racks in data centers and server closets. These routers can connect segments to backbones and can provide an entire private internetwork with access to computers in their branch offices, on the Internet, or both.

However, there are also much smaller and less expensive routers on the market. In fact, if you use the Internet Connection Sharing (ICS) feature in the current versions of Microsoft Windows to connect your home network to the Internet, you are actually using your computer as a router. Other software-based router products let you share dial-up, cable television network, and Digital Subscriber Line (DSL) Internet connections with a small network. There are also small hardware routers that can be used to connect a LAN to the Internet and include features such as network address translation (NAT) and Dynamic Host Configuration Protocol (DHCP) servers.

For private internetworking, you can use any hardware router, or you can use a Windows Server 2003 or Windows 2000 system with two network interfaces to route IP traffic between networks. Every computer with a TCP/IP client has a routing table in it, even those that are not strictly functioning as routers. For example, when you use a computer on a LAN to connect to the Internet with a dial-up connection, the computer uses its routing table to determine whether requests for network resources should go to the network interface adapter providing the LAN connection or to the modem providing the Internet connection. Even though the system is not providing Internet access to the LAN, it still uses the routing table.

> **NOTE** Demonstration Video   Run the Bridges_and_Routers video located in the Demos folder on the CD-ROM accompanying this book for a demonstration of the difference between a bridge and a router.

Switching

Another type of data-link layer connection device, called a switch, has largely replaced hubs and bridges in many of today's LANs. Switches are also replacing routers in many instances. A switch is a box with multiple cable jacks, similar in appearance to a hub. In fact, some manufacturers make hubs and switches of comparable size that are virtually identical in appearance, except for their markings. The difference between a hub and a switch is that a hub forwards every incoming packet out through all of its ports, and a switch forwards each incoming packet only to the port that provides access to the destination system, as shown in Figure 3-16.

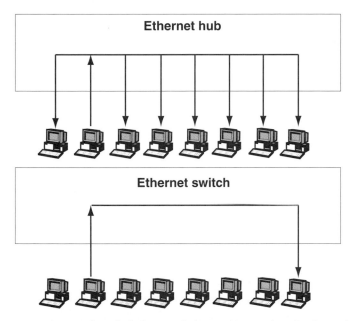

Figure 3-16 A switch forwards incoming packets only to the port that provides access to the destination system.

> **MORE INFO** **Demonstration Video** Run the Hubs_and_Switches video located in the Demos folder on the CD-ROM accompanying this book for a demonstration of the difference between a hub and a switch.

Because they forward packets to a single port only, switches basically convert the LAN from a shared network medium to a dedicated one. In a small network that uses a switch instead of a hub (such a switch is sometimes called a *switching hub*), each packet takes a dedicated path from the source computer to the destination, forming a separate collision domain for those two computers. Switches still forward broadcast messages to all of their ports, but not unicasts and multicasts. No computers receive packets destined for other systems, and no collisions occur during unicast transmissions because every pair of computers on the network has what amounts to a dedicated cable segment connecting them. Thus, a switch practically eliminates unnecessary traffic congestion on the network.

Another advantage of switching is that each pair of computers has the full bandwidth of the network dedicated to it. A standard Ethernet LAN using a hub might have 20 or more computers sharing the same 10 Mbps of bandwidth. Replace the hub with a switch, and every pair of computers has its own dedicated 10-Mbps channel. This can greatly improve the overall performance of the network without requiring any workstation modifications. In addition, some switches provide ports that operate in full-duplex mode, which effectively doubles the throughput of a 10-Mbps network to 20 Mbps.

> **NOTE Switch Prices**   In general, switches are more expensive than repeating hubs and less expensive than routers. As with hubs, you can purchase switches that range from small standalone units to large rack-mounted models.

Installing Switches

Switches generally aren't needed on small networks that only use a single hub. They are more often found on larger networks, where they're used instead of bridges or routers. If you take a standard enterprise internetwork consisting of a backbone and a series of segments and replace the routers with switches, the effect is profound. On the routed network, the backbone must carry the internetwork traffic generated by all the segments. This can lead to heavy traffic on the backbone, even if it uses a faster medium than the segments. On a switched network, you connect the computers to individual workgroup switches, which are in turn connected to a high-performance backbone switch, as shown in Figure 3-17. As a result, any computer on the network can open a dedicated channel to any other computer, even when the data path runs through several switches.

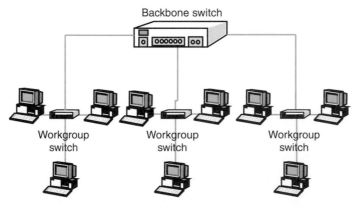

Figure 3-17   Switching enables computers to communicate directly with other computers, without the need for a shared backbone network.

There are many different ways to use switches on a complex internetwork; you don't have to replace all of the hubs and routers with switches at one time. For example, you can continue to use your standard shared network hubs and connect them all to a multiport switch instead of to routers. This increases the efficiency of your internetwork traffic. On the other hand, if your network generates more traffic within the individual LANs than between them, you can replace the workgroup hubs with switches to increase the available intranetwork bandwidth for each computer, leaving the routed backbone network intact.

Switches and Broadcasts

The problem with replacing all of the routers on a large internetwork with switches is that you create one huge broadcast domain instead of several small ones. The issue of collision domains is no longer a problem because there are far fewer collisions. However, switches relay every broadcast generated by a computer anywhere on the network to every other computer, which increases the number of unnecessary packets processed by each system. Several technologies address this problem, including the following:

- **Virtual LANs (VLANs)**   With a **virtual LAN** you can create subnets on a switched network that exist only in the switches themselves. The physical network is still switched, but you can specify the addresses of the systems that belong to a specific subnet. These systems can be located anywhere because the subnet is virtual and is not constrained by the physical layout of the network. When a computer on a particular subnet transmits a broadcast message, the packet goes only to the computers in that subnet, rather than being propagated throughout the entire network. Communication between subnets can be either routed or switched, but all traffic within a VLAN is switched.

- **Layer 3 switching**   Layer 3 switching is a variation on the VLAN concept that minimizes the amount of routing needed between the VLANs. When systems on different VLANs need to communicate, a router establishes a connection between the systems and then the switches take over, a process sometimes called "route once, switch many." Routing occurs only when absolutely necessary. Unlike data-link layer switches, which can read only the contents of the data-link layer protocol header in the packets they process, layer 3 switches can read the addresses in the network layer protocol header as well.

> **NOTE   Network+ Exam Objectives**   Objective 3.3 for the Network+ exam requires students to "identify the main characteristics of VLANs."

Switch Types

There are two basic types of switches: cut-through and store-and-forward. A *cut-through switch* forwards packets immediately by reading the destination address from their data-link layer protocol headers as soon as they're received and relaying the packets out through the appropriate port, with no additional processing. The switch does not wait for the entire packet to arrive before it begins forwarding it. In most cases, cut-through switches use a hardware-based mechanism consisting of a grid of I/O circuits that enable data to enter and leave the switch through any port. This is called *matrix switching* or *crossbar switching*. This type of switch is relatively inexpensive and minimizes the delay that happens while the switch processes the packets. (This delay time is called *latency*.)

A *store-and-forward switch* waits until an entire packet arrives before forwarding it to its destination. This type of switch can be a shared-memory switch, which has a common memory buffer that stores the incoming data from all of the ports, or a bus architecture switch, with individual buffers for each port, connected by a bus. While the packet is stored in the switch's memory buffers, the switch verifies the data by performing a CRC check. The switch also checks for other problems peculiar to the data-link layer protocol involved—problems that could result in malformed frames and detrimental conditions such as runts, giants, and jabber.

There are two drawbacks to store-and-forward switches:

- CRC and error checking naturally introduces additional latency into the packet forwarding process.

- The additional functions make store-and-forward switches more expensive than cut-through switches.

Test your knowledge of switches and their applications by completing Exercise 3-3, "Using Switches," now.

The advantage to store-and-forward switching is that a higher quality of service is maintained through the checking process.

Using Gateways

In computer networking, the term **gateway** can be confusing because it is used to refer to devices that are similar in theory but fundamentally different in application. The term *router* always refers to a hardware or software device that connects two networks at the network layer of the OSI model, forming an internetwork. In TCP/IP terminology, however, routers are often called gateways. For example, when you configure a TCP/IP client, you supply the address of a default gateway, which is actually a router on the local network that the system uses to access other networks.

Technically speaking, a gateway is a device that enables two computers to communicate, even though they are running different protocols at some layer of the OSI model. A router can be called a gateway because it enables computers running different data-link layer protocols to communicate. However, there are also gateways that operate at the application layer, providing an interface between two programs or operating systems. For example, the Gateway Service for NetWare included in Microsoft Windows 2000 Server enables Windows clients to access IPX-based NetWare servers without having to run a NetWare client or the IPX protocols themselves.

> **NOTE   Network+ Exam Objectives**   Objective 1.6 for the Network+ exam requires students to "identify the purpose, features, and functions of the following network components: hubs, switches, bridges, routers, gateways, CSU/DSUs, network interface cards/ISDN adapters/system area network cards, wireless access points, [and] modems."

SUMMARY

- A network interface adapter provides the link between a computer and the network medium.

- The network interface adapter and its driver implement the data-link layer protocol on the computer.

- Hardware resource configuration issues or device conflicts cause most network interface card (NIC) installation problems.

- Ethernet hubs, also called multiport repeaters, are physical layer devices that forward incoming traffic out through all other ports simultaneously. You connect Ethernet hubs together by cabling the uplink port on one hub to a standard port on the other.

- Token Ring hubs, called multistation access units (MAUs), forward packets out through each port in turn and wait for each packet to be returned. You connect Token Ring MAUs by using the Ring In and Ring Out ports.

- Bridges are data-link layer devices that selectively relay packets between network segments, depending on their data-link layer destination addresses. Bridges maintain a single broadcast domain and create separate collision domains.

- Transparent bridging and source route bridging are techniques that bridges use to gather information about the network segments they service. Local bridges connect network segments of the same type, translation bridges connect network segments of different types, and remote bridges connect network segments in distant locations.

- Routers connect networks at the network layer of the Open Systems Interconnection (OSI) reference model. Routers strip away the data-link layer frame of incoming packets and build a new frame using the data-link layer protocol of the outgoing network.

- Routers use internal tables, called routing tables, which contain information about the surrounding networks to forward packets to their destinations.

- Switches are data-link layer devices that improve on the function of bridges by forwarding packets only to their destination systems. Switches reduce the collisions on a network and increase the bandwidth available to each computer. Several types of switches are available, from relatively simple and inexpensive workgroup units to complex enterprise network switches.

- Virtual local area networks (VLANs) can be used to create multiple broadcast domains on a switched network.

- A gateway is a device that enables two computers to communicate, even though they are running different protocols at some layer of the OSI model. While a router can be called a gateway, there are also gateways that operate at the application layer, providing an interface between two programs or operating systems.

EXERCISES

Exercise 3-1: Hub Concepts

Match the concept in the left column with the definition that best describes it in the right column.

1. Token Ring MAU	a. Amplifies signals
2. Intelligent hub	b. Used to send reports to a network management console
3. Uplink port	
4. Loopback port	c. Used to connect MAUs
5. Repeater	d. Forwards packets serially
6. Ring In and Ring Out ports	e. Excluded from a Token Ring network
	f. Used to connect one Ethernet hub to a standard port on another Ethernet hub

Exercise 3-2: Bridging Concepts

Match the bridging concepts in the left column with the appropriate descriptions in the right column.

1. Translation bridge	a. Used to select one of the bridges on a network segment while the others remain idle
2. Source route bridging	
3. Transparent bridging	b. Enables bridges to compile their own address tables
4. Remote bridge	c. Connects two network segments using a WAN link
5. STA	d. Joins two network segments using different data-link layer protocols
	e. Enables computers to select the bridge they will use

Exercise 3-3: Using Switches

Study the network diagram below. Then, for each question, specify which device (or devices) you could replace with switches—with a minimum of expense—to achieve the results described in the question.

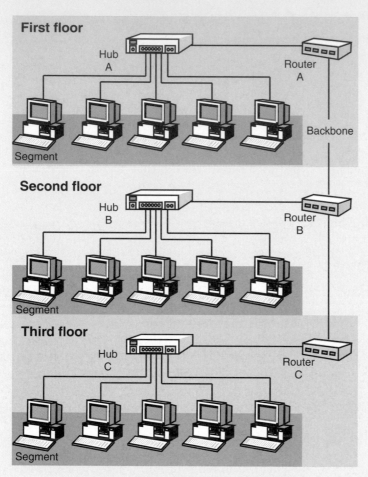

1. Which of the following devices would you replace with switches to reduce the number of collisions on the backbone?

   a. Hub A

   b. Routers A, B, and C, and Hubs A, B, and C

   c. Hubs A, B, and C

   d. Routers A, B, and C

2. Which of the following devices would you replace with switches to reduce traffic on the first-floor segment?

    a. Hub A

    b. Router A

    c. Router A and Hub A

    d. Routers A, B, and C

3. Which of the following devices would you replace with switches to create a single broadcast domain for the entire network?

    a. Router B and Hub B

    b. Routers A, B, and C

    c. Hubs, A, B, and C

    d. Routers A, B, and C, and Hubs A, B, and C

REVIEW QUESTIONS

1. Which of the following hardware resources do network interface adapters usually require? (Select two correct answers.)

    a. DMA channel

    b. I/O port address

    c. IRQ

    d. Memory address

2. What is the name of the process that a network interface adapter uses to determine when it should transmit its data over the network?

3. Which bus type should you use for a NIC that will be connected to a Fast Ethernet network?

4. A passive hub does not do which of the following?

    a. Transmit management information using SNMP

    b. Function as a repeater

    c. Provide a crossover circuit

    d. Store and forward data

5. What must you do to connect two Ethernet hubs together?

   a. Purchase a special crossover cable

   b. Connect the uplink ports on the two hubs together

   c. Connect any standard port on one hub to a standard port on the other

   d. Connect the uplink port on one hub to a standard port on the other

6. Which term describes a port in a Token Ring MAU that is not part of the ring?

   a. Passive

   b. Loopback

   c. Crossover

   d. Intelligent

7. A hub that functions as a repeater inhibits the effect of what type of signal degradation?

8. Which of the following can you use to connect two Ethernet computers, using UTP cable?

   a. An Ethernet hub

   b. A multiport repeater

   c. A crossover cable

   d. Any of the above

9. At what layer of the OSI reference model does a bridge function?

   a. Physical

   b. Data-link

   c. Network

   d. Transport

10. What does a bridge do when it receives a packet that is destined for a system on the same network segment from which the packet arrived?

   a. Discards it

   b. Relays it

   c. Broadcasts it

   d. Unicasts it

11. What type of bridge connects network segments using different data-link layer protocols?

    a. Transparent

    b. Remote

    c. Translation

    d. Source route

12. What type of domain do two network segments connected by a bridge share?

    a. Collision

    b. Broadcast

    c. Source route

    d. Unicast

13. What technique is used to prevent bridge loops?

    a. Transparent bridging

    b. Packet filtering

    c. Translation bridging

    d. The STA

14. Which of the following protocols is source route bridging associated with?

    a. Ethernet

    b. Token Ring

    c. FDDI

    d. TCP/IP

15. What happens when you replace the routers in a segment/backbone network with switches?

    a. The speed of the network increases.

    b. The traffic on the backbone increases.

    c. The number of LANs increases.

    d. The bandwidth available to workstations increases.

16. When you use switches instead of routers and hubs, what is the effect on the number of collisions on the network?

    a. They increase.

    b. They decrease.

    c. They stay the same.

17. When you replace the routers on an internetwork consisting of three segments connected by one backbone with switches, how many broadcast domains do you end up with?

    a. None

    b. One

    c. Three

    d. Four

18. What type of switch immediately relays signals from the incoming port to the outgoing port?

    a. A cut-through switch

    b. A shared memory switch

    c. A bus architecture switch

    d. A store-and-forward switch

19. On a switched network, VLANs are used to create multiples of what?

    a. Collision domains

    b. Broadcast domains

    c. Internetworks

    d. All of the above

20. Which of the following devices does not have buffers to store data during processing?

    a. A repeating hub

    b. A local bridge

    c. A cut-through switch

    d. All of the above

21. At what layer of the OSI reference model do routers operate?

   a. Physical

   b. Data-link

   c. Network

   d. Transport

CASE SCENARIOS

Scenario 3-1: Segmenting a Network

You are the network administrator responsible for a 10-Mbps Ethernet LAN that consists of 45 computers connected to three standard repeating hubs. Recently, you've received complaints that the network's performance is diminished during certain hours of the day. When you monitor the network, you notice that traffic levels have increased substantially, as have the number of collisions occurring on the network. You have determined that the increase in traffic is the source of the problem. Answer the following questions.

1. Which of the following is the most inexpensive way to reduce the overall traffic level on the network?

   a. Split the network into three LANs and connect them using dedicated hardware routers.

   b. Replace the three hubs with switches.

   c. Install a transparent bridge between two of the hubs.

   d. Upgrade the network to 100 Mbps by installing Fast Ethernet network interface adapters and hubs.

2. Which of the following will not increase the bandwidth available to each workstation?

   a. Splitting the network into three LANs and connecting them using dedicated hardware routers

   b. Replacing the three hubs with workgroup switches

   c. Installing a transparent bridge between two of the hubs

   d. Upgrading the network to 100 Mbps by installing Fast Ethernet network interface adapters and hubs

3. Which of the following will eliminate the shared network medium from the network?

   a. Splitting the network into three LANs and connecting them using dedicated hardware routers

   b. Replacing the three hubs with workgroup switches

   c. Installing a transparent bridge between two of the hubs

   d. Upgrading the network to 100 Mbps by installing Fast Ethernet network interface adapters and hubs

4. Which of the following will increase network performance without reducing the number of collisions?

   a. Splitting the network into three LANs and connecting them using dedicated hardware routers

   b. Replacing the three hubs with workgroup switches

   c. Installing a transparent bridge between two of the hubs

   d. Upgrading the network to 100 Mbps by installing Fast Ethernet network interface adapters and hubs

Scenario 3-2: Boosting Network Performance

A large campus internetwork currently consists of a fiber optic backbone connecting all of the buildings together and separate Ethernet LANs for each of the scholastic departments, all connected to the backbone by routers. Each department LAN has its own servers and workstations connected to a single hub, and the majority of the traffic on the internetwork is generated by workstations accessing their local departmental servers. However, there are also campus-wide e-mail and accounting services that are implemented on servers connected to the LAN in the university's computer center, which are accessed by users throughout the installation.

1. Which one of the following modifications to the current internetwork configuration will most likely provide the greatest increase in network performance?

   a. Splitting each LAN in two by installing a local transparent bridge

   b. Replacing the routers connecting each LAN to the backbone with a multiport switch

   c. Replacing the hub on each departmental LAN with a switch

   d. Moving the e-mail and accounting servers from the computer center LAN to the backbone

CHAPTER 4
DATA-LINK LAYER PROTOCOLS

Upon completion of this chapter, you will be able to:

- List the Ethernet physical layer standards.

- Describe the functions of the Ethernet frame.

- Describe the Carrier Sense Multiple Access with Collision Detection (CSMA/CD) Media Access Control (MAC) mechanism.

- List the physical layer options for Token Ring networks.

- Diagram the Token Ring frames.

- Describe the token-passing MAC mechanism.

- Describe the characteristics of the Fiber Distributed Data Interface (FDDI) protocol.

- Distinguish among the various types of FDDI network connections.

- Diagram a FDDI frame.

- Describe the two basic wireless topologies.

- List the Institute of Electrical and Electronics Engineers (IEEE) 802.11 physical layer options.

- Describe the Carrier Sense Multiple Access with Collision Avoidance (CSMA/CA) MAC mechanism.

In the design of a local area network (LAN), the protocol operating at the data-link layer of the Open Systems Interconnection (OSI) reference model is the most significant defining element of the network. The data-link layer protocol determines how fast the network transmits data, what types of network media you can install, how large the network can be, and how many computers you can connect to it. An understanding of the data-link layer protocols is essential to any study of computer networking because they have a profound effect on virtually all aspects of network administration.

> **MORE INFO   Data-Link Layer WAN Protocols**   This chapter covers only the data-link layer protocols that are used on LANs. For more information about the protocols that wide area networks (WANs) use at the data-link layer, see Chapter 10, "Remote Network Access."

ETHERNET

Ethernet is the most popular LAN protocol operating at the data-link layer and has been for decades. In most cases, when people talk about a LAN, they are referring to an Ethernet LAN. The Ethernet protocol was conceived and developed in the 1970s and has since been upgraded repeatedly to satisfy the changing requirements of networks and network users. Today's Ethernet networks run at speeds of 10, 100, and 1000 Mbps (1 Gbps), and soon even 10 Gbps, enabling them to fill roles ranging from home and small business networks to high-capacity backbones.

> **NOTE   Network + Exam Objectives**   Objective 1.2 for the Network+ exam states that students should be able to "specify the main features of 802.2 (LLC), 802.3 (Ethernet), 802.5 (Token Ring), 802.11b (wireless) and FDDI networking technologies, including speed, access method, topology, [and] media."

Ethernet Standards

The standards on which the Ethernet protocol is based have been developed and published by two different organizations over the years, as described in the following sections.

DIX Ethernet

The original conception for the Ethernet protocol was patented by employees of Xerox Corporation in 1977; in 1980, a consortium of the vendors Digital Equipment Corporation (DEC), Intel, and Xerox published a document called "The Ethernet, A Local Area Network: Data-Link Layer and Physical Layer Specifications." Taken from the initials of the three vendors, this document is usually referred to as **DIX Ethernet**.

The original DIX Ethernet standard defined a network running at 10 Mbps and using RG-8 coaxial cable in a bus topology. This physical layer specification was variously known as thick Ethernet, ThickNet, or 10Base5. Version 2 of the standard, published in 1982 and often referred to as DIX Ethernet II, added a second physical layer option to the protocol, also using RG-58 coaxial cable. This standard was known as thin Ethernet, ThinNet, Cheapernet, or 10Base2.

> **NOTE** **Ethernet Designations**   The terms "10Base5" and "10Base2" are designations for specific Ethernet physical layer specifications. The number 10 refers to the speed of the network (10 Mbps); the word "Base" refers to the use of baseband signaling on the network; and the numbers 5 and 2 refer to the maximum length of a cable segment, which is 500 meters for thick Ethernet and 200 (actually 185) meters for thin Ethernet. Subsequent designations have used letters representing the cable type, rather than numbers indicating cable lengths. For example, the "T" in 10Base-T refers to the use of twisted pair cable. The designations beginning with 10Base-T also include a hyphen, to prevent people from pronouncing it "bassett."

IEEE 802.3 Ethernet

Around the same time that the DIX Ethernet standards were published, an international standards-making body called the **Institute of Electrical and Electronics Engineers (IEEE)** began creating an international standard to define this type of network—a standard that would not be privately owned, as was the DIX Ethernet standard. In 1980, the IEEE assembled a working group within its Local and Metropolitan Networks (LAN/MAN) Standards Committee. The committee, which has always used the designation 802 for all of its standards, called the people working on Ethernet standardization the 802.3 working group.

The original document published in 1985 by the 802.3 working group, called "IEEE 802.3 Carrier Sense Multiple Access with Collision Detection (CSMA/CD) Access Method and Physical Layer Specifications," defines basically the same thick Ethernet network as that defined in the DIX Ethernet standard. However, the IEEE document, and all of its subsequent revisions, have scrupulously avoided using the term "Ethernet." Although Xerox no longer held a trademark on the name, the IEEE wanted to avoid any hint of collusion with a specific commercial interest; therefore, it has always referred to its standards as **IEEE 802.3**. The rest of the world, however, still uses the term "Ethernet," even though virtually all of the networks using this technology today are actually IEEE 802.3 networks.

Contrasting the DIX Ethernet and IEEE 802.3 Standards

The primary difference between the DIX Ethernet standards and the IEEE 802.3 standards is that the 802.3 working group has continued to revise its documents, while development of the DIX Ethernet standards stopped at version 2. The other main difference between the DIX Ethernet standards and the IEEE 802.3 standards is that the DIX standards are stand-alone documents, while the IEEE

802.3 standard is one of several documents published by the 802 committee. The 802 standards encompass the physical and data-link layers of the OSI reference model. For organizational purposes, the committee has created the following four subdivisions of those layers, as shown in Figure 4-1.

- Logical Link Control (LLC)
- Media Access Control (MAC)
- Physical signaling
- Media specifications

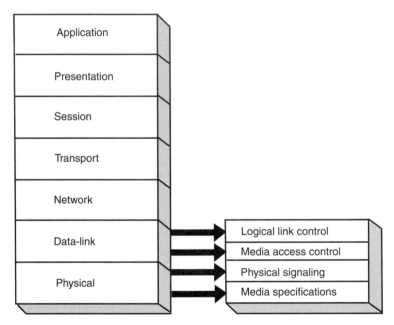

Figure 4-1   IEEE 802 sublayers of the OSI physical and data-link layers

Of these four sublayers, the last three are defined in a specific protocol standard, such as IEEE 802.3. The LLC sublayer is defined in a separate document, called "IEEE 802.2-1998, IEEE Standard for Information Technology–Telecommunications and Information Exchange Between Systems–Local and Metropolitan Area Networks–Specific Requirements–Part 2: Logical Link Control." The **IEEE 802.2** standard defines a mechanism for specifying which network layer protocol generates the data carried in a data-link layer frame.

> **MORE INFO   LLC and Ethertype**   In the DIX Ethernet standards, the protocol generating the contents of an Ethernet frame is specified by an Ethertype field in the frame itself, as contrasted with the IEEE 802.2 standard for the LLC sublayer. For more information on the differences in the frame formats of the two standards, see "The Ethernet Frame," later in this chapter.

LLC is defined in a separate document because it is equally applicable to a number of other MAC protocols, also standardized by the IEEE 802 committee. The current architecture of the 802 family of standards is shown in Figure 4-2. Of the four original MAC standards, numbered 802.3 to 802.6, only 802.3 (CSMA/CD) and 802.5 (Token Ring) are still in general use. The 802.11 and 802.12 standards were added to the architecture much later.

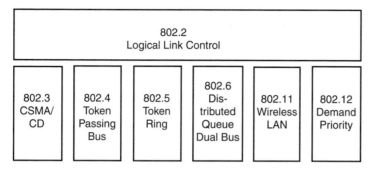

Figure 4-2   The IEEE 802 family of standards

IEEE 802.3 Revisions

All of the physical layer specifications that you can use on an Ethernet network beyond the original 10Base2 are the result of revisions to the 802.3 document. Each of the following revisions, named with a letter or letters following the 802.3 document number, adds one or more physical layer specifications to the standard.

- **802.3a–1988**   10Base2 (thin Ethernet)
- **802.3b–1985**   10Broad36
- **802.3c–1985**   10 Mbps repeater specifications
- **802.3d–1987**   Fiber Optic Inter-Repeater Link (FOIRL)
- **802.3e–1987**   1Base5
- **802.3i–1990**   10Base-T (unshielded twisted pair)
- **802.3j–1993**   10Base-FP, 10Base-FB, and 10Base-FL (fiber optic)
- **802.3u–1995**   100Base-T (Fast Ethernet)
- **802.3x–1997**   Full duplex operation
- **802.3z–1998**   1000Base-X (Gigabit Ethernet on fiber optic)
- **802.3ab–1999**   1000Base-T (Gigabit Ethernet on twisted pair)
- **802.3ae–2002**   10 Gbps Ethernet
- **802.3ak (unapproved draft)**   10Gbase-CX4 (10 Gbps Ethernet)

Test your knowledge of the IEEE 802 standards by doing Exercise 4-1, "IEEE Standards and Technologies," now.

All of these revisions (except the last two, which are too recent) have been incorporated into the main 802.3 standard, which is now a document over 1500 pages long, called "IEEE 802.3-2002, IEEE Standard for Information Technology–Telecommunications and Information Exchange Between Systems–Local and Metropolitan Area Networks–Specific Requirements–Part 3: Carrier Sense Multiple Access with Collision Detection (CSMA/CD) Access Method and Physical Layer Specifications."

> **MORE INFO**   *Obtaining IEEE Standards*   IEEE standards are available for purchase, in both printed and electronic formats, from the IEEE Web site at *standards.ieee.org.*

Ethernet Components

Both the IEEE 802.3 and DIX Ethernet standards consist of the following three basic components:

- **Frame format**   Specifies the size, function, and sequence of the fields that comprise the Ethernet protocol data unit

- **MAC mechanism**   Defines the CSMA/CD mechanism that all Ethernet systems use to regulate access to the network

- **Physical layer specifications**   Define the components that the computers and other devices (referred to as *stations* in the standards) use to generate communications signals, as well as the physical medium that carries those signals

The Ethernet Frame

One of the primary functions of the Ethernet protocol is to encapsulate the data it receives from the network layer protocol in a frame, in preparation for transmission across the network. The frame consists of a header and a footer that are divided into fields containing specific information needed to get each packet to its destination. Standard Ethernet, Fast Ethernet, and Gigabit Ethernet all use the same frame format, which is shown in Figure 4-3.

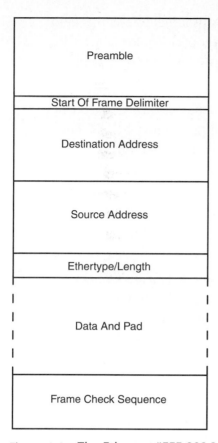

Figure 4-3   The Ethernet/IEEE 802.3 frame

The functions of the Ethernet frame fields are as follows:

- **Preamble (7 bytes)**   Contains 7 bytes of alternating 0s and 1s, which the communicating systems use to synchronize their clock signals.

- **Start Of Frame Delimiter (1 byte)**   Contains 6 bits of alternating 0s and 1s, followed by two consecutive 1s, which is a signal to the receiver that the transmission of the actual frame is about to begin.

- **Destination Address (6 bytes)**   Contains the 6-byte hexadecimal MAC address of the network interface adapter on the local network to which the packet will be transmitted.

- **Source Address (6 bytes)**   Contains the 6-byte hexadecimal MAC address of the network interface adapter in the system generating the packet.

- **Ethertype/Length (2 bytes)**   In the DIX Ethernet frame, this field contains a code identifying the network layer protocol for which the data in the packet is intended. In the IEEE 802.3 frame, this field specifies the length of the data field (excluding the pad).

- **Data And Pad (46 to 1500 bytes)**   Contains the data received from the network layer protocol on the transmitting system, which is sent to the same protocol on the destination system. Ethernet frames (including the header and footer, except for the Preamble and Start Of Frame Delimiter) must be at least 64 bytes long; therefore, if the data received from the network layer protocol is less than 46 bytes, the system adds padding bytes to bring it up to its minimum length.

- **Frame Check Sequence (4 bytes)**   The frame's footer is a single field that comes after the network layer protocol data and contains a 4-byte checksum value for the entire packet. The sending computer computes this value and places it into the field. The receiving system performs the same computation and compares it to the field to verify that the packet was transmitted without error.

Ethernet Addressing

The Destination Address and Source Address fields in the Ethernet frame use the 6-byte hardware addresses coded into network interface adapters to identify stations on the network. Every network interface adapter has a unique hardware address (also called a MAC address), which consists of a 3-byte value called an **organizationally unique identifier (OUI),** which is assigned to the adapter's manufacturer by the IEEE, plus another 3-byte value assigned by the manufacturer itself. Hardware addresses are typically expressed in one of the following forms:

```
00-D0-59-83-B1-52
00D05983B152
```

Ethernet, like all data-link layer protocols, is concerned only with transmitting packets to another system on the local network. If the packet's final destination is another system on the LAN, the Destination Address field contains the address of that system's network adapter. If the packet is destined for a system on another network, the Destination Address field contains the address of a router on the local network that provides access to the destination network. It is then up to the network layer protocol to supply the address of the system that is the packet's ultimate destination.

> **NOTE**   **Network + Exam Objectives**   *Objective 2.1 for the Network+ exam states that students should be able to give an example of and identify a MAC address.*

Protocol Identification

For any network that uses more than one protocol at the network layer, the data-link layer protocol must somehow identify which network layer protocol generated the data in a particular packet. This is necessary so that when a packet arrives at its destination, the data-link layer protocol on the receiving system can pass the data frame up to the correct network layer protocol. The way in which an Ethernet system performs this protocol identification is the primary difference between the DIX Ethernet and IEEE 802.3 standards.

In the DIX Ethernet frame, the two-byte field immediately following the Source Address field contains a value called an Ethertype, which is a code identifying a particular network layer protocol. The most common Ethertype values are listed in Table 4.1. The IEEE 802.3 frame, however, uses the two bytes following the Source Address field as a Length field, which specifies the amount of payload data in the frame.

> **NOTE**   **Ethernet Field Interpretation**   *Ethernet systems interpret the function of the Ethertype/Length field based on its value. Because the Data field is limited to 1500 bytes, Ethernet systems assume that any value greater than or equal to 1536 (0600 hexadecimal) is an Ethertype value. If the value of this field is less than 1536, it is assumed to be a Length value.*

Table 4-1   **Common Ethertype Values, in Hexadecimal**

Network Layer Protocol	Ethertype Value
IP	0800
Address Resolution Protocol (ARP)	0806
Reverse ARP	8035
AppleTalk on Ethernet	809B
NetWare Internetwork Packet Exchange (IPX)	8137

The utility of the Ethertype field is virtually the only reason why the DIX Ethernet standard has not faded into complete obsolescence. Some upper layer protocols still rely on the Ethertype field for protocol identification at the data-link layer, most noticeably TCP/IP, which was developed on DIX Ethernet networks in the 1970s. However, some of the protocols that were developed later (such as AppleTalk) use the IEEE 802.3 protocol identification method instead.

The IEEE 802.3 method involves the IEEE 802.2 standard for the LLC sublayer, discussed earlier in this chapter. The 802.2 standard defines an additional 3-byte or 4-byte subheader (shown in Figure 4-4) that is carried within the 802.3 Data field and contains *service access points (SAPs)* for the source and destination systems. These SAPs perform a function similar to that of the Ethertype field, by identifying locations in memory where the source and destination systems store the packet data.

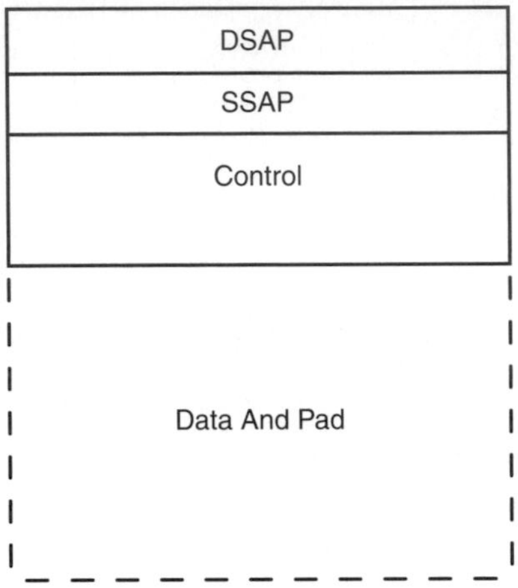

Figure 4-4   The LLC subheader

To provide the exact same function as the Ethertype field (using the Ethertype values), the LLC subheader can use a destination service access point (DSAP) value of 170, which points the receiving system to a second subheader called the *Subnetwork Access Protocol (SNAP)*. The SNAP subheader is 5 bytes long and contains a 2-byte Local Code field that performs the same function as the Ethertype field in the DIX Ethernet header.

When an IEEE 802.3 packet contains the additional subheaders generated by LLC and SNAP, the amount of network layer protocol information in the frame's Data field is reduced by the total number of bytes in the subheaders. It might seem odd for the IEEE to have created a protocol identification mechanism this complex when the Ethertype value works perfectly well, but you must consider the fact that the 802 committee was developing a collection of data-link layer protocols, all of which needed a protocol identification mechanism. The Ethertype field might function perfectly in the IEEE 802.3 protocol, but the other protocols under development did not necessarily have an equivalent, and a universal solution for all of the 802 protocols was needed.

In most cases, network users and administrators do not have to be concerned about which frame format their systems are using. Most operating systems and network interface adapters automatically negotiate a frame type, so no manual configuration is necessary.

CSMA/CD Mechanism

The CSMA/CD MAC mechanism is the single most defining element of an Ethernet network. CSMA/CD is the primary reason why the Ethernet standards have to include physical layer specifications, because for the MAC mechanism to function properly, network timing is essential. The mechanism is the same on both the DIX Ethernet and IEEE 802.3 networks.

When an Ethernet station has data to transmit, it first listens to the network media to see if it is in use by another system. This is called the *carrier sense* phase of the media access control process. If the network media is busy, the station does nothing for a given period and then checks again. If the network is free, the station transmits the data packet. This is called the *multiple access* phase because all of the stations on the network are contending for access to the same network medium.

> **NOTE** **Demonstration Video** For a demonstration of the carrier sense and multiple access phases, run the CSMA video located in the Demos folder on the CD-ROM accompanying this book.

Even though an initial check is performed during the carrier sense phase, it is still possible for two systems on the LAN to transmit at the same time, resulting in a signal quality error (SQE), or as it is more commonly known, a *collision*. For example, if Computer A performs its carrier sense, and Computer B has already begun transmitting but its signal has not yet reached Computer A, a collision will occur if Computer A transmits. When a collision occurs, both packets are discarded and the systems must retransmit them. These collisions are a normal and expected part of Ethernet networking; they are not a problem unless there are too many of them or the computers cannot detect them.

> **NOTE** **Demonstration Video** For a demonstration of a collision, run the Collision video located in the Demos folder on the CD-ROM accompanying this book.

The *collision detection* phase of the transmission process is the most important part of the CSMA/CD process. If the systems cannot tell when their packets collide, corrupted data might reach the destination system and be treated as valid. To avoid this potential problem, Ethernet networks are designed so that packets are large enough to fill the entire network cable with signals before the last bit leaves the transmitting computer. Ethernet packets must be at least 64 bytes long; systems pad out short packets to 64 bytes before transmission. The Ethernet physical layer guidelines also impose strict limitations on the lengths of cable segments.

The amount of time it takes for a transmission to propagate to the farthest end of the network and back again is called the network's *round trip delay time*. A collision can occur only during this round trip time. Once the signal arrives back at the transmitting system, that system is said to have captured the network. No other station can transmit on the network while it is captured because the system will detect the traffic during the carrier sense phase.

On a UTP or fiber optic network, a computer assumes that a collision has occurred if it detects signals on both its transmit and receive wires at the same time. On a coaxial network, a voltage spike indicates the occurrence of a collision. If the network cable is too long, if the packet is too short, or if there are too many hubs, a system might finish transmitting before the collision occurs and be unable to detect it.

> **NOTE** **Late Collisions** Although it is not a normal condition, it is conceivable that collisions might occur after the last bit of data has left the transmitting system. These are called *late collisions*, and they indicate a serious problem, such as a malfunctioning network interface adapter or cable lengths that exceed the protocol specifications. While regular collisions are normal and no cause for concern, you should diagnose and correct late collisions as quickly as possible.

When a system detects a collision, it immediately stops transmitting data and starts sending a jam pattern instead. The jam pattern serves as a signal to the other stations on the network that a collision has taken place, that they should discard any partial packets they may have received, and that they should not attempt to transmit any data until the network has cleared. After transmitting the jam pattern, the system waits a specified period of time before attempting to transmit again. This is called the *backoff period*. Both of the systems involved in a collision compute the length of their own backoff periods, using a randomized algorithm called *truncated binary exponential backoff*. They do this to try to avoid causing another collision by backing off for the same period of time.

Because of the way CSMA/CD works, the more systems you have on a network or the more data the systems transmit over the network, the more collisions occur. Collisions are a normal part of Ethernet operation, but they cause delays because systems have to retransmit the damaged packets. When the number of collisions is minimal, the delays aren't noticeable; but when network traffic increases, the number of collisions increases and the accumulated delays can begin to have a noticeable effect on network performance. You can reduce the traffic on the LAN by installing a bridge or switch or by splitting it into two LANs and connecting them with a router.

Using CSMA/CD might seem to be an inefficient way of controlling access to the network medium, but the process by which the systems contend for access to the network and recover from collisions occurs many times per second—so rapidly that the delays caused by a moderate number of collisions are negligible.

Test your knowledge of the CSMA/CD MAC mechanism by completing Exercise 4-2, "CSMA/CD Procedures," now.

MORE INFO   *Demonstration Video*   For a demonstration of how Ethernet systems contend for access to the network, run the Contention video located in the Demos folder on the CD-ROM accompanying this book.

Physical Layer Specifications

The physical layer specifications included in the Ethernet standards describe the types of cables you can use to build the network, define the topology, and provide other crucial guidelines, such as the maximum cable lengths and the number of repeaters you can use. The basic specifications for the Ethernet physical layer options are listed in Table 4-2. All of these specifications are defined in the IEEE 802.3 standard, except for 10Base5 and 10Base2, which are defined in both the DIX and IEEE standards.

Table 4-2   **Ethernet Physical Layer Specifications**

Designation	Cable Type	Physical Topology	Speed	Maximum Segment Length
10Base5	RG-8 coaxial	Bus	10 Mbps	500 meters
10Base2	RG-58 coaxial	Bus	10 Mbps	185 meters
FOIRL	62.5/125 multimode fiber optic	Star	10 Mbps	1000 meters
10Broad36 (seldom implemented)	75-ohm coaxial	Bus	10 Mbps	3600 meters
1Base5 (seldom implemented)	CAT3 UTP	Star	1 Mbps	250 meters
10Base-T	CAT3 UTP	Star	10 Mbps	100 meters

Table 4-2   **Ethernet Physical Layer Specifications (Continued)**

Designation	Cable Type	Physical Topology	Speed	Maximum Segment Length
10Base-FL	62.5/125 multimode fiber optic	Star	10 Mbps	2000 meters
10Base-FB (seldom implemented)	62.5/125 multimode fiber optic	Star	10 Mbps	2000 meters
10Base-FP (never implemented)	62.5/125 multimode fiber optic	Star	10 Mbps	500 meters
100Base-TX	CAT5 UTP	Star	100 Mbps	100 meters
100Base-T4 (seldom implemented)	CAT3 UTP	Star	100 Mbps	100 meters
100Base-T2 (never implemented)	CAT3 UTP	Star	100 Mbps	100 meters
100Base-FX	62.5/125 multimode fiber optic	Star	100 Mbps	412 meters
1000Base-LX	9/125 singlemode fiber optic	Star	1000 Mbps	5000 meters
1000Base-LX	50/125 or 62.5/125 multimode fiber optic	Star	1000 Mbps	550 meters
1000Base-SX	50/125 multimode fiber optic (400 MHz)	Star	1000 Mbps	500 meters
1000Base-SX	50/125 multimode fiber optic (500 MHz)	Star	1000 Mbps	550 meters

Table 4-2 **Ethernet Physical Layer Specifications (Continued)**

Designation	Cable Type	Physical Topology	Speed	Maximum Segment Length
1000Base-SX	62.5/125 multimode fiber optic (160 MHz)	Star	1000 Mbps	220 meters
1000Base-SX	62.5/125 multimode fiber optic (200 MHz)	Star	1000 Mbps	275 meters
1000Base-CX	150-ohm shielded, balanced copper cable	Star	1000 Mbps	25 meters
1000Base-T	CAT5 (or CAT5e) UTP	Star	1000 Mbps	100 meters

Several of the physical layer specifications listed in the table were seldom, if ever, implemented as commercial products, and many are considered to be obsolete, although there might still be some existing installations still in use. The following sections examine the Ethernet specifications for each of the three main cable types: coaxial, UTP, and fiber optic.

> **MORE INFO** **Ethernet Cables** *For more information about the actual cables used to build Ethernet networks, see Chapter 2, "Network Cabling."*

Coaxial Ethernet

The coaxial Ethernet specifications (**10Base5**, **10Base2**, and **10Broad36**) are the only ones that call for a physical bus topology. The maximum segment length indicates the length of the entire bus, from one terminator to the other, with all of the computers in between, as shown in Figure 4-5. A cable segment like this, which connects more than two computers, is called a **mixing segment**. The mixing segments on a 10Base5 network can have no more than 100 stations on them, and 10Base2 mixing segments are limited to 50 stations.

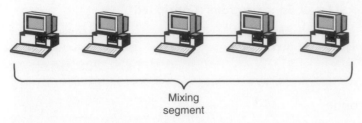

Mixing
segment

Figure 4-5   Ethernet's coaxial cable specifications use a mixing segment to connect multiple computers to the network.

Because 10Base5 networks use external transceivers that connect directly to the coaxial trunk, each system must also have an additional Attachment Unit Interface (AUI) cable (called a *transceiver cable* in the DIX Ethernet standard). This cable connects the transceiver to the network interface adapter, and it can be no more than 50 meters long. The 10Base2 network interface adapters have internal transceivers, so the coaxial cable must run right up to the adapter and attach to it with a T-connector.

> **NOTE   Dueling Nomenclatures**   *One of the other defining characteristics of the IEEE 802.3 documents is their insistence on replacing perfectly serviceable terminology from the DIX Ethernet standard with more complicated-sounding terms of their own. Thus, a transceiver cable becomes an Attachment Unit Interface cable and a collision becomes a signal quality error.*

The coaxial specifications are no longer used for new networks, although some coaxial cable networks (mostly thin Ethernet) are still in use. Coaxial cable is more difficult to install and maintain than UTP, and it has no upgrade path beyond its maximum speed of 10 Mbps.

UTP Ethernet

Except for the coaxial cable specifications, all Ethernet physical layer implementations use the star topology, in which a separate cable segment connects each computer to a central hub or switch. A cable segment that connects only two devices is called a **link segment**. UTP is by far the most popular type of cable used on Ethernet networks today because it is inexpensive, easy to install, and upgradeable from 10 Mbps to 100 and even 1000 Mbps.

10Base-T

The first Ethernet physical layer specification using twisted pair cable to achieve any serious market acceptance was **10Base-T**, which was added to the IEEE 802.3 document in 1990. Designed for use with the CAT3 UTP cables commonly employed for telephone installations at the time, a 10Base-T network consists of link segments up to 100 meters long, connecting stations to a repeating hub. The repeating action of the hub enables the incoming signals to go out to a station another 100 meters away, as shown in Figure 4-6

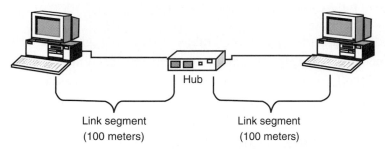

Link segment
(100 meters)

Link segment
(100 meters)

Hub

Figure 4-6   UTP cables can connect Ethernet systems to a hub 100 meters away, and the hub repeats the signal to another hub or computer.

Some early 10Base-T implementations used external transceivers, the same as the transceivers used in 10Base5 networks, to provide an upgrade path from a coaxial to a UTP network. Administrators had to replace the network cables and the external transceivers during the upgrade, but they could continue to use their original 10Base5 network interface adapters. Each station still required an AUI cable that plugged into the adapter's 15-pin AUI port at one end and connected to the 10Base-T cable at the other end. The use of external transceivers with 10Base-T was a relatively short-lived phenomenon, however. Soon after its introduction, the widespread acceptance of 10Base-T led manufacturers to integrate the transceiver into the network interface adapter, as on 10Base2 equipment—a practice that has continued to this day.

10Base-T uses one wire pair for transmitting data and one pair for receiving it. In each pair, one wire carries a positive amplitude of approximately +2.5 volts and the other a negative amplitude of −2.5 volts. The other two wire pairs in the cable are not used.

NOTE   Unused Wire Pairs   Even though there are two pairs of unused wires on many UTP Ethernet networks, do not be tempted to run voice telephone or other signals over those other two pairs while the data network is in use. This practice could lead to excessive signal interference due to cross talk between the wires. An earlier twisted pair specification called 1Base5 was designed to co-exist with telephone signals on the other two cable pairs, but it never achieved wide acceptance, due in part to its slow 1-Mbps transmission speed.

Today, virtually all UTP networks use CAT5 cable, which is perfectly acceptable for 10Base-T and also provides an upgrade path to the UTP-based Fast Ethernet and Gigabit Ethernet technologies.

100Base-T

The Fast Ethernet specifications (**IEEE 802.3u**), which were added to the 802.3 standard in 1995, include two UTP cable specifications known collectively as **100Base-T**. The two UTP Fast Ethernet variants are 100Base-TX and 100Base-T4

Both 100Base-TX and 100Base-T4 retain the 100-meter maximum segment length from the 10Base-T specification. This was one of the primary requirements for the developers of the standard, because they knew that the initial success of Fast Ethernet depended largely on the availability of a simple upgrade path from 10Base-T. The two specifications were designed to provide upgrades for networks running newer CAT5 cables, as well as older CAT3 installations.

100Base-TX, like 10Base-T, uses two of the four wire pairs in the UTP cable, but to support its greater transmission speed, it requires a higher grade of cable: CAT5 instead of CAT3. Today, virtually all of the UTP cable installed is CAT5 or better, and as a result, 100Base-TX has become the current industry standard for LAN installations. 100Base-TX also uses a different signal encoding scheme than the 10-Mbps Ethernet specifications, replacing the Manchester encoding method with one called 4B/5B, which was adapted from the FDDI standard.

100Base-T4 was designed as an upgrade path for older networks running CAT3 UTP cable. Because the lower grade of cable cannot support the same transmission techniques as 100Base-TX, the specification calls for the use of all four wire pairs in the cable. As with 10Base-T and 100Base-TX, one wire pair is used for transmitting signals and one for receiving them. The other two pairs are bidirectional and can be used for traffic running in either direction as needed.

The creation of the 100Base-T4 specification was a good idea in theory, but in practice, it was not really needed. 100Base-TX rapidly became the dominant Ethernet technology, and few products supporting the 100Base-T4 specification were ever produced.

1000Base-T

The first physical layer specifications for Gigabit Ethernet called for fiber optic cable, but less than a year after the adoption of these standards, the **1000Base-T** specification (IEEE 802.3ab) was ratified. The 1000Base-T specification provided support for UTP cables at 1000 Mbps. Just as with 100Base-T, the 1000Base-T specification was designed as an upgrade path for existing UTP cable installations with a maximum segment length of 100 meters.

The 1000Base-T specification calls for CAT5 cable, but it is better implemented by using the CAT5e or Category 6 (CAT6) UTP cable grades that are now available.

CAT5e cable runs at the same frequency as CAT5 but is more resistant to certain types of cross talk that are particularly problematic in Gigabit Ethernet communications. CAT6 runs at a higher frequency (250 MHz), and is even more resistant to cross talk than CAT5e.

1000Base-T achieves its great speed by using all four wire pairs, like 100Base-T4 does, and by using a different signaling scheme called Pulse Amplitude Modulation-5 (PAM-5) .

Fiber Optic Ethernet

Fiber optic cable has been an Ethernet physical layer option since its early days. In fact, the original Ethernet fiber optic specification, called **Fiber Optic Inter-Repeater Link (FOIRL)**, was standardized in **IEEE 802.3d** in 1987, three years before 10Base-T was approved. Fiber optic cable was first used on Ethernet networks to connect repeaters (or hubs) together over long distances, up to 1000 meters. This application was particularly valuable when the repeaters were located in different buildings because fiber optic cable is immune to the effects of lightning strikes and electromagnetic interference.

10Base-F

Eventually, manufacturers recognized the need for a fiber optic specification to connect stations to hubs, and some manufacturers began producing FOIRL products that could do this, even before there was a standard in place. The IEEE eventually revised the FOIRL specification to include station-to-repeater connections, as well as repeater-to-repeater connections, and gave that standard the new designation **10Base-F.** The new specification was published as **IEEE 802.3j** in 1993.

10Base-F is a collective designation for three separate fiber optic specifications, as follows:

- **10Base-FL**   Defines a fiber link standard that is an updated version of the FOIRL specification. 10Base-FL equipment is interoperable with FOIRL and can be used to link repeaters to repeaters, stations to stations, or repeaters to stations. A network using all 10Base-FL equipment can have cable segments up to 2000 meters long; if the network uses any FOIRL equipment, cable segments are subject to the FOIRL 1000-meter length limitation.

- **10Base-FB**   Defines a fiber backbone standard that can connect multiple repeaters in series, with individual cable segments up to 2000 meters long.

- **10Base-FP**   Defines a fiber passive standard for a mixing segment up to 500 meters long and containing up to 33 stations, using an unpowered signal coupler.

In practice, the 10Base-F specifications did little more than standardize what FOIRL equipment manufacturers were already doing in the first place. The 10Base-FB specification was hardly ever implemented commercially, and 10Base-FP not at all. There are 10Base-FL products available, but today there is little reason to implement a 10-Mbps network using an expensive medium that can easily support 100 Mbps or more.

100Base-FX

The **100Base-FX** specification was introduced, together with all of the other Fast Ethernet specifications, in the 802.3u standard in 1995. 100Base-FX is included in the 100Base-T designation, which is a collective term for all of the Fast Ethernet specifications, and also in the **100Base-X** designation, which consists of 100Base-FX and 100Base-TX, both of which use the 4B/5B signal encoding method.

The 100Base-FX specification calls for 62.5/125 multimode fiber optic, just like 10Base-FL, but limits the maximum length of a cable segment to 412 meters when the network is operating in half-duplex mode. When the network is operating in full-duplex mode, cable segments can be as long as 2000 meters. It is also possible to use single-mode fiber optic cable for 100Base-FX segments that span 20 km or more, in full-duplex mode.

1000Base-X

The designation **1000Base-X** encompasses all of the physical layer specifications for Gigabit Ethernet that use the 8B/10B signal encoding scheme, originally used on Fibre Channel networks. This includes all of the Gigabit Ethernet specifications except for 1000Base-T. Published as **IEEE 802.3z** in 1998, the 1000Base-X fiber optic specifications are as follows:

- **1000Base-SX**   A specification that calls for short wavelength (850 nanometer [nm]) transmissions over any one of four multimode cable types, with varying segment lengths up to a maximum of 550 meters.

- **1000Base-LX**   A specification that calls for long wavelength (1300 nm) transmissions over any one of three multimode cable types, with a maximum segment length of 550 meters, or for long wavelength transmissions over 9/125 singlemode cable, with a maximum segment length of 5000 meters.

> **NOTE   1000Base-CX**   The 1000Base-X designator also includes a copper cable specification called 1000Base-CX. 1000Base-CX is intended for short cable runs no longer than 25 meters, such as connections within data centers, using a special type of 150-ohm shielded twisted pair (STP) cable (not UTP or IBM Type I or II) with either 8-pin High Speed Serial Data Connectors or DB-9 connectors. The cables for 1000Base-CX connections must be specially constructed at a specific length, and you cannot connect two cables together to extend the length of the connection without unbalancing the signals and degrading performance. There are few, if any, 1000Base-CX products on the market.

In addition to the three official 1000Base-X specifications defined in the IEEE 802.3z document, there are also some proprietary variations on the market that have not been ratified by the IEEE. Several vendors, including Cisco Systems, market Gigabit Ethernet products using the following designations:

- **1000Base-LH**   A specification based on 1000Base-LX, which extends the maximum length for a single-mode fiber segment to 10 km

- **1000Base-ZX**   A specification that uses extended wavelength (1550 nm) transmissions and single-mode cables to provide segment lengths of up to 100 km

> **NOTE   Network + Exam Objectives**   Objective 1.3 for the Network+ exam states that students should be able to specify the characteristics (speed, length, topology, cable type, etc.) of the following 802.3 standards: 10Base-T, 100Base-TX, 10Base2, 10Base5, 100Base-FX, and Gigabit Ethernet.

Cable Installation Guidelines

Two factors have made obvious the need for cabling restrictions on an Ethernet network: the limitations of the network medium itself, and the requirements of the CSMA/CD mechanism. All network media are subject to degradation of the signals passing over them, for a variety of reasons. Chief among these is attenuation, the tendency of the signal to weaken the farther away it gets from the point of transmission. All network media are subject to attenuation, with some suffering more than others. Signals on copper cables, for example, always attenuate more than those on fiber optic cables. This is one reason why, as a general rule, fiber optic networks can have longer segment lengths than copper-based networks can.

Other reasons for signal degradation are particular to specific media. Twisted-pair cables, because they contain multiple wires in a single sheath, are subject to cross talk, which is when the signals on one wire interfere with those on another. There are many different types of cross talk, and many other factors, both internal and external, that can affect the quality of the signals on a network medium. The greater the interference, the shorter the maximum cable length the network can support.

As explained earlier, the functionality of CSMA/CD depends largely on its ability to detect collisions, and the collision detection mechanism is dependent on the network's round trip delay time. An improperly configured network can have a round trip time that is too large, causing collisions to go undetected. The round trip time for a network is obviously affected by its transmission speed, so there are different cabling guidelines for standard, Fast, and Gigabit Ethernet, as described in the following sections. Other significant factors in calculating a network's round trip time are the cable lengths and the number of repeaters on the network.

Standard Ethernet Cabling Guidelines

Repeating is an essential part of most Ethernet networks, and the standards include rules regarding the number of repeaters that can be used on a single LAN. For the original 10-Mbps Ethernet standard, the use of repeaters is governed by the **5-4-3 rule**, which states that you can have up to five cable segments, connected by four repeaters, with no more than three of these segments being mixing segments. In the days of coaxial cable networks, this rule meant that you could have up to three mixing segments of 500 or 185 meters each (for 10Base5 and 10Base2, respectively), populated with multiple computers and connected by two repeaters. You could also add two additional repeaters to extend the network with another two cable segments of 500 or 185 meters each, as long as these were link segments connected directly to the next repeater in line with no intervening computers, as shown in Figure 4-7. A 10Base2 network could therefore span up to 925 meters and a 10Base5 network up to 2500 meters.

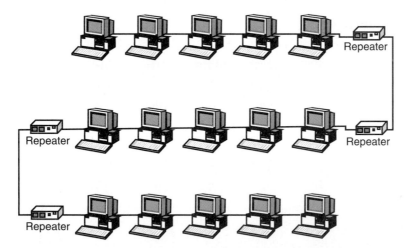

Figure 4-7   Coaxial Ethernet networks consist of up to three mixing segments and two link segments, all connected by repeaters.

NOTE **Repeaters and Hubs** For information about repeaters and their functions, see Chapter 3, "Network Connection Hardware."

On networks using the star topology, all of the segments are link segments, meaning that you can connect up to four repeating hubs using their uplink ports and still adhere to the 5-4-3 rule, as shown in Figure 4-8. As long as the traffic between the two most distant computers doesn't pass through more than four hubs, the network is configured properly. Because the hubs function as repeaters, each 10Base-T cable segment can be up to 100 meters long, for a maximum network span of 500 meters.

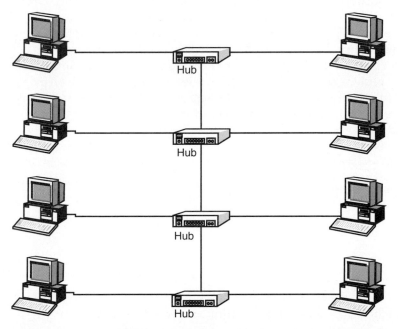

Figure 4-8   10Base-T Ethernet networks can have up to four repeating hubs connected together.

Fast Ethernet Cabling Guidelines

Because Fast Ethernet networks run at higher speeds, they cannot support as many hubs as 10-Mbps Ethernet networks do. The IEEE 802.3u standard defines two types of hubs, Class I and Class II. Every hub produced must be marked with the appropriate Roman numeral in a circle. Class I hubs connect Fast Ethernet cable segments of different types, such as 100Base-TX to 100Base-T4 or UTP to fiber optic, while Class II hubs connect segments of the same type. You can have as many as two Class II hubs on a single LAN, with a total cable length (for all three segments) of 205 meters for UTP cable and 228 meters for fiber optic cable. Because Class I hubs must perform an additional signal translation, which slows down the transmission process, you can have only one hub on the network, with maximum cable lengths of 200 and 272 meters for UTP and fiber optic, respectively.

Gigabit Ethernet Cabling Guidelines

The 1000Base-T cabling guidelines are simple: because of the high transmission speed, only one repeater is permitted on the network. Although Gigabit Ethernet theoretically supports half-duplex operation with the use of hubs, there are no products like this on the market. All Gigabit Ethernet implementations are full-duplex and use switches to connect the network nodes together.

> **NOTE   Calculating Round Trip Delay Times**   The Ethernet hub configuration rules supplied in this chapter are general guidelines that, in most cases, result in a network that functions properly. In designing an Ethernet network, a certain amount of leeway in real-world configuration practices is generally acceptable. For example, if all of your cable segments in a 10Base-T network are substantially shorter than 100 meters (and they usually are), you can probably get away with adding a fifth hub. However, as the speed of the network increases, the amount of leeway decreases. You might be able to use an additional hub on most 10Base-T networks, but the Fast Ethernet and Gigabit Ethernet cabling guidelines are more stringent. To ensure that your network conforms to the specifications, you can achieve greater accuracy by calculating the precise round trip delay time for your network, which is the time it takes for a packet to travel between the two most distant systems. You calculate the round trip delay time by adding together specific values for each meter of cable and each type of hub.

TOKEN RING

Token Ring is a protocol that contains the same basic elements as Ethernet: physical layer specifications, a frame format, and a MAC mechanism. However, Token Ring approaches the tasks of transmitting and receiving data on a shared network medium in a completely different manner. IBM originally designed Token Ring, but it was standardized in the **IEEE 802.5** document, the current version of which is titled "IEEE 802.5, 1998 Edition, IEEE Standard for Information Technology–Telecommunications and Information Exchange Between Systems–Local and Metropolitan Area Networks–Specific Requirements–Part 5: Token Ring Access Method and Physical Layer Specification." Many manufacturers now produce Token Ring hardware.

Token Ring networks were originally designed to run at 4 Mbps, but later implementations increased the speed to 16 Mbps. Most of the Token Ring network interface adapters sold today support both speeds. The 16-Mbps speed is faster than standard Ethernet speed, but nowhere near the 100-Mbps speed of Fast Ethernet. However, it's important to note that under normal circumstances, Token Ring networks experience no collisions–unlike Ethernet networks–which improves the network's overall efficiency.

Token Ring is used much less often than Ethernet, and one of the main reasons is the price of Token Ring hardware, which is substantially higher than that of Ethernet equipment.

Physical Layer Specifications

As described in Chapter 2, "Network Cabling," Token Ring networks use a ring topology that is implemented logically inside the MAU, the Token Ring equivalent of a hub. The network cables take the form of a star topology, but the MAU forwards incoming data to the next port only, not to all of the ports at the same time as in an Ethernet hub. This topology enables data packets to travel around the network from one workstation to the next until they arrive back at the system that originally generated them.

Token Ring networks still use a shared medium, however, meaning that every packet is circulated to every computer on the network. When a system receives a packet from the MAU, it reads the destination address from the Token Ring header to determine if it should pass the packet up through that computer's networking stack. But no matter what the address, the system returns the packet to the MAU so that it can be forwarded to the next computer on the ring.

The physical layer specifications for Token Ring networks are not as numerous as those for Ethernet, nor are they as precisely standardized. The IEEE 802.5 document contains no physical layer specifications at all. Cabling guidelines are derived from practices established by IBM, and they can differ when you are working with products made by other manufacturers. Most Token Ring networks use one of the two cable types described in the following sections.

IBM Type 1 Cable

Originally, the medium for Token Ring networks was IBM Type 1 cable, also called the IBM Cabling System. Type 1 is a heavy STP cable that is sold in various lengths, generally with connectors attached. The cables have IBM data connectors (IDCs) at the MAU end and standard DB-9 connectors at the other end to attach to network interface adapters. Cables with one IDC and one DB-9 connector, which are used to connect a computer to a MAU, are called *lobe cables*. Cables with IDC connectors at both ends, used for connecting MAUs together, are called *patch cables*.

Type 1 cable is thick, relatively inflexible, and difficult to install in walls and ceilings because of its large, preattached connectors. Type 1 MAUs also require a special IDC "key," which is a separate device that you plug into each MAU port and remove to initialize the port before connecting a lobe cable to it.

CAT5 UTP

Today, most Token Ring networks use CAT5 UTP cable with standard RJ-45 connectors at both ends, known in the Token Ring world as Type 3 cabling. Type 3 networks use the same connectors for both computers and MAUs, so only one type of cable is needed. In addition, with Type 3 cable, it is possible to install the network cables inside walls and ceilings, using bulk cable, and then attach the connectors afterward. Type 3 MAUs also don't require a separate key because the ports are self-initializing.

The only advantages Type 1 networks have over Type 3 networks are that Type 1 can span longer distances and connect more workstations. A Type 1 lobe cable can be up to 300 meters long, whereas Type 3 cables are limited to 150 meters. Type 1 networks can have up to 260 connected workstations, whereas Type 3 networks can have only 72.

Token Passing

The MAC mechanism of a Token Ring LAN, called token passing, is the single most defining element of the network, just as CSMA/CD is for Ethernet. Token passing is an inherently more efficient MAC mechanism than is CSMA/CD because each system on the network has an equal opportunity to transmit its data without generating any collisions and without diminished performance at high traffic levels. Other data-link layer protocols, such as FDDI, also use token passing as their MAC mechanism.

Token passing works by circulating a special packet called a *token* around the network. The token is only 3 bytes long and contains no useful data. Its only purpose is to designate which system on the network is allowed to transmit its data. In their idle state, computers on a Token Ring network are said to be in *repeat mode*. While in this state, the computer systems receive packets from the network and immediately forward them back to the MAU for transmission to the next port. If a system doesn't return the packet, the ring is effectively broken and network communication ceases. After a designated system (called the *active monitor*) generates it, the token circulates around the ring from system to system. When a computer has data to transmit, it must wait for a free token to arrive before it can send its data. No system can transmit unless it possesses the token, and because there is only one token, only one system on the network can transmit at any one time. This means that there can be no collisions on a Token Ring network unless something is seriously wrong.

MORE INFO **Demonstration Video** For a demonstration of how token passing works, run the TokenPassing video located in the Demos folder on the CD-ROM accompanying this book.

When a computer takes possession of the token, it changes the value of one bit (called the *monitor setting bit*) and forwards the packet back to the MAU for transmission to the next computer on the ring. At this point, the computer enters transmit mode. The new value of the monitor setting bit informs the other computers that the network is in use and that they can't take possession of the token themselves. Immediately after the computer transmits this "network busy" token, it transmits its data packet.

As with the token frame transmitted immediately before it, the MAU forwards the data packet to each computer on the ring in turn. Eventually, the packet arrives back at the computer that generated it. At the same time that the sending computer goes into transmit mode, its receive wire pair goes into stripping mode. When the data packet traverses the entire ring and returns to its source, it is the responsibility of the sending computer that generated the packet to strip it from the network. This prevents the packet from circulating endlessly around the ring.

MORE INFO **Demonstration Video** For a step-by-step illustration of the path that packets take on a Token Ring network, run the TokenRingNetwork video located in the Demos folder on the CD-ROM accompanying this book.

In the original Token Ring network design, the system transmitting its data packet had to wait for the last bit of data to return before it could generate a new token. Today, most 16-Mbps Token Ring networks have a feature called *early token release*, which enables workstations to transmit a free token immediately after they finish sending their data packets. This way, another system on the network can receive a data packet, take possession of the token, and begin transmitting its own data frame before all of the data from the first packet has returned to its source. There are parts of two data frames on the network at the same time, but there is never more than one free token.

Token Ring Frames

Unlike Ethernet, which uses one frame format for all communications, Token Ring uses four different frames:

- The data frame
- The token frame
- The command frame
- The abort delimiter frame

The Data Frame

The largest and most complex of the Token Ring frames is the data frame, shown in Figure 4-9. This frame is similar to the Ethernet frame because it encapsulates the data received from the network layer protocol, using a header and a footer. The other three frames are used strictly for control functions, such as ring maintenance and error notification.

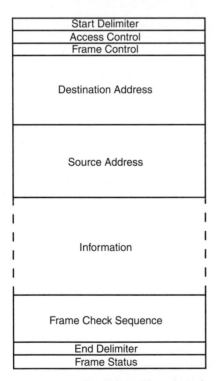

Figure 4-9   The Token Ring data frame

The functions of the fields in the data frame are as follows:

- **Start Delimiter (1 byte)**   Contains a bit pattern that signals the beginning of the frame to the receiving system

- **Access Control (1 byte)**   Contains bits that can be used to prioritize Token Ring transmissions, enabling certain systems to have priority access to the token frame and the network

- **Frame Control (1 byte)**   Contains bits that specify whether the frame is a data or a command frame

- **Destination Address (6 bytes)**   Contains the 6-byte hexadecimal address of the network interface adapter on the local network to which the packet will be transmitted

- **Source Address (6 bytes)**   Contains the 6-byte hexadecimal address of the network interface adapter in the system generating the packet

- **Information (up to 4500 bytes)**   Contains the data generated by the network layer protocol, including a standard LLC header as defined in IEEE 802.2

- **Frame Check Sequence (4 bytes)**   Contains a 4-byte checksum value for the packet (excluding the Start Delimiter, End Delimiter, and Frame Status fields) that the receiving system uses to verify that the packet was transmitted without error

- **End Delimiter (1 byte)**   Contains a bit pattern that signals the end of the frame, including a bit that specifies if there are further packets in the sequence yet to be transmitted and a bit that indicates if the packet has failed the error check

- **Frame Status (1 byte)**   Contains bits that indicate whether the destination system has received the frame and copied it into its buffers

The Token Frame

The token frame is 3 bytes long, as shown in Figure 4-10, and contains only the Start Delimiter, Access Control, and End Delimiter fields. The Start Delimiter and End Delimiter fields use the same format as that in the data frame, and the token bit in the Access Control field is set to a value of 1.

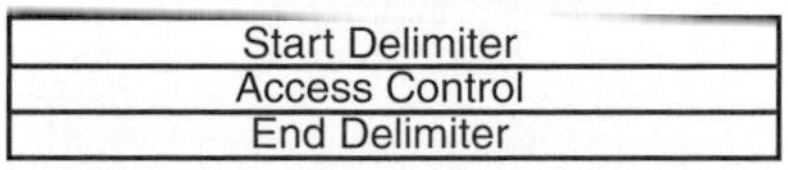

| Start Delimiter |
| Access Control |
| End Delimiter |

Figure 4-10   The Token Ring token frame

The Command Frame

The command frame (also called a MAC frame because it operates at the MAC sublayer, while the data frame operates at the LLC sublayer) uses the same basic format as that in the data frame, differing only in the value of the Frame Control field and the contents of the Information field. The Information field, instead of containing network layer protocol data, contains a 2-byte major vector ID, which specifies the control function the packet is performing, followed by the actual control data itself, which can vary in length. The following major vector IDs indicate some of the most common control functions performed by these packets:

- **0010—Beacon**   Beaconing is a process by which systems on a Token Ring network indicate that they are not receiving data from their nearest active upstream neighbor, presumably because a network error has occurred. Beaconing enables you to more easily locate a malfunctioning computer on the network.

- **0011—Claim Token**   The active monitor system uses this vector ID to generate a new token frame on the ring.

- **0100—Ring Purge**   If an error occurs, the active monitor system uses this vector ID to clear the ring of unstripped data and to return all of the systems to repeat mode.

The Abort Delimiter Frame

Test your knowledge of the benefits and drawbacks of the Ethernet and Token Ring protocols by completing Exercise 4-3, "Selecting a Data-Link Layer Protocol," now.

The Abort Delimiter frame consists of only 2 bytes—the same Start Delimiter and End Delimiter fields—and uses the same values for those fields as the data and command frames do. When a problem occurs, such as an incomplete packet transmission, the active monitor system generates an Abort Delimiter frame to flush all existing data from the ring.

FIBER DISTRIBUTED DATA INTERFACE (FDDI)

Until the introduction of Fast Ethernet, FDDI (pronounced "fiddy") was the only data-link layer protocol that offered 100-Mbps transmission speeds over fiber optic cable. Standardized by the American National Standards Institute (ANSI), FDDI was commonly used on backbone networks in the 1990s; there was also a desktop version of the protocol, designed to use copper cables, called Copper Distributed Data Interface (CDDI, or "siddy") that never achieved widespread deployment. Like Token Ring, FDDI networks are cabled using a ring topology and use the token passing MAC mechanism, but there are several important differences between FDDI and Token Ring, as described in the following sections.

Physical Layer Specifications

Apart from its speed, which was unprecedented at the time of its introduction, the use of fiber optic cable was the primary reason for FDDI's commercial success. Like other fiber optic protocols, FDDI networks can span much longer distances than copper-based networks, and they are completely resistant to electromagnetic interference. FDDI supports several different types of fiber optic cable, including the 62.5/125 multimode cable that is the industry standard for fiber optic LANs. If multimode cable is used, the network segments can be up to 100 kilometers long with up to 500 workstations placed as far as 2 kilometers apart. Single-mode fiber optic cable allows for even longer segments, with up to 60 kilometers between workstations.

The original FDDI standard calls for a ring topology, but unlike Token Ring networks, this ring is not a logical one implemented in the hub. The computers are actually cabled together in a physical ring. To provide fault tolerance in case of a cable break, the standard also defined a double ring topology that consists of two independent rings, a primary and a secondary, with traffic flowing in opposite directions. A computer that is connected to both rings is called a *dual attachment station (DAS)*. If one of the rings is broken by a cable fault, the computer switches to the other ring, thus providing continued access to the entire network. A double ring FDDI network in this condition is called a *wrapped ring*.

It's also possible to cable a FDDI network in a star topology, using a hub called a *dual attachment concentrator (DAC)*. The DAC creates a single logical ring, like a Token Ring MAU. A computer connected to the DAC is called a *single attachment station (SAS)*. A FDDI network can be deployed using the double ring, the star topology, or both. The double ring is better suited for use as a backbone network, and the star is better suited to a segment network connecting desktop computers. To construct an entire enterprise network using FDDI, you create a double ring backbone, to which you connect the servers and other vital computers as DAS's. You then connect one or more DACs to the double ring, which you use to attach your workstations, as shown in Figure 4-11.

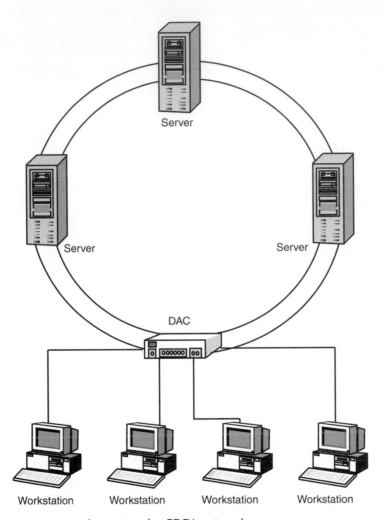

Figure 4-11   An enterprise FDDI network

The arrangement shown in Figure 4-11 is sometimes called a *dual ring of trees*. The DAS servers have full advantage of the double ring's fault tolerance, as do the DACs, while the SAS computers attached to the DACs are connected to the primary ring only. If a cable connecting a workstation to a DAC fails, the DAC can remove it from the ring without disturbing communications to the other computers, just as the MAU on a Token Ring network can. To expand the network further, you can connect additional DACs to ports in existing DACs without limit, as long as you stay within the maximum number of computers permitted on the network.

The FDDI Frames

Like Token Ring, FDDI uses several different types of frames in its communications. The most commonly used frame on a FDDI network is the data frame, shown in Figure 4-12.

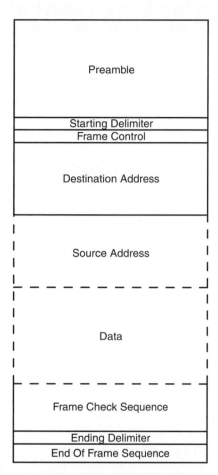

Figure 4-12   The FDDI data frame

The functions of the fields in the FDDI data frame are as follows:

- **Preamble (PA, 8 bytes)**   Contains a series of alternating 0s and 1s, used for clock synchronization

- **Starting Delimiter (SD, 1 byte)**   Indicates the beginning of the frame

- **Frame Control (FC, 1 byte)**   Indicates the type of data found in the Data field. Some of the most common values are

  - ❏ **41, 4F—Station Management (SMT) Frame.** Indicates that the Data field contains an SMT protocol data unit (PDU)

  - ❏ **C2, C3—MAC Frame.** Indicates that the frame is either a MAC Claim frame (C2) or a MAC Beacon frame (C3), which are used to recover from token passing errors

  - ❏ **50, 51—LLC Frame.** Indicates that the Data field contains application data in a standard IEEE 802.2 LLC frame

- **Destination Address (DA, 6 bytes)**   Specifies the hardware address of the computers that will receive the frame

- **Source Address (SA, 6 bytes)**   Specifies the hardware address of the system sending the frame

- **Data (variable)**   Contains network layer protocol data, or an SMT header and data, or MAC data, depending on the function of the frame

- **Frame Check Sequence (FCS, 4 bytes)**   Contains a cyclical redundancy check (CRC) value, used for error detection

- **Ending Delimiter (ED, 4 bits)**   Indicates the end of the frame

- **End of Frame Sequence (FS, 12 bits)**   Contains three indicators that can be modified by intermediate systems when they retransmit the packet:

  - ❏ **E (Error).** Indicates that an error has been detected, either in the FCS or in the frame format

  - ❏ **A (Acknowledge).** Indicates that the intermediate system has determined that the frame's destination address applies to itself

  - ❏ **C (Copy).** Indicates that the intermediate system has successfully copied the contents of the frame into its buffers

Test your knowledge of the FDDI protocol by completing Exercise 4-4, "FDDI Concepts," now.

Because it is a token passing protocol, FDDI also must have a token frame, which contains only the Preamble, Starting Delimiter, Frame Control, and Ending Delimiter fields, for a total of 3 bytes. The token passing mechanism used by FDDI is virtually identical to that of Token Ring, except that the early token release feature that is optional in Token Ring is standard equipment for the FDDI protocol. The third type of frame used on FDDI networks is the station management frame, which is responsible for ring maintenance and network diagnostics.

WIRELESS NETWORKING

When describing data networks, we typically think of a cable as the network medium. However, wireless data networking technologies offer another option, and they have been available for several years. Until recently, wireless LANs (WLANs) were usually synonymous with slow transmission speeds and unreliable service, but the wireless LAN technologies now available provide reasonably reliable service at speeds that are acceptable to the average user accustomed to a cable network.

Wireless Networking Standards

Until recently, wireless networking was based on standards defining physical layer technologies. While reasonably effective, these technologies were much slower than the average network and not altogether reliable. These technologies were also expensive and difficult to implement. In 1999, the IEEE defined a new series of technologies for the WLAN physical layer and released the first standard in the 802.11 working group, called "Wireless LAN Medium Access Control (MAC) and Physical Layer (PHY) Specifications," For the wireless networking industry, the breakthrough document in this series of standards is IEEE 802.11b, "Wireless LAN Medium Access Control (MAC) and Physical Layer (PHY) Specifications–Amendment 2: Higher-Speed Physical Layer (PHY) Extension in the 2.4 GHz Band."

The 802.11b standard defines a physical layer specification that enables WLANs to run at speeds up to 11 Mbps, slightly faster than a standard Ethernet network. When products conforming to this standard arrived on the market, they quickly became a popular solution, both for home and business use. Prices dropped accordingly and, for the first time, wireless networking became a major force in the industry.

Development has continued on standards that are designed to provide even higher WLAN transmission speeds. The 802.11a standard, "Wireless LAN Medium Access Control (MAC) and Physical Layer (PHY) Specifications: Amendment 1: High-Speed Physical Layer in the 5 GHz Band" defines a medium with speeds running up to 54 Mbps, while 802.11g, "Wireless LAN Medium Access Control (MAC) and Physical Layer (PHY) Specifications–Amendment 4: Further Higher Data Rate Extension in the 2.4 GHz Band," calls for 54-Mbps transmission speeds, using the same 2.4-GHz frequencies as 802.11b.

The IEEE 802.11 Physical Layer

As mentioned in Chapter 2, "Network Cabling," wireless LANs support two topologies, an ad hoc topology and an infrastructure topology. The ad hoc or independent topology is one in which computers equipped with wireless network interface adapters communicate directly with each other on a peer-to-peer basis; there is no cabled network involved. This type of network is designed to support only a limited number of computers, such as those in a home or small business. The infrastructure topology is designed to extend the range and flexibility of a normal cabled network by enabling wireless-equipped computers to connect to it using a specialized module called an *access point.*

An access point can be a computer with a wireless network interface adapter as well as a standard adapter connecting it to a standard cabled LAN, or it can be a dedicated device. The wireless clients communicate with the cabled network using the access point as an intermediary. The access point is essentially a translation bridge because it connects the wireless network to the cabled network, while preserving the single broadcast domain.

As with all wireless communication technologies, distance and environmental conditions can have significant effects on the performance realized by the mobile workstations. A single access point can typically support 10 to 20 clients, depending on how heavily they use the LAN, as long as they remain within an approximate 100- to 200-foot radius of the access point. Intervening walls and other sources of interference can diminish this performance substantially.

To extend the range of the wireless part of the network and provide support for more clients, you can use multiple access points in different locations, or you can use an extension point. An extension point is essentially a wireless signal repeater that functions as a way station between wireless clients and an access point. An IEEE 802.11 LAN is divided into cells, each of which is controlled by a base station. The 802.11 standard refers to each cell as a basic service set (BSS) and to each base station as an access point. If the network uses multiple access points, they are connected by a backbone, which the standard calls a *distribution system (DS)*. The DS is usually a cabled network, but it could conceivably be wireless as well.

MORE INFO   **Demonstration Video**   For a demonstration of the ad hoc and infrastructure topologies, run the WirelessLANs video located in the Demos folder on the CD-ROM accompanying this book.

The IEEE 802.11 standard supports three different types of signals at the physical layer, as follows:

- **Direct Sequence Spread Spectrum (DSSS)**   A radio transmission method in which the outgoing signals are modulated with a digital code (called a *chipping code*) that uses a redundant bit pattern. The end result is that each bit of data is converted into multiple bits, enabling the signal to be spread out over a wider frequency band. The use of DSSS in combination with a technique called *complementary code keying (CKK)* enables IEEE 802.11b systems to achieve their 11-Mbps transmission rates.

- **Frequency Hopping Spread Spectrum (FHSS)**   A radio transmission method in which the transmitter continuously performs rapid frequency shifts according to a preset algorithm. The receiver performs the exact same shifts to read the incoming signals. IEEE 802.11a systems can use FHSS, but IEEE 802.11b doesn't support it.

- **Infrared**   Infrared communications use high frequencies, just below the visible light spectrum. Infrared is a "line of sight" technology, meaning that the signals cannot penetrate through opaque walls and objects. This restriction severely limits the utility of infrared technology and explains why the technology is rarely used for LAN communications, except for simple links between computers and peripherals such as printers and handheld devices.

The IEEE 802.11 MAC Layer

Like all of the protocols developed by the IEEE 802 working groups, IEEE 802.11 splits the data-link layer into two sublayers: LLC and MAC. The LLC sublayer, which is used to package the network layer data to be transmitted, is the same for all of the IEEE 802 protocols. The IEEE 802.11 protocol's MAC sublayer defines the data, control, and management frames used by the protocol, as well as its MAC mechanism. IEEE 802.11 uses a variation on the CSMA/CD MAC mechanism used by Ethernet, called **Carrier Sense Multiple Access with Collision Avoidance (CSMA/CA).**

CSMA/CA is similar to CSMA/CD in that computers check the network to see if it is in use before they send their data; if the network is free, the transmission proceeds. Also like CSMA/CD, two computers can transmit at the same time on a CSMA/CA network, causing a collision. The difference between the two MAC mechanisms is that in a wireless environment, the CSMA/CD collision detection mechanism would be impractical because it would require full-duplex communications. A computer on a twisted-pair Ethernet network assumes that a collision has occurred when an incoming signal arrives over its receive wire pair while it's sending data over the transmit wire pair. Wireless LAN devices usually cannot transmit and receive simultaneously, so the CSMA/CD MAC mechanism would be difficult or impossible to implement.

Test your knowledge of Wireless LAN concepts by completing Exercise 4-5, "IEEE 802.11 Concepts," now.

Instead of detecting collisions as they occur, the receiving computer on a CSMA/CA network performs a CRC check on the incoming packets and, if no errors are detected, transmits an acknowledgment message to the sender. This acknowledgment indicates that no collision has occurred. If the sender does not receive an acknowledgment for a particular packet, it automatically retransmits the packet until it either receives an acknowledgment or times out. If the sender still doesn't receive an acknowledgment after a specific number of retransmissions, it abandons the effort and leaves the error correction process to the protocols at the upper layers of the networking stack.

SUMMARY

- There are two sets of Ethernet standards: DIX Ethernet and Institute of Electrical and Electronics Engineers (IEEE) 802.3, which differ primarily in their frame formats.

- Ethernet supports many different physical layer configurations, using various types of cables: coaxial, twisted pair, and fiber optic.

- Ethernet uses the Carrier Sense Multiple Access with Collision Detection Media Access Control (CSMA/CD MAC) mechanism, which relies on the ability of the computers to detect packet collisions when they occur.

- Token Ring supports two physical layer options: a shielded twisted pair (STP) cable called Type 1 and an unshielded twisted pair (UTP) cable called Type 3.

- Token Ring uses the token passing MAC mechanism, in which only the system in possession of a special token frame is permitted to transmit data.

- Token Ring uses four different types of frames, while Ethernet uses only one.

- Fiber Distributed Data Interface (FDDI) is a token passing data-link layer protocol that was at one time a popular solution for backbone networks.

- FDDI uses either a physical double ring topology or a star topology.

- A FDDI workstation attached to both rings of a double ring is called a dual attachment station (DAS), and one that is attached to a single ring is called a single attachment station (SAS).

- Wireless LAN technologies enable wireless computers to communicate among themselves or with a standard cabled network.

- The IEEE 802.11 protocol supports three physical layer options and provides transmission speeds up to 54 Mbps.

- IEEE 802.11 splits the data link layer into Logical Link Control (LLC) and MAC sublayers and uses Carrier Sense Multiple Access with Collision Avoidance (CSMA/CA) as its MAC mechanism.

EXERCISES

Exercise 4-1: IEEE Standards and Technologies

Match the standard in the left column with the most suitable technology in the right column.

1.	IEEE 802.2	a.	Gigabit Ethernet
2.	IEEE 802.3	b.	Fast Ethernet
3.	IEEE 802.3u	c.	Thick Ethernet
4.	IEEE 802.3z	d.	LLC
5.	IEEE 802.3ab	e.	10Base-T
6.	IEEE 802.5	f.	Thin Ethernet
7.	DIX Ethernet	g.	1000Base-T
8.	DIX Ethernet II	h.	Token Ring

Exercise 4-2: CSMA/CD Procedures

Put the following steps of the CSMA/CD transmission process in the proper order:

1. The system begins transmitting data. *3*
2. The system retransmits data. *8*
3. The system detects incoming signal on receive wires. *4*
4. The system backs off. *7*
5. The system listens to the network. *1*
6. The system stops transmitting data. *5*
7. The system transmits a jam pattern. *6*
8. The system detects no network traffic. *2*

Exercise 4-3: Selecting a Data-Link Layer Protocol

For each of the following scenarios, specify which data-link layer protocol you think is preferable—Ethernet or Token Ring—and give reasons why. In some cases, either protocol would be suitable; the reasons you provide are more significant than the protocol you select.

1. A family with two computers in the home wants to network them to share a printer and an Internet connection.

2. A small graphics design firm wants to build a 10-node network to handle the extremely large image files that they must transfer between systems and to a print server.

3. A company with a 50-node LAN used by its order entry staff will be going public in the near future and is expected to grow enormously over the next year.

Exercise 4-4: FDDI Concepts

Match the acronyms in the left column with the correct definitions in the right column.

1. DAS   **a.** A version of FDDI that uses copper cable
2. DAC   **b.** A computer connected to a FDDI network using the star topology
3. SAS   **c.** A FDDI frame that performs ring management functions
4. CDDI   **d.** The hub used in a FDDI star network
5. SMT   **e.** A computer connected to both rings of a double ring

Exercise 4-5: IEEE 802.11 Concepts

Match the concepts in the left column with the correct definitions in the right column.

1. Extension point   **a.** An access point
2. BSS   **b.** A backbone connecting access points
3. Base station   **c.** Another term for a cell
4. DS   **d.** A repeater for wireless signals

REVIEW QUESTIONS

1. What does an Ethernet system generate when it detects a collision?

   a. A jam signal

   b. An error message

   c. A beacon frame

   d. None of the above

2. Which of the following is not a required component of a 10Base-T Ethernet network?

    a. Network interface adapters

    b. Cables

    c. A hub

    d. Computers

3. To achieve 100-Mbps speed over CAT3 cable, what does 100Base-T4 Ethernet use?

    a. PAM-5 signaling

    b. Quartet signaling

    c. CSMA/CD

    d. All four wire pairs

4. Which of the following standards defines Gigabit Ethernet?

    a. IEEE 802.2

    b. IEEE 802.3

    c. IEEE 802.3u

    d. IEEE 802.3z

5. List the hardware components that you have to replace when upgrading a 10-year-old 10Base-T network to 100Base-TX.

6. How could you upgrade a 10-year-old 10Base-T network to Fast Ethernet without replacing the cables?

7. Which Fast Ethernet physical layer option is best suited for a connection between two campus buildings 200 meters apart? Why?

8. Which of the following is a valid MAC address?

    a. 00:B0:A1:8C:32:65:BB

    b. 01:DB:7F:86:E4:6G

    c. 00:D0:B7:AD:1A:7B

    d. 03:BC:5A:E6:E4

9. What is the Frame Check Sequence field in a data-link layer protocol header used for?

10. Which data-link layer protocol is preferred on a network with high levels of traffic: Ethernet or Token Ring? Why?

11. Which of the following Token Ring cables has both IDC and DB-9 connectors?

    a. A Type 3 cable

    b. A lobe cable

    c. A patch cable

    d. A token cable

12. Most Token Ring networks today run at what speed?

    a. 4 Mbps

    b. 16 Mbps

    c. 100 Mbps

    d. 1000 Mbps

13. A Token Ring system that is waiting to capture a free token is said to be in what mode?

    a. Transmit mode

    b. Passive mode

    c. Stripping mode

    d. Repeat mode

14. What is the term for a FDDI double ring network that has experienced a cable failure?

    a. A wrapped ring

    b. A truncated ring

    c. A bifurcated ring

    d. A dual ring of trees

15. Which FDDI physical layer option supports the longest network segments?

    a. The double ring topology

    b. The star topology

    c. Single-mode fiber optic

    d. Multimode fiber optic

16. Which of the following fields identifies the type of data carried in a FDDI data frame?

    a. Starting Delimiter

    b. Frame Control

    c. Source Address

    d. Frame Check Sequence

17. What MAC mechanism does an IEEE 802.11 network use?

    a. CSMA/CA

    b. FHSS

    c. DSSS

    d. CSMA/CD

18. Which of the following terms describes a wireless LAN that does not use access points?

    a. Infrastructure

    b. Distribution

    c. Ad hoc

    d. Basic

19. Which of the following is not a physical layer option supported by IEEE 802.11?

    a. DSSS

    b. BSS

    c. Infrared

    d. FHSS

CASE SCENARIOS

Scenario 4-1: Troubleshooting an Ethernet Network

You are a network consultant who has been called in to resolve a communications problem on a newly installed Ethernet network. Users are experiencing intermittent connection failures and marginal network performance, even under the best conditions. After testing the network with a protocol analyzer, you determine that a large number of late collisions are occurring. You ask to see the plans for the network's design, and you are shown a sketch that calls for five Class II 100Base-TX Fast Ethernet hubs scattered around the site. The entire network uses CAT5 cable, and all of the cable runs are far less than 100 meters long. Which of the following could possibly be the cause of the problem?

1. The network is using the wrong hubs. Class II hubs are used only for 100Base-T4 networks.

2. The network is not in conformance with the 5-4-3 rule, because all of the hubs are using linking segments.

3. The network has too many hubs. No more than two Class II hubs are permitted on a Fast Ethernet network.

4. There is too much traffic on the network, as evidenced by the large number of late collisions.

Scenario 4-2: Designing an Ethernet Network

You have been asked to design a mission-critical network that runs at 100 Mbps and that can support consistently high traffic levels with no degradation of performance. The network must also be able to tolerate a cable break anywhere without any loss of connectivity. You design a fiber optic network using 100Base-FX with two Class II hubs. Which of the network design goals have you achieved?

1. Your design achieves all of the goals required by the client.

2. Your design provides 100-Mbps transmission speeds, but it fails to support high traffic levels adequately and does not meet the fault tolerance requirement.

3. Your design provides adequate speed and fault tolerance but fails to support high traffic levels.

4. Your design fails to achieve any of the network design requirements.

CHAPTER 5
NETWORK LAYER PROTOCOLS

Upon completion of this chapter, you will be able to:

- Describe the functions of the Internet Protocol (IP) protocol and the various IP header fields.

- Understand the basics of IP addressing, routing, and fragmentation.

- Understand the function of a subnet mask and how to create subnets on a network.

- Describe the functions of the Internetwork Packet Exchange (IPX) protocol and the various IPX header fields.

- Understand the function of the Network Basic Input/Output System (NetBIOS) in the Microsoft Windows operating systems.

- Describe the NetBIOS Extended User Interface (NetBEUI) Frame format.

- Understand AppleTalk addressing.

INTERNET PROTOCOL (IP)

The protocols operating at the data-link layer are concerned only with transmitting packets to other systems on the local area network (LAN). By contrast, the protocols operating at the network layer of the Open Systems Interconnection (OSI) reference model are responsible for the end-to-end transmission of data across an internetwork. The network layer protocols are therefore a crucial element of any network consisting of more than a single LAN. This chapter examines the most commonly used network layer protocols:

- IP, from the Transmission Control Protocol/Internet Protocol (TCP/IP) suite

- The IPX protocol developed by Novell for its NetWare operating system

- NetBEUI, the protocol used by early versions of Windows

- Apple Computer's Datagram Delivery Protocol (DDP), part of its AppleTalk protocol suite

IP is the cornerstone of the TCP/IP protocol suite. Generally, a discussion of a network layer protocol or its functions is referring to IP. The TCP/IP suite is named for a combination of two protocols—IP at the network layer and the Transmission Control Protocol (TCP) at the transport layer; together, these two protocols provide one of the most frequently used network transport services. TCP data is encapsulated within IP, as are most of the other protocols in the TCP/IP suite. IP essentially functions as the envelope that delivers TCP/IP data to its destination.

IP Standards

The TCP/IP protocols are defined in documents called **Requests for Comments (RFCs)**, which are published by a body called the **Internet Engineering Task Force (IETF)**. These documents can then wend their way through a ratification process that eventually results in their publication as Internet standards. Unlike most networking standards, TCP/IP specifications are released to the public domain and are freely available on the Internet at many different sites, including the IETF home page at *www.ietf.org*.

The IP specification was published as RFC 791, "Internet Protocol: DARPA Internet Program Protocol Specification," in September 1981 and was later ratified as Internet Standard 5. RFC 791 is a relatively brief document that concentrates primarily on IP's addressing and fragmentation functions.

Other important functions of the IP protocol are defined in other RFC documents, including the following:

- RFC 894, "Standard for the Transmission of IP Datagrams over Ethernet Networks," April 1984

- RFC 950, "Internet Standard Subnetting Procedure," August 1985

- RFC 1042, "A Standard for the Transmission of IP Datagrams over IEEE 802 Networks," February 1988

- RFC 1812, "Requirements for IP Version 4 Routers," June 1995

The IP protocol is also in the midst of a migration to an upgraded standard, from version 4 (IPv4) to version 6 (IPv6). These upgrades are defined in many additional RFCs, such as the following:

- RFC 1881, "IPv6 Address Allocation Management," December 1995

- RFC 1887, "An Architecture for IPv6 Unicast Address Allocation," December 1995

- RFC 2460, "Internet Protocol Version 6 (IPv6) Specification," December 1998

- RFC 3513, "Internet Protocol Version 6 (IPv6) Addressing Architecture," April 2003

- RFC 3596, "DNS Extensions to Support IP Version 6," October 2003

> **MORE INFO   IPv6**   For more information on the IPv6 standard, see "IPv6 Addressing" later in this chapter.

IP Functions

On a TCP/IP internetwork, IP is the protocol responsible for transmitting data from its source to its final destination. Like most network layer protocols, IP is a connectionless protocol, meaning that it transmits messages to a destination without first establishing a connection to the receiving system. IP is connectionless because it carries data generated by other protocols, only some of which require connection-oriented service.

The TCP/IP suite includes both connection-oriented and connectionless services at the transport layer, making it possible for applications to select one or the other, depending on the quality of service they need. Because TCP provides connection-oriented service at the transport layer, there is no need to implement that same service at the network layer. The network layer can remain connectionless, thus reducing the amount of control overhead generated by the protocol stack.

IP performs several functions that are essential to the internetworking process, including the following:

- **Data encapsulation**   The packaging of the transport layer data into a datagram

- **IP addressing**   The identification of systems in the network by using unique addresses

- **IP routing**   The selection of the most efficient path through the internetwork to the destination system

- **Fragmentation**   The division of data into fragments of an appropriate size for transmission over the network

- **Protocol identification**   The specification of the transport layer protocol that generated the data in the datagram

These functions are discussed in the following sections.

Data Encapsulation

Just as a data-link layer protocol, such as Ethernet, packages network layer data for transmission over a LAN, a transport layer protocol, such as TCP or the User Datagram Protocol (UDP), passes data down to the network layer. At the network layer, IP encapsulates the data by adding a header, thus creating a datagram (also known as a packet), shown in Figure 5-1. The datagram is addressed to the computer that will ultimately use the data, whether that computer is located on the local network or on another network far away. Except for a few minor modifications, the datagram remains intact throughout the packet's journey to its destination. Once it has created the datagram, IP passes it down to a data-link layer protocol for transmission over the network.

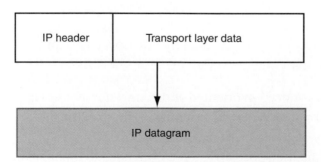

Figure 5-1   IP encapsulates transport layer data into units called datagrams.

> **NOTE** **Protocol Data Units** *Protocols operating at different layers of the OSI reference model use different names for the protocol data units (PDUs) they create. For example, network layer protocols create datagrams or packets, while data-link layer protocols create frames. The term PDU is generic and can refer to the data structure created by any protocol.*

During the transportation process, various systems might encapsulate the datagram in different data-link layer protocol frames, but the datagram itself remains intact. The process is similar to the delivery of a letter by the post office, with IP functioning as the envelope. The letter might be placed into different mailbags and transported by various trucks and planes during the course of its journey, but the envelope remains sealed. Only the addressee is permitted to open it and use the contents.

The IP Datagram Format

The header that IP applies to the data it receives from the transport layer protocol is typically 20 bytes long and contains information needed to route the datagram to its destination, just like addresses on an envelope. The IP datagram format is shown in Figure 5-2.

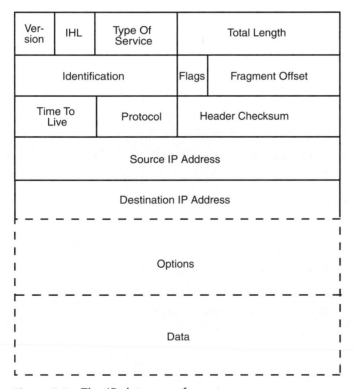

Figure 5-2 The IP datagram format

The IP datagram fields perform the following functions:

- **Version (4 bits)**   Specifies the version of the IP protocol used to create the datagram. The version currently in use on most networks is IPv4, but IPv6 is in the process of being deployed.

- **Internet Header Length (IHL, 4 bits)**   Specifies the length of the datagram's header (exclusive of the Data field), in 32-bit (4-byte) words. The typical length of a datagram header is five words (20 bytes), but if the datagram includes additional options, it can be longer, which is the reason for the existence of this field.

- **Type Of Service (1 byte)**   Contains a code that specifies the service priority for the datagram. This is a feature that enables a system to assign a priority to a datagram that routers observe while forwarding it through an internetwork. Of the eight bits in the field, the first, second, third, and eighth are not used. The fourth through seventh bits contain one of the following values:

    - ❑ 0000. Default
    - ❑ 0001. Minimize monetary cost
    - ❑ 0010. Maximize reliability
    - ❑ 0100. Maximize throughput
    - ❑ 1000. Minimize delay
    - ❑ 1111. Maximize security

    These values and their usage are defined in RFC 2474, "Definition of the Differentiated Services Field (DS Field) in the IPv4 and IPv6 Headers."

- **Total Length (2 bytes)**   Specifies the length of the entire datagram, including the Data field and all of the header fields, in bytes.

- **Identification (2 bytes)**   Contains a value that uniquely identifies the datagram. The destination system uses this value, along with the contents of the Flags and Fragment Offset fields, to reassemble datagrams that have been fragmented during transmission.

- **Flags (3 bits)**   Contains bits used to regulate the datagram fragmentation process, as follows:

    - ❏ Bit 1. Unused.

    - ❏ Bit 2. Don't fragment. When this bit has a value of 1, systems receiving the datagram are instructed never to fragment it.

    - ❏ Bit 3. More fragments. A value of 0 for this bit notifies the receiving system that the last fragment of the datagram has been transmitted. A value of 1 for this bit indicates that there are still more fragments to be transmitted.

- **Fragment Offset (13 bits)**   When a datagram is fragmented, this field contains a value (in 8-byte units) that identifies the fragment's place in the datagram.

- **Time To Live (TTL, 1 byte)**   Specifies the number of networks that the datagram should be permitted to travel through on the way to its destination. Each router that forwards the datagram reduces the value of this field by 1. If the value reaches 0, the datagram is discarded. The value currently recommended by the Internet Assigned Numbers Authority (IANA) for the Time To Live field is 64, but many IP implementations use larger values.

- **Protocol (1 byte)**   Contains a code identifying the protocol that generated the information found in the Data field.

- **Header Checksum (2 bytes)**   Contains a checksum value computed on the IP header fields only (and not the contents of the Data field) for the purpose of error detection.

- **Source IP Address (4 bytes)**   Specifies the IP address of the system that generated the datagram.

- **Destination IP Address (4 bytes)**   Specifies the IP address of the system for which the datagram is destined.

- **Options (variable)**   Present only when the datagram contains one or more of the 16 available IP options. The size and content of the field depend on the number and the nature of the options.

- **Data (variable)**   Contains the information generated by the protocol specified in the Protocol field, usually a transport layer protocol. The size of the field depends on the data-link layer protocol used by the network over which the system will transmit the datagram.

IP Options

IP options are additional header fields that enable datagrams to carry extra information and, in some cases, to accumulate information as they travel through an internetwork on the way to their destinations. To include options, the datagram contains an additional subheader, as shown in Figure 5-3.

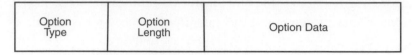

Figure 5-3   **The IP option subheader**

The functions of the fields in the IP option subheader are as follows:

- **Option Type (1 byte)**   Contains three subfields that specify the function of the option, as follows:

    - Copied Flag (1 bit). When the datagram is fragmented, this flag specifies whether the option should be copied to each fragment.

    - Option Class (2 bits). Specifies the basic function of the option. A value of 0 indicates a control option, and a value of 2 indicates a debugging and measurement option.

    - Option Number (5 bits). Contains a number uniquely identifying the option, assigned and published by the IANA.

- **Option Length (1 byte)**   Specifies the total length of the option subheader, including the Option Type, Option Length, and Option Data fields.

- **Option Data (Option Length value minus 2)**   Contains option-specific information to be delivered to the destination system.

> **MORE INFO**   **IP Options List**   *The current list of IP options is available at www.iana.org/assignments/ip-parameters.*

Table 5-1 contains some of the most commonly used IP options, along with the values for their Option Type subfields and an option value that is often used to identify the option. All of the options listed in this table are defined in RFC 791, but there are other options defined in various other RFCs.

Table 5-1 **Commonly Used IP Options**

Copied Flag	Option Class	Option Number	Option Value	Option Name	Designation
0	0	0	0	End Of Options List	EOOL
0	0	1	1	No Operation	NOP
1	0	3	131	Loose Source Routing	LSR
0	2	4	68	Internet Timestamp	TS
0	0	7	7	Record Route	RR
1	0	9	137	Strict Source Routing	SSR

The functions of the options listed in the table are as follows:

- **End Of Options List (EOOL)**   Functions as a delimiter that indicates the end of the Options field in a datagram. When a datagram includes multiple options, there is only one EOOL option included, not one for each option. EOOL is one of two options that consists only of an Option Type field. There is no Option Length or Option Data field in this option.

- **No Operation (NOP)**   Functions as a padding byte between options to align the beginning of the subsequent option on the boundary of a 32-bit word. As with EOOL, the NOP option consists only of an Option Type field.

- **Loose Source Routing (LSR)**   Provides a means for a sending system to include routing information in a datagram. In the LSR option, the Option Data field contains a pointer plus the IP addresses of selected gateways on the internetwork that the datagram must pass through on the way to its destination. The pointer contains a value (in number of bytes relative to the beginning of the option) that indicates which IP address in the option field should be processed next. In loose source routing, the datagram must be processed by the specified gateways, but it can also pass through other gateways as well.

- **Internet Timestamp (TS)**   Provides a means for gateways to add timestamps indicating when they processed the datagram. In the TS option, the Option Data field contains the following subfields:

  - ❏ Pointer (1 byte). Specifies the location (in number of bytes relative to the beginning of the option) where the next timestamp should be recorded.

  - ❏ Overflow (4 bits). Specifies the number of gateways that cannot record their timestamps because the Option Data field is full. The size of the Option Data field for the TS option specified by the sending system must be sufficient to hold all of the expected timestamp information because this field cannot be expanded while the datagram is en route.

❏ Flag (4 bits). Specifies the nature of the information stored in the rest of the Option Data field. A value of 0 indicates that the field contains 32-bit timestamps only. A value of 1 indicates that each timestamp is preceded by the IP address of the gateway that added it. A value of 3 indicates that the IP addresses of the gateways that are to record their timestamps are already specified in the Option Data field.

❏ IP Addresses/Timestamps. Contains the timestamp information (or IP address and timestamp information, depending on the value of the Flag field) recorded by the gateways processing the datagram.

■ **Record Route (RR)**   Provides a means for a datagram to record the IP addresses of the gateways processing the packet on the way to its destination. In the RR option, the Option Data field initially contains a pointer specifying the location (in number of bytes relative to the beginning of the option) where the next gateway address should be written. As the datagram travels through the internetwork, each gateway system adds its IP address to the Option Data field and increments the value of the pointer by 4.

■ **Strict Source Routing (SSR)**   Provides a means for a sending system to include routing information in a datagram. In the SSR option, the Option Data field contains a pointer, and the field also must contain the IP addresses of all gateways on the internetwork that the datagram must pass through on the way to its destination. The pointer contains a value (in number of bytes relative to the beginning of the option) that indicates which IP address in the option field should be processed next. In strict source routing, the datagram must include a complete route to the destination because no gateways other than those specified in the datagram are permitted to process the packet.

IP Addressing

IP is unique among network layer protocols because it has its own self-contained addressing system, which it uses to uniquely identify computers on almost any size of internetwork. Other network layer protocols (such as IPX) use the hardware addresses coded into network interface adapters to identify computers, with a separate address for the network, while NetBEUI assigns a name to each computer on the LAN and has no network addresses. Because IP addresses do not rely on hardware addresses or any other characteristics of the network interface, they are suitable for use on any type of network or computing platform. IPX, by contrast, is designed primarily for use on LANs because it relies on the properties of a data-link layer LAN protocol, and NetBEUI can only be used on single-segment networks because the names it uses for addresses are not routable.

IP addresses are 32 bits long and contain both a network identifier and a host identifier. In TCP/IP parlance, the term *host* refers to a network interface found in a computer or other device. In most cases, each computer on a network has one IP address, but it is actually the network interface that the address represents, not the computer itself. A computer with two network interfaces, whether they are provided by network interface adapters or wide area network (WAN) devices such as modems, will actually have two IP addresses, one for each interface.

> **MORE INFO** **IP Addressing** For more information about the structure and assignment of IP addresses, see "IP Addressing," later in this chapter.

The IP addresses that a computer inserts into the Source IP Address and Destination IP Address fields of the IP header identify, respectively, the computer that created the packet and the one that will eventually receive it. If the packet is intended for a computer on the local network, the Destination IP Address refers to the same computer as the Destination Address in the data-link protocol header. However, if the packet's destination is a computer on another network, the Destination IP Address refers to a different computer because IP is an end-to-end protocol that is responsible for the entire journey of the data to its ultimate destination, not just for a single network hop as is the case with the data-link layer protocol.

Data-link layer protocols cannot work with IP addresses, so to actually transmit the datagram, IP has to supply the data-link layer protocol with the hardware address of a system on the local network. To do this, IP uses another TCP/IP protocol, called **Address Resolution Protocol (ARP)**. ARP works by generating broadcast messages that contain an IP address on the local network. The system using that IP address must respond to the broadcast, and the reply message contains the system's hardware address. If the datagram's destination system is located on the local network, the transmitting system generates an ARP message containing the IP address of that destination. The destination system then responds with an ARP reply message containing its hardware address. If the destination system is located on another network, IP generates an ARP message containing the address of a router on the local network instead. Once it has received the ARP reply, the IP protocol on the original system can pass the datagram down to the data-link layer protocol and provide it with the hardware address it needs to build the frame.

> **MORE INFO   Understanding ARP**   *For more information on how ARP supplies hardware addresses to data-link layer protocols, see Chapter 7, "TCP/IP."*

IP Routing

Routing is the most important and the most complex function of the IP protocol. When a TCP/IP system has to transmit data to a computer on another network, the packets must travel through the routers (called *gateways* in TCP/IP terminology) that connect the networks together. The source and final destination computers in a case like this are called end systems and the routers are called intermediate systems, as shown in Figure 5-4. When the packets pass through an intermediate system, they travel up through the protocol stack only as high as the network layer, where IP is responsible for deciding where to send the packet next. If the router is connected to the network where the destination system is located, the system can transmit the packet directly to its final destination. If the destination system is located on another network, the router sends the packet to another router, which brings the packet one hop closer to its destination. Depending on the complexity of the internetwork, a packet might pass through dozens of routers on the way to its destination.

> **NOTE   IP Routing**   *Intermediate systems use their own internal routing tables to determine where to send each packet they receive, and the most complicated part of the routing process is the compiling of the routing tables. For more information about routing tables and the other complexities of IP routing, see "Understanding IP Routing," later in this chapter.*

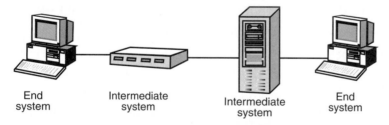

| End | Intermediate | Intermediate | End |
| system | system | system | system |

Figure 5-4   Packets can travel through multiple intermediate systems to reach an end system.

Because packets reach only as high as the network layer in an intermediate system, the router never accesses the information in a datagram's Data field. The router strips off the data-link layer frame and later builds a new one, but the datagram "envelope" remains sealed until it reaches its destination. However, each intermediate system does make some changes to the IP header. The most important of these changes is to the TTL field, which is set with a predetermined value by the end system that generated the packet. Each router, as it processes the packet, reduces this value by one. If the TTL value reaches 0, the router discards the packet. This mechanism prevents packets from circulating endlessly around an internetwork in the event of a routing problem.

When a router discards a packet with a TTL value of 0, it generates an error message called a Time To Live Exceeded In Transit message, using the **Internet Control Message Protocol (ICMP)**, and sends it to the end system where the packet originated. This message informs that system that the packet has not reached its destination. A utility called Traceroute (included with most TCP/IP implementations) uses the TTL field to display a list of the routers that packets are using to reach a particular destination. By generating a series of packets with successively larger TTL values, each router in turn generates an ICMP error message identifying the router that discarded the packet. Traceroute assembles the router addresses from the error messages and displays the entire route to the destination. For more information about Traceroute, see Chapter 11, "Network Troubleshooting Tools."

Fragmentation

IP routers can connect networks that use different media types and different data-link layer protocols, but to forward packets from one network to another, routers must often repackage the datagrams into different data-link layer frames. In some cases, this is simply a matter of stripping off the old frame and adding a new one, but in other cases the data-link layer protocols are different enough to require more extensive repackaging. For example, when a router connects a Token Ring network and an Ethernet network, it must contend with the fact that datagrams arriving from the Token Ring network can be up to 4500 bytes long, while the datagrams in Ethernet packets can be no larger than 1500 bytes.

To overcome this problem, the router splits the datagram arriving from the Token Ring network into multiple fragments, as shown in Figure 5-5. Each fragment has its own IP header and is transmitted in a separate data-link layer frame. The size of each fragment is based on the size of the largest PDU allowed on the outgoing network, which is called its **maximum transmission unit (MTU)**. Once the fragments are transmitted, if they encounter a network with an even smaller MTU, a router can split them into still smaller fragments. Once a datagram is fragmented, the individual parts are not reassembled until they reach the end system, which is their final destination.

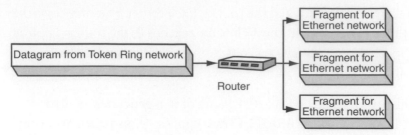

Figure 5-5   Routers can split datagrams into fragments for transmission over networks with smaller MTUs.

When IP fragments a datagram, it splits the contents of the Data field and attaches an IP header to each fragment. The Identification field in each fragment's header contains the same value as the datagram's original header, which enables the destination system to associate the fragments that make up a particular datagram. The system performing the fragmentation leaves the rest of the IP header fields intact, with the following exceptions:

- **Internet Header Length**   Modified to reflect the length of the header in each fragment, due to the possible removal of certain IP options.

- **Total Length**   Modified to reflect the length of each fragment.

- **Flags**   The value of the More Fragments bit is changed from 0 to 1 in all of the fragments except the last one. The value of 1 in this bit indicates that there are more fragments coming for that datagram. The destination system uses this bit to determine when it has received all of the fragments and can begin to assemble them back into the whole datagram.

- **Fragment Offset**   Modified to reflect each fragment's place in the original datagram. The first fragment has a value of 0 in this field, and the value in the second fragment is the size (in bytes) of the first fragment. The third fragment's offset value is the size of the first two fragments, and so forth. The destination system uses these values to reassemble the fragments in the proper order.

- **Header Checksum**   Recomputed to reflect the modified values in the other header fields.

- **Options**   Some IP options must be reproduced in every fragment, while others need only be present in the first fragment for a particular datagram. The LSR and SSR options must be copied to every fragment. The RR and TS options are copied only to the first datagram. The EOOL and NOP options can be copied to one, all, or none of a datagram's fragments, as needed.

Another bit in the Flags field, called the Don't Fragment bit, instructs routers to discard a datagram rather than fragment it. When a router receives a datagram that requires fragmentation, but the value of this bit is set to 1, the router discards the packet instead of fragmenting it and returns an ICMP Fragmentation Needed and Don't Fragment Was Set error message to the source end system.

The size of the fragments created by a router is left up to the individual implementation of the IP protocol. Some routers create fragments based on the MTU of the outgoing network, while others always create 576-byte fragments, because the IP standard states that "every internet destination must be able to receive a datagram of 576 [bytes] either in one piece or in fragments to be reassembled." Fragmentation is not a desirable process, but it is a necessary evil. Obviously, fragmenting a datagram increases the amount of traffic on the network, because what was originally one packet with a single data-link layer frame and IP header is now many packets, each with its own frame and header.

In addition, once a datagram is fragmented, if any one of the fragments is lost or damaged in transit, all of the fragments must be retransmitted. This is necessary because the source end system has no knowledge of the fragmentation processes performed by the intermediate systems on the way to the destination, and because there is no mechanism for recreating and retransmitting one fragment out of many.

Protocol Identification

For the destination system to process the incoming datagram properly, it must know which protocol generated the information carried in the Data field. The Protocol field in the IP header provides this information, using codes that are defined by the IANA and published on their Web site at *www.iana.org/assignments/protocol-numbers*.

Some of the most commonly used values for the Protocol field are as follows:

- **1**   ICMP
- **2**   Internet Group Management Protocol (IGMP)
- **3**   Gateway-to-Gateway Protocol (GGP)
- **4**   IP in IP (encapsulation)
- **6**   TCP
- **8**   Exterior Gateway Protocol (EGP)
- **17**   UDP

> **NOTE** **The Protocol File** Every TCP/IP system has a text file called Protocol that also contains a partial list of the protocol codes expected to be recognized or used by that system.

Test your knowledge of the functions performed by the IP protocol by completing Exercise 5-1, "IP Functions," now.

The protocols that you most expect to see in the list are TCP and UDP, which are the transport layer protocols that account for much of the IP traffic on a TCP/IP network. However, IP also carries other types of information in its datagrams, including ICMP messages, which notify systems of errors and other network conditions, and messages generated by routing protocols like GGP and EGP, which TCP/IP systems use to automatically update their routing tables.

Understanding IP Addressing

The self-contained IP addressing system is one of the most important elements of the TCP/IP protocol suite. IP addresses enable computers running any operating system on any platform to communicate by providing unique identifiers for the computer itself and for the network on which it is located. Understanding how IP addresses are constructed and how they should be assigned is an essential part of TCP/IP network administration.

An IPv4 address is a 32-bit value that contains both a network identifier and a host identifier. The address is notated by using four decimal numbers ranging from 0 to 255, separated by periods, as in 192.168.1.44. This is known as *dotted decimal notation*. Each of the four values is the decimal equivalent of an 8-bit binary value. For example, the binary value 10101010 is equal to the decimal value 170. To properly understand some of the concepts of IP addressing, you must remember that the familiar decimal numbers are only convenient equivalents of binary values.

> **NOTE** **Octets, Bytes, and Quads** In TCP/IP terminology, each of the 8-bit values that make up an IP address is called an *octet* (or sometimes even a *quad*), and the combination of four octets is called a *word*. The developers of the TCP/IP protocols deliberately avoided the more traditional term *byte* because at the time, some computing platforms used a 7-bit rather than an 8-bit byte. Today, either octet or byte is appropriate.

As mentioned earlier, IP addresses represent network interfaces, and a computer can have more than one network interface. A router, for example, has interfaces to at least two networks and must therefore have an IP address for each of those interfaces. Workstations on a LAN typically have only a single interface, but in some cases they use a modem to connect to another network, such as the Internet. In this case, the modem interface has its own separate IP address (usually assigned by the server at the other end of the modem connection) in addition to that of the LAN connection. If other systems on the LAN access the Internet through that computer's modem, that system is actually functioning as a router.

IP Address Assignments

Hardware addresses are hard-coded into network interface adapters at the factory, but IP addresses must be assigned by network administrators to the systems on their networks, either manually or dynamically using the Dynamic Host Configuration Protocol (DHCP). It is essential for each network interface to have its own unique IP address; when two systems have the same IP address, they cannot communicate with the network properly.

As mentioned earlier, IP addresses consist of two parts: a network identifier and a host identifier. All of the network interface adapters on a particular subnet have the same network identifier but different host identifiers. For systems on the Internet, the IANA assigns network identifiers to ensure that there is no address duplication on the Internet. When an organization registers its network, it is assigned a network identifier. It is then up to the network administrators to assign unique host identifiers to each of the systems on that network. This two-tiered system of administration is one of the basic organizational principles of the Internet. Domain names are assigned in the same way.

> **NOTE**   *Obtaining Network Addresses*   Although the IANA is ultimately responsible for the assignment of all Internet network addresses, network administrators seldom deal with the address registrar directly. Instead, they obtain a network address from an Internet service provider (ISP). The ISP might have obtained the network address from a local, national, or regional Internet registry (LIR, NIR, and RIR, respectively); the IANA assigns pools of addresses to these registries. But it is also possible that the ISP obtained the address from its own service provider. Internet addresses often pass through several layers of service providers in this way before they get to the organization that actually uses them.

IP Address Classes

You have already learned that an IP address contains a network identifier and a host identifier, which means that some of the 32 bits in the address specify the network on which the host is located and the rest of the bits identify the specific host on that network. The most complicated aspect of an IP address is that the division between the network identifier bits and the host identifier bits is not always in the same place. In a network interface adapter's hardware address, for example, the first three bytes are always the organizationally unique identifier (OUI) assigned to the manufacturer of the network adapter and the last three bytes are the value that the manufacturer itself assigns to the adapter. However, IP addresses can have various numbers of bits assigned to the network identifier, depending on the size and organization of the network.

RFC 791 defines three classes of IP addresses, which provide support for networks of different sizes, as shown in Figure 5-6.

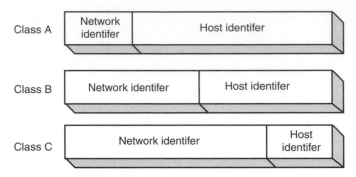

Figure 5-6   The three classes of IP addresses have differently sized network and host identifiers.

The characteristics of these three address classes are listed in Table 5-2.

Table 5-2   **IP Address Classes and Parameters**

IP Address Class	Class A	Class B	Class C
First bit values (binary)	0	10	110
First byte value (decimal)	0–127	128–191	192–223
Number of network identifier bits	8	16	24
Number of host identifier bits	24	16	8
Number of possible networks	126	16,384	2,097,152
Number of possible hosts	16,777,214	65,534	254

> **NOTE   Additional IP Address Classes**   In addition to Classes A, B, and C, RFC 791 also defines two additional address classes, Class D and Class E. Class D addresses begin with the bit values 1110, and Class E addresses begin with the values 11110. The IANA has allocated Class D addresses for use as multicast identifiers. A *multicast address* identifies a group of computers on a network, all of which possess a similar trait. Multicast addresses enable TCP/IP applications to send traffic to computers that perform specific functions (such as all the routers on the network), even if they are located on different subnets. Class E addresses are defined as experimental and are as yet unused.

The "First bit values" row in Table 5-2 specifies the values that the first one, two, or three bits of an address in each class must have. Some TCP/IP implementations use these bit values to determine the class of an address. The binary values of the first bits of each address class limit the possible decimal values for the first byte of the address. For example, because the first bit of Class A addresses must be 0, the possible binary values of the first byte in a Class A address range from 00000000 to 01111111, which in decimal form are values ranging from 1 to 127. Thus, when you see an IP address in which the first byte is a number from 1 to 127, you know that this is a Class A address.

In a Class A address, the network identifier is the first 8 bits of the address and the host identifier is the remaining 24 bits. Thus, there are only 126 possible Class A networks (network identifier 127 is reserved for diagnostic purposes), but each network can have up to 16,777,214 network interface adapters on it. Class B and Class C addresses devote more bits to the network identifier, which means that they support a greater number of networks, but at the cost of having fewer host identifier bits. This tradeoff reduces the number of hosts that can be created on each network.

The values in Table 5-2 for the number of networks and hosts supported by each address class might appear low. For example, an 8-bit binary number can have 256 (that is, 28) possible values, not 254, as shown in the table for the number of hosts on a Class C address. The value 254 is used because the original IP addressing standard states that you cannot assign the "all zeros" or "all ones" addresses to individual networks or hosts. Today, most routers and operating systems let you use all zeros for a network identifier, but you must be sure that all your equipment supports these values before you decide to use them. The "all ones" identifier always signifies a broadcast address, and it can never be assigned to an individual network or host. Therefore, to compute the number of possible network or host addresses you can create with a given number of bits, you use the formula $2x - 2$, where x is the number of bits.

Subnet Masking

It may at first seem odd that the IP address classes are defined as they are. After all, there aren't any private networks that have 16 million hosts on them, so it makes little sense even to have Class A addresses. However, it's possible to subdivide network addresses even further by creating subnets on them. A **subnet** is simply a subdivision of a network address that can be used to represent a part of a larger network, such as one LAN on an internetwork or the client of an ISP. Thus, a large ISP might have a Class A address registered to it, and it might allocate sections of the address to its clients in the form of subnets. In many cases, a large ISP's clients are smaller ISPs, which in turn supply addresses to their own clients.

To understand the process of creating subnets, you must understand the function of the **subnet mask**. When you configure the TCP/IP client on a computer, you assign it an IP address and a subnet mask. Simply put, the subnet mask specifies which bits of the IP address are the network identifier and which bits are the host identifier. For a Class A address, for example, the default subnet mask value is 255.0.0.0. When expressed as a binary number, a subnet mask's 1 bits indicate the network identifier, and its 0 bits indicate the host identifier. A mask of 255.0.0.0 in binary form is as follows:

11111111 00000000 00000000 00000000

This mask indicates that the first 8 bits of a Class A IP address are the network identifier bits and the remaining 24 bits are the host identifier. The default subnet masks for the three main address classes are as follows:

- **Class A**   255.0.0.0
- **Class B**   255.255.0.0
- **Class C**   255.255.255.0

> **MORE INFO**   **Demonstration Video**   For a demonstration of subnet masking, run the SubnetMasking video located in the Demos folder on the CD-ROM accompanying this book.

Subnetting a Network Address

If all of the IP addresses in a particular class used the same number of bits for the network and host identifiers, there would be no need for a subnet mask. The value of the first byte of the address would indicate its class. However, you can create multiple subnets, using a single address of a given class, by applying a different subnet mask. If, for example, you have a Class B address, the default subnet mask of 255.255.0.0 would allocate the first 16 bits for the network identifier and the last 16 bits for the host identifier. However, if you use a mask of 255.255.255.0 with a Class B address, you allocate an additional 8 bits to the network identifier, which you are borrowing from the host identifier. The third byte of the address thus becomes a *subnet identifier*, as shown in Figure 5-7.

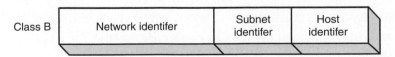

Figure 5-7   By changing the subnet mask, you can create multiple subnets out of one network address.

By subnetting in this way, you can create up to 254 subnets using that one Class B address, with up to 254 network interface adapters on each subnet. An IP address of 131.107.67.98 would therefore indicate that the network is using the Class B address 131.107.0.0, and that the interface is host number 98 on subnet 67. A large corporate network might use this scheme to create a separate subnet for each of its LANs.

> **NOTE Subnet Notation** You are likely to see IP address assignments notated in the form of a network address, followed by a slash and the number of 1-bits in the subnet mask. For example, the address 192.168.42.0/24 refers to a network address of 192.168.42.0 with a subnet mask of 255.255.255.0. Addresses for the three classes are therefore sometimes referred to as "/8s" for Class A, "/16s" for Class B, and "/24s" for Class C.

Subnetting Between Bytes

To complicate matters further, the boundary between the network identifier and the host identifier does not have to fall between two bytes. An IP address can use any number of bits for its network address, and more complex subnet masks are required in this type of environment. Suppose, for example, you have a Class C network address of 192.168.65.0 that you want to subnet. There are already 24 bits devoted to the network address, and you obviously can't allocate the entire fourth byte as a subnet identifier or there would be no bits left for the host identifier. You can, however, allocate part of the fourth byte. If you use 4 bits of the last byte for the subnet identifier, you have 4 bits left for your host identifier. To do this, the binary form of your subnet mask must appear as follows:

```
11111111 11111111 11111111 11110000
```

The decimal equivalent of this binary value is 255.255.255.240 because 240 is the decimal equivalent of 11110000. This leaves a 4-bit subnet identifier and a 4-bit host identifier, which means that you can create up to 14 subnets with 14 hosts on each one. (Subnet identifiers are subject to the same rules about not using all ones or all zeroes as are network identifiers and host identifiers.) Figuring out the correct subnet mask for this type of configuration is relatively easy. Figuring out the IP addresses you must assign to your workstations is harder. To do this, you have to increment the 4 subnet bits separately from the 4 host bits. Once again, this is easier to understand when you look at the binary values. The 4-bit subnet identifier can have any one of the following 14 values:

```
0001 0010 0011 0100 0101 0110 0111 1000 1001 1010 1011 1100 1101 1110
```

Each one of these subnets can have up to 14 workstations, with each host identifier having one of the values from that same set of 14 values. Thus, to calculate the value of the IP address's fourth byte, you must combine the binary values of the subnet and host identifiers and convert them to decimal form. For example, the first host (0001) on the first subnet (0001) would have a fourth-byte binary value of 00010001, which in decimal form is 17. Thus, the IP address for this system would be 192.168.65.17 and its subnet mask would be 255.255.255.240.

The last host on the first subnet would use 1110 as its host identifier, making the value of the fourth byte 00011110 in binary form, or 30 in decimal form, for an IP address of 192.168.65.30. Then, to proceed to the second subnet, you would increment the subnet identifier to 0010 and the host identifier back to 0001, for a binary value of 00100001, or 33 in decimal form. As you can see, the IP addresses you use on a network like this do not increment normally. The numbers 31 and 32 cannot be used because they represent the broadcast address of the first subnet and the network address of the second subnet, respectively. You must compute them carefully to create the correct values.

> **NOTE**   **Exam Objectives**   Objective 2.9 for the Network+ exam states that students should be able to identify the purpose of subnetting and default gateways.

Converting Binaries and Decimals

Part of the difficulty in calculating IP addresses and subnet masks is converting between decimal and binary numbers. The easiest way to do this, of course, is to use a calculator. Most scientific calculators are able to work with binary as well as decimal numbers and can usually convert between the two. However, it is also useful to be able to perform the conversions by hand.

> **TIP**   **IP Subnet Calculators**   A number of software tools are available that can simplify the process of calculating IP addresses and subnet masks for complex subnetted networks. One of these, available as freeware, is Wild Packets' IP Subnet Calculator, available for download at www.wildpackets.com/products/ipsubnetcalculator. However, you should be aware that tools like these are not permitted when you are taking MCP exams, so you must be capable of performing the calculations manually.

To convert a binary number to a decimal, you assign a numerical value to each bit, starting at the right with 1 and proceeding to the left, doubling the value each time. The values for an 8-bit number are therefore as follows:

128   64   32   16   8   4   2   1

You then line up the values of your 8-bit binary number with the eight conversion values as follows:

```
1     1     1     0     0     0     0     0
128   64    32    16    8     4     2     1
```

Finally, you add together the conversion values for the 1 bits only:

```
1     1     1     0     0     0     0     0
128   +64   +32   +0    +0    +0    +0    +0  =224
```

Therefore, the decimal equivalent of the binary value 11100000 is 224.

At times, it might be necessary to convert decimal numbers into binaries. To do this you use the same basic process in reverse, by subtracting the conversion values from the decimal you want to convert, working from left to right. For example, to convert the decimal number 202 into binary form, you subtract the conversion value 128 from 202, leaving a remainder of 74. Because you were able to subtract 128 from 202, you put a value of 1 in the first binary bit as follows:

```
1
128   64    32    16    8     4     2     1
```

You then subtract 64 from the remaining 74, leaving 10, so the second binary bit has a value of 1 also:

```
1     1
128   64    32    16    8     4     2     1
```

You cannot subtract 32 or 16 from the remaining 10, so the third and fourth binary bits are 0:

```
1     1     0     0
128   64    32    16    8     4     2     1
```

You can subtract 8 from 10, leaving 2, so the fifth binary bit is a 1:

```
1     1     0     0     1
128   64    32    16    8     4     2     1
```

You cannot subtract 4 from 2, so the sixth binary bit is a 0, but you can subtract 2 from 2, so the seventh bit is a 1. There is now no remainder left, so the eighth bit is a 0, completing the calculation as follows:

```
1     1     0     0     1     0     1     0
128   64    32    16    8     4     2     1
```

Therefore, the binary value of the decimal number 202 is 11001010.

Calculating IP Addresses Using the Subtraction Method

Manually calculating IP addresses by using binary values can be a slow and tedious task, especially if you are going to have hundreds or thousands of computers on your network. However, when you have the subnet mask for the network and you understand the relationship between subnet and host identifier values, you can calculate IP addresses without having to convert them to binary values.

To calculate the network address of the first subnet, begin by taking the decimal value of the octet in the subnet mask that contains both subnet and host identifier bits and subtracting it from 256. For example, with a Class C network address of 192.168.42.0 and a subnet mask of 255.255.255.224, the result of 256 minus 224 is 32. The network address of the first subnet is therefore 192.168.42.32. To calculate the network addresses of the other subnets, you repeatedly increment the result of your previous subtraction by itself. For example, if the network address of the first subnet is 192.168.42.32, the addresses of the remaining five subnets are as follows:

```
192.168.42.64
192.168.42.96
192.168.42.128
192.168.42.160
192.168.42.192
```

Practice calculating subnet masks by completing Exercise 5-2, "Calculating Subnet Masks," now.

To calculate the IP addresses in each subnet, you repeatedly increment the host identifier by one. The IP addresses in the first subnet are therefore 192.168.42.33 to 192.168.42.62. The 192.168.42.63 address is omitted because this address has a binary host identifier value of 11111, which is a broadcast address. The IP address ranges for the subsequent subnets are as follows:

```
192.168.42.65 to 192.168.42.94
192.168.42.97 to 192.168.42.126
192.168.42.129 to 192.168.42.158
192.168.42.161 to 192.168.42.190
192.168.42.193 to 192.168.42.222
```

Registered and Unregistered Addresses

For a computer to be accessible from the Internet, it must have a public IP address that is registered with the IANA. However, not every computer that can access the Internet has to be accessible from the Internet. For security reasons, networks typically use a firewall of some type to protect their private networks from intrusion by outside computers. These firewalls use various techniques to provide workstations with access to Internet resources without making them accessible to other systems on the Internet.

The computers on a private network typically use unregistered, private IP addresses, which the network administrator can freely assign without obtaining them from an ISP or the IANA. RFC 1918, "Address Allocation for Private Internets," defines a range of network addresses for each class that are intended for use on private networks and are not registered to anyone. When building a private network, you should use these addresses rather than simply choosing an address at random.

The unregistered addresses for each class are as follows:

- **Class A**   10.0.0.0 through 10.255.255.255

- **Class B**   172.16.0.0 through 172.31.255.255

- **Class C**   192.168.0.0 through 192.168.255.255

> **NOTE**   **Exam Objectives**   *Objective 2.10 for the Network+ exam states that students should be able to identify the differences between public versus private networks.*

Obtaining IP Addresses

If you need only a few registered IP addresses for your network, you can usually obtain them individually from your ISP, although you might have to pay an extra monthly fee for them. If the computers requiring the registered address are all on the same LAN and must communicate with each other, be sure that you obtain addresses in the same subnet. If you need a large number of registered IP addresses, you can obtain a network address from the ISP and use it to create as many host addresses as you need.

A network address is the network identifier portion of an IP address. For example, if your ISP assigns you the network address 131.107.118.0, with a subnet mask of 255.255.255.0, you could assign IP addresses ranging from 131.107.118.1 to 131.107.118.254 to your computers. The network address you receive from the ISP depends on the class of the address and on the number of computers you have requiring registered addresses.

IPv6 Addressing

When the IP protocol was originally designed, no one could have predicted the growth that the Internet has experienced in recent years. The 32-bit address space allotted to IP, which once seemed so enormous, is now in danger of being depleted. To address this problem, work is proceeding on an upgraded version of the Internet Protocol (currently at version 4), known as IP version 6, or **IPv6**. In IPv6, the address space is increased from 32 to 128 bits, which is large enough to provide a minimum of 1564 addresses for each square meter of the Earth's surface.

IPv6 addresses are notated as follows:

`XX:XX:XX:XX:XX:XX:XX:XX`

Each X is a hexadecimal representation of a single byte. Some examples of IPv6 are as follows:

`3FFE:2900:D005:3210:FEDC:BA98:7654:3210`

`3FFE:FFFF:0:0:8:800:200C:417A`

Leading zeros can be omitted from individual byte values, and repeated zero-byte values can be replaced with the "::" symbol (but only once in an address). Thus, the second address listed above could also be expressed as follows:

`3FFE:FFFF::8:800:200C:417A`

The IPv6 unicast addresses assigned to registered computers are split into six variable-length sections instead of the two or three sections used in IPv4 addresses. These sections are as follows:

- **Format prefix**   Specifies the type of address, such as provider-based unicast or multicast. (There is also a new type of address called an *anycast* that causes a message to be sent to only one of a specified group of interfaces.)

- **Registry ID**   Identifies the Internet address registry that assigned the Provider ID.

- **Provider ID**   Identifies the ISP that assigned this portion of the address space to a particular subscriber.

- **Subscriber ID**   Identifies a particular subscriber to the service provided by the ISP specified in the Provider ID field.

- **Subnet ID**   Identifies all or part of a specific physical link on the subscriber's network. Subscribers can create as many subnets as needed.

- **Interface ID**   Identifies a particular network interface on the subnet specified in the Subnet ID field.

> **NOTE Exam Objectives**   Objective 2.8 for the Network+ exam states that students should be able to identify IP addresses (IPv4, IPv6) and their default subnet masks.

INTERNETWORK PACKET EXCHANGE (IPX)

When Novell created its NetWare operating system, the company designed its own suite of protocols, which is generally referred to as IPX, or Internetwork Packet Exchange/Sequenced Packet Exchange (IPX/SPX). Internetwork Packet Exchange (IPX) is the name of the suite's network layer protocol, and IPX/SPX refers to the combination of IPX and the suite's connection-oriented transport layer protocol, Sequenced Packet Exchange (SPX). The IPX protocols have never been published as public standards like TCP/IP and Ethernet. These protocols remain the property of Novell, and NetWare's core file and print services used them exclusively until 1998, when Novell incorporated TCP/IP into its native communications architecture.

> **NOTE   NetWare Defaults**   Novell added support for TCP/IP to NetWare many years ago, but the TCP/IP protocols could only be used with applications designed for them. It was not possible to share NetWare files and printers using TCP/IP without using a process called tunneling, in which IPX packets were carried inside IP datagrams. It was only with the release of NetWare version 5 in 1998 that a NetWare network could function without using the IPX protocols at all. TCP/IP is now the default protocol on NetWare servers, although IPX is still included with the operating system.

IPX Functions

IPX is based on a protocol called Internetwork Datagram Packet (IDP), which was designed for an early networking system called Xerox Network System (XNS). IPX is a connectionless protocol that is similar to IP in that it functions at the network layer of the OSI reference model and provides services to a variety of protocols operating at the upper layers of the OSI reference model. The location of IPX in the protocol stack and its relationship with the other IPX protocols is illustrated in Figure 5-8.

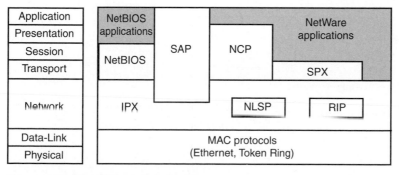

Figure 5-8   The IPX protocol suite

IPX and the other protocols in the IPX suite are designed for use on LANs only, while the TCP/IP protocols were designed for what is now the Internet. Despite this, however, IPX performs many of the same functions as IP, including the following:

- **Data encapsulation**   The packaging of transport layer data into an IPX datagram

- **IPX addressing**   The identification of systems and networks, using unique addresses

- **IPX routing**   The selection of the most efficient path to the destination system through the internetwork

These functions are discussed in the following sections.

IPX Data Encapsulation

Like IP, IPX creates datagrams by adding a header to the data it receives from transport layer protocols. The IPX header is longer than that of IP—30 bytes as opposed to 20. The format of the IPX header is shown in Figure 5-9.

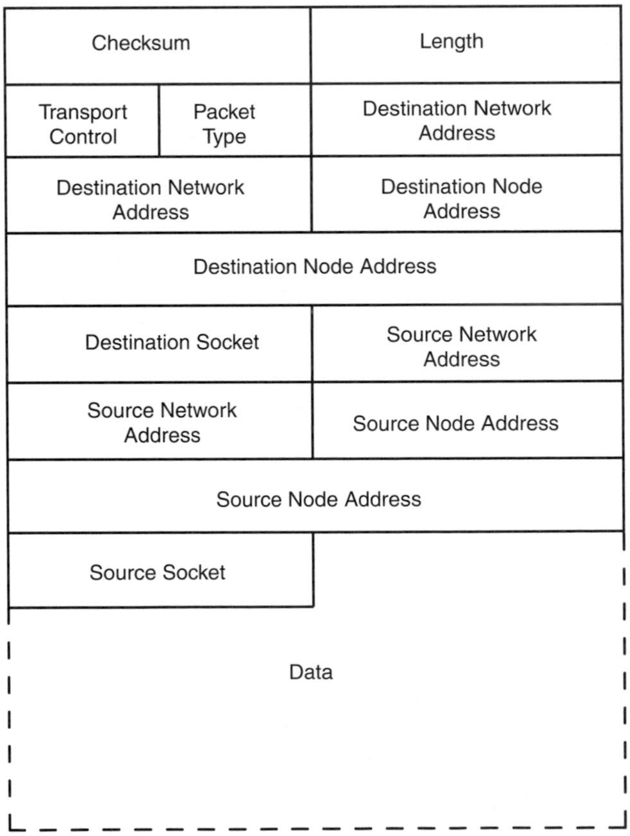

Figure 5-9   The IPX header format

The fields of an IPX datagram perform the following functions:

- **Checksum (2 bytes)**   Originally used by IDP to carry a cyclical redundancy check (CRC) value for error detection purposes, this field was not used in early versions of NetWare and always contained the hexadecimal value *FFFF*. Today, NetWare again uses this field to carry a CRC value.

- **Length (2 bytes)**   Specifies the length (in bytes) of the entire datagram, including all of the header fields and the data.

- **Transport Control (1 byte)**   Specifies the number of routers that the datagram has passed through on the way to its destination.

- **Packet Type (1 byte)**   Specifies the type of service offered or required by the packet, using one of the following hexadecimal values:

    - ❑ 0x00. NetWare Link Services Protocol (NLSP)

    - ❑ 0x01. Routing Information Protocol (RIP)

    - ❑ 0x04. Service Advertising Protocol (SAP)

    - ❑ 0x05. SPX

    - ❑ 0x11. NetWare Core Protocol (NCP)

    - ❑ 0x14. NetBIOS

- **Destination Network Address (4 bytes)**   Identifies the network on which the destination node is located. When set to a value of 0x00000000, the destination node is assumed to be on the same network as the source node.

- **Destination Node Address (6 bytes)**   Specifies the hardware address of the destination system. The value 0xFFFFFFFFFFFF is a broadcast address, used to transmit a packet to all of the nodes on the network.

- **Destination Socket (2 bytes)**   Specifies the process or application on the destination system for which the datagram is intended, using values such as the following:

    - ❑ 0x451. NCP

    - ❑ 0x452. SAP

    - ❑ 0x453. RIP

    - ❑ 0x455. Novell NetBIOS

    - ❑ 0x456. Diagnostics

❑ 0x9001. NLSP

❑ 0x9004. IPXWAN protocol

Test your knowledge of the IPX header format by completing Exercise 5-3, "IPX Properties," now.

■ **Source Network Address (4 bytes)**   Identifies the network on which the node that generated the datagram is located. When set to a value of 0x00000000, the source network is assumed to be unknown.

■ **Source Node Address (6 bytes)**   Specifies the hardware address of the source system.

■ **Source Socket (2 bytes)**   Specifies the process or application on the source system that generated the datagram, using the same values as the Destination Socket field.

■ **Data (variable)**   Contains the information generated by the upper layer protocols.

IPX Addressing

IPX, unlike IP, does not have its own self-contained node addressing system. Instead, IPX uses the same hardware addresses that data-link layer protocols use to identify the computers on the network. This is possible with NetWare because the operating system is intended for use with LAN-based computers, while IP has to accommodate all of the different types of computers found on the Internet. Because the Ethernet and Token Ring network interface adapters used on most of today's LANs have 6-byte hardware addresses, the Destination Node Address and Source Node Address fields are each 6 bytes long. However, IPX can function with LAN technologies that use shorter hardware addresses.

Another important difference between IPX and IP addressing is that a single IP address identifies both a network and a host on that network, while IPX uses hardware addresses to identify nodes only. For a router on a NetWare network to forward packets properly, it must know which network the destination system is on, and this requires some means to identify particular networks.

NetWare uses separate network addresses that an administrator or the operating system setup program assigns to the networks when they install the NetWare servers. Because NetWare is designed for private LANs, there's no reason to register network addresses, as with IP. The network administrator only needs to ensure that every network is assigned a unique address. IPX network addresses are four bytes long, and the IPX header uses them in the Destination Network Address and Source Network Address fields. The combination of the network address and the node (or hardware) address identifies a specific network interface on an internetwork.

IPX Routing

IPX routes traffic between networks in much the same way as IP, except that it uses its own network and node addresses instead of IP addresses. Novell NetWare servers that function as routers maintain routing tables containing information about other networks, and the servers use that information to transmit packets to the appropriate destinations.

The traditional method that IPX routers use to compile their routing tables is to run **Routing Information Protocol (RIP)**, which is an IPX version of the dynamic routing protocol of the same name often used on TCP/IP networks. A RIP router broadcasts the contents of its routing table at regular intervals so that other routers on the network can add the information to their own routing tables. NetWare servers also use Service Advertising Protocol (SAP) along with RIP to enable IPX systems to locate servers providing specific services.

The chief complaint that administrators have regarding RIP and SAP is the large amount of broadcast traffic they generate, which is caused by the servers having to frequently retransmit their information to keep their routing tables current. In response to these complaints, Novell created another dynamic routing protocol, called **NetWare Link Services Protocol (NLSP)**. Based on the Intermediate-System-to-Intermediate-System (IS-IS) routing protocol developed by the International Organization for Standardization (ISO), NLSP enables NetWare servers to exchange routing and service information without the high broadcast overhead generated by RIP and SAP. Instead of periodically retransmitting its information every few minutes like RIP and SAP, NLSP only transmits every two hours, or when there is a change in a route or service, making it much more suitable for use over a WAN.

The Transport Control field in the IPX header is similar to the Time To Live field in the IP header, except that the Transport Control field starts at a value of 0 and is incremented by each router that forwards the datagram. If the value of the field reaches 16, the packet is discarded, except when the NetWare servers are using NLSP for dynamic routing, in which case the servers can be configured to use up to 127 hops. The IP TTL field, by contrast, starts at a value specified by the system generating the datagram and is decremented by each router. The difference in the functionality of these two fields is indicative of the differences between IPX and IP, as they were originally conceived. IP has almost unlimited scalability, as demonstrated by the fact that a system can be configured with a relatively large TTL value. Windows-based systems, for example, use a default value of 128 for this field. IPX, which is designed for use on private networks, was originally limited to 16 hops, more than enough for most corporate networks but not sufficient for Internet communications.

NETBIOS EXTENDED USER INTERFACE (NETBEUI)

The default protocol for Windows operating systems today is TCP/IP, but the early versions of Microsoft Windows NT and Microsoft Windows for Workgroups relied on another protocol called NetBIOS Extended User Interface (NetBEUI). All of the Windows operating systems can still use NetBEUI (although Microsoft Windows Server 2003 does not include the files needed to install NetBEUI with the product), and some of its elements are an integral part of Windows networking, whether you use the NetBEUI protocol or not.

Network Basic Input/Output System (NetBIOS) is a programming interface that applications use to communicate with the networking hardware in the computer and, through that hardware, with the network. NetBEUI was designed in the mid-1980s to transport NetBIOS information across a network. Microsoft adopted NetBEUI for use with Windows at a time when the company was first adding networking capabilities to its operating systems. As with NetWare, the initial networking market was for small workgroup LANs, and it is in this environment that NetBEUI excels. However, no other commercial operating systems besides Windows ever implemented the protocol.

For a small stand-alone network, NetBEUI provides excellent performance, requires no configuration, and is self-adjusting. There's no need to supply a NetBEUI client with an address or other configuration parameters, as with TCP/IP. NetBEUI, however, does not support Internet communications; this requires TCP/IP. If the computers on a NetBEUI network are to access the Internet, they must run TCP/IP as well (or instead). The need for Internet access is the primary reason why few networks use NetBEUI today.

> **NOTE   Transporting NetBIOS Information**   NetBEUI is not the only means of transporting NetBIOS information across a network. Both the TCP/IP and IPX protocols can transport NetBIOS information as well. As a matter of fact, the Windows operating systems continued to rely on NetBIOS for some of their vital communications functions long after NetBEUI was dropped as the default protocol for Windows in favor of TCP/IP.

NetBEUI differs substantially from IP and IPX in several important ways. The primary differences are that NetBEUI uses names, rather than addresses, to identify computers, and that the protocol has no network identifiers, so it is not routable. Therefore, NetBEUI is not suitable for use on large internetworks.

> **NOTE**   **Troubleshooting with NetBEUI**   If you have problems getting a
> Windows-based system to communicate with the other systems on a
> TCP/IP network, installing NetBEUI on the systems involved is a good way
> of isolating the problem. If the systems can communicate using NetBEUI,
> you know that the networking hardware and the network interface
> adapter drivers are all functioning properly and the problem most likely
> lies with the TCP/IP configuration on one or both systems.

NetBEUI Standards

Unlike TCP/IP and IPX, there are no official standards, public or private, that
define the nature of a NetBEUI implementation. NetBIOS was originally designed
for IBM PC networks, and the closest thing there is to a standard is IBM
document number SC30-3587-01, published in 1996, called "LAN Technical
Reference: IEEE 802.2 and NetBIOS [Application Programming Interfaces] APIs,"
available at *http://publibz.boulder.ibm.com/cgi-bin/bookmgr_OS390/Shelves/
BK80BK03?filter=netbios&SUBMIT=Find.* This document accurately describes
how NetBEUI traffic is encapsulated for transmission over IEEE 802–based
LANs, but it provides little insight into the internal structure of NetBEUI
messages as they are implemented on Windows networks.

NetBIOS Naming

One of the primary attributes of NetBIOS is that it includes its own namespace,
which NetBEUI uses to identify computers on the network, just as IP uses its own
IP addresses and IPX uses hardware addresses. In versions of Windows prior to
Microsoft Windows 2000, the computer name that you specify during the
operating system installation is, in reality, a NetBIOS name, which must be unique
on the network. Today, Windows relies primarily on the Domain Name System
(DNS) for its computer names, but Windows 2000 and later versions still contain
NetBIOS equivalents for their DNS names, for backward compatibility reasons.

A NetBIOS name is 16 characters long. Windows reserves the last character for
a code that identifies the type of resource using the name, leaving 15 assignable
alphanumeric characters. Different codes can identify NetBIOS names as
representing computers, domain controllers, users, groups, and other resources.
If you assign a name of fewer than 15 characters to a computer, the system pads
it out to 15 so that the identification code always falls on the sixteenth character.

NetBIOS names perform the same function as host identifiers in IP and node
addresses in IPX; they uniquely identify a specific resource on the network. All of
the NetBIOS names on a network must be unique. Because NetBEUI is intended
for use only on small LANs, there is no central name registration authority. It is

up to the network administrator to see to it that the network does not have computers with duplicate names.

NetBIOS names are stored in a flat-file database; there is no hierarchy among the names. IP and IPX both use a hierarchical system of addressing in which one value identifies the network interface and another value identifies the network on which the interface is located. NetBIOS names are associated with computers, not interfaces, and they have no network identifiers. This is why NetBEUI is not routable; it has no means of addressing packets to specific networks or maintaining routing tables containing information about networks. NetBEUI deals solely with computer identifiers, which means that all of the computers must be accessible from the one network.

The NetBEUI Frame

The NetBEUI Frame (NBF) protocol is a multipurpose protocol that Windows-based computers use for a variety of purposes, including registration and resolution of NetBIOS names, establishment of sessions between computers on the network, and transport of file and print data using the Windows Server Message Block (SMB) protocol. All of these functions use a single frame format, as diagrammed in Figure 5-10.

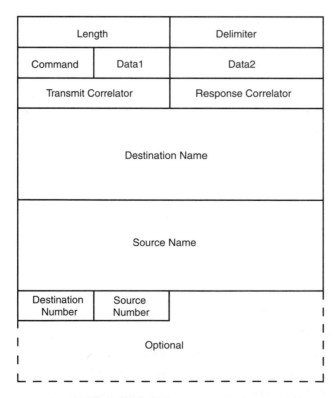

Figure 5-10   The NBF format

The functions of the NBF fields are as follows:

- **Length (2 bytes)** Specifies the length of the NBF header (in bytes)

- **Delimiter (2 bytes)** Signals the receiving system that the message should be delivered to the NetBIOS interface

- **Command (1 byte)** Identifies the function of the NBF message, using one of the following values:

    - 00. Add Group Name Query

    - 01. Add Name Query

    - 02. Name In Conflict

    - 03. Status Query

    - 07. Terminate Trace (remote)

    - 08. Datagram

    - 09. Datagram Broadcast

    - 0A. Name Query

    - 0D. Add Name Response

    - 0E. Name Recognized

    - 0F. Status Response

    - 13. Terminate Trace (local and remote)

    - 14. Data Ack

    - 15. Data First Middle

    - 16. Data Only Last

    - 17. Session Confirm

    - 18. Session End

    - 19. Session Initialize

    - 1A. No Receive

    - 1B. Receive Outstanding

    - 1C. Receive Continue

    - 1F. Session Alive

- **Data1 (1 byte)**   Contains optional data specific to the message type specified by the Command field

- **Data2 (2 bytes)**   Contains optional data specific to the message type specified by the Command field

- **Transmit Correlator (2 bytes)**   Contains a value that the receiving system will duplicate in the same field of its reply messages, enabling the sending system to associate the requests and replies

- **Response Correlator (2 bytes)**   Contains the value that the sending system expects to receive in the Transmit Correlator field of the reply to this message

- **Destination Name (16 bytes)**   Contains the NetBIOS name of the system that will receive the packet

- **Source Name (16 bytes)**   Contains the NetBIOS name of the system sending the packet

- **Destination Number (1 byte)**   Contains the number assigned to the session by the destination system

- **Source Number (1 byte)**   Contains the number assigned to the session by the source system

- **Optional (variable)**   Contains the actual data payload of the packet

Four separate protocols use the NetBEUI Frame, as follows:

- Name Management Protocol (NMP)

- Session Management Protocol (SMP)

- User Datagram Protocol (UDP)

- Diagnostic and Monitoring Protocol (DMP)

These protocols are discussed in the following sections.

Name Management Protocol (NMP)

Computers running Windows use NMP to register and resolve NetBIOS names on the network. When a system first starts up, it generates an Add Name Query message containing its NetBIOS name and transmits it to the other NetBIOS systems on the network. The function of this message is to ensure that no other system is using that same name. If there is a duplication, the computer already using the name must reply with an Add Name Response message, and the querying system displays an error message. If the system receives no response, the name is registered to that system.

Name resolution is the process of converting a NetBIOS name into the hardware address needed for a system to transmit data-link layer frames to it. When a NetBEUI system has data to transmit to a particular system or wants to establish a session with another system, it begins by generating a Name Query message containing the name of the target system in the Destination Name field and sending it to all of the NetBIOS systems on the network. All of the systems on the network with registered NetBIOS names are required to respond to Name Query messages containing their name. The system with the requested name responds by transmitting a Name Recognized message back to the sender as a unicast message. The sender, on receiving this message, extracts the hardware address of the system holding the requested name and can then transmit subsequent packets to it as unicasts.

One of the drawbacks of NetBEUI, and one of the reasons it is only suitable for relatively small networks, is the large number of broadcast packets it generates. These Name Query requests are actually transmitted to a special NetBIOS address, but on a Windows-based network, this is the functional equivalent of a broadcast. On a large network or a network with high traffic levels, systems must process a large number of these name resolution broadcasts for no reason, because they are intended for other systems.

Session Management Protocol (SMP)

The NBF messages used by NMP use NetBEUI's connectionless service. These messages are part of brief request and response transactions that don't require additional services such as packet acknowledgment. For more extensive data transfers, however, a connection-oriented, reliable service is required, and to do this, the two communicating systems must first create a session between them. The systems use the NBF SMP messages to establish a session, transmit data, and then break down the session afterward.

The session establishment begins with a standard name resolution exchange, followed by the establishment of a session at the Logical Link Control (LLC) layer. Then the client system initiating the session transmits a Session Initialize message to the server system, which responds with a Session Confirm message. At this point, the session is established, and the systems can begin to transmit application data using Data First Middle and Data Only Last messages, which contain data generated by other protocols such as SMB. The system receiving the data replies with Receive Continue or Data Ack messages that serve as acknowledgments of successful transmissions.

During the session, when no activity is taking place, the systems transmit periodic Session Alive messages, which prevent the session from timing out. When the exchange of data packets is completed, the client generates a Session End message, which terminates the session.

User Datagram Protocol (UDP)

To exchange small amounts of data, systems can also use the same connectionless service as NMP. This is sometimes referred to as UDP, but it is important not to confuse this protocol with the TCP/IP transport layer protocol of the same name. UDP is the simplest of the NBF protocols, consisting of only two message types: the Datagram message and the Datagram Broadcast message. Systems can transmit various kinds of information using these messages, including SMB data.

Diagnostic and Monitoring Protocol (DMP)

NetBEUI systems use DMP to gather status information about systems on the network. A NetBEUI system generates a Status Query message and transmits it to all of the NetBIOS systems on the network. The systems reply with Status Response messages containing the requested information.

Test your knowledge of the functions performed by the NetBEUI Frame protocols by completing Exercise 5-4, "NBF Protocols," now.

APPLETALK

Like NetBEUI, **AppleTalk** is a protocol stack that was designed to provide small groups of computers with basic networking capabilities. Apple Macintosh systems have had integrated networking hardware and software almost since their introduction and, although AppleTalk does not have the flexibility of TCP/IP, it is simple to set up and use and provides adequate performance for standard networking tasks, such as file and printer sharing. AppleTalk does not support Internet communications, however, which is the main reason why it has been largely replaced by TCP/IP.

AppleTalk originally used its own data-link layer protocol, called Apple LocalTalk, and the adapter for LocalTalk was built into the Macintosh computer. LocalTalk ran at only 230 Kbps, however, and it was replaced by Apple EtherTalk at 10 Mbps (or Fast EtherTalk at 100 Mbps) and, to a lesser extent, by TokenTalk at 4 or 16 Mbps and FDDITalk at 100 Mbps. The latter three protocols are adaptations of the Ethernet, Token Ring, and Fiber Distributed Data Interface (FDDI) protocols, respectively.

Like IP and IPX, AppleTalk uses a hierarchical addressing system to identify the computers on a network. Every AppleTalk computer has a unique 8-bit node ID that it randomly selects and assigns to itself as it connects to the network. After transmitting a broadcast message to make sure that no other computer is using the same ID, the system stores the address for future use each time it reconnects. Because the number is only 8 bits long, a single AppleTalk network can have no more than 254 nodes (28 − 2, because 0 and 255 are not used for node IDs). AppleTalk also uses 16-bit network numbers to identify the LANs in an internetwork for routing purposes. A computer connecting to the network uses the Zone Information Protocol (ZIP) to obtain the network number value for the LAN. As with IP and IPX, AppleTalk networks can be connected together with routers that read the destination network numbers and node IDs in each packet and forward them to the appropriate LAN.

To identify specific processes running on a computer, AppleTalk uses an 8-bit socket number, which performs the same function as the Protocol field in the IP header. The combination of network number, node ID, and socket is expressed as three decimal numbers separated by periods, as in 2.12.50, meaning network 2, node 12, and socket 50. AppleTalk reconciles the data-link hardware addresses coded into network interface adapters with the node IDs and network numbers by using the AppleTalk Address Resolution Protocol (AARP), which functions remarkably like the ARP in the TCP/IP suite.

In addition to the node IDs and network numbers, AppleTalk computers have friendly names that make it easier to locate specific resources on the network. Computers have their own names, and groups of computers are gathered into units called *zones*. A zone is a logical grouping that makes it easier to locate specific resources on the network.

At the network layer, AppleTalk uses DDP. Like IP and IPX, DDP is a connectionless protocol that encapsulates data generated by an upper layer protocol. DDP provides many of the same services as IP and IPX, including packet addressing, routing, and protocol identification. A simple AppleTalk network that consists of only one network number and one zone is called a *nonextended network*. A network that consists of multiple network numbers and zones is called an *extended network*. The extended network uses the long-format DDP header shown in Figure 5-11.

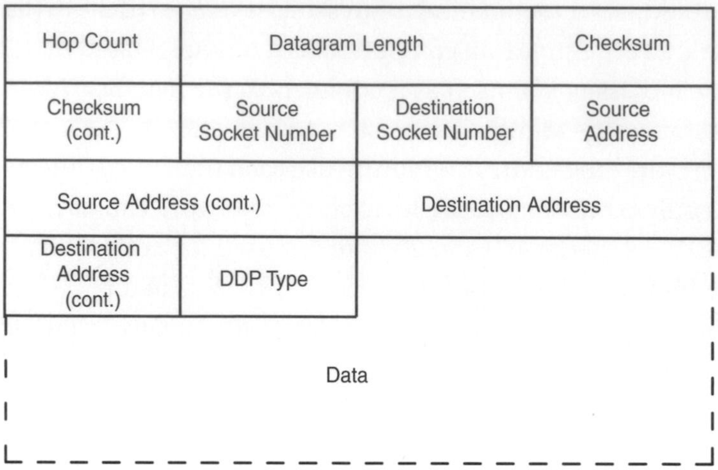

Figure 5-11   The DDP long-format header

The functions of the DDP header fields are as follows:

- **Hop Count (1 byte)**   Specifies the number of routers that have processed the packet on the way to its destination

- **Datagram Length (2 bytes)**   Specifies the length of the DDP datagram; used for basic error detection

- **Checksum (2 bytes)**   Optional field containing a checksum computed on the entire datagram; used for more extensive error detection

- **Source Socket Number (1 byte)**   Specifies the socket number of the application or process that generated the information in the data field

- **Destination Socket Number (1 byte)**   Specifies the socket number of the application or process to which the information in the data field is to be delivered

- **Source Address (3 bytes)**   Specifies the network number and node ID of the computer generating the packet

- **Destination Address (3 bytes)**   Specifies the network number and node ID of the computer that is to receive the packet

- **DDP Type (1 byte)**   Identifies the upper layer protocol that generated the information carried in the data field

- **Data (variable, up to 586 bytes)**   Contains information generated by an upper layer protocol

On a nonextended network, DDP uses the short-format header, which includes only the four source and destination fields, plus the Datagram Length and DDP Type fields.

> **NOTE   Exam Objectives**   Objective 2.3 for the Network+ exam states that students should be able to differentiate between the following network protocols in terms of routing, addressing schemes, interoperability, and naming conventions: TCP/IP, IPX/SPX, NetBEUI, and AppleTalk.

SUMMARY

- Internet Protocol (IP) is a connectionless protocol in the Transmission Control Protocol/Internet Protocol (TCP/IP) suite that is used to carry information generated by several other protocols in units called datagrams.

  - The primary functions of IP are data encapsulation, IP addressing, IP routing, fragmentation, and protocol identification.

  - IP has its own addressing system that it uses to identify networks and the hosts on those networks.

  - IP routes packets by repackaging them to use different data-link layer frames.

  - When data-link layer protocols have different maximum transfer units (MTUs), IP can split datagrams into smaller fragments to facilitate transmission.

  - IP addresses are 32 bits long and are expressed as four decimal numbers separated by periods. They consist of a network identifier and a host identifier. Every network interface adapter on a TCP/IP network must have its own unique IP address.

  - The Internet Assigned Numbers Authority (IANA) assigns IP network addresses in three classes, and network administrators assign the host addresses to each individual system.

  - The subnet mask specifies which bits of an IP address identify the network and which bits identify the host. Modifying the subnet mask for an address in a particular class enables you to create subnets by "borrowing" some of the host bits to create a subnet identifier.

- Internetwork Packet Exchange (IPX) is the NetWare equivalent of IP.

  - To identify systems, IPX uses the hardware addresses coded into network interface adapters.

  - To identify networks, IPX uses network addresses assigned during the NetWare installation.

  - IPX uses socket numbers to identify the processes that generate datagrams.

- NetBIOS Extended User Interface (NetBEUI) is a network layer protocol used by small Windows networks for local area network (LAN) networking services.

  - NetBEUI differs from IP and IPX primarily in that it has no network identifiers and is therefore not routable.

  - The NetBEUI Frame provides transport services for four protocols: the Name Management Protocol (NMP), the Session Management Protocol (SMP), the User Datagram Protocol (UDP), and the Diagnostic and Monitoring Protocol (DMP).

- AppleTalk networks can use any one of several protocols at the data-link layer, including LocalTalk, EtherTalk, TokenTalk, and FDDITalk.

  - Computers on an AppleTalk network have 8-bit node IDs that they assign to themselves, and the networks have 16-bit network numbers.

  - Processes on AppleTalk computers are identified by 8-bit socket numbers.

EXERCISES

Exercise 5-1: Understanding IP Functions

Match the IP functions in the left column with the descriptions in the right column.

1. Fragmentation
2. Encapsulation
3. Routing
4. Protocol identification
5. Addressing

a. Uses assigned numbers
b. The primary function of intermediate systems
c. Generates datagrams
d. Uses 32-bit values
e. Used when transmitting over a network with a smaller MTU

Exercise 5-2: Calculating Subnet Masks

Specify the subnet mask value you would use for each of the following network configurations:

1. A Class C network address with a 2-bit subnet identifier

2. A Class A network address with a 16-bit host identifier

3. A Class B network address with a 6-bit subnet identifier

4. A Class A network address with a 21-bit host identifier

5. A Class B network with a 9-bit host identifier

Exercise 5-3: Understanding IPX Properties

Match the IPX header fields in the left column with the appropriate functions in the right column.

1. Transport Control

2. Source Socket

3. Destination Network Address

4. Checksum

5. Source Hardware Address

a. Contains a value assigned by the network administrator or the NetWare installation program

b. Always contains the value FFFF in older NetWare versions

c. Has a maximum value of 16

d. Contains a 6-byte value

e. Identifies the application that generated the packet

Exercise 5-4: NBF Protocols

For each of the NBF message types listed, specify which of the four NBF protocols—NMP, SMP, UDP, or DMP—is primarily associated with it.

1. Datagram Broadcast

2. Data First Middle

3. Name Query

4. Status Response

5. Add Name Response

REVIEW QUESTIONS

1. What does the Protocol field in the IP header identify?

    a. The physical layer specification of the network that will carry the datagram

    b. The data-link layer protocol that will carry the datagram

    c. The transport layer protocol that generated the information in the Data field

    d. The application that generated the message carried in the datagram

2. Which of the following IP header elements is never modified during the IP fragmentation process?

    a. The Identification field

    b. The More Fragments bit

    c. The Fragment Offset field

    d. The Time To Live field

3. What does an IP address identify?

    a. A network

    b. A computer

    c. A network interface

    d. A network and a network interface

4. Which IP header field makes the Traceroute utility possible?

    a. Version

    b. Type Of Service

    c. Identification

    d. Time To Live

5. Which two protocols carried within IP datagrams operate at the transport layer of the OSI model?

    a. IMCP

    b. TCP

    c. UDP

    d. IGMP

6. Which IP address class provides for the largest number of hosts?

   a. Class A

   b. Class B

   c. Class C

   d. All three classes provide the same number of hosts.

7. What kind of IP address must a system have to be visible from the Internet?

   a. Subnetted

   b. Registered

   c. Class A

   d. Binary

8. Which of the following statements about subnet masks is not true?

   a. Subnet masks can have the same range of values as IP addresses.

   b. The subnet mask specifies which bits of an IP address are the network identifier and which bits are the host identifier.

   c. The dividing line between network bits and host bits can fall anywhere in a subnet mask.

   d. Subnet masks are assigned by the IANA, but they can be modified by network administrators.

9. What IPX header field performs the same function as the Time To Live field in the IP header?

   a. Packet Type

   b. Transport Control

   c. Checksum

   d. Source Socket

10. Which of the following statements about IPX is not true?

   a. IPX routes datagrams between different types of networks.

   b. IPX has its own network addressing system.

   c. IPX uses a checksum to verify the proper transmission of data.

   d. The IPX header is smaller than the IP header.

11. How many bytes long is the information that IPX uses to identify the datagram's destination computer on a particular network?

    a. 2

    b. 4

    c. 6

    d. 10

12. What is the maximum number of RIP routers that an IPX datagram can pass through on the way to its destination?

    a. 0

    b. 15

    c. 127

    d. 255

13. How does a NetBEUI network prevent two systems from using the same NetBIOS name?

14. Give two reasons why NetBEUI is not suitable for use on a large internetwork.

15. Place the following phases of an NBF session in the proper order:

    a. Session Alive

    b. Session Initialize

    c. LLC session establishment

    d. Name resolution

    e. Session End

    f. Session Confirm

16. Which of the following protocols can provide connection-oriented service?

    a. IP

    b. IPX

    c. NetBEUI

    d. None of the above

17. Which of the following network layer protocols is not routable?

    a. IP

    b. IPX

    c. NetBEUI

    d. DDP

18. Which of the following DDP fields identifies the upper layer protocol that generated the information in the data field?

    a. Source Socket Number

    b. Checksum

    c. Source Address

    d. DDP Type

19. At what speed does a LocalTalk network transmit data?

    a. 56 Kbps

    b. 230 Kbps

    c. 10 Mbps

    d. 16 Mbps

CASE SCENARIOS

Case Scenario 5-1: Choosing a Network Layer Protocol

The Lee family is building a new home, and they want it wired with Category 5 (CAT5) unshielded twisted pair (UTP) cable for a Fast Ethernet computer network. Mr. Lee travels frequently for his business, and he has a laptop running Microsoft Windows XP with him at all times. Mrs. Lee runs an interior design business out of her home office and uses a desktop computer running Microsoft Windows 2000 Professional. The kids share a Macintosh computer in the family room. Which of the following network layer protocols should the Lees use on their three computers to enable them all to communicate with each other without having to purchase additional software?

    a. IP

    b. IPX

    c. NetBEUI

    d. AppleTalk

Case Scenario 5-2: Subnetting a Class C Address

A company consists of 30 small offices scattered around the country, each with no more than 5 computers. As the network consultant for the company, you have obtained a Class C network address for them, which you want to use to connect all of the offices to the Internet. To create a separate subnet for each of the offices, what is the minimum number of bits you would have to allocate from the Class C address for a subnet identifier?

1. 3
2. 4
3. 5
4. 6

Case Scenario 5-3: Calculating a Subnet Mask

You work for a large corporation that has a Class A network address, which has been subnetted by allocating 6 bits to the subnet address. This allows the corporation to use a different subnet for each of its 50 offices around the world. Which subnet mask would you use when configuring a computer on one of these subnets?

1. 255.255.255.252
2. 255.255.252.0
3. 255.252.0.0
4. 252.0.0.0

CHAPTER 6
TRANSPORT LAYER PROTOCOLS

■ Describe the services provided by Transmission Control Protocol (TCP) and the User Datagram Protocol (UDP) and understand the functions of the various TCP and UDP header fields.

■ Describe the services provided by the Sequenced Packet Exchange (SPX) and NetWare Core Protocol (NCP) protocols and identify the functions of the SPX and NCP header fields.

The protocols that operate at the transport layer of the Open Systems Interconnection (OSI) reference model work with the network layer protocols to provide a unified quality of service for the applications using them. Both the Transmission Control Protocol/Internet Protocol (TCP/IP) and the Internetwork Packet Exchange (IPX) suites have multiple protocols at the transport layer that provide various levels of service. This chapter examines the options available to applications at this layer and describes the mechanisms that the protocols use to provide the services they supply.

TCP/IP AND THE TRANSPORT LAYER

In Chapter 1, "Networking Basics," you learned how the OSI reference model calls for the network and transport layers to provide a flexible quality of service by supporting both connection-oriented and connectionless protocols. In practice, however, the protocol suites actually in use on networks all use a connectionless protocol at the network layer, such as Internet Protocol (IP) or IPX, and provide both connection-oriented and connectionless service only at the transport layer.

The TCP/IP suite uses two protocols at the transport layer to provide different levels of service for applications: the **Transmission Control Protocol (TCP)** and User Datagram Protocol (UDP). Both TCP and UDP generate protocol data units (PDUs) that are carried inside IP datagrams. TCP is a connection-oriented protocol that provides reliable service with guaranteed delivery, packet acknowledgment, flow control, and error correction and detection. TCP is designed for transmitting data that requires perfect bit accuracy, such as program and data files. UDP is a connectionless protocol that provides unreliable service. UDP is used for short transactions that consist of a single request and reply; it is also used for data transmissions that can survive the loss of a few bits, such as audio and video streams. Not surprisingly, TCP generates much more control traffic than UDP does as it provides all of these services, while the UDP overhead is quite low.

> **NOTE   Reliable and Unreliable Protocols**   The term *reliable*, in the context of a protocol's service, refers to its ability to deliver data with acknowledgment from the recipient. It is not a reflection of the protocol's relative value. In fact, *unreliable* protocols, though they do not allow for guaranteed delivery, usually deliver their messages to the destination without error. One of the most common analogies used to describe reliable and unreliable protocols is that of a certified letter to a postcard.

Transmission Control Protocol (TCP)

TCP/IP gets its name from the combination of the TCP and IP protocols, which together provide the service that accounts for the majority of traffic on a TCP/IP network. Internet applications such as Web browsers and e-mail clients depend on the TCP protocol to retrieve large amounts of data from servers, without error. TCP is defined in Request for Comments (RFC) 793, "Transmission Control Protocol: DARPA Internet Program Protocol Specification," published in 1981 by the Internet Engineering Task Force (IETF) and ratified as Internet Standard 7.

The TCP Header

Transport layer protocols encapsulate data that they receive from the application layer protocols operating above them by applying a header, just as the protocols at the lower layers do. In many cases, the application layer protocol passes more data to TCP than can fit into a single packet, so TCP splits the data into smaller pieces. Each piece is called a *segment*, and the segments that comprise a single transaction are known collectively as a *sequence*. Each segment receives its own TCP header, as illustrated in Figure 6-1, and is passed down to the network layer for transmission in a separate datagram. When all of the segments arrive at the destination, the receiving computer reassembles them into the original order, using the Sequence Number field as a guide.

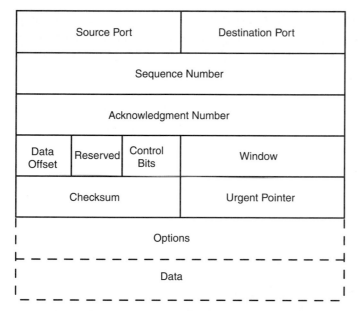

Figure 6-1   The TCP message format

The functions of the TCP message fields are as follows:

- **Source Port (2 bytes)**   Identifies the process or application on the transmitting system that generated the information carried in the Data field

- **Destination Port (2 bytes)**   Identifies the process on the receiving system for which the information in the Data field is intended

- **Sequence Number (4 bytes)**   Identifies the location of the data in this segment in relation to the entire sequence

- **Acknowledgment Number (4 bytes)**   In acknowledgment (ACK) messages, specifies the sequence number of the next segment expected by the receiving system

■ **Data Offset (4 bits)**   Specifies the number of 4-byte words in the TCP header

■ **Reserved (6 bits)**   Unused

■ **Control Bits (6 bits)**   Contains six flag bits that identify the functions of the message, as follows:

  ❑ URG.   Indicates that the segment contains urgent data. When this flag is present, the receiving system reads the contents of the Urgent Pointer field to determine which part of the Data field contains the urgent information.

  ❑ ACK.   Indicates that the message is an acknowledgment of a previously transmitted segment. When this flag is present, the system receiving the message reads the contents of the Acknowledgment Number field to determine what part of the sequence it should transmit next.

  ❑ PSH.   Indicates that the receiving system should forward the data it has received in the current sequence to the process identified in the Destination Port field immediately, rather than waiting for the rest of the sequence to arrive.

  ❑ RST.   Causes the receiving system to reset the TCP connection and discard all of the segments of the sequence it has received thus far.

  ❑ SYN.   Synchronizes the systems' respective Sequence Number values during the establishment of a TCP connection.

  ❑ FIN.   Terminates a TCP connection.

■ **Window (2 bytes)**   Specifies how many bytes the computer can accept from the connected system.

■ **Checksum (2 bytes)**   Contains the results of a cyclical redundancy check (CRC) performed by the transmitting system. These results are used by the receiving system to detect errors in the TCP header, data, and parts of the IP header.

■ **Urgent Pointer (2 bytes)**   When the urgent (URG) control bit is present, indicates which part of the data in the segment the receiver should treat as urgent.

■ **Options (variable)**   Contains information related to optional TCP connection configuration features.

Test your understanding of the functions of the TCP header fields by completing Exercise 6-1, "TCP Header Fields," now.

■ **Data (variable)**   Contains one segment of an information sequence generated by an application layer protocol.

> **MORE INFO   Port Number Values**   For more information on the values used for the Source Port and Destination Port fields, see "Ports and Sockets," later in this chapter.

TCP Options

TCP has an Options field that can carry various types of data. The Options field consists of a subheader, shown in Figure 6-2.

Figure 6-2   The TCP Options subheader

The Options subheader consists of the following three fields:

■ **Option Kind (1 byte)**   Specifies the function of the option

■ **Option Length (1 byte)**   Specifies the length of the Options field, including all three subfields

■ **Option Data (variable)**   Contains information specific to the option's function

> **MORE INFO   TCP Options List**   The current list of TCP options is available at www.iana.org/assignments/tcp-parameters.

Some of the most commonly used TCP options are listed in Table 6-1, along with their Option Kind and Option Length values.

Table 6-1   **Commonly Used TCP Options**

Option Kind	Option Length	Option Name
0	Not applicable	End Of Options List
1	Not applicable	No Operation
2	4	Maximum Segment Size
3	3	WSOPT – Window Scale
4	2	SACK Permitted
5	Variable	SACK
8	10	TSOPT – Timestamp

The functions of these options are listed below.

- **End Of Options List**   Indicates the end of the Options field in a datagram. When a datagram includes multiple options, there is only one End Of Options List option included, not one for each option. This is one of two options that consists only of an Option Kind field. There is no Option Length or Option Data field in this option.

- **No Operation**   Functions as a padding byte between options to align the beginning of the subsequent option on the boundary of a 32-bit word. As with the End Of Options List option, this option consists only of an Option Type field.

- **Maximum Segment Size**   In segments containing the SYN control bit, specifies the size of the largest segment the system can receive.

- **WSOPT – Window Scale**   Enables the systems involved in a TCP connection to expand the functionality of the Windows field from 16 to 32 bits. In segments containing the SYN control bit, this option informs the other system that the sender supports the window scale extension. This option is defined in RFC 1323, "TCP Extensions for High Performance."

- **Selective Acknowledgment (SACK Permitted/SACK)**   Enables a TCP system receiving data to acknowledge individual segments that have arrived successfully so that specific segments that have been dropped can be retransmitted individually. The SACK Permitted option is included in segments containing the SYN control bit and informs the other system that the sender supports selective acknowledgment. The SACK option contains a list of the segments that have been received successfully. These options are defined in RFC 2018, "TCP Selective Acknowledgment Options."

- **TSOPT – Timestamp**   Enables systems receiving TCP data packets to include timestamps in their acknowledgments, which allows the sender of the data to measure the round trip time for the two systems. This option is defined in RFC 1323, "TCP Extensions for High Performance."

TCP Communications

TCP is a connection-oriented protocol, which means that before two systems can exchange application layer data, they must first establish a connection. This connection ensures that both computers are present, operating properly, and ready to receive data. The systems also exchange information about their capabilities, which determines how subsequent communications will proceed. The TCP connection remains active during the entire exchange of data, after which the systems close it in an orderly manner.

In most cases, a TCP connection exists for the duration of a single file transmission. For example, when a Web browser connects to a server on the Internet, it first establishes a connection with the server, then it transmits a Hypertext Transfer Protocol (HTTP) request message specifying the file it wants to download, and finally it receives the file from the server. After the file is transferred, the systems terminate the connection. As the browser processes the downloaded file, it might detect links to graphic images, audio clips, or other files needed to display the Web page. The browser then establishes a separate connection to the server for each of the linked files, retrieves them, and displays them as part of the downloaded page. Thus, downloading a single Web page might require the browser to create many separate TCP connections to the server to download the individual files.

Establishing a Connection

The process that TCP uses to establish a connection is known as a *three-way handshake*. This process consists of an exchange of three messages (as shown in Figure 6-3), none of which contain any application layer data. The purpose of these messages, apart from determining that the other computer actually exists and is ready to receive data, is to exchange the sequence numbers that the computers will use to number the messages they transmit. At the start of the handshake, each computer selects an *initial sequence number (ISN)* for the first TCP message it transmits. The computers then increment the sequence numbers for each subsequent message. The computers select an ISN using an incrementing algorithm that makes it highly unlikely for connections between the same two computers to use identical sequence numbers at the same time. Each computer maintains its own sequence numbers, and, during the handshake, each informs the other of the numbers it will use.

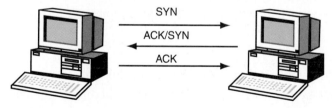

Figure 6-3   TCP uses a three-way handshake to establish a connection between two systems.

> **NOTE TCP Connectivity**   The connection established by two TCP systems is only a logical connection, not a permanent channel between the two as is the case on a circuit-switching network. The individual TCP messages are still carried within IP datagrams, using IP's connectionless service. The messages might take different routes to the destination and

might even arrive in a different order from that in which they were transmitted. TCP accounts for all of these possibilities. The sequence numbers in each segment enable the receiving system to rearrange the data segments into the proper order.

The messages that contain the ISN for each computer have the SYN flag set in the Control Bits field. In a typical TCP transaction, a client computer transmits a SYN message, with its ISN in the Sequence Number field. The client then enters the SYN-SENT state, indicating that it is waiting to receive an acknowledgment from the server. The server is initially in the LISTEN state as it waits for a connection from a client. When the server receives the client's SYN message, it generates a response that performs two functions. First, the ACK flag is set so that the message functions as an acknowledgment of the client's SYN message. Second, when the client receives the acknowledgment from the server, the client enters the ESTABLISHED state because the client-to-server connection is now active.

In addition to the ACK control bit, the server's response message also has the SYN flag set and includes its own ISN in the Sequence Number field. After transmitting this message, the server enters the SYN-RECEIVED state. When the client computer receives the server's ACK/SYN message, it generates a response of its own, which contains the ACK flag in response to the server's SYN. Once the server receives the client's acknowledgment, the server enters the ESTABLISHED state because the server-to-client connection is active. Both systems are now ready to exchange messages containing application data. Thus, a TCP connection is actually two separate connections running in opposite directions. TCP is therefore known as a *full-duplex protocol* because the systems establish each connection separately and later terminate each one separately.

> **MORE INFO   Demonstration Video**   *For a demonstration of the TCP connection establishment process, run the TCPConnection video located in the Demos folder on the CD-ROM accompanying this book.*

Another function of the SYN messages generated by two computers during the three-way handshake is for each system to inform the other of its *maximum segment size (MSS)*. Each system uses the other system's MSS to determine how much data it should include in each segment it transmits. The MSS value for each system depends on which data-link layer protocol is used by the network on which each system resides. The MSS is included as a TCP option in the two SYN packets.

If the two systems have different MSS values, the TCP standard leaves the process of selecting an appropriate segment size up to the individual TCP implementations. In some cases, the systems use the smaller of the two MSS values, while others default to 536 bytes. According to the IP standard, 536 bytes is the minimum datagram size that all TCP/IP systems must support (576 bytes minus 40 bytes for the IP and TCP headers).

Some TCP implementations also use a special technique to determine the *path maximum transmission unit (MTU)* for the connection. The path MTU is the largest packet size permitted on any network connecting the two systems. For example, if both end systems are on Ethernet networks, they both support the same 1500-byte packet size. However, if the two Ethernet networks are connected by the Internet, some or all of the intermediate networks are probably limited to the 576-byte minimum datagram size. Therefore, the path MTU for this connection is 536 bytes. Determining the path MTU before the systems begin sending data prevents IP routers from having to fragment packets during their journey.

Transmitting Data

After the connection has been established between the two systems, each computer has all of the information it needs for TCP to begin transmitting application data, as explained below.

- **Port number**   The client is already aware of the well-known port number for the server, which it needed to initiate the connection. The messages from the client to the server contain the ephemeral port number (in the Source Port field) that the server must use in its replies.

- **Sequence number**   Each system uses the other system's sequence numbers in the Acknowledgment Number field of its own messages.

- **MSS**   Using the information in the MSS option, the systems know how large to make the segments of each sequence.

The application determines whether the client or the server transmits its data first. A transaction between a Web browser client and a Web server begins with the client sending a request to a server, typically requesting a site's home page. Other client/server transactions might begin with the server sending data to the client.

Acknowledging Packets

The Sequence Number and Acknowledgment Number fields are the key to TCP's packet acknowledgment and error correction systems. During the three-way handshake, when the server replies to the client's SYN message, the server's SYN/ACK message contains its own ISN in the Sequence Number field, and it also contains a value in its Acknowledgment Number field. This Acknowledgment Number value is the equivalent of the client's ISN plus 1. The function of the Acknowledgment Number field is to inform the other system what value is expected in the next message's Sequence Number field. For example, if the client's ISN is 1000000, the server's SYN/ACK message contains the value 1000001 in its Acknowledgment Number field. When the client sends its first data message to the server, that message will have the value 1000001 in its Sequence Number field, which is what the server expects.

> **NOTE** **Sequence Numbering** You might wonder why the client's first data message has the Sequence Number value 1000001 when it previously had to send an ACK message in response to the server's SYN. It may seem as though the ACK message should have used Sequence Number 1000001, but in fact, messages that function solely as acknowledgments do not increment the sequence number counter. The server's SYN/ACK message does increment the counter because it includes the SYN flag.

When the systems begin to send data, they increment their Sequence Number values for each byte of data they transmit. When a Web browser sends its request to a Web server, for example, the Sequence Number value in the request's TCP header is its ISN plus 1 (1000001), as expected by the server. If the actual file or Web page requested by the client is 500 bytes (not including the IP and TCP headers), the server responds to the request message with an ACK message that contains the value 1000501 in its Acknowledgment Number field. This indicates that the server received 500 bytes of data successfully and expects the client's next data packet to have the Sequence Number 1000501. Because the client transmitted 500 bytes to the server, the client increments its Sequence Number value by that amount, and the next data message it sends will use the value that the server expects (assuming there are no transmission errors).

The same sequence numbering process also occurs simultaneously in the other direction. The server has transmitted no data yet, except for its SYN/ACK message, so the ACK generated by the client during the handshake contains the server's ISN plus 1. The server's acknowledgment of the client's request contained no data, so the Sequence Number field was not incremented. Thus, when the server responds to the client's request, its first data message will use the same ISN-plus-1 value in its Sequence Number field, which is what the client expects (see Figure 6-4).

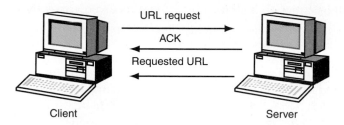

Figure 6-4   **Web client/server communications**

In the example described above, the client's request is small and requires only one TCP message, but in most cases, the Web server responds by transmitting a Web page, which will likely require a sequence of TCP messages consisting of multiple segments. The server divides the Web page (which becomes the sequence it is transmitting) into segments no larger than the client's MSS value. When the server begins to transmit the segments, it increments its Sequence Number value according to the amount of data in each message. If the server's ISN is 20000, the Sequence Number of its first data message will be 20001. If the client's MSS is 1000, the server's second data message will have a Sequence Number of 21001, the third will be 22001, and so on.

Once the client begins receiving data from the server, it is responsible for acknowledging the data. TCP uses a system called *delayed acknowledgments*, which means that the systems do not have to generate a separate acknowledgment message for every data message they receive. The intervals at which the systems generate their acknowledgments is determined by the individual TCP implementation. Each acknowledgment message that the client sends in response to the server's data messages has the ACK flag, and the value of its Acknowledgment Number field reflects the number of bytes in the entire sequence that the client has successfully received.

If the client receives messages that fail the CRC check, or if the client fails to receive messages containing some of the segments in the sequence, it notifies the server, using the Acknowledgment Number field in the ACK messages. The Acknowledgment Number value reflects the number of bytes from the beginning of the sequence that the destination system has received correctly. For example, if a sequence consists of 10 segments and all are received correctly except the seventh segment, the recipient's acknowledgment message will contain an Acknowledgment Number value that reflects the number of bytes in the first six segments only. Segments 8 through 10, even though they were received correctly, are discarded and must be retransmitted along with segment 7. This is called *positive acknowledgment with retransmission* because the destination system acknowledges only the messages that were sent correctly. A protocol that uses *negative acknowledgment* assumes that all messages were received correctly except for those that the destination system explicitly listed as having errors.

> **NOTE** **Selective Acknowledgment** The selective acknowledgment TCP option, as defined in RFC 2018, prevents systems from having to retransmit segments that were actually received without error, as described in the example above. In a TCP connection using selective acknowledgment, the recipient would acknowledge the successful receipt of segments 1 through 6 and 8 through 10, leaving only segment 7 to be retransmitted.

The source system maintains a queue of the messages that it has transmitted and deletes messages for which acknowledgments have arrived. Messages that remain in the source system's queue for a predetermined period of time are assumed to be lost or discarded, and the system automatically retransmits them.

After the server transmits all of the segments in the sequence that contains the requested Web page and the client acknowledges that it has received all of the segments correctly, the systems terminate the connection. This termination procedure is described in "Terminating the Connection," later in this chapter. If the segments arrive at their destination out of sequence, the receiving system uses the Sequence Number values to reassemble them in the proper order. The client system then processes the data it received to display the Web page.

The page will probably contain links to images or other elements, and the client will have to make additional connections to the server to download more data. This is the nature of the Web client/server process. However, other types of applications might maintain a single TCP connection for a much longer period of time and perform repeated exchanges of data in both directions. In a case like this, both systems can exchange data messages and acknowledgments, with the error detection and correction processes occurring on both sides.

Detecting Errors

Two things can go wrong during a TCP transaction: messages can arrive in a corrupted state, or they can fail to arrive at all. When messages fail to arrive, the lack of acknowledgments from the destination system causes the sender to retransmit the missing messages. If a serious network problem prevents the systems from exchanging any messages, the TCP connection eventually times out and the entire process must start again.

When messages arrive at their destination, the receiving system checks them for accuracy by performing the same checksum computation that the sender performed before transmitting the data. The receiving system then compares the results with the value in the Checksum field. If the values don't match, the system discards the message. This is a crucial element of the TCP protocol because it is the only end-to-end checksum performed on the actual application layer data. IP includes an end-to-end checksum, but only on its header data, and data-link layer protocols such as Ethernet and Token Ring contain a checksum, but only for one hop at a time. If the packets pass through a network that doesn't provide a checksum, such as a Point-to-Point Protocol (PPP) link, there is a potential for errors to be introduced that can't be detected at the data-link or network layer.

The checksum performed by TCP is unusual because it is calculated not only on the entire TCP header and the application data but also on a *pseudo-header*. The pseudo-header consists of the IP header's Source IP Address, Destination IP Address, Protocol, and Length fields, plus 1 byte of padding, to bring the total number of bytes to an even 12 (three 4-byte words), as shown in Figure 6-5. Including the pseudo-header ensures that the datagrams are delivered to the correct computer and to the correct transport layer protocol on that computer.

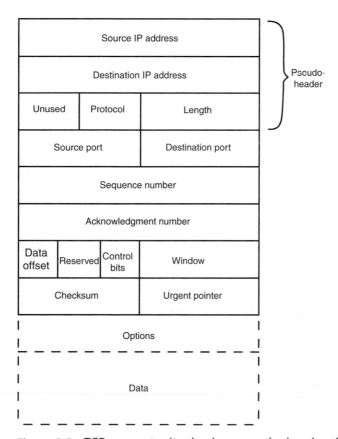

Figure 6-5   TCP computes its checksum on the header, the data, and a pseudo-header derived from the IP header.

Flow Control

Flow control is the process by which the destination system in a TCP connection provides information to the source system that enables that source system to regulate the speed at which it transmits data. Each system has a limited amount of buffer space to store incoming data. The data remains in the buffer until the receiving system generates messages acknowledging that data. If the system transmitting the data sends too much information too quickly, the receiver's buffers could fill up, forcing it to discard data messages. The system receiving the data uses the Window field in its acknowledgment messages to let the sender know how much buffer space it has available at the time of each message's transmission. The transmitting system uses the Window value along with the Acknowledgment Number value to determine what data in the sequence the system is permitted to transmit. For example, if an acknowledgment message contains an Acknowledgment Number value of 150000 and a Window value of 500, the sending system knows that all of the data in the sequence through byte 150000 has been received correctly at the destination, and that it can now transmit bytes 150001 through 150500. If the sender has received no additional acknowledgments by the time it transmits those 500 bytes, it must stop transmitting until the next acknowledgment arrives.

This type of flow control is called a *sliding window* technique. The *offered window* (shown in Figure 6-6) is the series of bytes that the receiving system has permitted the transmitting system to send. As the receiving system acknowledges the incoming bytes, the left side of the window moves to the right. As the system passes the acknowledged bytes up to the application layer process indicated by the Destination Port number, the right side of the window moves to the right. Thus the window can be said to be sliding along the incoming byte stream, from left to right.

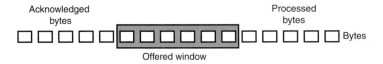

Figure 6-6   The sliding window technique

Terminating the Connection

Once the systems in a TCP connection have finished exchanging data, they terminate the connection by using control messages, much like those used in the three-way handshake that established the connection. As with the establishment of the connection, the application generating the data determines which system initiates the termination sequence. In the case of the Web client/server transaction used as an example earlier in this section, the server begins the termination process by setting the FIN flag in the Control Bits field of its last data message. In other cases, the system initiating the termination process might use a separate message containing the FIN flag and no data. The system then enters the FIN-WAIT-1 state, indicating that it is waiting for a FIN message from the other system or an acknowledgment of its own FIN message.

The system that receives the FIN flag transmits an acknowledgment message and then generates its own message containing a FIN flag, after which it enters the CLOSING state. The other system then must respond with an ACK message, and then it enters the CLOSED state. This acknowledgment is necessary because the connection runs in both directions, so both systems must terminate their respective connections, using a total of four messages (see Figure 6-7). Unlike the connection establishment procedure, the computers can't combine the FIN and ACK flags in the same message, which is why four messages are needed instead of three. When the final ACK message arrives, both systems enter the CLOSED state, which is actually a null condition, because the connection no longer exists. In some cases, only one of the two connections is terminated and the other is left open. This is called a *half close*.

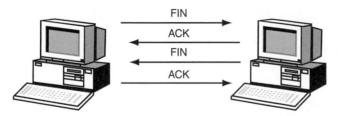

Figure 6-7   The TCP connection termination process

User Datagram Protocol (UDP)

UDP is defined in RFC 768, "User Datagram Protocol." Unlike TCP, UDP is a connectionless protocol, so it provides no packet acknowledgment, flow control, segmentation, or guaranteed delivery. As a result, UDP is far simpler than TCP and generates much less overhead. The UDP header is much smaller than that of a TCP header—8 bytes as opposed to 20 bytes or more—and there are no separate control messages, such as those used to establish and terminate connections. UDP is designed for transactions that consist of only two messages: a request and a reply, with the reply functioning as a tacit acknowledgment. For this reason, many of the applications that use UDP transport only amounts of data small enough to fit into a single message. Domain Name System (DNS) and Dynamic Host Configuration Protocol (DHCP) are two of the most common application layer protocols that use UDP.

Some applications do use UDP to transmit large amounts of data, such as streaming audio and video, but UDP is appropriate for these purposes because this type of data can survive the loss of an occasional packet, while a program or data file cannot. In these cases, the application splits the data stream into small enough segments to fit into UDP messages.

The format of a UDP message is shown in Figure 6-8.

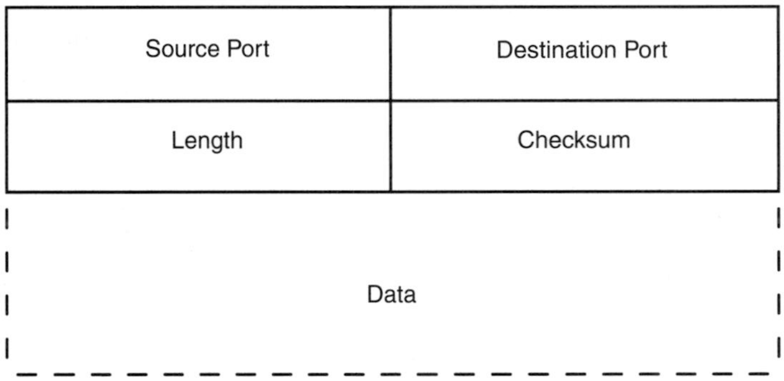

Source Port	Destination Port
Length	Checksum

Data

Figure 6-8   The UDP message format

The functions of the UDP message fields are as follows:

- **Source Port (2 bytes)**   Identifies the process on the transmitting system that generated the information carried in the Data field. This field performs the same function as in the TCP header.

- **Destination Port (2 bytes)**   Identifies the process on the receiving system for which the information in the Data field is intended. This field performs the same function as in the TCP header.

- **Length (2 bytes)** Specifies the length of the UDP header and data in bytes. By subtracting the known length of the header, this field can specify how much data is included in the message.

- **Checksum (2 bytes)** Contains the results of a CRC performed by the transmitting system and is used by the receiving system to detect errors in the UDP header, the data, and parts of the IP header. The Checksum value is computed using the message header, the data, and the IP pseudo-header, just as in TCP. The UDP standard specifies that the use of the checksum is optional. The transmitting system fills the Checksum field with zeroes if it is unused. There has been a great deal of debate about whether UDP messages should include checksums. RFC 768 requires all UDP systems to be capable of using checksums to check for errors, and most current implementations include the checksum computations.

- **Data (variable)** Contains the information generated by the application layer process specified in the Source Port field.

Ports and Sockets

As with data-link and network layer protocols, one of the important functions of a transport layer protocol is to identify the protocol or process that generated the data it carries so that the receiving system can deliver the data to the correct application. Both TCP and UDP do this by specifying the number of a port that has been assigned to a particular process by the Internet Assigned Numbers Authority (IANA). These port numbers are published at *www.iana.org/ assignments/port-numbers*, and a list of the most common ports is included with every TCP/IP client in a text file called Services. When a TCP/IP packet arrives at its destination, the transport layer protocol receiving the IP datagram from the network layer reads the value in the Destination Port field and delivers the information in the Data field to the program or protocol associated with that port.

All of the common Internet applications have particular port numbers associated with them, called **well-known ports** (or sometimes contact ports). Table 6-2 lists the most commonly used well-known ports. For example, Web servers use port 80, and DNS servers use port 53. TCP and UDP both maintain their own separate lists of well-known port numbers. For example, the File Transfer Protocol (FTP) uses TCP ports 20 and 21. Because FTP uses only TCP (and not UDP) at the transport layer, a different application layer protocol can use the same ports (20 and 21) with the UDP protocol. However, in some cases, a protocol can use either one of the transport layer protocols. DNS, for example, is associated with both TCP port 53 and UDP port 53.

Test your knowledge of the well-known port numbers used by TCP and UDP by completing Exercise 6-3, "Port Numbers," now.

Table 6-2 **Well-Known Port Numbers**

Service Name	Port Number	Protocol	Function
ftp-data	20	TCP	FTP data channel; used for transmitting files between systems
ftp	21	TCP	FTP control channel; used by FTP-connected systems for exchanging commands and responses
telnet	23	TCP	Telnet; used to execute commands on network-connected systems
smtp	25	TCP	Simple Mail Transport Protocol (SMTP); used to send e-mail messages
domain	53	TCP and UDP	DNS; used to receive host name resolution requests from clients
bootps	67	TCP and UDP	Bootstrap Protocol (BOOTP) and DHCP servers; used to receive TCP/IP configuration requests from clients
bootpc	68	TCP and UDP	BOOTP and DHCP clients; used to send TCP/IP configuration requests to servers
http	80	TCP	HTTP; used by Web servers to receive requests from client browsers
pop3	110	TCP	Post Office Protocol 3 (POP3); used to receive e-mail requests from clients
snmp	161	TCP and UDP	Simple Network Management Protocol (SNMP); used by SNMP agents to transmit status information to a network management console

When one TCP/IP system addresses traffic to another, it uses a combination of an IP address and a port number. The combination of an IP address and a port is called a **socket**. To specify a socket in a Uniform Resource Locator (URL), you enter the IP address first and then follow it with a colon and the port number. For example, the socket 192.168.2.10:21 addresses port 21 on the system with the address 192.168.2.10. Because the port number for the FTP control port is 21, this socket addresses the FTP server running on that computer. In most cases, however, URLs contain DNS names, not IP addresses; the format remains the same, but with the DNS name replacing the IP address (for example, ftp.adatum.com:21).

You usually don't have to specify the port number when you're typing a URL because most programs assume that you want to connect to the well-known port.

Your Web browser, for example, addresses all the URLs you enter to port 80, the HTTP Web server port, unless you specify otherwise. The IANA port numbers are recommendations, not ironclad rules, however. You can configure a Web server to use a port number other than 80; in fact, many Web servers assign alternate ports to their administrative controls so that only users who know the correct port number can access them. For example, you can create a semisecret Web site of your own by configuring your server to use port 81 instead of 80. Users would then have to type a URL such as *http://www.myserver.com:81* into their browsers instead of just *http://www.myserver.com* to access your Web site.

Test your understanding of the functions of the TCP and UDP protocols by completing Exercise 6-2, "TCP and UDP Functions," now.

The well-known ports published by the IANA refer mostly to servers. Because it is the client that usually initiates communication with the server, rather than the other way around, clients don't need permanently assigned port numbers. Instead, a client program typically selects a port number at random, called an **ephemeral port number**, to use while communicating with a particular server. The IANA only manages port numbers from 1 to 1023, so ephemeral port numbers always have values higher than 1024. A server receiving a packet from a client uses the value in the TCP header's Source Port field to address its reply to the correct ephemeral port in the client system.

> **NOTE** **Exam Objectives**   Objective 2.6 for the Network+ exam requires students to be able to "define the function of TCP/UDP ports and identify well-known ports."

NOVELL NETWARE AND THE TRANSPORT LAYER

Like TCP/IP, the Novell IPX protocol suite includes multiple protocols at the transport layer that provide varying levels of service. Interestingly, the transport layer protocol most frequently associated with IPX, called the Sequenced Packet Exchange (SPX) protocol, is actually used far less frequently by Novell NetWare than is the NetWare Core Protocol (NCP).

Sequenced Packet Exchange (SPX)

SPX is NetWare's connection-oriented transport layer protocol. It provides many of the same services as TCP, including packet acknowledgment and flow control. Unlike TCP, however, SPX is rarely used. NetWare servers use SPX for communication between print queues, print servers, and printers; and for specialized applications that require the SPX services, such as Rconsole (a remote console program) and network backups.

Like IPX, SPX is based on a Xerox Network System (XNS) protocol called Sequenced Packet Protocol (SPP). SPX messages are carried within IPX datagrams, using the message format, shown in Figure 6-9.

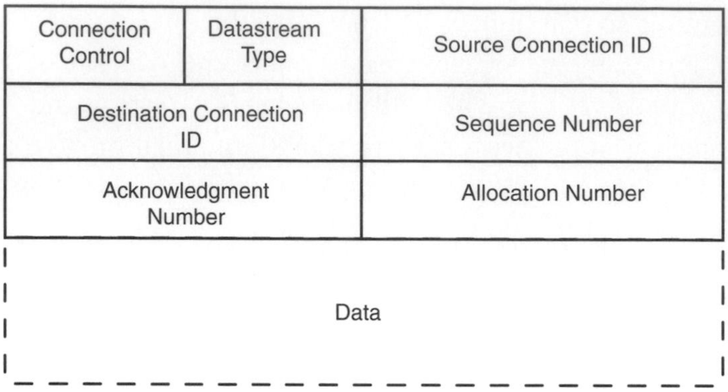

Connection Control	Datastream Type	Source Connection ID
Destination Connection ID		Sequence Number
Acknowledgment Number		Allocation Number
Data		

Figure 6-9   The SPX message format

The functions of the SPX message fields are as follows:

- **Connection Control (1 byte)**   Contains a code that identifies the message as performing a certain control function, such as the following:

    - ❏ 10. End Of Message

    - ❏ 20. Attention

    - ❏ 40. Acknowledgment Required

    - ❏ 80. System Packet

- **Datastream Type (1 byte)**   Identifies the type of information found in the Data field, or contains a code used during the connection termination sequence, such as the following:

    - ❏ FE. End-of-Connection

    - ❏ FF. End-of-Connection Acknowledgment

- **Source Connection ID (2 bytes)**   Contains the number used by the transmitting system to identify the current connection

- **Destination Connection ID (2 bytes)**   Contains the number used by the receiving system to identify the current connection

- **Sequence Number (2 bytes)**   Specifies the location of this message in the sequence

- **Acknowledgment Number (2 bytes)**   Contains the Sequence Number value that the system expects to find in the next packet it receives, thus acknowledging successful receipt of all the previous packets

- **Allocation Number (2 bytes)**   Specifies, for flow control purposes, the number of packet receive buffers that are available on the transmitting system

- **Data (variable)**   Contains the information generated by an application or an upper layer protocol

NetWare Core Protocol (NCP)

NetWare Core Protocol (NCP) is responsible for all of the file-sharing traffic generated by Novell NetWare clients and servers, and it also has many other functions. As a result, NCP is far more frequently used than SPX. The wide variety of network functions that use NCP make it difficult to pinpoint the protocol's place in the OSI reference model. File transfers between clients and servers place the protocol firmly in the transport layer, but NCP also includes functions that span the session, presentation, and application layers. However, for all of these services, NCP messages are carried within IPX datagrams, which affirms its dominant presence at the transport layer.

Unlike SPX and the TCP/IP transport layer protocols, NCP uses different formats for client request and server reply messages. In addition, there is another form of NCP message called the *NetWare Core Packet Burst (NCPB) protocol*, which enables systems to transmit multiple messages with only a single acknowledgment. NCPB was developed relatively recently to address a shortcoming of NCP, which requires an individual acknowledgment message for each data packet.

The NCP Request message format is illustrated in Figure 6-10.

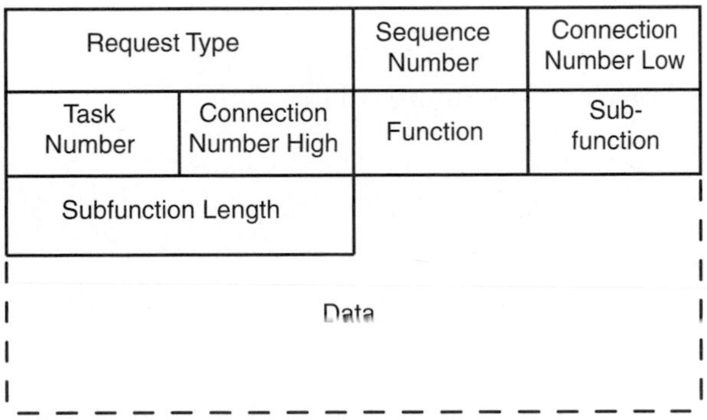

Request Type		Sequence Number	Connection Number Low
Task Number	Connection Number High	Function	Sub-function
Subfunction Length			
Data			

Figure 6-10   The NCP Request message format

The NCP Request message fields perform the following functions:

- **Request Type (2 bytes)**   Specifies the basic type of request performed by the message, using codes that represent the following functions:

    - ❑ Create a Service Connection

    - ❑ File Server Request

    - ❑ Connection Destroy

    - ❑ Burst Mode Protocol Packet

- **Sequence Number (1 byte)**   Contains a value that indicates this message's place in the current NCP sequence

- **Connection Number Low (1 byte)**   Contains the number of the client's connection to the NetWare server

- **Task Number (1 byte)**   Contains a unique value that the connected systems use to associate requests with replies

- **Connection Number High (1 byte)**   Unused

- **Function (1 byte)**   Specifies the exact function of the message

- **Subfunction (1 byte)**   Further describes the function of the message

- **Subfunction Length (2 bytes)**   Specifies the length of the Data field

- **Data (variable)**   Contains information that the server will need to process the request, such as a file location

> **NOTE   NCP Functions**   The NCP Request format has three fields that describe the function of the message. This might seem redundant, but there are more than 200 combinations of function and subfunction codes that cover virtually all of the services provided by NetWare servers.

The NCP Reply message format is illustrated in Figure 6-11.

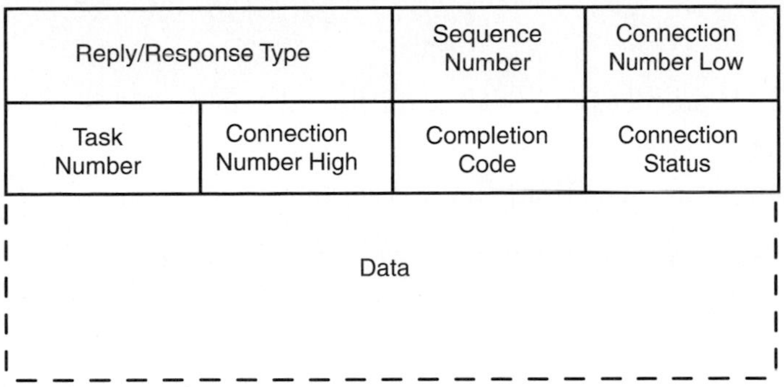

Reply/Response Type		Sequence Number	Connection Number Low
Task Number	Connection Number High	Completion Code	Connection Status

Data

Figure 6-11   The NCP Reply message format

The functions of the NCP Reply message fields are as follows:

- **Reply/Response Type (2 bytes)**   Specifies the type of reply in the message, using codes that represent the following functions:

  - ❑ File Server Reply

  - ❑ Burst Mode Protocol

  - ❑ Positive Acknowledgment

- **Sequence Number (1 byte)**   Contains a value that indicates this message's place in the current NCP sequence

- **Connection Number Low (1 byte)**   Contains the number of the client's connection to the NetWare server

- **Task Number (1 byte)**   Contains a unique value that the connected systems use to associate requests with replies

- **Connection Number High (1 byte)**   Unused

- **Completion Code (1 byte)**   Indicates whether the request associated with this reply has been successfully completed

- **Connection Status (1 byte)**   Indicates whether the connection between the client and the server is still active

- **Data (variable)**   Contains information sent by the server in response to the request

SUMMARY

- Transmission Control Protocol (TCP) is a connection-oriented protocol that provides services such as packet acknowledgment, flow control, error detection and correction, and segmentation.

  - ❏ Establishing a TCP connection between two systems requires a three-way handshake. During the three-way handshake, each computer supplies the other with the initial sequence number (ISN) it will assign to its messages, plus its maximum segment size (MSS).

  - ❏ To transmit large amounts of data over a TCP connection, a system divides a byte stream into multiple segments, each of which is transmitted in a separate message.

  - ❏ The system receiving the data segments acknowledges them with acknowledgment messages. Unacknowledged messages are eventually retransmitted.

  - ❏ Acknowledgment messages inform the other system how much data it can transmit. This is called flow control.

  - ❏ TCP messages contain a checksum that the receiving system uses to detect transmission errors.

  - ❏ Closing a TCP connection requires the systems to exchange termination (FIN) messages and acknowledgments.

- User Datagram Protocol (UDP) is a connectionless protocol that provides error detection through checksums, but it provides none of the other services found in TCP.

- Sequenced Packet Exchange (SPX) is NetWare's connection-oriented protocol, which includes most of the same features as TCP. However, it is used far less often than NetWare Control Protocol (NCP).

- NCP is the transport layer protocol most often used by NetWare systems because it supports many functions, including client/server file sharing and Novell Directory Service (NDS) communications.

EXERCISES

Exercise 6-1: TCP Header Fields

Match the TCP header field in the left column with the correct description in the right column.

1. Source Port
2. Sequence Number
3. Checksum
4. Window
5. Urgent Pointer
6. Data Offset
7. Destination Port
8. Acknowledgment Number
9. Control Bits
10. Data

a. Specifies how many bytes the sender can transmit

b. Specifies the number of bytes in the sequence that have been successfully transmitted

c. Specifies the functions of messages used to initiate and terminate connections

d. Contains information for the application layer

e. Specifies which of the bytes in the message should receive special treatment from the receiving system

f. Identifies the application or protocol that generated the data carried in the TCP message

g. Used to reassemble segments that arrive at the destination out of order

h. Specifies the length of the TCP header

i. Contains error detection information

j. Specifies the application that will use the data in the message

Exercise 6-2: TCP and UDP Functions

Specify whether each of the following statements describes TCP, UDP, or both.

1. Provides flow control: _____

2. Used for DNS communications: _____

3. Detects transmission errors: _____

4. Used to carry DHCP messages: _____

5. Divides data to be transmitted into segments: _____

6. Acknowledges transmitted messages: _____

7. Used for Web client/server communications: _____

8. Requires a connection establishment procedure: _____

9. Contains a Length field: _____

10. Uses a pseudo-header in its checksums: _____

Exercise 6-3: Port Numbers

Specify the application or service associated with each of the following well-known port numbers:

1. 23

2. 21

3. 80

4. 25

5. 110

6. 53

7. 20

REVIEW QUESTIONS

1. In TCP, what does "delayed acknowledgment" mean?

    a. A predetermined time interval must pass before the receiving system can acknowledge a data packet.

    b. Data segments are not acknowledged until the entire sequence has been transmitted.

    c. The receiving system doesn't have to generate a separate acknowledgment message for every segment.

    d. A data segment must be acknowledged before the next segment is transmitted.

2. What does the Data Offset field in the TCP header specify?

    a. The length of the TCP header

    b. The location of the current segment in the sequence

    c. The length of the Data field

    d. The checksum value used for error detection

3. What is the combination of an IP address and a port number called?

   a. A sequence number

   b. A checksum

   c. A data offset

   d. A socket

4. Which of the following TCP/IP systems uses an ephemeral port number?

   a. The client

   b. The server

   c. The system initiating the TCP connection

   d. The system terminating the TCP connection

5. What flag does the first message transmitted in any TCP connection contain?

   a. ACK

   b. SYN

   c. FIN

   d. PSH

6. What TCP header field provides flow control?

   a. Window

   b. Data Offset

   c. Acknowledgment

   d. Sequence Number

7. Which of the following services does UDP provide?

   a. Flow control

   b. Guaranteed delivery

   c. Error detection

   d. None of the above

8. Which of the following is not true about the SPX protocol?

   a. It is connection-oriented.

   b. It operates at the transport layer only.

   c. Clients use it to access server files.

   d. It provides flow control.

9. At which layers of the OSI reference model does NCP provide functions?

10. Which of the following protocols requires the receiving system to transmit a separate acknowledgment message for each packet received?

   a. IPX

   b. SPX

   c. NCP

   d. NCPB

CASE SCENARIOS

Case Scenario 6-1: Troubleshooting TCP

The manager of your company's Sales department calls the help desk and reports a general slowdown of the Sales network and intermittent failures when users try to access files on the Sales server. As part of your troubleshooting process, you use a protocol analyzer to capture a sample of the network's traffic. While analyzing the traffic sample, you notice the server is transmitting large numbers of TCP packets with the same Sequence Number value.

Judging from this information, which of the following statements are true? (Choose all answers that are correct.)

1. The server is failing to receive acknowledgments of its transmissions from clients.

2. The server is failing to receive clients' file access requests.

3. Clients are sending multiple file request messages with the same Sequence Number value to the server.

4. Clients are sending multiple acknowledgment messages with the same Acknowledgment Number value to the server.

Case Scenario 6-2: Using Port Numbers

While you are installing an Internet Web server on a client's network, the owner of the company tells you that he also wants to build a Web server for internal use by the company's employees. This intranet Web server will not contain confidential information, but it should not be accessible from the company's Internet Web site. To do this, you create a second site on the Web server. The Internet site uses the well-known port number for Web servers, which is 80. For the intranet site, you select the port number 283. Assuming that the Web server's IP address on the internal network is 10.54.3.145, what will the users on the company network have to do to access the intranet Web site with Microsoft Internet Explorer?

1. Type http://283:10.54.3.145 in the Address field.

2. Type http://10.54.3.145:283 in the Address field.

3. Type http://10.54.3.145 in the Address field and then specify the port number in the company home page.

4. Configure Internet Explorer to use port 283 in its Options dialog box and then type http://10.54.3.145 in the Address field.

CHAPTER 7
TCP/IP

Upon completion of this chapter, you will be able to:

■ List the layers of the Transmission Control Protocol/Internet Protocol (TCP/IP) protocol stack and locate the TCP/IP protocols in the Open Systems Interconnection (OSI) reference model.

■ Understand the function of the Address Resolution Protocol (ARP).

■ Describe the functions of the Internet Control Message Protocol (ICMP).

■ Describe the properties of TCP/IP's application layer protocols.

■ Understand the functions of a router and describe the information in a routing table.

■ Distinguish between static and dynamic routing.

■ Create a static route in a routing table.

■ Understand the operation of routing protocols.

■ Manually configure TCP/IP client parameters on Microsoft Windows, Novell NetWare, and UNIX/Linux computers.

Because of the explosive growth of the Internet in recent years, Transmission Control Protocol/Internet Protocol (TCP/IP) is now used on more networks than any other suite of protocols. In Chapter 5, "Network Layer Protocols," and Chapter 6, "Transport Layer Protocols," you learned about some of the major protocols in the TCP/IP suite. In this chapter, you learn about how the protocols in the suite work together as a whole. Because the TCP/IP protocols are required for Internet communications, virtually all networks use them, so it is vital for you to understand how they work and how to configure a computer to use them.

INTRODUCING TCP/IP

The TCP/IP protocols were developed in the 1970s specifically for use on a packet-switching network built for the United States Department of Defense. That network was known as the ARPANET, which evolved into what is now the Internet. Since early in their development, the TCP/IP protocols have also been associated with the UNIX operating systems. Thus, the TCP/IP protocols predate the personal computer, the Open Systems Interconnection (OSI) reference model, the Ethernet protocol, and most of the other elements that are considered the foundations of computer networking. Unlike other protocol suites that perform some of the same functions, such as Novell's Internetwork Packet Exchange (IPX), TCP/IP was never the product of a single company. TCP/IP was a collaborative effort, with the resulting standards being released to the public domain.

TCP/IP Development

Development of the core TCP/IP protocols began in 1975, when the ARPANET was officially declared to be an operational, rather than experimental, network. In 1983, the protocols were ratified as official standards and were required on all ARPANET systems. By the time development of the TCP/IP protocols began, the developers had enough experience with the ARPANET to understand the basic design principles that should be observed when creating a new protocol suite. These principles are discussed in the following sections.

Platform Independence

One of the main design principles for the TCP/IP protocols—indeed, the guiding factor for the entire project—was that the protocols must be wholly independent of any particular vendor, computing platform, or hardware specification. Platform independence means that a computer can use any type of processor, run any operating system, and connect to a TCP/IP network using any physical medium available, such as a leased phone line or a dial-up connection.

Before the personal computer (PC) became the predominant computing platform, the ARPANET consisted of a wide variety of computers that used many different technologies to connect to the network. As local area networking became more prevalent, and as the ARPANET evolved into the Internet, data-link layer protocols such as Ethernet and Token Ring became more popular. The physical layer specifications included with these protocols were also assimilated into the TCP/IP networking standards.

Because TCP/IP adapts to any hardware platform, the protocols effectively insulate the applications running on the networked computers from the physical aspect of the network. A client application on one Ethernet network can use the Internet to connect to a server on another Ethernet network, but the signal might pass through a dozen or more different network types during the journey.

The decision to create protocols that are platform independent naturally led the developers to other design principles that became the hallmarks of the TCP/IP protocols. Essentially, creating an independent protocol suite means that no assumptions can be made regarding the computers that will be connected to the network, except that they all must have some physical means to make the required connection. All of the other elements needed for computers to communicate with each other had to be provided by the protocols. These elements include the following:

- Each system must have some way to uniquely identify itself to the other systems on the network.

- Each system must be able to create an interface between the new protocols and the physical medium used to connect to the network.

- Each system must have a programming interface that enables the requests for network resources issued by the system's applications to be serviced by use of the new protocols.

- The growth potential of the network should not be limited by the new protocols.

- The standards that define the new protocols should be formatted so that new computing platforms can be easily accommodated.

- Use of the new protocol standards should not be limited by trademarks, copyrights, or other publishing restrictions.

Addressability

A computer on a TCP/IP data communications network must be capable of generating the following three types of data transmissions:

- **Broadcasts** Transmissions that are sent to every system on the network

- **Multicasts** Transmissions that are sent to a group of systems

- **Unicasts** Transmissions that are sent to a single system on the network

Broadcast transmissions are the easiest to implement because the data only needs to circulate around the entire network. However, this is also the least efficient method when a transmission is actually intended for only one or a few other systems. The Internet would never have become what it is today if it relied exclusively on broadcast transmissions. The use of unicast and multicast transmissions introduces a critical problem, however. To transmit data to a single destination system or group of systems, there must be a way to uniquely identify that system or group of systems by means of a name or an address. Many of the computing platforms used on the Internet already have an addressing system. For example, Ethernet and Token Ring systems both have unique hardware addresses hard-coded into their network interface adapters. These addresses would work well on the Internet, except for the fact that not every type of computer has them.

Because different types of hardware addresses are used on local networks, the developers of the TCP/IP protocols decided to implement their own addressing system. IP addresses are unique 32-bit binary numbers that are assigned to every interface on the network, in addition to any other hardware addressing system that is in place. This IP address identifies both the network on which the computer is located and the individual host system on that network.

The efficiency of this IP addressing system has been demonstrated, along with many of TCP/IP's other features, by the explosive growth of the Internet. At the time of their inception, no one expected the TCP/IP protocols to have to support a network containing the millions of systems in use today, but they are continuing to function very well.

Another issue that no one anticipated is that all of the possible network addresses would be allocated. That situation is rapidly approaching, however, and the IP address space is currently being upgraded from 32 to 128 bits.

Modularity

When TCP/IP was being developed, it became clear that no single monolithic protocol would be able to support all of the different computing platforms being used on the ARPANET. The new protocols had to work with existing standards and accommodate all of the different physical media used by the networked computers, as well any new physical standards that might be developed in the future. The protocols also needed to support a number of different application programming interfaces (APIs) so that programs running on different platforms could all request access to the same network resources.

The result of these requirements was a series of separate standard documents that define a collection of protocols functioning in four distinct operational layers. Separate protocols were defined for the various physical standards and APIs being used. This method of documenting the protocols has several advantages:

- **Task delegation**   Separating the support for different physical media and APIs into discrete protocols allows the development tasks to be delegated to people according to their areas of expertise. With separate teams working on the standards for different connection types, the individual protocols can be developed independently, without the need to assemble a group of engineers familiar with both technologies.

- **Quality of service**   Having multiple protocols operating at the same layer enables applications to select the protocol that provides only the level of service required.

- **Scalability**   Additional standards documents that adapt the protocols to emerging technologies support a steadily increasing number of systems and a growing number of system types. Additional protocol standards that support new physical media and APIs can be developed without modifying the existing protocols.

- **Simultaneous development**   By using independent teams to work simultaneously on separate areas of the project, the schedule for developing the protocols is accelerated.

Mutability is one of the basic tenets on which the Internet and the TCP/IP protocols are based. The computing and networking industries are constantly advancing, and technologies are expected to change. The TCP/IP standards are acknowledged to be works-in-progress, with new versions of the documents regularly obsolescing older ones.

TCP/IP Standards

Another important aspect of the TCP/IP standards is that the documents are freely available to the public, with no limitations on their use, distribution, or re-publication. This makes it easy for the average administrator to access the source information used to create the TCP/IP implementations found in specific products and operating systems. The standards documents can be very valuable, both as learning and troubleshooting tools.

Because the TCP/IP standards were designed for use on the fledgling Internet, they were developed and ratified as part of the Internet standardization process, even though they are now used on many private networks. To become an official

Internet standard, a document defining a protocol or other technical aspect of TCP/IP must undergo an evaluation and ratification process. During this process, anyone who is interested in contributing to the effort has the opportunity to test it and comment on its contents. The standardization process is governed by the Internet Society (ISOC), which is concerned with all aspects of the Internet's growth and evolution. ISOC is composed of several subgroups, as follows:

- **Internet Architecture Board (IAB)**   Technical advisors to ISOC, and the highest level committee involved in the standard ratification process. Consisting of 12 voluntary members, this board performs the final review of a potential standards document before its ratification.

- **Internet Engineering Task Force (IETF)**   Falling under the jurisdiction of the IAB, the IETF is the group most directly involved in the technological development and review of potential standards as they proceed through the ratification process. The IETF is composed of eight areas, each of which has one or more Area Directors. Each area is composed of Working Groups that investigate specific technical areas that might result in the development of a standards document or simply work to address a problem. The eight areas of the IETF are as follows:

  - Applications
  - Internet
  - Network Management
  - Operational Requirements
  - Routing
  - Security
  - Transport
  - User Services

- **Internet Engineering Steering Group (IESG)**   Composed of the Chairman of the IETF and the Area Directors of all of the Working Groups, the IESG is responsible for moving standards documents through the formal ratification process. The final ratification of an Internet standard comes from the IAB, based on recommendations submitted by the IESG.

- **Internet Assigned Numbers Authority (IANA)**   An organization devoted to the registration of numerical values that uniquely identify certain protocol specifications used by all implementations of a standard. For example, the IANA assigns the standard port numbers for particular services and prevents those numbers from being duplicated. The IANA also assigns identifying numbers to MIBs (Management Information Bases), protocols, and other elements defined in Internet standards documents.

- **Internet Research Task Force (IRTF)**   An organization that performs long-term investigations of technological issues that are not necessarily involved in the standards ratification process. The issues might involve emerging technologies that will eventually be passed to the IETF for development of a standard.

IETF Membership and Activities

Most of the people working in these organizations are volunteers; membership, particularly in the IETF, can be fluid. IETF meetings are held three times annually, and any interested person can register for and attend a meeting or participate in the discussions on the IETF's Internet mailing lists. Although many of the people in the IETF are employed by firms that are important to the industry surrounding the Internet, their involvement is strictly individual. They do not participate as representatives of their employers, but simply as people interested in the development and well-being of the Internet.

The actual activities of the IETF Working Groups consist of discussions, conducted both by mailing lists and in person, that try to achieve what has become the unofficial IETF motto: "Rough consensus and running code." This means the group tries to come to a general agreement about how to achieve their goal, and then tries to realize that goal in concrete terms, to prove that it is a viable solution.

> **MORE INFO**   **IETF Information**   For more information on the IETF, and to access IETF publications and mailing lists, see *www.ietf.org/*. For a general introduction to the IETF, see Request for Comments (RFC) 3160, "The Tao of IETF—A Novice's Guide to the Internet Engineering Task Force."

Requests for Comments (RFCs)

The published product of the IETF's work, as well as that of the other bodies governed by ISOC, is a series of documents known as Requests for Comments (RFCs). The IETF maintains a master index of RFCs, which currently lists over 3600 documents dating back to 1969. All of the documents are text files, except for a few that are also available in PostScript (PS) or Adobe Acrobat (PDF) format to facilitate the inclusion of graphical material. All of the documents are available for download from the IETF Web site, and from dozens of mirror sites around the world.

When the IETF publishes an RFC, it assigns a number to the document and lists it in the index. Once an RFC is assigned a number, the version of the document that number represents never changes. When a document is revised, it receives a new number and is republished in its entirety, and older versions are always available. The RFC index is extensively cross-referenced, so you can see when new RFCs make other documents obsolete or when they have been made obsolete by other documents.

> **MORE INFO   Accessing the RFC Index**   The most current version of the RFC index is available at www.ietf.org/iesg/1rfc_index.txt.

All of the official Internet standards are published as RFCs, but not all RFCs define Internet standards. There are six status indicators for RFCs: three that are devoted to the development and ratification of standards, and three that are used for documents that are not intended to be standards. The latter three RFC status indicators are as follows:

- **Informational**   A document that is considered to be of general interest to the Internet community but has no implicit endorsement or recommendation from the IETF or any of its related bodies. While some informational RFCs are technical in nature, many are not, and some are even quite amusing.

- **Experimental**   A document resulting from a research project (conducted by the IRTF or another body) that is not intended or not yet ready for development into a standard.

- **Historic**   A document that has been made obsolete by another specification and is now of purely historical interest.

> **NOTE   Historical Hysteria**   The IETF, in RFC 2026, "The Internet Standards Process—Revision 3," acknowledges that the term for the historic document type should properly be *historical*, not *historic*, but to quote its author, Scott Bradner, "at this point the use of 'historic' is historical."

Informational and experimental documents can be the product of one of the Internet governing bodies, or they can come from outside sources of any type. Before an outside document is published as an informational or experimental RFC, it is reviewed by the RFC Editor and the IESG. The purpose of this review is to prevent misuse of the RFC publishing process by people who might want to introduce a document and make it appear to be a ratified Internet standard, when it is in fact the product of an outside company or organization.

The Standardization Process

Most of the RFCs that define specific TCP/IP protocols are official Internet standards. Documents that are said to be "on the standards track" are revised and published several times before they are ratified as standards. With these works-in-progress available to the public, they can receive the greatest possible amount of feedback from users. Real-world testing is a major part of the standards development process.

Before becoming RFCs, preliminary versions of standards documents are often published in a separate directory called Internet-Drafts. This directory is a series of temporary documents that are posted for a period of not less than two weeks and not more than six months while being considered for advancement to the standards track. Internet draft documents are removed from the directory when they are approved by the IESG for publication as RFCs. Once published as an RFC, a standard goes through three changes of status on its way to ratification, as follows:

- **Proposed standard**   The elevation of a document to proposed standard status indicates that it is on the standards track and that the technology defined in the document is complete and generally stable. However, a proposed standard has not usually been implemented or tested in the field yet. It is recommended that implementations based on the proposed standard be used only in a lab environment because the technology might change significantly before the standard advances to the next stage. A document must remain a proposed standard for at least six months, and two implementations are required before it can be advanced to draft standard status.

- **Draft standard**   Before a proposed standard can be elevated to draft standard status, it must have two implementations that include all features and options, and the features and options must be completely interoperable. The technology should also have had sufficient field testing to demonstrate that the document is mature and ready to become an Internet standard with only a minimum of modification. It is usually safe to develop and deploy production software based on a draft standard because changes will be made only to address specific problems. A document must remain a draft standard for at least four months before it can be granted full Internet standard status.

- **Internet standard**   Once a draft standard has had sufficient time to demonstrate its stability in extensive operational testing, it can be declared a fully ratified Internet standard. A ratified standard document is assigned another number, called an STD number, which is independent of the RFC number and remains with the standard even when it is updated by a new RFC. The document is made available in a separate directory that contains only ratified standards.

Each entry in the RFC index is annotated with the document's current status, and with its STD number if the document is an Internet standard. Another way to track the progress of the standardization process is to consult an RFC called "Internet Official Protocol Standards." This document contains information about the current status of all of the RFC documents on the standards track and how to obtain them. This RFC is updated frequently to reflect the latest changes and is always assigned an RFC number that is a multiple of 100. The current version of this document as of this writing is RFC 3600, published in November, 2003.

The TCP/IP Protocol Stack

The development of the TCP/IP protocols began years before the documents defining the OSI reference model were published, but the protocols use layers in much the same way. Instead of the seven layers used by the OSI model, TCP/IP has its own four-layer networking model, which is defined in RFC 1122, "Requirements for Internet Hosts—Communication Layers." The layers are roughly analogous to the OSI model, as shown in Figure 7-1.

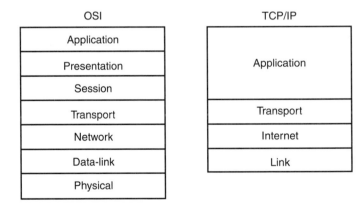

Figure 7-1   The four TCP/IP protocol layers, compared with the seven-layer OSI reference model

> **MORE INFO**   *Understanding the OSI Reference Model*   *For more information on the OSI model and the functions of its layers, see Chapter 1, "Networking Basics."*

The four TCP/IP layers, from bottom to top, are discussed in the following sections.

The Link Layer

The TCP/IP protocol suite includes two link layer protocols: Serial Line Internet Protocol (SLIP) and Point-to-Point Protocol (PPP). SLIP and PPP are used for most wide area network (WAN) connections. However, TCP/IP does not include physical layer specifications of any kind or complex local area network (LAN) protocols such as Ethernet and Token Ring. Therefore, although TCP/IP does maintain a layer that is comparable to the OSI model's data-link layer, in many cases the protocol operating at that layer is not part of the TCP/IP suite.

When a TCP/IP system uses SLIP or PPP at the link layer, the protocol stack assumes the presence of a network medium providing the physical connection, because SLIP and PPP do not include physical layer specifications. When the link layer functionality is provided by a non-TCP/IP protocol, such as on a LAN, TCP/IP assumes the presence of both a valid network medium and a protocol that provides an interface to that medium. While the TCP/IP standards do not define the link layer protocol itself on a LAN, there are TCP/IP standards that define the interaction between the internet layer protocol (IP) and the protocol providing the link layer functionality. For example, the use of Ethernet with TCP/IP is governed by standards such as the following:

- **RFC 826**   "Ethernet Address Resolution Protocol: Or Converting Network Protocol Addresses to 48-bit Ethernet Address [sic] for Transmission on Ethernet Hardware"

- **RFC 894**   "A Standard for the Transmission of IP Datagrams over Ethernet Networks"

While the functionality defined in the four layers of the TCP/IP protocol stack can encompass the OSI model from data-link to application layer, the TCP/IP protocol stack does not include a physical layer specification. Therefore, it is not a complete networking solution.

The Internet Layer

The TCP/IP internet layer is exactly equivalent to the network layer of the OSI reference model. Internet Protocol (IP) is the primary protocol operating at this layer. IP provides connectionless services to the protocols operating at the transport layer above it, including data encapsulation, routing, addressing, type of service specification, fragmentation, and limited error detection.

Two additional protocols, the Internet Control Message Protocol (ICMP) and the Internet Group Management Protocol (IGMP), also operate at the internet layer, as do some specialized dynamic routing protocols.

> **NOTE   Internet Capitalization**   In this context, the term "internet"
> is a generic reference to an internetwork and uses a lowercase "i," as
> opposed to the public, packet-switching Internet, with an uppercase
> "I." Be careful not to confuse the two.

The Transport Layer

The TCP/IP transport layer is equivalent to the transport layer in the OSI model. The TCP/IP suite includes two protocols at this layer: the Transmission Control Protocol (TCP) and the User Datagram Protocol (UDP). TCP and UDP provide connection-oriented and connectionless data transfer services, respectively.

The Application Layer

The TCP/IP application layer is roughly analogous to the presentation and application layers of the OSI model. The TCP/IP protocols at the application layer take two distinct forms, as follows:

- **User protocols**   Provide services directly to users, as in the case of the File Transfer Protocol (FTP) and Telnet protocols

Test your knowledge of the TCP/IP model layers by completing Exercise 7-1, "TCP/IP Layers and Protocols," now.

- **Support protocols**   Provide common system functions, as in the case of the Dynamic Host Configuration Protocol (DHCP) and Domain Name System (DNS) protocols

The TCP/IP standards define many application layer protocols, some of which are discussed later in this chapter.

TCP/IP PROTOCOLS

The following sections examine some of the protocols that operate at the various layers of the TCP/IP protocol stack.

Link Layer Protocols

SLIP and PPP are link layer protocols that systems use for wide area connections using telephone lines and many other types of physical layer technologies. SLIP is defined in RFC 1055, "A Nonstandard for Transmission of IP Datagrams over Serial Lines." PPP is more complex than SLIP and uses additional protocols to establish a connection between two systems. These protocols are defined in separate documents, including the following:

- RFC 1661, "The Point-to-Point Protocol"
- RFC 1662, "PPP in HDLC-Like Framing"

MORE INFO   **Using SLIP and PPP**   *For more information about SLIP and PPP, see Chapter 10, "Remote Network Access."*

Address Resolution Protocol (ARP)

The Address Resolution Protocol (ARP), as defined in RFC 826, "Ethernet Address Resolution Protocol," occupies an unusual place in the TCP/IP suite. ARP provides a service to IP, which seems to place it in the link layer (or the data-link layer of the OSI model). However, ARP has its own Ethertype value and its messages are carried directly within data-link layer frames, not encapsulated in IP datagrams, which justifies its placement at the internet (or network) layer protocol. Whatever its place in the protocol stack, however, ARP provides an essential service when TCP/IP is running on a LAN.

The TCP/IP protocols rely on IP addresses to identify networks and hosts, but when the computers are connected to an Ethernet or Token Ring LAN, the IP datagrams containing the IP addresses must eventually be encapsulated within data-link layer frames for transmission over the LAN. Because the data-link layer protocol uses its own hardware addresses (also called Media Access Control, or MAC, addresses) to identify other computers on the network, there must be an interface between the two addressing systems.

When IP constructs a datagram, it knows the IP address of the end system that is the packet's ultimate destination. That address identifies a computer connected to the local network or a system on another network. If the destination end system is on another network, IP uses the information in its routing table to determine what intermediate system should receive the datagram next. IP determines what system on the local network should next receive the datagram, but at this point IP only knows that system's IP address. Before Ethernet (or another data-link layer protocol) can actually transmit the datagram over the network, that destination IP address must be converted to a hardware address. ARP performs this conversion, so ARP provides the interface between the IP addressing system used at the internet (or network) layer and the hardware addresses used by the data-link layer protocols.

The ARP Message Format
To determine the hardware address of the system on the local network that will receive each datagram, IP generates an ARP message and broadcasts it over the LAN. The format of the ARP message is shown in Figure 7-2.

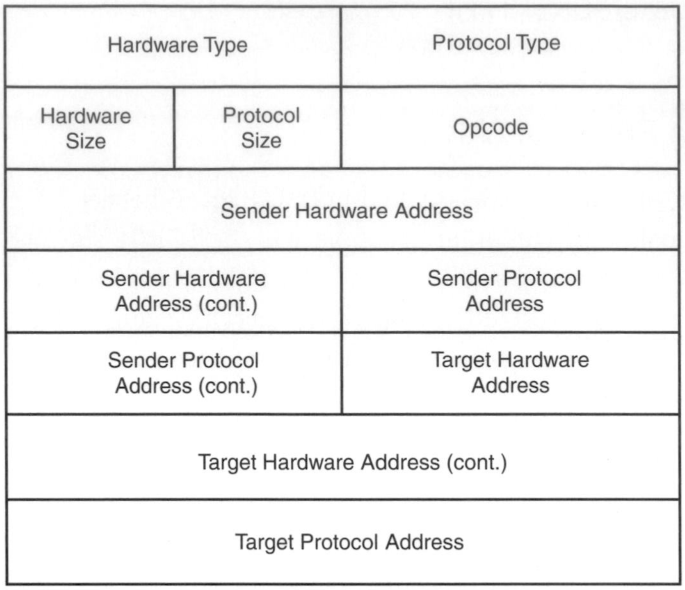

Hardware Type		Protocol Type	
Hardware Size	Protocol Size	Opcode	
Sender Hardware Address			
Sender Hardware Address (cont.)		Sender Protocol Address	
Sender Protocol Address (cont.)		Target Hardware Address	
Target Hardware Address (cont.)			
Target Protocol Address			

Figure 7-2   The ARP message format

The functions of the ARP message fields are as follows:

- **Hardware Type (2 bytes)**   Identifies the type of hardware addresses in the Sender Hardware Address and Target Hardware Address fields. For Ethernet and Token Ring networks, the value is 1.

- **Protocol Type (2 bytes)**   Identifies the type of addresses in the Sender Protocol Address and Target Protocol Address fields. The hexadecimal value for IP addresses is 0800 (the same as the Ethertype code for IP).

- **Hardware Size (1 byte)**   Specifies the size, in bytes, of the addresses in the Sender Hardware Address and Target Hardware Address fields. For Ethernet and Token Ring networks, the value is 6.

- **Protocol Size (1 byte)**   Specifies the size, in bytes, of the addresses in the Sender Protocol Address and Target Protocol Address fields. For IP addresses, the value is 4.

- **Opcode (2 bytes)**   Specifies the function of the packet, using one of the following values:

  - ❏ 1 ARP Request

  - ❏ 2 ARP Reply

  - ❏ 3 RARP Request

  - ❏ 4 RARP Reply

- **Sender Hardware Address (6 bytes)**   Contains the hardware address of the system generating the ARP message.

- **Sender Protocol Address (4 bytes)**   Contains the IP address of the system generating the ARP message.

- **Target Hardware Address (6 bytes)**   Contains the hardware address of the system for which the message is destined. In ARP Request messages, this field is blank.

- **Target Protocol Address (4 bytes)**   Contains the IP address of the system for which the message is intended.

> **NOTE**   *Understanding the Reverse Address Resolution Protocol (RARP)*   *RARP performs the opposite function of ARP. It enables a system to discover its IP address by transmitting its hardware address to an RARP server. RARP is a progenitor of the* **Bootstrap Protocol (BOOTP)** *and DHCP, which are used to automatically configure TCP/IP clients. RARP was once used by diskless workstations, but it is rarely if ever used today.*

ARP Communications

The process by which IP uses ARP to discover the hardware address of the destination system is as follows:

1. IP packages transport layer information into a datagram, inserting the IP address of the destination system into the Destination IP Address field of the IP header.

2. IP compares the network identifier in the destination IP address to its own network identifier and determines whether to send the datagram directly to the destination host or to a router on the local network. If it will send the datagram to a router, IP uses the information in its routing table to determine the IP address of the router that should receive the datagram.

3. IP generates an ARP Request packet containing its own hardware address and IP address in the Sender Hardware Address and Sender Protocol Address fields, respectively. The Target Protocol Address field contains the IP address of the datagram's next destination (host or router), as determined in step 2. The Target Hardware Address Field is left blank.

4. The system passes the ARP Request message down to the data-link layer protocol, which encapsulates it in a frame and transmits it as a broadcast to the entire local network.

5. The systems on the LAN receive the ARP Request message and read the contents of the Target Protocol Address field. If the Target Protocol Address value does not match the system's own IP address, the system silently discards the message and takes no further action.

6. If the system receiving the ARP Request message recognizes its own IP address in the Target Protocol Address field, it generates an ARP Reply message. The system copies the two sender address values from the ARP Request message into the respective target address values in the ARP Reply and copies the Target Protocol Address value from the request into the Sender Protocol Address field in the reply. The system then inserts its own hardware address into the Sender Hardware Address field.

7. The system transmits the ARP Reply message as a unicast message back to the computer that generated the request, using the hardware address in the Target Hardware Address field.

8. The system that originally generated the ARP Request message receives the ARP Reply and uses the newly supplied value in the Sender Hardware Address field to encapsulate the datagram in a data-link layer frame and transmit it to the desired destination as a unicast message.

ARP Caching

The ARP specification requires TCP/IP systems to maintain a cache of hardware addresses that the system has recently discovered by using the ARP protocol. This cache prevents systems from flooding the network with separate ARP Request broadcasts for each datagram transmitted. For example, when a system transmits a file in a sequence of TCP segments, usually only one ARP transaction is required because ARP, after it discovers the hardware address of the destination system for the sequence, stores that address in the cache. For each of the subsequent segments in the sequence, IP checks the ARP cache for a hardware address before generating a new ARP request. The individual TCP/IP implementation determines the length of time that unused ARP information remains in the cache, but it is usually relatively short to prevent the system from using outdated address information.

> **NOTE   Using Arp.exe**   Nearly all TCP/IP implementations include a command or utility that enables you to view and manipulate the contents of the ARP cache on a computer. For more information on working with the ARP cache, see Chapter 11, "Network Troubleshooting Tools."

Internet Protocol (IP)

IP is the internet (or network) layer protocol responsible for carrying the data generated by nearly all of the other TCP/IP protocols from the source system to its ultimate destination. IP is a connectionless protocol that provides two of the TCP/IP protocol stack's most important functions: addressing and routing. IP also provides fragmentation and error detection. For detailed information about IP and its functions, see Chapter 5, "Network Layer Protocols."

Internet Control Message Protocol (ICMP)

ICMP, as defined in RFC 792, "Internet Control Message Protocol," is, like ARP, a protocol that performs vital network administration tasks for IP. ICMP is considered to be an internet (or network) layer protocol, despite the fact that it carries no application data and its messages are carried within IP datagrams. In essence, ICMP is a partner to IP, because many of its functions are performed in response to IP activities.

ICMP uses only one message format for all its functions, which is illustrated in Figure 7-3.

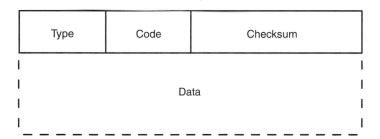

Figure 7-3   The ICMP message format

The functions of the ICMP message fields are as follows:

- **Type (1 byte)**   Contains a code that specifies the basic function of the message

- **Code (1 byte)**   Contains a code that indicates the specific function of the message with a given type

- **Checksum (2 bytes)**   Contains a checksum computed on the entire ICMP message that is used for error detection

- **Data (variable)**   Contains information related to the specific function of the message

ICMP Error Messages

ICMP performs many different functions, which can be divided into two basic categories: error messages and queries. Table 7-1 lists the ICMP error messaging functions, along with the Type and Code values for each function.

Table 7-1   **ICMP Error Messaging Functions**

Type	Code	Function
3	0	Net Unreachable
3	1	Host Unreachable
3	2	Protocol Unreachable
3	3	Port Unreachable
3	4	Fragmentation Needed And Don't Fragment Was Set
3	5	Source Route Failed
3	6	Destination Network Unknown
3	7	Destination Host Unknown
3	8	Source Host Isolated
3	9	Communication With Destination Network Is Administratively Prohibited
3	10	Communication With Destination Host Is Administratively Prohibited
3	11	Destination Network Unreachable For Type Of Service
3	12	Destination Host Unreachable For Type Of Service
4	0	Source Quench
5	0	Redirect Datagram For The Network (Or Subnet)
5	1	Redirect Datagram For The Host
5	2	Redirect Datagram For The Type Of Service And Network
5	3	Redirect Datagram For The Type Of Service And Host
11	0	Time To Live Exceeded In Transit
11	1	Fragment Reassembly Time Exceeded
12	0	Pointer Indicates The Error
12	1	Missing A Required Option
12	2	Bad Length
31	0	Datagram Conversion Error
32	0	Mobile Host Redirect

The primary function of ICMP is to report errors of various types. IP is a connectionless protocol, so no internet/network layer acknowledgments are returned to the sending system. TCP's connection-oriented transport layer service does return acknowledgments to the source end system, which could conceivably contain error messages, but these acknowledgments are generated only by the destination end system. If a problem occurs while a packet is being processed by an intermediate system (that is, a router), there is no mechanism built into IP or the transport layer protocol to inform the sender. ICMP provides this mechanism.

ICMP essentially functions as a monitor of internet layer communications, enabling both intermediate and end systems to return error messages to the sender. For example, when a router has a problem processing a datagram during the journey to its destination, it usually discards the packet. It relies on the transport layer protocol at the destination end system to detect the packet's absence and have it retransmitted. ICMP enables the router to generate a message informing the source end system of the problem. The source system can then take action to solve the problem in response to the ICMP message.

The Data field in an ICMP error message contains the entire 20-byte IP header of the datagram that caused the problem, plus the first 8 bytes of the datagram's own Data field. In most cases, the datagram contains TCP or UDP data, so the first 8 bytes contain some or all of the TCP or UDP header, including the Source Port and Destination Port numbers and, in the case of TCP, the segment's Sequence Number value. The inclusion of this data enables the source system receiving the ICMP message to identify the packet that caused the problem.

All TCP/IP systems must be able to generate ICMP error messages, but there are certain situations where the ICMP standard explicitly prohibits ICMP transmissions. The primary reason for these prohibitions is to prevent ICMP from generating large amounts of network traffic unnecessarily. These situations are as follows:

- TCP/IP systems must not generate ICMP error messages in response to other ICMP error messages. This rule prevents two systems from endlessly bouncing error messages back and forth. Systems can generate ICMP errors in response to ICMP queries, however.

- When a datagram is split into fragments, a TCP/IP system must generate an ICMP error message for the first fragment only.

- TCP/IP systems must never generate ICMP error messages in response to broadcast or multicast transmissions, transmissions with a source IP address of 0.0.0.0, or transmissions addressed to the loopback address.

ICMP error messages are informational only. The source end system receiving an ICMP error message does not respond to it, and it is not required to take action to correct the condition that caused the problem generating the error.

The following sections examine some of the most important ICMP error messages.

Destination Unreachable Messages

When an intermediate or end system attempts to forward a datagram to a resource that is inaccessible, it usually generates an ICMP Destination Unreachable message and transmits it back to the source system. Destination Unreachable messages all have a Type value of 3; the Code value specifies exactly what resource is unavailable, using the values shown in Table 7-1. For example, when a router fails to transmit a datagram to the destination system on a local network, it returns a Destination Host Unreachable message to the sender. If the router can't transmit the datagram to another router, it generates a Destination Network Unreachable message. If the datagram reaches the destination system but the designated transport layer or application layer protocol is unavailable, the system returns a Protocol Unreachable or Port Unreachable message.

Source Quench Messages

Source Quench messages function as rudimentary flow control mechanisms for the internet layer. When a router's memory buffers are nearly full, it can send a Source Quench message to the source system, which instructs it to slow down its transmission rate. When the Source Quench messages cease, the sending system can gradually increase the rate again. Source Quench messages have a Type value of 4.

Redirect Messages

Routers generate ICMP Redirect messages to inform a host or another router that there is a more efficient route to a particular destination. Many internetworks have a matrix of routers that enables packets to take different paths to a single destination, as shown in Figure 7-4. If System 1 sends a packet to Router A in an attempt to get it to System 2, Router A forwards the packet to Router B, but it also transmits an ICMP Redirect message back to System 1, informing it that it can send packets destined for System 2 directly to Router B.

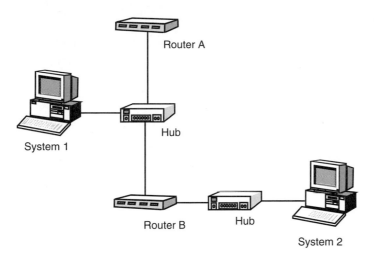

Figure 7-4   ICMP Redirect messages enable routers to inform other systems of more efficient routes.

The Data field in the ICMP Redirect message contains the usual 28 bytes from the datagram in question (the 20-byte IP header plus the first 8 bytes of the Data field) plus an additional 4-byte Gateway Internet Address field. The Gateway Internet Address field contains the IP address of the router that the system should use from now on when transmitting datagrams to that particular destination. By changing the router, the source system saves a hop on the packet's path through the internetwork and reduces the processing burden on Router A.

Time Exceeded Messages

When a TCP/IP system creates an IP datagram, it inserts a value in the IP header's Time To Live (TTL) field. Each router that processes the datagram reduces this value by 1 during the packet's journey through the internetwork. If the TTL value reaches 0 during the journey, the last router to receive the packet discards it and transmits an ICMP Time Exceeded (Type 11, Code 0) message to the sender, informing it that the packet has not reached its destination and telling it why. This is called a Time To Live Exceeded In Transit message.

> **NOTE   ICMP and Traceroute**   The Time To Live Exceeded In Transit message is the basis for the **Traceroute** program included in most TCP/IP implementations. For more information about Traceroute, see Chapter 11, "Network Troubleshooting Tools."

Another type of Time Exceeded message is used when a destination system is attempting to reassemble datagram fragments and one or more fragments fail to arrive in a timely manner. The system then generates a Fragment Reassembly Time Exceeded (Type 11, Code 1) message and sends it back to the source system.

ICMP Query Messages

The other function of ICMP messages is to carry requests to another system for some type of information and also to return the replies containing that information. Table 7-2 lists the ICMP query functions, along with the Type and Code values for each function.

Table 7-2   **ICMP Query Functions**

Type	Code	Function
0	0	Echo Reply
8	0	Echo Request
9	0	Router Advertisement
10	0	Router Solicitation
13	0	Timestamp
14	0	Timestamp Reply
15	0	Information Request
16	0	Information Reply
17	0	Address Mask Request
18	0	Address Mask Reply
30	0	Traceroute
33	0	IPv6 Where-Are-You
34	0	IPv6 I-Am-Here
35	0	Mobile Registration Request
36	0	Mobile Registration Reply

The ICMP query messages are not reactions to an outside process, as error messages are. However, external programs, such as the TCP/IP **Ping** utility, can generate query messages.

Because query messages aren't generated in response to an external problem, their Data fields do not contain the IP header and data from another datagram. Instead, the various types of query messages include more diverse information in the Data field, according to their functions. The following sections examine the most important query message types.

Echo Request and Echo Reply Messages

The Echo Request (Type 8, Code 0) and Echo Reply (Type 0, Code 0) messages form the basis for the Ping utility and are essentially a means to test whether another TCP/IP system on the network is up and running. Both messages contain 2-byte Identifier and 2-byte Sequence Number subfields in the Data field. These fields are used to associate requests and replies, plus a certain amount of padding, as dictated by the Ping utility. Ping generates a series of Echo Request messages and transmits them to a destination system specified by the user. When the destination system receives the messages, it reverses the values of the Source IP Address and Destination IP Address fields, changes the Type value from 8 to 0, recalculates the checksum, and transmits the messages back to the sender. When Ping receives the Echo Reply messages, it assumes that the destination system is functioning properly.

> **NOTE** **ICMP and Ping**   For more information about Ping, see "TCP/IP Utilities," in Chapter 11, "Network Troubleshooting Tools."

Router Solicitation and Router Advertisement Messages

Strictly speaking, Router Solicitation (Type 10, Code 0) and Router Advertisement (Type 9, Code 0) messages cannot truly be called routing protocols, because they don't provide information about the efficiency of particular routes, but they do enable a TCP/IP system to discover the address of a default gateway on the local network. The process begins when a workstation broadcasts a Router Solicitation message to the local network. The routers on the network respond with unicast Router Advertisement messages containing the router's IP address and other information. The workstation then uses the information in these replies to configure the default gateway entry in its routing table.

TCP/IP Transport Layer Protocols

TCP and UDP are the transport layer protocols that provide connection-oriented and connectionless service to the other protocols in the TCP/IP stack. All application layer protocols use either TCP or UDP to transmit data across the network, depending on the services they require. For more information about TCP and UDP, see Chapter 6, "Transport Layer Protocols."

Application Layer Protocols

The protocols that operate at the application layer of the TCP/IP model are not concerned with the network communication issues addressed by the link, internet, and transport layer protocols. An application-layer protocol is concerned solely with the communication between a client program and a server program on another computer; the protocol assumes that there is a connection between the two systems that provides an appropriate quality of service.

Application layer protocols use different combinations of protocols at the lower layers to achieve the level of service they require. For example, when servers use Hypertext Transfer Protocol (HTTP) and FTP to transmit entire files to client systems, the files must be received without error. These protocols, therefore, use a combination of TCP and IP to achieve connection-oriented, reliable communications. On the other hand, DHCP and DNS servers exchange small messages between clients and servers that can easily be retransmitted if necessary, so they use the connectionless service provided by UDP and IP.

Application Layer Communications

Many application layer protocols use a communications method that differs from that of the protocols in the TCP/IP suite discussed so far. The protocols at the lower layers of the TCP/IP model use a message format based on fields containing codes that perform specific functions. For example, the function of an ICMP message is indicated by the values of its Type and Code fields. By contrast, many application layer protocols use text commands rather than function codes. When you use a client program to log on to an FTP server, for example, the client sends the following commands in clear text:

```
USER username
PASS password
```

The *username* and *password* variables contain the name of the account the client will use to access the server and the password associated with that account. In response, the FTP server sends text-based reply codes that indicate whether the client's commands succeeded or failed. As the FTP session proceeds, the client can send commands requesting the server to perform file management and transfer operations.

Application Layer Protocol Functions

Some of the most important TCP/IP application layer protocols are as follows:

- **Domain Name System (DNS)**   A system used by TCP/IP systems to resolve Internet host names to the IP addresses they need to communicate.

- **Dynamic Host Configuration Protocol (DHCP)**   A protocol that workstations use to request TCP/IP configuration parameter settings, such as IP addresses and subnet masks, from a server.

- **File Transfer Protocol (FTP)**   A protocol used to transfer files between TCP/IP systems. An FTP client can browse through the directory structure of a connected server and select files to download or upload. FTP is unique in that it uses two separate ports for its communications. When an FTP client connects to a server, it uses TCP port 21 to establish a control connection. When the user initiates a file download, the program opens a second connection, using port 20 for the file transfer. This data connection is closed when the file transfer is complete, but the control connection remains open until the client terminates it.

- **Hypertext Transfer Protocol (HTTP)**   A protocol used by Web clients and servers to exchange file requests and files. A client browser opens a TCP connection to a server and requests a particular file. The server replies by sending that file, which the browser displays as a home page. HTTP messages can also contain fields containing information about the communicating systems.

- **Internet Mail Access Protocol 4 (IMAP4)**   A protocol that e-mail clients use to access e-mail messages on a server. Unlike Post Office Protocol 3 (POP3), IMAP can store messages permanently on the server, which enables clients to create e-mail folders and manage their messages directly on the server.

- **Network Time Protocol (NTP)**   A protocol that enables computers to synchronize their clocks with other computers on the network by exchanging time signals.

- **Post Office Protocol 3 (POP3)**   A protocol that e-mail clients use to access e-mail messages on a server. Unlike IMAP, POP3 provides temporary mail storage only. Clients typically retrieve their messages from a POP3 server and immediately delete them from the server, relying on the client program for permanent mail storage.

- **Secure Hypertext Transfer Protocol (S-HTTP or HTTPS)**   A security protocol that works with HTTP to provide user authentication and data encryption services to Web client/server transactions.

- **Simple Mail Transfer Protocol (SMTP)**   A protocol used by e-mail applications to transmit messages across a network. All e-mail between servers uses SMTP, and clients use the protocol to send their outgoing messages to an e-mail server.

- **Simple Network Management Protocol (SNMP)**   A network management protocol used to gather information about network components. Remote programs called *agents* gather information and transmit it to a central network management console, using SNMP messages.

Test your knowledge of the protocols in the TCP/IP suite by completing Exercise 7-2, "TCP/IP Protocols," now.

- **Telnet**   A command-line terminal emulation program that lets a user log in to a remote computer on the network and execute commands there, using what is called a *network virtual terminal.*

- **Trivial File Transfer Protocol (TFTP)**   A minimized, low-overhead version of FTP that can transfer files across a network. TFTP uses UDP instead of TCP and does not include FTP's authentication and user interface features. TFTP was originally designed for use on diskless workstations that had to download an executable system file from a network server in order to boot.

> **NOTE   Exam Objectives**   Objective 2.5 for the Network + exam requires students to be able to define the purpose, function, and/or use of the following protocols within TCP/IP: IP, TCP, UDP, FTP, TFTP, SMTP, HTTP, HTTPS, POP3/IMAP4 , TELNET, ICMP, ARP, and NTP.

IP ROUTING

Routing is one of the most important and most complex operations performed by TCP/IP. The protocols were designed with scalability in mind, but no one in the 1970s could have predicted the massive growth of the Internet that would occur two decades later. While packets might pass through a handful of routers on a private internetwork, Internet packets routinely pass through a dozen or more routers on the way to their destinations. Some of the routers on the Internet have to maintain information about many different networks, and the process of compiling and maintaining this information makes the Internet routing process very complex.

Understanding Routing

A router is a system connected to two or more networks that forwards packets from one network to another. Routers operate at the network layer of the OSI reference model, so they can connect networks running different data-link layer protocols and different network media. On a small internetwork, a router's job can be quite simple. For example, when two LANs are connected by one router, the router simply receives packets from one network and forwards only those destined for the other network. On a large internetwork, however, routers must forward packets to several different networks, and in many cases, networks have more than one router connected to them, as shown in Figure 7-5. This redundant router arrangement enables packets to take different paths to a given destination. If one router on the network fails, packets can bypass it and still reach their destinations.

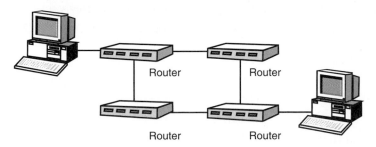

Figure 7-5   Internetworks with redundant routers provide multiple paths between two end systems.

On a complex internetwork, an important part of a router's job is to select the most efficient route to a packet's destination. Usually, this is the path that gets a packet to its destination by using the fewest hops (that is, by passing through the smallest number of routers). Routers share information about the networks to which they are attached with other routers in the immediate vicinity. As a result, a composite picture of the internetwork eventually develops, but on a large internetwork such as the Internet, no single router has the entire image. Instead, the routers work together by passing each packet from router to router, one hop at a time.

> **NOTE**   **Understanding Packet Routing**   For more information about the packet-routing process, see Chapter 3, "Network Connection Hardware."

Router Products

A router can be a stand-alone hardware device or a regular computer. Server operating systems such as Microsoft Windows 2003 Server, Microsoft Windows 2000, Microsoft Windows NT, NetWare, and many UNIX/Linux distributions can route IP traffic. Creating a router out of a computer running one of these operating systems is simply a matter of installing two network interface adapters, connecting the computer to two different networks, and configuring it to route traffic between those networks. In TCP/IP terminology, a computer with two or more network interfaces is called a **multihomed** system.

Most versions of Windows also include a feature called Internet Connection Sharing (ICS), which enables other computers on the LAN to access the Internet through one computer's dial-up or broadband connection to an Internet service provider (ISP). There are also third-party software products that provide Internet connection sharing. In essence, these products are software routers that enable your computer to forward packets between the local network and the network run by your ISP. Using these products, all of the computers on a LAN installed in a home or a small business can share a single computer's connection to the Internet, whether it uses a dial-up modem, cable modem, or some other type of connection.

When you use a computer as an IP router, each network interface adapter must have its own IP address that is appropriate for the network to which it is attached. When one of the two networks is an ISP connection, the ISP's server typically supplies the address for that interface. The other IP address is the one that you assign to your network interface adapter when you install it.

A stand-alone router is a hardware device that is essentially a special-purpose computer. The device has multiple built-in network interface adapters, a processor, and memory for storing its routing information and temporary packet buffers. Routers are available at a wide range of prices and with a variety of capabilities. You can use an inexpensive stand-alone router that lets you share an Internet connection with a small network for less than a hundred dollars, or you can use enormously expensive rack-mounted models that connect the LANs of a large internetwork or provide wide area connectivity to remote offices or ISPs.

Understanding Routing Tables

The routing table is the heart of any router; without it, all that's left is the mechanics of packet forwarding. The routing table holds the information that the router uses to forward packets to the proper destinations. However, not only routers have routing tables; every TCP/IP system has a routing table, which it uses to determine where to send its packets. Routing is essentially the process of determining what data-link layer protocol address the system should use to reach a particular IP address. If a system wants to transmit a packet to a computer on the local network, for example, the routing table instructs it to address the packet directly to that system. This is called a *direct route*. In this case, the Destination IP Address field in the IP header and the Destination Address field in the data-link layer protocol header refer to the same computer.

If a packet's destination is on another network, the routing table contains the address of the router that the system should use to reach that destination. In this case, the Destination IP Address and Destination Address fields specify different systems because the data-link layer address has to refer to a system on the local network, and for the packet to reach a computer on a different network, that local system must be a router. Because the two addresses refer to different systems, this is called an *indirect route*.

Routing Table Format

A routing table is essentially a list of network (and possibly host) addresses, plus the addresses of routers that the system can use to reach them. The arrangement of the information in the routing table can differ, depending on the operating system. The routing table for a Red Hat Linux system is shown in Figure 7-6.

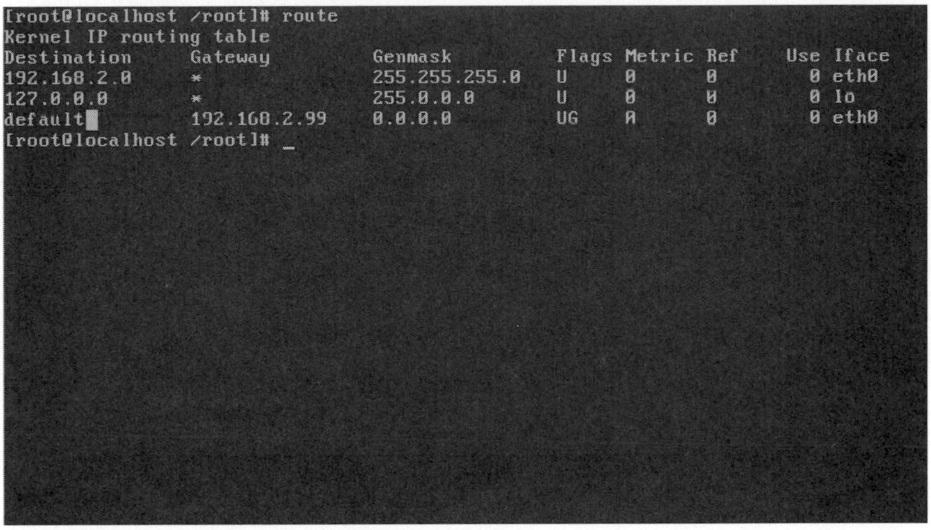

```
[root@localhost /root]# route
Kernel IP routing table
Destination     Gateway         Genmask         Flags Metric Ref    Use Iface
192.168.2.0     *               255.255.255.0   U     0      0        0 eth0
127.0.0.0       *               255.0.0.0       U     0      0        0 lo
default         192.168.2.99    0.0.0.0         UG    A      0        0 eth0
[root@localhost /root]# _
```

Figure 7-6   A Red Hat Linux routing table

The routing table for a Microsoft Windows XP workstation is shown in Figure 7-7.

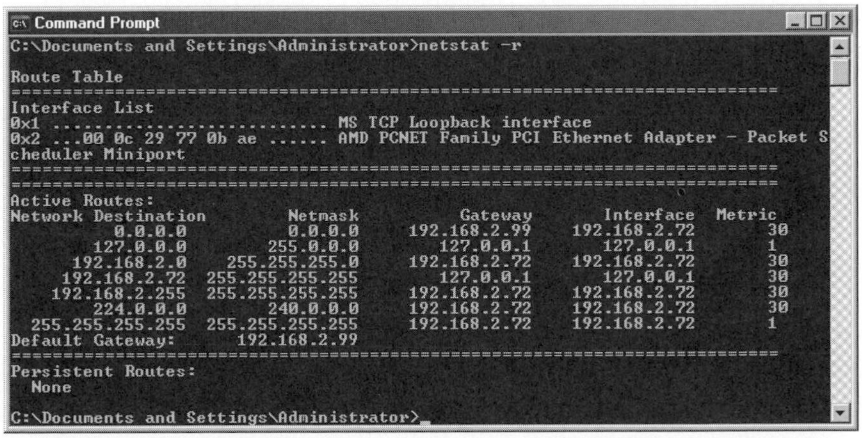

```
Command Prompt                                                    _ □ ×
C:\Documents and Settings\Administrator>netstat -r

Route Table
===========================================================================
Interface List
0x1 ........................... MS TCP Loopback interface
0x2 ...00 0c 29 77 0b ae ...... AMD PCNET Family PCI Ethernet Adapter - Packet S
cheduler Miniport
===========================================================================
===========================================================================
Active Routes:
Network Destination        Netmask          Gateway       Interface  Metric
          0.0.0.0          0.0.0.0     192.168.2.99   192.168.2.72      30
        127.0.0.0        255.0.0.0       127.0.0.1      127.0.0.1       1
      192.168.2.0    255.255.255.0    192.168.2.72   192.168.2.72      30
     192.168.2.72  255.255.255.255       127.0.0.1      127.0.0.1      30
    192.168.2.255  255.255.255.255    192.168.2.72   192.168.2.72      30
        224.0.0.0        240.0.0.0    192.168.2.72   192.168.2.72      30
  255.255.255.255  255.255.255.255    192.168.2.72   192.168.2.72       1
Default Gateway:       192.168.2.99
===========================================================================
Persistent Routes:
  None

C:\Documents and Settings\Administrator>
```

Figure 7-7   A Windows XP routing table

The functions listed in the Windows routing table are as follows:

- **Network Destination**   Specifies the IP address of the network or host for which routing information is provided.

■ **Netmask**   Specifies the subnet mask for the value in the Network Destination column. As with any subnet mask, the system uses the Netmask value to determine which parts of the Network Destination value are the network identifier, the subnet identifier (if any), and the host identifier.

■ **Gateway**   Specifies the IP address of the router that the system should use to send datagrams to the network or host identified in the Network Destination column. On a LAN, the hardware address for the system identified by the Gateway value will become the Destination Address value in the packet's data-link layer protocol header.

■ **Interface**   Specifies the IP address of the network interface that the computer should use to transmit packets to the system identified in the Gateway column.

■ **Metric**   Contains a value that specifies the efficiency of the route. Metric values are relative—a lower value indicates a more efficient route than a higher value. When a routing table contains multiple routes to the same destination, the system always uses the table entry with the lower Metric value.

> **NOTE   Routers and Gateways**   In TCP/IP terminology, the term "gateway" is synonymous with the term "router." However, this is not the case in other networking disciplines, where a gateway can refer to a different device that connects networks at the application layer instead of the network layer.

Default Routing Table Entries

The sample Windows XP routing table shown in Figure 7-7 contains the typical entries for a workstation that is not functioning as a router. The functions of each entry in the sample routing table are as follows:

■ **Entry 1**   The value 0.0.0.0 in the Network Destination column, found in the first entry in the table, identifies the default gateway entry. The default gateway is the router on the LAN that the system uses when there are no routing table entries that match the Destination IP Address of an outgoing packet. Even if multiple routers are available on the local network, a routing table can have only one functional default gateway entry. On a typical workstation that is not a router, the majority of packets go to the default gateway; the only packets that do not use this router are those destined for systems on the local network. The Gateway column contains the IP address of a router on the local network, and the Interface column contains the IP address of the network interface adapter that connects the system to the network.

- **Entry 2**   The IP address in the Network Destination column, 127.0.0.0, is designated by the IP standard as a TCP/IP loopback address. IP automatically routes all packets destined for any address on the 127.0.0.0 network back to the incoming packet queue on the same computer. The packets never reach the data-link layer or leave the computer. This entry ensures the loopback functionality by specifying that the system should use its own loopback address (127.0.0.1) as the "router" to the destination.

- **Entry 3**   The IP address of the network interface adapter in the computer to which this routing table belongs is 192.168.2.72. Therefore, the third entry in the sample routing table contains the address of the local network on which the computer is located. The Network Destination and Netmask values indicate that it is a Class C network with the address 192.168.2.0. This is the entry that the system uses for direct routes when it transmits packets to other systems on the local network. The Gateway and Interface columns both contain the IP address of the computer's network interface adapter, indicating that the computer should use itself as the gateway. In other words, the computer should transmit the data-link layer frames to the same computer identified by the Destination IP Address value in the datagrams.

- **Entry 4**   The fourth entry in the sample routing table contains the host address of the computer itself. Routing tables can contain host address entries, as well as network address entries. This entry instructs the system to transmit data addressed to itself to the loopback address (127.0.0.1). IP always searches the routing table for host address entries before searching for network address entries; therefore, when processing any packets addressed to the computer's own address (192.168.2.72), IP would select this entry before the entry above it, which specifies the system's network address.

- **Entries 5 and 7**   The fifth and seventh entries in the sample routing table contain broadcast addresses, both the generic IP broadcast address (255.255.255.255) and the local network's broadcast address (192.168.2.255). In both of these cases, packets are transmitted to the computers on the local network, so the system again uses itself as a gateway.

■ **Entry 6**   The sixth entry in the sample routing table contains the network address for the multicast addresses designated by the IANA for specific purposes.

The routing table on a router is often considerably more complex than this sample because it contains entries for all of the networks to which it is attached, as well as entries provided either manually by administrators or dynamically by routing protocols. A router also makes more use of the value in the Interface column. On a workstation with one network interface adapter, there is only one interface to use, so the Interface column is actually superfluous. Routers and multihomed systems have at least two network interfaces, so the value in the Interface column is a crucial part of transmitting a packet correctly.

> **NOTE** **Exam Objectives**   *Objective 2.9 for the Network + exam requires students to be able to identify the purpose of subnetting and default gateways.*

Selecting a Routing Table Entry

When a TCP/IP system has data to transmit, the IP protocol selects a route for each packet, using the procedure shown in Figure 7-8.

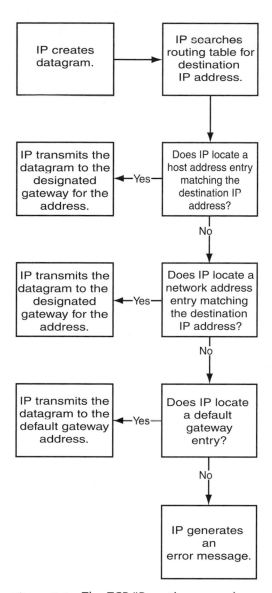

Figure 7-8   The TCP/IP routing procedure

The procedure illustrated in Figure 7-8 is described in the following steps:

1. After packaging the transport layer information into a datagram, IP compares the Destination IP Address for the packet with the routing table, looking for a host address with the same value. A host address entry in the table has a full IP address in the Network Destination column and the value 255.255.255.255 in the Netmask column.

2. If there is no host address entry that exactly matches the Destination IP Address value, the system then scans the routing table's Network Destination and Netmask columns for an entry that matches the address's network and subnet identifiers. If there is more than one

entry in the routing table that contains the desired network and subnet identifiers, IP selects the entry with the lower value in the Metric column.

3. If there are no table entries that match the network and subnet identifiers of the Destination IP Address value, the system searches for a default gateway entry that has a value of 0.0.0.0 in the Network Destination and Netmask columns.

4. If there is no default gateway entry, the system generates an error message. If the system transmitting the datagram is a router, it transmits an ICMP Destination Unreachable message back to the end system that originated the datagram. If the system transmitting the datagram is itself an end system, the error message gets passed back up to the application that generated the data.

5. When the system locates a viable routing table entry, IP prepares to transmit the datagram to the router identified in the Gateway column. The system obtains the hardware address of the router by accessing the ARP cache or performing an ARP procedure.

Test your knowledge of the process by which a TCP/IP system uses its routing table by completing Exercise 7-3, "Routing Tables," now.

6. Once the system has discovered the router's hardware address, IP passes it and the datagram down to the data-link layer protocol associated with the address specified in the Interface column. The data-link layer protocol constructs a frame, using the router's hardware address in its Destination Address field, and transmits the frame out over the designated interface.

Building Routing Tables

Now that you have learned how TCP/IP systems use the routing table to determine the destination for a packet, the next thing to consider is how the information gets into the routing table. The sample routing table shown in Figure 7-7 contains only the default entries created automatically by a workstation. This is known as *minimal routing*. Routers can have many more entries, depending on the size of the internetwork and the method used to create the table.

Static and Dynamic Routing

There are two techniques for updating the routing table: static routing and dynamic routing. In **static routing,** a network administrator manually creates routing table entries, using a program designed for this purpose. In **dynamic routing,** routing table entries are automatically created by specialized routing protocols that run on the router systems. Two examples of these dynamic protocols are the Routing Information Protocol (RIP) and the Open Shortest Path

First (OSPF) protocol, both of which are discussed later in this chapter. Routers use these protocols to exchange messages containing routing information with other nearby routers. Each router is, in essence, sharing its routing table with other routers.

It should be obvious that although static routing can be an effective routing solution on a small internetwork, it isn't a suitable solution for a large installation. If you have a network with a configuration that never changes, or one with only one possible route to each destination, running a routing protocol can be a waste of energy and bandwidth.

The advantage of dynamic routing, in addition to reducing the network administrator's workload, is that it automatically compensates for changes in the network infrastructure. For example, if a particular router goes down, its failure to communicate with the other routers nearby means that it will eventually be deleted from their routing tables, and packets will take different routes to their destinations. When that router comes back online, it will resume communications with the other routers and will be again added to their tables. On an internetwork as large as the Internet, for which the IP routing system was designed, dynamic routing is essential; it would be all but impossible for administrators to keep up with the constant changes occurring on the network without dynamic routing.

Managing Static Routes

Static routes are created by using a utility supplied with the TCP/IP protocol stack to create, modify, or delete entries in the routing table. In most cases, the utility runs from the command line. Stand-alone routers run their own proprietary software that uses a command set created by the manufacturer. The utilities for various operating systems capable of static routing are described in the following sections.

Managing Static Routes in Windows

All Windows operating systems include a command line program called Route.exe, which you can use to modify the contents of the system's routing table. The syntax for Route.exe is as follows:

```
ROUTE [-f] [-p] [command [destination] [MASK netmask] [gateway] [METRIC metric]
[IF interface]
```

- **-f** Deletes all entries from the routing table. When used with the ADD command, deletes the entire table before adding the new entry.

- **-p**   When used with the ADD command, creates a persistent entry in the routing table. A *persistent route* is one that remains in the table permanently, even after the system is restarted. When -p is used with the PRINT keyword, the system displays only the persistent routes in the table.

- ***command***   Contains one of the following keywords that specifies the function of the command:

    - PRINT Displays the contents of the routing table. When used with the -p parameter, displays only the persistent routes in the routing table.

    - ADD Creates a new entry in the routing table.

    - DELETE Deletes an existing entry from the routing table.

    - CHANGE Modifies the parameters of an entry in the routing table.

- ***destination***   Specifies the network or host address of the table entry being managed.

- **MASK *netmask***   Specifies the subnet mask to be applied to the address specified by the *destination* variable.

- ***gateway***   Specifies the IP address of the router that the system should use to reach the host or network specified by the *destination* variable.

- **METRIC *metric***   Specifies a value that indicates the relative efficiency of the route in the table entry.

- **IF *interface***   Specifies the number of the network interface adapter that the system should use to reach the router specified by the *gateway* variable.

For example, if you were using the network configuration shown in Figure 7-9 to create an entry that informs Router A of the existence of Router B on the same LAN, you would execute a Route.exe command like the following at the Router A system's command line:

```
ROUTE ADD 192.168.5.0 MASK 255.255.255.0 192.168.2.7 IF 1 METRIC 1
```

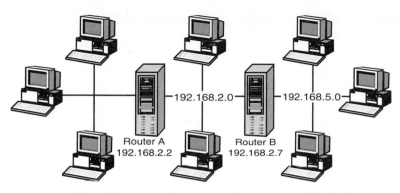

Figure 7-9   By adding a static route to the routing table in the Router A system, Router A can forward packets to Router B.

The functions of the Route.exe parameters in this particular command are as follows:

- **ADD**   Indicates that the program should create a new entry in the existing routing table.

- **192.168.5.0**   The address of the other network to which Router B provides access.

- **MASK 255.255.255.0**   The subnet mask to be applied to the destination address, which in this case indicates that the address represents an unsubnetted Class C network.

- **192.168.2.7**   The address of the network interface adapter that connects both Router A and Router B to the same network.

- **IF 1**   The number of the network interface adapter in Router A that provides access to the network it shares with Router B.

- **METRIC 1**   Indicates that the destination network is one hop away.

This new routing table entry essentially tells Router A that when it has traffic to send to any computer on the network with the address 192.168.5.0, it should send the traffic to the router with the address 192.168.2.7, using the Router A network interface adapter designated by the system as interface 1.

On a computer running Windows 2003 Server or Windows 2000 Server that is functioning as a router, you can also use the Routing And Remote Access console to create static routing table entries, using the interface shown in Figure 7-10.

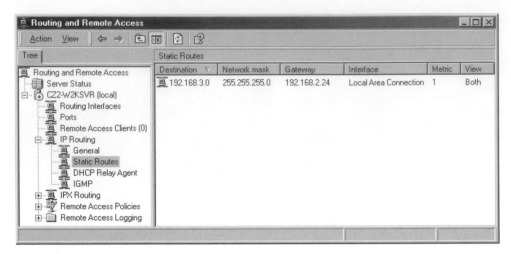

Figure 7-10   Creating static routes using the Routing And Remote Access console

However, the functionality for editing routing tables in this console is limited. You can create new entries in the routing table and manage or delete the static routes you have already created using the console, but you cannot manage the default routing table entries or static routes created with Route.exe. Route.exe is the more comprehensive tool because it can manage all of the routing table's entries, whatever their source.

Managing Static Routes in UNIX/Linux

Most UNIX and Linux distributions use a daemon called *routed* (pronounced route-dee) to route IP traffic. To modify the contents of the routed routing table, you use a tool called *route*, which uses the following syntax:

```
route command [-net|-host] destination [netmask netmask] [gw gateway]
[metric metric] [mss bytes] [dev interface]
```

- ***command***   Contains one of the following keywords that specifies the function of the command:

  - ❑ add Creates a new entry in the routing table

  - ❑ del Deletes an existing entry from the routing table

- ***destination***   Specifies the network or host address value of the table entry being managed.

- **-net|-host**   Specifies whether the value of the *destination* variable is a network or host address.

- **netmask *netmask***   Specifies the subnet mask to be applied to the address specified by the *destination* variable.

- **gw *gateway***   Specifies the IP address of the router that the system should use to reach the host or network specified by the *destination* variable.

- **metric *metric***   Specifies a value that indicates the relative efficiency of the route in the table entry.

- **mss *bytes***   Specifies the maximum segment size (mss) for packets using this route.

- **dev *interface***   Specifies the device name of the network interface adapter the system should use to reach the router specified by the *gateway* variable. When this is the final parameter in the command line, the word **dev** is optional.

Therefore, the UNIX/Linux route command for creating the same static route specified in the Windows Route.exe example provided earlier would be as follows:

```
route add -net 192.168.5.0 mask 255.255.255.0 gw 192.168.2.7 metric 1 eth0
```

Managing Static Routes in NetWare

On a NetWare server, you can create static routes from the server command prompt by using the Routecon.nlm utility, or you can use the menu-driven Inetcfg.nlm program. The syntax for Routecon.nlm is as follows:

```
routecon command [-net|-host] destination gateway [-netmask netmask]
```

- ***command***   Contains one of the following keywords that specifies the function of the command:
    - ❏ add Creates a new entry in the routing table
    - ❏ delete Deletes an existing entry from the routing table
    - ❏ change Modifies the parameters of an entry in the routing table
    - ❏ get Displays an entry in the routing table

- **-net|-host**   Specifies whether the value of the *destination* variable is a network or host address

- ***destination***   Specifies the network or host address value of the table entry being managed

- ***gateway***   Specifies the IP address of the router that the system should use to reach the host or network specified by the *destination* variable

■ **netmask** *netmask*   Specifies the subnet mask to be applied to the address specified by the *destination* variable

Routecon.nlm cannot display the system's entire routing table. When you run the program with the get command, you must specify a destination value identifying a specific entry in the table, which then appears as shown in Figure 7-11.

```
Destination   : 192.168.2.0
Gateway       : 192.168.2.73
Interface     : PCNTNW_2_EII
Flags         : UP STATIC
MTU           : 1500
Hop count     : 1
Netmask       : 255.255.255.0

get net 192.168.2.0 gateway 192.168.2.73

<Press any key to exit>_
```

Figure 7-11   A NetWare routing table entry as displayed by Routecon.nlm

Inetcfg.nlm is a menu-driven tool that you load from the server command prompt. This tool enables you to configure a wide variety of networking parameters for a NetWare server, including static routing table entries. You can display the contents of the routing table, as shown in Figure 7-12, and create new routing table entries, using the interface shown in Figure 7-13.

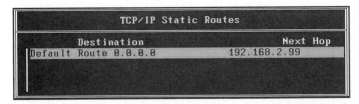

```
                 TCP/IP Static Routes

          Destination                    Next Hop
Default Route 0.0.0.0                 192.168.2.99
```

Figure 7-12   A NetWare routing table as displayed by Inetcfg.nlm

```
                 Static Route Configuration

Route Type:                   Network
IP Address of Network/Host:   (Not Specified)
Subnetwork Mask:              (Not Specified)
Next Hop Router on Route:     (Not Specified)

Metric for this route:        1
Type of route:                Passive
```

Figure 7-13   Creating a static route using Inetcfg.nlm

Dynamic Routing

A router only has direct knowledge of the networks to which it is connected. When an internetwork has two or more routers connected to it, dynamic routing enables each of the routers to know about the others and create routing table entries that specify the networks to which the other routers are connected. Dynamic routing uses special application layer protocols that are designed only for router-to-router communications.

Consider the example network shown in Figure 7-14:

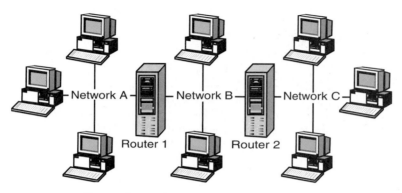

Figure 7-14   Dynamic routing

- Router 1 has direct knowledge of Networks A and B because the system is connected to both.

- Router 2 has knowledge of Networks B and C for the same reason.

- Router 1 has no direct knowledge of Network C because it is not connected to it.

- By using a dynamic routing protocol, Router 2 can share its knowledge of Network C with Router 1.

- After Router 2 shares its routing table information for Network C with Router 1, Router 1 can add an entry for the distant Network C to its routing table.

On a larger internetwork, the process is repeated throughout the enterprise. Routers compile information about the networks to which they are connected and share it with other routers, using a routing protocol. By sharing their information in this way, routers can obtain information about distant networks and can route packets more efficiently as a result.

There are many different routing protocols in the TCP/IP suite. On a private internetwork, a single routing protocol such as RIP is usually sufficient to keep all of the routers updated with the latest network information. On the Internet, however, routers use various protocols, depending on their place in the network hierarchy. Routing protocols are generally divided into two categories: *Interior Gateway Protocols (IGPs)* and *Exterior Gateway Protocols (EGPs)*. On the Internet, a collection of networks that fall within the same administrative domain is called an *autonomous system (AS)*. The routers within an AS all communicate using an IGP selected by the administrators. EGPs are used for communications between AS's, as shown in Figure 7-15.

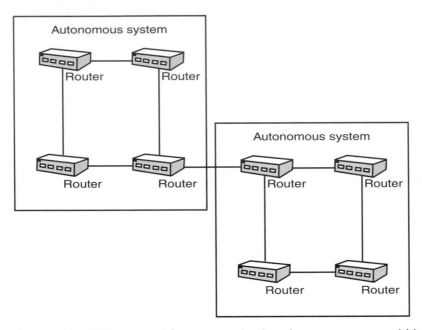

Figure 7-15   IGPs are used for communications between routers within an AS, and EGPs are used for communications between routers in different autonomous systems.

The following sections examine some of the most common dynamic routing protocols.

Routing Information Protocol (RIP)

RIP is one of the most commonly used IGPs in the TCP/IP suite and on networks around the world. Originally designed for UNIX systems, RIP was eventually ported to many other platforms and was standardized in RFC 1058 in 1988. Some years later, RIP was updated to a version 2, which was published as RFC 2453.

Most RIP exchanges are based on two message types, requests and replies, both of which are packaged in UDP packets addressed to well-known port number 520. When a RIP router starts, it generates a RIP request and transmits it as a broadcast over all of its network interfaces. Upon receiving the broadcast, every other router on either network that supports RIP generates a reply message that contains its routing table information. A reply message can contain up to 25 routes, each of which is 20 bytes long. If the routing table contains more than 25 entries, the router generates multiple reply messages until it has transmitted its entire routing table. When the router that sent the request receives the replies, it integrates the routing information in the reply messages into its own routing table. The RIP reply message is shown in Figure 7-16.

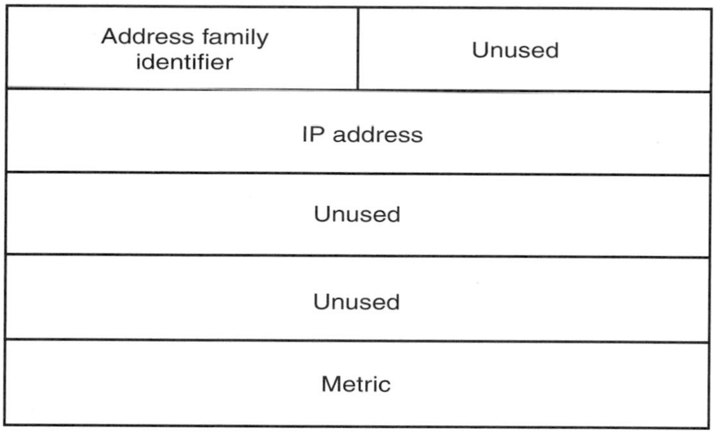

Address family identifier	Unused
IP address	
Unused	
Unused	
Metric	

Figure 7-16 A RIP version 1 route

The metric value included with each RIP route determines the efficiency of the route, based on the number of hops required to reach the destination. When routers receive routing table entries from other routers using RIP, they increment the value of the metric for each route to reflect the additional hop required to reach the destination. The maximum value for a metric in a RIP message is 15. A routing protocol that uses metrics based on the number of hops to the destination is called a **distance vector protocol**.

After their initial exchange of RIP messages, the routers transmit updates every 30 seconds to ensure that all of the other routers on the networks to which they are connected have current information. If a RIP-supplied routing table entry is not refreshed every three minutes, the router assumes that the entry is no longer viable, increases its metric value to 16 (an illegal value), and eventually removes the entry from the table completely.

This frequent retransmission of routing data is the main criticism leveled at RIP. The protocol generates a large amount of redundant broadcast traffic. In addition, the RIP version 1 (RIP v1) message format cannot include a subnet mask for each route. Instead, RIP applies the subnet mask of the interface it receives from each route, which may not always be accurate. RIP version 2 (RIP v2) addresses both of these problems.

The primary difference between RIP v1 and RIP v2 is the format of the routes included in the reply messages. The RIP v2 message is no larger than that of RIP v1, but it uses the unused fields from the RIP v1 format to include additional information about each route. The format of a RIP v2 route is shown in Figure 7-17.

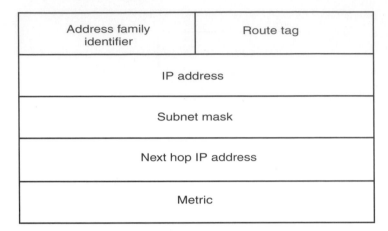

Figure 7-17   A RIP v2 route

The functions of the RIP v2 route fields are as follows:

- **Address Family Identifier (2 bytes)**   Contains a code that identifies the protocol for which routing information is being provided. The code for IP is 2. (RIP supports other protocols besides IP.)

- **Route Tag (2 bytes)**   Contains an AS number that enables RIP to communicate with EGPs.

- **IP Address (4 bytes)**   Specifies the address of the network or host for which routing information is being provided.

- **Subnet Mask (4 bytes)**   Contains the subnet mask that the router should apply to the IP Address value.

- **Next Hop IP Address (4 bytes)**   Specifies the address of the gateway that the router should use to forward traffic to the network or host specified in the IP Address field.

- **Metric (4 bytes)**   Contains a value that specifies the relative efficiency of the route.

The other main differences between RIP v1 and RIP v2 are that RIP v2 supports the use of multicast transmissions and can authenticate routes. A multicast address is a single address that represents a group of computers. By using a multicast address that represents all of the routers on the network, instead of broadcasts, RIP v2 can significantly reduce the amount of extraneous traffic to be processed by the other computers.

Open Shortest Path First (OSPF)

Test your knowledge of static and dynamic routing by completing Exercise 7-4, "Static and Dynamic Routing," now.

Judging routes by the number of hops required to reach a destination is not always efficient. A hop can refer to anything from a 1000-Mbps Gigabit Ethernet connection to a 33.6-Kbps dial-up line, so it is possible for traffic moving over a route with a smaller number of hops to take longer than one with more hops. There is another type of routing protocol, called a **link-state protocol**, that measures the actual properties of each connection and stores the information in a database that is shared among the routers on the network. The most common IGP that uses this method is the **Open Shortest Path First (OSPF)** protocol, as defined in RFC 2328. OSPF has many other advantages over RIP, including updating routing tables more quickly when changes occur on the network (called *convergence*), balancing the network load by splitting traffic between routes with equal metrics, and authenticating routing protocol messages.

CONFIGURING TCP/IP

Understanding the theory behind the TCP/IP suite is important, but that theory must eventually be put into practice. This section examines the procedures for configuring a TCP/IP client on the three main operating system platforms: Windows, UNIX/Linux, and NetWare. All of these operating systems use TCP/IP by default, and the operating system installation usually installs TCP/IP automatically when it detects a network interface in the system.

Before a computer can communicate using TCP/IP, the TCP/IP client must be configured with values for some or all of the following parameters:

- **IP address**   Identifies the network to which the computer is connected and the host on the network. The IP address is the only TCP/IP parameter that is absolutely required for the system to function on the network.

- **Subnet mask**   Specifies which bits in an IP address are the network identifier and which bits are the host identifier.

- **Default gateway**   Specifies the IP address of a router on the local network that provides access to other networks.

- **DNS server addresses**   Specifies the IP addresses of DNS servers the system will use to resolve host and domain names into IP addresses.

- **WINS server addresses**   Specifies the IP addresses of Windows Internet Name Service (WINS) servers on the network that the system will use to resolve Network Basic Input/Output System (NetBIOS) names into IP addresses.

- **NetBIOS/host name**   Specifies a friendly name by which the system will be known on the network.

The following sections examine the tools and procedures you use to configure these parameters in various operating systems.

Configuring TCP/IP in Windows

The Windows operating systems provide support for the TCP/IP protocol suite in the form of a single component called Internet Protocol (TCP/IP). This one component installs all of the basic protocols needed to transmit data across the network, including IP, TCP, and UDP. Microsoft's TCP/IP client also supports ancillary protocols, such as ICMP and ARP, as well as DHCP, DNS, and WINS clients. In addition, the Microsoft TCP/IP stack includes utilities such as Arp.exe, Route.exe, Ping.exe, and Tracert.exe, as well as FTP and Telnet client programs.

All of the current versions of Windows use the TCP/IP protocols by default. If the operating system's installation program detects a network interface adapter in the computer, the program identifies it and installs the appropriate network interface adapter driver, using plug and play (PnP). The installation program then installs the following networking modules:

- Client For Microsoft Networks
- File And Printer Sharing For Microsoft Networks
- Internet Protocol (TCP/IP)

Once installed, these modules appear in the Windows Control Panel, in the Local Area Connection Properties dialog box for each network connection, as shown in Figure 7-18.

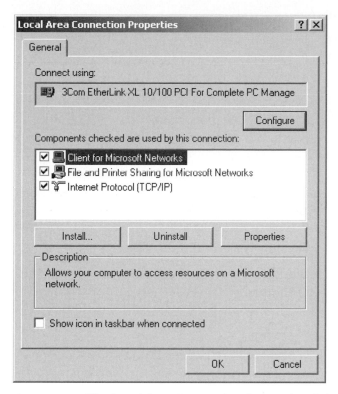

Figure 7-18   The Local Area Connection Properties dialog box

The configuration settings for these networking components are stored in a system database called the Windows registry. Windows loads the parameters from the registry whenever the system starts. When you modify the parameters, using Control Panel, you are actually changing the values stored in the registry.

Using DHCP to Configure TCP/IP

By default, the Windows operating systems configure the Microsoft TCP/IP client to use its DHCP client capabilities to request configuration settings from a DHCP server on the network. A DHCP server maintains a pool of IP addresses and allocates them to clients that request them, along with settings for other TCP/IP parameters. If your network has properly configured DHCP servers, then there is no need to manually configure TCP/IP parameters.

> **MORE INFO**   **Using DHCP**   For more information on DHCP, see Chapter 8, "Networking Software."

Configuring Essential TCP/IP Properties

In Windows, you manually configure the TCP/IP client in the Local Area Connection Properties dialog box (where the networking components were installed during the operating system setup). Use the following procedure to access the TCP/IP client's configuration interface on a Windows XP workstation and configure the TCP/IP parameters.

> **CAUTION   Avoiding TCP/IP Conflicts**   If you plan to experiment with this TCP/IP configuration procedure on a live network, be sure that the values you supply for the TCP/IP parameters, particularly the IP address, are correct for your computer and your network. Some TCP/IP parameters, when incorrectly set, can prevent your computer from communicating with the network, and others can cause conflicts with other computers on the network, preventing them from communicating. If you want to avoid explaining to your boss why she couldn't retrieve e-mail this morning, check with your network's administrator before you begin experimenting.

▶ Configuring TCP/IP Client Settings

1. Click Start, select Settings, and then select Network Connections.

   The Network Connections window appears.

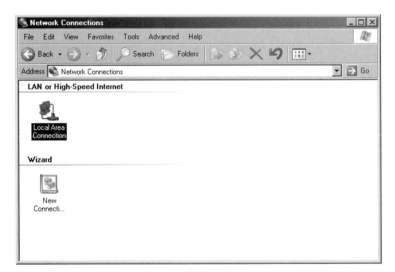

2. Right-click the Local Area Connection icon in the Network Connections window, and then select Properties.

   The Local Area Connection Properties dialog box appears.

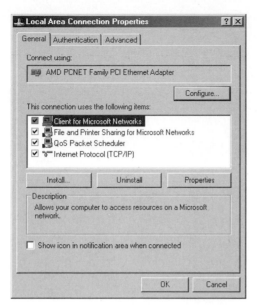

3. Select the Internet Protocol (TCP/IP) module in the components list, and then click Properties.

The Internet Protocol (TCP/IP) Properties dialog box appears.

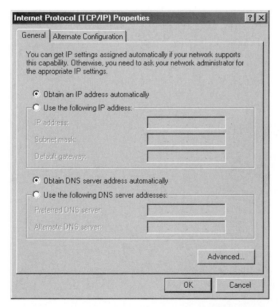

4. Select the Use The Following IP Address option to activate the IP Address, Subnet Mask, and Default Gateway text boxes.

These text boxes provide the dialog box's manual configuration capability. Although the dialog box does not say so, it is the Obtain An IP Address Automatically option that activates the DHCP client.

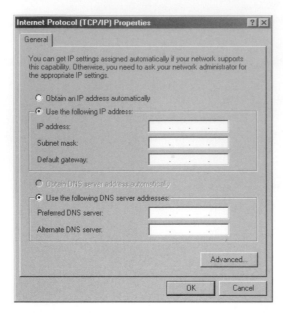

5. In the IP Address text box, enter a valid IP address, using the standard dotted decimal notation.

   The address must be unique on the network and it must conform to the subnet configuration used on your network. If you don't know anything about the addresses used on your network, ask an administrator to give you an IP address you can use. Do not simply select one at random or change the last number of the address used by another computer.

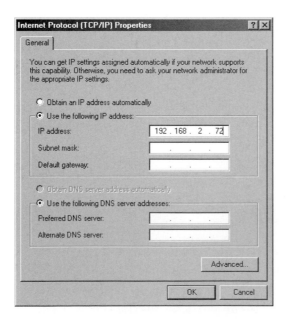

6. In the Subnet Mask text box, enter an appropriate mask for the IP address you supplied.

Windows XP supplies a subnet mask based on the value of the first byte in your IP address. However, if your network is subnetted, the subnet mask value supplied by the operating system might not be correct.

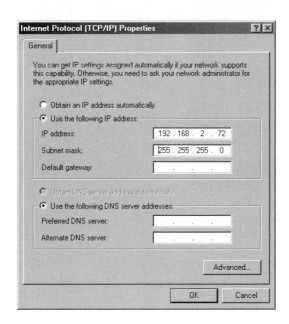

NOTE   Subnet Masking   Windows XP determines its value for the Subnet Mask text box by examining the first three bits of the 32-bit IP address you have supplied. If the first bit of the address is a 0, Windows XP supplies the subnet mask for a Class A address (255.0.0.0). If the first two bits are 10, Windows XP assumes the use of a Class B address and supplies a subnet mask of 255.255.0.0. If the first three bits are 110, the subnet mask value is for a Class C address (255.255.255.0). For more information about IP addresses and subnet masking, see Chapter 5, "Network Layer Protocols."

7. The Default Gateway text box should contain the IP address of the router on the local network that the computer should use to send TCP/IP traffic to destinations on other networks. If the computer is connected to a LAN that is not part of an internetwork and is not connected to the Internet, leave this text box blank.

On a private internetwork, the default gateway is a router that provides access to the other networks. On a stand-alone LAN connected to the Internet, the default gateway refers to the system that provides the shared Internet connection.

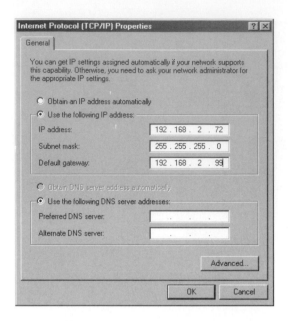

NOTE   Routing Tables and the Default Gateway   The address that you enter into the Default Gateway text box becomes an entry in the computer's routing table with a Network Destination value of 0.0.0.0. You can also create, delete, or modify the default gateway (or any other routing table entry) manually, using Route.exe, as explained earlier in this chapter.

8. In the Preferred DNS Server and Alternate DNS Server text boxes, enter the IP addresses of the DNS servers that your computer will use to resolve DNS names into IP addresses.

When you select the Use The Following IP Address option in the Internet Protocol (TCP/IP) Properties dialog box, Windows XP deactivates the DHCP client completely; as a result, the Obtain DNS Server Address Automatically option becomes unavailable.

The Microsoft TCP/IP client uses the Alternate DNS Server address only if the primary DNS server is unreachable. If your network is connected to the Internet, you must supply at least one DNS server address to convert the DNS names in your Uniform Resource Locators (URLs) into IP addresses.

If your computer is part of an Active Directory domain, you need to supply the address of the DNS server that is hosting the zone for your network's Active Directory installation. If you are not using Active Directory directory service, the DNS server can be located either on your internetwork or that of your ISP.

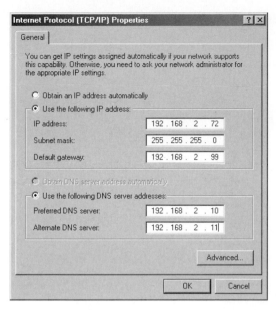

9. Click OK to close the Internet Protocol (TCP/IP) Properties dialog box, and then click OK again to close the Local Area Connection Properties dialog box.

Configuring Advanced TCP/IP Properties

In many cases, a Windows system needs only the TCP/IP parameters configured in the preceding procedure. However, the Internet Protocol (TCP/IP) Properties dialog box also has an Advanced button that opens the Advanced TCP/IP Settings dialog box, in which you can configure a more complete set of TCP/IP parameters, discussed in the following sections.

The IP Settings Tab

The IP Settings tab of the Advanced TCP/IP Settings dialog box lets you specify multiple IP addresses and subnet masks for the network interface adapter in your computer, as well as multiple default gateway addresses. Most computers with multiple IP addresses have multiple network interfaces, with one address allotted to each interface. However, in certain situations a computer can use more than one IP address for a single network interface adapter, such as when a single physical network hosts multiple TCP/IP subnets. In such cases, a computer needs an IP address on each of the two subnets to participate on both. Windows XP supports an unlimited number of IP address/subnet mask combinations for each network interface adapter in the computer. The IP Settings tab is shown in Figure 7-19

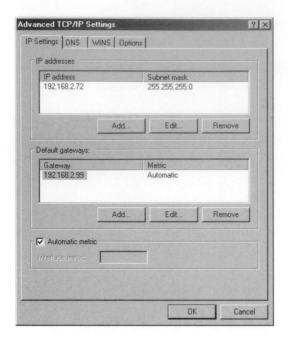

Figure 7-19   The IP Settings tab of the Advanced TCP/IP Settings dialog box

As noted earlier in this chapter, a computer can use only one default gateway at a time, so the ability to specify multiple default gateways in the Advanced TCP/IP Settings dialog box is simply a fault-tolerance mechanism. If the first default gateway in the list is unavailable for any reason, Windows XP sends packets to the second address listed. This practice assumes that the computer is connected to a LAN that has multiple routers on it, each of which provides access to the rest of the internetwork.

The DNS Tab

The DNS tab of the Advanced TCP/IP Settings dialog box also provides a fault-tolerance mechanism for the Windows XP DNS client. You can specify more than the two DNS server addresses provided in the main Internet Protocol (TCP/IP) Properties dialog box, and you can modify the order in which the computer uses them if one or more of the servers is unavailable. The DNS tab is shown in Figure 7-20.

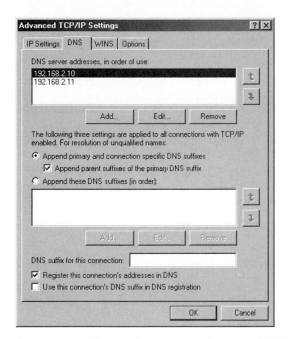

Figure 7-20   The DNS tab of the Advanced TCP/IP Settings dialog box

The other controls in the DNS tab control how the TCP/IP client resolves unqualified names. An *unqualified name* is an incomplete DNS name that does not specify the domain in which the host resides. The Windows TCP/IP client can still resolve these names by appending a suffix to the unqualified name before sending it to the DNS server for resolution. For example, with a properly configured TCP/IP client, you can supply only the name *www* as a URL in your Web browser, and the client appends your company's domain name (for example, *adatum.com*) to the URL as a suffix, resulting in the fully qualified DNS name *www.adatum.com*, which is presumably the name of your network's intranet Web server.

The DNS controls let you configure the client to append the primary and connection-specific DNS suffixes to unqualified names, or you can create a list of suffixes that the client will append to unqualified names, one after the other, until the name resolution process succeeds. The primary DNS suffix is the domain name you specify for the computer in the Network Identification tab of the System dialog box, accessed from the Control Panel. This suffix applies to all of the computer's network interfaces. You can also create a connection-specific suffix by entering a domain name in the DNS Suffix For This Connection text box. To create a list of suffixes, select the Append These DNS Suffixes (In Order) option and add a series of suffixes, using the controls provided.

You can use the two check boxes at the bottom of the DNS tab to specify whether the computer should register its DNS name with its designated DNS server. This option requires a DNS server that supports dynamic updates, such as the DNS

Server service supplied with Windows 2003 Server. If you select the Register This Connection's Addresses In DNS check box, Windows XP will use the system's primary DNS suffix to register the addresses. If you select the Use This Connection's DNS Suffix In DNS Registration check box, the computer will use the connection-specific suffix you entered in the DNS Suffix For This Connection text box.

The WINS Tab

Windows XP includes a WINS client for NetBIOS name resolution, but on a network that uses the Active Directory, WINS is not needed because Active Directory uses DNS names for the computers on the network and relies on DNS for its name resolution services. However, if you run Windows systems that use Windows NT domains or no directory service at all, you can use the WINS tab in the Advanced TCP/IP Settings dialog box to configure the Microsoft TCP/IP client to use WINS, as shown in Figure 7-21.

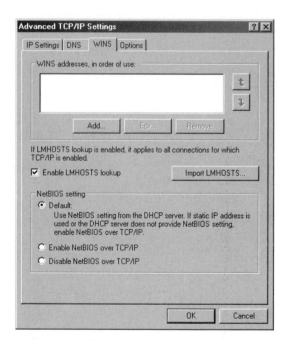

Figure 7-21   The WINS tab of the Advanced TCP/IP Settings dialog box

Select Add in the WINS tab to open the TCP/IP WINS Server dialog box, in which you can specify the address of a WINS server on your network. You can create a list of WINS servers and specify the order in which Windows XP should use them. As with the default gateway and DNS server settings, supplying multiple WINS server addresses is a fault-tolerance feature.

The Enable Lmhosts Lookup check box forces the computer to use a file called Lmhosts to resolve NetBIOS names before contacting the designated WINS server. Lmhosts is a text file located, by default, in the \Windows\System32\ Drivers\Etc folder on the computer's local drive, which contains a list of NetBIOS names and their equivalent IP addresses. Lmhosts functions in much the same way as the Hosts file, which was used for host name resolution before the advent of DNS. Because each computer must have its own Lmhosts file, Windows XP enables you to import a file from a network drive to the local computer. To do this, select Import Lmhosts and browse for the desired file.

Using the options at the bottom of the WINS tab, you can specify whether the computer should or should not use NetBIOS Over TCP/IP (NetBT), or whether the computer should rely on a DHCP server to specify the NetBIOS setting. On a network that uses Active Directory, you can disable NetBT because the computers use DNS names instead of NetBIOS names.

> **MORE INFO**   **Using WINS**   For more information about NetBIOS naming and WINS, see Chapter 8, "Networking Software."

The Options Tab

The Options tab in the Advanced TCP/IP Settings dialog box contains a list of additional features included with the Microsoft TCP/IP client. You can select any item in the list and click Properties to open a dialog box that enables you to configure that option.

Test your knowledge of TCP/IP configuration parameters by completing Exercise 7-5, "Microsoft Windows TCP/IP Configuration Requirements" now.

Windows XP includes only one option: TCP/IP Filtering. The TCP/IP Filtering option is essentially a rudimentary form of firewall that you can use to control what kinds of network and transport layer traffic can pass over the computer's network interface adapters. If you select the TCP/IP Filtering option and click Properties, the TCP/IP Filtering dialog box opens, as shown in Figure 7-22. In this dialog box, you can specify which protocols and which ports the computer can use. Selecting the Enable TCP/IP Filtering (All Adapters) check box activates three separate selectors: one for TCP ports, one for UDP ports, and one for IP protocols. By default, all three selectors permit all traffic to pass through the filters, but you can select the Permit Only option on any selector to build a list of permitted ports or protocols. The filters prevent traffic generated by all unlisted ports and protocols from passing through any of the computer's network interface adapters in either direction.

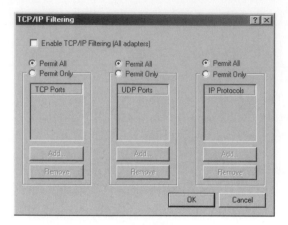

Figure 7-22   The TCP/IP Filtering dialog box

Configuring TCP/IP in UNIX/Linux

Compared to Windows, UNIX and Linux take a more basic approach to TCP/IP configuration. Instead of storing the TCP/IP configuration parameters in a registry, UNIX and Linux typically use plain text files. Scripts that run at boot time contain commands that configure the TCP/IP client with the appropriate settings. There are dozens of different UNIX and Linux distributions, and the default names and locations of the text and script files can vary, so you might have to consult the online manuals (commonly called man pages) or other documentation for your operating system to locate these files.

Configuring TCP/IP Parameters

On a Red Hat Linux system, the etc/sysconfig/network-scripts directory contains a file called ifcfg-eth0, shown in Figure 7-23, which contains commands that configure the basic TCP/IP parameters for the Ethernet network interface adapter in the system.

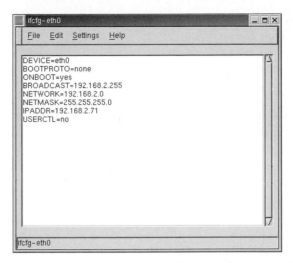

Figure 7-23   A network interface configuration file on a Red Hat Linux system

The commands found in this file on a typical workstation are as follows:

- **DEVICE=eth0**   Specifies the device name of the network interface adapter installed in the computer

- **BOOTPROTO=none**   Specifies whether the system should use DHCP to obtain TCP/IP configuration parameters

- **ONBOOT=yes**   Specifies whether the system should configure and initialize the network interface when the system boots

- **BROADCAST=192.168.2.255**   Specifies the broadcast address for the network interface

- **NETWORK=192.168.2.0**   Specifies the network address for the network interface

- **NETMASK=255.255.255.0**   Specifies the subnet mask to be applied to the network interface's IP address

- **IPADDR=192.168.2.71**   Specifies the IP address for the network interface

- **USERCTL=no**   Specifies whether the user should be permitted to deactivate the interface.

Most of these parameters are also interactively configurable with the ifconfig program, using a syntax like the following:

```
ifconfig interface address_family [up|down] [broadcast address] [netmask mask]
ipaddress
```

- ***interface***   Specifies the device name of the network interface adapter installed in the computer.

- ***address_family***   Specifies the type of address to assign to the interface. For IP addresses, the correct value is inet.

- **up|down**   Activates or deactivates the network interface.

- **broadcast *address***   Specifies the broadcast address for the network interface.

- **netmask *mask***   Specifies the subnet mask to be applied to the interface's IP address.

- ***ipaddress***   Specifies the IP address for the network interface.

> **NOTE   Using ifconfig**   The ifconfig tool also has many other command line arguments, which you can use to configure many parameters for a network interface.

An example of a properly formatted ifconfig command is as follows:

```
ifconfig eth0 inet up broadcast 192.168.2.255 netmask 255.255.255.0 192.168.2.71
```

Configuring DNS Server Addresses

The addresses of the DNS servers that the system will use are usually located in a file called resolv.conf, shown in Figure 7-24, which is typically located in the etc directory.

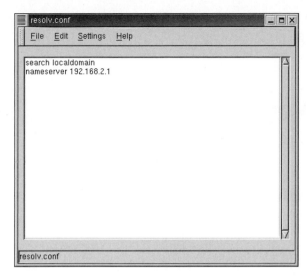

Figure 7-24   A resolv.conf file on a Red Hat Linux system

A typical resolv.conf file for a workstation contains the following commands:

- **search localdomain**   Specifies the name of a domain that the system should search by default when a host name is not fully qualified (that is, when it does not include a domain name)

- **nameserver 192.168.2.1**   Specifies the IP address of a DNS server that the system should use to resolve host and domain names into IP addresses

A resolv.conf file can contain as many search and nameserver commands as needed. You can modify the DNS server address configuration by editing the file directly.

Configuring Default Gateway Addresses

As you learned earlier in this chapter, the computer's default gateway address is really just another entry in the routing table. In many cases, UNIX and Linux network configuration scripts contain commands that call the route utility to create the default gateway table entry. As with any other static route, you can modify the default gateway at any time by using the route command.

Using Graphical TCP/IP Configuration Tools

Many UNIX and Linux distributions include tools that allow you to use a graphical interface to configure TCP/IP parameters. In most cases, these tools are just shells that modify the system's configuration scripts or execute command line programs in the background. However, they provide a simplified interface for the user, who doesn't have to remember a series of complex command line arguments.

The graphical configuration tools included with the various UNIX and Linux distributions vary greatly in appearance and capabilities. For example, Red Hat Linux includes a Network Configurator utility that lets you configure a network interface, as shown in Figure 7-25.

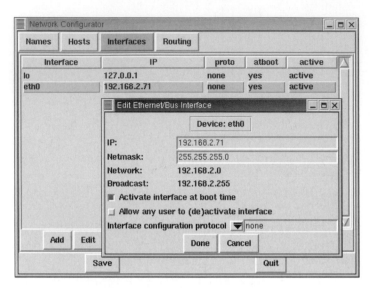

Figure 7-25   Configuring TCP/IP parameters in the Red Hat Linux Network Configurator tool

You can also use Network Configurator to configure the system's host name, add entries to the hosts file, specify a default gateway address, and create static routes, as shown in Figure 7-26.

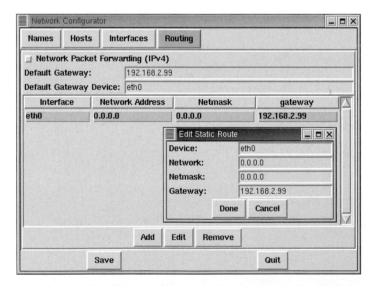

Figure 7-26   Configuring the default gateway in the Red Hat Linux Network Configurator tool

Configuring TCP/IP in NetWare

From the perspective of TCP/IP configuration, NetWare servers function similarly to UNIX and Linux, in that they store the system's TCP/IP configuration parameters in script files that the server loads each time it starts. For example, the Autoexec.ncf file shown in Figure 7-27 contains commands that load the network adapter driver (called Pcntnw.lan) and the TCP/IP module.

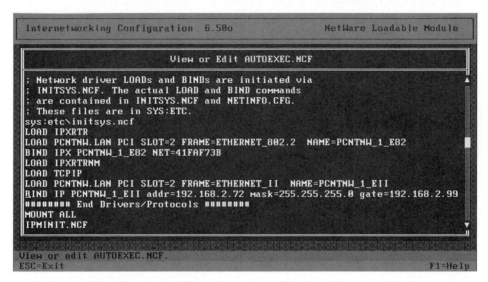

```
Internetworking Configuration  6.50o              NetWare Loadable Module

                      View or Edit AUTOEXEC.NCF

; Network driver LOADs and BINDs are initiated via
; INITSYS.NCF. The actual LOAD and BIND commands
; are contained in INITSYS.NCF and NETINFO.CFG.
; These files are in SYS:ETC.
sys:etc\initsys.ncf
LOAD IPXRTR
LOAD PCNTNW.LAN PCI SLOT=2 FRAME=ETHERNET_802.2  NAME=PCNTNW_1_E82
BIND IPX PCNTNW_1_E82 NET=41FAF73B
LOAD IPXRTRNM
LOAD TCPIP
LOAD PCNTNW.LAN PCI SLOT=2 FRAME=ETHERNET_II  NAME=PCNTNW_1_EII
BIND IP PCNTNW_1_EII addr=192.168.2.72 mask=255.255.255.0 gate=192.168.2.99
######## End Drivers/Protocols ########
MOUNT ALL
IPMINIT.NCF

View or edit AUTOEXEC.NCF.
ESC=Exit                                                        F1=Help
```

Figure 7-27   The Autoexec.ncf file on a NetWare server

Then a Bind command joins the network adapter driver and the TCP/IP module and uses the following command line parameters to configure the TCP/IP client. To modify the settings for an interface, you can also run the Unbind and Bind commands interactively from the server command prompt, using the same parameters.

■ **addr**   Specifies the IP address for the network interface

■ **mask**   Specifies the subnet mask to be applied to the interface's IP address

■ **gate**   Specifies the default gateway address for the network interface

NetWare also includes utilities that automate the process of editing the system configuration files. The most comprehensive of these is Inetcfg.nlm, which enables you to control the binding of the TCP/IP protocols to a network interface interactively, as shown in Figure 7-28, as well as to edit Autoexec.ncf and other configuration files.

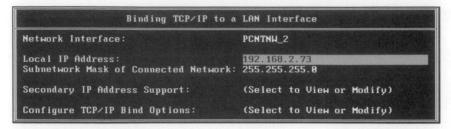

Figure 7-28   Controlling bindings on a NetWare server with Inetcfg.nlm

Inetcfg.nlm can also modify the computer's routing table, including the default gateway address, as shown in Figure 7-29.

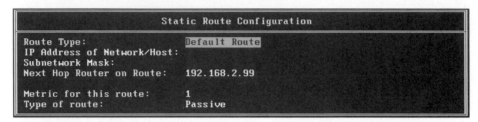

Figure 7-29   Specifying a default gateway address on a NetWare server with Inetcfg.nlm

NetWare also includes a Web-based server configuration tool called NetWare Remote Manager (NRM) that provides a graphical interface in which you can configure TCP/IP parameters and other settings, as shown in Figure 7-30.

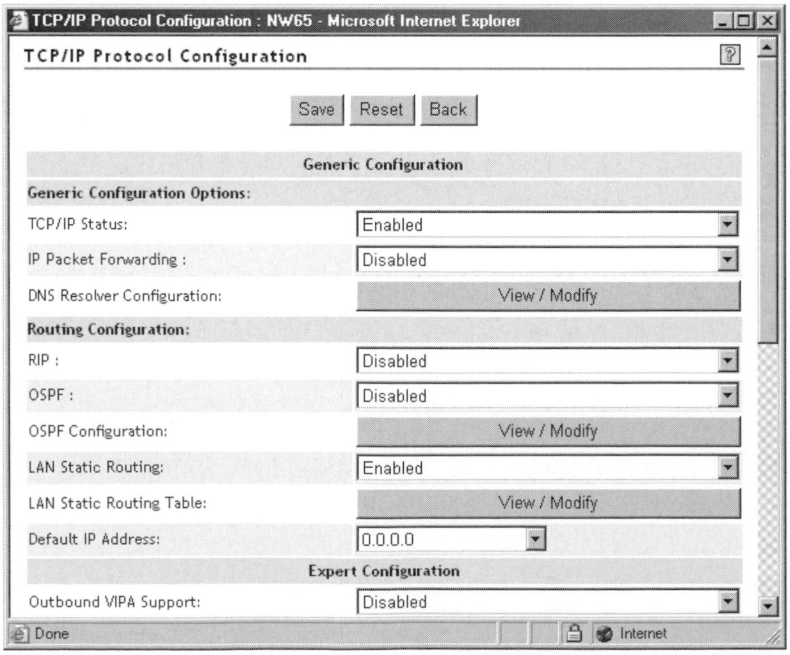

Figure 7-30   The NetWare Remote Manager interface

NOTE   Exam Objectives   Objective 3.11 for the Network + exam requires students to be able to select the appropriate network interface card (NIC) and network configuration settings (DHCP, DNS, WINS, protocols, NETBIOS/host name, etc.) for a given network configuration.

SUMMARY

- The Transmission Control Protocol/Internet Protocol (TCP/IP) protocols were developed for use on the ARPANET, later to become the Internet, and are designed to support systems using any computing platform or operating system. The TCP/IP protocol stack consists of four layers: link, internet, transport, and application.

- The Address Resolution Protocol (ARP) protocol is used by Internet Protocol (IP) to resolve IP addresses into the hardware addresses needed for data-link layer protocol communications.

- The Internet Control Message Protocol (ICMP) protocol performs many functions at the internet layer, including reporting errors and querying systems for information.

- Application layer protocols are not involved in the data transfer processes performed by the lower layers; instead, they enable specific programs and services running on TCP/IP computers to exchange messages.

- Routing is one of the most complicated functions of IP. Routers receive packets and forward them on to their destinations. A router can be a stand-alone hardware device, an operating system, or a separate software product. Complex internetworks can have redundant routers that provide multiple paths to the same destination. The job of a router is to use the most efficient path to forward packets.

- Routers store information about the network in a routing table. When forwarding a packet, the router searches the table for a route to each destination and transmits the packet to the appropriate destination. When a router fails to locate a route to a particular destination in the table, it sends the packet to the designated default gateway.

- Information gets into the routing table in two ways: by using static routing, which is the manual creation and maintenance of table entries; or by using dynamic routing, which uses specialized routing protocols to update the table.

- Windows operating systems implement the TCP/IP protocol suite as a single module. You install and configure TCP/IP in Windows using the Local Area Connections Properties dialog box.

- UNIX and Linux computers use text files to store TCP/IP configuration parameters and scripts to configure network interfaces when the system starts. UNIX and Linux distributions have various command line and graphical tools that you can use to modify these text files and scripts.

- NetWare computers also use text files and scripts to store TCP/IP configuration parameters. The two primary TCP/IP configuration tools are Inetcfg.nlm and NetWare Remote Manager.

EXERCISES

Exercise 7-1: TCP/IP Layers and Protocols

Specify the layer of the TCP/IP protocol stack at which each of the following protocols operates:

1. DHCP
2. ARP
3. IP
4. UDP
5. POP3
6. ICMP
7. SMTP
8. TCP
9. DNS
10. SLIP

Exercise 7-2: TCP/IP Protocols

Match each of the protocols in the left column with its appropriate description in the right column.

1. DHCP   **a.** Transmits e-mail messages between servers

2. ARP   **b.** Routes datagrams to their final destination

3. IP   **c.** Provides connection-oriented service at the transport layer

4. POP3   **d.** Resolves host names into IP addresses

       CHAPTER **e.** Connects two systems at the link layer
          S
          N
          M
          P

5. ICMP   **f.** Converts IP addresses into hardware addresses

6. TCP   **g.** Automatically configures TCP/IP clients

7. DNS   **h.** Provides communications between e-mail clients and servers

8. PPP   **i.** Carries network management data to a central console

9. SMTP   **j.** Carries error messages from routers to end systems

Exercise 7-3: Routing Tables

Place the following steps of the routing table search process in the proper order.

1. Default gateway search

2. Host address search

3. Network address search

Exercise 7-4: Static and Dynamic Routing

Specify whether each of the following terms is associated with static routing, dynamic routing, both, or neither.

1. Routed

2. Default gateway

3. Convergence

4. Route.exe

5. Link-state routing

6. Routing And Remote Access

7. Distance vector routing

8. route add

9. Autonomous system

10. Metric

Exercise 7-5: Windows TCP/IP Configuration Requirements

For each of the network scenarios (numbered 1 to 5), specify which of the following TCP/IP parameters (a, b, c, d, and e) you must configure to provide a computer running Windows XP with full communications capabilities. Choose all answers that are correct.

1. A private internetwork using Windows NT domains

2. A single peer-to-peer LAN

3. A corporate internetwork using Active Directory

4. A peer-to-peer LAN using a shared Internet connection

5. A Windows NT internetwork with a router connected to the Internet

   a. IP address

   b. Subnet mask

   c. Default gateway

   d. DNS server address

   e. WINS server address

REVIEW QUESTIONS

1. Which of the following fields is blank in an ARP Request message?

    a. Sender Hardware Address

    b. Sender Protocol Address

    c. Target Hardware Address

    d. Target Protocol Address

2. Which ICMP message type is the basis for the Traceroute utility?

    a. Echo Request

    b. Time To Live Exceeded In Transit

    c. Host Unreachable

    d. Fragment Reassembly Time Exceeded

3. Why are ARP Request messages transmitted as broadcasts?

4. Which ICMP message type performs a rudimentary form of flow control?

    a. Source Quench

    b. Router Solicitation

    c. Redirect

    d. Echo Request

5. Which of the following fields in an ARP Reply message contains a value supplied by the system transmitting the message?

    a. Sender Hardware Address

    b. Sender Protocol Address

    c. Target Hardware Address

    d. Target Protocol Address

6. How does ARP minimize the number of broadcasts it generates?

7. Which application layer protocol uses two port numbers at the server?

   a. SMTP

   b. HTTP

   c. DHCP

   d. FTP

8. What type of route does a packet use if the Destination IP Address and the data-link layer Destination Address values refer to different computers?

   a. The default gateway

   b. A direct route

   c. The default route

   d. An indirect route

9. What is a TCP/IP system with interfaces to two different networks called?

   a. A bridge

   b. Multihomed

   c. A switch

   d. All of the above

10. In a Windows routing table, what column contains the address of the router that should be used to reach a particular network or host?

    a. Network Destination

    b. Netmask

    c. Gateway

    d. Interface

11. What does a router do when it fails to find a routing table entry for a particular network or host?

12. In a Windows routing table, what is the Network Destination value for the default gateway entry?

   a. 0.0.0.0

   b. The address of the network to which the router is connected

   c. 255.255.255.255

   d. The address of the router's network interface

13. Which of the following is not a dynamic routing protocol?

   a. OSPF

   b. RIP

   c. ICMP

   d. EGP

14. What is the name for the use of metrics based on the number of hops between a source and a destination?

   a. Distance vector routing

   b. Loose source routing

   c. Link-state routing

   d. OSPF routing

15. What is the primary difference between OSPF and RIP?

16. Which of the following fields is not included in a RIP v1 route?

   a. Metric

   b. Subnet mask

   c. IP address

   d. Address family identifier

17. What is the primary criticism leveled at RIP?

18. What is the name of the process of updating routing tables to reflect changes in the network?

   a. Divergence

   b. Link-state routing

   c. Minimal routing

   d. Convergence

19. The Next Hop IP Address in a RIP v2 route ends up in which column of a Windows routing table?

    a. Network Destination

    b. Netmask

    c. Gateway

    d. Interface

20. Which of the following components is not installed by default during the Windows 2000 setup process when a PnP network interface adapter is in the computer?

    a. NetBEUI

    b. Internet Protocol (TCP/IP) module

    c. Client For Microsoft Networks

    d. File And Printer Sharing For Microsoft Networks

21. Which of the following services is not used on a Windows 2000 Active Directory network?

    a. DHCP

    b. WINS

    c. DNS

    d. IPSec

22. What is the function of a DNS suffix?

23. Which Windows utility can you use to specify a default gateway address?

    a. Tracert.exe

    b. Arp.exe

    c. Ipconfig.exe

    d. Route.exe

24. Which of the following UNIX/Linux tools can you use to configure a computer's subnet mask?

    a. routed

    b. route

    c. ifconfig

    d. resolv.conf

25. Which of the following is a valid reason for assigning more than one IP address to a single network interface adapter?

    a. To balance the network traffic load between the addresses

    b. To support multiple subnets on one network

    c. To provide fault tolerance

    d. To support both TCP and UDP traffic

CASE SCENARIOS

Case Scenario 7-1: Creating Static Routes

On your corporate internetwork, there are two computers running Windows 2003 Server that have been configured to function as routers, called Server A and Server B. Both servers have two network interface adapters installed in them, and neither is running any routing protocols. The network interface adapters on Server A have been assigned Internet Protocol (IP) addresses 192.168.42.1 and 192.168.65.1. Server B is configured to use IP addresses 192.168.65.8 and 192.168.12.1. All four addresses use the same subnet mask, 255.255.255.0. What Route.exe command should you execute on Server A to enable it to route traffic to both of the networks that Server B is connected to?

    a. route add 192.168.65.0 mask 255.255.255.0 192.168.65.1 if 1 metric 1

    b. route add 192.168.65.0 mask 255.255.255.0 192.168.65.8 if 1 metric 1

    c. route add 192.168.12.0 mask 255.255.255.0 192.168.65.8 if 1 metric 1

    d. route add 192.168.12.0 mask 255.255.255.0 192.168.12.1 if 1 metric 1

Case Scenario 7-2: Choosing a Routing Method

Two small businesses, Adventure Works and Blue Yonder Airlines, have decided to merge. Both companies have made substantial investments in their networking equipment, and Blue Yonder intends to move its entire headquarters operation to Adventure Works' office building.

Adventure Works has a Token Ring internetwork that consists of 12 LANs, all located in the one office building and all connected to a single backbone. These LANs have network addresses ranging from 172.16.0.0 through 172.27.0.0, with a subnet mask of 255.255.0.0.

Blue Yonder has an Ethernet internetwork that consists of 3 LANs at their headquarters and 15 other LANs located in branch offices around the country, which are connected to the headquarters by means of routers and WAN links of various types, ranging from dial-up connections to high-speed leased lines. The Blue Yonder networks have network addresses ranging from 192.168.1.0 through 192.168.18.0, with a subnet mask of 255.255.255.0.

The new company has plans to open several other offices during the next year. After moving Blue Yonder's headquarters network to the new location, the owners intend to connect it to the Adventure Works network, using a computer running Windows 2003 Server configured to function as a router. Which of the following router configuration solutions would best suit this network environment?

     a. Use static routing.

     b. Install RIP v1 on all of the network's routers.

     c. Install RIP v2 on all of the network's routers.

     d. Install OSPF on all of the network's routers.

Case Scenario 7-3: Configuring TCP/IP Clients

Mark is setting up a small Ethernet network in his home by installing network adapters in three computers running Windows XP and connecting them to a hub. Mark only uses one of the computers to access the Internet with a modem, but he wants to be able to access files and his printer from any one of the three systems. When the hardware is installed, he notes that the default networking components have been installed on all three systems, and he sets about configuring their TCP/IP configuration parameters manually. Which of the following TCP/IP parameters must Mark configure in order to achieve the network connectivity he desires? Choose all answers that are correct.

    a. IP address

    b. Subnet mask

    c. Default gateway

    d. Preferred DNS server

CHAPTER 8
NETWORKING SOFTWARE

Upon completion of this chapter, you will be able to:

- Describe the basic networking capabilities of the Microsoft Windows, Novell NetWare, UNIX/Linux, and Apple Macintosh operating systems.

- Describe the client capabilities of the major operating systems.

- Identify the directory services provided with major operating systems.

- Describe the difference between a flat file directory and a hierarchical directory.

- List the fault-tolerance and security features of the major directory services.

- Explain how Dynamic Host Configuration Protocol (DHCP) assigns Transmission Control Protocol/Internet Protocol (TCP/IP) configuration settings to workstations.

- Understand the history of name resolution on the Internet.

- Understand the functions of the Domain Name System (DNS) and the Windows Internet Naming Service (WINS).

This chapter examines the various software elements that provide network connectivity. You might need hardware, such as network interface adapters and cables, to physically connect your computers together into a network, but software is also an important component. The various software elements that provide network connectivity include operating systems, clients, directory services, and applications. These components implement the protocols that make up the networking stack and provide the services that computers need to communicate effectively. Although you might be very familiar with some of the components discussed in this chapter, there might be others you have never used, and you should become familiar with them.

CLIENT/SERVER AND PEER-TO-PEER NETWORKING

Computers can interact with each other on a network in different ways and fulfill different roles. Two primary networking models define this interaction: client/server and peer-to-peer.

In **client/server networking**, certain computers act as servers and others act as clients. A server is simply a computer (or more precisely, an application running on a computer) that provides a service to other computers. The most basic network functions are file sharing and printer sharing; the machines that do this are called *file servers* and *print servers*. There are many other types of servers as well: application servers, e-mail servers, Web servers, database servers, and so on. A client is a computer that uses the services provided by servers.

> **NOTE   Server Computers and Server Applications**   Although servers are often thought of as computers, they are actually applications. A single computer can run several different server applications at the same time and, in most cases, perform client operations as well.

At one time, it was common for computers to be limited to either client or server roles. Novell NetWare, which was the most popular network operating system for many years, consists of a separate server operating system and clients that run on Windows or other workstations. The NetWare server computer functions only as a server and the clients function only as clients. The most popular network operating systems today, however, include both client and server functions. For example, all of the current versions of Windows and all UNIX and Linux systems can function as both clients and servers. How to use each system is up to the network administrator.

You can construct a client/server network by designating one or more of the networked computers as a server and the rest as clients, even when all of the computers can perform both functions. A client/server network typically uses a directory service to store information about the network and its users. Users log on to the directory service instead of logging on to individual computers, and administrators can control access to the entire network, using the directory service as a central resource.

In **peer-to-peer networking**, every computer is an equal and functions as both a client and a server. This means that any computer can share its resources with the network and access the shared resources on other computers. You can therefore use any of the Windows or UNIX/Linux versions for this type of network, but you cannot use a dedicated client/server operating system like

NetWare. Peer-to-peer networks should generally be limited to 10 or 15 nodes or fewer on a single local area network (LAN), because each system has to maintain its own user accounts and other security settings, and because the administrative overhead becomes prohibitive as the network grows larger.

USING SERVER OPERATING SYSTEMS

In the past, there was a significant difference between a stand alone operating system and a network operating system. The typical stand-alone operating system provided no networking capabilities, and you had to purchase and install networking software to run on it. Today, virtually all operating systems are network operating systems because they include the software needed to connect to a network. The following sections are concerned primarily with the server functions of today's operating systems, although in some cases you can also use the server system as a client or a member of a peer-to-peer network.

> **NOTE** **Exam Objectives** *Objective 3.1 for the Network+ exam calls for students to be able to identify the basic capabilities (such as client support, interoperability, authentication, file and print services, application support, and security) of the following server operating systems: UNIX/Linux, NetWare, Windows, and Macintosh.*

Microsoft Windows

Windows is the most popular operating system used today, with an installed user base that far outnumbers its closest competitors. Originally, Windows was a shell program that ran on top of the MS-DOS operating system, providing a **graphical user interface (GUI)** and access to common device drivers. In 1993, however, Microsoft released the first version of Microsoft Windows NT (called version 3.1), which did not use the DOS kernel and which was designed from the outset to be a server operating system. From that time forward, Microsoft maintained both Windows product lines, with the DOS operating systems aimed at the workstation market and the Windows NT line aimed at servers.

The DOS-based workstation operating systems progressed from Microsoft Windows for Workgroups, which was the first Windows version to include networking capabilities, to Microsoft Windows 95, Microsoft Windows 98, and finally Microsoft Windows Me, which is the last version of Windows based on the DOS kernel. The original motivation for retaining DOS as the underlying operating system for Windows was backward compatibility with the DOS applications in general use at the time. As those applications were gradually retired, however, there was less need to retain the DOS kernel, which imposed certain restrictions on the operating system architecture that were best left behind.

With the release of Windows NT 4.0, Microsoft split the Windows NT operating system into two product lines: Windows NT Workstation and Windows NT Server, a practice that has continued to this day. Both versions are based on the same kernel; the differences between the two consist primarily of the applications and services included with the product. The version history of Windows is illustrated in Figure 8-1.

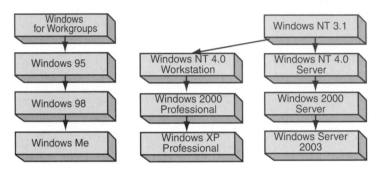

Figure 8-1   Microsoft Windows version history

Today, Microsoft Windows Server 2003 is the current server version of Windows, and Microsoft Windows XP is the workstation version. Both of these operating systems are based on the same NT kernel. In fact, Windows Server 2003 is similar in appearance to Windows NT 4.0, as shown in Figure 8-2.

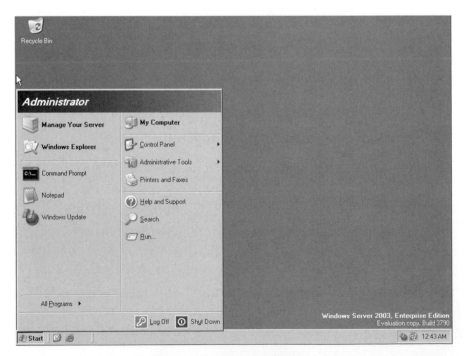

Figure 8-2   The Windows Server 2003 user interface

Windows XP, however, has undergone revisions to the user interface to make it simpler and more intuitive for the average user, as shown in Figure 8-3.

Figure 8-3   The Windows XP Professional user interface

Both Windows XP and Windows Server 2003 are available in multiple versions. These versions are discussed in the following sections.

Windows XP Versions

Windows XP is available in Home and Professional editions. Windows XP Home Edition, as the name implies, is intended for stand-alone systems and includes a variety of features that simplify common tasks. Home Edition also disables some of the operating system's more advanced security features by default, and it cannot participate in an Active Directory network. Windows XP Professional is designed for the business market, where security and networking capabilities are more important. The operating system can participate in an Active Directory domain and has a variety of security features that are more appropriate for business use.

Windows Server 2003 Versions

The different editions of Windows Server 2003 support various hardware platforms and server roles. In addition to the four basic editions of Windows Server 2003—Web, Standard, Enterprise, and Datacenter—it is also available in versions that support 64-bit processor platforms and embedded systems.

MORE INFO   New Features in Windows Server 2003   For more information on the Windows Server 2003 platform and a complete list of its new features and capabilities, see the Microsoft Web site for Windows Server 2003 at http://www.microsoft.com/windowsserver2003.

The four main Windows Server 2003 editions have different hardware requirements. Table 8-1 lists the system requirements for each, as well as hardware recommendations.

Table 8-1   **Windows Server 2003 System Requirements**

	Web Edition	**Standard Edition**	**Enterprise Edition**	**Datacenter Edition**
Minimum processor speed	133 MHz	133 MHz	133 MHz	400 MHz
Recommended processor speed	550 MHz	550 MHz	733 MHz	733 MHz
Minimum RAM	128 MB	128 MB	128 MB	512 MB
Recommended minimum RAM	256 MB	256 MB	256 MB	1 GB
Maximum RAM	2 GB	4 GB	32 GB	64 GB
Symmetric multiprocessing (SMP) support	Up to 2 processors	Up to 4 processors	Up to 8 processors	Up to 32 processors
Minimum disk space	1.5 GB	1.5 GB	1.5 GB	1.5 GB

The following sections discuss the Windows Server 2003 editions in greater detail.

Web Edition

To position Windows Server 2003 more competitively against other Web servers, Microsoft released a special-purpose edition of Windows Server 2003 that was designed specifically to function as a Web server. The Web Edition is a subset of the standard operating system that enables customers to deploy Web sites, Web applications, and Web services with a minimum of expense and administrative overhead. The operating system supports a maximum of 2 GB of memory and up to two processors—half the capacity of the Standard Edition.

The Web Edition of Windows Server 2003 does not contain any features that are not found in the other Windows Server 2003 editions, but it does omit some components that are typically not needed on a Web server, such as the following:

- A computer running the Web Edition can be a member of an Active Directory domain, but it cannot function as a domain controller.

- The standard Client Access License model does not apply to computers running the Web Edition. The operating system supports an unlimited number of Web connections, but it is limited to 10 simultaneous Server Message Block (SMB) connections. This means that no more than 10 internal network users can access the server's file and print resources at any one time.

- The Internet Connection Firewall (ICF) and Internet Connection Sharing (ICS) features are not included with the Web Edition. This prevents the computer from functioning as an Internet gateway.

- A computer running the Web Edition cannot function as a Dynamic Host Configuration Protocol (DHCP) server, fax server, Microsoft SQL Server, or terminal server, although it does support Remote Desktop for Administration.

- The Web Edition cannot run non–Web-serving applications.

Web Edition does include all of the standard components that a Web server needs, including Microsoft Internet Information Services (IIS) 6, Network Load Balancing (NLB), and Microsoft ASP.NET.

Obviously, the Web Edition is not a suitable platform for a general-purpose network server, nor is it intended to be one. However, it does enable organizations to deploy dedicated Web servers without having to provide support for a lot of components that the computer doesn't need.

> **NOTE** **Purchasing the Web Edition** The Web Edition is not sold through retail channels. The product is available only to Microsoft customers with Enterprise and Select licensing agreements, to service providers with a service provider licensing agreement (SPLA), and through Microsoft original equipment manufacturers (OEMs) and System Builder partners.

Standard Edition

Windows Server 2003, Standard Edition, is a multipurpose server platform that can provide directory, file, print, application, multimedia, and Internet services for small- to medium-sized businesses. Among the many features included with the operating system are the following:

- **Directory services**   The Standard Edition includes full Active Directory support, enabling the computer to function as a member server or a domain controller. Administrators can use the tools included with the operating system to deploy and manage Active Directory objects, group policies, and other Active Directory–based services.

- **Internet services**   The Standard Edition includes IIS 6, which provides Web and File Transfer Protocol (FTP) services as well as other components used by Web server deployments, such as NLB. NLB enables multiple Web servers to host a single Web site, sharing the incoming client requests among up to 32 servers and thus providing fault tolerance.

- **Infrastructure services**   The Standard Edition includes the Microsoft DHCP Server, Domain Name System (DNS) Server, and Windows Internet Name Service (WINS) server, which provide important services for internal network and Internet clients.

- **TCP/IP routing**   A computer running the Standard Edition can function as a router in a variety of configurations, including LAN and wide area network (WAN) routing, Internet access routing, and remote access routing. To facilitate these roles, the operating system's Routing And Remote Access Service (RRAS) also includes support for Network Address Translation (NAT), Internet Authentication Service (IAS), Routing Information Protocol (RIP), and the Open Shortest Path First (OSPF) routing protocol.

- **File and print services**   Users on the network can access shared drives, folders, and printers on a Standard Edition server. A Client Access License (CAL) is needed for each client that attempts to access server shares. The Standard Edition is typically sold with a package of 5, 10, or more CALs. To add more users, you must purchase additional CALs.

- **Terminal Server**   A computer running the Standard Edition can function as a terminal server, enabling computers and other devices to access the Windows desktop and applications running on the server. Terminal Server is essentially a remote control mechanism that enables clients to access a Windows session on the server. All application execution takes place on the server, and only keyboard, mouse, and display information is transmitted over the network. Terminal Server clients require a license that is separate from the standard Windows Server 2003 CAL, although the Standard Edition does include a two-user license for Remote Desktop for Administration, which is a Terminal Server–based remote administration tool.

■ **Security services** The Standard Edition includes a variety of security features that administrators can deploy as needed, including Encrypting File System (EFS), which protects files on server drives by storing them in an encrypted format; IP Security (IPSec) extensions, which digitally sign and encrypt data before transmitting it over the network; ICF, which regulates the traffic admitted onto the network from the Internet; and the Public Key Infrastructure (PKI), which provides security based on public key encryption and digital certificates.

Enterprise Edition

Windows Server 2003, Enterprise Edition, is a powerful server platform for medium- to large-sized businesses. The Enterprise Edition differs from the Standard Edition primarily in terms of degree. For example, the Enterprise Edition supports up to eight processors, compared with four for the Standard Edition, and up to 32 GB of memory, compared with 4 GB for the Standard Edition.

The Enterprise Edition also includes some important additional features that are not supplied with the Standard Edition, including the following:

■ **Microsoft Metadirectory Services (MMS)** A metadirectory is essentially a directory of directories—a means of integrating multiple information sources into a single, unified directory. MMS makes it possible to combine Active Directory information with other directory services to create a unified view of all available information about a given resource. The Enterprise Edition only includes support for MMS, not the actual MMS software. You must obtain the actual MMS software from a Microsoft Consulting Service (MCS) or via an MMS partner agreement.

■ **Server clustering** A server cluster is a group of servers that function as a single entity, providing high availability for a particular set of applications. High availability in this case means that application processing is distributed among the servers in the cluster, reducing the load on each computer and providing fault tolerance if any of the servers fails. The servers in a server cluster are called *nodes*. Nodes have shared access to a common data source, usually in the form of a storage area network (SAN), thus enabling all of the nodes to maintain a current information base. The Enterprise Edition supports server clusters of up to eight nodes.

- **Hot Add Memory**   The Enterprise Edition includes software support for a hardware feature called Hot Add Memory, which enables administrators to add or replace memory in the computer without powering it down or restarting. To use this capability, the computer must have the appropriate hardware support.

- **Windows System Resource Manager (WSRM)**   This feature enables administrators to allocate system resources to specific applications or processes, based on the needs of the computer's users, and to maintain accounting records of the resources used by those applications or processes. This enables businesses to set resource limits for specific processes or to bill customers based on their resource usage.

Datacenter Edition

Windows Server 2003, Datacenter Edition, is designed for high-end, high-traffic application servers that require huge amounts of system resources. The Datacenter Edition is nearly identical to the Enterprise Edition in its feature set but provides even greater hardware scalability, supporting up to 64 GB of RAM and up to 32 processors. The Datacenter Edition does omit a few Enterprise Edition features, such as ICS and ICF, primarily because high-end servers such as those supporting the Datacenter Edition are not expected to serve in the roles that use these features.

> **NOTE   Purchasing the Datacenter Edition**   Like the Web Edition, the Datacenter Edition is not available through standard retail channels. You can obtain it only through an OEM as part of a high-end server hardware package.

64-Bit Editions

Both the Enterprise Edition and the Datacenter Edition are available in versions that support computers equipped with Intel Itanium processors. Itanium is a processing platform that provides 64-bit addressing (while Intel's standard x86 processors are 32-bit), a greatly enlarged virtual address space and paged pool area, and enhanced floating point performance. It is specifically designed for processor-intensive tasks, such as massive database applications, scientific analysis, and heavily accessed Web servers.

The system requirements for the Itanium versions of the Enterprise Edition and the Datacenter Edition are slightly different from those of the x86 versions, as summarized in Table 8-2. Also, some features of the x86 editions are not available in the Itanium editions. Most notably, the Itanium editions do not support 16-bit Windows applications, real-mode applications, POSIX applications, or print services for Apple Macintosh clients.

Table 8-2   Special System Requirements for Itanium Versions of Windows Server 2003

	Enterprise Edition	Datacenter Edition
Minimum processor speed	733 MHz	733 MHz
Maximum RAM	64 GB	512 GB
Minimum disk space	2 GB	2 GB

File and Printer Sharing

Sharing files and printers is one of the main reasons for networking computers, and all network operating systems include a service that makes file and printer sharing possible. All versions of Windows can share their files and printers with other computers running Windows, and all versions of Windows can access the files and printers shared by other computers running Windows. To do this, the Windows operating systems rely on the Server Message Blocks (SMB) protocol.

SMB is an application layer protocol that Windows uses to perform file management and authentication tasks on remote computers. For example, when a Windows workstation attempts to access a file on a Windows server, the two systems first exchange SMB messages that establish a session between the computers and authenticate the client's access to the file.

To make the files and printers on a Windows server available to network clients, a system administrator creates shares by selecting resources, giving them names, and then assigning permissions that specify who can access the resources. These shares appear to network users as they browse the network, allowing them to access the resources by using file management utilities such as Windows Explorer or any other appropriate application.

One of the most important elements of file sharing is the ability to restrict access to the server files. All of the Windows NT–based operating systems include the NTFS file system (NTFS) that is specifically designed for this purpose. The MS-DOS–based versions of Windows use the file allocation table (FAT) file system exclusively, and the Windows NT–based versions support FAT as well as NTFS. You can share FAT drives with other users on the network, but the FAT file system's security capabilities are extremely limited. When you create NTFS drives during a Windows Server 2003, Microsoft Windows 2000, or Windows NT installation, you can grant access permissions for specific files and folders to the users and groups on your network with great precision, using the controls shown in Figure 8-4. NTFS also supports larger amounts of storage than FAT drives do.

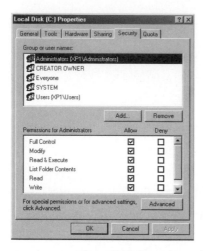

Figure 8-4   The NTFS file system lets you control access to files and folders on Windows server drives.

For example, if you store your company's accounting spreadsheets on an NTFS drive, you can grant the bookkeepers full Read/Write access to the files, grant Read-Only access to other company executives, and prevent any other users from even seeing that the files exist. Maintaining these permissions is an important part of the network administrator's job.

> **NOTE**   **NTFS Drive Access**   NTFS drives can be read only by the Windows operating systems that support NTFS. For example, if you were to use an MS-DOS boot disk to boot a computer with NTFS drives, the drives would be invisible. However, this compatibility issue has nothing to do with access to the drives over the network. Any operating system can access shared NTFS drives, as long as the appropriate permissions are in place.

Application Support

In Windows terminology, a service is an application that runs continuously in the background while other operations are running at the same time, as shown in Figure 8-5. Unlike regular applications, services can load when the computer starts and before a user logs on, so they are available whenever the system is running. Most of the networking capabilities in Windows, and particularly the server functions, are provided by services.

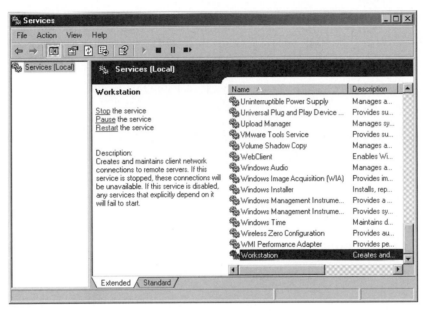

Figure 8-5   The Windows operating systems include a variety of services that you can configure to load at boot time.

The following services are the core of Windows' networking capabilities:

- **Server**   Enables the system to share its resources, such as files and printers

- **Workstation**   Enables the system to access the shared resources on another computer

- **Computer Browser**   Maintains a list of the shared resources on a network from which users can choose

- **Messenger**   Enables the system to display pop-up messages about the activities on other network systems

- **Alerter**   Works with the Messenger service to notify selected users of administrative alerts that occur on the system

- **Netlogon**   Provides secure channels between computers running Windows for communications related to the authentication process

The services listed above are available on all computers running Windows, whether they are workstations or servers. The server versions of the operating system, however, include many other networking services that are optional, but which provide important support for clients on the network. Some of these services are listed below.

- **Internet Information Services (IIS)**   Provides Internet services, such as Web and FTP servers

- **Windows Internet Name Service (WINS)**   Resolves the Network Basic Input/Output System (NetBIOS) names of pre–Windows 2000 computers into Internet Protocol (IP) addresses

- **Domain Name System (DNS) Server**   Resolves DNS host and domain names into IP addresses

- **Dynamic Host Configuration Protocol (DHCP) Server**   Automatically configures Transmission Control Protocol/Internet Protocol (TCP/IP) settings on multiple client systems

- **Routing and Remote Access (RRAS)**   Enables a server to route traffic between two LANs or a WAN and a LAN, and provides support for various routing protocols

- **Distributed file system (DFS)**   Enables shared drives on servers all over the network to appear to clients as a single combined share

Authentication and Security

Over the years, security has become increasingly important to computer network administration, and each ensuing version of Windows has increased the security capabilities of the operating systems. Today, many of the security capabilities of Windows are aided or implemented by the **Active Directory directory service**, an enterprise directory service that stores all account information in a proprietary database and provides authentication services to users and computers. Active Directory uses the **Kerberos** protocol for authentication, which enables clients and servers to exchange confidential information without transmitting it over the network in a penetrable form.

> **MORE INFO**   **Understanding Active Directory**   For more information about Active Directory and Windows security, see "Directory Services," later in this chapter.

Test your knowledge of the Windows Server 2003 editions by completing Exercise 8-1, "Selecting an Operating System," now.

In addition to Active Directory, the current versions of Windows include many other security mechanisms, including IPSec, which digitally signs and encrypts packets before transmitting them over the network; and EFS, which stores files on disk in encrypted form.

Novell NetWare

Novell NetWare was the first commercially successful network operating system, and in the early 1990s, the product dominated the business LAN market. Although the Windows operating systems have eclipsed its popularity, NetWare still remains a viable networking platform. Unlike Windows or UNIX, NetWare is strictly a client/server operating system. Any computer running Windows, whether it is a server or a workstation edition, can share its own resources and access shared resources on other computers running Windows. A computer running the NetWare operating system, by contrast, is dedicated solely to server operations. A NetWare server cannot run client applications or access resources on client computers. NetWare clients can communicate with NetWare servers, but not with other clients. For example, to transfer files from one workstation to another using NetWare, you must copy them from the first workstation to a server, and then you must use the other workstation to access those files on the server.

There is no dedicated NetWare client operating system. NetWare clients typically run some version of Windows, using either the client software included with Windows or a client supplied by Novell. Other operating systems can also function as NetWare clients.

> **NOTE**   **NetWare and Windows Clients**   It is possible for a computer running a NetWare client to function as a Windows server and client at the same time, enabling it to perform Windows as well as NetWare networking functions.

Because they do not have to perform workstation operations, NetWare servers have always had a simple, menu-driven, character-based interface, as shown in Figure 8-6.

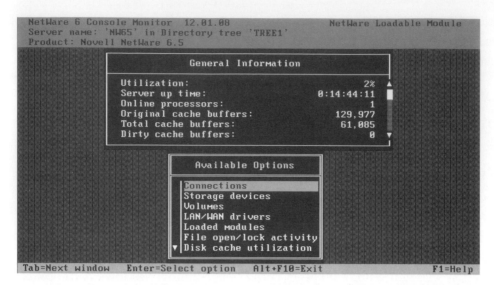

Figure 8-6   The classic NetWare server console is character-based, but uses keyboard-driven menus.

There is no real need for a graphical interface on a dedicated server, but Novell has added a Java-based server console application to its most recent NetWare versions, as shown in Figure 8-7, to make the interface more familiar to users accustomed to Windows.

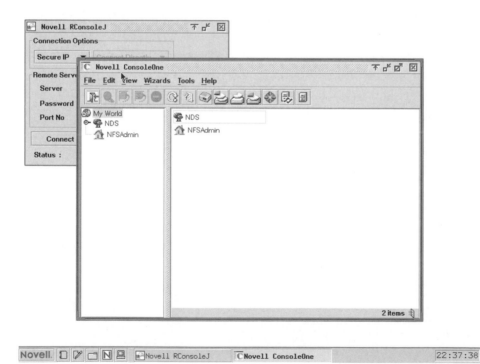

Figure 8-7   The Java-based graphical NetWare server console

NetWare Versions

Novell began releasing networking products in the early 1980s, and for many years, the NetWare product was synonymous with local area networking. The history of NetWare releases can be divided into two distinct phases, as follows:

- **Bindery-based NetWare** The original NetWare products stored user account information in a simple flat database called the **bindery**. Each NetWare server maintained its own bindery and performed its own user authentications. The 3.*x* versions of NetWare were enormously popular and continued to be used by many installations for years after directory-based NetWare appeared. NetWare 3.12, released in 1993, was intended to be the final bindery-based version, but there was still a sufficiently large user base in the late 1990s to warrant a 3.2 release, for Y2K compatibility reasons. Novell finally discontinued its support for version 3.2 in February 2002.

- **Directory-based NetWare** NetWare 4.0, released in April 1993, was the first commercial operating system to be based on a hierarchical directory service, which Novell then called NetWare Directory Services (NDS). NDS eventually came to stand for Novell Directory Services, until the name was changed again to Novell eDirectory in 2002. Directory-based NetWare uses a centralized, replicated, partitioned directory service database to store information about many types of network resources, including users, computers, and applications. Instead of logging on to individual servers, as with bindery-based NetWare, users log on to the directory service and can access resources anywhere on the network. The current version of NetWare is 6.5.

NetWare Protocols

When NetWare was first developed in the mid-1980s, networking was more of a proprietary venture; interoperability between products made by different manufacturers was less of a concern than it is today. Novell, therefore, developed its own set of networking protocols, which have come to be named after the main network layer protocol, called Internetwork Packet Exchange (IPX).

> **NOTE** **Understanding the IPX Protocol Suite** For more information about the IPX protocol suite, see Chapter 5, "Network Layer Protocols," and Chapter 6, "Transport Layer Protocols."

Unlike the Windows operating systems, which began using TCP/IP as their default protocols in the mid-1990s, and UNIX, which has always used TCP/IP, NetWare remained committed to the IPX protocols until the release of NetWare 5 in 1999. Versions earlier than NetWare 5 could use TCP/IP for specific applications, such as Web servers, but NetWare's core file and print functionality still used IPX. For a period of time, it was possible to run TCP/IP with NetWare for file and print services using a technique called *tunneling*, but IPX was still required, because tunneling was just the encapsulation of IPX packets in IP datagrams.

For the IPX-based versions of NetWare, client computers had to have support for IPX to connect to a NetWare server. For this purpose, Microsoft developed its own version of the IPX protocols, called NWLink, which was compatible with IPX. All of the Windows operating systems can use NWLink to access shared resources on IPX-based NetWare servers.

Beginning with version 5, NetWare servers could use the TCP/IP suite as their native protocols, finally eliminating the need for IPX entirely. The current version of NetWare, version 6.5, installs TCP/IP by default, but the operating system still includes IPX support, which can run instead of or in addition to TCP/IP.

File and Print Services

NetWare is a network operating system that was originally designed primarily to provide clients with access to file and print services, and these have always been NetWare's primary strengths. Like the Windows server operating systems, NetWare has its own file system that lets you control access to server resources with great precision. The NetWare file system consists of volumes that you create on server drives. NetWare 6.5 includes several technologies that provide storage-related services, including the following:

- **Novell Storage Services (NSS)**   A 64-bit, indexed storage service that enables administrators to use the storage space on multiple drives to create an unlimited number of logical volumes up to eight terabytes in size. (One terabyte equals 1,099,511,627,776 bytes.)

- **Native File Access**   Enables Windows, Macintosh, and UNIX/Linux users to store and access files on NetWare servers using the operating systems' native formats.

- **iSCSI**   Provides NetWare with SAN capabilities, so that servers can maintain volumes that are physically located in separate hardware devices on an IP network.

- **iFolder**   A data synchronization service that enables users to access their data from a central repository that continually updates local copies of their files, using Hypertext Transfer Protocol (HTTP) connections.

The NetWare print architecture includes the following components:

- **Novell Distributed Print Services (NDPS)**   The network printing architecture that replaced NetWare's traditional queue-based printing with a single object in the directory service that provides simplified, centralized printer administration

- **iPrint**   Enables users to send print jobs to any printer on the Internet, using the Internet Printing Protocol (IPP)

Application Support

Although it was once the most popular network operating system in the industry, NetWare's dwindling market share has, in recent years, led many application developers to abandon the platform. Today, compared with Windows, there are relatively few applications available for NetWare servers, outside of those created by Novell itself.

Prior to 1996, NetWare included a collection of utilities, but no major applications. In 1996, Novell released a version of NetWare called intraNetWare, which consisted of NetWare 4.11 plus a collection of TCP/IP applications, including Web and FTP servers, for virtually the same price as the operating system alone. This was the only release of intraNetWare, but from that point on, the NetWare product included a collection of applications, as well as the core operating system.

Although the types of applications included with the operating system have remained fairly stable, the actual applications themselves have changed several times over the years. For example, intraNetWare included Novell Web Server, which was developed by Novell itself. Subsequent NetWare products included various Web servers licensed from other manufacturers. Today, Novell places greater emphasis on open source applications. NetWare 6.5 includes the following:

- **Apache Web Server**   Industry-standard open source application for hosting Web sites and Web-based applications for intranet or Internet clients

- **MySQL**   An open source database application that can be used for Internet sites and business applications

- **NetWare FTP Server**   Enables the NetWare server to act as a host for FTP clients on the local network or on the Internet

- **NetWare Web Search Server 3.0**   Provides Web site searching capabilities for intranet or Internet installations

- **Novell DNS/DHCP Services**   Enables the NetWare server to automatically configure TCP/IP clients on the network and resolve DNS host and domain names

UNIX and Linux

UNIX is a TCP/IP-based network operating system that was originally developed in the 1970s by Bell Labs, a division of AT&T. It is now available in dozens of different versions and variants, generally referred to as *distributions*. Unlike Windows and NetWare, UNIX is not the product of one particular company. A variety of different development teams worked on their own UNIX versions during the decades following the original release. These UNIX versions were released under many different names, including the following:

- **UNIX System V**   The descendant of the original UNIX development program started by AT&T in the 1970s. The UNIX trademark has changed hands several times over the years, and the UNIX System V source code is now owned by The Santa Cruz Operation, Inc. (SCO).

- **Berkeley Software Distribution (BSD) UNIX**   BSD UNIX was one of the first variants to splinter off from the original AT&T development effort, and it has become one of the most consistently popular UNIX products. The most popular BSD UNIX versions today are FreeBSD, OpenBSD, and NetBSD, all of which are open source products, which means that the operating systems and their source code are available free of charge.

- **Sun Solaris**   Sun Microsystems markets Solaris, one of the most popular and user-friendly commercial UNIX operating systems available. Solaris is essentially a modified version of BSD UNIX with elements of SVR4, one of the progenitors of UNIX System V. Solaris also includes Open Windows, one of the better graphical interfaces for UNIX.

- **Hardware-specific UNIX variants**   Several hardware manufacturers have developed their own UNIX variants, designed specifically to run on their computers. These include Hewlett Packard's HP-UX and IBM's Advanced Interactive Executive (better known as AIX).

- **Linux**   Linux is a UNIX-based subculture unto itself, in that there are many different Linux versions, both free and commercial. Originally developed as a school project by a Swedish student named Linus Torvalds, Linux is the quintessential open source operating system because its development and maintenance was, until recently, almost a completely noncommercial collaboration among enthusiasts communicating over the Internet. There are now some Linux distributions sold as commercial products with documentation and technical support, but others are still available free of charge.

> **NOTE   UNIX Processor Support**   While Windows and NetWare run solely on computers with Intel-based processors, the various UNIX operating systems run on computers with a wide variety of processors, including Intel, Sun Microsystems' proprietary SPARC processor, and others.

The UNIX and Linux operating systems are all built around the TCP/IP protocol suite. While all have similarities, they vary greatly in their appearance and capabilities due to the additional software included with the operating system and the commercial (or noncommercial) nature of the various products. Some UNIX variants are commercial products marketed by large software companies, such as Hewlett Packard, Sun Microsystems, and IBM. Others are developed and maintained as part of the open source movement, in which volunteer programmers work on the software in their spare time, usually communicating with their colleagues over the Internet, and freely releasing their work to the public domain. There are many different UNIX operating systems that you can download from the Internet free of charge, such as FreeBSD, NetBSD, and various Linux distributions.

This noncommercial side of UNIX development is based on the fact that many of the development teams freely post the source code for the operating system. Users with programming expertise can then modify the code to suit their particular needs and post the revised code for use by others. This is in stark contrast to the work of companies such as Microsoft and Novell, who zealously guard the source code for their operating systems.

Deploying UNIX/Linux

UNIX is primarily an application server platform, typically associated with Internet services, such as Web, FTP, and e-mail servers. As with Windows, all UNIX systems can function as both servers and clients simultaneously. You can use UNIX or Linux as a general-purpose LAN server, but the ease or difficulty of the server deployment process depends on the distribution you select. Commercial UNIX and Linux products frequently have automated graphical setup programs that detect system hardware and install the appropriate drivers and other components, making the server installation process similar to that of Windows and NetWare. Other distributions are less automated, requiring you to select and locate the proper drivers and then create startup scripts that load them from the command prompt.

UNIX/Linux Interfaces

UNIX and Linux are, in general, less intuitive operating systems than either Windows or NetWare. Although most distributions now include GUIs, UNIX and Linux are still primarily character based. While the Windows operating systems based on the NT kernel were all developed to use a graphical interface from the outset, UNIX and Linux (as well as NetWare) rely on the command line for their full capabilities. The GUIs available with most UNIX and Linux distributions today are just shells that insulate the user from the command line; they are not an integral part of the operating system, as with Windows. In fact, many UNIX and Linux distributions are equipped with multiple GUIs, so users can select the one they prefer.

To UNIX enthusiasts, the operating system's emphasis on the command prompt is not a shortcoming. The UNIX/Linux command interface requires a good deal of study and practice to use effectively. There are dozens of command line tools, each of which can have dozens of arcane switches and arguments. However, the command interface also provides a greater degree of power and flexibility than virtually any other operating system. While UNIX and Linux might not be suitable for unsophisticated users, it is a boon for programmers and power users.

File and Print Services

File and printer sharing are not primary functions of UNIX and Linux, as they are with Windows and NetWare. There are several mechanisms that UNIX and Linux can use to share files, but none of them are as ubiquitous or integral as Windows or NetWare file sharing.

FTP and Telnet

All UNIX and Linux distributions use TCP/IP, and all include both client and server functionality for the FTP and Telnet application layer protocols. Because FTP and Telnet are TCP/IP standards, the clients and servers supplied with different operating systems are completely interoperable. You can use FTP and Telnet with computers running different UNIX or Linux distributions, or even different operating system platforms. For example, in many cases, FTP and Telnet are the only way for a Windows client to access files on a UNIX server without installing special software.

FTP provides a client with rudimentary access to the file system on a server. The client can navigate the directory tree, list the contents of directories, and copy files to or from the server drives. However, unlike the file sharing in Windows or NetWare, FTP does not enable a client to open a file from its location on the server. For example, if you want to use your word processor to open a document on a server drive, and you only have FTP access to that drive, you must use your FTP client to connect to the server, then download the file to your computer, and then open the local copy in the word processor. If you modify the document and want to make it available to the rest of the network, you must upload the new version back to the server. For this reason, FTP is generally the last resort when it comes to UNIX/Linux file sharing.

Telnet is a remote terminal application that enables a client to execute commands on a remote server. You can therefore use Telnet to edit a file on a server drive by running an editor in the Telnet session and opening the file. However, Telnet does not provide the same file sharing functionality found in Windows and NetWare. When you work with a server file using Telnet, you are actually running an application on the remote server. If you want to use Telnet to open a server document in a word processor, the word processor application must be installed on the server. You cannot use an application installed on the client computer to open a server file by using Telnet.

Network File System (NFS)

The most commonly used file sharing mechanism in the UNIX/Linux world is the **Network File System (NFS)**, which was developed by Sun Microsystems in the 1980s. NFS has now been standardized by the Internet Engineering Task Force (IETF) as Request for Comments (RFC) 1813, "NFS Version 3 Protocol Specification." Releasing the NFS standard to the public domain made it possible for other manufacturers to implement it; as a result, most UNIX and Linux distributions support NFS file sharing. All NFS implementations that conform to the standard are interoperable, making it possible for different UNIX and Linux distributions to access each other's file systems. In addition, NFS support is also available for Windows, NetWare, and Macintosh, although in some cases you must purchase a separate product.

NFS is a platform-independent, client/server application in which a server exports a part of its file system, and clients access the shared resource by mounting it into their own file systems. The result is that the shared server directories appear as though they are part of the client's local file system, and users can open the server files in their own applications, just as though they were stored on a local drive.

Compared with the file sharing mechanisms in Windows and NetWare, NFS is relatively simple, with the clients performing the bulk of the file system integration. NFS servers simply supply files to clients; it is up to the client implementations to integrate the files they receive from the server into the local file system. NFS servers are also stateless, meaning that they do not keep track of the files individual clients have open. If an NFS server fails, clients can simply retry their requests until the server is back in operation. If an NFS client fails, there is no damaging effect on the server and no need for a complex reconnection sequence.

Samba

Samba is a collection of applications, developed and distributed using the open source model, that enable non-Windows operating systems to communicate by using the Windows SMB protocol. Installing Samba on a UNIX or Linux server enables Windows clients on the network to access the files and printers on the server, just as though they were hosted by another Windows system.

> **MORE INFO**   **Learning About Samba**   *For more information about Samba, see the Samba home page at us2.samba.org/samba/samba.html.*

Line Printer Remote (LPR) and Line Printer Daemon (LPD)

The LPR and LPD programs are the client and server halves, respectively, of the most commonly used network printing solution on the UNIX/Linux platform. In UNIX terminology, a **daemon** is a program that runs continuously in the background, much like a service in Windows. LPD runs on a computer functioning as a print server and LPR runs on client systems. The client uses LPR to send print jobs to the print server, and LPD is responsible for queuing them and feeding them to the printer itself.

Virtually all UNIX and Linux distributions include LPR and LPD, as do other operating systems, including Windows.

Applications Support

The UNIX and Linux operating systems are based on a small kernel, with relatively few functions being integrated into the operating system itself. Instead, most of the operating system's capabilities are implemented as separate tools that call the functions provided by the kernel. Many of the basic command line tools traditionally associated with UNIX and Linux are implemented in virtually all distributions, but the inclusion of larger applications is left up to individual developers.

In most cases, the decision to include applications in a particular UNIX or Linux distribution is based on its cost and distribution channel. A commercial distribution will likely include a large assortment of applications, while a free one might include few or none. In either case, however, the open source model upon which much of the UNIX and Linux community is based carries over to application development as well. Many of the best and most popular UNIX/Linux applications (such as the Apache Web server, for example) are open source and available without charge.

Apple Macintosh

Apple Macintosh computers have included networking capabilities virtually since their inception. Early Macintosh computers include a network interface called a *LocalTalk adapter* as part of their standard equipment, and the Mac OS operating system uses a proprietary networking protocol suite called *AppleTalk*. AppleShare is a file and printer sharing solution that enables a Macintosh computer to function as a server and provides the security features needed to password-protect data resources and to monitor network activity. The computers on a Macintosh network are divided into *zones*, which are essentially organizational units that make it easier to locate network resources. Together, these components provide basic networking capabilities that are suitable for joining a handful of Apple computers into a network and sharing files and printers. The performance of an all-Apple network is rudimentary and not designed for heavy traffic, but it does enable Macintosh computers to share resources.

As the years passed, Apple, along with the rest of the computer networking industry, moved away from their proprietary solutions and toward recognized standards. Macintosh computers now have Ethernet network interface adapters built into them and use the industry-standard TCP/IP protocols for network communications. The AppleTalk protocols from the presentation and application layers of the Open Systems Interconnection (OSI) reference model—Apple Filing Protocol (AFP) and AppleShare—were retained and now use the services of the TCP/IP protocols at the network and transport layers, and Ethernet at the data-link layer. This version of AppleShare is now known as *AppleShare IP*.

The latest version of the Macintosh operating system, called Mac OS X, is based on the UNIX kernel, though it retains the familiar Macintosh interface. The operating system includes Samba and NFS to provide Windows and UNIX connectivity, so virtually any client can access file and printer resources on a Macintosh computer. Also, for the first time, a server version of the Macintosh operating system is available, called *Mac OS X Server*.

Test your
knowledge of
operating
systems by
completing
Exercise 8-2,
"Network
Operating
System
Products,"
now.

As a server platform, Macintosh lacks the broad-based application support found in Windows and UNIX/Linux, but with the proper hardware, it can be a good performer. In most cases, however, Macintosh computers are used as servers only on all-Macintosh networks. It is rare to see a Windows or UNIX shop use Macintosh computers as servers.

CONNECTING CLIENTS

A client is a software component that enables a computer to access the resources provided by a server. Clients can take many forms, and they can either be included as part of an operating system or distributed as a separate product. In its simplest form, a client is a stand-alone program that sends requests to and receives replies from a server. For example, a Web browser such as Microsoft Internet Explorer is a client that communicates with Web servers on a local network or on the Internet. In the same way, FTP, e-mail, and newsreader programs are all clients, as are programs that provide access to databases and other resources on a local network. These clients run as applications on a computer and use application layer protocols to communicate with their corresponding servers. Clients of this type are highly specialized—they only communicate with one type of server. Application layer clients contain no lower layer protocols of their own, relying instead on protocols such as Transmission Control Protocol (TCP), IP, and Ethernet, which are already installed on the computer, to provide network communications services.

The other main type of client enables you to access shared resources on the local network, such as files and printers. This type of client is more tightly integrated with the operating system—you don't have to launch a special program and you can access files and printers through your regular applications, just as if they were part of your local computer environment. This type of client is specific to the platform used by the server. There are clients for Windows networks, clients for NetWare, and clients for UNIX systems. In some cases, the client is supplied as part of the operating system, while in other cases you must install a separate client software package.

At one time, interoperability between computers running different operating systems was a major problem for network administrators. Client capabilities for particular combinations of operating systems could be insufficient, or even non-existent. Today, however, just about any operating system can function as a client of any server platform, and in many cases, no special software installation or configuration is required. Table 8-3 lists the types of clients that can be used to access each of the major server operating systems from each of the major workstation operating systems. These client solutions are discussed in the following sections.

Table 8-3 **Client/Server Operating System Interoperability Solutions**

	Windows Client	UNIX/Linux Client	Macintosh Client
Windows Server	SMB (native) FTP/Telnet	Microsoft Windows Services for UNIX Samba LPR/LPD FTP/Telnet	Microsoft Windows Services for Macintosh Samba FTP/Telnet
NetWare Server	Microsoft Client Service for NetWare Novell Client Novell Native File Access for Windows FTP	Novell NetWare NFS Services Novell Native File Access for UNIX FTP	Novell Native File Access for Macintosh NetWare Client for Mac OS (third party) FTP
UNIX/ Linux Server	Samba Microsoft Windows Services for UNIX LPR/LPD FTP/Telnet	NFS (native) LPR/LPD FTP/Telnet	MacNFS (third party) FTP
Macintosh Server	Samba (Mac OS X) FTP	NFS (Mac OS X) LPR/LPD FTP	AppleShare IP (native) FTP

> **NOTE Exam Objectives** *Objective 3.2 for the Network+ exam calls for students to be able to identify the basic capabilities of client workstations, such as client connectivity, local security mechanisms, and authentication.*

Microsoft Windows Client Capabilities

All versions of Windows—except Windows 3.1 and earlier—include both client and server capabilities with the operating system. This means that you can share the files and printers on any Windows systems and also use the client capabilities to access shared files and printers on other computers. Only Windows 3.1 and earlier versions shipped with no network client at all.

All Windows versions Windows 95 and later include everything you need to connect to a Windows network, including a complete client networking stack. The stack, shown in Figure 8-8, consists of the following major components:

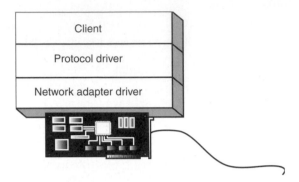

Figure 8-8   The Windows networking stack consists of several components that work together to provide client access to network resources.

- **Clients**   What the Windows operating systems call a "client" is actually a component called a *redirector*. A redirector is a module that receives requests for file system resources from an application and determines whether the requested resource is located on a local or network drive. It is the redirector that enables you to open a network file in your word processing program as easily as you would open a local file.

- **Protocol drivers**   The Windows protocol drivers implement the protocol suites required for network communications, such as Transmission Control Protocol/Internet Protocol (TCP/IP), IPX, or NetBIOS Enhanced User Interface (NetBEUI). In Windows terminology, the singular term *protocol* is used to refer to components such as TCP/IP and IPX, both of which are actually suites consisting of many different protocols. There are also other software components running on the system (for example, Ethernet) that Windows doesn't refer to as protocols, but that actually are.

- **Network interface adapter drivers**   The network interface adapter driver is a Windows device driver that provides the connection between the network interface adapter and the rest of the networking stack. The combination of the network interface adapter and its driver implement the data-link layer protocol used by the system, such as Ethernet or Token Ring. Windows supports network interface adapters that conform to the Network Driver Interface Specification (NDIS). Different operating systems use different NDIS driver versions.

- **Services**   Although they are not essential to client functionality, Windows includes services that provide additional networking capabilities. For example, to share resources on a Windows system, you must install the File and Printer Sharing for Microsoft Networks service.

Together with the network interface adapter, these software components provide the functions of all seven layers of the OSI model. A system can have more than one of each component installed, providing alternative paths through the networking stack for different applications. For example, most Windows operating systems include two redirectors: one for Windows networking, and one for connecting to NetWare servers. The operating systems include multiple protocol drivers for the same purpose. Connecting with older NetWare servers requires the IPX protocols, for example, while a Windows network uses TCP/IP. Windows and NetWare systems can share the same network medium, so a single data-link layer protocol implementation can provide services for both protocol stacks. It is also possible to install two network interface adapters, each with its own driver, and connect the computer to two networks—one for Windows and one for NetWare—but this is not often done.

> **NOTE   Using Windows for Workgroups**   Although the drivers can take different forms, all Windows operating systems contain the same set of basic networking components, with the exception of Windows for Workgroups. Windows for Workgroups was developed in the early days of Microsoft networking and is rarely used today. That operating system includes a redirector for Windows networking and NetBEUI and IPX, but it does not include a NetWare client or TCP/IP. However, you can add NetWare support by installing a client supplied by Novell, and you can add TCP/IP support by downloading and installing the TCP/IP-32 update, available from Microsoft at *ftp://ftp.microsoft.com/peropsys/windows/ public/tcpip/wfwt32.exe.*

Connecting to Windows Servers

In most cases, no special configuration is required for a Windows client to access resources on a Windows server. When the Windows installation program detects a network interface adapter in the computer, it automatically installs the following networking components:

- **Client for Microsoft Networks**   A client redirector that forwards requests for network resources to the protocol stack

- **File and Printer Sharing for Microsoft Networks**   A service that enables the computer to share its own files and printers

- **Internet Protocol (TCP/IP)**   A protocol module that implements the entire TCP/IP protocol stack

The SMB protocol, running at the application layer, uses these components to communicate with other computers running Windows on the network. To make Windows resources available to other computers on the network, the server administrator must create file or printer shares, which clients can then access by browsing the network, by using Windows Explorer, or by using some another application.

Connecting to NetWare Servers

When Microsoft first introduced its own network operating systems (Windows for Workgroups and Windows NT) in 1993, NetWare ruled the local area networking industry. To successfully compete with Novell, Microsoft knew that its operating systems had to be able to access NetWare resources, but early negotiations to have Novell supply a NetWare client for the Windows operating systems failed. As a result, Microsoft developed its own IPX protocol stack and its own NetWare clients for Windows. Some time later, Novell released clients of their own for Windows, which shipped with the NetWare product. Both companies have continued to update their software. For connectivity with IPX-based NetWare servers, you can choose either the Client Service for NetWare (CSNW) that ships with Windows or Novell's client, which you can download from Novell's Web site.

Using Microsoft Clients for NetWare

The NetWare clients provided by Microsoft fit into the same networking architecture as the client for Windows networking. For example, to access IPX-based NetWare resources in Windows XP, you must install CSNW and the NWLink IPX/SPX/NetBIOS Compatible Transport Protocol (NWLink) module, which is a reverse-engineered version of Novell's IPX protocols. To install CSNW and NWLink, you use the Local Area Connection Properties dialog box, accessible from the Windows Control Panel, as shown in Figure 8-9.

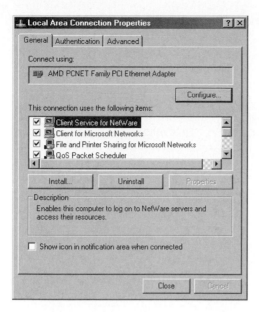

Figure 8-9   NetWare client modules in Windows XP

The CSNW module is a second redirector that you can use along with—or instead of—the Microsoft networking client. When an application requests access to a network resource, the system determines whether the request is for a Windows or NetWare file and sends it to the appropriate redirector. In most cases, Windows systems use the IPX protocols only to access NetWare servers. When both Windows and NetWare clients are installed, the NetWare redirector is connected to the NWLink protocol module, and the Microsoft redirector uses TCP/IP. The modules for both protocols are then connected to the same network interface adapter driver, as shown in Figure 8-10.

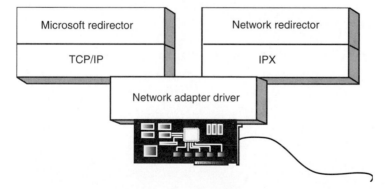

Figure 8-10   Microsoft's NetWare client functions as a second redirector within the Windows networking architecture, using its own version of the IPX protocols.

NOTE   *Using the Gateway Service for NetWare*   The CSNW included with most Windows operating systems provides basic NetWare connectivity, but Microsoft Windows 2000 Server and Windows NT Server include the Gateway Service for NetWare (GSNW), which expands this functionality. In addition to providing client access to NetWare servers, GSNW also enables Windows systems without an installed NetWare client to access NetWare resources. Once you've installed GSNW, the service's client can connect to NetWare servers. You can then configure GSNW to share those NetWare resources using the system's Microsoft networking capabilities. When a Windows client accesses the share on the Windows NT or Windows 2000 server, the server accesses the files on the NetWare server and relays them to the client.

The main limitation of the NetWare clients included with Windows is that they are designed only to access IPX-based NetWare servers. Current versions of NetWare use TCP/IP by default, and the Microsoft NetWare clients cannot communicate with them.

Using Novell Clients for NetWare

Novell continues to maintain its own client software packages for NetWare, which you can use instead of the ones included with Windows. The Novell clients included with the NetWare product are

■ Novell Client for Windows 95/98

■ Novell Client for Windows NT/2000/XP

Novell's clients provide full access to all NetWare features, including TCP/IP-based servers and the eDirectory directory service. Novell also provides a client application called ConsoleOne that enables administrators to manage the eDirectory tree from a workstation.

Once you install the Novell client on a Windows workstation, the Windows Login dialog box is replaced with a NetWare equivalent (as shown in Figure 8-11), which lets you log on to eDirectory and an Active Directory domain simultaneously.

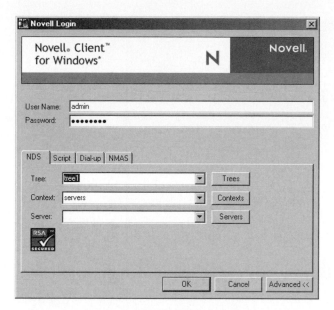

Figure 8-11   The Novell Login dialog box

Using Novell Native File Access for Windows

One of the most welcome additions to recent versions of NetWare is a feature
called Novell Native File Access, which enables Windows, Macintosh, and UNIX
workstations to access NetWare servers using their respective native protocols,
with no additional client software required. The Native File Access for Windows
feature enables the NetWare server to communicate using the SMB protocol and
the Common Internet File System (CIFS). With this capability installed on the
server, Windows clients can browse to NetWare servers and access their
resources, using standard Windows tools such as Windows Explorer, as
shown in Figure 8-12.

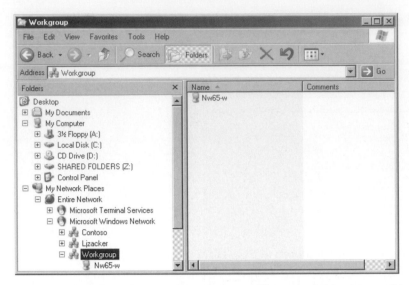

Figure 8-12   Novell Native File Access enables a NetWare server (Nw65-w) to appear in Windows Explorer without requiring additional client software.

Connecting to UNIX/Linux Servers

The only way to access a UNIX or Linux server by using a Windows workstation, without installing additional software, is to use tools such as the Windows FTP and Telnet clients for file system access and LPR for remote printer access. However, you can install additional software, either on the server or the client, to implement a fully functional file and printer access solution.

Windows systems use the SMB/CIFS protocols for resource sharing, and most UNIX and Linux systems use NFS. Therefore, the objective is either to provide Windows with NFS capabilities or to provide UNIX/Linux with SMB/CIFS capabilities. As noted earlier, you can install Samba on a UNIX or Linux system to provide it with SMB communication capabilities. This enables a Windows client to access the UNIX/Linux server's resources just as if they were hosted by a Windows server.

Another option is to implement NFS services on the computer running Windows, using Microsoft Windows Services for UNIX. Windows Services for UNIX is a separate product that includes the following NFS capabilities:

- **NFS server**   Enables a computer running Windows to export file system resources as NFS shares so that UNIX or Linux systems with NFS client capabilities can access it.

- **NFS client**   Enables a computer running Windows to access file system resources exported by NFS servers, such as UNIX and Linux systems. Users can browse and access NFS resources just as if they were Windows shares.

- **NFS gateway**   Enables a computer running Windows to function as a gateway between shared NFS resources and Windows network clients. The system functioning as the gateway accesses the NFS shares, using its NFS client capability, and then publishes the NFS resources to the network as Windows shares. This enables other network computers running Windows that do not have Windows Services for UNIX installed to access the NFS resources.

Connecting to Macintosh Servers

As is the case with Windows and UNIX/Linux, Windows and Macintosh systems use different native protocols for resource sharing. To achieve connectivity between a Macintosh server and a Windows client, you need to either implement AFP in Windows or SMB in Mac OS. Microsoft Services for Macintosh enables a computer running Windows to function as a file and print server for Macintosh clients using AFP, but it does not enable Windows clients to access a Macintosh server.

Macintosh OS X and OS X Server, however, include an implementation of Samba, which enables Windows clients to access Macintosh servers using their native SMB/CIFS protocols, with no additions or modifications needed at the client. To Windows clients, the Macintosh resources are integrated into the network, just as if they were Windows shares, and users can use standard Windows tools to browse and access those resources.

UNIX/Linux Client Capabilities

Virtually all UNIX and Linux operating systems include NFS client and server capabilities, which the computers use to access each other's file systems. In most cases, the ability of other operating systems to host UNIX and Linux clients is provided by NFS implementation.

Connecting to Windows Servers

As noted earlier, Samba enables you to implement SMB on a UNIX or Linux computer, and Microsoft Services for UNIX enables you to implement NFS on a computer running Windows. Both of these solutions are bidirectional, so you can take either course to provide UNIX and Linux clients with Windows server connectivity.

To implement NFS server capabilities on computers running Windows, you must buy a copy of the Windows Services for UNIX product for each computer that you want UNIX or Linux clients to access. You must also have the appropriate client access licenses for the UNIX clients accessing the Windows servers. Once you install the NFS server component on the Windows systems, UNIX and Linux clients can access the servers with no modifications.

To implement SMB on UNIX/Linux systems, you install the Samba package on each UNIX or Linux client. Samba is free. Once it is installed, you use the tools supplied with the package to mount Windows shares to the UNIX or Linux file system.

Connecting to NetWare Servers

To enable UNIX and Linux clients to access NetWare server resources, you must implement NFS on the server. Novell has two NFS implementations you can use, depending on your needs and on the NetWare version you are using.

NetWare NFS Services is a stand-alone product that enables a NetWare server to function as both an NFS server and an NFS gateway. Using the NFS server capability, UNIX and Linux clients can access NetWare file system resources by mounting them into their native file systems, just as they would with another UNIX or Linux system. The NFS gateway enables NFS resources exported on UNIX and Linux systems to appear to other (non-NFS) NetWare clients as NetWare resources.

Native File Access for UNIX is a similar product that is included with the current NetWare version (6.5) and is available as a separate product for earlier versions as far back as NetWare 5.1. Native File Access for UNIX provide only NFS server capabilities, enabling UNIX and Linux clients to access NetWare server resources with no additional client software. An NFS gateway for NetWare 6.5 is in development, and it will likely be available as a separate product.

Connecting to Macintosh Servers

In addition to including Samba for Windows connectivity, Mac OS X and OS X Server also include an NFS implementation that enables UNIX and Linux clients to access file system resources on Macintosh servers. The operating system also supports LPR and LPD, enabling UNIX and Linux clients to access Macintosh printers.

Macintosh Client Capabilities

As discussed earlier, Macintosh systems use AFP for resource sharing among themselves. Originally, AFP used AppleTalk, but it now runs over TCP/IP. To connect a Macintosh client to a server running another operating system, you can either implement AFP on the server or implement the server operating system's native resource-sharing protocol on Mac OS.

Connecting to Windows Servers

The Mac OS X operating system includes native support for SMB, so Macintosh clients can browse and access shared Windows resources with no special software installation or configuration. For earlier Mac OS versions, you must install Microsoft Windows Services for Macintosh on the Windows servers.

Services for Macintosh is an AFP implementation that runs on computers running Windows. It supports Macintosh client connections using either AppleTalk or TCP/IP. With Services for Macintosh installed on a Windows server, Macintosh clients can access Windows shares, store their files on the Windows server, and access Windows printers.

Connecting to NetWare Servers

There are two ways to give Macintosh clients access to NetWare servers. The first is to use Novell's Native File Access for Macintosh. Included with NetWare 6 and available for NetWare versions 5.1 and later, Native File Access for Macintosh is similar to the Native File Access implementations for Windows and UNIX. Native File Access implements AFP on the NetWare server, enabling Macintosh clients to access NetWare resources with no special client software. Native File Access supports AFP using TCP/IP. Earlier versions of NetWare include support for the AppleTalk protocols, but NetWare 6.5 does not.

The second way for Macintosh systems to access a NetWare server is to install a client on the workstation. Originally, Macintosh clients accessed NetWare servers by using a client that was installed on the Macintosh system. Novell originally developed this client but sold it many years ago to a company called Prosoft Engineering, Inc. (*www.prosofteng.com*). Prosoft has continued to market this client and now has the following two products available:

- **NetWare Client for Mac OS Classic–IPX Edition**   Enables Macintosh systems running Mac OS versions 7.6.1 to 9.2.2 to access NetWare servers using IPX. This is currently the only client that provides Macintosh connectivity to IPX-based NetWare networks.

- **NetWare Client for Mac OS X–IP Edition**   Enables Macintosh systems running Mac OS X versions 10.1.5 and later to access NetWare servers using TCP/IP. Unlike Novell Native File Access for Macintosh, which uses AFP for authentication and does not send a password to the NetWare server, the Client for Mac OS X performs a secure authentication by using public key encryption.

Connecting to UNIX/Linux Servers

The NFS capability included in Mac OS X is server-only; it does not enable the Macintosh system to access NFS resources exported by other systems, such as UNIX or Linux servers. To use a Macintosh workstation as an NFS client, you must use a third-party utility, such as MacNFS, by Thursby Software (*www.thursby.com*).

> **NOTE** **Exam Objectives**   Objective 4.4 for the Network+ exam calls for students to be able to configure a client to connect to the following servers, given specific parameters: UNIX/Linux, NetWare, Windows, and Macintosh.

UNDERSTANDING DIRECTORY SERVICES

A **directory service** is a database of user accounts and other information that network administrators use to control access to shared network resources. When users connect to a network, they have to be authenticated before they can access network resources. Authentication is the process of checking the user's credentials (usually a user name and a password) against the directory. Users who supply the proper credentials are permitted access according to the permissions specified by the network administrator.

As explained at the beginning of this chapter, on a peer-to-peer network, each computer maintains its own user accounts and security settings, while client/ server networks rely on a centralized security database or directory service. Directory services range from simple, flat file databases containing a list of accounts to complex, hierarchical databases that store information about a network's hardware, software, and human resources.

Flat file directory services are suitable for relatively small installations, but for large enterprise networks, they are difficult to maintain. For this reason, both Novell and Microsoft have developed hierarchical directory services that can support networks of virtually any size and have the fault tolerance and security capabilities needed for large installations.

The NetWare Bindery

The bindery, included in all versions of NetWare earlier than and including version 3.2, is a simple database that contains a list of user and group accounts, basic information about those accounts, and little else. The bindery even stretches the definition of a directory service because it is not a centralized storehouse of information for an entire network. Every bindery-based NetWare server maintains its own list of accounts, which it uses to authenticate users trying to access its resources. If network users need to access files or printers on more than one NetWare server, they must have an account on each server, and each server performs its own separate user authentication.

In the early days of NetWare, LANs were relatively small and users generally required access to only one or two servers, so the bindery was all they needed. In fact, there are still some NetWare shops that don't feel the need for an enterprise directory service, which is why the final bindery-based version of NetWare (version 3.2) was only removed from the market in late 2000, seven years after the first release of the NDS version of NetWare. However, as a network grows larger, the bindery grows increasingly impractical. If a user requires access to 10 different servers, an administrator must create an account for the user on each one, and every time the user's information changes, an administrator must modify each bindery account individually.

Novell eDirectory

NetWare 4.0, released in 1993, was the first version of NetWare to include NDS, which at that time stood for NetWare Directory Services. The name was later changed to Novell Directory Services, and then changed again to eDirectory. eDirectory was the first hierarchical directory service to be a commercial success. In the years since its initial release, it has matured into a robust enterprise network solution.

A hierarchical directory service is composed of objects, which are arranged in a treelike structure, much like a file system directory tree, as shown in Figure 8-13. There are two basic kinds of objects in a directory service: container objects and leaf objects. Container objects are the equivalent of directories in a file system; they hold other objects. Leaf objects represent network resources, such as users, groups, computers, and applications. All objects are composed of attributes (which eDirectory calls *properties*), the nature of which depends on the object's type. For example, the properties of a user object can specify the user's name, password, telephone number, e-mail address, and other pertinent information.

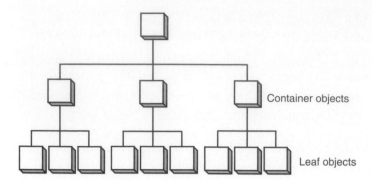

Figure 8-13   eDirectory and other hierarchical directory services consist of objects arranged in a tree structure.

NOTE **X.500 and Directory Services**   The basic components of the hierarchical directory services in NetWare and Windows, such as objects and attributes, container objects and leaf objects, and the tree structure, are derived from the X.500 directory service standard, which was developed by the International Telecommunications Union (ITU) and the International Organization for Standardization (ISO). X.500 is not a commercial directory services product. Rather, it is a model for a global directory that is designed to enable users to search for people and objects by providing an object naming standard and a hierarchical tree structure.

The types of objects that you can create in the eDirectory tree and the properties of those object types are determined by the directory schema. Network applications can modify the schema to create their own specialized object types or to add new properties to existing object types. The capability for schema modification makes the directory service a flexible tool for application developers. For example, a network backup program can create an object type used to represent a job queue, which contains a list of backup jobs waiting to be executed as one of its properties.

Deploying the directory service is a matter of designing and building an eDirectory tree, which is a hierarchy of containers into which administrators put the various leaf objects. The tree design can be based on the geographical layout of the network, with containers representing buildings, floors, and rooms, or it can be based on the structure of the organization using the network, with containers representing divisions, departments, and workgroups. An eDirectory tree can also use a combination of the two, or any other organizational paradigm the administrator chooses. The important part of the design process is grouping users with similar network access requirements, to simplify the process of assigning them permissions. Permissions flow down through the eDirectory tree and are inherited by the objects beneath, like on a file system. Granting a container object permission to access a particular resource means that all of the objects in that container receive the same permission.

Unlike the NetWare bindery, which is server-specific, there is usually only one eDirectory database for the entire network. When a user logs on, he logs on to eDirectory, not a specific server, and one authentication can grant the user access to resources located anywhere on the network. This means that administrators need to create and maintain only one account for each user instead of one for each server the user accesses, as in bindery-based NetWare.

Because the entire NetWare network relies on eDirectory, the directory has features that ensure its availability at all times. You can split the eDirectory database into partitions, which are stored on different servers, to make it easy for a user to log on using a nearby server. In addition, you can create replicas of the partitions and store those on different servers. In this way, if a server containing all or part of the eDirectory tree fails, users can still access the directory from another server.

Windows NT Domains

Windows NT uses a directory service that is more capable and more complex than the NetWare bindery, but it is still not suitable for a large enterprise network. Windows NT networks are organized into **domains**, which contain accounts that represent the users, groups, and computers on the network. A domain is a flat file database like a bindery, but it is not server specific. The domain directory is stored on Windows NT servers that have been designated as **domain controllers** during the operating system installation.

> **NOTE** **Windows NT and Internet Domains**   A Windows NT domain is not the same as an Internet domain (such as those used by DNS). Windows NT domains are named using a single word, while DNS domains have names that are at least two words long and are separated by periods (such as microsoft.com). Be sure not to confuse the two.

A Windows NT server can be a Primary Domain Controller (PDC) or a Backup Domain Controller (BDC). Most domains have at least two domain controllers, for fault-tolerance purposes. Each domain has one (and only one) PDC, which contains the main copy of the domain directory. Domains can have any number of BDCs, each of which contains a replica of the domain. Whenever network administrators modify the directory by adding, deleting, or modifying accounts, they are making changes to the files on the PDC, which holds the master copy of the data. At periodic intervals, the PDC replicates the directory database to the BDCs, thus keeping the BDCs updated with the latest information. This process, called **single master replication**, is shown in Figure 8-14.

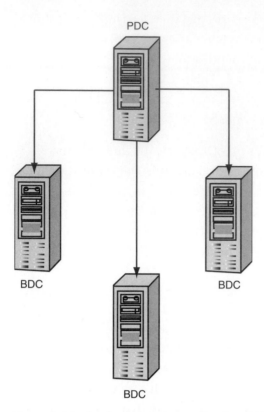

Figure 8-14   In single master replication, Windows NT domain controllers keep their information updated by replicating in one direction, from the PDC to the BDCs.

> **NOTE   Creating Domain Controllers**   You can only designate a Windows NT server as a domain controller during the operating system installation. Once Windows NT is installed, you can promote a BDC to a PDC or demote a PDC to a BDC, but you can't convert a regular server into a domain controller, nor can you convert a domain controller into a regular server.

It is common for larger Windows NT networks to have multiple domains that can communicate with each other. For this to occur, administrators must create trust relationships between the domains, using the User Manager For Domains utility. Trust relationships operate in one direction only. If Domain A trusts Domain B, users from Domain B can access resources in Domain A (assuming they have the appropriate permissions). For Domain A users to access Domain B resources, an administrator must create a trust running in that direction.

Because you have to create trust relationships manually, managing a large enterprise Windows NT network with many domains can be extremely labor intensive. Users who have to access resources in multiple domains must have a separate account in each domain, just as users of bindery-based NetWare need a separate account on each server.

Active Directory

Microsoft first introduced an enterprise directory service in the Windows 2000 Server product line, calling it Active Directory. Active Directory is similar in structure to eDirectory in that it uses a hierarchical tree design comprised of container and leaf objects. The fundamental unit of organization in Active Directory is still the domain, but now you can group domains together into a tree and even group multiple trees together into a forest. Domains that are in the same tree automatically have bidirectional trust relationships established between them, eliminating the need for administrators to create them manually. The trust relationships are also transitive, meaning that if Domain A trusts Domain B and Domain B trusts Domain C, then Domain A trusts Domain C.

In Windows NT, the domain structure is completely separate from the concept of the DNS domain, but the Active Directory architecture is fully integrated into the DNS namespace. Computers on an Active Directory network use DNS names instead of NetBIOS names, and workstations use DNS requests to locate the domain controllers on the network. Domains in the same tree are named with multiword domain names (just as in DNS) that reflect the tree structure of the directory. For example, if the root domain in a tree is called adatum.com, the other domains beneath the root could have names like sales.adatum.com and engineering.adatum.com.

The Active Directory architecture still uses domain controllers, like Windows NT does, but you have a great deal more flexibility in their configuration. In Windows 2000 Server and Windows Server 2003, you can promote any server to a domain controller at any time or demote it back to a standard member server. In addition, there are no more PDCs and BDCs; all domain controllers on an Active Directory network function as peers. Administrators can make changes to the Active Directory data on any domain controller, and the servers propagate those changes to the other domain controllers throughout the network, as shown in Figure 8-15. This is called **multiple master replication**.

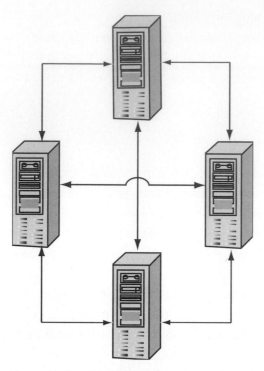

Figure 8-15   The Active Directory architecture uses multiple master replication to keep all its domain controllers updated.

With these features, Active Directory can support networks of virtually any size, including corporate networks with sites located across in the world. You can configure the replication of data between domain controllers to occur only at specific times (to minimize the traffic on expensive WAN links), create a directory hierarchy that reflects the locations of the branch offices, and even create links between separate trees or forests built by different companies, in the event of a merger.

Network Information System (NIS)

Network Information System (NIS) is a relatively simple directory service, originally created by Sun Microsystems. The service was originally called Yellow Pages (and many of the commands used to administer the service still begin with yp), but the name had to be changed to avoid conflict with registered trademarks. NIS is basically a service that stores frequently replicated configuration files in a central location, where they can be accessed by any system that needs them. For example, rather than create and maintain an identical /etc/passwd file containing user account information on every computer, NIS enables administrators to maintain a single file stored on an NIS server. NIS clients can then access the server file when authenticating users.

In an NIS deployment, there are three possible roles, as follows:

- **Server** Stores the master copies of the centralized configuration files. All modifications to the files are applied to the server copy.

- **Slave** Stores duplicate copies of the centralized configuration files, for fault tolerance purposes. The files on the slave are updated whenever an administrator modifies the master copies on the server.

- **Client** Accesses the configuration files on an NIS server or slave, rather than using the copies on the local drive.

NIS+ is an enhanced version of NIS, also created by Sun Microsystems, that uses a hierarchical directory structure, much like Active Directory and eDirectory. Network nodes are represented by objects in the NIS+ directory. There are six types of nodes: directory, entry, group, link, table, and private. NIS+ also supports data encryption and secure authentication using the remote procedure call (RPC) protocol.

Test your knowledge of directory services by completing Exercise 8-3, "Directory Service Concepts," now.

Most UNIX and Linux distributions include NIS client and server support. NIS+ has only been implemented by Sun Microsystems. NIS+ client support is available for Linux, and a project to develop a NIS+ server for Linux was begun but has since been abandoned.

UNDERSTANDING TCP/IP SERVICES

In addition to its communication capabilities, the TCP/IP suite includes a number of applications that range from helpful tools to essential services. This section examines some of the most important of these services and some of the tools that network administrators use to maintain and troubleshoot TCP/IP systems.

The core protocols that TCP/IP uses to provide communication between computers—IP, TCP, and the User Datagram Protocol (UDP)—rely on several other services to perform their functions. Some of these services are independent protocols, such as the Address Resolution Protocol (ARP), which runs on every TCP/IP computer and enables IP to discover the hardware address of a computer using a particular IP address. Other services, such as DHCP and DNS, are both protocols and applications that run on their own servers.

NOTE **Exam Objectives** Objective 2.7 for the Network+ exam calls for students to be able to identify the purpose of the following network services: DHCP/BOOTP, DNS, NAT/ICS, WINS, and SNMP.

Using Dynamic Host Configuration Protocol (DHCP)

In Chapter 5, "Network Layer Protocols," you learned about the advantages of TCP/IP's self-contained addressing system and about the nature of IP addresses themselves. Although there are many advantages in IP addressing, there are also several significant problems with it— for example, every computer on the network must have a unique IP address. This requirement complicates the process of configuring the TCP/IP client. The administrator of a TCP/IP network must be sure that every computer is configured properly, which means keeping track of the IP address assignments so that no duplication occurs. On a small network, configuring the individual TCP/IP workstations and keeping track of IP addresses is relatively painless, but on a large corporate internetwork, it can be a monumental task.

DHCP Origins

Over the years, the developers of the TCP/IP protocols have created several solutions that address the problem of configuring the TCP/IP settings for large numbers of workstations. The first of these was the Reverse Address Resolution Protocol (RARP), which was designed for diskless workstations that had no way to permanently store their TCP/IP settings. RARP is essentially the opposite of ARP, and uses the same message format. While ARP broadcasts an IP address in an effort to discover its equivalent hardware address, RARP broadcasts the hardware address, as shown in Figure 8-16. A RARP server then responds by transmitting the IP address assigned to that client computer. RARP was suitable for use with diskless workstations on early TCP/IP networks, but it isn't sufficient for today's needs because it can only supply the computer with an IP address. It provides none of the other settings needed by a typical workstation now, such as a subnet mask and a default gateway.

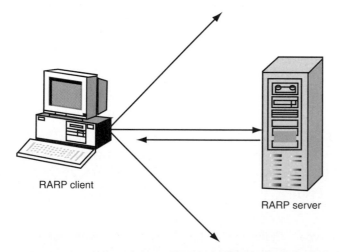

RARP client

RARP server

Figure 8-16   A workstation that uses RARP receives an IP address from an RARP server in response to a broadcast message containing the client's hardware address.

MORE INFO   **Understanding ARP and RARP**   *For more information about ARP and RARP, see Chapter 7, "TCP/IP."*

The next automatic TCP/IP configuration mechanism was called the Bootstrap Protocol (BOOTP). BOOTP does more than RARP, which is why it is still sometimes used today, while RARP is not. BOOTP enables a TCP/IP workstation to retrieve settings for all of the configuration parameters it needs to run, including an IP address, subnet mask, default gateway, and DNS server addresses. A workstation can also download an executable boot file from a BOOTP server, using the Trivial File Transfer Protocol (TFTP), which shows that BOOTP, like RARP, was designed for diskless workstations. The drawback of BOOTP is that although it can perform all the TCP/IP client communication tasks required by today's computers, an administrator must still manually specify the settings for each workstation on the BOOTP server. There is no mechanism for automatically assigning a unique IP address to each computer, nor is there any way to prevent two computers from receiving the same IP address as a result of administrator error.

The **Dynamic Host Configuration Protocol (DHCP)** was created for the express purpose of addressing the shortcomings in RARP and BOOTP. DHCP is based on BOOTP to a great extent, but instead of simply supplying predetermined configuration parameters to TCP/IP clients, DHCP can dynamically allocate IP addresses from a pool and reclaim them when they are no longer in use. This prevents workstations from being assigned duplicate IP addresses. It also enables administrators to move computers around among subnets without manually reconfiguring them. In addition, DHCP can deliver a wide range of configuration parameters to TCP/IP clients, including platform-specific parameters added by third-party developers.

DHCP Architecture

The basic components of DHCP are defined in RFC 2131, "Dynamic Host Configuration Protocol," published by the IETF in March 1997. RFC 2132, "DHCP Options and BOOTP Vendor Extensions," defines additional options and extensions that can supply other types of information to client computers.

DHCP consists of three components: a client, a server, and the protocol that they use to communicate with each other. DHCP is integrated into the networking client on most current TCP/IP implementations, even if the operating system doesn't specifically refer to it as such. For example, on a Windows XP system, in the Internet Protocol (TCP/IP) Properties dialog box, when you select Obtain An IP Address Automatically, you are actually activating the DHCP client.

The DHCP server is an application that services requests from DHCP clients. All of the current Windows and NetWare server operating systems include a DHCP server implementation, as do many UNIX and Linux distributions. Because DHCP is an Internet standard, any DHCP client can retrieve configuration settings from a DHCP server running on any platform.

The core function of DHCP is to assign IP addresses to clients. This is the most complicated part of the service, because the IP address must be unique for each client computer. The DHCP standard defines three types of IP address allocation, as follows:

- **Manual allocation** An administrator assigns a specific IP address to a computer in the DHCP server, and the server provides that address to the computer when it is requested.

- **Automatic allocation** The DHCP server supplies clients with IP addresses taken from a common pool of addresses, and the clients retain the assigned addresses permanently.

- **Dynamic allocation** The DHCP server supplies IP addresses to clients from a pool on a leased basis. The client must periodically renew the lease or else the address returns to the pool for reallocation.

Manual allocation is the functional equivalent of a BOOTP address assignment. This option requires more labor from network administrators, but it is necessary for systems that require permanently assigned IP addresses, such as Internet servers that have DNS names associated with specific addresses. Administrators could conceivably configure the TCP/IP clients of these computers directly, but using the DHCP server to assign IP addresses prevents them from being accidentally duplicated.

Automatic allocation is a fitting solution for networks on which administrators rarely move workstations between subnets. Assigning IP addresses from a pool (called a *scope*) eliminates the need to furnish a specific address for each computer and prevents address duplication. Permanently assigning those addresses minimizes the network traffic generated by DHCP client/server communications.

Once the server is configured, dynamic allocation completely automates the TCP/IP client configuration process, enabling administrators to add, remove, and relocate computers as needed. When a computer boots, the server leases an address to the computer for a given period of time, renews the lease if the computer remains active, and reclaims the address when it is no longer in use, returning it to the pool

DHCP Message Format

Communications between DHCP clients and servers use a single message format, which is illustrated in Figure 8-17. All DHCP messages are carried within UDP datagrams, using the well-known port numbers 67 at the server and 68 at the client, as established by the Internet Assigned Numbers Authority (IANA).

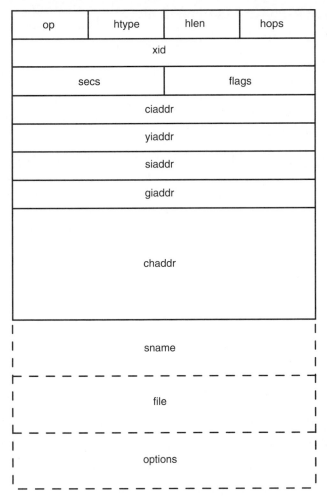

Figure 8-17   The DHCP message format

The functions of the fields in the DHCP message are as follows:

- **op (1 byte)**   Specifies whether the message originated at a client or a server

- **htype (1 byte)**   Specifies the type of hardware address in the chaddr field

- **hlen (1 byte)**   Specifies the length of the hardware address in the chaddr field, in bytes

- **hops (1 byte)**   Specifies the number of routers in the path between the client and the server

- **xid (4 bytes)**   Contains a transaction identifier used to associate requests and replies

- **secs (2 bytes)**   Specifies the elapsed time (in seconds) since the beginning of an address allocation or lease renewal process

- **flags (2 bytes)**   Indicates whether DHCP servers and relay agents should use broadcast transmissions to communicate with a client instead of unicast transmissions

- **ciaddr (4 bytes)**   Contains the client computer's IP address when it is in the bound, renewal, or rebinding state

- **yiaddr (4 bytes)**   Contains the IP address being offered to a client by a server

- **siaddr (4 bytes)**   Specifies the IP address of the next server in a bootstrap sequence; used only when the DHCP server supplies an executable boot file to a diskless workstation

- **giaddr (4 bytes)**   Contains the IP address of a DHCP relay agent located on a different network, when necessary

- **chaddr (16 bytes)**   Contains the hardware address of the client system, using the type and length specified in the htype and hlen fields

- **sname (64 bytes)**   Contains either the host name of the DHCP server or overflow data from the options field

- **file (128 bytes)**   Contains the name and path to an executable boot file for diskless workstations

- **options (variable)**   Contains a series of DHCP options, which specify the configuration parameters for the client computer

The options field is where the DHCP message carries all of the TCP/IP parameters assigned to a client, except for the IP address. Each option consists of three subfields, as shown in Figure 8-18.

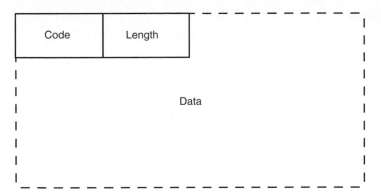

Figure 8-18   The DHCP option format

The functions of the option subfields are as follows:

- **Code (1 byte)**   Specifies the function of the option
- **Length (1 byte)**   Specifies the length of the data field
- **Data (variable)**   Contains information specific to the option type

The DHCP Message Type option is required. This option contains a code that specifies the function of each message. There are eight possible values for this option, as follows:

- **1 DHCPDISCOVER**   Used by clients to request configuration parameters from a DHCP server
- **2 DHCPOFFER**   Used by servers to offer IP addresses to requesting clients
- **3 DHCPREQUEST**   Used by clients to accept or renew an IP address assignment
- **4 DHCPDECLINE**   Used by clients to reject an offered IP address
- **5 DHCPACK**   Used by servers to acknowledge a client's acceptance of an offered IP address
- **6 DHCPNAK**   Used by servers to reject a client's acceptance of an offered IP address
- **7 DHCPRELEASE**   Used by clients to terminate an IP address lease
- **8 DHCPINFORM**   Used by clients to obtain additional TCP/IP configuration parameters from a server

DHCP Communications

DHCP clients initiate communication with servers when they boot for the first time, as illustrated in Figure 8-19. The client generates a series of DHCPDISCOVER messages, which it transmits as broadcasts. At this point, the client has no IP address and is said to be in the init state. Like all broadcasts, these transmissions are limited to the client's local network, but administrators can install a DHCP Relay Agent service on a computer on the LAN, which relays the messages to DHCP servers on other networks. This enables a single DHCP server to service clients on multiple LANs.

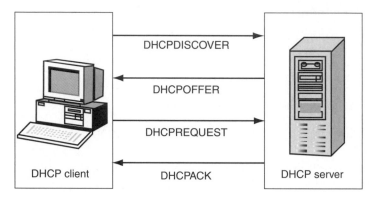

Figure 8-19   DHCP client/server communications

When a DHCP server receives a DHCPDISCOVER message from a client, it generates a DHCPOFFER message containing an IP address and whatever other optional parameters the server is configured to supply. In most cases, the server transmits this as a unicast message directly to the client. Because the client broadcasts its DHCPDISCOVER messages, it might receive DHCPOFFER responses from multiple servers. After a specified period of time, the client stops its broadcasting and accepts one of the offered IP addresses. To signal its acceptance, the client generates a DHCPREQUEST message. The DHCPREQUEST message contains the address of the server from which it is accepting the offer, along with the offered IP address. Because the client has not yet configured itself with the offered parameters, it transmits the DHCPREQUEST message as a broadcast. This broadcast notifies the server that the client is accepting the offered address and also notifies the other servers on the network that the client is rejecting their offers.

When the server receives the DHCPREQUEST message, it commits the offered IP address and other settings to its database, using a combination of the client's hardware address and the offered IP address as a unique identifier for the assignment. This is known as the *lease identification cookie*. To conclude its part of the transaction, the server sends a DHCPACK message to the client, acknowledging that the process is complete. If the server cannot complete the assignment (because it has already assigned the offered IP address to another system, for example), it transmits a DHCPNAK message to the client and the whole process begins again.

As a final test, the client transmits an ARP Request message to ensure that no other system on the network is using the assigned IP address. If the client does not receive a response, the DHCP transaction is completed and the client enters what is known as the *bound* state. If another system does respond, the client can't use the IP address, and it transmits a DHCPDECLINE message to the server, nullifying the transaction. The client can then reissue a series of DHCPDISCOVER messages, restarting the whole process.

DHCP Leasing

The process that a DHCP server uses to assign configuration parameters to a client is the same whether the server uses manual, automatic, or dynamic allocation. With manual and automatic allocation, this process is the end of the DHCP client/server communications. The client keeps the settings assigned to it by the server until someone explicitly changes them or forces a reassignment. However, when the server dynamically allocates settings, the client leases its IP address for a certain period of time and must renew the lease to continue using it.

The length of the IP address lease is configured at the server. It is typically measured in days and is generally based on whether computers are frequently moved around the network or whether IP addresses are in short supply. Shorter leases generate more network traffic but enable servers to reclaim unused addresses faster. For a relatively stable network, longer leases reduce the amount of traffic that DHCP generates.

The lease renewal process, illustrated in Figure 8-20, begins when a bound client reaches what is known as the *renewal time value*, or *T1 value*, of its lease. By default, the renewal time value is 50 percent of the lease period. When a client reaches this point, it enters the renewing state and begins generating DHCPREQUEST messages. The client transmits the messages to the server that holds the lease as unicasts, unlike the broadcast DHCPREQUEST messages the client generates while in the init state. If the server is available to receive the message, it responds with either a DHCPACK message, which renews the lease and restarts the lease time clock, or a DHCPNAK message, which terminates the lease and forces the client to begin the address assignment process again from the beginning.

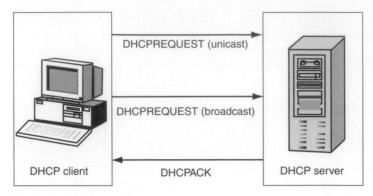

Figure 8-20   The DHCP lease renewal process

If the server does not respond to the DHCPREQUEST unicast message, the client continues to send them until it reaches what is known as the *rebinding time value* or *T2 value*, which defaults to 87.5 percent of the lease period. At this point, the client enters the rebinding state and begins transmitting DHCPREQUEST messages as broadcasts, soliciting an address assignment from any DHCP server on the network. Again, a server can respond with either a DHCPACK or DHCPNAK message. If the lease time expires with no response from any DHCP server, the client's IP address is released and all of its TCP/IP communications cease, except for the transmission of DHCPDISCOVER broadcasts.

Releasing an IP Address

A client can also terminate an IP address lease at any time by transmitting a DHCPRELEASE message containing the lease identification cookie to the server. On Windows XP, for example, you can do this manually, using the Ipconfig.exe utility. For more information about Ipconfig.exe, see Chapter 11, "Network Troubleshooting Tools."

Test your understanding of the DHCP communications process by completing Exercise 8-4, "DHCP Message Types," now.

> **MORE INFO**   **Demonstration Video**   For a demonstration of DHCP address assignment, run the DHCP video located in the Demos folder on the CD-ROM accompanying this book.

Host Files

IP addresses might be an excellent way for computers to recognize and communicate with each other, but they are not exactly user friendly. Imagine having to remember the IP address for every site that you visit while surfing the Web or for every computer on the local network that has drives or printers you want to access. To make TCP/IP more user friendly, its developers devised the concept of host names.

Host names enable administrators to assign friendly names to the computers on a network and resolve them into IP addresses as needed. A host name is simply a name that represents a computer. In the early days of TCP/IP, the names of the hosts on a network were stored in a text file called hosts on each computer. The hosts file also contained the IP address of the computer associated with each of those names, as in the following example:

```
172.16.94.97      server1      # source server
10.25.63.10       client23     # x client host
127.0.0.1         localhost
```

The host table on any TCP/IP operating system consists of three columns, the functions of which are as follows, from left to right:

- **IP address**   The IP address of a particular system on the network.

- **Host name**   The host name associated with the IP address in the first column.

- **Comments**   Everything after the # symbol is ignored by the computer when it scans the host table. Administrators use this space to add comments, such as a description of the system that the IP address and host name in the first two columns represent.

When an application encountered a reference to a host name, it consulted the computer's hosts file, searched for the name, and read the IP address associated with that name. The process of converting a name into its equivalent IP address is called *name resolution*. The name resolution process is essential because an IP datagram must use an IP address, not a name, to identify its destination.

Every TCP/IP computer still contains a host table, although few of them actually use it anymore. There are two advantages in using a host table for name resolution:

- It is simple and very fast because the table is stored on the computer's local drive.

- No network communication is required.

You can modify the host table on a TCP/IP computer and use it to resolve frequently used names.

Although host tables are useful, their disadvantages as a general-purpose name resolution mechanism outweigh their advantages. In the early days of the ARPANET, the entire network consisted of a few dozen computers. The operators of those computers each chose their own host name. The host table was small and easily maintained, with the network's users informally notifying each other of new names to be added to their tables. As the network began to grow, the ARPANET's administrators decided to create a central registry for the host names. The Network Information Center (NIC) at Stanford Research Institute (SRI) in Menlo Park, California, was chosen to maintain the master hosts file for all the computers on the ARPANET. System administrators all over the network would send their new host names, which they still chose themselves, to SRI, and SRI would add them to the master host table. Network users would then download the latest version of the hosts file periodically and copy it to their systems.

Although this was a good solution at first, it gradually became inadequate as the network continued to grow. The number of additions to the master host table increased, making it difficult for SRI to keep up with the changes, and the number of users downloading the file created an excessive amount of network traffic. Name conflicts also became a problem when users assigned host names to their computers without checking to see whether another computer was already using the same name.

In hindsight, it is easy to see why using host tables for name resolution could only be a temporary solution. A single host table listing the names and IP addresses of all the computers on the Internet today would be colossal and would change thousands of times per second. Clearly, a more efficient solution was needed, and this led to the development of DNS.

Understanding the Domain Name System (DNS)

When the Internet outgrew the hosts file, it also outgrew the flat namespace the file used. There were too many systems on the Internet to assign each a unique single name. To address these problems, the TCP/IP developers created the **Domain Name System (DNS)**. DNS enables administrators to assign hierarchical names to the computers on a network and resolve them into IP addresses as needed. DNS is defined in two primary IETF standards: RFC 1034, "Domain Names: Concepts and Facilities," and RFC 1035, "Domain Names: Implementation and Specification." Many additional RFCs provide updates and augmentations to DNS.

The developers responsible for the ARPANET decided that maintaining an extensive list of IP addresses and hosts required a distributed database, one that would prevent the maintenance and traffic problems inherent in a single data store. One of their objectives was to create a means for administrators to assign host names to their computers without duplicating the names of other systems. Another objective was to store those names in a database distributed among servers all over the network, to avoid creating a traffic bottleneck or a single point of failure. In addition to finding a means for managing host names, these developers also recognized the need for a standardized system for naming hosts and for accessing electronic mailboxes. They wanted to satisfy both needs with a single solution.

At its core, DNS is still a list of names and their IP addresses, but instead of storing all the information in one place, DNS distributes it among servers all over the Internet. DNS consists of the following three elements:

- **The DNS namespace** A specification for a tree-structured namespace in which each branch of the tree identifies a domain. Each domain contains an information set that consists of host names, IP addresses, and other information. Query operations are attempts to retrieve specific information from a particular information set.

- **Name servers** Applications running on server computers that maintain information about the domain tree structure and contain authoritative information about specific areas of that structure. The application can respond to queries for information about the areas for which it is the authority, and it also has pointers to other name servers that enable it to access information about any other area of the tree.

- **Resolvers** Client programs that generate requests for DNS information and send them to name servers for fulfillment. A **resolver** has direct access to at least one name server and can also process referrals to direct its queries to other name servers when necessary.

In its most basic form, the DNS name resolution process consists of a resolver submitting a name resolution request to its designated DNS server. If the server does not possess authoritative information about the requested name, it forwards the request to another DNS server on the network. The second server generates a response containing the IP address of the requested name and returns it to the first server, which in turn relays the information to the resolver, as shown in Figure 8-21. In practice, however, the DNS name resolution process can be considerably more complex, as you will learn later in this chapter.

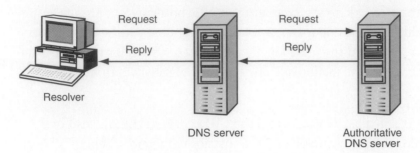

Figure 8-21   DNS servers relay requests and replies to other DNS servers.

What Is a Domain?

For DNS to function in this manner, it was necessary to divide the namespace in a way that would distribute it among many servers. A methodology also had to be devised to enable a server to systematically locate the authoritative source for a particular name. To accomplish these goals, the developers of DNS created the concept of the domain. In the context of DNS, a domain is an administrative entity that consists of a group of hosts that are usually computers. The DNS namespace consists of a hierarchy of domains, and each domain has DNS name servers that supply information about the hosts in that domain. The designated name servers for a particular domain are the authoritative sources of information about that domain. When a DNS server is the authoritative source for a domain, it possesses information about the hosts in that domain, which it stores in resource records.

Resource Records

The **resource record** is the fundamental data storage unit in all DNS servers. When DNS clients and servers exchange name and address information, they do so in the form of resource records. The most basic common resource record is the Host (A) resource record, which consists of the host name and its equivalent IP address. However, DNS servers can also store other types of resource records, including the following:

- **Start of Authority (SOA)**   Indicates that the name server is the authoritative source for the domain
- **Name Server (NS)**   Identifies the DNS servers in the domain

- **Address (A)**   Contains a name-to-address mapping for a computer in the domain

- **Canonical Name (CNAME)**   Used to create an alternative (or alias) name for a computer already represented by an Address record

- **Pointer (PTR)**   Contains an address-to-name mapping in in-addr.arpa for a computer in the domain

- **Mail Exchange (MX)**   Identifies the computer that processes e-mail traffic addressed to the domain

DNS Name Structure

As a result of adding domains to the host naming system, the full name for a computer in DNS consists of two basic parts: a host name and a domain name. The host name, as in earlier versions of DNS, is a single word that identifies a specific computer or other TCP/IP device on the network. However, current host names do not have to be unique in the entire namespace; a host name has to be unique only in its domain. For example, when you browse the Web and access a server with a name like www.adatum.com, the host name of the Web server computer is www, and the domain name is adatum.com. Of course, there are thousands of Web servers on the Internet with the host name www, and this is permissible only if each host with that name is in a different domain.

> **NOTE   DNS Names and IP Addresses**   When you study the structure of a DNS name, notice the similarity between the DNS names and IP addresses, which also consist of two parts: a network identifier and a host identifier. This two-part hierarchy is a recurring theme in TCP/IP network architecture because it distributes administrative responsibilities throughout the network. In the same way that administrators receive network identifiers for their IP addresses and are responsible for assigning the host identifiers on that network, administrators also receive DNS domain names and are responsible for assigning host names within that domain.

The domain name part of a DNS name is hierarchical and consists of two or more words, separated by periods. The domain namespace takes the form of a tree that, much like a file system, has its root at the top. Just beneath the root is a series of top-level domains, and beneath each top-level domain is a series of second-level domains. At minimum, the complete DNS name for a computer on the Internet consists of a host name, a second-level domain name, and a top-level domain name, written in that order and separated by periods. The complete DNS name for a particular computer is called its *fully qualified domain name (FQDN)*.

Unlike an IP address, which places the network identifier first and follows it with the host, the notation for an FQDN places the host name first, followed by the domain name, with the top-level domain name last. In the example cited earlier, the FQDN www.adatum.com consists of a host (or computer) called www in the adatum.com domain. In the adatum.com domain name, com is the top-level domain and adatum is the second-level domain. Technically, every FQDN should end with a period, representing the root of the DNS tree, as follows:

```
www.adatum.com.
```

However, the period is rarely included in FQDNs today.

Domain Hierarchy Levels

The hierarchical nature of the DNS domain namespace allows any DNS server on the Internet to use a minimum number of queries to locate the authoritative source for any domain name. This efficiency is possible because the domains at each level maintain information about the domains at the next lower level. Each level of the DNS domain hierarchy has name servers, which are responsible for the individual domains at that level.

At the top of the domain hierarchy are the root name servers. The **root name servers** are the highest-level DNS servers in the entire namespace, and they maintain information about the top-level domains. All DNS name server implementations are preconfigured with the IP addresses of the root name servers because these servers are the ultimate source for all DNS information. When a computer attempts to resolve a DNS name, it begins at the top of the namespace hierarchy with the root name servers, and works its way down through the levels until it reaches the authoritative server for the domain in which the name is located.

Just beneath the root name servers are the top-level domains. There are seven primary top-level domains in the DNS namespace:

- com
- net
- org
- edu
- mil
- gov
- int

> **NOTE** **Other Top-Level Domains**   In addition to the seven main top-level domains, there are also two-letter international domain names representing most of the countries in the world, such as it for Italy and de for Germany (Deutschland). There are also a number of newer top-level domains promoted by Internet entrepreneurs, such as biz and info, which have yet to see widespread commercial use.

The top two levels of the DNS hierarchy—the root and the top-level domains—are represented by servers that exist primarily to respond to queries for information about other domains. There are no hosts in the root or top-level domains, except for the name servers themselves. For example, you will never see a DNS name consisting of only a host and a top-level domain, such as www.com. The root name servers respond to millions of requests by sending the addresses of the authoritative servers for the top-level domains, and the top-level domain servers do the same for the second-level domains.

Each top-level domain has its own collection of second-level domains. Individuals and organizations can buy these domains for their own use. For example, the second-level domain adatum.com belongs to a company that bought the name from one of the many Internet registrars that are in the business of selling domain names. For an annual fee, you can buy the rights to a second-level domain.

To use the domain name, you must supply the registrar with the IP addresses of the DNS servers that you want to be the authoritative sources for information about this domain. The administrators of the top-level domain servers then create resource records pointing to these authoritative sources, so any DNS server for the com top-level domain that receives a request to resolve a name in the adatum.com domain can reply with the addresses of the adatum.com servers.

> **NOTE** **Domains and DNS Servers**   To create authoritative sources for your Internet domain, you can use your own DNS servers, using Windows Server 2003 or another operating system, or you can pay to use your ISP's DNS servers. If you decide to host an Internet domain on your own DNS servers, those servers must be accessible from the Internet and therefore must have registered IP addresses.

Once you buy the rights to a second-level domain, you can create as many hosts as you want in that domain, simply by creating new resource records on the authoritative servers. You can also create as many additional domain levels as you want. For example, you can create the subdomains sales.adatum.com and marketing.adatum.com, and then populate each of these subdomains with hosts, such as www.sales.adatum.com and ftp.marketing.adatum.com. The only limitations to the subdomains and hosts you can create in your second-level domain are that each domain name can be no more than 63 characters long, and that the total FQDN, including the trailing period, can be no more than 255 characters long. For the convenience of users and administrators, most domain names do not even approach these limitations.

The DNS Name Resolution Process

To help explain the relationship of the DNS servers for various domains in the namespace, a diagram of the Internet name resolution process is shown in Figure 8-22.

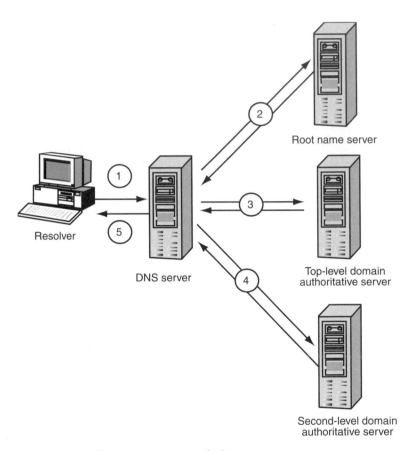

Figure 8-22   The DNS name resolution process

The following explains how a DNS name on the Internet is resolved:

1. An application running on the client computer has a name to resolve and passes it to the DNS resolver running on that system. The resolver generates a DNS name resolution request message and transmits it to the DNS server address specified in its TCP/IP configuration.

2. Upon receiving the request, the client's DNS server checks its own database and cache for the requested name. If the server has no

information about the requested name, it forwards the request message to one of the root name servers on the Internet. The root name server, in processing the request, reads only the top-level domain of the requested name and then generates a reply message containing the IP address of an authoritative server for that top-level domain. The root name server then transmits the reply back to the client's DNS server.

3. The client's DNS server now has the IP address of an authoritative server for the requested name's top-level domain, so it transmits the same name resolution request to that top-level domain server. The top-level domain server reads only the second-level domain of the requested name, and it then generates a reply containing the IP address of an authoritative server for that second-level domain. The top-level server then transmits the reply to the client's DNS server.

4. The client's DNS server now finally has the IP address of an authoritative server for the second-level domain that actually contains the requested host, so it forwards the name resolution request to that second-level domain server. The second-level domain server reads the host in the requested name and transmits a reply containing the A resource record for that host back to the client's DNS server.

5. The client's DNS server receives the A resource record from the second-level domain server and forwards it to the resolver on the client computer. The resolver then supplies the IP address associated with the requested name to the original application. After the original application receives the requested name, direct communication between the client and the intended destination can begin.

MORE INFO   **Demonstration Video**   For a demonstration of the DNS name resolution process, run the DNSNameResolution video located in the Demos folder on the CD-ROM accompanying this book.

Speeding Up DNS

The name resolution process described earlier might seem to be incredibly long and tedious, but it actually proceeds very quickly. There are also DNS mechanisms that help to shorten the name resolution process, such as combined DNS servers and name caching.

Combined DNS Servers

In the name resolution process described above, the process of resolving the top-level and second-level domain names is portrayed as a series of steps, but this is not always the case. The most commonly used top-level domains, such as com, net, and org, are actually hosted by the root name servers, which eliminates one entire referral from the name resolution process.

Name Caching

Most DNS server implementations maintain a cache of information they receive from other DNS servers. When a server has information about a requested FQDN in its cache, it responds directly, using the cached information, rather than sending a referral to another server. This is called *name caching*. For example, if a DNS server on your network just successfully resolved the name www.adatum.com for a user by contacting the authoritative server for the adatum.com domain, a second user trying to access the same host a few minutes later would receive an immediate reply from the local DNS server's cache, rather than having to wait for the entire referral process to be repeated, as shown in Figure 8-23. DNS information only remains cached for a limited amount of time, as specified by the authoritative server for the domain.

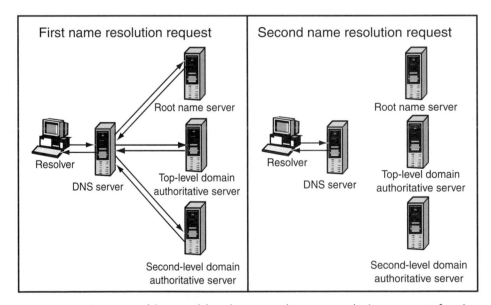

Figure 8-23   Name caching enables the second name resolution request for the same name to bypass the referral process.

Caching is a critical part of the DNS because it reduces the amount of network traffic generated by the name resolution process and reduces the burden on the root name and top-level domain servers.

Referrals and Queries

The process by which one DNS server sends a name resolution request to another DNS server is called a *referral.* Referrals are essential to the DNS name resolution process. The DNS client is not involved in the name resolution process at all, except for sending one query and receiving one reply. The client's DNS server might have to send referrals to several servers before it reaches the one that has the information it needs.

DNS servers recognize two types of name resolution requests:

- **Recursive query**   In a recursive query, the DNS server receiving the name resolution request takes full responsibility for resolving the name. If the server has information about the requested name, it replies immediately to the requestor. If the server has no information about the name, it sends referrals to other DNS servers until it gets the information it needs. TCP/IP client resolvers always send recursive queries to their designated DNS servers.

- **Iterative query**   In an iterative query, the server that receives the name resolution request immediately responds to the requestor with the best information it has. This information could be cached or authoritative and it could be a resource record containing a fully resolved name or a reference to another DNS server. DNS servers use iterative queries when communicating with each other. It would be improper to configure one DNS server to send a recursive query to another DNS server. For example, if DNS servers started sending recursive queries to the root name servers, instead of iterative queries, the additional burden on the root name servers would be immense and would probably cause the entire Internet to grind to a halt. The only time a DNS server does send recursive queries to another server is in the case of a special type of server called a *forwarder,* which is specifically configured to interact with other servers in this way.

Reverse Name Resolution

The name resolution process converts DNS names into IP addresses. However, there are occasions when a computer must convert an IP address into a DNS name. This is called **reverse name resolution**. Because the domain hierarchy is based on domain names, there is no apparent way to resolve an IP address into a name by using iterative queries. The only exception would be to forward the reverse name resolution request to every DNS server on the Internet in search of the requested address, which would be impractical.

To overcome this problem, the developers of DNS created a special domain called in-addr.arpa that is specifically designed for reverse name resolution. The in-addr.arpa second-level domain contains four additional levels of subdomains, with each level consisting of subdomains that are named using the numerals 0 to 255. For example, beneath in-addr.arpa, there are 256 third-level domains, which have names ranging from 0.in-addr.arpa to 255.in-addr.arpa. Each of the 256 third-level domains can have 256 fourth-level domains below it, numbered from 0 to 255. This is also true of each fourth-level domain, which can have 256 fifth-level domains, numbered from 0 to 255, as shown in Figure 8-24, and each fifth-level domain, which can have up to 256 hosts in it, numbered from 0 to 255.

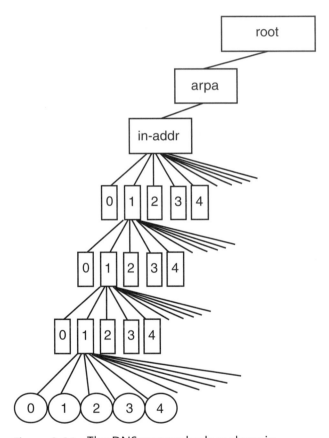

Figure 8-24   The DNS reverse lookup domain

Using this hierarchy of subdomains, it is possible to express the first three bytes of an IP address as a DNS domain name, and to create a resource record named for the fourth byte in the appropriate fifth-level domain. For example, to resolve the IP address 192.168.89.34 into a name, a DNS server would locate a domain named 89.168.192.in-addr.arpa in the usual manner and read the contents of a special type of resource record named 34 in that domain. Address-to-name mappings use a special type of resource record called a Pointer (PTR).

> **NOTE** **Reverse Lookup Domains** In the in-addr.arpa domain, the IP address is reversed in the domain name because IP addresses have the least pertinent bit, that is, the host identifier, on the right. In DNS FQDNs, the host name is on the left.

Windows Internet Name Service (WINS)

If computers on your network are running versions of Windows earlier than Windows 2000, they are using NetBIOS names and must have a way to resolve those names into IP addresses. When Microsoft originally incorporated networking capabilities into Windows, it relied on NetBIOS names to identify computers and on NetBEUI for communications. NetBEUI uses these names exclusively; it has no other addressing system. Later, Microsoft adopted TCP/IP as its default protocol but continued to use NetBIOS to provide friendly names for computers until the release of Active Directory with Windows 2000.

> **NOTE** **NetBIOS Compatibility** Windows operating systems earlier than Windows 2000 can interact with computers running Windows 2000 and later versions because the computers maintain a NetBIOS-compatible equivalent for every Active Directory name.

WINS is similar to DNS in that it resolves computer names into IP addresses. However, WINS is designed specifically for pre–Active Directory versions of Windows networks, and WINS resolves NetBIOS names rather than the DNS names used on the Internet. The NetBIOS namespace that Windows uses to provide friendly names for computers is not hierarchical like that of DNS, but the problem of using TCP/IP with these names is the same. A computer must resolve the name of the computer it wants to communicate with into an IP address before it can send IP datagrams to it.

If all the computers on your network are running Windows 2000 or later and Active Directory has been installed, the network is not using NetBIOS names, and you don't have to run WINS servers for NetBIOS name resolution. You can also disable the NetBIOS Over TCP/IP (NetBT) protocol on your computers by using the controls in the NetBIOS Settings box, which are located in the WINS tab in the Internet Protocol (TCP/IP) Properties/Advanced TCP/IP Settings dialog box.

Windows has several ways of resolving NetBIOS names into IP addresses, so WINS is not an essential part of a Windows network. Without WINS, a computer resolves NetBIOS names either by looking them up in a text file similar to Hosts, called Lmhosts, or by transmitting broadcast messages containing the desired name on the LAN, and then waiting for the computer using that name to respond with its IP address. WINS increases the efficiency of the network by reducing the amount of broadcast traffic. Instead of broadcasting a request, a WINS client transmits a request to its designated WINS server as a unicast message, and the server responds with the IP address associated with the requested name.

> **NOTE** **NetBIOS Naming**   For more information about NetBIOS names, see Chapter 5, "Network Layer Protocols."

Unlike DNS, which requires administrators to create resource records manually, WINS automatically registers clients as they boot and then adds their names and IP addresses to its database. WINS is also designed for use on large internetworks. You can run multiple WINS servers to provide fault tolerance and service thousands of clients. WINS servers can also communicate with each other to replicate their database information. This allows you to maintain a composite picture of the entire network on all of your servers.

> **NOTE** **Exam Objectives**   Objective 4.9 for the Network+ exam calls for students to be given a scenario and then to be able to predict the impact of modifying, adding, or removing network services (such as DHCP, DNS, or WINS) on network resources and users.

SUMMARY

- The Windows, Macintosh, and UNIX/Linux operating systems all include both server and client functionality. NetWare is strictly a client/server network operating system.

- Early versions of NetWare used a bindery to store a simple list of user and group accounts maintained on each server. Later versions use Novell Directory Services (NDS), later renamed eDirectory.

- UNIX and Linux are available in many different distributions, both commercial and noncommercial.

- Most Windows versions include a client for NetWare networks created by Microsoft, but you can also use a client supplied by Novell.

- Windows operating systems use the Server Message Block (SMB) protocol for resource sharing, UNIX/Linux operating systems use Network File System (NFS), and Mac OS uses Apple Filing Protocol (AFP). Achieving client connectivity is usually a matter of implementing one of these protocols on a system that does not support it natively.

- The latest versions of NetWare and Mac OS both include native support for Windows, UNIX/Linux, and Macintosh clients.

- Novell eDirectory was the first hierarchical directory service to achieve commercial success.

- Windows NT stores user account information in domains that are stored on servers called domain controllers. Active Directory expands on the domain concept by adding administrative units called trees and forests.

- Dynamic Host Configuration Protocol (DHCP) is a combination of a client, a server, and a protocol that can automatically configure the Transmission Control Protocol/Internet Protocol (TCP/IP) clients on computers all over the network. DHCP can lease IP addresses from a common pool to client computers, reclaiming them when they are no longer in use, and then returning them to the pool for reassignment.

- Domain Name System (DNS) enables users to identify computers on a network by using friendly names instead of IP addresses. DNS servers resolve the names into the IP addresses that computers need to communicate, using TCP/IP. The DNS namespace is hierarchical; a computer's DNS name consists of a host name followed by two or more domain names, separated by periods.

■ Windows Internet Name Service (WINS) is a Windows service that converts Network Basic Input/Output System (NetBIOS) names into IP addresses.

EXERCISES

Exercise 8-1: Selecting an Operating System

For each of the Windows Server 2003 versions in the left column, specify which description or descriptions in the right column apply.

1. Web Edition   **a.** Supports 512 GB of memory

2. Standard Edition   **b.** Supports eight-node server clusters

3. Enterprise Edition   **c.** Cannot run 16-bit Windows applications

4. Datacenter Edition   **d.** Supports 32-node NLB clusters

5. Datacenter Edition (64-bit)   **e.** Supports computers with four processors

Exercise 8-2: Network Operating System Products

Match the network operating system in the left column with the phrase in the right column that best describes it.

1. Linux   **a.** Uses a bindery to store user accounts

2. Windows NT   **b.** The current version of the original AT&T UNIX

3. Macintosh

4. UNIX System V   **c.** Available in Web, Standard, Enterprise, and Datacenter editions

5. NetWare 3.*x*

6. Windows Server 2003   **d.** The first version of Windows that was not based on MS-DOS

e. Originally used a proprietary data-link layer protocol

f. An open source UNIX version

Exercise 8-3: Directory Service Concepts

Match the directory service concepts in the left column with the correct descriptions in the right column.

1. Schema
2. Partition
3. Multiple master replication
4. Windows NT domain
5. Leaf object

a. Represents a network resource
b. Uses single-word domain names
c. Enables administrators to apply updates to the directory service on any domain controller
d. Determines the types of objects in a directory service
e. Used to split a directory service database into pieces stored on different servers

Exercise 8-4: DHCP Message Types

1. In what order are the following DHCP message types used during a successful IP address assignment procedure?

    a. DHCPACK
    b. DHCPOFFER
    c. DHCPREQUEST
    d. DHCPDISCOVER

2. In what order are the following DHCP message types used for an unsuccessful attempt to renew an IP address lease?

    a. DHCPDISCOVER
    b. DHCPREQUEST (broadcast)
    c. DHCPREQUEST (unicast)
    d. DHCPNAK

REVIEW QUESTIONS

1. What is the name of the file system in Windows NT that enables administrators to assign permissions to individual files?

    a. Active Directory

    b. eDirectory

    c. FAT

    d. NTFS

2. Which of the following network services configures TCP/IP clients?

    a. DNS

    b. NFS

    c. DHCP

    d. NIS

3. What is a program called that runs in the background on a UNIX system?

    a. A service

    b. A daemon

    c. An application

    d. A domain

4. What protocol was originally associated with NetWare networking?

    a. NetBEUI

    b. IPX

    c. TCP/IP

    d. Ethernet

5. What Windows component enables an application to access a network resource in the same way as it accesses a local one?

    a. A redirector

    b. A protocol

    c. A client

    d. A service

6. Which of the following Windows network components is not required for client functionality?

    a. A redirector

    b. A service

    c. A protocol

    d. A network interface adapter driver

7. Which network clients are included with Windows Server 2003? Choose all answers that are correct.

    a. Client Service for NetWare

    b. Gateway Service for NetWare

    c. Client for Microsoft Networks

    d. Client Service for UNIX

8. Which directory service requires users to have a separate account for each server?

    a. Windows NT domains

    b. Active Directory

    c. NetWare bindery

    d. eDirectory

9. Which of the following provides communication between Windows NT domains?

    a. Trust relationships

    b. Single master replication

    c. Multiple master replication

    d. Partitioning

10. On an Active Directory network, a tree is composed of multiples of what?

    a. Servers

    b. Partitions

    c. Forests

    d. Domains

11. What determines the types of objects you can create in an eDirectory tree?

    a. The number of partitions

    b. The directory schema

    c. The number of containers

    d. The X.500 directory service

12. Which of the following terms does not describe the trust relationships between Active Directory domains in the same tree?

    a. Transitive

    b. Bidirectional

    c. Automatic

    d. Single master

13. Which of the following ITU standards is the basis for eDirectory and Active Directory?

    a. X.25

    b. X.400

    c. X.500

    d. X.5

14. Which of the following directory services uses multiword names for its domains?

    a. The NetWare bindery

    b. eDirectory

    c. Windows NT domains

    d. Active Directory

15. What is the term for splitting an eDirectory tree into pieces and storing those pieces on different servers?

    a. Replication

    b. Partitioning

    c. Establishing trust relationships

    d. Creating a tree

16. Which of the following statements is not true?

    a. Containers are composed of objects.

    b. Trees are composed of domains.

    c. Objects are composed of attributes.

    d. Forests are composed of trees.

17. What does the first word in an FQDN identify?

    a. The top-level domain

    b. The second-level domain

    c. The DNS server

    d. The host

18. What happens to a DHCP client when its attempts to renew its IP address lease fail and the lease expires?

19. Which of the following message types is not used during the DHCP lease assignment process?

    a. DHCPDISCOVER

    b. DHCPRELEASE

    c. DHCPOFFER

    d. DHCPREQUEST

20. What is the DNS resource record type that contains the basic name-to-address mapping used for name resolution?

    a. Address

    b. Pointer

    c. Canonical Name

    d. Start of Authority

21. What is the name of the DNS domain that contains address-to-name mappings?

22. Name one method other than WINS that computers running Windows can use to resolve NetBIOS names into IP addresses.

23. What is the name of the time during the lease renewal process when a DHCP client begins broadcasting DHCPREQUEST messages?

    a. Lease identification cookie

    b. Rebinding time value

    c. Renewal time value

    d. Init value

24. What is the function of a WINS server?

    a. To convert IP addresses into hardware addresses

    b. To convert host names into IP addresses

    c. To convert IP addresses into host names

    d. To convert NetBIOS names into IP addresses

CASE SCENARIOS

Case Scenario 8-1: Deploying eDirectory

A network administrator is rolling out Novell eDirectory on a corporate internetwork with LANs in Atlanta, Chicago, and Philadelphia, connected by three T-1 lines. The goals of the plan are to use the partitioning and replication capabilities of eDirectory to eliminate authentication traffic from the T-1 connections under normal conditions, and to provide fault tolerance so that the failure of the T-1 lines in any single office will not prevent users from accessing the entire eDirectory database. To do this, the administrator creates three partitions, one in each office, containing the users and other objects located in that office. Then the administrator creates a replica of each partition on a server in a different city. Which of the following statements is true about this directory service configuration?

    a. This configuration fails to accomplish both of the stated goals.

    b. This configuration accomplishes the goal of eliminating authentication traffic from the T-1 connections, but it fails to accomplish the fault tolerance goal.

    c. This configuration fails to accomplish the goal of eliminating authentication traffic from the T-1 connections, but it does accomplish the fault tolerance goal.

    d. This configuration successfully accomplishes both of the stated goals.

Case Scenario 8-2: Troubleshooting DHCP

While you are troubleshooting a DHCP problem on a client's network, you capture a sample of the DHCP traffic. When you examine the traffic sample, you notice that there are a significant number of DHCPDECLINE messages in the sample. Which of the following scenarios could be the cause of these messages?

    a. The DHCP scope has not been activated.

    b. The DHCP clients are rejecting the offered IP addresses because they are addresses for a different subnet.

    c. The DHCP scope contains IP addresses that have already been assigned to other computers on the network.

    d. The IP address leases for the DHCP clients are expiring.

CHAPTER 9
NETWORK SECURITY AND AVAILABILITY

Upon completion of this chapter, you will be able to:

- Describe how you can use packet filtering to protect a network from unauthorized access.

- Understand how Network Address Translation (NAT) enables networked computers to use unregistered Internet Protocol (IP) addresses and still participate on the Internet.

- Understand how proxy servers protect networked computers at the application layer and how you can use them to restrict users' Internet access.

- Describe how IP security (IPSec) secures local area network (LAN) communications.

- Understand how Layer 2 Tunneling Protocol (L2TP) is used in virtual private networking.

- Describe how Secure Sockets Layer (SSL) can secure Web client/server communications.

- Understand how Kerberos provides secure single network logons.

- Understand the mechanisms used to make network data continuously available.

- Describe how clustering ensures the constant availability of vital network servers.

- Understand how to use redundant equipment to provide fault-tolerant network communications.

- Describe the types of hardware used to perform backups.

- Understand the capabilities of software backup products.

- Distinguish among full, incremental, and differential backups.

The primary function of a network administrator is to ensure that users have access to the services they need when they need them. Two of the main factors that can interfere with that access are security breaches and hardware failures. This chapter discusses some of the technologies you can use to protect your network from intrusion by unauthorized users and from lost time and productivity due to hardware malfunctions.

UNDERSTANDING FIREWALLS

Security is a part of every network administrator's job, whether there is confidential data stored on the network computers or not. Even protecting vital operating system and application files from accidental deletion is a security function. Various mechanisms are used to provide security on a network because different types of protection are needed. Network administrators routinely use permissions and other mechanisms to control access to network resources. This prevents internal users from accessing restricted resources. However, there is a whole world of potential security hazards outside the private internetwork, and the Internet connection that most networks have today is the door through which these hazards can enter. A **firewall** is a hardware or software product that protects a network from unauthorized access by outside parties, while letting appropriate traffic through, as shown in Figure 9-1. If your network is connected to the Internet, you must have some sort of firewall to protect it, because intruders can wreak havoc on the network that you have so carefully designed and constructed.

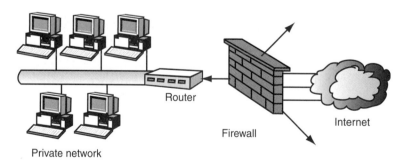

Figure 9-1   A firewall blocks unauthorized network traffic.

NOTE   Deploying Internal Firewalls   Firewalls are usually deployed to protect a private network or internetwork from unauthorized access through the Internet. However, you can also use a firewall internally to protect one section of the network from the rest of it. For example, you can use a firewall to isolate the LAN used by your company's accounting department to prevent other users from accessing confidential financial records.

A firewall is essentially a barrier between two networks that evaluates all incoming or outgoing traffic to determine whether it should be permitted to pass to the other network. A firewall can take many different forms and can use different criteria to evaluate the network traffic it receives. Some firewalls are dedicated hardware devices, essentially routers with additional software that monitors incoming and outgoing traffic. In other cases, firewalls are software products that run on a standard computer. At one time, all firewalls were complex, extremely expensive, and used only in professional network installations. These high-end products still exist, but now you can also buy inexpensive firewall software products that protect a small network or even an individual computer from unauthorized access through an Internet connection.

Firewalls can use several methods to examine network traffic and detect potential threats. Most firewall products use more than one of these methods and often provide other services as well. For example, one firewall product—a proxy server—not only allows users to access Web pages with complete safety, but also can cache frequently used pages for quicker retrieval by other systems. Some of the most common firewall technologies are covered in the following sections.

Packet Filtering Firewalls

A **packet filter** is the most basic type of firewall, one in which the system implementing the filter examines each packet as it arrives and decides if it meets the criteria for admission to the network. Packets that do meet the admission criteria are processed by the system in the normal manner; those that do not are silently discarded. For example, Internet e-mail servers typically use the Simple Mail Transfer Protocol (SMTP) for outgoing traffic and the Post Office Protocol 3 (POP3) for incoming traffic. These protocols use the well-known port numbers 25 and 110, respectively. You can create a packet filter that permits only packets addressed to port numbers 25 and 110 to pass through the firewall, as shown in Figure 9-2. Packets with any other port numbers are discarded before they can do any damage.

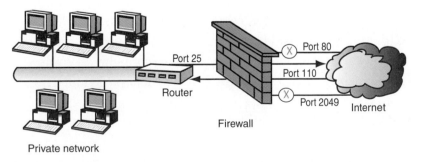

Figure 9-2   A firewall filtering out all ports except 25 and 110.

NOTE   Real World Packet Filtering   While the example illustrated in Figure 9-2 makes packet filtering sound simple, that is rarely the case. In reality, an e-mail server probably does receive legitimate traffic that uses ports other than 25 and 110. This traffic uses different port numbers, and for the server to function properly, its packet filters must admit all legitimate traffic while blocking everything else. Implementing packet filters, therefore, requires a careful analysis of a computer's traffic patterns, and trial and error, before you can implement a workable filtering solution.

Packet Filtering Implementations

Packet filtering is used primarily by routers and firewalls that connect a private network to the Internet. However, you can also use packet filtering inside a private network, to isolate one part of the network from the others. Most routers have packet filtering capabilities built into them, so you can implement filters at the boundaries between networks. The problem with integrating packet filters into a router is that the filters can introduce a large amount of overhead, slowing down the router's performance. The router must examine each incoming packet, compare it against all the filters, and then decide whether to admit the packet to the network. If you have a large, complex system of filters, the amount of time needed for the router to process each packet can become a major network performance bottleneck.

When considering the processing overhead of packet filtering, you must decide where that overhead can best be managed. Implementing packet filters on a target server, for example, does not degrade overall network performance as router packet filtering does, but it can degrade the performance of that particular server's functions.

Many operating systems have packet filtering capabilities built into them as well. All of the current Microsoft Windows versions have a rudimentary packet filtering implementation built into the Transmission Control Protocol/Internet Protocol (TCP/IP) client, as described in Chapter 7, "TCP/IP," which is limited to filtering protocols and port numbers. The Routing And Remote Access Service (RRAS) in Microsoft Windows Server 2003 and Microsoft Windows 2000 Server includes a packet filtering mechanism that is more comprehensive than that of the TCP/IP client, but you can use it only when you have configured Windows Server 2003 to function as a router. As with the TCP/IP client packet filtering mechanism, you can create different filters for each network interface on the computer. However, RRAS packet filtering has a number of capabilities that

TCP/IP client filtering does not have, such as the following:

- Creating filters based on the Internet Protocol (IP) addresses, protocols, and port numbers of a packet's source or destination

- Creating inclusive or exclusive filters

- Creating filters for inbound or outbound traffic

- Creating filters for Internet Control Message Protocol (ICMP) messages, specified by the message type and code values

- Creating multiple filters of the same type

The interface you use to create packet filters in the Routing And Remote Access console is shown in Figure 9-3.

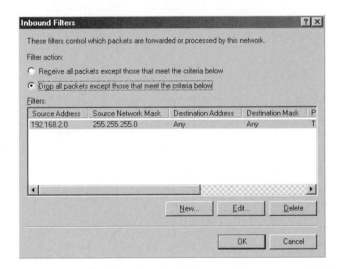

Figure 9-3   The Routing And Remote Access console's Inbound Filters dialog box

NOTE   Using Basic Firewall   Windows Server 2003 also includes a new feature called Basic Firewall, which is an automated packet filtering implementation that prevents computers on a public network from accessing a private network. For example, when RRAS is configured as a Network Address Translation (NAT) router, enabling Basic Firewall causes the system to use dynamic packet filters to prevent any access to the private network through the public interface, unless the communication was initiated by a computer on the private network. The type of protection is called a *stateful firewall*, because the system examines the current state of the connection between the communicating computers, and not just the contents of the individual packets, before permitting traffic to pass. A firewall that cannot analyze the connection traffic in this way is called a *stateless firewall*.

Most UNIX and Linux distributions have packet filtering built into the kernel, although the various operating systems have different tools for managing the filtering rules. For example, Berkeley Software Distribution (BSD) UNIX uses a tool called ipfw, while Linux uses iptables. Both of these are command line tools with extensive sets of arguments and parameters.

A Novell NetWare 6.5 server can function as a router and can filter IP, Internetwork Packet Exchange (IPX), and AppleTalk traffic by using a utility called Filtcfg.nlm to create and manage the filters. The interface that Filtcfg.nlm uses to create packet filters is shown in Figure 9-4. Packet filtering is also implemented in the Novell BorderManager firewall product.

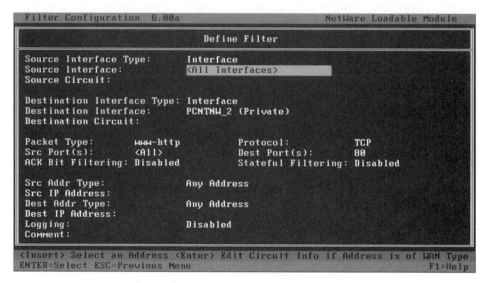

Figure 9-4   The Novell NetWare Filtcfg.nlm utility

In addition to routers and servers, separate firewall products are also likely to have packet filtering capabilities. Firewall-based filters have the following two advantages:

- **Better performance**   By implementing the routing and filtering functions on different systems, you are less likely to experience degraded network performance.

- **Increased filtering capabilities**   Dedicated firewall products are likely to have more advanced packet filtering capabilities, such as preset filter configurations designed to protect against specific types of attacks.

> **NOTE   Packet Filtering Implementation Products**   The basic capabilities of most packet filtering implementations are roughly the same; what differs is the interface and the configurability of the filters. Two products might have the same packet filtering capabilities, but one with preset configurations and detailed documentation will be easier to use than one that requires you to design filter configurations yourself and fully understand the TCP/IP communications processes that are affected by the filters you are creating.

Packet filtering is not a perfect security solution. Intruders can still attack a server using the ports and protocols the firewall lets through, or find a clever new way to bypass the filters you have in place. The trick to using packet filters effectively is to strike a balance between providing sufficient access to legitimate users and blocking enough traffic to provide protection.

In some cases, the creation of packet filters can be an ongoing battle of wits between the protector and a determined attacker. Every time the attacker finds a way to penetrate the filters, the system administrator modifies them to close the opening that is being exploited. Advanced packet filtering requires a detailed understanding of the TCP/IP protocols and the applications that use them.

Packet Filtering Criteria

Creating packet filters is a matter of selecting the specific criteria you want the system to examine and specifying the values that are allowed or denied passage through the filter. Packet filters can be inclusive or exclusive. With an inclusive packet filter, you start with a network connection that is completely blocked and use filters to specify what traffic can pass through. With an exclusive packet filter, you start with a completely open connection and specify the types of traffic you want to block. An inclusive packet filter is inherently more secure; however, it can be more difficult to debug because you must make sure all the traffic that needs to pass through the filters is getting through.

> **NOTE   Bidirectional Filtering**   Packet filtering can work in either direction. For example, you can use filters to prevent users on the Internet from accessing your private network, or you can use them to limit the Internet access granted to your internal users.

The criteria most commonly used in packet filtering are as follows:

- **Port numbers**   Filtering by port numbers, also known as **service-dependent filtering**, is the most common type of packet filtering and the most flexible. Because port numbers represent specific applications, you can use them to prevent traffic generated by these applications from reaching a network. For example, to protect a perimeter network containing your company's Web servers, you can create filters that allow only traffic using port 80 to enter from the Internet, blocking all other application ports.

  > **MORE INFO   Well-Known Port Numbers**   For more information on the well-known port numbers assigned to specific applications and services, see Chapter 6, "Transport Layer Protocols."

- **Protocol identifiers**   The Protocol field in every packet's IP header contains a code that identifies the next protocol in the destination's networking stack that should receive the packet. In most cases, the code represents a transport layer protocol, such as Transmission Control Protocol (TCP) or User Datagram Protocol (UDP). However, IP datagrams frequently carry ICMP messages as well. Filtering using protocol identifiers is not very precise because it blocks or allows all the traffic that uses a particular protocol. However, for certain applications, blocking an entire protocol is necessary, and it is easier than anticipating the specific applications an attacker might use. For example, if you have a network that contains only Internet Web and File Transfer Protocol (FTP) servers, you could use protocol filters to limit incoming traffic to TCP packets. Because these servers rely on TCP for their primary functions, you could block all UDP and ICMP traffic, preventing attacks from using any applications that rely on these protocols.

  > **NOTE   Filtering and Denial of Service (DoS) Attacks**   One simple type of denial of service (DoS) attack uses the Ping utility on several computers to send a continuous stream of Echo Request messages to a particular server. The server is then so busy replying to the Ping requests that its performance is severely degraded, thus preventing it from performing its primary function. To prevent this type of attack, you can filter out all ICMP traffic, which prevents the Ping requests from reaching the server.

■ **IP addresses**   IP address filtering lets you limit network access to specific computers. For example, if you have an Internet Web server on a local area network (LAN) with other computers, and you want Internet clients to be able to access only the Web server, you can create a filter permitting only those packets addressed to the Web server to enter the network from the Internet. You can also use IP address filtering to protect part of a private network. You can create filters that give only certain computers access to the protected LAN, while preventing all others from accessing it.

> **NOTE**   **IP Address Filtering Limitations**   Filtering using IP addresses is not secure if potential attackers have a way to discover the IP addresses of the computers on your network, such as access to Domain Name System (DNS) records. Once an attacker finds out the IP addresses the filter allows to access the network, it is simple to impersonate another computer by using the impersonated computer's IP address. This is called *spoofing*.

■ **Hardware addresses**   Hardware addresses, also called Media Access Control (MAC) addresses, are coded into network interface adapters at the factory. Filtering based on hardware addresses provides the same basic functionality as IP address filtering. However, it is much more difficult to spoof a hardware address than an IP address, so hardware address filters are inherently more secure than IP address filters. Hardware address filtering is rarely used on Internet routers or firewalls, but for internal filtering, hardware addresses are a useful means of restricting access to specific resources.

The four criteria listed above correspond to the application, transport, network, and data-link layers of the Open Systems Interconnection (OSI) reference model, as shown in Figure 9-5. Filters get more specific as you move up in the OSI model. Filtering by port numbers enables you to specify which applications you want to permit through the filter, while filtering by IP addresses and hardware addresses enables you to block access by entire computers.

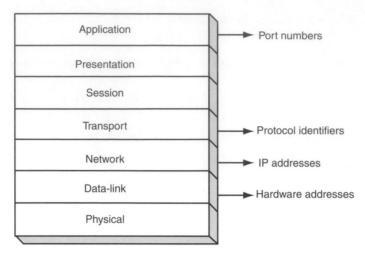

Figure 9-5   Packet filtering criteria and OSI model layers

The real strength of using packet filtering as a security mechanism comes when you combine different types of filters to create a composite solution. For example, you might want to open up the Telnet port (port 23) so administrators can remotely manage the company Web servers from home, using the Internet. However, leaving this port open is an invitation for unauthorized Internet users to access your servers. You could add an additional filter that limits port 23 access to only your administrators' IP addresses. This would protect the network without compromising the functionality the administrators need.

There are two main drawbacks to using packet filtering as a security mechanism:

- Packet filtering requires a detailed understanding of TCP/IP communications and the ways of the criminal mind. Using packet filters to protect your network means participating in an ongoing battle with attackers. Intruders are constantly inventing new techniques to defeat standard packet filter configurations, and you must be ready to modify your filters to counteract these techniques.

- Packet filters can only detect attacks implemented in the packet headers; they do not examine the application data inside the packets. For example, you might configure the packet filters on your firewall to allow all port 80 traffic into the network so Internet users can access your Web server, but at the same time, you could be admitting packets that are designed to attack the Web service itself. To examine the application layer data in the packets, you must use a proxy server. Proxy servers are discussed in more detail later in this chapter.

Stateful Packet Inspection Firewalls

Some packet filtering firewalls include additional security capabilities, typically in the form of a technique called **stateful packet inspection.** Stateful packet inspection is a generic term for a process in which a router examines the incoming packets from the Internet more carefully than usual. In a typical packet filtering firewall, the router is concerned only with the basic criteria listed earlier, such as port and protocol numbers and IP addresses, when it examines packets. A firewall that supports stateful packet inspection examines other network and transport layer header fields as well, looking for patterns that indicate damaging behaviors, such as IP spoofing, SYN floods, and teardrop attacks. SYN floods and teardrop attacks are two forms of DoS attacks in which a target is bombarded with large numbers of packets containing TCP SYN flags or datagrams requiring fragmentation, respectively.

The router also tracks the connections between the systems generating packets by examining the Sequence Number values in the TCP headers. This allows the router to determine the current state of each connection. To gain admittance to the network, packets not only must meet the requirements of the packet filters, but they must also be part of a connection listed in the router's state table.

Because the router must examine each packet more carefully, firewalls that use stateful packet inspection are necessarily slower than simple packet filtering firewalls. Firewalls with stateful packet inspection are usually also more expensive than firewalls without stateful packet inspection. While there are some free stateful packet inspection firewalls, such as the Linux netfilter module, most commercial products are quite costly. However, most commercial products include a graphical configuration interface and better documentation, which makes it easier to set up and maintain the firewall. Different manufacturers implement stateful packet inspection in different ways, so not all routers with this capability offer the same degree of protection.

> **NOTE   Exam Objectives**   Objective 3.8 for the Network+ exam requires students to be able to identify the characteristics of a firewall and identify the purpose and benefits of using a firewall.

USING NETWORK ADDRESS TRANSLATION (NAT)

Network Address Translation (NAT) is a routing technique that enables computers with unregistered IP addresses to access the Internet. If you connect a network to the Internet without firewall protection of any kind, you must use registered IP addresses for your computers so that they can communicate with other systems. However, registered IP addresses are visible from the Internet. This means that any user on the Internet can access your network's computers and, with a little ingenuity, wreak havoc on your network. NAT prevents this from happening by enabling you to assign unregistered IP addresses to your computers.

As you learned in Chapter 5, "Network Layer Protocols," the Internet Assigned Numbers Authority (IANA) has designated three address ranges for use on private networks. These address ranges are not registered to any Internet user, so they are not visible from the Internet. You can safely deploy them on your computer without the danger of Internet intruders accessing them. However, this also means that Internet servers, once they receive requests from the private network computers, cannot send replies to them. NAT solves this problem by functioning as an intermediary between the Internet and a client computer on an unregistered network. For each packet generated by a client, the NAT router substitutes a registered address for the client's unregistered address.

NAT Communications

Under normal conditions, routers do not modify datagrams any more than the postal service modifies envelopes. A NAT router, however, modifies each datagram it receives from an unregistered client computer by changing the value of the Source IP Address field in its IP header. The following steps explain this process:

1. When a client sends a request message to an Internet server, the datagram containing the request first goes to a NAT router.

2. NAT substitutes a registered IP address for the client computer's unregistered address in the datagram and then forwards it to the destination server on the Internet. The NAT router also maintains a table of those unregistered addresses and the public address assigned to them in order to keep track of the datagrams it has processed.

3. When the destination server receives the request, it processes it in the normal manner and generates its reply. However, because the Source IP Address value in the request datagram is the NAT router's registered address, the destination server addresses its reply to the NAT router, not to the original client.

4. When the NAT router receives the reply from the Internet server, it modifies the datagram again, substituting the client's unregistered address for the Destination IP Address in the datagram's IP header, and forwards the packet to the client on the private network.

The NAT router's processes are invisible both to the client and the server. The client generates a request and sends it to a server, and the client eventually receives a reply from that server. The server receives a request from the NAT router and transmits its reply to the same router. Both the client and the server function normally, unaware of the NAT router's intervention. More importantly, the client computer remains invisible to the Internet and is protected from most types of unauthorized access.

Because NAT functions at the network layer, it works with any application that communicates using IP. Client computers on the private network can run Internet e-mail clients, Web browsers, FTP clients, or any other Internet application, and NAT provides protection against intruders.

MORE INFO **Demonstration Video** Run the NAT video located in the Demos folder on the CD-ROM accompanying this book for a demonstration of NAT.

NAT Types

There are three basic types of NAT:

- **Static NAT** Static NAT translates a number of unregistered IP addresses to an equal number of registered addresses, as shown in the following figure. This allows each client to always use the same registered address. This type of NAT does not conserve IP address space, because you need the same number of registered addresses as unregistered addresses. Static NAT is also not as secure as the other NAT types, because each computer is permanently associated with a particular registered address. This makes it possible for Internet intruders to direct traffic to a particular computer on your network using that registered address.

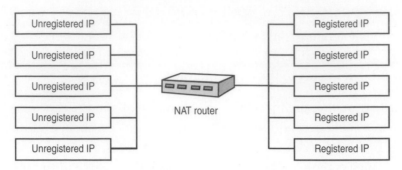

■ **Dynamic NAT**   Dynamic NAT is used if you have fewer registered IP addresses than unregistered computers, as shown in the following figure. Dynamic NAT translates each unregistered address to one of the available registered addresses. Because the registered address assigned to each client changes frequently, it is more difficult for intruders on the Internet to associate a registered address with a particular computer, as in static NAT. The main drawback of dynamic NAT is that it can support only the same number of simultaneous users as the number of available registered IP addresses. If all the registered addresses are in use, a client attempting to access the Internet receives an error message.

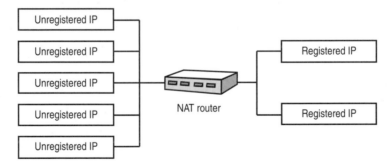

■ **Masquerading**   *Masquerading*, also known as port address translation (PAT), translates all the unregistered IP addresses on your network using a single registered IP address, as shown in the following figure. The NAT router uses port numbers to differentiate between packets generated by and destined to different computers, so multiple clients can access the Internet simultaneously. Masquerading provides the best security of the NAT types because the association between the unregistered client and the registered IP address/port number combination in the NAT router lasts only for a single connection.

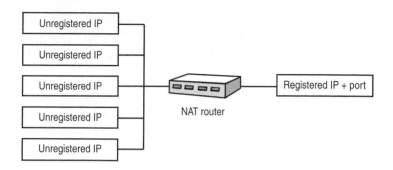

NAT Security

Most NAT implementations today rely on masquerading because it minimizes the number of registered IP addresses needed, and it maximizes the security provided by NAT. However, NAT by itself, even if it uses masquerading, is not a true firewall, and it does not provide ironclad security for high-risk environments. NAT effectively blocks unsolicited requests and other probes from the Internet, meaning that it prevents intruders from searching for unprotected file shares, open ports, and private Web or FTP servers on the private network. However, NAT does not prevent users on the Internet from launching directed DoS attacks against specific computers or from using other more complex tactics to compromise your network security.

NAT also does not prevent users from inadvertently running dangerous programs that initiate contact with servers on the Internet. A *Trojan horse* is an application disguised as an innocuous file that functions as a client, enabling intruders on the Internet to establish contact with a computer, even if it has an unregistered IP address. Remember, NAT can only prevent unsolicited communication from the Internet to an unregistered computer. If the unregistered computer initiates the communication, intentionally or not, the system is vulnerable. Using private addresses provides a distinct advantage over using public addresses, but it is not a perfect solution.

Port Forwarding

Because the NAT router functions are invisible to unregistered computers, users can access the Internet with any client application. However, the one thing you can't do with a standard NAT implementation is run an Internet server. The client must initiate the client/server transaction, and a client computer on the Internet has no way to contact a server running on an unregistered computer first.

However, you can host a Web server or other Internet server application on an unregistered system using a technique called *port forwarding*. Port forwarding occurs when the NAT router creates a mapping between a specific registered IP address and port number and a specific unregistered address on the private network. This mapping enables traffic that the NAT router would ordinarily block to pass through to its destination.

Another benefit of port forwarding is that the router can manipulate translation to provide additional functionality, such as load balancing. A NAT server can receive requests destined for one particular registered address and distribute them among several unregistered addresses. If your Web site receives a lot of traffic, you can deploy multiple, identical Web servers and split the incoming traffic load among them.

NAT Implementations

NAT is implemented in a variety of products, both hardware and software. Most of the hardware routers that provide shared Internet access support NAT, particularly the low-end devices intended for home or small business use. These devices typically provide a complete home networking and Internet access solution, including

- Automatic assignment of unregistered IP address and other TCP/IP configuration settings using Dynamic Host Configuration Protocol (DHCP).
- A NAT implementation, often with port forwarding and other features.
- An administration interface provided by an integrated Web server.

Many operating systems support NAT as well. The Windows operating systems have two different NAT implementations. In the Windows server operating systems, including Windows Server 2003 and Windows 2000 Server, NAT is integrated into the RRAS service, enabling a computer functioning as a router to translate IP addresses between any two network interfaces. The workstation operating systems, including Microsoft Windows XP and Microsoft Windows 2000 Professional, have a feature called Internet Connection Sharing (ICS), which is similar to the NAT/DHCP implementations in stand-alone router products. With ICS, a computer can share a network connection to an Internet service provider (ISP) with other computers on the LAN, allowing them to access the Internet using the ISP-connected computer as a router.

UNIX and Linux typically implement NAT as part of the operating system kernel. In Linux, NAT is integrated into the same netfilter component that provides packet filtering capabilities. You use the same iptables tool to configure both the NAT process and packet filtering. In the NetWare operating system beginning with intraNetWare, the Novell Internet Access Server (NIAS) component includes basic NAT functions, and a more complete implementation is included in Novell BorderManager.

> **NOTE**   **Exam Objectives**   *Objective 2.7 for the Network+ exam requires students to be able to identify the purpose of the NAT/ICS service.*

USING A PROXY SERVER

NAT provides some security for unregistered computers while giving them access to the Internet. Because NAT operates at the network layer, it permits clients to use any TCP/IP application. NAT does not provide much true firewall protection, except in the case of routers that also support stateful packet inspection. If you want more protection than NAT and stateful packet inspection can provide, and you want more control over your users' Internet activities, you can use a proxy server.

A **proxy server** is somewhat similar to NAT in that it acts as an intermediary between client computers on a private network and servers on the Internet. Unlike NAT, however, a proxy server is an independent software product that runs at the application layer and is not incorporated into a router. When an unregistered client wants to send a request to an Internet server, the computer forwards the request datagram to a proxy server instead. The proxy server sends an identical request to the destination server, receives a reply, and then sends the results back to the client. For the proxy server to communicate with Internet servers, it must have a registered IP address and a private network interface.

The main difference in using a proxy server instead of NAT or a packet filtering router is that the proxy server never permits a connection to be established between the private network client and the Internet server. Both systems think they are communicating only with the proxy server. There is no datagram manipulation at the network or transport layers either; proxy servers are concerned only with application layer communications.

Proxy Packet Inspection

The real protection provided by the proxy server is the result of the application layer data inspection that the proxy server performs as it processes packets. Proxy servers can perform a more complete inspection than either packet filtering or stateful packet inspection routers. Because it examines the actual application layer data, and not just the protocol header fields, a proxy server can have rules based on any type of information included in the packet. For example, proxy servers can do any of the following:

- Identify specific types of attachments included in e-mail messages

- Identify Java or JavaScript code in a Web page

- Check the name or IP address of a Web site request against a list of permitted or denied destinations

- Scan a downloaded FTP file for viruses or other dangerous code

- Cache frequently accessed Internet sites for quick access

In any of these cases, you can configure the proxy server to permit or deny the client access to the server, filter out unacceptable code from the packets, or log the activities of the client for later examination. This gives you a greater degree of supervision and control over users' Internet activities than any of the other firewall types discussed here. You can use the proxy server to limit user access to specific Web sites, or to specific times of the day, and prevent them from inadvertently downloading and running code that could damage the network.

> **NOTE**   **Exam Objectives**   *Objective 3.9 for the Network+ exam requires students to identify the purpose and characteristics of a proxy server and the benefits of using it.*

Adaptive Proxy

Not surprisingly, this type of detailed packet inspection can be costly. Proxy servers can be slower than any other type of firewall, depending on how elaborate an inspection it is configured to perform. To increase the speed, some proxy server products use a technique called *adaptive proxy* (or sometimes *dynamic proxy*), which combines the proxy server's application layer inspection capabilities with stateful packet inspection and packet filtering at the lower layers. A server using adaptive proxy examines packets at the application layer, but it also constructs state tables to associate the packets involved in a particular transaction. Once the server has determined, from an application layer inspection, that the first few packets of a transaction are safe, the rest of the packets in that transaction pass with packet filtering only. Adaptive proxy can speed up the proxy server's processing enormously, because only a fraction of the packets arriving at the server require a full inspection.

Proxy Server Implementations

Proxy servers are also more expensive than the other firewall technologies discussed in this chapter. Proxy servers are not free, and they are generally not integrated into operating systems. Some proxy server solutions cost thousands of dollars and require special hardware as well. Microsoft has a proxy server product called Microsoft Internet Security and Acceleration (ISA) Server 2000 and Novell includes proxy services in its BorderManager product, but most proxy servers are produced by third parties. Products are available that support all of the major Windows, UNIX, Linux, and NetWare platforms.

Unlike firewall solutions that operate at the lower layers of the OSI model, proxy servers do not process all TCP/IP traffic. Proxy servers work only with specific applications, and the clients must be configured to use the proxy server instead of contacting Internet servers directly. At one time, administrators had to manually configure the applications on each client computer to access the proxy server, using an interface like the one shown in Figure 9-6. Today, however, client applications can detect a proxy server on the network and configure themselves to use it.

Figure 9-6   The Internet Explorer proxy server configuration interface

> **NOTE**   **Exam Objectives**   *Objective 3.10 for the Network+ exam requires students, given a scenario, to be able to predict the impact of a particular security implementation on network functionality (such as blocking port numbers or using encryption).*

UNDERSTANDING SECURITY PROTOCOLS

Applications and operating systems can use security protocol standards to protect data as it is transmitted over the network. These protocols generally use specific types of data encryption and define how the communicating computers exchange the information needed to read each other's encrypted transmissions. Some of these protocols are discussed in the following sections.

IPSec

IPSec is the term used to describe a series of draft standards published by the Internet Engineering Task Force (IETF) that define a methodology for securing data as it is transmitted over a network. Most of the security protocols that encrypt transmitted data are designed for use on the Internet or for specialized traffic between specific types of clients and servers. Until IPSec was developed, there was no standard to provide comprehensive protection for data as it was transmitted over a LAN.

IPSec protects data by digitally signing and encrypting it before transmission. IPSec **encrypts** the information in IP datagrams by encapsulating it, so that even if the packets are captured, the information inside remains uncompromised. Using IPSec protects your network against a variety of threats, including password penetration, compromise of encryption keys, IP address spoofing, and data modification. An unauthorized user with a network monitor application can still capture packets as they are transmitted over the network, but the user cannot do the following:

- Read a packet's contents, because it is encrypted
- Modify a packet's contents without being detected
- Successfully spoof a recipient by assuming another user's identity
- Discover passwords and keys, or reuse encrypted packets
- Use DoS attacks to inhibit network functionality

IPSec operates as an extension to the IP protocol at the network layer, so it provides end-to-end encryption, meaning that the source computer encrypts the data, and it is not decrypted until it reaches its final destination. Intermediate systems, such as routers, treat the encrypted part of the packets purely as payload, so they do not have to perform any decryption; they just forward the encrypted payload as is. The routers do not have to possess the keys needed to decrypt the packets, and they do not have to support the IPSec extensions in any way.

> **NOTE** Data-Link Layer Encryption By contrast, encrypting network traffic at the data-link layer would require each router receiving an encrypted packet to decrypt it and then encrypt it again before transmitting it to its next destination. This would add a tremendous amount of processing overhead to each router and would slow down the entire network.

Because IPSec operates at the network layer, it can encrypt any traffic that takes the form of IP datagrams, no matter what kind of information they contain. To the transport layer protocols encapsulated in the IP datagrams, such as TCP and UDP, and to the applications generating the traffic, IPSec is completely invisible because the data is encrypted after it leaves the transmitting application and is packaged in the transport layer protocol and decrypted before it arrives at the transport layer or the destination application on the receiving system.

> **NOTE** IPSec Acceleration Encryption is, by nature, a highly processor-intensive task, and implementing IPSec can create a large amount of additional overhead for the computers that are encrypting and decrypting traffic. For that reason, a variety of IPSec acceleration products are now available. These products offload the IPSec-specific processing tasks to an external processor, which is located on a network interface adapter or other expansion card.

Taken together, these protection mechanisms prevent potential intruders from using any of the methods listed earlier in this chapter to compromise the security of the network.

IPSec Standards

IPSec is based on a series of Requests for Comments (RFCs) that are in the process of being ratified as standards by the IETF. RFC 2411, "IP Security Document Roadmap," explains how the technologies defined in the other documents work together. There are dozens of RFCs concerned with IPSec topics. The most important are as follows:

- **RFC 2401** "Security Architecture for the Internet Protocol"
- **RFC 2402** "IP Authentication Header"
- **RFC 2406** "IP Encapsulating Security Payload (ESP)"
- **RFC 2409** "The Internet Key Exchange (IKE)"
- **RFC 2411** "IP Security Document Roadmap"
- **RFC 3585** "IPSec Configuration Policy Information Model"
- **RFC 3586** "IP Security Policy (IPSP) Requirements"

IPSec Protocols

The IPSec standards define two protocols that provide different types of security for network communications: **IP Authentication Header (AH)** and **IP Encapsulating Security Payload (ESP)**. These protocols are discussed in the following sections.

IP Authentication Header

The IP Authentication Header protocol does not encrypt the data in IP packets, but it does provide the following services:

- **Mutual authentication**   Before two computers can communicate using IPSec, they must authenticate each other to establish a trust relationship. Once the computers have authenticated each other, the cryptographic checksum in each packet functions as a digital signature, preventing anyone from spoofing or impersonating one of the computers.

- **Anti-replay**   In some cases, intruders can analyze network traffic patterns, determine the functions of certain packets, and use data from captured packets to wage an attack, even when the data in the packets is encrypted. For example, the first few packets that two computers exchange during a secured transaction are likely to be authentication messages. By retransmitting these same packets, still in their encrypted form, attackers can sometimes use them to gain access to secured resources. IPSec prevents packet replays from being effective by assigning a sequence number to each packet. A system using IPSec will not accept a packet that has an incorrect sequence number.

- **Integrity**   IPSec uses cryptographic keys to calculate a checksum for the data in each packet, called a *hash message authentication code (HMAC)*, and then transmits it with the data. If anyone modifies the packet while it is in transit, the HMAC calculated by the receiving computer will be different from the one in the packet. This prevents attackers from modifying the information in a packet or adding information to it.

A system using IPSec can use AH by itself or in combination with ESP. Using AH alone provides basic security services, with relatively low overhead. However, AH by itself does not prevent unauthorized users from reading the contents of captured data packets. Using AH does, however, guarantee that no one has modified the packets en route, and that the packets did actually originate at the system identified by the packet's source IP address.

On a TCP/IP network, a normal packet has a format like that shown in Figure 9-7. A message generated by an application is encapsulated by a transport layer protocol (TCP or UDP) or ICMP, which is in turn encapsulated by IP at the network layer and by a protocol such as Ethernet at the data-link layer.

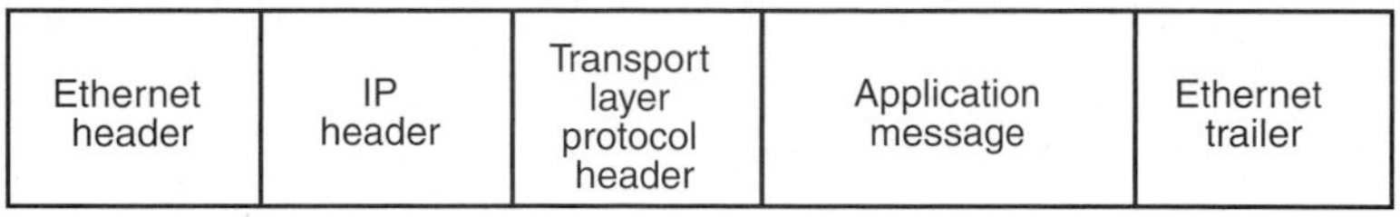

Ethernet header	IP header	Transport layer protocol header	Application message	Ethernet trailer

Figure 9-7   A typical TCP/IP data packet

When a computer uses AH to protect its transmissions, the system inserts an AH header into the IP datagram, immediately after the IP header and before the transport layer protocol header, as shown in Figure 9-8.

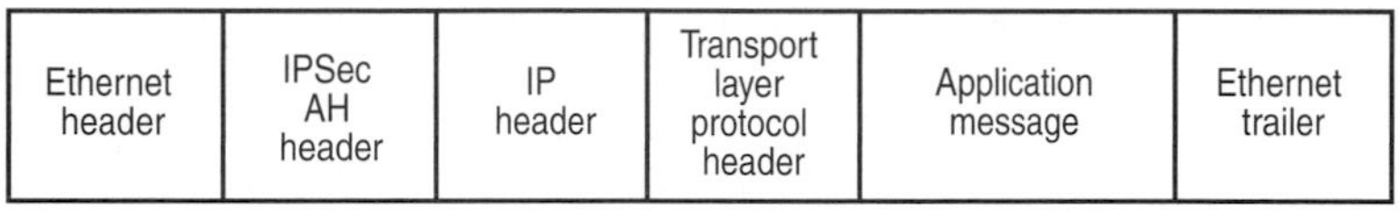

Ethernet header	IPSec AH header	IP header	Transport layer protocol header	Application message	Ethernet trailer

Figure 9-8   The AH header location

IP Encapsulating Security Payload

The IP Encapsulating Security Payload (ESP) protocol encrypts the data in an IP datagram, preventing intruders from reading the information in packets they capture from the network. ESP also provides authentication, integrity, and anti-replay services. Unlike AH, which inserts only a header into the IP datagram, ESP inserts a header and a trailer, which surround the datagram's payload, as shown in Figure 9-9. ESP encrypts all the data following the ESP header, up to and including the ESP trailer. Therefore, someone who captures a packet encrypted with ESP can read the contents of the IP header but cannot read any part of the datagram's payload, including the TCP, UDP, or ICMP header.

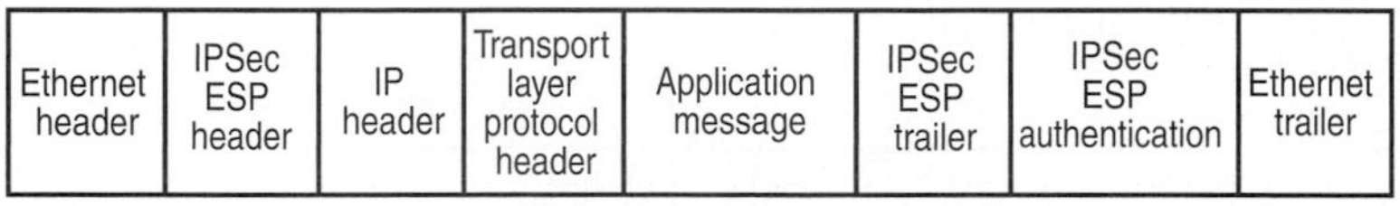

Ethernet header	IPSec ESP header	IP header	Transport layer protocol header	Application message	IPSec ESP trailer	IPSec ESP authentication	Ethernet trailer

Figure 9-9   The ESP header and trailer locations

An IPSec packet can use ESP by itself or in combination with AH. When a packet uses both protocols, the ESP header follows the AH header, as shown in Figure 9-10. Although AH and ESP perform some of the same functions, using both protocols provides the maximum possible security for a data transmission.

Ethernet header	IPSec AH header	IPSec ESP header	IP header	Transport layer protocol header	Application message	IPSec ESP trailer	IPSec ESP authentication	Ethernet trailer

Figure 9-10   An IP datagram using AH and ESP

Transport Mode and Tunnel Mode

IPSec can operate in two modes: transport mode and tunnel mode. Transport mode protects communications between computers on a LAN. In transport mode, the two end systems must support IPSec, but intermediate systems, such as routers, do not have to support IPSec. All the discussion of the AH and ESP protocols so far in this chapter applies to transport mode.

Tunnel mode provides security for gateway-to-gateway wide area network (WAN) connections, and particularly virtual private network (VPN) connections, which use the Internet as a communications medium. In tunnel mode, the end systems do not support IPSec; instead, the routers at both ends of the WAN connection use IPSec to secure the data passing over the WAN connection. IPSec, in essence, forms a protected tunnel through an unprotected medium. The internal network traffic between the end systems and the routers use standard, unprotected TCP/IP communications.

IPSec uses a different packet structure in tunnel mode. In transport mode, IPSec modifies the existing IP datagram by adding its own headers. In tunnel mode, the IPSec implementation creates an entirely new datagram and uses it to encapsulate the existing datagram, as shown in Figure 9-11. The "inner" IP header is the header from the original datagram, which remains unchanged. The ESP header and trailer surround the original datagram and are themselves preceded by a new, "outer" IP header. This outer header is designed to get the packet only from one router to the other. Although the source IP address and destination IP address of the inner IP header contain the ultimate source and destination of the packet, the outer header contains the IP addresses of the two gateways that form the endpoints of the tunnel.

New IP header	IPSec ESP trailer	Original IP header	Transport layer protocol header	Application message	IPSec ESP trailer	IPSec ESP authentication

Figure 9-11   An IPSec tunnel mode packet

Tunnel mode communications proceed as follows:

1. Computers on one of the private networks transmit their data using standard, unprotected IP datagrams.

2. The packets reach the router that provides access to the WAN, and then the router encapsulates them by using IPSec, encrypting and hashing data as needed.

3. The router transmits the protected packets through the secure tunnel to a second router at the other end of the WAN connection.

4. The second router verifies the packets by calculating and comparing integrity check values, and decrypts the packets if necessary.

5. The second router repackages the information in the packets into standard, unprotected IP datagrams and transmits them to their destinations on the private network.

IPSec Implementations

The commercial implementation of IPSec is incomplete at this point. All of the current Windows operating systems support IPSec in transport mode, with the server operating systems supporting tunnel mode as well. In the UNIX/Linux world, only a few operating systems, such as Sun Microsystems' Solaris, include IPSec support, but there are a number of third-party implementations, both commercial and open source, for various distributions. Novell BorderManager supports IPSec in tunnel mode for VPNs. A number of routers also support IPSec in tunnel mode for VPNs.

Layer Two Tunneling Protocol (L2TP)

As explained earlier in this chapter, tunneling is the process of creating a secure communications conduit through an inherently insecure network. IPSec forms tunnels and encrypts the data passing through them. However, you can also use another protocol, such as the **Layer Two Tunneling Protocol (L2TP)**, to form the tunnel, while IPSec continues to provide the data encryption service.

L2TP is a protocol defined in RFC 2661, "Layer Two Tunneling Protocol 'L2TP'." L2TP is a combination of the **Point-to-Point Tunneling Protocol (PPTP)** and the Cisco Systems Layer Two Forwarding (L2F) protocol. L2TP encapsulates PPP frames, such as those used by WAN connections, inside UDP datagrams, as shown in Figure 9-12. It doesn't matter whether the original data being transmitted through the tunnel uses TCP or UDP at the transport layer; each separate datagram is packaged in another UDP datagram before transmission. In fact, the PPP frame can even contain IPX or NetBIOS Extended User Interface (NetBEUI) data.

Figure 9-12   L2TP with ESP packet format

L2TP can encapsulate datagrams to form a tunnel, but it cannot encrypt them. L2TP relies on IPSec's ESP protocol to encrypt and authenticate the UDP datagrams it creates to protect them from compromise by unauthorized users. Although it is possible to create L2TP tunnels without encryption, this defeats the reason for creating a VPN connection in the first place, because the data inside the tunnel would not be secured.

Secure Sockets Layer (SSL)

Secure Sockets Layer (SSL) is a special-purpose security protocol that protects the data transmitted by servers and their clients. Unlike IPSec, SSL operates at the application layer and can protect only the data generated by the specific applications for which it is implemented. Originally used to protect the Hypertext Transfer Protocol (HTTP) data exchanged by Web servers and browsers, SSL is now used to protect other types of traffic, such as e-mail data using SMTP and articles exchanged by newsreaders and servers using the Network News Transfer Protocol (NNTP).

SSL protects application layer data in the following three ways:

- **Authentication**   Clients and servers can exchange credentials to confirm their identities.

- **Encryption**   Data exchanged by clients and servers is encrypted using public key encryption to prevent the data in intercepted packets from being compromised.

- **Data integrity**   Packets are signed with HMAC, which the receiver uses to ensure the data has not been modified in transit.

Virtually all current Web servers and browsers support SSL, as do many other Internet applications. When you access a secured site on the Internet, your browser points to a Uniform Resource Locator (URL) with an https:// prefix, instead of the usual http://. This prefix causes the browser to send its request to TCP port 443 instead of the standard HTTP port 80. The server responds to the client's request by sending its digital certificate and public key. After the two systems negotiate a mutually agreeable encryption level, the client generates a session key, which it encrypts with the server's public key and transmits to the server. The server then decrypts the session key and uses it to encrypt all subsequent data transmissions.

Kerberos

Kerberos is an authentication protocol that uses tickets to coordinate the authentication of network clients and servers. Named for the three-headed dog guarding the entrance to Hades in Greek mythology, a Kerberos implementation consists of the following three components:

- **Clients**   Users or applications that must be authenticated before they can access network resources
- **Servers**   Systems hosting resources that clients need to access
- **Key Distribution Center (KDC)**   An authentication server that functions as an intermediary between clients and servers by issuing tickets to clients, which they can use to access server resources

Kerberos was developed at the Massachusetts Institute of Technology in the early 1980s and is now standardized by the IETF in RFC 1510, "The Kerberos Network Authentication Service (V5)." Kerberos has been implemented in various UNIX and Linux distributions for years, and it is now the default authentication protocol used by the Active Directory directory service included in Windows Server 2003 and Windows 2000 Server.

When a client logs on to a network that uses Kerberos, it sends a request message to an authentication server, which already possesses the account name and password associated with that client. The authentication server responds by sending a ticket-granting ticket (TGT) to the client. The TGT is encrypted using a key based on the client's password. Once the client receives the TGT, it prompts the user for the password and uses it to decrypt the TGT. Because only that user (presumably) has the password, this process serves as an authentication. Now that the client possesses the TGT, it can access network resources by sending a request to a Ticket-Granting Server (TGS), which might or might not be the same as the authentication server. The request contains an encrypted copy of the TGT. The TGS, after it has decrypted the TGT and verified the user's status, creates a server ticket and transmits it to the client.

Test your knowledge of security protocols and their functions by completing Exercise 9-1, "Security Protocols," now.

The server ticket allows a specific client to access a specific server for a limited length of time. The ticket also includes a session key, which the client and the server can use to encrypt the data transmitted between them, if necessary. The client transmits the server ticket (which was encrypted by the TGS using a key that the server already possesses) to that server. After the server decrypts the server ticket, the server grants the client access to the desired resource.

> **NOTE   Exam Objectives**   Objective 2.13 for the Network+ exam requires students to be able to identify the following security protocols and describe their purpose and function: IPSec, L2TP, SSL, and Kerberos.

PROVIDING FAULT TOLERANCE

Many organizations rely heavily on computers, and once the computers are networked, they come to rely on those network communications as well. Depending on the type of organization using the network, an equipment failure or other service interruption can mean lost productivity, lost revenue, and, in some cases, even lost lives. This is why many networks have built-in fault-tolerance mechanisms. When the functions of a network are absolutely critical, such as in hospitals or airport control towers, the fault-tolerance mechanisms can be incredibly elaborate. In most cases, however, only a few key components are protected from outages due to hardware or software faults. This section examines some of the systems that you can use to protect your network from such disasters.

Data Availability

The most commonly implemented fault tolerance measures are designed to keep an organization's vital data available at all times. Many organizations must have their data available all the time in order to function. If a drive on a server fails, its data might be restorable from a backup, but the time lost replacing the drive and restoring from the backup can mean lost productivity that costs the company dearly. Hard disk drives are more susceptible to failure than most other computer components because they have moving parts that operate at extremely close tolerances.

To provide a higher degree of data availability, there are a variety of hardware technologies that work in different ways to ensure that network data is continuously accessible. Most of these technologies use multiple disk drives, combining their storage space to create a single network volume. A volume is a fixed amount of data storage space on a hard disk or other storage device. On a typical computer, the hard disk drive can be broken up into multiple volumes to separate data into discrete storage units. For example, if you have a C drive and a D drive on your computer, these two letters can refer to volumes on two different hard drives or to two volumes on a single drive. You can also combine the storage space on two hard disks into a single volume. Network file servers often use this capability to provide fault tolerance, simplify users' access to files, or increase performance. Some of the data storage technologies frequently used on network file servers are as follows:

- **Drive spanning**   When you use drive spanning, you combine the storage space on multiple hard disks to create a single logical volume. You can use drive spanning to make the storage space on all of the drives in a server appear to users as a single entity. The disadvantage of drive spanning is that if one of the hard drives containing part of the volume fails, the entire volume is lost. Drive spanning does not provide fault tolerance or increased performance, but it can help users locate the data they need more easily.

- **Disk striping**   When you use disk striping, you create a single volume by combining the storage space on multiple hard disks and configuring the system to write data alternately to each disk. Normally, when a spanned volume stores data, entire files are stored on each of the disks. When you use disk striping, the computer splits each file into multiple segments and writes alternate segments to each of the disks. This speeds up data access by enabling one drive to read a segment while the other drive's heads are moving to the next segment. When you consider that network servers might need to process dozens of file access requests at once (from various users), the speed improvement provided by disk striping can be significant. However, striped volumes do not provide fault tolerance, and they are subject to the same problem as spanned volumes—if one drive in the stripe set fails, the entire volume is lost.

- **Disk mirroring**   Disk mirroring is an arrangement in which two identical hard disk drives connected to a single host adapter always contain identical data. The two drives appear to users as one logical volume, and whenever anyone saves data to the volume, the computer writes it to both of the drives in the mirror set simultaneously. If one hard drive unit fails, the other can take over immediately until the malfunctioning drive is replaced. Many operating systems and storage hardware solutions support disk mirroring, which is also known as redundant array of independent disks (RAID) Level 1. Disk mirroring has two main disadvantages:

❑ The server provides only half of its available disk space to users.

❑ Although mirroring protects against a drive failure, a failure of the host adapter or the computer can still render the data unavailable.

■ **Disk duplexing**   Disk duplexing provides a higher degree of data availability than disk mirroring by using duplicate host adapters as well as disk drives. Identical disk drives on separate host adapters maintain exact copies of the same data, creating a single logical drive, just as in disk mirroring, but in this case, the server can survive either a disk failure or a host adapter failure and still make its data available to users.

■ **Redundant Array of Independent Disks (RAID)**   RAID is a comprehensive data availability technology with levels that provide functions like striping and mirroring, as well as more advanced configurations. Higher RAID levels store error correction information (called *parity*) along with the data, so that if a drive in a RAID array fails, its data still remains available from the other drives. RAID provides complete fault tolerance while using as little as one-third of the available disk space to store redundant data. Although RAID is available as a software product that works with standard disk drives and is incorporated into some operating systems, many high-end servers use dedicated RAID drive arrays, which consist of multiple hard drives in a single housing, often with hot swap capability. Hot swapping allows you to remove and replace a malfunctioning drive without shutting down the other drives in the array. This enables the data to remain continuously available to network users, even when the support staff is dealing with a drive failure. The various RAID levels and their functions are listed in Table 9-1.

Table 9-1   **RAID Levels**

RAID Level	RAID Technology	Description
0	Disk striping	Enhances performance by writing data to multiple disk drives, one block at a time; provides no fault tolerance.
1	Disk mirroring and disk duplexing	Provides fault tolerance by maintaining duplicate copies of all data on two drives. Disk mirroring uses two drives connected to the same host adapter, and disk duplexing uses two drives connected to different host adapters.
2	Hamming error-correcting code (ECC)	Ensures data integrity by writing error-correcting code to a separate disk drive; rarely implemented.
3	Parallel transfer with shared parity	Provides fault tolerance by striping data at the byte level across a minimum of two drives and storing parity information on a third drive. If one of the data drives fails, its data can be restored using the parity information.
4	Independent data disks with shared parity	Identical to RAID 3, except that the data is striped across the drives at the block level.
5	Independent data disks with distributed parity	Provides fault tolerance by striping both data and parity across three or more drives, instead of using a dedicated parity drive, as in RAID 3 and RAID 4. A RAID 5 installation can therefore survive the loss of any drive in the array.
6	Independent disks with two-dimensional parity	Provides additional fault tolerance by striping data and two complete copies of the parity information across three or more drives.
7	Asynchronous RAID	A proprietary hardware solution that consists of a striped data array and a separate parity drive, plus a dedicated operating system that coordinates the disk storage activities.
10	Striping of mirrored disks	Combines RAID 0 and RAID 1 by striping data across mirrored pairs of disks, thus providing both fault tolerance and enhanced performance.

Table 9-1   **RAID Levels (Continued)**

RAID Level	RAID Technology	Description
53	Striped array of arrays	Stripes data across multiple RAID 5 arrays, providing the same fault tolerance as RAID 5 with additional performance enhancement.
0+1	Mirroring of striped disks	Combines RAID 0 and RAID 1 in a different manner by mirroring the data stored on identical striped disk arrays.

Test your knowledge of data availability concepts by completing Exercise 9-2, "Data Availability Technologies," now.

> **NOTE   Data Availability and Backups**   None of the data availability techniques described in this section are intended to replace regular backups using a device such as a tape drive. For more information about backing up network data, see "Backups" later in this chapter.

Network Attached Storage (NAS)

Network attached storage (NAS) is a relatively new hardware technology that implements fault tolerant storage solutions independent of the existing network servers. A NAS device is a drive array that connects directly to the network and is actually a dedicated file server with its own embedded operating system. In most cases, NAS devices give clients access to stored data using the two primary file sharing protocols used on today's networks: Server Message Blocks (SMB), used by Windows, and Network File System (NFS), used by UNIX and Linux. Offloading storage-related services, such as security and RAID calculations, to a separate device reduces the burden on the network's general purpose servers.

> **NOTE   Exam Objectives**   Objective 3.4 for the Network+ exam requires students to be able to identify the main characteristics of NAS.

Storage Area Networks (SANs)

Unlike a NAS device, which connects directly to the LAN, a storage area network (SAN) is a separate network that is dedicated solely to traffic between servers and network storage devices, such as stand-alone drive arrays. SANs typically use a high speed serial networking protocol called Fibre Channel to communicate, but they can theoretically use any network medium and protocol. By moving the storage-related traffic to a separate network, the client/server LAN is not overloaded with traffic between servers and their storage devices. A SAN also enables multiple servers to access the same storage resources, which can be used to implement a fault tolerance mechanism called *clustering*.

Server Availability

Data availability techniques are useful, but they do no good if the server that contains the disks malfunctions. In addition to specialized data availability techniques, there are similar technologies designed to make servers more reliable. For example, some servers take the concept of hot swapping to the next level by providing redundant components, such as fan assemblies and various types of drives, that you can remove and replace without shutting down the computer. Of course the ultimate solution for server fault tolerance is to have more than one server. There are various solutions that enable multiple computers to operate as one, so that if one server fails, another can immediately take its place.

Novell NetWare SFT III was one of the first commercially successful server duplication technologies. NetWare SFT III was a version of NetWare that consisted of two copies of the network operating system, plus a proprietary hardware connection that was used to link the two separate server computers, as shown in Figure 9-13. The servers ran an application that synchronized their activities. For example, when a user saved data to one server volume, the data was written to both servers at the same time. If one of the servers malfunctioned for any reason, the other server instantaneously took its place.

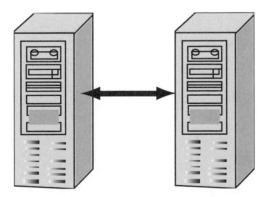

Figure 9-13   Novell NetWare SFT III connected two servers, using one as a failover backup to the other.

SFT III was designed solely to provide fault tolerance, but the next generation of server duplication technology does more. Clustering is a technique for interconnecting multiple computers to form a unified computing resource, as shown in Figure 9-14. In addition to providing fault tolerance, a cluster can also distribute the processing load for specific tasks among the various computers or balance the processing load by allocating client requests to different computers in turn. To increase the speed and efficiency of the cluster, you can simply connect another computer to the group, which adds its capabilities to those of the others. Clustering solutions are available for all of the major server operating systems.

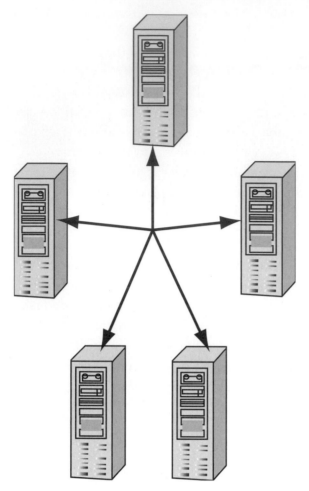

Figure 9-14   A server cluster provides fault-tolerance, load-balancing, and process distribution services.

Network Redundancy

Service interruptions on a network are not always the result of a computer or drive failure. Sometimes the network itself is to blame. For this reason, many larger internetworks include redundant components that enable traffic to reach a given destination in more than one way. If a network cable is cut or broken, or if a router or switch fails, redundant equipment enables data to take another path to its destination. There are several ways to provide redundant paths. Typically, you have at least two routers or switches connected to each network, so that the computers can use either one as a gateway to the other segments. For example, you can build an internetwork with two backbones, as shown in Figure 9-15. Each workstation can use either of the routers on its local segment as a gateway. You can also use this arrangement to balance the traffic on the two backbones by configuring half of the computers on each LAN to use one of the routers as their default gateway and the other half to use the other router.

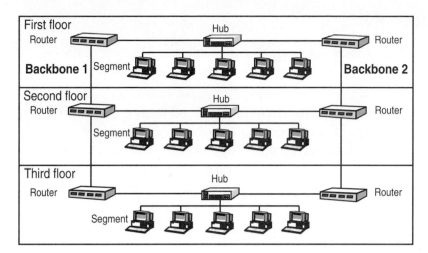

Figure 9-15 Building a network with two backbones provides both fault tolerance and load balancing.

> **NOTE** **Exam Objectives** Objective 3.5 for the Network+ exam requires students to be able to identify the purpose and characteristics of fault tolerance.

PERFORMING BACKUPS

It might not happen today or tomorrow, but someday you will lose a hard drive containing essential network data. The drive might be stolen along with the computer, it might be destroyed in a fire or other catastrophe, or it might simply fail. Whatever happens, the data is gone and it's up to you, as the network administrator, to get it back. When this happens, you will thank yourself for all the effort you took to set up a network backup strategy. If you don't have a backup strategy in place, you might have to start working on your résumé.

Backups are simply copies of your data that you make on a regular basis. If a storage device fails or is damaged and the data stored there is lost, you can restore it from the backup in a timely manner. A backup is the ultimate fault-tolerance measure. Even if you have other storage technologies in place that provide fault tolerance, such as mirrored disks or a RAID array, you still need a backup solution. Networks both complicate and simplify the process of making regular backups. The process is more complicated because you have data stored on multiple devices that must be protected, and it is simpler because you can use the network to access those devices. A network backup strategy specifies what data you back up, how often you back it up, and what medium you use to store the backups. The decisions you make regarding the backup hardware, software, and administrative policies you will use depend on how much data you have to back up, how much time you have to back it up, and how much protection you need.

Backup Hardware

You can perform backups by using any type of storage device. One of the main objectives in developing an effective backup strategy, however, is to automate as much of the process as possible. Although you can back up 1 GB of data to 1.44-MB floppy disks, you probably don't want to sit around feeding 695 disks into a floppy drive. You should select a device that can store all of your data without frequent media changes so you can schedule backup jobs to run unattended. This doesn't mean, however, that you have to buy a drive that can hold all of the data stored on all of your network's computers. You can be selective about which data you want to back up, so it's important to determine how much of your data needs to be protected before you decide on the capacity of your backup device.

You should also consider the speed at which the drive writes data to the medium. Backup jobs typically run when the network is not otherwise in use. This ensures that all of the data on the network is available for backup. The amount of time that you have to perform your backups is sometimes called the *backup window*. The backup device that you choose should depend in part on the amount of data you have to protect and the amount of time that you have to back it up. For example, if you have 10 GB of data to back up and your company closes from 5:00 P.M. until 9:00 A.M., you have a 16-hour backup window—plenty of time to copy your data, using a medium-speed backup device. However, if you have 100 GB of data to back up and your company closes from 7:00 A.M. to 8:00 A.M. only, you will have to use a much faster device or, in this case, several devices.

Cost is always a factor in selecting a hardware product. Backup drives are available in many different speeds, and the faster ones are generally more expensive. You can buy a low-end backup drive for $100 to $200, which is suitable for backing up a home computer where speed isn't a major factor. However, as the speed and capacity of the drives increase, the prices increase exponentially. High-end backup drives, suitable for network backups, can command prices that run into five figures.

When you evaluate backup devices, you must also be aware of the product's extended costs. Backup devices use a removable medium, such as a tape or disk cartridge. This enables you to store copies of your data offsite, such as in a bank's safe deposit vault. If the building where your network is located is destroyed by a fire or other disaster, you still have your data, which you can use to restart operations elsewhere. Therefore, in addition to buying the drive, you must also buy storage media. Some products might seem at first to be economical because the drive is inexpensive, but in the long run they might not be, because the media are so expensive. A good way to evaluate various backup devices is to determine the cost per megabyte or gigabyte of storage it provides. Divide the price of the medium by the number of megabytes or gigabytes it can store, and use this figure to compare the relative cost of various devices. Of course, in some cases you might need to sacrifice economy for speed or capacity.

Magnetic Tape Drives

The most common hardware device used to back up data is a magnetic tape drive, like the one shown in Figure 9-16. Unlike hard disk, floppy disk, and CD/DVD-ROM drives, tape drives are not random-access devices. This means that the drive cannot move the read/write heads to a particular file on a backup tape without spooling through all of the files before it. As with other types of tape drives, such as audio and video, the drive unwinds the tape from a spool and pulls it across the heads until it reaches the point in the tape where the data you want is located. As a result, you can't mount a tape drive in a computer's file system, assign it a drive letter, and copy files to it, as you can with a hard disk drive. You need to use a special software program to address the drive and send the data to it for storage. This also means that tape drives are useless for anything other than backups, while other media, such as writable CDs and DVDs, can be used for other things.

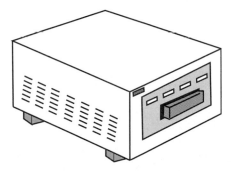

Figure 9-16   An external magnetic tape drive

Magnetic tape drives are well suited for backups—they're fast, they hold a lot of data, and their media cost is low, often less than one-half cent per megabyte. There are many different types of magnetic tape drives that differ greatly in speed, capacity, and price. At the low end are quarter-inch cartridge (QIC) drives, which cost as little as $200 and store anywhere from 150 MB to 20 GB on a single cartridge. At the high end are digital linear tape (DLT) and linear tape-open (LTO) drives, which cost thousands of dollars and store as much as 100 GB on a single tape. The most common magnetic tape technologies used for backups are listed in Table 9-2.

Table 9-2 **Magnetic Tape Technologies**

Type	Tape Width	Cartridge Size	Capacity (Uncompressed)	Speed
QIC, Travan	.25 inch	4 × 6 × 0.625 inches (data cartridge); 3.25 × 2.5 × 0.6 inches (minicartridge)	50 GB	600 MB/min
Digital audio tape (DAT)	4 mm	2.875 × 2.0625 × 0.375 inches	20 GB	360 MB/min
8 mm	8 mm	3.7 × 2.44 × 0.59 inches	100 GB	1,400 MB/min
DLT, Super DLT	.50 inch	4.16 × 4.15 × 1 inches	160 GB	960 MB/min
LTO, Ultrium	.50 inch	4.0 × 4.16 × 0.87 inches	200 GB	3,600 MB/min

NOTE *Compression and Magnetic Tape Capacities*   The capacities of magnetic tape drives are generally specified using two figures, such as 40 GB to 80 GB. These numbers refer to the capacity of a tape without compression and with compression. Most tape drives have hardware-based data compression capabilities built into them, but you can get additional capacity depending on the type of data you are storing. The capacity figures assume an average compression ratio of 2:1, which is about right for most application files. Some types of files, however, such as image files using uncompressed BMP or TIF formats, can compress at much higher ratios, as high as 8:1. Files that are already compressed, such as GIF or JPG image files or ZIP archives, cannot be compressed further and are stored at a 1:1 compression ratio.

Writable CD-ROM and DVD-ROM drives are becoming increasingly popular as personal backup devices. Although the capacity of a CD is limited to approximately 650 MB, the low cost of CDs can make them an economical solution, even if they can only be used once, as is the case with CD-Rs. Now that prices for writable DVD-ROM drives are coming down, DVDs are more suitable than CDs because of their greater capacity (over 4 GB). The biggest advantage of using CD-ROMs or DVD-ROMs for backup is that most computers already have the drives installed for other purposes, eliminating the need to purchase a dedicated backup drive.

For network backups, CD-ROMs and DVD-ROMs are usually inadequate because most networks have many gigabytes of data to back up, which would require many disc changes. DVD-ROMs reduce the number of media changes and might be suitable for smaller networks, but they still do not have the capacity required to efficiently back up a large enterprise network. In addition, network backup software products do not usually recognize CD-ROM and DVD-ROM drives as backup devices. Although these drives often come with software that provides limited backup capabilities (intended for relatively small, single-system backups), this software usually does not provide the features needed to back up a network effectively.

Cartridge Drives

Another commonly used storage device that can be easily used for backups is a removable cartridge drive. Products such as Iomega's Zip and Jaz drives provide performance that approaches that of a hard disk drive, but they use removable cartridges. These drives mount into a computer's file system, which means that you can assign them a drive letter and copy files to them just as you can with a hard drive.

Zip cartridges hold no more than 750 MB, which makes them not much more practical than CDs for backups. However, Jaz drives are available in 1 GB and 2 GB drives, which is sufficient for a backup device, even on a small network. The drawback of using this type of drive for backups is the extremely high cost of the media. A 2 GB Jaz cartridge can cost as much as $125, which is more than 6 cents per megabyte—far more than virtually any other storage device.

Autochangers

In some cases, even the highest capacity drive isn't big enough to back up a large network with constantly changing data. To create an automated backup solution with a greater capacity than that provided by a single drive, you can buy a device called an *autochanger*. An autochanger is a unit that contains one or more drives (usually magnetic tape drives, but optical disk and CD-ROM autochangers are also available) and a robotic mechanism that swaps the media in and out of the drives. Sometimes these devices are called *jukeboxes* or *tape libraries*. When a backup job fills one tape (or other storage medium), the mechanism extracts it from the drive and inserts another, and the job continues. The autochanger tracks which tapes are available and automatically loads the appropriate tape to perform a restore job. An autochanger is shown in Figure 9-17.

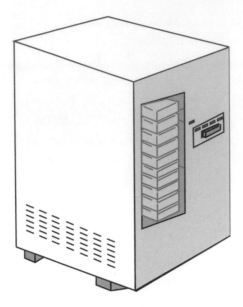

Figure 9-17   A tape autochanger

Some autochangers are small devices with a single drive and an array that holds four or five tapes, while others are enormous devices with as many as four drives and an array of 100 tapes or more. If you buy a large enough autochanger, you can create a long-term backup strategy that can run backups completely unattended for weeks at a time. However, before you decide to get a refrigerator-sized autochanger, be aware that the cost of these devices can be astonishingly high, reaching as much as six figures in some cases.

Selecting a Drive Interface

Backup devices can use any of the standard computer interfaces, such as Integrated Drive Electronics (IDE), universal serial bus (USB), and Small Computer System Interface (SCSI). Some backup drives even connect to the computer's parallel port, although this is just a form of SCSI that uses a different port.

The most common interface used in high-end network backup solutions is SCSI. SCSI devices operate more independently than those using IDE, which means that the backup process, which often involves reading from one device while writing to another on the same interface, is more efficient. When multiple IDE devices share a channel, only one operates at a time. Each drive must receive, execute, and complete a command before the other drive can receive its next command. On the other hand, SCSI devices can maintain a queue of commands that they have received from the host adapter and can execute them sequentially and independently.

Magnetic tape drives require a consistent stream of data to write to the tape with maximum effectiveness. If there are constant interruptions in the data stream, as can be the case with IDE, the tape drive must repeatedly stop and start the tape, which is called *shoeshining*. Shoeshining reduces the drive's speed and overall storage capacity. A SCSI drive can often operate continuously without pausing to wait for the other devices on the channel.

A SCSI backup device is more expensive than a comparable IDE alternative, because the drive requires additional electronics and because you must have a SCSI host adapter installed in the computer. Most SCSI devices are available as internal or external units. External units have their own power supplies, which also adds to the cost. However, a reliable network backup solution is worth the additional expense.

Backup Software

Apart from the hardware, the other primary component in a network backup solution is the software that you use to perform the backups. Storage devices designed for use as backup solutions are not treated like the other storage subsystems in a computer; a specialized software product is required to package the data and send it to the drive. Depending on the operating system you're using, you might already have a backup program that you can use with your drive, but in many cases an operating system's own backup program provides only basic functionality and lacks features that are useful in a network environment.

The primary functions of a good backup software product are examined in the following sections.

Target Selection and Filtering

The most basic function of a backup software program is to let you select the data that you want to back up, which is sometimes called the *target*. A good backup program gives you many options for selecting the target. You can select entire computers to back up, specific drives on those computers, specific directories on the drives, or specific files in specific directories. Most backup programs let you select the targets from a directory tree display. Figure 9-18 shows the interface that the Windows Server 2003 Backup program uses to select backup targets.

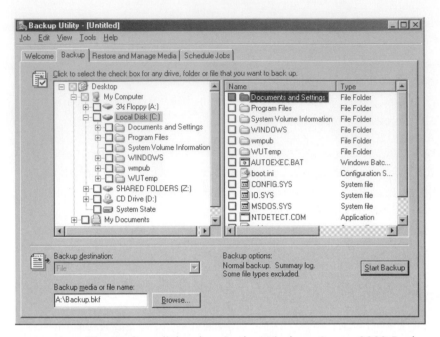

Figure 9-18   The Backup dialog box in the Windows Server 2003 Backup program

In most cases, you don't need to back up all of the data on a computer's drives. If a hard drive is completely erased or destroyed, you will likely have to reinstall the operating system before you can restore files from a backup tape, so it might not be worthwhile to back up all of the operating system files each time you run a backup job. The same is true for applications. You can reinstall an application from the original distribution media, so you might want to back up only your data files and configuration settings for that application. In addition, most operating systems today create temporary files as they run, which you do not need to back up. Windows, for example, creates a temporary file for memory paging that can be several gigabytes in size. Because this file is re-created each time you start the computer, you can save space on your backup tapes by omitting files like this from your backup jobs. Carefully selecting backup targets can mean the difference between fitting an entire backup job onto one tape or staying late after work to insert a second tape into the drive.

Individually selecting the files, directories, and drives that you want to back up can be quite tedious, though, so many backup programs provide other ways to specify targets. One common method is to use filters that enable the software to evaluate each file and directory on a drive and decide whether to back it up. A good backup program uses filters that allow you to select targets based on file and directory names, extensions, sizes, dates, and attributes. For example, you can configure the software to back up a computer running Windows Server 2003 and use filters to exclude Pagefile.sys, which is the memory paging file; the

\Temporary Internet Files folder, which contains Microsoft Internet Explorer's browser cache; and all files with a .tmp extension, which are temporary files created by various applications. None of these files are necessary when you restore the system from a backup tape, so backing them up wastes time and space.

You can also use filters to limit your backups only to files that have changed recently, using either date or attribute filters. The most common type of filter used by backup programs is the one for the archive attribute, which enables the software to back up only the files that have changed since the last backup. This filter is the basis for incremental and differential backups.

Incremental and Differential Backups

The most basic type of backup job is a full backup, which copies the entire contents of a computer's drives to the backup medium. You can perform a full backup every day or each time that you back up that particular computer. However, this practice can be wasteful, both in terms of time and tape. When you perform a full backup every day, the majority of the files you are writing to the tape are exactly the same as they were yesterday. The program files that make up the operating system and your applications do not change. The only files that change on a regular basis are data files and perhaps files that store configuration settings, along with special resources like the Windows Registry and directory service databases.

To save tape and shorten the backup time, many network administrators perform full backups only once a week, or even less frequently. In between the full backups, they perform special types of filtered jobs that back up only the files that have recently been modified. These types of jobs are as follows:

- **Incremental backup**   A job that backs up only the files that have changed since the last backup job of any kind

- **Differential backup**   A job that backs up only the files that have changed since the last full backup

The backup software filters the files for these jobs by using a special file attribute called the *archive bit*, which every file on the computer possesses. File attributes are 1-bit flags, stored with each file on a drive, that perform various functions. For example, the read-only bit, when activated, prevents any application from modifying or deleting that particular file, and the hidden bit prevents that file from appearing in a directory listing. The archive bit for a file is activated by any application that modifies that file. When the backup program scans the target drive during an incremental or differential job, it selects only the files with active archive bits for backup.

During a full backup, the software backs up the entire contents of a computer's drives, and also resets (that is, removes) the archive bit on all of the files. Immediately after the job is completed, you have a complete copy of the drives on tape, and none of the files on the target drive has an active archive bit. The next time applications or the operating system modify files, they activate the archive bits for those files. The next day, you can run an incremental or differential backup job, which is also configured to back up the entire computer, except that it filters out all files that do not have an active archive bit. This means that all of the program files that make up the operating system and the applications are skipped, along with all data files that have not changed. When compared to a full backup, an incremental or differential backup job is usually much smaller, so it takes less time and less tape.

Running incremental or differential jobs can make it possible to automate your backups without spending too much on hardware. If your full backup job totals 50 GB, for example, you might be able to buy a 20 GB drive. You'll have to manually insert two additional tapes during your full backup jobs, once a week, but you can run incremental or differential jobs the rest of the week using only one tape, which means that the jobs can run unattended.

Using Incremental Jobs

The difference between an incremental and a differential job lies in the behavior of the backup software when it either resets or does not reset the archive bits of the files it copies to tape. Incremental jobs reset the archive bits, and differential jobs don't. This means that when you run an incremental job, you're only backing up the files that have changed since the last backup, whether it was a full backup or an incremental backup. This uses the least amount of tape, but it also lengthens the restore process. If you have to restore an entire computer, you must first restore the last full backup tape, and you must then restore each of the incremental jobs performed since the last full backup. For example, suppose that you run a full backup job on a particular computer every Monday evening and incremental jobs every evening from Tuesday through Friday. If the computer's hard drive fails on a Friday morning, you must restore the previous Monday's full backup, and you must then restore the incremental jobs from Tuesday, Wednesday, and Thursday, in that order. The order of the restore jobs is essential if you want the computer to have the latest version of every file.

Using Differential Jobs

Differential jobs do not reset the archive bit on the files they back up. This means that every differential job backs up all of the files that have changed since the last full backup. If you perform a full backup on Monday evening, Tuesday evening's differential job will back up all files changed on Tuesday, Wednesday evening's differential job will back up all files changed on Tuesday and Wednesday, and Thursday evening's differential backup will back up all files changed on Tuesday, Wednesday, and Thursday. Differential backups use more tape, because some of the same files are backed up each day, but differential backups also simplify the restore process. To completely restore a computer that fails on a Friday morning, you only have to restore Monday's full backup tape and the most recent differential backup, which was performed Thursday evening. Because the Thursday tape includes all of the files modified on Tuesday, Wednesday, and Thursday, no other tapes are needed. The archive bits for these changed files are not reset until the next full backup job is performed.

Test your knowledge of backup job types by completing Exercise 9-3, "Incremental and Differential Backups," now.

MORE INFO   **Demonstration Video**   Run the Backups video located in the \Demos folder on the CD-ROM accompanying this book for a demonstration of incremental and differential backups.

Drive Manipulation

When you have selected what you want to back up, the next step is to specify where to send the data. The backup software typically enables you to select a backup device (if you have more than one) and prepare to run the job by configuring the drive and the storage medium. If you are backing up to a tape drive, this part of the process can include any of the following tasks:

- Formatting a tape
- Supplying a name for the tape you're creating
- Specifying whether you want to append the backed-up files to the tape or overwrite the tape
- Turning on the drive's compression feature

Scheduling

All backup products let you create a backup job and execute it immediately, but the key to automating a backup routine is being able to schedule jobs to execute unattended. This way, you can configure your backup jobs to run when the office is closed and the network is idle, so that all resources are available for backup, and user productivity is not affected. Not all of the backup programs supplied with operating systems or designed for stand-alone computers support scheduling, but all network backup software products do.

Backup programs use various methods to automatically execute backup jobs, but no matter which mechanism the backup software uses, the process of scheduling them is usually the same. You specify whether you want to execute the job once or repeatedly at a specified time each day, week, or month, using an interface like that shown in Figure 9-19. The idea of scheduling is to create a logical sequence of backup jobs that execute by themselves at regular intervals. After this is done, the only thing that you need to do is to change the tape in the drive each day. If you have an autochanger, you can even eliminate this part of the job and create a backup job sequence that runs for weeks or months without any manual intervention at all.

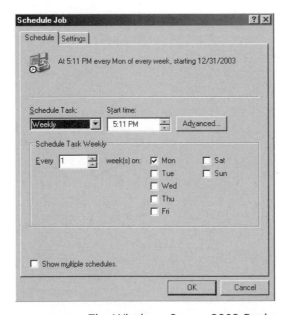

Figure 9-19   The Windows Server 2003 Backup program's Schedule Job dialog box

Logging and Cataloging

When a backup job runs, the software accesses the specified targets and feeds the data to the backup drive in the appropriate manner. Because of the nature of the media typically used for backups, it is important for the data to arrive at the storage device in a consistent manner and at the proper rate of speed. The software, therefore, must be designed to address specific drives in the manner appropriate for that device.

As the software feeds the data to the drive, it also keeps track of the software's activities. Most backup software products maintain a log of the backup process as it occurs. You can often specify a level of detail for the log, such as whether it should list every file backed up or just record the major events that occur during the job. Periodically checking the logs is an essential part of administering a network backup program. The logs tell you when selected files are skipped for any reason, for example, if the files are locked open by an application or if the computers on which they are stored are turned off. The logs also let you know when errors occur on either the backup drive or one of the computers involved in the backup process. Some software products can generate alerts when errors occur, notifying you by sending a status message to a network management console, by sending you an e-mail message, or by other methods.

> **NOTE** **Checking Backup Logs** You must also watch the size of your log files, particularly when you configure them to maintain a high level of detail. These files can grow huge very quickly and can consume all of the available disk space on the drive on which they are stored.

In addition to logging their activities, backup software programs also catalog the files they back up, thus facilitating the process of restoring files later. The catalog is essentially a list of every file that the software has backed up during each job. To restore files from the backup medium, you browse through the catalog and select the files, directories, or drives that you want to restore. Different backup software products store the catalog in different ways. Some products store the catalog for each tape on the tape itself. The problem with this method is that you have to insert a tape into the drive to read the catalog and browse the files on that tape.

More elaborate network backup software programs maintain a database of the catalogs for all of your backup tapes on the computer where the backup device is installed. This database enables you to browse through the catalogs for all of your tapes and select any version of any file or directory for restoration. In some cases, you can view the contents of the database in several different ways, such as by the computer, drive, and directory where the files were originally located, by the backup job, or by the tape or other media name. After you make your selection, the program specifies which tape contains the file or directory. Insert that tape into the drive, and the job proceeds.

The database can use a lot of the computer's disk space and processor time, but it makes the software easier to use, particularly in a network environment.

> **NOTE   Backup Database Storage**   Backup software products that rely on a database typically store a copy of the database on your tapes as well as on the computer's hard drive. This is done so that if the drive on the computer you use to run the backups fails, you can restore the database later.

Media Rotation

Some network administrators use new tapes for every backup job and store them all permanently. However, this can become extremely expensive. It's more common to reuse backup tapes. To do this properly, however, you must have a carefully planned media rotation scheme, so that you don't inadvertently reuse a tape you'll need later. You can always create such a scheme yourself, but some backup software products do it for you. One of the most common media rotation schemes is called Grandfather-Father-Son, which refers to backup jobs that run monthly, weekly, and daily. You have one set of tapes for your daily jobs, which you reuse every week; a set of weekly tapes, which you reuse every month; and a set of monthly tapes, which you reuse each year. There are other schemes that vary in complexity and utility, depending on the software product.

When the software program implements the rotation scheme, it provides a basic schedule for the jobs (which you can modify), tells you what name to write on each tape as you use it and, once you begin to reuse tapes, tells you which tape to put in the drive for each job. The end result is that you maintain a perpetual record of your data while using the minimum number of tapes without fear of overwriting a tape you need.

Restoring

Restoring data from your backups is, of course, the reason for making them in the first place. The ease with which you can locate the files you need to restore is an important feature of any backup software product. It is absolutely essential that you perform periodic test restores from your backup tapes or other media to ensure that you can recover data. Even if all your jobs complete successfully and your log files show that all of your data has been backed up, there is no better way to test the backup than to perform an actual restore. There are plenty of horror stories of network administrators who dutifully perform their backups every day for a year, only to find out when disaster strikes that all their carefully labeled tapes are blank due to a malfunctioning drive.

Although making regular backups is usually thought of as protection against a disaster that causes you to lose an entire hard drive, the majority of the restore jobs you will perform in a network environment are of one or a few files that a user has inadvertently deleted. The program's cataloging capability is a critical part of the restoration process. If a user needs to have one particular file restored and you have to insert tape after tape into the drive to locate it, everyone's time is wasted. A backup program with a database that lets you search for a particular file makes your job much easier and enables you to restore any file in minutes.

Restore jobs are similar to backup jobs, in that you typically select the files or directories that you want to restore, using an interface like that shown in Figure 9-20. You then specify whether you want to restore the files to the locations they originally came from or to another location. If you restore them to a different location, you can usually configure the software to put all of the restored files into one directory or re-create the directory structure from which the files were backed up.

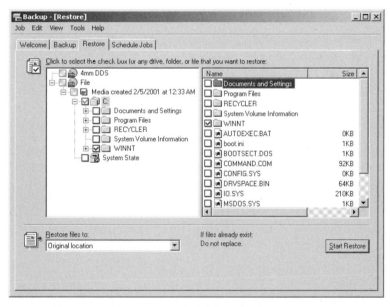

Figure 9-20   The Windows Server 2003 Backup program's Restore dialog box

Disaster Recovery

One of the problems with the typical backup software product is that, like any application, it requires an operating system to run. What happens if the drive in the computer hosting the backup drive fails? You might have a complete backup of the computer, but to restore it, you first have to reinstall the entire operating system and the backup software, which can be a time-consuming task. To address this problem, many backup software products provide a disaster recovery feature that creates a boot disk that loads just enough of the operating system and the backup application to perform a restore. A restore from a full backup will then provide all of the software needed to restart the computer in the normal manner.

> **NOTE   Exam Objectives**   *Objective 3.6 for the Network+ exam requires students to be able to identify the purpose and characteristics of disaster recovery.*

Network Backup Functions

It is particularly important that you choose a backup software product that is designed for network use. The primary difference between network backup software and an application designed for stand-alone systems is that the network backup software can back up other computers on the network. This means you can buy one backup drive and use it to protect your entire network. Many stand-alone backup products can access drives on networked computers, but a fully functional network backup product can also back up important operating system features on other computers, such as the Windows Registry and directory service databases. This type of remote backup might require you to install a software component, called an *agent,* on the target computer.

Many network backup products also have optional add-on components that let you perform specialized backup tasks, such as backing up live databases or computers running other operating systems. These can be a critical part of your network backup solution. For example, if you have database or e-mail servers that run around the clock, you might not be able to fully back them up using a standard software product because the database files are locked open. As a result, your backup job protects the program files for the database engine (the part that's easily replaceable) but leaves your actual data unprotected. To back up a database of this type, you either have to close it by shutting it down or use a specialized piece of software that creates temporary database files (called *delta files*) that the server can use while the database itself is closed for the duration of the backup process.

SUMMARY

- Firewalls protect networks from outside interference by using a variety of techniques to limit the traffic passing between the internal network and the Internet.

- Packet filtering is a technique in which a router determines whether to allow network access to each packet based on the contents of its protocol headers.

- Network address translation (NAT) enables the computers on a private network to use unregistered Internet Packet (IP) addresses and still access the Internet normally through a special router that modifies the contents of the IP header in each packet.

- Proxy servers are application layer products that act as intermediaries between network clients and Internet servers. Client applications must be configured to use proxy servers, and administrators can configure the servers to limit users' access to specific Internet resources.

- IP Security (IPSec) is a series of Transmission Control Protocol/Internet Protocol (TCP/IP) standards that provides authentication and encryption services for local area network (LAN) communications.

- Layer 2 Tunneling Protocol (L2TP) creates tunnels for virtual private networks (VPNs) that can be encrypted by using IPSec.

- Secure Sockets Layer (SSL) is a security protocol used by Web servers and browsers to encrypt and authenticate their transmitted data.

- Kerberos is an authentication protocol used by directory services to provide clients with single logon access to network resources.

- Networks often use data storage techniques such as mirroring, duplexing, spanning, striping, redundant array of independent disks (RAID), network attached storage (NAS), and storage area networks (SANs) to increase the efficiency and fault tolerance of the network storage subsystem.

- Magnetic tape is the most popular storage medium for backups because it is fast and inexpensive, and it holds a lot of data. Tape drives are available in a variety of speeds and capacities to suit the needs of different installations.

- Backup software lets you select the data you want to back up and sends it to the tape drive or other device you use for your backups. Daily backup jobs can be full backups, which copy all of the data on a computer, or incremental or differential backups, which copy only the data that has recently changed.

■ A good backup software program lets you schedule jobs to execute at any time, and it maintains both a tape version and a hard disk version of a catalog of all of the files that have been backed up. The software also enables you to back up data from computers anywhere on the network. It might also provide optional features such as live database backups.

EXERCISES

Exercise 9-1: Identifying Security Protocols

Match the security protocols in the left column with the correct descriptions in the right column.

1. SSL   a. Provides encryption for IPSec

2. ESP   b. Encapsulates PPP frames in UDP datagrams

3. L2TP   c. Provides authentication services to Active Directory

4. AH   d. Provides encryption for specific applications

5. Kerberos   e. Provides authentication services for IPSec

Exercise 9-2: Data Availability Technologies

Which disk technology (mirroring, duplexing, spanning, or striping) applies to each of the following statements? Choose all answers that are correct.

1. Enables a server to survive a drive failure

2. Uses multiple hard drives to create a single logical hard drive

3. Enables a server to survive a disk host adapter failure

4. Stores a single file on multiple drives

5. Causes an entire volume to be lost when one drive fails

Exercise 9-3: Distinguishing Between Incremental and Differential Backups

1. If you back up your network by performing a full backup every Wednesday at 6:00 P.M. and differential backups in the evening on the other six days of the week, how many jobs are needed to completely restore a computer with a hard drive that failed on a Tuesday at noon?

2. If you back up your network by performing a full backup every Wednesday at 6:00 P.M., how many jobs are needed to completely restore a computer with a failed hard drive if you performed incremental backups in the evenings of the other six days of the week?

3. For a complete restore of a computer that failed at noon on Tuesday, how many jobs are needed if you performed full backups at 6:00 A.M. every Wednesday and Saturday and incremental backups at 6:00 A.M. on the other five days of the week?

REVIEW QUESTIONS

1. Service-dependent packet filtering allows or denies access to a network based on what criterion?

    a. Port numbers

    b. IP addresses

    c. Hardware addresses

    d. Protocol identifiers

2. Which type of firewall operates at the application layer?

3. At which layer of the OSI model does NAT operate?

    a. The data-link layer

    b. The network layer

    c. The transport layer

    d. The application layer

4. Where is a firewall typically located?

    a. At the boundary between your ISP's network and the Internet

    b. On your private network

    c. On the Internet

    d. At the boundary between your private network and your ISP's network

5. Which of the following protocols does L2TP use to encrypt VPN data?

    a. L2TP (itself)

    b. AH

    c. ESP

    d. SSL

6. What mode does IPSec use to secure LAN communications?

    a. AH mode

    b. Transport mode

    c. ESP mode

    d. Tunnel mode

7. Which of the following is the first element that a client receives during the Kerberos authentication process?

    a. A TGT

    b. A TGS

    c. A session key

    d. A server ticket

8. Which of the following storage services cannot be provided by RAID?

    a. Data striping

    b. Tape backup

    c. Disk mirroring

    d. Error correction

9. What additional hardware can you install to create redundant paths through the network?

   a. Network interface adapters

   b. Hubs

   c. Servers

   d. Routers

10. Which of the following types of backup jobs does not reset the archive bits of the files it backs up?

    a. Full

    b. Incremental

    c. Differential

    d. Supplemental

11. Which of the following is the criterion most commonly used to filter files for backup jobs?

    a. Filename

    b. File extension

    c. File attributes

    d. File size

12. How does an autochanger increase the overall storage capacity of a backup solution?

13. What are the three elements in the Grandfather-Father-Son media rotation system?

    a. Hard disk drives, CD-ROM drives, and magnetic tape drives

    b. Incremental, differential, and full backup jobs

    c. Monthly, weekly, and daily backup jobs

    d. QIC, DAT, and DLT tape drives

14. Which drive interface is most commonly used by network backup devices?

    a. IDE

    b. SCSI

    c. USB

    d. Parallel port

CASE SCENARIOS

Case Scenario 9-1: Designing a Network Backup Solution

You are a network consultant for a client who wants to install a new network backup system. The client's network has five file servers containing company data, with a total capacity of 100 GB. Roughly a third of the data consists of databases that are updated continually during business hours. The rest is archival data that seldom changes. The company works two shifts during the week, so there is a relatively small backup window of five hours, from 1:00 A.M. to 6:00 A.M. The company is closed on weekends. The client wants all new data to be protected every night. Which of the following backup solutions will allow the company to back up its data with the greatest convenience and the lowest cost?

1. Buy one 20-GB DAT drive and use it to perform a full backup on the weekends and an incremental backup every night.

2. Buy one 40-GB DLT drive and use it to perform a full backup on the weekends and an incremental backup every night.

3. Buy a LTO drive and use it to perform a full backup every night.

4. Buy a DAT autochanger and use it to perform a full backup every night.

Case Scenario 9-2: Recovering from a Disaster

You are the network administrator for a company that uses the Grandfather–Father–Son media rotation method to back up the network. You come into the office on Thursday morning and discover that the hard drive on one of the servers has failed, causing all of its data to be lost. The first thing you do is to install a new hard drive into the server and load the operating system. Then, checking the backup logs, you see that the last "Grandfather" job was a full backup performed three weeks ago, on the first day of the month. The most recent "Father" job was a full backup performed the previous Sunday. The "Son" jobs are incremental backups that are performed every weeknight. All of the incrementals for that week were performed successfully, except for Tuesday night's job, which failed because you did not put the appropriate tape into the backup job. What do you need to do to completely restore all of the lost data on the failed drive?

1. Restore the most recent "Grandfather" job, then the most recent "Father" job, then the most recent "Son" incremental.

2. Restore the most recent "Father" job, and then restore the most recent "Son" incremental.

3. Restore the most recent "Father" backup, and then restore all of the "Son" incrementals performed since that full backup.

4. There is no way to restore all of the lost data, because one of the "Son" incremental jobs failed.

CHAPTER 10
REMOTE NETWORK ACCESS

Upon completion of this chapter, you will be able to:

- Describe the types of technologies used to connect remote computers to networks.

- Describe the characteristics of a leased line.

- Understand how frame relay provides flexible wide area network (WAN) solutions.

- List the optical carrier (OC) levels provided by the Synchronous Optical Network (SONET).

- Describe the characteristics of the Asynchronous Transfer Mode (ATM) protocol.

- Describe the Serial Line Internet Protocol (SLIP) and Point-to-Point Protocol (PPP) frame formats.

- Diagram the process for establishing a PPP connection.

Although most people associate the phrase "computer networking" with local area networks (LANs), other types of computer connections are networks as well. For example, when you use a dial-up modem to connect to the Internet, you are actually connecting to a remote network. In this case, the bus slot or serial port on your computer is the network interface and the telephone system is the network medium. Your computer accesses the Internet by connecting to a network run by your Internet service provider (ISP). You can use the same type of dial-up connection to connect to other networks, such as the LAN in your office, when you are at home or traveling.

There are many technologies that you can use to connect a stand-alone computer to a network at a remote location, or to connect two remote networks together. From the network layer up, a remote connection is no different from a direct LAN connection, but the physical and data-link layers can take different forms. This chapter examines some of the most common connection types and protocols used for remote networking and discusses the issues involved in installing and configuring them.

REMOTE CONNECTION REQUIREMENTS

To establish a remote network connection, the computers involved must have the following elements:

- **Physical layer connection**   The computers must be connected using a wide area networking (WAN) technology as a physical medium. In nearly all cases, a WAN link uses a service provider, such as a telephone company, to furnish the connection.

- **Common protocols**   The two computers to be connected must use the same protocols at the data-link layer and above. This means that you must configure both computers to use a data-link layer protocol suitable for point-to-point connections. The computers must also use the same network and transport layer protocols, such as Transmission Control Protocol/Internet Protocol (TCP/IP), Internetwork Packet Exchange (IPX), or NetBIOS Extended User Interface (NetBEUI).

- **TCP/IP configuration**   If a computer will use TCP/IP to communicate with a remote network, the computer must be assigned an Internet Protocol (IP) address and other configuration parameters appropriate for that network. You can configure the TCP/IP settings if someone familiar with the host network supplies them to you, but most remote networking solutions enable the network server to assign configuration parameters automatically using the Dynamic Host Configuration Protocol (DHCP) or some other mechanism.

- **Host and remote software**   Each of the computers to be connected must be running an application appropriate to its role. The remote (or client) computer needs a client program that can use the physical layer medium to establish a connection, such as by instructing a modem to dial a number. The host (or server) computer must have a program that can respond to a connection request from the remote computer and provide access to the network. For example, the Microsoft Windows operating systems use an application called Remote Access Service (RAS). The RAS server is incorporated into the Routing and Remote Access Service (RRAS) in Microsoft Windows Server 2003 and Microsoft Windows 2000 Server. The RAS client is built into Microsoft Windows 95 and all later Windows operating systems. In Microsoft Windows XP, you create a connection to a RAS server from the Network Connections window in Control Panel.

WAN CONNECTION TYPES

Many different WAN technologies are used for remote network access, and they provide varying amounts of speed, security, and flexibility. The interface that links the WAN to the computer can vary from a serial port to a universal serial bus (USB) port to a standard network interface adapter, but the actual network medium is the WAN service that carries the signals for most of their journey. The following sections examine some of the physical layer options that you can use for remote network connections. Many of the technologies discussed in this chapter have various applications, such as connecting a computer to a private network, connecting two private networks, or connecting a computer or a private network to an ISP. The connection you choose for a particular installation depends on your networking requirements and your budget.

Public Switched Telephone Network

The Public Switched Telephone Network (PSTN) is just a technical name for the standard, analog telephone system you use every day, also known as the **Plain Old Telephone Service (POTS)**. This voice-based system, found all over the world, can be used with asynchronous modems to transmit data between computers at virtually any location. The PSTN service in your home or office probably uses copper-based twisted-pair cable, as do most LANs, and RJ-11 jacks. RJ-11 jacks are the same as the RJ-45 jacks used on twisted-pair LANs, except that RJ-11 jacks have four (or sometimes six) electrical contacts instead of eight. The PSTN connection leads to a central office belonging to the telephone company, which can route calls from there to any other telephone in the world. Unlike a LAN, which is digital and uses packet switching, the PSTN is an analog, circuit-switched network.

> **NOTE** **Packet Switching and Circuit Switching** For more information about packet switching and circuit switching, see Chapter 1, "Networking Basics."

To transmit computer data over the PSTN, the digital signals generated by your computer must be converted to analog signals that the telephone network can carry. A device called a *modulator/demodulator*, more commonly known as a **modem**, handles this conversion. A modem takes the digital signals fed to it through a serial port, a USB port, or the system bus, converts them to analog signals, and then transmits them over the PSTN, as shown in Figure 10-1. At the other end of the PSTN connection, another modem performs the same process in reverse, converting the analog data back into its digital form and sending it to another computer. The combination of the interfaces to the two computers, the two modems, and the PSTN connection forms the physical layer of the networking stack.

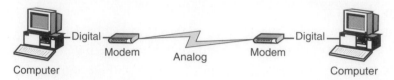

Figure 10-1   Modems convert digital signals to analog signals that the PSTN can carry, and they then convert the analog signals back to digital signals.

The first modems used proprietary protocols for the digital/analog conversions. This meant that users had to use the same manufacturer's modems at each end of the PSTN connection. To standardize modem communications, organizations like the Comité Consultatif International Télégraphique et Téléphonique (CCITT), now known as the International Telecommunication Union (ITU), began developing specifications for the communication, compression, and error-detection protocols that modems use when generating and interpreting their analog signals. Today, virtually all the modems on the market support a long list of protocols that have been ratified at various times throughout the history of modem communications. The current industry-standard modem communication protocol is V.92, which defines the 56 kilobytes per second (Kbps) data transfer mode that most modem connections use today.

The PSTN was designed for voice transmissions, not data transmissions. As a result, connections are relatively slow, with a maximum speed of only 33.6 Kbps when both communicating devices use analog PSTN connections. A 56-Kbps connection requires that one of the connected devices have a digital connection to the PSTN. The quality of PSTN connections varies widely, depending on the locations of the modems and the state of the cables connecting the modems to their central offices. In some areas, the PSTN cabling is many decades old, and connections suffer as a result. When modems detect errors while transmitting data, they revert to a slower transmission speed. This is one reason that the quality of modem connections can vary from minute to minute.

Dedicated, permanent PSTN connections between two locations, called *leased lines*, are also available, in both analog and digital forms. Leased lines provide a more consistent quality of service, but they lack the flexibility of dial-up connections and they are quite expensive. For more information on leased lines, see "Leased Lines," later in this chapter.

Integrated Services Digital Network (ISDN)

Although it achieved only modest popularity in the United States in the late 1990s, the **Integrated Services Digital Network (ISDN)** has been around for several decades and has been a popular solution in Europe, where leased telephone lines are prohibitively expensive. ISDN is a digital communications service that uses the same network infrastructure as the PSTN. It was designed as a complete digital replacement for the analog telephone system, but it had few supporters in the United States until the need for faster Internet connections led people to explore its capabilities. However, other high-speed Internet access solutions, such as Digital Subscriber Line (DSL) and cable television (CATV) networks, have recently become available. These other solutions are generally faster and less costly than ISDN and have largely eclipsed it in popularity.

ISDN is a dial-up service, like the PSTN, but its connections are digital, so no modems are required. Although ISDN can support specially made telephones, fax machines, and other devices, most ISDN installations in the United States are used only for computer data transmissions. Because it is a dial-up service, you can use ISDN to connect to different networks. For example, if you have an ISDN connection to the Internet, you can change ISPs simply by dialing a different number. No intervention from the telephone company is required. This is not possible with other high-speed WAN technologies. However, because ISDN needs special equipment, it cannot be used in mobile devices, such as laptop computers, when traveling away from the service location.

ISDN also delivers greater transmission speeds than the PSTN. The ISDN **Basic Rate Interface (BRI)** service consists of two 64-Kbps channels (called *B channels*) that carry the actual user data, plus one 16-Kbps channel (called a *D channel*) that carries only control traffic. Because of these channel names, the BRI service is sometimes called *2B+D*. The B channels can function separately or can be combined into a single 128-Kbps connection. A higher grade of service, called **Primary Rate Interface (PRI)**, consists of 23 B channels and one 64-Kbps D channel. The total bandwidth is the same as that of a T-1 leased line. PRI is used primarily to terminate a large number of ISDN BRI connections from remote sites into a single site such as a data center or headquarters location. ISDN is also often used to provide a redundant solution to leased line connectivity.

ISDN uses the same wiring as the PSTN, but additional equipment is required at the terminal locations. The telephone company provides what is called a *U interface*, which connects to a device called a **Network Terminator 1 (NT-1)**. The NT-1 can provide a four-wire connection, called an **S/T interface**, for up to seven devices, which are collectively called *terminal equipment* (TE). Digital devices designed for use with ISDN, such as ISDN telephones and fax machines, connect directly to the S/T interface and are called TE1 devices. A device that cannot connect directly to the S/T interface is called a *TE2 device*, and it requires a **terminal adapter**, which connects to the S/T interface and provides a jack for the TE2 device, as shown in Figure 10-2.

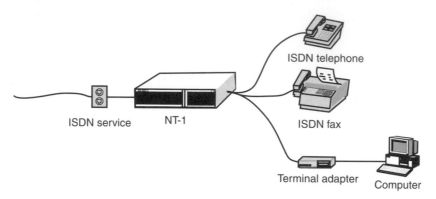

Figure 10-2   The NT-1 provides connectors for the terminal equipment that will use the ISDN service.

> **NOTE   ISDN Distance Limitations**   *Because of the increased speed at which ISDN operates, the length of the connection is limited. Your home or office must be within 18,000 feet of the telephone company's nearest central office (or a suitable repeating device).*

When you plan to connect multiple devices to the ISDN service, you buy an NT-1 as a separate unit. However, most ISDN installations in the United States use the service solely for Internet access, so there are products that combine an NT-1 and a terminal adapter into a single unit. These combined ISDN solutions can be expansion cards that plug into a bus slot or separate units that connect to the computer's serial port.

ISDN has never become hugely popular in the United States, partly because of its reputation for being expensive and for installation and reliability problems. Most telephone companies that provide ISDN charge both a monthly subscription fee and a per-minute rate (usually about 1 cent per minute). If you connect to the Internet using ISDN, you must also pay a monthly fee to an ISP for high-speed Internet access. Because of these added costs, using ISDN can be quite expensive when compared to services such as DSL and CATV. However, unlike these other services, an ISDN link can be disconnected when it is not in use. This prevents you from paying for bandwidth you are not using, and eliminates a potential window through which intruders can access your network.

Digital Subscriber Line (DSL)

Digital Subscriber Line (DSL) is a blanket term for a variety of digital communication services that use standard telephone lines and provide data transfer speeds much greater than the PSTN or even ISDN. Each of the various DSL service types has a different descriptive word or phrase added to its name, which is why some sources use the generic abbreviation *x*DSL. Some of the many DSL services are shown in Table 10-1.

Table 10-1   DSL Services and Their Properties

Service	Transmission Rate	Link Length	Applications
High-bit-rate Digital Subscriber Line (HDSL)	Up to 1.544 Mbps	12,000 feet	Used by large networks as a substitute for T-1 leased line connections, LAN and Private Branch Exchange (PBX) interconnections, or frame relay traffic aggregation
Symmetric digital subscriber line (SDSL)	Up to 2.3 Mbps	10,000 feet	Same as HDSL
Multirate Symmetric DSL (MSDSL)	Up to 2 Mbps	29,000 feet	A variant of SDSL that can use more than one transfer rate, set by the service provider
Asymmetric digital subscriber line (ADSL)	Up to 8.448 Mbps downstream; up to 800 Kbps upstream	18,000 feet	Internet/intranet access, remote LAN access, virtual private networking, video on demand, voice over IP
Rate-Adaptive Digital Subscriber Line (RADSL)	Up to 7 Mbps downstream; up to 1.088 Mbps upstream	18,000 feet	Same as ADSL, except that the transmission speed is dynamically adjusted to accommodate the link length and signal quality
ADSL Lite	Up to 1 Mbps downstream; up to 512 Kbps upstream	18,000 feet	Internet/intranet access, remote LAN access, IP telephony, videoconferencing

Table 10-1   DSL Services and Their Properties (Continued)

Service	Transmission Rate	Link Length	Applications
Very high-rate digital subscriber line (VDSL)	Up to 51.84 Mbps downstream; up to 16 Mbps upstream	4500 feet	Multimedia Internet access, high-definition television delivery
Internet digital subscriber line (IDSL)	Up to 144 Kbps	18,000 feet	Internet/intranet access, remote LAN access, IP telephony, videoconferencing

As noted by the transmission rates listed in Table 10-1, many DSL services run at different upstream and downstream speeds. These types of services are described as *asymmetrical*. The different speeds occur because some DSL signals cause greater levels of crosstalk in the data traveling from the customer site to the central office than in the other direction. For end-user Internet access, this asymmetrical behavior is usually not a problem, because Web surfing and other common activities generate far more downstream traffic than upstream traffic. However, if you will use DSL to connect your own servers to the Internet, make sure that you obtain a service that is symmetrical or that offers sufficient upstream bandwidth for your needs. DSL services are also subject to distance restrictions, just like ISDN.

DSL provides higher transmission rates by using high frequencies that standard telephone services do not use and by using special signaling schemes. For this reason, in many cases, you can use your existing telephone lines for a DSL connection and for voice traffic at the same time. The most common DSL services are HDSL, used by phone companies and large corporations for WAN links, and **ADSL**, which is used by ISPs to provide Internet access to end users. DSL is an excellent Internet access solution, and you can use it to connect a home user to an office LAN, as long as the upstream bandwidth suits your needs.

An ADSL connection requires additional hardware called an **ADSL Termination Unit-Remote (ATU-R)**, which is sometimes called a *DSL transceiver* or a *DSL modem*. You will also need a line splitter if you will also use the line for voice traffic. A DSL modem is not really a modem because it does not convert signals between digital and analog formats. (All DSL communications are digital.) The ATU-R connects to your computer using either a standard Ethernet network interface adapter or a USB port. At the other end of the link at the ISP's site is a more complicated device called a **Digital Subscriber Line Access Multiplexer (DSLAM)**, shown in Figure 10-3.

Figure 10-3   An ADSL connection is a direct link between your home or office and an ISP or other network site.

Unlike ISDN connections, DSL connections are direct, permanent links between two sites that remain connected at all times. This means that if you use DSL to connect to the Internet, the telephone company activates the DSL connection between your home or office and the ISP's site. If you want to change your ISP, the phone company must install a new link. In many cases, however, telephone companies are themselves offering DSL Internet access, which eliminates one party from the chain.

Cable Television (CATV) Networks

All of the remote connection technologies described up to this point rely on cables installed and maintained by telephone companies. However, the cable television (CATV) industry has also been installing a vast network infrastructure throughout most of the United States over the past few decades. In recent years, many CATV systems have started taking advantage of their networks to provide Internet access to their customers through the same cable used for the TV service. CATV Internet access is very fast—sometimes as fast as 512 Kbps or more—and is usually quite inexpensive. CATV networks use broadband transmissions, meaning that the one network medium carries many discrete signals at the same time.

Each TV channel you receive over cable is a separate signal, and all the signals arrive over the cable simultaneously. (If you have two or more TVs in your home, you prove this every day by watching two different programs at the same time using the same CATV connection.) By devoting some of this bandwidth to data transmissions, CATV providers can deliver Internet data at the same time as the television signals. If you already have CATV, installing the Internet service is simply a matter of connecting a splitter to the cable and running it to a device called (again, erroneously) a *cable modem*, which is connected to an Ethernet network interface adapter in your computer, as shown in Figure 10-4.

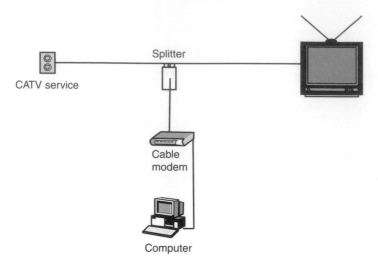

Figure 10-4   CATV data connections use the same cable that delivers television signals to carry Internet data.

CATV data connections are different from both ISDN and DSL connections because they are not dedicated links. In effect, you are connecting to a metropolitan area network (MAN) run by your cable company. If you run Windows on your computer and try to browse the network, you might see your neighbors' computers on the same network as yours. This arrangement has two disadvantages:

- **Bandwidth sharing**   With a CATV connection, you are sharing your Internet bandwidth with all the other users in your area. During peak usage periods, you might notice a significant slowdown in your Internet downloads. ISDN and DSL, by contrast, are not shared connections, so the full bandwidth to the service provider's nearest point of presence is available at all times.

- **Security**   If you share a drive on your computer without protecting it with passwords, anyone else on the network can access, modify, or even delete your files. The installers from the cable company usually disable file sharing on your computer, however, and you can use personal firewall products for additional protection.

Like most DSL services, CATV data connections are asymmetrical. CATV networks carry signals primarily in one direction, from the provider to the customer. There is a small amount of upstream bandwidth, which some systems use for purposes such as ordering pay-per-view movies from a remote control. Part of this upstream bandwidth is allocated for Internet traffic. In most cases, the upstream speed of a CATV connection is far less than the downstream speed. This makes the service unsuitable for hosting your own Internet servers, but it is still faster than a PSTN connection.

Test your knowledge of low-end WAN connections by completing Exercise 10-1, "Remote Connection Technologies," now.

CATV connections are an inexpensive and fast Internet access solution, but you cannot use them to connect your home computer to your office LAN, unless you use a virtual private network (VPN) connection through the Internet. If you plan to implement VPNs, be sure that the cable modem you use supports them.

Leased Lines

A **leased line** is a permanent telephone connection between two locations that provides a predetermined amount of bandwidth at all times. Leased lines can be analog or digital, although most of the leased lines used today are digital. The most common leased line configuration in the United States is called a **T-1**, which runs at 1.544 Mbps. The European equivalent of a T-1 is called an **E-1**, which runs at 2.048 Mbps. Many organizations use T-1 lines to connect their networks to the Internet or to connect remote networks together. For applications requiring more bandwidth, a **T-3** connection runs at 44.736 Mbps and an **E-3** runs at 34.368 Mbps. These designations are collectively known as T-carrier and E-carrier services, respectively.

> **NOTE   LAN and WAN Speeds**   When discussing the transmission capabilities of WAN links, *high-speed* is a relative term. All of the WAN technologies discussed in this chapter run at much faster speeds than PSTN connections, but most of them are also considerably slower than even a modest LAN. The reason for the discrepancy is that a WAN link nearly always involves an outside service provider that charges a fee based on the bandwidth used, while LANs are wholly owned by their operators and incur no bandwidth charges. For this reason, hardware and software products that are used on WANs tend to have features that enable you to minimize the amount of traffic passing over the WAN link.

Leased line services are split into 64-Kbps channels. A T-1, for example, consists of 24 channels that can be used as a single data pipe or as individual 64-Kbps links. You can also install a leased line that uses part of a T-1. This is called a *fractional T-1* service, and you can use it to specify exactly the amount of bandwidth you need. For data transmission purposes, a leased line is typically left as a single channel using all of the available bandwidth. However, T-1s and other leased line services are used for standard telephone communications as well. When a large organization installs its own telephone system, the PBX or switchboard is connected to one or more T-1 lines. Each T-1 line is split into the 64-Kbps channels, and each channel can function as one voice telephone line. The PBX allocates the channels to the various users of the telephone system as needed.

A T-3 connection is the equivalent of 672 channels of 64 Kbps each, or 28 T-1 lines. This much bandwidth is usually required only by large corporate networks, ISPs, and other service providers with a need for huge amounts of bandwidth.

To install a leased line, you contract with a telephone provider to furnish a link between two specific sites, running at a particular bandwidth. Prices depend on the amount of bandwidth and the distance between the sites, but a T-1 connection can easily cost $1,000 to $2,000 per month, plus installation and equipment fees at both ends. At each end of the connection, you must have a device called a **channel service unit/data service unit (CSU/DSU)**, which you connect to your data network using a router (or a PBX, in the case of a voice network), as shown in Figure 10-5.

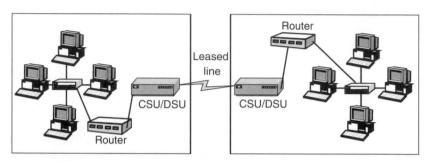

Figure 10-5   A CSU/DSU is required at both ends of a leased line.

A CSU/DSU is actually two devices that are always combined into a single unit that looks something like an external modem. In fact, CSU/DSUs are sometimes called *digital modems*, a term that is incorrect when the leased line is digital because no modulation or demodulation occurs. The CSU part of the device provides the terminus for the digital link and keeps the link alive when no traffic is passing over it. The CSU also provides diagnostic and testing functions. The DSU part of the device translates the signals generated by the LAN equipment into the bipolar digital signals used by the leased line.

> **NOTE   Identifying Modems**   Any external device providing a connection to a WAN service is commonly called a *modem*, regardless of whether the service is analog or digital. References to DSL modems, cable modems, and ISDN modems are common, mainly because all of these devices are little boxes with flashing lights on them. Most professionals aware of the distinction have given up trying to explain the differences.

Leased lines are a popular WAN solution, but they do have a significant disadvantage. Because the link is permanently connected, you pay for a specific amount of bandwidth 24 hours a day. If your applications do not run around the clock, you might end up paying premium prices for bandwidth you are not using. At one time, the bandwidth of a leased line was set at a particular rate. If your bandwidth needs exceeded the capacity of the line, the only way to augment your connection was to install another line. Today, flexible-rate connections are available from most service providers. You pay for a particular rate and can burst to a higher rate during peak traffic periods, paying extra when you do. Leased line connections are also upgradable, by changing the CSU clocking at both ends.

As a result, leased lines are excellent solutions for some applications but can be less cost effective for others.

> **NOTE** **Exam Objectives** *Objective 1.6 for the Network+ exam requires students to be able to identify the purpose, features, and functions of CSU/DSU and modems.*

Frame Relay

Frame relay is a WAN solution that provides bandwidth similar to that of a leased line, but with greater flexibility. Frame relay services range from 56 Kbps all the way up to T-3 speeds, but the subscriber is not permanently locked into a specific transmission rate, as with a leased line. When you enter into a contract with a frame relay provider, you agree on a specific amount of bandwidth, called the *committed information rate* (CIR), which is the base speed of your link. However, the frame relay service can provide additional bandwidth (called *bursts*) during your high-traffic periods by borrowing it from other circuits that are not operating at full capacity. In addition to the CIR, you also negotiate a *committed burst information rate* (CBIR), which is the maximum amount of bandwidth that the provider agrees to furnish during burst periods. Your contract specifies the duration of the bursts you are permitted. If you exceed the bandwidth agreed on, you are charged extra.

A frame relay connection is not a permanent link between two points, as a leased line is. Instead, each of the two sites is connected to the service provider's nearest point of presence, usually using a standard leased line. The provider's network takes the form of a frame relay cloud, which enables the leased line at one site to be connected to the line at the other site, as shown in Figure 10-6. This connection through the cloud from one point of presence to another is called a *permanent virtual circuit* (PVC).

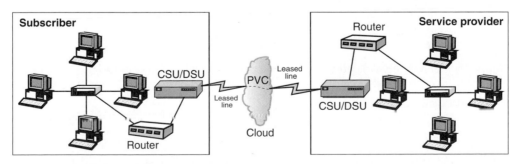

Figure 10-6   A frame relay connection

Because each site uses a local telephone provider for its leased line to the cloud, the cost is generally less than it would be to have a single leased line connecting the two different sites.

The hardware device that provides the interface between the LAN at each site and the connection to the cloud is called a *frame relay assembler/disassembler* (FRAD). A FRAD is a network layer device that strips off the LAN's data-link layer protocol header from each packet and repackages it for transmission through the cloud. One of the main advantages of frame relay is that you can use a single connection to a frame relay provider to replace several dedicated leased lines. For example, if a corporation has five offices located in different cities, it would take ten leased lines to connect each office to every other office.

Using frame relay, you can create a mesh WAN topology connecting the networks at all five sites by using a single leased line at each location to connect to a common cloud. Because the connections in a frame relay cloud are ephemeral, a single network can simultaneously establish multiple PVCs to different destinations, as shown in Figure 10-7.

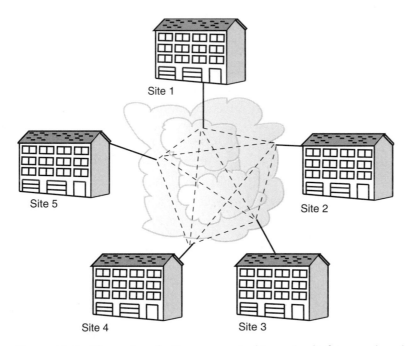

Figure 10-7   Five network sites connected to a single frame relay cloud

In a frame relay connection, you pay for only the PVC bandwidth you use (although you must pay for the leased line bandwidth, whether or not you use it). In addition, if you select the right provider, you can use frame relay to connect each of your sites to a local point of presence, reducing the cost of the leased lines.

SONET/Synchronous Digital Hierarchy

The **Synchronous Optical Network (SONET)** is a physical layer standard that defines a method for building a synchronous telecommunications network based on fiber optic cables. First ratified by the American National Standards Institute (ANSI), SONET was then adapted by ITU, which called it the *Synchronous Digital Hierarchy* (SDH). Intended as a replacement for the T-carrier and E-carrier services used in the United States and Europe, SONET provides connections at various optical carrier (OC) levels running at different speeds. The idea behind SONET is to create a standardized series of transmission rates and formats, eliminating the problems that currently affect connections between different types of carrier networks. The OC levels are listed in Table 10-2.

Table 10-2 **SONET OC Levels**

OC Level	Data Transmission Rate (in Mbps)
OC1	51.84
OC3	155.52
OC6	311.04
OC9	466.56
OC12	622.08
OC18	933.12
OC24	1244.16
OC36	1866.24
OC48	2488.32
OC96	4976.640
OC192	9953.280

Asynchronous Transfer Mode (ATM)

Asynchronous Transfer Mode (ATM) is a protocol that was originally designed to carry voice, data, and video traffic on both LANs and WANs. Today, ATM is most commonly used in WAN connections. Unlike most data-link layer protocols, ATM uses fixed-length, 53-byte frames (called *cells*) and provides a connection-oriented, full-duplex, point-to-point service between devices. Because the cells are a uniform size, unlike the variable-sized packets used by most networking protocols, ATM can provide a guaranteed, predefined quality of service.

There are no broadcast transmissions in ATM, and data is relayed between networks by switches, not routers. ATM speeds range from a 25.6-Mbps service, intended for desktop LAN connections, to a 2.46-Gbps service. Physical media include standard multimode fiber optic and unshielded twisted-pair (UTP) cables on LANs, and SONET or T-carrier services for WAN connections.

Test your knowledge of higher-end WAN connections by completing Exercise 10-2, "WAN Concepts," now.

On an internetwork where ATM is implemented on both the LANs and the WAN connections, cells originating at a workstation can travel all the way to a destination at another site through switches without having to be reencapsulated in a different data-link layer protocol. ATM never gained popularity on the desktop, however, because at the time of its introduction, Fast Ethernet provided better transmission rates and a simpler upgrade procedure. In the same way, Gigabit Ethernet has become the predominant high-speed backbone protocol, largely displacing most ATM backbones. Today, therefore, ATM has largely been relegated to use on WANs.

> **NOTE   Exam Objectives**   Objective 2.11 for the Network+ exam requires students to be able to "identify the basic characteristics (e.g., speed, capacity, and media) of the following WAN technologies: packet switching vs. circuit switching, ISDN, FDDI, ATM, Frame Relay, SONET/SDH, T-1/E-1, T-3/E-3, [and] OCx."

REMOTE NETWORKING PROTOCOLS

Unlike LANs, which use a shared network medium, the WAN links used for remote networking are nearly always end-to-end connections involving two systems only. For this reason, the data-link layer protocols used for WAN connections are substantially different from those used on LANs. For example, the Ethernet protocol devotes a large part of its header to the source and destination addresses of the communicating systems and to information Ethernet uses to implement its Media Access Control (MAC) mechanism. On a WAN link between two systems, there is no need to include the addresses of both systems in every packet, and there is no need for MAC at all. Therefore, the packet header on a WAN can be reduced, conserving expensive bandwidth.

The Serial Line Internet Protocol (SLIP) and the Point-to-Point Protocol (PPP) are data-link layer protocols, but they are part of the TCP/IP protocol suite, unlike Ethernet and Token Ring. SLIP and PPP are not designed to connect systems to a LAN that uses a shared network medium. As a result, these protocols are far simpler than LAN protocols. SLIP and PPP also do not include physical layer specifications; they operate strictly at the data-link layer. Another standard, such as one of the WAN technologies described earlier in this chapter, provides the physical layer.

The following sections examine some of the data-link layer protocols used for remote networking with WAN connections.

Serial Line Internet Protocol (SLIP)

SLIP is so simple that it hardly deserves to be called a protocol. In fact, although there is no official SLIP standard, there is a Request for Comments (RFC) published by the Internet Engineering Task Force (IETF) called RFC 1055, "A Nonstandard for Transmission of IP Datagrams over Serial Lines," which defines the protocol's function. Created in the early 1980s, SLIP transmits signals over a serial connection (which in most cases means a modem and a telephone line) in the simplest possible manner and with the lowest possible amount of control overhead. For example, compared with the 18 bytes of header information that Ethernet adds to every packet, SLIP adds only 1 byte. Of course, with only 1 byte of overhead, SLIP cannot provide functions such as error detection, network layer protocol identification, security, or anything else.

SLIP transmits an IP datagram received from the network layer over the network medium and follows it with a single framing byte called an *End Delimiter*, as shown in Figure 10-8.

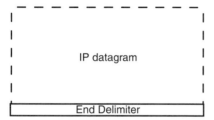

Figure 10-8   SLIP uses an End Delimiter to mark the end of each data packet.

The End Delimiter byte serves as notice to the receiving system that it has finished receiving the data portion of the packet. In some cases, the system surrounds the datagram with two End Delimiter fields, making it possible for the receiving system to easily ignore any line noise that occurs outside the frame.

Because of its utter simplicity, SLIP is easy to implement and provides the ultimate in efficiency, as far as traffic overhead is concerned. However, because SLIP supplies no additional information to the receiving system, the protocol has many critical shortcomings, including the following:

- **No addresses**   SLIP has no way of supplying the IP address of each system involved in a connection to the other. Each of the connected computers must be preconfigured with the IP address of the other computer.

- **No protocol identification**   SLIP has no way of identifying the network layer protocol that generated the data carried in the frame. Therefore, it is impossible for SLIP to multiplex network layer protocols (such as IP and IPX) using a single connection.

- **No error detection/correction**   A system receiving data using SLIP has no way of determining whether the datagram in the frame has been damaged in transit. It is left to the upper layer protocols to identify damaged packets and arrange for their retransmission.

Because of these shortcomings, SLIP is rarely used today.

Point-to-Point Protocol (PPP)

The Point-to-Point Protocol (PPP) has, in nearly all cases, replaced SLIP as the data-link layer protocol used in remote networking over WAN connections. PPP is more complex than SLIP and provides a number of services that SLIP lacks. These include the ability of the systems to exchange IP addresses, carry data generated by multiple network layer protocols, and support different authentication protocols. Still, PPP does all this while adding only 8 bytes to a network layer datagram, which is larger than the SLIP header but still less than half the size of the Ethernet frame.

PPP Communications

As small as it is, the PPP frame cannot possibly provide all of the functions that SLIP lacks. Instead, the protocol performs many of these functions by performing an elaborate connection establishment procedure when two systems first communicate. The connection establishment procedure includes separate transactions performed by other, subordinate protocols, including the following:

- **Link Control Protocol (LCP)**   Negotiates the parameters the systems will use during the connection, such as authentication, compression, and packet size. LCP messages inform each computer of the other system's capabilities so that they can agree on a set of parameters that both support.

- **Authentication protocols**   Authentication in a PPP connection is optional, but when it does occur, the two systems agree on the use of a specific authentication protocol, such as the Password Authentication Protocol (PAP) or the Challenge Handshake Authentication Protocol (CHAP).

- **Network control protocols**   For each network layer protocol that the systems will use to communicate, the system must perform a separate transaction using the appropriate network control protocol (NCP), such as the Internet Protocol Control Protocol (IPCP) and the Internetwork Packet Exchange Control Protocol (IPXCP).

This method of exchanging information is more efficient than increasing the size of the PPP header because there is no need to include it in every packet. For example, it is beneficial for the two communicating systems to know each other's IP addresses, but there is no need to include address fields in every packet header, as in Ethernet, because only two computers are involved and they have to identify themselves only once. The same is true for functions like authentication.

Unlike SLIP, PPP is standardized, but the specifications are divided among several different RFCs. Some of the documents that define the protocols used during PPP communications are as follows:

- **RFC 1661**   "The Point-to-Point Protocol (PPP)"

- **RFC 1662**   "PPP in HDLC-Like Framing"

- **RFC 1663**   "PPP Reliable Transmission"

- **RFC 1332**   "The PPP Internet Protocol Control Protocol (IPCP)"

- **RFC 1552**   "The PPP Internetwork Packet Exchange Control Protocol (IPXCP)"

- **RFC 1994**   "PPP Challenge Handshake Authentication Protocol (CHAP)"

- **RFC 1989**   "PPP Link Quality Monitoring"

The PPP Frame

The PPP frame is illustrated in Figure 10-9.

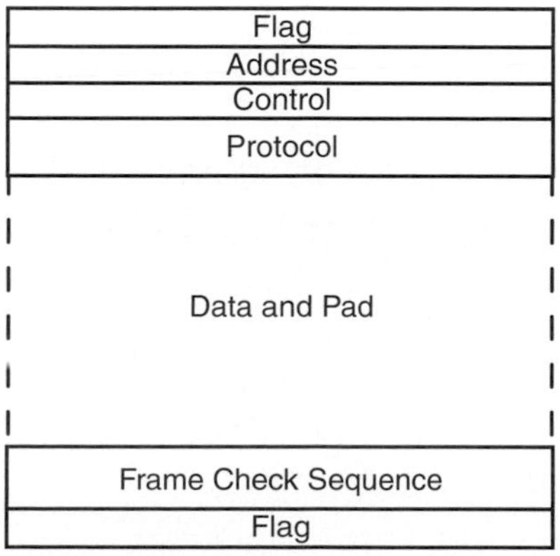

Flag
Address
Control
Protocol
Data and Pad
Frame Check Sequence
Flag

Figure 10-9   The PPP frame

The functions of the fields in the PPP frame are as follows:

- **Flag (1 byte)**   Contains a hexadecimal value of 7e and functions as a packet delimiter, like SLIP's End Delimiter.

- **Address (1 byte)**   Contains a hexadecimal value of ff, indicating the packet is addressed to all stations.

- **Control (1 byte)**   Contains a hexadecimal value of 03, identifying the packet as containing an unnumbered information message.

- **Protocol (2 bytes)**   Contains a code identifying the protocol that generated the information in the data field. Code values in the 0xxx to 3xxx range identify network layer protocols, values from 4xxx to 7xxx identify low-volume network layer protocols with no corresponding network control protocol, values from 8xxx to bxxx identify network layer protocols with corresponding network control protocols, and values from cxxx to fxxx identify link layer control protocols like LCP and the authentication protocols. The permitted codes, as specified by the Internet Assigned Numbers Authority (IANA), include the following:

  - ❑ **0021**   Uncompressed IP datagram (used when Van Jacobson compression is enabled)

  - ❑ **002b**   Novell IPX datagram

  - ❑ **002d**   IP datagrams with compressed IP and TCP headers (used when Van Jacobson compression is enabled)

  - ❑ **002f**   IP datagrams containing uncompressed TCP data (used when Van Jacobson compression is enabled)

  - ❑ **8021**   IPCP

  - ❑ **802b**   802b IPXCP

  - ❑ **c021**   LCP

  - ❑ **c023**   PAP

  - ❑ **cc23**   CHAP

- **Data And Pad (variable, up to 1500 bytes)**   Contains the payload of the packet, up to a default maximum receive unit (MRU) of 1500 bytes. The field can contain meaningless bytes to bring its size up to the MRU.

- **Frame Check Sequence (FCS) (2 or 4 bytes)**   Contains a cyclical redundancy check (CRC) value calculated on the entire frame, excluding the flag and frame check sequence fields, for error-detection purposes.

- **Flag (1 byte)**   Contains the same value as the Flag field at the beginning of the frame. When a system transmits two packets consecutively, one of the Flag fields is omitted, since two would be mistaken as an empty frame.

> **NOTE   PPP Frame Modifications**   Some of the fields in the PPP frame can be changed as a result of LCP negotiations between the two systems. For example, the length of the Protocol and FCS fields and the MRU for the data field could be changed.

Establishing a PPP Connection

During the PPP connection establishment procedure, the following phases occur before the systems can exchange any application data:

1. **Link Dead phase**   The two systems begin and end the PPP session in the Link Dead phase, with no communication or physical layer connection between them. To begin the link establishment process, one of the systems initiates a physical layer connection by triggering a hardware process, such as by running a program that causes a modem to dial. Once the hardware connection process is complete, both systems enter the Link Establishment phase.

2. **Link Establishment phase**   The Link Establishment phase begins when the system that initiated the connection transmits a PPP frame containing an LCP Configure Request message. This message contains options specifying the protocols and parameters the system wants to use during the session, such as an authentication protocol, link quality protocol, network layer protocols, or a different MRU value. The other system replies to the message, either accepting the offered conditions or specifying its own list of LCP options. Eventually, the two systems agree on a list of options they have in common, and one receives an LCP Configure Ack message in response to its Configure Request. Both systems then begin the next part of the process.

3. **Authentication**   If the systems agreed to use a particular authentication protocol during the Link Establishment phase, they then exchange PPP frames containing messages specific to that protocol. If the systems agreed not to authenticate, this phase is skipped. PPP computers commonly use PAP or CHAP, but other authentication protocols are also available. The authentication messages contain user credentials or whatever other information the authentication protocol requires. If the authentication is successful, the computers move on to the next part of the process. If the authentication

fails, what happens next depends on the authentication protocol. For example, the systems might be allowed to try again, or they might go directly to the Link Termination phase.

4. **Link quality monitoring**   If the two systems negotiated the use of a link quality monitoring protocol during the Link Establishment phase, the computers exchange messages relevant to that protocol. The only such protocol that has been standardized is the Link Quality Report Protocol, and the messages exchanged during this phase enable the systems to agree on how often they should transmit their link quality statistics. Once this negotiation is complete, the systems proceed to the next part of the process.

5. **Network layer protocol configuration**   A PPP connection can support multiple network layer protocols simultaneously. For each network layer protocol that the systems agreed to use, the systems must perform a separate network layer connection establishment procedure, using the appropriate network control protocol. These procedures are similar to LCP messages, except that the options are unique to the specific protocol. For example, during the IPCP message exchange, the systems exchange IP addresses. Once the network control protocol exchanges are complete, the systems proceed to the Link Open phase.

6. **Link Open Phase**   Once the systems reach the Link Open phase, the PPP connection is fully established. The systems can begin exchanging packets containing network layer application data.

7. **Link termination**   When the two systems have finished communicating, they sever the PPP connection by exchanging LCP termination messages. The systems then return to the Link Dead phase.

Test your knowledge of the PPP connection establishment process by completing Exercise 10-3, "PPP Connection Establishment," now.

Point-to-Point Protocol over Ethernet

Point-to-Point Protocol over Ethernet (PPPoE) is a TCP/IP standard, defined in RFC 2516, "A Method for Transmitting PPP Over Ethernet (PPPoE)." PPPoE provides a way to create individual PPP connections between computers on an Ethernet LAN and external services connected to the LAN by using a broadband device such as a cable or DSL modem. Broadband remote network access devices can easily support multiple computers, and Ethernet is the most common protocol used to network the computers and connect them to the broadband device. However, a shared Ethernet LAN does not enable each computer to access remote services using individual parameters for functions such as access control and billing. The object of PPPoE is to connect multiple computers to a remote network using an Ethernet LAN and broadband technology, while establishing a separate PPP connection between each computer and a given remote service. Each PPP connection has all of the PPP components, such as LCP negotiation, authentication, and network control protocol configuration.

Virtual Private Networks (VPNs)

One of the advantages of using the PSTN to connect a computer to a distant network is that no special service installation is required and the only hardware you need is a modem and a telephone jack. This means that users working remotely can dial in to their office networks from wherever they happen to be. However, dialing in to a distant network using the PSTN can be expensive, especially when a company has many remote network users. One way to minimize these long-distance telephone charges is to use what is known as a **virtual private network (VPN)** connection.

A VPN is a connection between a remote computer and a server on a private network that uses the Internet as its network medium. The network is permanently connected to the Internet and has a server that is configured to receive incoming VPN connections through the Internet. The remote user connects to the Internet by using a modem to dial in to a nearby ISP. Many ISPs offer national and even international service, so the user can connect to the Internet with a local telephone call. The remote computer and the network server then establish a secured connection that protects the data exchanged between them, using the Internet as the network medium. This technique is called **tunneling**, because the connection runs across the Internet inside a secure conduit, protecting the data in the way that a tunnel under a river protects cars from the water around it.

The primary protocol that makes tunneling possible is the Point-to-Point Tunneling Protocol (PPTP). PPTP works with PPP to establish a connection between the client computer and a server on the target network, both of which are connected to the Internet. The connection process begins when the client computer dials up and connects to a local ISP using the standard PPP connection establishment process. When the computer is connected to the Internet, it uses TCP to establish a control connection to the server. This control connection is the PPTP tunnel through which the computers transmit and receive all subsequent data.

When the tunnel is in place, the computers send their data through it by encapsulating the PPP data that they would normally transmit over a dial-up connection within IP datagrams. The computer then sends the datagrams through the tunnel to the other computer. This violates the rules of the Open Systems Interconnection (OSI) model—a data-link layer frame is actually carried within a network layer datagram.

The PPP frames are encapsulated by IP, but at the same time, they can also contain other IP datagrams that contain the user data that one computer is sending to the other. Thus, the messages transmitted through the TCP connection that forms the tunnel are IP datagrams that contain PPP frames, with the PPP frames containing messages generated by IP or any network layer protocol. In other words, because the PPP user data is secured within the IP datagrams, that data can be another IP datagram or an IPX or NetBEUI message, as shown in Figure 10-10. Because the tunnel is encrypted and secured with an authentication protocol, the data is protected from interception. After the IP datagrams pass through the tunnel to the other computer, the PPP frames are extracted and processed by the receiver in the normal manner.

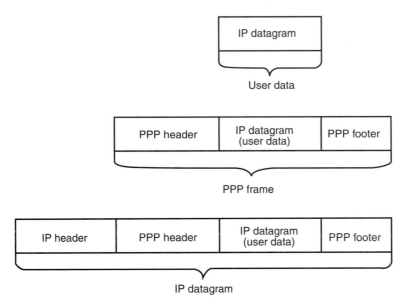

Figure 10-10   PPTP violates data encapsulation rules by carrying PPP frames within IP datagrams.

Terminal Connections

Another type of remote connection that some networks use within a single site, instead of between sites, is called *thin client computing*. In thin client computing, a terminal client program runs on a low-end computer or a dedicated network client device that communicates with a terminal server elsewhere on the network. The client provides the interface to the operating system and nothing more; the actual operating system and all applications run on the terminal server. The client and the server communicate using a specialized protocol, such as the *Independent Computing Architecture* (ICA), developed by Citrix Systems, Inc. ICA carries keystrokes, mouse actions, and screen updates between the client and the server, enabling a user at the client side to work as though the applications were running locally, when they are actually running at the server. Thin client computing enables a network to use inexpensive machines for its clients, leaving most of the computing environment on the server, where administrators can easily monitor and maintain it.

> **NOTE** **Exam Objectives**   Objective 3.7 for the Network+ exam requires students to be able to configure the connection in a remote connectivity scenario (such as IP, IPX, dial-up, PPPoE, authentication, or physical connectivity).

SUMMARY

- To connect computers to a network at a remote location, you can use any one of several different wide area network (WAN) technologies.

- Public Switched Telephone Network (PSTN) connections use modems and standard telephone lines to transmit data. They are relatively slow but also flexible and universal.

- Integrated Services Digital Network (ISDN) is a digital dial-up service provided by telephone companies that offers faster speeds and greater dial-up flexibility than PSTN, but it is also more expensive.

- Digital Subscriber Line (DSL) is a point-to-point connection that uses standard telephone lines to carry digital signals at much higher speeds than PSTN connections.

- Cable television (CATV) networks use CATV technology to provide users with economical, high-speed Internet access. However, CATV is a shared service, which means that bandwidth can diminish as more local users concurrently access the Internet.

- Leased lines are dedicated, permanent, point-to-point connections that telephone carriers provide between two sites.

- Frame relay is a service that provides flexible amounts of bandwidth between sites using a cloud of virtual circuits.

- Synchronous Optical Network (SONET) is a fiber optic telecommunications network standard consisting of a series of optical carrier levels.

- Asynchronous Transfer Mode (ATM) is a switched, connection-oriented service that was designed for use on both local area networks (LANs) and WANs.

- WAN connections use data-link layer protocols that are quite different from LAN protocols, such as Ethernet and Token Ring. Serial Line Internet Protocol (SLIP) and Point-to-Point Protocol (PPP) are Transmission Control Protocol/Internet Protocol (TCP/IP) data-link layer protocols that can be used with most types of WAN connections.

- SLIP is a simple protocol that enables two systems connected through their serial ports to exchange messages with very little control overhead.

- PPP is a more complicated end-to-end protocol that enables two systems to negotiate the use of optional features such as authentication protocols and multiple network layer protocols.

- Virtual private networks (VPNs) are secure tunnels through the Internet that enable remote computers to communicate with their networks without using long-distance telephone connections.

- PPPoE is a method for creating individual PPP connections between computers on an Ethernet LAN and external services connected to the LAN by using a broadband device such as a cable or DSL modem.

- In a terminal connection, a terminal client program running on a low-end computer or a dedicated network client device communicates with a terminal server elsewhere on the network. The client provides the interface to the operating system only; the actual operating system and all applications run on the terminal server.

EXERCISES

Exercise 10-1: Remote Connection Technologies

Specify which of the following remote connection technologies (PSTN, ISDN, DSL, or CATV) are associated with each of the following concepts.

1. Asymmetrical transfer rates

2. Uses standard telephone lines

3. Slowest of the connection types discussed

4. Uses an NT-1

5. Also called POTS

6. Uses an ATU-R

7. Uses analog signals

8. Requires the nearest central office to be relatively near

Exercise 10-2: WAN Concepts

Match the WAN technologies in the left column with the appropriate concepts in the right column.

1. Frame relay   **a.** International equivalent of SONET

2. T-1   **b.** Uses 53-byte cells

3. ATM   **c.** Provides bursts of additional bandwidth

4. SDH   **d.** Consists of 24 channels providing 64 Kbps of bandwidth each

5. E-3

   e. Runs at 34.368 Mbps

Exercise 10-3: PPP Connection Establishment

Put the following steps of the PPP connection establishment process in the correct order.

1. Link Open phase

2. Link termination

3. Network layer protocol configuration

4. Authentication

5. Link quality monitoring

6. Link Establishment phase

7. Link Dead phase

REVIEW QUESTIONS

1. Why are cable modems and DSL modems not really modems?

2. Which DSL type is most commonly used to provide Internet access to end users?

   a. HDSL

   b. ADSL

   c. SDSL

   d. VDSL

3. An ISDN installation in the United States provides you with a connection using which interface?

   a. BRI

   b. S/T

   c. U

   d. PRI

4. Which of the following protocols can be transmitted through a PPTP tunnel?

   a. IP only

   b. IP and NetBEUI

   c. IP and IPX

   d. IP, IPX, and NetBEUI

5. Which of the following is not the name of an ISDN service?

   a. BRI

   b. 2B+D

   c. PRI

   d. VDSL

6. What three new hardware components are required to install CATV Internet access on the computer of an existing cable TV customer?

7. Name one of the data-link layer protocols that computers can use with a PSTN connection.

8. Which device enables you to use a computer with an ISDN connection?

   a. A terminal adapter

   b. An NT-1

   c. Terminal equipment

   d. A U interface

9. What is the name of the device that connects a user site to a frame relay network via a leased line?

    a. A CSU/DSU

    b. A FRAD

    c. A cell

    d. An OC3

10. For which of the following services do you negotiate a CBIR?

    a. T-3

    b. E-3

    c. ATM

    d. Frame relay

11. What type of cable does a SONET network use at the physical layer?

    a. UTP

    b. Shielded twisted pair (STP)

    c. Coaxial

    d. Fiber optic

12. What protocol do systems use to exchange their IP addresses during the PPP connection establishment procedure?

    a. CHAP

    b. LCP

    c. IPCP

    d. NCP

13. How large is the End Delimiter field used during SLIP communications?

    a. 1 byte

    b. 2 bytes

    c. 5 bytes

    d. 18 bytes

14. Which of the following connection elements are configured by the LCP? Choose three correct answers.

   a. The network layer protocols that will be used during the connection

   b. The authentication protocol that will be used during the establishment of the connection

   c. The application layer protocols that will be used to generate the data transmitted during the connection

   d. The link quality protocol that will be used during the establishment of the connection

CASE SCENARIOS

Case Scenario 10-1: Selecting a WAN Technology

Consolidated Messenger has its headquarters in the state capital and has 10 branch offices located throughout the state. Each office has its own LAN, and the company wants to connect them all into a single internetwork using WAN links. Once the WAN links are installed, the company will buy a proprietary tracking software product that allows each of the offices to keep in constant communication with all of the others, simultaneously. The traffic on the internetwork will be very heavy during normal business hours, tapering off to nearly nothing at night. After consulting with several different networking consultants, the company has received four proposals, each of which calls for a different WAN technology. The WAN technologies called for by the four proposals are as follows:

   a. Install a single ISDN connection at each site, enabling users to dial in to the other offices.

   b. Install a leased line at each site, connecting it to a frame relay cloud.

   c. Install separate leased lines connecting each office to every other office.

   d. Connect all of the sites to the Internet service provided by the local CATV company and use VPN connections between the offices.

Based on this information, answer the following questions.

1. Which of these four proposals will successfully enable the users on one LAN to keep in constant touch with all of the other LANs simultaneously? Choose all answers that are correct.

2. Which of these four proposals would provide the *worst* network performance under heavy traffic conditions?

3. Which of the four proposals would provide the *best* performance at the lowest cost?

CHAPTER 11
NETWORK TROUBLESHOOTING TOOLS

Upon completion of this chapter, you will be able to:

- Understand the functions of light-emitting diodes (LEDs) on Ethernet equipment.

- List the types of error messages and event logs used by network operating systems.

- Understand the architecture of a Simple Network Management Protocol (SNMP)–based network management product.

- List the tools used to monitor system and network performance in the major network operating systems.

- Understand the functions of a protocol analyzer.

- Describe the troubleshooting functions of crossover cables and loopback connectors.

- Understand the uses of a tone generator and a locator.

- List the capabilities of more elaborate cable testing equipment.

- Understand the functions and recognize the output displays of the primary Transmission Control Protocol/Internet Protocol (TCP/IP) utilities.

A key aspect of network troubleshooting is having the proper tools. Although you will need basic hand tools, such as screwdrivers, and some more specialized tools, such as the cabling tools discussed in Chapter 2, "Network Cabling," the primary network troubleshooting tool is information. Finding, gathering, interpreting, and using information properly are all essential skills. This chapter explains how to gather information about the products you use on your network, the current condition of your hardware, and the status of your software.

LOGS AND INDICATORS

One of the first and most important factors in maintaining a network is knowing when something is wrong. Networks perform many important processes automatically and in the background, and it is your job to make sure that what is supposed to have been done has been done, without error and without problems. The following sections examine some of the tools that network administrators use to check the performance of network components and to find indications of trouble.

Power and Drive Lights

Many devices have lights that signal that a piece of equipment is switched on and operational. One of the most basic signs that something has gone wrong on your network is when these lights are not lit. An unlit light could be the result of a power failure, a tripped circuit breaker, or something as mundane as the electrical plug falling out of the socket. However, the device could have experienced a power supply failure, or a drive light could be out because a drive inside the computer has failed or become disconnected. It is a good idea to become familiar with the light-emitting diode (LED) displays of your equipment during normal operation so that you can quickly determine when something is wrong.

Link Pulse LEDs

As mentioned in Chapter 3, "Network Connection Hardware," most of the Ethernet network interface adapters designed to use unshielded twisted pair (UTP) cable have a link pulse LED on them, which is lit when the adapter is connected to a functioning hub or switch. A link pulse LED is shown in Figure 11-1.

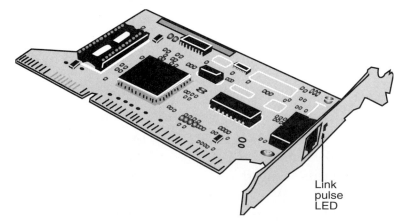

Link
pulse
LED

Figure 11-1   The link pulse LED on an Ethernet network interface adapter

A hub usually has an LED for each port as well, as shown in Figure 11-2, which enables you to tell from either end of the patch cable whether the devices are connected. However, although these link pulse lights can tell you whether a computer is wired to the hub properly, it is also important to know what these lights do *not* do.

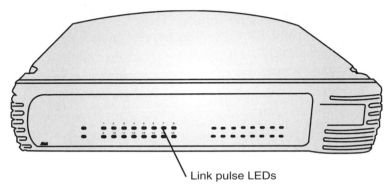
Link pulse LEDs

Figure 11-2   The link pulse LEDs on an Ethernet hub

When you connect a UTP network interface adapter to a hub or a switch, the link pulse lights on both devices should light, as long as both are connected to a power source. The network interface adapter must be installed in the computer and the computer must be plugged into a power socket, but the computer does not have to be turned on, the network interface adapter driver does not have to be installed, and you do not need to be logged on to the network to activate the link pulse LED.

> **NOTE   LEDs and System Power**   Link pulse LEDs light up when the computer is switched off because newer computers draw a minimal amount of power whenever they are plugged in, even when they are not switched on. This enables certain special features to function, such as Remote Wake-on-LAN, which enables you to power up a computer from a remote location by sending a special signal to its network interface adapter. Obviously, some power is required for the network interface adapter to receive the signal. Older computers without these features might power completely down when switched off, disabling the link pulse LEDs as well.

When an Ethernet adapter and a hub are properly connected, they exchange link pulse signals every 16.8 milliseconds to test the connection. These signals occur only when the network is not busy transmitting data, so they do not interfere with normal operations. When the LEDs at both ends of the connection are lit, this indicates that the normal link pulse (NLP) signals generated by each device are reaching the other device.

If you accidentally use a crossover cable to connect a computer to a hub, the signals sent over the transmit wires do not reach the receive contacts in the other device, and the LEDs will not light. For the same reason, if you connect two network interface adapters by using a straight-through cable and no hub, the LEDs will not light. If the LED lights on one device, but not on the other, there is a fault in the cable connection. The cable itself could be faulty, one of the devices' connectors could be broken, or the cable might not be properly seated into the jack at one or both ends. Try reseating the cable connectors into the jacks, or replace the cable with one that you know is functioning properly, and then see if both link pulse lights come on.

> **MORE INFO**   *Connecting Twisted Pair Cables*   For more information about straight-through connections and crossover connections, see Chapter 2, "Network Cabling."

It is important to understand that the link pulse LEDs indicate only that the network connection is wired properly. Just because the LEDs are lit does not mean that the connection can carry actual Ethernet traffic. Link pulse signals run far more slowly than Ethernet data signals and are not affected by electromagnetic interference (EMI), such as crosstalk, the way that actual Ethernet data signals are. For example, if you use a silver satin–type telephone cable to connect a network interface adapter to a hub, the link pulse LEDs will usually light. However, in this type of cable, the wire pairs are not twisted, which results in high levels of crosstalk. When Ethernet signals are transmitted over this type of cable, crosstalk causes the signals to bleed over from one wire pair to the others, causing the network interface adapters to receive signals simultaneously over both the transmit and receive wire pairs.

UTP Ethernet adapters interpret simultaneous signals on both wire pairs as an indication that a collision has occurred. In fact, even though there has been no real collision, the adapters behave as though there has been one. They discard the packets and begin the data retransmission process. This is called a *phantom collision*, and if it occurs frequently enough, it can seriously degrade the efficiency of the network. Thus, you can use the link pulse LEDs as an indication that you have wired your network correctly, but do not mistake them for a true diagnostic test of the network's transmission capabilities.

Speed Indicator LEDs

Twisted-pair Fast Ethernet and Gigabit Ethernet equipment that supports multiple speeds uses **fast link pulse (FLP)** signals. FLP signals differ from the **normal link pulse (NLP)** signals used by 10Base-T devices in that they include a 16-bit data packet that the devices use to autonegotiate their connection speed. The data packet contains a *link code word* that consists of a selector field and a technology ability field. The devices use these fields to advertise their capabilities, including the speeds they can run at and whether they support full-duplex (that is, simultaneous bidirectional) communications. By examining the link code word supplied by the other device, the network interface adapter and the hub both configure themselves to use the best transmission mode that they have in common, using the following priorities:

1. 1000Base-T (full-duplex)

2. 1000Base-T

3. 100Base-TX (full-duplex)

4. 100Base-T4

5. 100Base-TX

6. 10Base-T (full duplex)

7. 10Base-T

FLP signals are fully compatible with the NLP signals that are used by devices that cannot operate at multiple speeds. For example, if you connect a computer with a 10/100 dual-speed Fast Ethernet adapter to a standard 10Base-T hub, the adapter receives the NLP signal from the hub and determines that 10 Mbps half-duplex is the fastest speed they have in common, and the adapter configures itself accordingly. The 10Base-T hub, receiving the FLP signal from the adapter, cannot interpret the link code word and sees the signal only as a normal NLP link test. No autonegotiation occurs at the hub because none is possible.

Some multiple speed devices also have LEDs that indicate the speed at which the device is configured to run. Some devices have separate LEDs to indicate the different speeds, while others have a single LED that changes color, depending on the speed. Do not confuse the speed indicator LED with the link pulse LED.

Collision LEDs

Many Ethernet hubs have an additional LED that flashes when a collision occurs. Some collisions are expected on an Ethernet network, but excessive numbers of collisions can indicate a problem. The collision LED does not provide enough information for you to determine how many collisions are occurring during a particular time interface, but if the LED is flashing constantly, you should take steps to determine why.

Error Displays

The most obvious indication that a problem has occurred on a computer is an error message that appears on the screen. Error messages are generated by applications and operating systems to inform you when something has gone wrong with the computer or the software. In most cases, error messages cannot give you specific information about a problem with the network itself because, except in special circumstances, there is no way for the computer to test or communicate with network components except for other computers. For example, an error message generated by an operating system might tell you that the computer was unable to communicate with another system on the network, but it cannot tell you why unless the problem is with the computer itself.

Error messages can be helpful, or they can just add to your confusion, depending on the information they provide. Many error messages are ambiguous or misleading, so you might need help interpreting them, either from the product documentation or from the manufacturer. The most important thing to do if you receive an error message you do not understand is to write down the exact message, including all number and letter codes, memory addresses, and other types of information. Even if you do not know what the information means, it could help the manufacturer's technical support department and could make the difference between successfully resolving the problem or not. You should also inform all users to do the same thing for any error messages they receive.

> **NOTE   Saving Error Messages**   One of the easiest ways to save a complex error message is to save an image of the entire screen. On a computer running Microsoft Windows, pressing the PRINT SCREEN key copies the current screen image to the clipboard. If you open the Paint program and select Paste from the Edit menu, the image is pasted into the program, and you can print it or save it to an image file. In UNIX and Linux, some of the graphical interfaces (such as KDE) let you capture screens, and there are many graphics applications on all platforms with similar capabilities. These techniques assume that the computer can still run programs. If a fatal error halts the system, you have no recourse other than to write down the error information.

When you receive error messages that you do not understand, it is helpful to have the product documentation on a searchable medium, such as a CD-ROM or a Web site. You can search for the entire message or for keywords or phrases much more easily than you can by poring through a printed manual.

> **NOTE   Exam Objectives**   Objective 4.6 for the Network+ exam requires that students, "given a network scenario, [be able to] interpret visual indicators (e.g., link lights, collision lights, etc.) to determine the nature of the problem."

Event Logs

An *event log* is a running record of processes that functions as an operational history of the product involved. Many applications, operating systems, and networking software components can maintain logs of their activities. Part of your job is to regularly check the logs for problems or even just for informational messages. Some products maintain their logs as text files and might or might not supply the means for you to view them. You might have to open these log files in a separate application to read the contents. Log files can grow very large, so to keep up with them you might have to use a text editor that can handle large files and that has searching capabilities.

Logging Options

In some cases, you can specify whether you want an application to log its activities and how much detail you want in the logs. When you are working with a newly installed or reconfigured application or device, it is a good idea to keep logs for a while. However, the amount of detail you want in the logs is an important consideration. Selecting the most detailed option might not always be best, because although you want to have an accurate picture of the product's activities, you do not want to spend hours slogging through log files. For example, most backup programs have a full detail logging option, which means that the log lists every file that the program backs up. This approach might be useful in some instances, but the log file is so large that is difficult to scan for basic information, such as whether a backup job has completed successfully. In a case like this, you are better off selecting a less detailed log unless you suspect a problem that requires more specific information.

Highly detailed log files also take up a lot of disk space, and you have to be careful that you do not let them grow unchecked. Many applications that keep logs let you set parameters that limit how large the files can grow. For example, Microsoft Internet Information Services (IIS) in Microsoft Windows Server 2003 lets you specify when each service should create a new log file—hourly, daily, weekly, or monthly—using the dialog box shown in Figure 11-3.

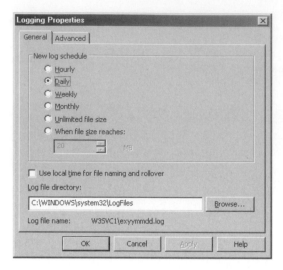

Figure 11-3   The IIS Logging Properties dialog box

You can also specify a maximum size for the log file or leave it with no limitations. By selecting the Advanced tab, you can choose what information the service should include in the log, as shown in Figure 11-4.

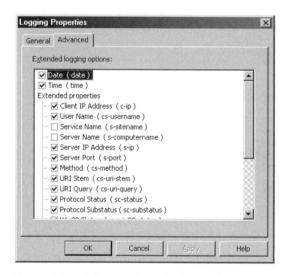

Figure 11-4   The IIS Extended Logging options

Using Windows Event Viewer

In some cases, logs are maintained and displayed by a separate application, such as the Event Viewer console included in all versions of Microsoft Windows NT. When you launch the Event Viewer console, the application displays the logs for the current system by default, but you can also view the logs of another computer running Windows by selecting Event Viewer in the left pane, and then selecting Connect To Another Computer from the Action menu.

The Event Viewer console maintains lists of messages generated by components of the operating system. Each log entry is listed as a separate item with the date and time that it was generated, the process that generated it, the event ID, and other important information, as shown in Figure 11-5.

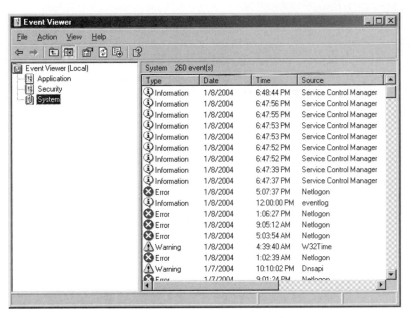

Figure 11-5   The Windows Server 2003 Event Viewer console

By default, a computer running Windows contains three different logs: Application, Security, and System, all of which are maintained independently. The server versions of Windows include these three logs, plus others, depending on the services installed. For example, an Active Directory domain controller also has Directory Service, DNS Server, and File Replication Service logs.

Each event in each log is assigned one of the following classifications and is marked with a corresponding icon:

- **Information**   Indicates that an event was successfully completed, such as launching a server application or loading a device driver. Information messages are a normal by-product of the computer's operations and do not indicate problems.

- **Warning**   Indicates a condition that is not necessarily a problem now, but might become a problem in the future. For example, a warning might appear when available memory or disk space drops below a certain level.

- **Error**   Indicates that a significant problem has occurred, causing a loss of system functionality or a loss of data. Error events require immediate attention, such as when a service fails to load or a drive goes offline.

When you double-click an entry in the main display of the Event Viewer console, you see an Event Properties dialog box, like that shown in Figure 11-6.

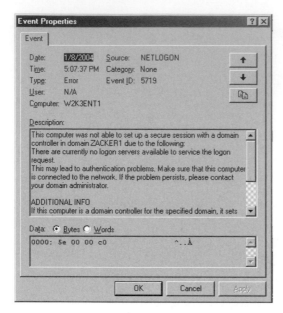

Figure 11-6   An Event Properties dialog box

This dialog box contains more detailed information about the entry, including a description and any data generated by the event. You can use the arrow buttons in the upper right corner of the dialog box to scroll up and down through the events in the log. One of the advantages of using the Event Viewer console is that you do not have to write down most error messages, because you can always view or print them later. You can click the third button in the upper right corner to copy the contents of the entry to the Windows clipboard, and then paste it into Notepad or another application for printing or faxing to a technical support representative.

While the Event Viewer console does provide a centralized logging resource for the Windows operating system, not all of the applications and services included with Windows use it. For example, the Dynamic Host Configuration Protocol (DHCP) Server service maintains its logs as text files, separate from the Event Viewer logs. To view the DHCP Server logs, you must open the log files in Notepad or some other text editor.

Using Syslogd
UNIX and Linux operating systems and applications, in most cases, maintain logs as individual text files, and they can be scattered in various directories throughout the system. One of the most common UNIX/Linux tools for logging system

activity is syslogd, a daemon that registers messages generated by applications and system processes and distributes them to appropriate log files. The syslogd daemon uses a configuration file called /etc/syslog.conf to determine where to save messages of various types. The syslog.conf file is a lookup table containing text strings the daemon should search for in the system messages it receives. Each text string is associated with a path to a log file where the program should place the message.

You can monitor the contents of the logs maintained by syslogd using any text viewer application. A graphical interface can simplify this process by letting you browse directories for the log files and loading them directly into a viewer or editor.

Depending on the UNIX or Linux distribution you are using, managing log files to prevent them from filling up the drive can be a strictly manual affair, or the task might already be automated for you. Some distributions include scripts that use tools like cron (which schedules actions to occur at specific times) and gzip (which compresses files into an archive) to automatically rename the log files once a day and compress them to save space.

Network Management Products

Error messages generated by operating systems and applications are usually easy to monitor, but it can be more difficult to monitor error messages from other network components, such as routers or computers at remote locations. For example, a stand-alone router does not have a screen to display error messages. However, many networking devices can supply you with information about their status. Network management products, such as HP's OpenView, provide you with a comprehensive view of network systems and processes, using a distributed architecture based on a specialized management protocol, such as the Simple Network Management Protocol (SNMP) or the **Remote Monitoring (RMON) protocol**.

SNMP is a TCP/IP application layer protocol and query language that specially equipped networking devices use to communicate with a central console. Many networking hardware and software products—including routers, switches, hubs, operating systems, and applications—have SNMP agents. An SNMP agent is a software module that gathers information about the product and delivers it to one computer that has been designated as the network management console. The agents gather specific information about the network devices and store them as managed objects in a **management information base (MIB)**. At regular intervals, the agents transmit their MIBs to the console using SNMP messages, which are carried inside User Datagram Protocol (UDP) datagrams.

The console collects the information that it receives from the agents and compiles a composite picture of the network and its processes. The console software can usually create a map of the interconnections between network devices and can display detailed log information for each device. If there is a serious problem, an agent can generate a special message called a *trap*, which it transmits immediately to the console, causing it to alert you to a potentially dangerous condition. In many cases, you can configure the console software to send alerts in a variety of ways, including pop-up messages, e-mails, faxes, and even pager signals.

Network management products often include other functions as well, including the following:

- Software distribution and metering
- Network diagnostics
- Network traffic monitoring
- Report generation

Many network management products for Windows and various UNIX/Linux distributions are available from third-party developers. Operating systems typically support SNMP, but you must buy the management console software separately. In addition, you must consider management capabilities when you are buying network hardware components, such as routers, switches, and network interface adapters. Network management products are usually not designed for small networks; they are intended for administrators of large networks who cannot possibly monitor all their network devices individually. Deploying a network management system is a complex and expensive undertaking. However, network management products can greatly simplify your job and help you identify significant problems before they cause serious outages.

Performance Monitors

Error messages, logs, and network management products generally inform you about what has already happened on your network. However, there are also products that can help you to know what is currently happening on your network. Monitoring tools like the Performance console in Windows NT display activities as they are occurring, some of which affect or are affected by network performance. Other operating systems have their own monitoring applications, as discussed in the following sections.

Using the Performance Console

The Performance console, included in all versions of Windows based on the NT kernel, is a graphical application that displays real-time statistics about a computer's activities. It can also maintain logs of those statistics and generate alerts when their values reach certain levels. The Performance console consists of the following two components:

- **System Monitor** Displays real-time performance data that is collected from configurable components called *performance counters*

- **Performance Logs And Alerts** Records data from performance counters over a period of time and executes specific actions when counters reach a certain value

In the System Monitor, shown in Figure 11-7, you can select the statistics you want to monitor and view them in a dynamic graph display.

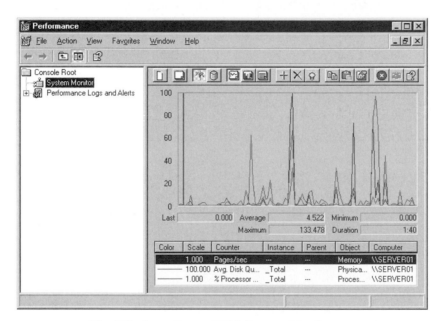

Figure 11-7 The Windows Server 2003 System Monitor

By default, three counters appear in System Monitor. The legend beneath the graph specifies the line color for each of the three counters, the scale of values for each counter, and other identifying information about each counter. When you select one of the counters in the legend, its current values appear in numerical form at the bottom of the graph. In addition to the line graph, System Monitor has two other views of the same data: a histogram view and a report view.

The histogram view is a bar graph with a separate vertical bar for each counter, as shown in Figure 11-8. In this view, it is easier to monitor large numbers of counters because the lines do not overlap.

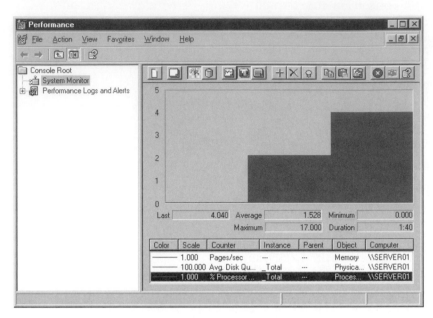

Figure 11-8   The System Monitor histogram view

The report view, as shown in Figure 11-9, displays the numerical value for each of the performance counters.

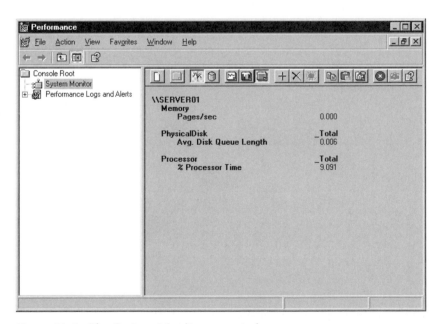

Figure 11-9   The System Monitor report view

These three default performance counters are useful gauges of the computer's performance, but System Monitor includes dozens of other counters that you can add to the display. To add counters to the System Monitor details pane, you use the Add Counters dialog box, as shown in Figure 11-10.

Figure 11-10   The Add Counters dialog box

To add a counter to the display, you have to specify the following four pieces of information in this dialog box:

- **Computer**   The name of the computer you want to monitor with the selected counter.

- **Performance object**   A category representing a specific hardware or software component in the computer. Each performance object contains performance counters related to that component.

- **Performance counter**   A statistic representing a specific aspect of the selected performance object's activities.

- **Instance**   An element representing a specific occurrence of the selected performance counter. For example, on a computer with two network interface adapters, each counter in the Network Interface performance object has two instances, one for each adapter, enabling you to track the performance of each adapter individually. Some counters also have instances such as Total or Average, enabling you to track the performance of all instances combined or the median value of all instances.

The performance objects, performance counters, and instances that appear in the Add Counters dialog box depend on the computer's hardware configuration, the software installed on the computer, and the computer's role on the network. For example, installing the Domain Name System (DNS) Server service on the computer adds the DNS performance object, which consists of a collection of counters that let you track the DNS server's activities.

The System Monitor console is a useful tool, but it can only display performance information in real time, so you must constantly watch the display to use it. You can also use the Performance Logs And Alerts feature of the Performance console to create log files containing the statistics of particular counters over a period of time. You can create alerts that are triggered when the value of a particular counter reaches a level that you specify, using the dialog box shown in Figure 11-11.

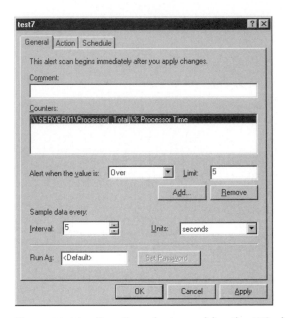

Figure 11-11   Creating alerts enables the Windows 2000 Performance console to notify you when specified conditions are met.

You can configure the alert to notify you by adding an entry to the event log, sending a network message, starting a performance data log, or executing a program that you specify.

Performance Monitoring in UNIX and Linux

In UNIX and Linux, performance monitoring is rarely as user friendly as it is in Windows, primarily because of the operating systems' greater reliance on the command line. Some of the graphical interfaces used on UNIX and Linux include their own network monitoring tools, but these vary in usefulness and are proprietary tools associated only with that interface. However, there are some standard UNIX and Linux tools that you can use to monitor certain aspects of a computer's network performance, such as top and netstat. (The netstat tool is covered later in this chapter.)

One of the most commonly used tools for performance monitoring in UNIX and Linux is the top utility. The basic function of top is to display information about the processes currently running on the system that are using the most processor time, as shown in Figure 11-12.

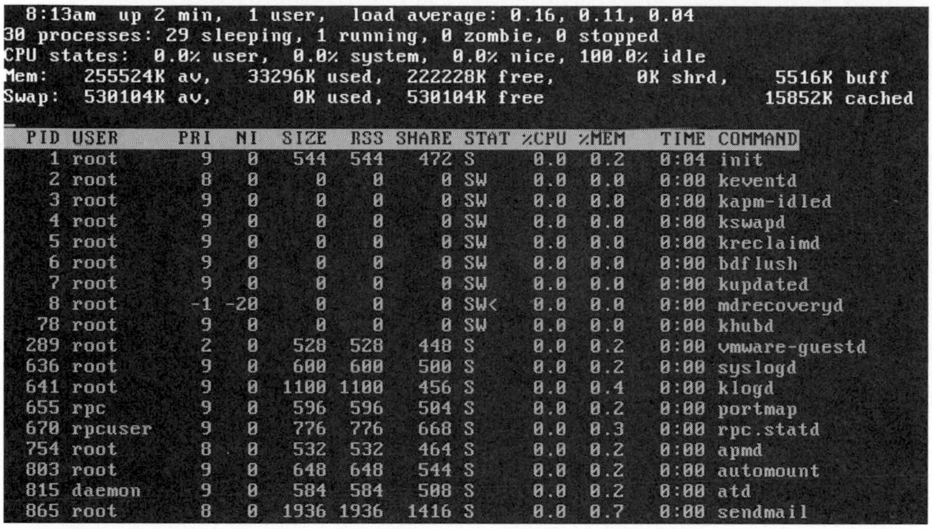

```
 8:13am  up 2 min,  1 user,   load average: 0.16, 0.11, 0.04
30 processes: 29 sleeping, 1 running, 0 zombie, 0 stopped
CPU states:   0.0% user,  0.0% system,  0.0% nice, 100.0% idle
Mem:    255524K av,   33296K used,  222228K free,       0K shrd,     5516K buff
Swap:   530104K av,       0K used,  530104K free                    15852K cached

  PID USER      PRI   NI  SIZE  RSS SHARE STAT %CPU %MEM   TIME COMMAND
    1 root        9    0   544  544   472 S     0.0  0.2  0:04 init
    2 root        8    0     0    0     0 SW    0.0  0.0  0:00 keventd
    3 root        9    0     0    0     0 SW    0.0  0.0  0:00 kapm-idled
    4 root        9    0     0    0     0 SW    0.0  0.0  0:00 kswapd
    5 root        9    0     0    0     0 SW    0.0  0.0  0:00 kreclaimd
    6 root        9    0     0    0     0 SW    0.0  0.0  0:00 bdflush
    7 root        9    0     0    0     0 SW    0.0  0.0  0:00 kupdated
    8 root       -1  -20     0    0     0 SW<   0.0  0.0  0:00 mdrecoveryd
   78 root        9    0     0    0     0 SW    0.0  0.0  0:00 khubd
  289 root        2    0   528  528   448 S     0.0  0.2  0:00 vmware-guestd
  636 root        9    0   600  600   500 S     0.0  0.2  0:00 syslogd
  641 root        9    0  1100 1100   456 S     0.0  0.4  0:00 klogd
  655 rpc         9    0   596  596   504 S     0.0  0.2  0:00 portmap
  670 rpcuser     9    0   776  776   668 S     0.0  0.3  0:00 rpc.statd
  754 root        8    0   532  532   464 S     0.0  0.2  0:00 apmd
  803 root        9    0   648  648   544 S     0.0  0.2  0:00 automount
  815 daemon      9    0   584  584   508 S     0.0  0.2  0:00 atd
  865 root        8    0  1936 1936  1416 S     0.0  0.7  0:00 sendmail
```

Figure 11-12   The default display of the UNIX/Linux top utility

The top display is interactive, refreshing itself every five seconds by default. As with most UNIX and Linux tools, top has many command line arguments that let you alter its default behavior. In addition, top has many interactive commands that can alter the display in real time. Although top is limited to processor monitoring, it can provide other useful information, such as the amount of processor time that is being consumed by daemons providing network services.

Using Monitor.nlm

The Novell NetWare Monitor.nlm utility is a performance monitoring application that runs on a NetWare server. Using NetWare's character-based interface, Monitor.nlm displays processor and memory statistics for the server, as well as information about the current client connections to the server, the system's network activity, and the number of packets transmitted over a particular interface, as shown in Figure 11-13.

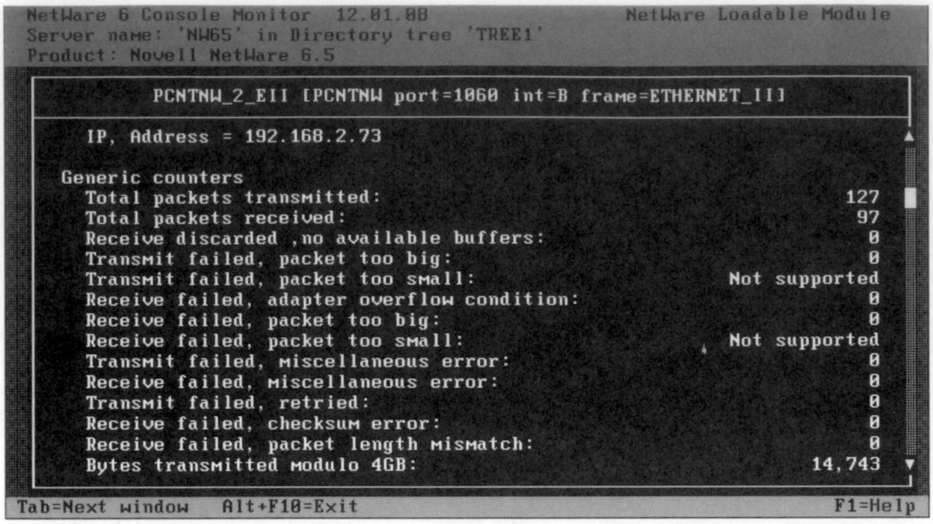

```
NetWare 6 Console Monitor  12.01.08              NetWare Loadable Module
  Server name: 'NW65' in Directory tree 'TREE1'
  Product: Novell NetWare 6.5

    ┌─────────────────────────────────────────────────────────────────────┐
    │       PCNTNW_2_EII [PCNTNW port=1060 int=B frame=ETHERNET_II]        │
    ├─────────────────────────────────────────────────────────────────────┤
    │   IP, Address = 192.168.2.73                                        ▲│
    │                                                                      ││
    │ Generic counters                                                     ││
    │   Total packets transmitted:                              127        ││
    │   Total packets received:                                  97        ││
    │   Receive discarded ,no available buffers:                  0        ││
    │   Transmit failed, packet too big:                          0        ││
    │   Transmit failed, packet too small:            Not supported        ││
    │   Receive failed, adapter overflow condition:               0        ││
    │   Receive failed, packet too big:                           0        ││
    │   Receive failed, packet too small:             Not supported        ││
    │   Transmit failed, miscellaneous error:                     0        ││
    │   Receive failed, miscellaneous error:                      0        ││
    │   Transmit failed, retried:                                 0        ││
    │   Receive failed, checksum error:                           0        ││
    │   Receive failed, packet length mismatch:                   0        ││
    │   Bytes transmitted modulo 4GB:                        14,743        ▼│
    ├─────────────────────────────────────────────────────────────────────┤
    │ Tab=Next window    Alt+F10=Exit                             F1=Help   │
    └─────────────────────────────────────────────────────────────────────┘
```

Figure 11-13   The NetWare Monitor.nlm utility

Unlike the Windows and UNIX/Linux tools discussed in this section, Monitor.nlm is not configurable, but it does provide a good picture of the server's performance in real time.

Protocol Analyzers

A protocol analyzer is one of the most powerful tools for learning about, understanding, and monitoring network communications. A protocol analyzer captures a sample of the traffic passing over the network, decodes the packets into the language of the individual protocols they contain, and lets you examine them in minute detail. Some protocol analyzers can also compile network traffic statistics, such as the number of packets using each protocol and the number of collisions that are occurring on the network. Using the protocol analyzer to capture and display network traffic is relatively easy, but interpreting the information that the analyzer presents and using it to troubleshoot your installation require a detailed understanding of the protocols running on the network. However, there is no better way to acquire this type of knowledge than to examine the actual data transmitted over a live network.

> **NOTE** **Analyzer Cautions**   Protocol analyzers are useful tools in the hands of experienced network administrators, but they can also be used for malicious purposes. In addition to displaying the information in the captured packets' protocol headers, the analyzer can also display

the data carried inside the packets. This can sometimes include confidential information, such as unencrypted passwords and personal correspondence. If possible, do not permit your users to run protocol analyzers unsupervised.

A protocol analyzer is typically a software product that runs on a computer connected to a network. Some network consultants who frequently work at different sites install a software-based protocol analyzer on a portable computer and can connect to virtually any type of network by simply changing PC Card network interface adapters. Protocol analyzers typically work by switching the network interface adapter they use to access the network into promiscuous mode. When a network interface adapter is in promiscuous mode, it reads and processes all the traffic that is transmitted over the network, not just the packets that are addressed to it. This means that the system can examine all of the traffic transmitted on the network from one computer.

The most commonly used protocol analyzer is the Microsoft Network Monitor application, mostly because it is included with the Windows Server 2003, Microsoft Windows 2000 Server, and Microsoft Windows NT Server. It is also included with Microsoft Systems Management Server (SMS). The version of Network Monitor in SMS supports promiscuous mode, but the version included with the server operating systems does not. This means that you can use the server version only to capture traffic addressed to or transmitted by the server on which Network Monitor is running.

Network Monitor is one of the few protocol analyzer applications included with an operating system. In most cases, you must obtain and install the application yourself. There are many protocol analyzer products available for Windows, UNIX, and Linux. The analyzers for Windows are all graphical and provide varying capabilities. For UNIX and Linux, both commercial and open source protocol analyzers are available, some of which are character-based (such as tcpdump), while others are graphical (such as Ethereal, which is also available in a Windows version).

The following sections examine the basic functions of a protocol analyzer, using Network Monitor as an example.

Capturing Traffic

The first step of a protocol analysis is to capture a sample of the network traffic. Network Monitor uses the window shown in Figure 11-14 to control the sampling process.

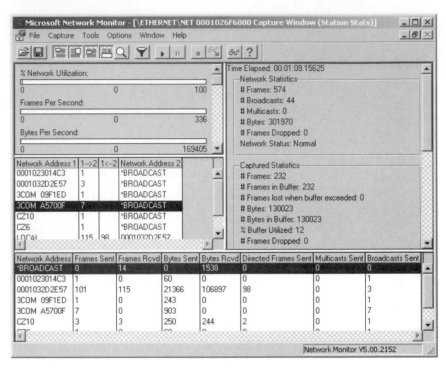

Figure 11-14   The Network Monitor Capture window

To start a packet capture, select the network interface that you want to use (if there is more than one), and then click the Start Capture button on the toolbar. The program reads the packets that arrive over the network interface and stores them in a buffer for later examination.

Protocol analyzers, like detailed log files and performance monitors, offer a huge amount of information, so the trick to using the tool effectively is zeroing in on what you actually need. On a busy network, a packet capture of only a few seconds can consist of thousands of packets generated by dozens of different systems. Protocol analyzers have filters that let you select the packets that you want to capture by using a number of different criteria, such as the source computer address, the destination computer address, the protocols used to build the packets, and the information found in the packets. For example, if you are having a problem establishing Hypertext Transfer Protocol (HTTP) connections to your Web server, you can use the Network Monitor Capture Filter SAPs And ETYPEs dialog box, shown in Figure 11-15, to capture TCP packets only, because TCP is the protocol used for HTTP connections.

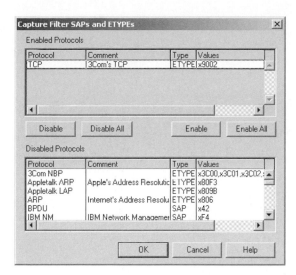

Figure 11-15   The Network Monitor Capture Filter SAPs And ETYPEs dialog box

You can then use the Address Expression dialog box, shown in Figure 11-16, to specify that you want to capture only the traffic arriving at your server from the other computers on the network.

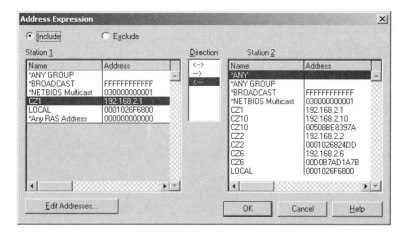

Figure 11-16   The Network Monitor Address Expression dialog box

In this case, the server is named CZ1 and has an IP address of 192.168.2.1. The source of traffic on the network can be any computer. The direction chosen is from ANY computer towards the server, CZ1.

When you specify capture filters, you get a much smaller traffic sample that contains less of the extraneous information generated by other network processes. For example, if you want to learn how much network traffic is generated by Address Resolution Protocol (ARP) transactions, you can create a filter configuration that captures only ARP traffic for a specific period of time, and work out the number of megabits per hour devoted to ARP from the size of your captured sample. The Capture Filter dialog box, shown in Figure 11-17, displays the combination of filters you have chosen, and enables you to save capture filter configurations to reuse later.

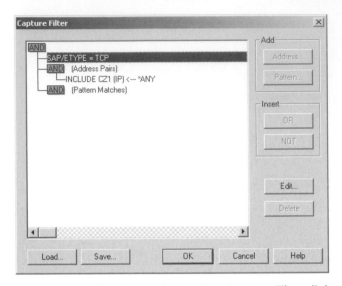

Figure 11-17   The Network Monitor Capture Filter dialog box

Displaying Captured Traffic

After you have captured a network traffic sample, click Display Captured Data to show your sample in the Capture Summary window, as shown in Figure 11-18.

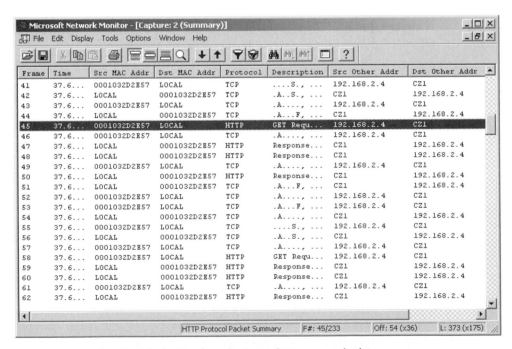

Figure 11-18   The Network Monitor Capture Summary window

This window displays a chronological list of the packets in your sample, including the following information:

- **Frame**   Shows the number of the frame (or packet) in the sample.

- **Time**   Indicates the time (in seconds) that the packet was captured, measured from the beginning of the sample.

- **Src MAC Addr**   Specifies the hardware address of the network interface in the computer that transmitted the packet. The computer on which the analyzer is running is identified as LOCAL.

- **Dst MAC Addr**   Specifies the hardware address of the network interface in the computer that received the packet.

- **Protocol**   Specifies the dominant protocol in the packet. Each packet contains information generated by protocols running at several different layers of the Open Systems Interconnection (OSI) reference model. The protocol specified here indicates the primary function of the packet. For example, an HTTP packet also uses the Transmission Control Protocol (TCP), Internet Protocol (IP), and Ethernet protocols, but the reason for the packet's existence is to deliver an HTTP message.

- **Description**   Specifies the function of the packet, using information specific to the protocol referenced in the Protocol field. For an HTTP packet, for example, this field indicates whether the packet contains an HTTP GET Request or a Response message.

- **Src Other Addr**   Specifies another address that identifies the computer that transmitted the packet. In the case of the TCP/IP protocols, this field contains the IP address.

- **Dst Other Addr**   Specifies another address (such as an IP address) that identifies the computer that received the packet.

- **Type Other Addr**   Specifies the type of address used in the Src Other Addr and Dst Other Addr fields.

From this main display, you can track the progress of transactions between specific pairs of computers on your network. For example, you can see that an exchange of messages between a Web browser and a Web server begins with the exchange of TCP messages that forms a three-way handshake and establishes a connection between the two computers. The browser then transmits an HTTP GET Request message, and the server replies with a series of responses.

To zero in on a particular message exchange, Network Monitor enables you to apply filters to samples that have already been captured as well as to samples obtained during the capture. The interface you use to create the filters is similar to the one you use to select capture filters. When you apply a filter, you see only the packets that conform to the parameters you have chosen. The other packets are still there in the sample; they are just not being displayed. You can modify the filter at any time to display more or less data.

When you double-click one of the packets listed in the main Capture Summary window, the display splits into three parts, as shown in Figure 11-19.

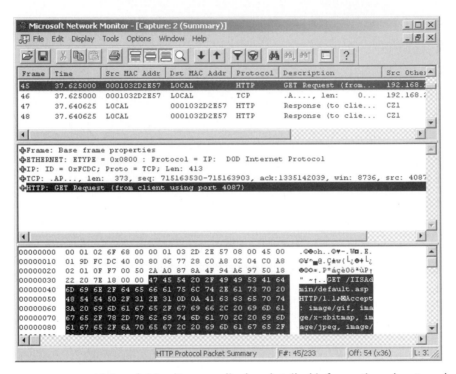

Figure 11-19   Network Monitor can display detailed information about each packet in both raw and interpreted forms.

The top section, called the Summary pane, contains the original capture summary, with the selected packet highlighted. The middle section, called the Detail pane, contains the contents of the selected packet, in a fully interpreted, expandable display. The bottom section, called the Hex pane, contains the raw, uninterpreted contents of the packet in hexadecimal and alphanumeric form.

The Detail pane is where you can learn the most about the contents of each packet. The analyzer interprets the data in the packet and separates it into the headers for the protocols operating at the various layers. Clicking the plus sign next to a protocol expands it to display the contents of the various header fields. For example, Figure 11-20 shows the expanded TCP header of an HTTP GET Request packet. The header fields display the source port and destination port numbers, the latter of which contains the protocol code for HTTP, plus the

sequence number and acknowledgment number values used to implement the
TCP packet acknowledgment and error detection mechanisms, and the other
header fields.

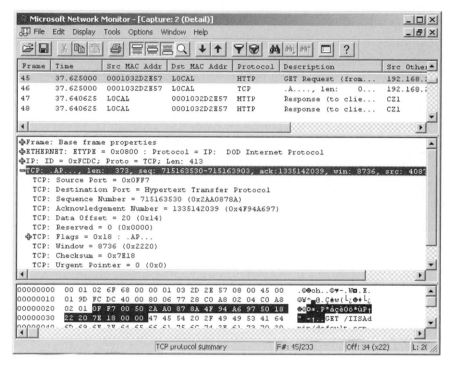

Figure 11-20   Network Monitor interprets the data in a packet and displays the
contents of the header fields in each protocol.

> **NOTE   Examining TCP Headers**   For more information about the
> structure of the TCP header and the functions of its fields, see Chapter
> 6, "Transport Layer Protocols."

Test your
knowledge of
concepts
related to
network
management
and status
indicators by
completing
Exercise 11-1,
"Network
Indicators,"
now.

The Hex pane is used primarily to view the application layer data carried as
the payload inside a packet. For example, when you look at an HTTP Response
packet transmitted by a Web server to a browser, you see the HTML code of the
Web page the server is sending to the browser, as shown in Figure 11-21.

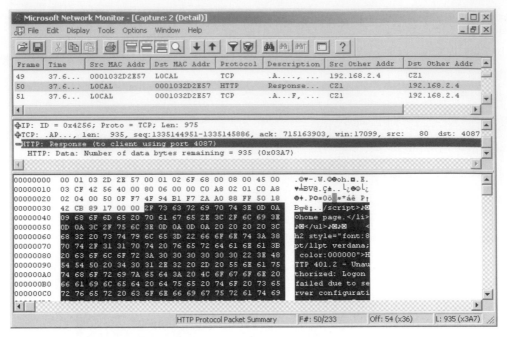

Figure 11-21   Network Monitor's raw data display shows the actual contents of a packet.

NETWORK TESTING AND MONITORING TOOLS

Not all of the tools used by network administrators are purely informational. Specialized physical tools (beyond the standard screwdrivers and pliers) can come in handy also. Most of these specialized tools are used to install and troubleshoot cables, primarily because cables are a component of the network that have no way to display error messages.

Crossover Cables

A crossover cable, which connects UTP Ethernet computers without a hub, is also a good tool for eliminating the hub and the cables as a possible source of a network communications problem. If you have two computers that seem to be properly connected using a hub and prefabricated cables (or an internal cable run and patch cables), and they are not communicating, try connecting the computers with a crossover cable that you know works properly. If the computers can communicate by using the crossover cable, you know that the problem is in your hub or the cables connecting the computer to the hub. If the computers fail to communicate using the crossover cable, the problem is in one or both of the computers or network interface adapters.

> **NOTE**   *Crossover Cable Construction*   A crossover cable is a UTP cable in which the transmit contacts in each of the RJ-45 connectors are connected to the receive contacts in the other connector, eliminating the need for a hub, which normally supplies the crossover circuit. For more information, see Chapter 2, "Network Cabling."

Hardware Loopback Connectors

A **loopback connector** is an inexpensive device that you plug into a jack. This connector redirects the outgoing signals from the device right back into it. For example, you can buy loopback connectors for parallel and serial ports that work with diagnostic software to check the transmission and reception capabilities of the ports. You can also buy a loopback connector that plugs into a UTP network interface adapter's RJ-45 port. Many adapters have a diagnostic utility built into their configuration programs. After plugging the loopback connector into the adapter port, you run the diagnostic program and it transmits a series of signals out through the adapter. If the adapter receives the signals back in exactly the same format as they were sent, the adapter passes the test.

Running a test using a loopback connector is completely different from transmitting packets to the TCP/IP loopback address (127.0.0.1). Even though using that address causes all transmitted traffic to return to the incoming buffers of the same computer, the signals never actually reach the network interface adapter. The loopback address is a feature of the IP protocol, and packets sent to it never travel below the network layer of the OSI reference model. In a loopback connector test, the packets travel down to the physical layer and out of the computer, only to be routed immediately back in by the loopback connector.

Tone Generators and Tone Locators

When you install UTP cable internally, you must test each of your connections. After you have pulled all of your cables, secured them in the walls and ceilings, punched them down, installed the wall plates, and cleaned everything up, you do not want to tear it all apart again because of an improperly wired connection.

One of the most basic ways to identify and test a cable connection is to use a **tone generator and locator**, as shown in Figure 11-22, also known as a *fox-and-hound* cable tester. The tone generator is a device that you connect to a cable at one end. It then transmits a signal over the cable. The tone locator is a separate device that has a probe that detects the generator's signal, either by touching it to the conductor in the cable, or simply by touching it to the insulation on the outside of the cable. When the locator detects the generator's signal, it emits an audible tone. You can use this type of device to test an entire cable or to test the individual wire connections inside a UTP cable.

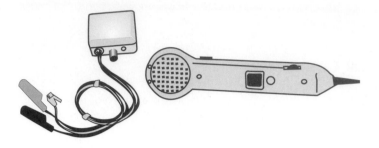

Figure 11-22   A tone generator and locator

A tone generator and locator is most commonly used to identify the cable belonging to a particular connection. For example, if you are performing an internal cable installation and you forget to label one of your cables, you can connect the tone generator at the wall plate end and touch the probe to each of the cables at the patch panel end until you find the one that produces a tone. Some cable installers omit the labeling process entirely and rely completely on this method for identifying their cable runs, but this is not recommended. The tool is also valuable for identifying one particular cable in a bundle in the middle of the connection.

You can also use a tone generator and locator to test the individual wire connections inside a UTP cable. You connect the generator to a single wire or connector contact by using alligator clips, and then touch the locator to each wire or contact at the other end of the cable. Using this method, you can test for any major wiring faults that affect internal UTP cable installations. For example, if you do not detect a signal on the contact to which you have the generator connected at the other end, you have an **open circuit**. If you detect a signal on the wrong contact, you have punched down the wires to the wrong contacts, resulting in transposed wires. If you detect a signal on two or more wires, you have a **short circuit**.

The tone generator and locator is the simplest and most inexpensive type of cable tester (at about $100), but this method of testing UTP cable connections is relatively unreliable and incredibly time-consuming. Testing each of the wires in a UTP cable individually is a slow and error-prone process. You also must have two people to use the equipment, one at the generator end and one at the locator end, who are in constant contact. Or you can do it all by yourself, if you do not mind running back and forth from one end of your cable connections to the other. For troubleshooting a single cable connection, the tone generator and locator is a useful tool. For testing a large number of newly installed cable runs, you can use a wire map tester instead that detects all the same faults by testing all of the wire connections in the cable at once.

Wire Map Testers

A **wire map tester** is a device that is similar in principle to a tone generator and locator, except that it tests all the wire connections in a UTP cable at once. A wire map tester also consists of two parts that you connect to the opposite ends of a cable. The unit at one end transmits signals over all the wires, which are detected by the unit at the other end. A wire map tester can detect transposed wires, opens, and shorts, just as a tone generator and locator can, but it does all the tests simultaneously and displays a simple readout telling you what, if anything, is wrong. However, a typical stand-alone wire map tester cannot detect a split pair.

A **split pair** is a wiring fault in which the wires are connected to the wrong contacts at both ends of the cable in exactly the same way. Each of the contacts is wired straight through to its corresponding contact at the other end, yielding a connection that appears to be correct to a normal wire map test. However, the wires that are actually carrying the signals are improperly paired. Normally, a UTP cable has one transmit wire and one receive wire, each of which is twisted into a separate pair with its corresponding ground wire. In a split pair, the transmit and receive wires can be twisted into one pair and their two ground wires into another pair. Having the two signal wires twisted into the same pair generates an excessive amount of crosstalk, which negatively affects communications. A basic wire map tester knows only that the signals it transmitted over each wire have reached the other end of the cable at the correct contact. You need a device that can measure crosstalk to detect split pairs.

Wire map testers are relatively inexpensive ($200 to $300) stand-alone devices. Some current products also include other functions, such as basic crosstalk testing capabilities and cable length measurement, which make it possible to detect split pairs and other faults. You can also find the same functions in a multifunction cable tester, which costs much more. For a small to medium-sized internal cable installation, a wire map tester is a good investment, both for installation and for troubleshooting purposes later. You can also use the tester to check your prefabricated cables for faults. For large installations or professional cable installers, a multifunction cable tester is a better idea.

Multifunction Cable Testers

Multifunction cable testers, also called *media testers,* *scanners,* or *certifiers,* are handheld devices that perform a variety of tests on a cable connection and compare the results to standard values that have been programmed into the unit. As a result, anyone can use these devices. You simply connect the unit to the cable and press a button, and the device comes up with a list of pass or fail ratings for the individual tests. A multifunction cable tester is shown in Figure 11-23.

Figure 11-23   A multifunction cable tester

In addition to the basic wire mapping tests described earlier, multifunction cable testers can also test any of the following:

- **Length**   The most common method for determining the length of a cable is a tool called a **time domain reflectometer (TDR)**, in which the device transmits a signal over the cable and measures how long it takes for the signal's reflection to return. Using the **nominal velocity of propagation (NVP)** for the cable, which is the speed at which signals travel through the cable (supplied by the manufacturer), the TDR can compute the length of the cable. A TDR can also find the location of a break in a cable.

- **Attenuation**   By comparing the strength of a signal at the far end of a cable to its strength when transmitted, the tester determines the cable's attenuation (measured in decibels).

- **Near end crosstalk (NEXT)**   Testing for NEXT is a matter of transmitting a signal over one of a cable's wires and then detecting the strength of the signal that bleeds over into the other wires near the end of the cable where the transmitter is located.

- **Power sum NEXT (PSNEXT)**   PSNEXT measures the crosstalk that is generated when three of the four wire pairs are carrying signals at once. This test is intended for networks using technologies like Gigabit Ethernet that transmit signals over several wire pairs simultaneously.

- **Equal level far end crosstalk (ELFEXT)**   ELFEXT measures the crosstalk at the opposite end of the cable from the transmitter, corrected to account for the amount of attenuation in the connection.

- **Power sum ELFEXT (PSELFEXT)**   PSELFEXT measures the crosstalk that is generated at the far end of the cable by three signal-carrying wire pairs, corrected for attenuation.

- **Propagation delay**   The propagation delay is the amount of time required for a signal to travel from one end of a cable to the other.

- **Delay skew**   Delay skew is the difference between the lowest and the highest propagation delay measurements for the wires in a cable. Because the wire pairs inside a UTP cable are twisted at different rates, their relative lengths can differ, and the delay skew measurement quantifies that difference.

- **Return loss**   Return loss measures the accumulated signal reflection caused by variations in the cable's impedance along its length. These impedance variations are typically caused by untwisting the wires when making connections.

Not all of these tests are required for every cable installation, but knowing the lengths of your cables and other measurements can help you keep your cable installation within the guidelines established for the protocol you will be using. It is also useful to measure elements such as attenuation and delay skew before you install the cables, so that you can be sure that you received the cable grade that you paid for.

In some ways, multifunction cable testers can be dangerous because of the very strengths they advertise. Much of the marketing material for these devices implies that you do not really have to know what all of these measurements mean; you can just plug your cables in and rely on the device to tell you if they are installed correctly. This is true as long as the tester is calibrated to the proper standards. If you do not know what the various tests represent, you are relying on the manufacturer of the device to set it to the proper standards. In some cases, official standards for certain cable types have not yet been ratified.

You can also reprogram the device with your own baseline standards, which can be a problem if you rely on someone else's tester to tell you that your installation has been performed properly. For example, an unscrupulous cable installer could make a few simple changes to the tester's settings, such as changing the NVP rating for the cable, and cause a network that would previously have failed certain tests to pass them. The bottom line for using these devices is that you should not trust the tester of an untrustworthy person, and if you purchase a tester of your own, you should familiarize yourself with all of its tests and the standards against which it compares its results.

The other drawback of multifunction cable testers is that most of them are very expensive. Prices of several thousand dollars are common, and top-of-the-line units (such as those that combine copper and fiber optic testing capabilities) cost $5,000 or more.

Fiber Optic Cable Testing

All of the testing devices discussed so far in this section are exclusively designed for copper cable connections. Fiber optic cable installations require their own separate testing tools and procedures. With copper cables, the testing and troubleshooting processes are primarily concerned with detecting and measuring the interference that can affect network communications. Fiber optic cables are immune to the interference caused by the different forms of crosstalk and most of the other conditions measured by copper-based testing devices.

The primary goal of fiber optic cable testing is to determine whether signals arrive at their destinations with sufficient strength to be read by the receiving system. To do this, you measure the amount of optical loss that a fiber optic cable run experiences as a result of attenuation. Optical loss is simply the difference in the strength of the signal at the source and at the destination. Some signal degradation results from the properties of the fiber optic cable itself. For example, multimode fiber experiences more signal degradation than singlemode. Signal strength is also affected by the connections created during the cable installation.

To test the optical loss in a fiber optic cable run, you use a tool called an *optical loss test set* (OLTS). An OLTS consists of a calibrated light source, which creates an optical signal of a specified strength, and a power meter that can measure the strength of the signal at the other end of the cable. You can buy a basic OLTS for a few hundred dollars, or you can buy a multifunction fiber optic tester that performs other tests as well, for several thousand dollars. More elaborate fiber optic tools are available, such as optical time domain reflectometers (OTDRs), which have prices that can easily run into five figures.

Test your
knowledge of
network testing
devices by
completing
Exercise 11-2,
"Network Testing
Equipment," now.

NOTE **Exam Objectives** *Objective 4.5 for the Network+ exam requires
that students, "given a wiring task, [be able to] select the appropriate
tool (e.g., wire crimper, media tester/certifier, punch down tool, tone
generator, optical tester, etc.)."*

TCP/IP UTILITIES

Virtually every operating system with networking capabilities includes support
for the TCP/IP protocols. In most cases, the TCP/IP stack includes utilities that
enable you to gather information about the various protocols and the network.
Traditionally, these utilities run from the command line, although there are some
graphical versions. In many cases, TCP/IP utilities use the same syntax, even on
different operating systems. This section examines some of the most common
TCP/IP utilities and their purposes.

Ping

Ping is the most basic of the TCP/IP utilities. Virtually every TCP/IP
implementation includes a version of it. On UNIX and Linux systems, the
program is called ping, and on Windows systems, it is called Ping.exe. NetWare
includes a server-based version called Ping.nlm, as shown in Figure 11-24.

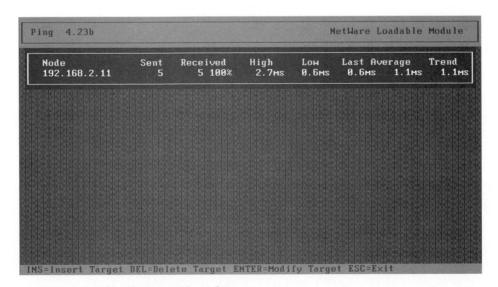

Figure 11-24   The NetWare Ping.nlm program

Ping can tell you if the TCP/IP stack of another system on the network is
functioning normally. The Ping program generates a series of Echo Request
messages using the Internet Control Message Protocol (ICMP) and transmits

them to the computer whose name or IP address you specify on the command line. The basic syntax of the Ping program is as follows:

```
ping target
```

The *target* variable contains the IP address or name of a computer on the network. You can use either DNS names or Network Basic Input/Output System (NetBIOS) names in Ping commands. Ping resolves the name into an IP address before sending the Echo Request messages, and it then displays the address in its readout. Most Ping implementations also have command-line switches that enable you to modify the operational parameters of the program, such as the number of Echo Request messages it generates and the amount of data in each message.

TCP/IP computers respond to any Echo Request messages they receive that are addressed to them by generating Echo Reply messages and transmitting them back to the sender. When the pinging computer receives the Echo Reply messages, it produces a display like the following:

```
Pinging cz1 [192.168.2.10] with 32 bytes of data:

Reply from 192.168.2.10: bytes=32 time<10ms TTL=128
Reply from 192.168.2.10: bytes=32 time<10ms TTL=128
Reply from 192.168.2.10: bytes=32 time<10ms TTL=128
Reply from 192.168.2.10: bytes=32 time<10ms TTL=128

Ping statistics for 192.168.2.10:
Packets: Sent = 4, Received = 4, Lost = 0 (0% loss),
Approximate round trip times in milli-seconds:
Minimum = 0ms, Maximum =  0ms, Average =  0ms
```

> **NOTE   Exam Objectives**   Objective 4.7 for the Network+ exam requires that students, "given output from a diagnostic utility (e.g. Tracert, Ping, or Ipconfig, etc.), [be able to] identify the utility and interpret the output."

In the case of this Ping implementation (from Microsoft Windows XP), the display shows the IP address of the computer receiving the Echo Requests, the number of bytes of data included with each request, the elapsed time between the transmission of each request and the receipt of each reply, and the value of the Time To Live (TTL) field in the IP header. In this particular example, the target computer was on the same local area network (LAN), so the time measurement is very short—less than 10 milliseconds. When pinging a computer on the Internet, the interval is likely to be longer. A successful use of Ping like this one indicates that the target computer's networking hardware is functioning properly, as are the protocols, at least as high as the network layer of the OSI model. If the Ping test fails, there is a problem in one or both of the computers or in the cabling connecting them.

Traceroute

Traceroute is a variant of the Ping program that displays the path that packets take to their destination. Because of the nature of IP routing, paths through an internetwork can change from minute to minute, and Traceroute displays a list of the routers that are currently forwarding packets to a particular destination. The program is called traceroute on UNIX and Linux systems, Tracert.exe on Windows, and Iptrace.nlm on NetWare.

Traceroute uses ICMP Echo Request and Echo Reply messages just like Ping, but it modifies the messages by changing the value of the TTL field in the IP header. The values in the TTL field prevent packets from getting caught in router loops that keep them circulating endlessly around the network. The computer generating the packet normally sets a relatively high value for the TTL field; on computers running Windows, the default value is 128. Each router that processes the packet reduces the TTL value by one. If the value reaches zero, the last router discards the packet and transmits an ICMP error message back to the original sender.

When you start Traceroute with the name or IP address of a target computer, Traceroute generates its first set of Echo Request messages with TTL values of 1. When the messages arrive at the first router on their path, the router decrements their TTL values to 0, discards the packets, and reports the errors to the sender. The error messages contain the router's address, which Traceroute displays as the first hop in the path to the destination. Traceroute's second set of Echo Request messages use a TTL value of 2, causing the second router on the path to discard the packets and generate error messages. The Echo Request messages in the third set have a TTL value of 3, and so on. Each set of packets travels one hop farther than the previous set before causing a router to return error messages to the source. The list of routers displayed by Traceroute as the path to the destination is the result of these error messages. The following is an example of a Traceroute display:

```
Tracing route to www.fineartschool.co.uk [173.146.1.1] over a maximum of 30 hops:
 1  <10 ms    1 ms <10 ms  192.168.2.99
 2  105 ms   92 ms  98 ms  qrvl-67terminal01.cpandl.com [131.107.24.67.3]
 3  101 ms  110 ms  98 ms  qrvl.cpandl.com [131.107.67.1]
 4  123 ms  109 ms 118 ms  svcr03-7b.cpandl.com [131.107.103.125]
 5  123 ms  112 ms 114 ms  clsm02-2.cpandl.com [131.107.88.26]
 6  136 ms  130 ms 133 ms  sl-gw19-pen-6-1-0-T3.fabrikam.com [157.54.116.5]
 7  143 ms  126 ms 138 ms  sl-bb10-pen-4-3.fabrikam.com [157.54.5.117]
 8  146 ms  129 ms 133 ms  sl-bb20-pen-12-0.fabrikam.com [157.54.5.1]
 9  131 ms  128 ms 139 ms  sl-bb20-nyc-13-0.fabrikam.com [157.54.18.38]
10  130 ms  134 ms 134 ms  sl-gw9-nyc-8-0.fabrikam.com [157.54.7.94]
11  147 ms  149 ms 152 ms  sl-demon-1-0.fabrikam.com [157.54.173.10]
12  154 ms  146 ms 145 ms  ny2-backbone-1-ge021.router.fabrikam.com [157.54.173.121]
13  230 ms  225 ms 226 ms  tele-backbone-1-ge023.router.adatum.co.uk [157.60.173.12]
14  233 ms  220 ms 226 ms  tele-core-3-fxp1.router.adatum.co.uk [157.60.252.56]
```

```
15  223 ms 224 ms 224 ms tele-access-1-14.router.adatum.co.uk [157.60.254.245]
16  236 ms 221 ms 226 ms tele-service-2-165.router.adatum.co.uk [157.60.36.149]
17  220 ms 224 ms 210 ms www.fineartschool.co.uk [206.73.118.65]
Trace complete.
```

In this example, Traceroute displays the path between a computer in Pennsylvania and one in the United Kingdom. Each of the hops contains the elapsed times between the transmission and reception of three sets of Echo Request and Echo Reply packets. In this trace, you can clearly see the point at which the packets begin traveling across the Atlantic Ocean. At hop 13, the elapsed times increase from approximately 150 to 230 milliseconds (ms) and stay in that range for the subsequent hops. This additional delay of only 80 ms is the time it takes the packets to travel the thousands of miles across the Atlantic Ocean.

You can use Traceroute to isolate the location of a network communications problem. Ping simply tells you whether or not a problem exists; it can't tell you where. A failure to contact a remote computer could be due to a problem in your workstation, in the remote computer, or in any of the routers in between. Traceroute can tell you how far your packets are going before they run into the problem.

> **NOTE** **Traceroute Shortcomings**   Because the configuration of the Internet is constantly changing, there is no guarantee that the route displayed by Traceroute is completely accurate. The IP datagrams that execute each step of the Traceroute process might in fact be taking different routes to the same destination, resulting in the display of a composite route between two points that does not actually exist. There is also no way of knowing what the return path is.
>
> Additionally, all routers deprioritize ICMP processes in favor of packet forwarding and other critical router tasks. When a router is busy, it might delay the processing of a Ping or Traceroute packet. The resulting latency numbers will be higher than the delay experienced by actual data packets crossing the network.

Ifconfig, Ipconfig.exe, and Winipcfg.exe

UNIX and Linux systems have a program called ifconfig (the name is derived from the words *interface configuration*) that you use to configure the properties of network interface adapters and assign TCP/IP configuration parameters to them. Running ifconfig with just the name of an interface displays the current configuration of that interface. Windows NT has a version of this program, Ipconfig.exe, which omits most of the configuration capabilities and retains the configuration display. Microsoft Windows Me, Microsoft Windows 95, and Microsoft Windows 98 include a graphical version of Ipconfig called Winipcfg.exe.

When you run Ipconfig.exe with the /all parameter at the Windows Server 2003 command line, you see a display like the following:

```
Windows IP Configuration
Host Name . . . . . . . . . . . . . : cz2-w2ksvr
Primary DNS Suffix  . . . . . . . : zacker2.com
Node Type . . . . . . . . . . . : Hybrid
IP Routing Enabled. . . . . . . . : Yes
WINS Proxy Enabled. . . . . . . . : No
DNS Suffix Search List. . . . . . : zacker2.com
Ethernet adapter Local Area Connection:
Connection-specific DNS Suffix  . :
Description . . . . . . . . . . . : HP NC7760 Gigabit Server Adapter
Physical Address. . . . . . . . . : 00-01-02-68-24-DD
DHCP Enabled. . . . . . . . . . . : No
IP Address. . . . . . . . . . . . : 192.168.2.2
Subnet Mask . . . . . . . . . . . : 255.255.255.0
Default Gateway . . . . . . . . . : 192.168.2.99
DNS Servers . . . . . . . . . . . : 206.73.118.15
                                    206.73.118.16
```

To run Winipcfg.exe, you must supply the filename in the Run dialog box or find the file in the \Windows directory and execute it because there is no shortcut on the Start menu. Running Winipcfg.exe produces a display like the one shown in Figure 11-25.

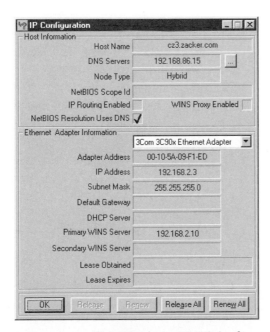

Figure 11-25   The Windows 98 Winipcfg.exe utility

Both Ipconfig.exe and Winipcfg.exe also have another function. These utilities are often associated with DHCP, because this is the easiest way in Windows to see what IP address and other parameters the DHCP server has assigned to your computer. However, these programs also enable you to manually release IP addresses obtained through DHCP and renew existing leases. By running Ipconfig.exe with the /release and /renew command-line parameters or by using the Release, Renew, Release All, or Renew All buttons in Winipcfg.exe, you can release or renew the IP address assignment of one of the network interfaces in the computer or for all of the interfaces at once.

ARP

The Address Resolution Protocol (ARP) enables a TCP/IP computer to convert IP addresses to the hardware addresses that data-link layer protocols need to transmit frames. IP uses ARP to discover the hardware address to which each of its datagrams will be transmitted. To minimize the amount of network traffic ARP generates, the computer stores the resolved hardware addresses in a cache in system memory. The information remains in the cache for a short time (usually between two and ten minutes), in case the computer has additional packets to send to the same address.

> **NOTE**   **Understanding ARP**   For more information about ARP and its function, see Chapter 7, "TCP/IP."

UNIX, Linux, and Windows include a command-line utility that you can use to manipulate the contents of the ARP cache. In UNIX and Linux, this utility is called arp; in Windows, it is called Arp.exe. You can use arp or Arp.exe to add the hardware addresses of computers you contact frequently to the cache, saving time and reducing network traffic during the connection process. Addresses that you add to the ARP cache manually are static, meaning that they are not deleted after the usual expiration period. The cache is stored in memory only, however, so it is erased when you reboot the computer. If you want to preload the cache whenever you boot your system, you can create a script containing arp or Arp.exe commands and execute it by using an rc file (in UNIX/Linux) or by placing it in the Startup program group (in Windows).

The arp and Arp.exe utilities use a similar syntax, with many identical command line arguments. This syntax and some of the most important command line arguments are as follows:

```
arp [-a {ipaddress}] [-n ipaddress] [-s ipaddress hwaddress {interface}]
[-d ipaddress {interface}]
```

- **-a {ipaddress}**   Displays the contents of the ARP cache. The optional *ipaddress* variable specifies the address of a particular cache entry to be displayed.

- **-n ipaddress**   Displays the contents of the ARP cache. The *ipaddress* variable identifies the network interface for which you want to display the cache.

- **-s ipaddress hwaddress {interface}**   Adds a new entry to the ARP cache. The *ipaddress* variable contains the IP address of the computer. The *hwaddress* variable contains the hardware address of the same computer. The *interface* variable contains the IP address of the network interface in the local system for which you want to modify the cache.

- **-d ipaddress {interface}**   Deletes the entry in the ARP cache that is associated with the computer represented by the *ipaddress* variable. The optional *interface* variable specifies the cache from which the entry should be deleted.

The ARP table of a computer running Microsoft Windows 2000, as displayed by Arp.exe, appears as follows:

```
Interface: 192.168.2.6 o--- 0x2
  Internet Address       Physical Address       Type
  192.168.2.10           00-50-8b-e8-39-7a       dynamic
  192.168.2.99           08-00-4e-a5-70-0f       dynamic
```

Netstat

Netstat is a command-line program that displays status information about the current network connections of a computer running TCP/IP and about the traffic generated by the TCP/IP protocols. In UNIX and Linux, the program is called netstat, and in Windows, it is called Netstat.exe. The command-line parameters differ for the various implementations of Netstat, but the information they display is roughly the same.

Using Netstat.exe on Windows

The syntax for Netstat.exe is as follows:

```
NETSTAT [interval] [-a] [-p protocol] [-n] [-e] [-r] [-s]
```

- **interval**   Refreshes the display every *interval* seconds until the user aborts the command.

- **-a**   Displays the current network connections and the ports that are currently listening for incoming network connections.

- **-p *protocol***   Displays the currently active connections for the protocol specified by the *protocol* variable.

- **-n**   When combined with other parameters, causes the program to identify computers using IP addresses instead of names.

- **-e**   Displays incoming and outgoing traffic statistics for the network interface. The statistics are broken down into bytes, unicast packets, nonunicast packets, discards, errors, and unknown protocols.

- **-r**   Displays the routing table plus the current active connections.

- **-s**   Displays detailed network traffic statistics for the IP, ICMP, TCP, and UDP protocols.

The default network connection listing displayed by Netstat.exe on a computer running Windows XP appears as follows:

```
Active Connections
Proto       Local Address         Foreign Address              State
TCP         cz8:3232              cz10.zacker.local:netbios-ssn  ESTABLISHED
TCP         cz8:3238              cz1.zacker.local:1025          ESTABLISHED
TCP         cz8:3571              crl.verisoon.net:http          CLOSE_WAIT
TCP         cz8:3949              zacker.com:ftp                 CLOSE_WAIT
TCP         cz8:4066              cz4.zacker.local:microsoft-ds  ESTABLISHED
TCP         cz8:4295              cz1.zacker.local:1164          ESTABLISHED
TCP         cz8:4431              zacker.com:ftp                 CLOSE_WAIT
```

The interface statistics on a computer running Windows XP look like this:

```
Interface Statistics

                         Received                Sent
Bytes                  2127854975           751579877
Unicast packets           3151802             2833248
Non-unicast packets         64418                 995
Discards                        0                   0
Errors                          0                   0
Unknown protocols            8465
```

The routing table display produced by Netstat.exe appears as follows:

```
Route Table
===============================================================================
Interface List
0x1 . . . . . . . . . . . . . . . .MS TCP Loopback interface
0x2 . . . .00 0d 60 11 44 e1 . . .Intel(R) PRO/1000 MT Mobile Connection - Packet

Scheduler Miniport
===============================================================================
Active Routes:
  Network Destination        Netmask          Gateway        Interface  Metric
          0.0.0.0          0.0.0.0     192.168.2.99    192.168.2.11     10
        127.0.0.0        255.0.0.0        127.0.0.1       127.0.0.1      1
      192.168.2.0    255.255.255.0     192.168.2.11    192.168.2.11     10
     192.168.2.11  255.255.255.255        127.0.0.1       127.0.0.1     10
    192.168.2.255   255.255.255.25     192.168.2.11    192.168.2.11     10
        224.0.0.0        240.0.0.0     192.168.2.11    192.168.2.11     10
  255.255.255.255  255.255.255.255     192.168.2.11    192.168.2.11      1
    Default Gateway:       192.168.2.99
===============================================================================
Persistent Routes:
None
```

Using Netstat on UNIX and Linux

The command-line parameters for the UNIX/Linux netstat tool are similar to those used in Netstat.exe, but they are not identical. The UNIX/Linux version has additional parameters. The default netstat display on a UNIX or Linux system is shown in Figure 11-26.

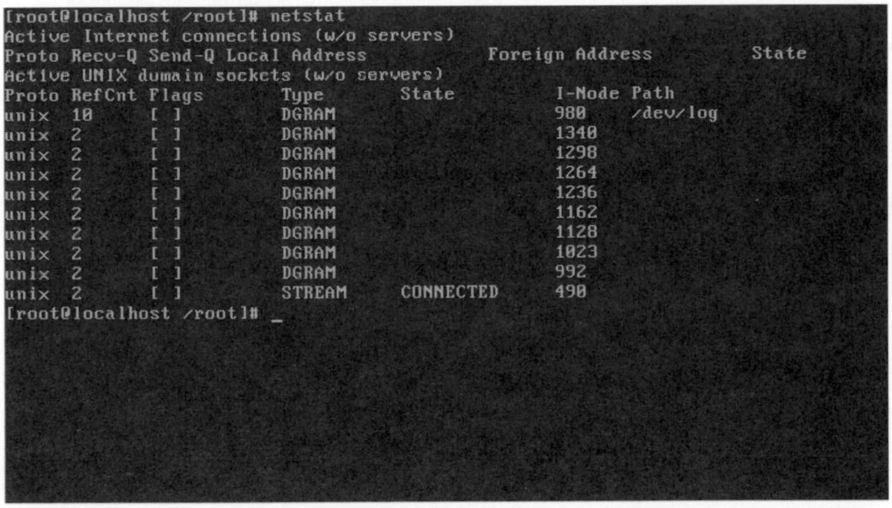

Figure 11-26 The default netstat display

To display the statistics for the system, you run netstat with the –s parameter. The statistics display is shown in Figure 11-27.

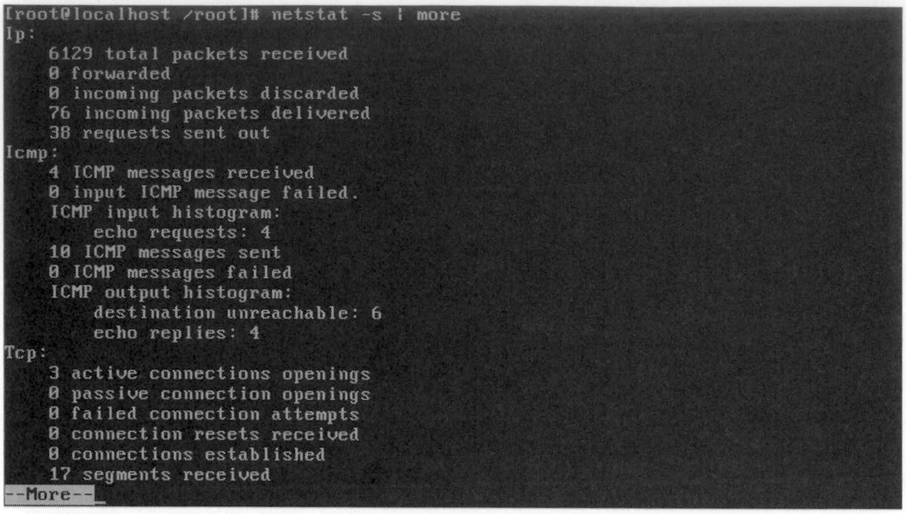

```
[root@localhost /root]# netstat -s | more
Ip:
    6129 total packets received
    0 forwarded
    0 incoming packets discarded
    76 incoming packets delivered
    38 requests sent out
Icmp:
    4 ICMP messages received
    0 input ICMP message failed.
    ICMP input histogram:
        echo requests: 4
    10 ICMP messages sent
    0 ICMP messages failed
    ICMP output histogram:
        destination unreachable: 6
        echo replies: 4
Tcp:
    3 active connections openings
    0 passive connection openings
    0 failed connection attempts
    0 connection resets received
    0 connections established
    17 segments received
--More--_
```

Figure 11-27   The netstat statistics display

To display the system's current connections, you run netstat with the –l parameter. The connections display is shown in Figure 11-28.

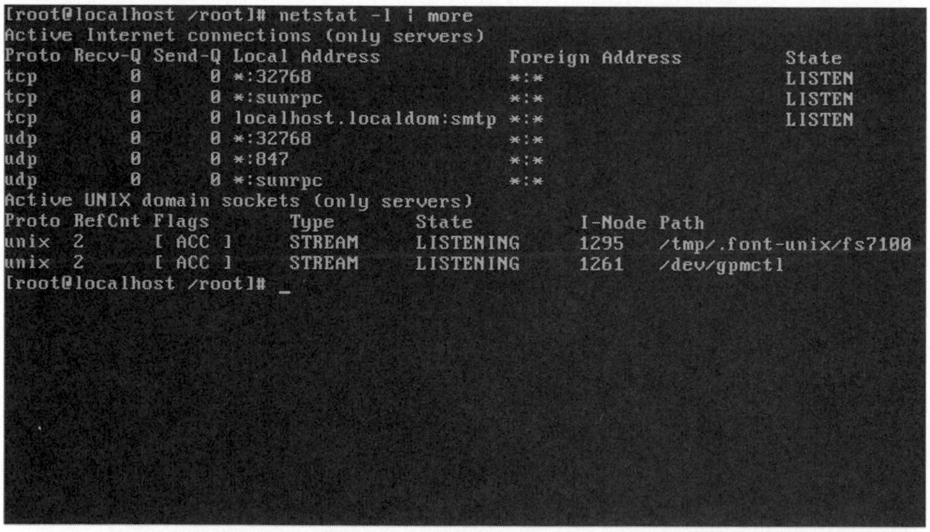

```
[root@localhost /root]# netstat -l | more
Active Internet connections (only servers)
Proto Recv-Q Send-Q Local Address           Foreign Address         State
tcp        0      0 *:32768                 *:*                     LISTEN
tcp        0      0 *:sunrpc                *:*                     LISTEN
tcp        0      0 localhost.localdom:smtp *:*                     LISTEN
udp        0      0 *:32768                 *:*
udp        0      0 *:847                   *:*
udp        0      0 *:sunrpc                *:*
Active UNIX domain sockets (only servers)
Proto RefCnt Flags       Type       State         I-Node Path
unix  2      [ ACC ]     STREAM     LISTENING     1295   /tmp/.font-unix/fs7100
unix  2      [ ACC ]     STREAM     LISTENING     1261   /dev/gpmctl
[root@localhost /root]# _
```

Figure 11-28   The netstat connections display

Nbtstat.exe

Nbtstat.exe is a Windows command-line program that displays information about the NetBIOS Over TCP/IP (NetBT) connections that Windows uses when communicating with other computers running Windows on the TCP/IP network. The syntax for Nbtstat.exe is as follows:

```
nbtstat [-a name] [-A ipaddress] [-c] [-n] [-r] [-R] [-s] [-S] [-RR]
```

- **-a** *name*   Displays the NetBIOS names registered on the computer identified by the name variable

- **-A** *ipaddress*   Displays the NetBIOS names registered on the computer identified by the *ipaddress* variable

- **-c**   Displays the contents of the local computer's NetBIOS name cache

- **-n**   Displays the NetBIOS names registered on the local computer

- **-r**   Displays the number of NetBIOS names registered and resolved by the local computer, using both broadcasts and Windows Internet Name Service (WINS)

- **-R**   Purges the local computer's NetBIOS name cache of all entries and reloads the Lmhosts file

- **-s**   Displays a list of the computer's currently active NetBIOS settings (identifying remote computers by name), their current status, and the amount of data transmitted to and received from each system

- **-S**   Displays a list of the computer's currently active NetBIOS settings (identifying remote computers by IP address), their current status, and the amount of data transmitted to and received from each system

- **-RR**   Sends name release requests to WINS, then starts refresh

NOTE   Using Nbtstat.exe Command-Line Parameters   Unlike most Windows utilities, the command-line parameters for Nbtstat.exe are case-sensitive.

The NetBIOS cache listing as displayed by Nbtstat.exe on a computer running Windows XP appears as follows:

```
Local Area Connection:
Node IpAddress: [192.168.2.11] Scope Id: []

                NetBIOS Remote Cache Name Table

    Name                  Type           Host Address     Life[sec]
    ---------------------------------------------------------------
    192.168.2.1     <20>    UNIQUE         192.168.2.1      602
    CZ1.ZACKER.LOCA <4C>    UNIQUE         192.168.2.1      602
    CZ4             <20>    UNIQUE         192.168.2.19     602
    CZ1             <20>    UNIQUE         192.168.2.1      582
```

The list of NetBIOS names registered by a computer appears as follows:

```
Local Area Connection:
Node IpAddress: [192.168.2.11] Scope Id: []

        NetBIOS Remote Machine Name Table

    Name               Type         Status
    ---------------------------------------------
    CZ8         <00>    UNIQUE       Registered
    ZACKER      <00>    GROUP        Registered
    CZ8         <03>    UNIQUE       Registered
    CZ8         <20>    UNIQUE       Registered
    ZACKER      <1E>    GROUP        Registered
    CRAIGZ      <03>    UNIQUE       Registered

    MAC Address = 00-0D-60-11-44-E1
```

Nslookup

The nslookup (in UNIX) and Nslookup.exe (in Windows NT) command-line utilities enable you to generate DNS request messages and transmit them to specific DNS servers on the network. The advantage of nslookup is that you can test the functionality and the quality of the information on a specific DNS server by specifying it on the command line.

The basic command-line syntax of nslookup is as follows:

```
nslookup DNSname DNSserver
```

- **DNSname**   Specifies the DNS name that you want to resolve

- **DNSserver**   Specifies the DNS name or IP address of the DNS server that you want to query for the name specified in the *DNSname* variable

There are also many additional parameters that you can include on the command line to control the server query process. The output generated by Nslookup.exe in Windows XP looks like the following:

```
C:\>nslookup www.microsoft.com 206.73.118.54
Server:         ns1-dlls.cpandl.com
Address:        206.73.118.54
Non-authoritative answer:
Name:           www2.microsoft.net
Addresses:      207.46.156.252, 207.46.244.188, 207.46.245.92, 207.46.249.29
                207.46.249.221, 207.46.134.157, 207.46.134.189, 207.46.134.221
Aliases:        www.microsoft.com, www.microsoft.net
```

Test your knowledge of TCP/IP tools and their functions by completing Exercise 11-3, "TCP/IP Utilities," now.

Test your familiarity with the output produced by TCP/IP utilities by completing Exercise 11-4, "Identifying TCP/IP Utility Output," now.

The nslookup utility has two operational modes: command-line and interactive. When you run nslookup with no command-line parameters, the program displays its own prompt from which you can issue commands to specify the default DNS server to query, resolve multiple names, and configure many other aspects of the program's functionality.

> **NOTE** **Replacing Nslookup**   In many UNIX and Linux distributions, nslookup has been replaced by the dig and host tools, which provide the same functionality with additional flexibility. Some distributions retain the nslookup tool for compatibility reasons, while others omit it entirely.

> **NOTE** **Exam Objectives**   Objective 4.1 for the Network+ exam requires that students, "given a troubleshooting scenario, [be able to] select the appropriate TCP/IP utility from among the following: Tracert, Ping, Arp, Netstat, Nbtstat, Ipconfig/Ifconfig, Winipcfg, [and] Nslookup."

SUMMARY

- The link pulse light-emitting diodes (LEDs) on Ethernet hubs and network interface adapters indicate when these devices are connected properly. Other LEDs can indicate the speed at which the equipment is operating.

- Network management products provide a centralized, comprehensive resource for information about the devices connected to a large enterprise network.

- Tools like the Performance console in Windows enable you to monitor ongoing computer and network operations in real time.

- Protocol analyzers capture network traffic and decode it for further study.

- Crossover cables can eliminate cable runs and hubs as possible sources of communication problems.

- A loopback connector tests the functionality of a network interface adapter by redirecting its outgoing signals back into it.

- A tone generator and locator is a simple cable-testing device that determines whether a cable is carrying a signal.

- Wire map testers test all four of the wire pairs in a unshielded twisted pair (UTP) cable at the same time.

- Multifunction cable testers perform a comprehensive battery of tests on a cable connection and compare the results to established standards.

- The ping, Ping.exe, and Ping.nlm utilities test whether one Transmission Control Protocol/Internet Protocol (TCP/IP) computer can communicate with another one.

- The traceroute, Tracert.exe, and Iptrace.nlm programs display the path that packets take through a network to reach their destinations.

- Ipconfig.exe and Winipcfg.exe are Windows programs that display information about the computer's TCP/IP configuration and manipulate Dynamic Host Configuration Protocol (DHCP) Internet Protocol (IP) address assignments. The ifconfig program is a UNIX/Linux program that can configure a network interface as well as display information about it.

- The arp and Arp.exe utilities enable you to view and modify the contents of the Address Resolution Protocol (ARP) cache maintained by a TCP/IP system.

- The netstat and Netstat.exe utilities display information about a computer's TCP/IP connections and the traffic passing over them.

- Nbtstat.exe displays information about NetBIOS connections and their traffic.

- The nslookup and Nslookup.exe utilities enable you to transmit Domain Name System (DNS) requests to specific servers.

EXERCISES

Exercise 11-1: Network Indicators

Define each of the following terms in relation to the concepts discussed in this chapter.

1. SNMP

2. NLP

3. Trap

4. Link code word

5. MIB

Exercise 11-2: Network Testing Equipment

For each of the devices listed in the left column, specify which of the faults in the right column it can detect.

1. Crossover cable	a. Cable short
2. RJ-45 loopback connector	b. Split pair
3. Tone generator and locator	c. Malfunctioning hub
4. Wire map tester	d. Excessive crosstalk
5. Multifunction cable tester	e. Transposed wires
	f. Faulty network interface adapter
	g. Untwisted cables
	h. Broken cable

Exercise 11-3: TCP/IP Utilities

Match the utilities in the left column with their functions in the right column.

1. Ipconfig.exe
2. Traceroute
3. Ping
4. Netstat
5. Winipcfg.exe
6. Nbtstat.exe
7. Arp
8. Ifconfig

a. Displays TCP/IP configuration in Windows 98

b. Creates cache entries containing IP and hardware addresses

c. Configures the network interface in UNIX

d. Tests communications between two computers

e. Displays network traffic statistics

f. Lists the routers forwarding packets to a particular destination

g. Releases and renews IP address assignments in Windows XP

h. Displays NetBIOS connection information

Exercise 11-4: Identifying TCP/IP Utility Output

Each of the following is an excerpt from the output produced by a particular TCP/IP utility. For each excerpt, specify the name of the utility that generated it and the functions being performed by that utility.

1.

```
Physical Address. . . . . . . . . : 00-01-02-68-24-DD
DHCP Enabled. . . . . . . . . . . : No
IP Address. . . . . . . . . . . . : 192.168.2.2
Subnet Mask . . . . . . . . . . . : 255.255.255.0
Default Gateway . . . . . . . . . : 192.168.2.99
DNS Servers . . . . . . . . . . . : 199.224.86.15
```

2.

```
Reply from 192.168.14.5: bytes=32 time=54ms TTL=128
Reply from 192.168.14.5: bytes=32 time=45ms TTL=128
Reply from 192.168.14.5: bytes=32 time=87ms TTL=128
Reply from 192.168.14.5: bytes=32 time=29ms TTL=128
```

3.

```
192.168.2.1        <20>       UNIQUE      192.168.2.1     602
CZ1.ZACKER.LOCA    <4C>       UNIQUE      192.168.2.1     602
CZ4                <20>       UNIQUE      192.168.2.19    602
CZ1                <20>       UNIQUE      192.168.2.1     582
```

4.

```
Server:       ns1-dlls.cpandl.com
Address:      206.73.118.54
Non-authoritative answer:
Name:         www.microsoft.com
Addresses:    207.46.156.252
```

5.

```
15 223 ms 224 ms 224 ms tele-access-1-14.router.adatum.com [206.73.118.245]
16 236 ms 221 ms 226 ms tele-service-2-165.router.adatum.com [206.73.118.149]
17 220 ms 224 ms 210 ms www.alpineskihouse.com [131.107.1.1]
```

REVIEW QUESTIONS

1. How does the FLP signal used by Fast Ethernet equipment differ from the NLP signal used by standard Ethernet?

2. How does the performance of a network interface adapter differ when it is in promiscuous mode?

3. Arrange the following Ethernet technologies in the order of priority established by the FLP signal.

   a. 100Base-T4

   b. 10Base-T full-duplex

   c. 100Base-TX

   d. 10Base-T

   e. 100Base-TX full-duplex

4. What are the individual elements measured by the Windows Server 2003 Performance console called?

   a. Counters

   b. Statistics

   c. Alerts

   d. Traps

5. Where do agents used by network management products store their information?

   a. SNMP

   b. MIB

   c. NNTP

   d. Console

6. A fox and hound tester is another name for what device?

   a. A crossover cable

   b. A tone generator and locator

   c. A wire map tester

   d. A multifunction cable tester

7. Which of the following cabling faults is a standard wire map tester unable to detect?

   a. Open pairs

   b. Split pairs

   c. Transposed pairs

   d. Shorts

8. Which of the following types of cable tester is the most expensive?

   a. Fox and hound

   b. Wire map

   c. Multifunction

   d. Loopback

9. Which TCP/IP utility should you use to most easily identify a malfunctioning router on your internetwork?

   a. Ifconfig

   b. Ping

   c. Traceroute

   d. Netstat

10. Which of the following protocols does the Ping program *never* use to carry its messages?

    a. Ethernet

    b. ICMP

    c. IP

    d. UDP

11. Which of the following commands displays the routing table on the local computer?

    a. Arp –r

    b. Netstat –r

    c. Nbtstat –r

    d. Telnet –r

12. Which command would you use to purge the NetBIOS name cache on the local computer?

    a. Nbtstat –p

    b. Nbtstat –P

    c. Nbtstat –r

    d. Nbtstat –R

CASE SCENARIOS

Case Scenario 11-1: Troubleshooting a Cable Installation

You are helping a friend perform an internal UTP cable installation. After pulling the cables through the walls and ceilings and punching them down into the wall plates and the patch panel, you and your friend begin to test the connections, using the only tools available to you: a tone generator and locator. Using this information, answer the following questions.

1. On one particular connection, your friend applies the tone generator to pin 3 at one end of the connection, but you do not detect a signal on pin 3 at the other end. After testing the other contacts, you finally detect a signal on pin 8. What type of cabling fault have you discovered?

    a. An open circuit

    b. A short

    c. Transposed wires

    d. A split pair

2. On another connection, the tone generator and locator fail to find any faults, but this connection still does not function correctly when a computer uses it to connect to the hub. Which one of the following cable faults could be the cause of the problem?

    a. An open circuit

    b. A short

    c. Transposed wires

    d. A split pair

CHAPTER 12

NETWORK TROUBLESHOOTING PROCEDURES

Upon completion of this chapter, you will be able to:

- Understand the steps involved in troubleshooting a network problem.

- List the rules for prioritizing problem calls.

- Describe the process of isolating the source of a network problem.

- Understand the progression of a technical support help call.

- Troubleshoot Internet access problems.

- Distinguish among network problems, computer problems, and user problems.

The process of troubleshooting network problems varies, depending on the size of the organization and the people involved. In medium-sized to large-sized organizations, there is usually a written procedure that determines how technical support calls are registered, addressed, and escalated. In smaller organizations, the process might be much more informal. This chapter describes the procedures commonly used for typical technical support calls. In some cases, the cause of the problem might be simple to identify, such as user error, and the procedures described here illustrate how you can handle even minor problems to everyone's satisfaction. In other cases, the problem itself might seem minor, but it might actually be a sign of a serious problem that affects the whole network.

TROUBLESHOOTING A NETWORK

One of the key elements of troubleshooting a network problem is having a plan of action. Many troubleshooting calls are from users who are improperly using software, and these can often be cleared up immediately with some remedial training. When you are faced with what appears to be a real problem, however, you should follow a set troubleshooting procedure, which consists of a series of steps similar to the following:

1. Establish the symptoms.

2. Identify the affected area.

3. Establish what has changed.

4. Select the most probable cause.

5. Implement a solution.

6. Test the result.

7. Recognize the potential effects of the solution.

8. Document the solution.

Each support technician can use slightly different steps or perform them in a slightly different order, but the overall process should be similar. The following sections examine each of these steps.

> **NOTE   Exam Objectives**   Objective 4.9 for the Network+ exam requires students, "given a network problem scenario, [to be able to] select an appropriate course of action based on a general troubleshooting strategy. This strategy includes the following steps: establish the symptoms, identify the affected area, establish what has changed, select the most probable cause, implement a solution, test the result, recognize the potential effects of the solution, [and] document the solution."

Establishing the Symptoms

The first step in troubleshooting a network problem is to determine exactly what is going wrong and to note how the problem affects the network so that it can be assigned a priority. In a large network, the network support staff often receives more calls for help than they can handle at one time. Therefore, it is essential to establish a system of priorities that dictates which calls get addressed first. As in the emergency department of a hospital, the priorities should not necessarily be based on who is first in line. The severity of the problem should determine who gets attention first. However, it is usually not wise to ignore the political reality that senior management problems are addressed before those of the rank and file.

You can use the following guidelines to establish priorities:

- **Shared resources take precedence over individual resources.** A problem with a server or another network component that prevents many users from working must take precedence over one that affects only a single user.

- **Network-wide problems take precedence over workgroup or departmental problems.** A problem with a resource that provides services to the entire network, such as an e-mail server, should take precedence over a problem with a departmental resource, such as a file or print server.

- **Departmental issues should be rated according to the function of the department.** A problem with a resource belonging to a department that is critical to the organization, such as order entry or customer service call centers, should take precedence over a problem with a resource belonging to a department that can better tolerate a period of down time, such as research and development.

- **System-wide problems take precedence over application problems.** A problem that puts an entire computer out of commission and prevents a user from getting any work done should take precedence over a problem a user is experiencing with a single device or application.

It is sometimes difficult to determine the exact nature of the problem from the description given by a relatively inexperienced user, but part of the process of narrowing down the cause of a problem involves obtaining accurate information about what has occurred. Users are often vague about what they were doing when they experienced the problem, or even what the indications of the problem were. For example, in many cases, users call the help desk because they received an error message, but they neglect to write down the wording of the message. Training users in the proper procedures for documenting and reporting problems is part of your job as well. It might not be any help now, but it can help the next time a user receives an error.

Begin by asking the user questions like the following:

- What exactly were you doing when the problem occurred?

- Have you had any other problems with your computer lately?

- Was the computer behaving normally just before the problem occurred?

- Has any hardware or software been installed, removed, or reconfigured recently?

- Did you or anyone else do anything to try to resolve the problem?

Identifying the Affected Area

The next step in troubleshooting a network problem is to see whether it can be duplicated. Network problems that can be reproduced are far easier to fix, primarily because you can easily test to see whether a solution was successful. However, many types of network problems are intermittent or might occur for only a short period of time. In these cases, you might have to leave the incident open until the problem occurs again. In some instances, having the user reproduce the problem can lead to the solution. User error is a common cause of problems that might seem to be hardware-related or network-related.

If you can duplicate a problem, you can set about finding the source of the difficulty. For example, if a user has trouble opening a file in a word processing application, the difficulty might lie in the application, in the user's computer, in the file server where the file is stored, or in any of the networking components in between. The process of isolating the location of the problem consists of logically and methodically eliminating the elements that are not the cause.

If you can duplicate the problem, you can begin to isolate the cause by reproducing the conditions under which the problem occurred. To do this, use a procedure like the following:

1. Have the user reproduce the problem on the computer repeatedly, to determine whether the user's actions are causing the error.

2. If possible, you should sit at the computer yourself and perform the same task. If the problem does not occur, the cause might lie in how the user is performing a particular task. Watch the user carefully to see if he is doing something wrong. It is entirely possible that you and the user are performing the same task in different ways and that the user's method is exposing a problem that yours does not.

3. If the problem recurs when you perform the task, log off from the user's account, log on using an account with administrative privileges, and repeat the task. If the problem does not recur, the user probably does not have the rights or permissions needed to perform the task.

4. If the problem recurs, try to perform the same task on another, similarly equipped computer connected to the same network. If you

cannot reproduce the problem on another computer, you know that the cause lies in the user's computer or its connection to the network. If the problem does recur on another computer, then there is a network problem, either in the server that the computer was communicating with or the hardware that connects the two.

Test your understanding of how to isolate a problem by completing Exercise 12-1, "Network Troubleshooting," now.

If you determine that the problem is in the network and not in the user's computer, the next step is to begin isolating the area of the network that is the source of the problem. For example, if the same problem occurs on a nearby computer, you can begin performing the same task on computers located elsewhere on the network. Again, proceed methodically and document the results. For example, try to reproduce the problem on another computer connected to the same hub, and then on a computer connected to a different hub on the same local area network (LAN). If the problem occurs throughout the LAN, try a computer on a different LAN. Eventually, you should be able to narrow down the source of the problem to a particular component, such as a server, router, hub, or cable.

Establishing What Has Changed

When a computer or other network component that used to work properly now does not, it stands to reason that some change has occurred. When a user reports a problem, it is important to determine how the computing environment changed immediately before the malfunction. Unfortunately, getting this information from the user can often be difficult. The response to the question "Has anything changed on the computer recently?" is nearly always "No." Only later will the user remember to mention that a major hardware or software upgrade was performed just before the problem occurred. On a network with properly established maintenance and documentation procedures, you should be able to determine whether the user's computer has been upgraded or modified recently. Official records are the first place to look for information like this.

Major changes, such as the installation of new hardware or software, are obvious possible causes of the problem, but you must be conscious of causes evidenced in more subtle changes as well. For example, an increase in network traffic levels, as disclosed by a protocol analyzer, can contribute to a reduction in network performance. Occasional problems noticed by several users of the same application, cable segment, or LAN can indicate the existence of a fault in a component of the network. Tracking down the source of a networking problem can often be a form of detective work, and learning to "interrogate" your "suspects" properly can be an important part of the troubleshooting process.

Selecting the Most Probable Cause

There's an old medical school axiom that says when you hear hoofbeats, think horses, not zebras. In the context of network troubleshooting, this means that when you look for the possible causes of a problem, start with the obvious cause first. For example, if a workstation cannot communicate with a file server, do not start by checking the routers between the two systems; check the simple things on the workstation first, such as whether the network cable is plugged into the computer. You also must work methodically and document everything so that you do not duplicate your efforts.

Implementing a Solution

After you have isolated the problem to a particular piece of equipment, try to determine whether hardware or software is the culprit. If it is a hardware problem, you might replace the unit that is at fault or use an alternative that you know is functioning properly. Communication problems, for example, might force you to start replacing network cables until you find one that is faulty. If the problem is in a server, you might need to replace components, such as hard drives, until the defective component is found. If you determine that the problem is caused by software, try running an application or storing data on a different computer or reinstalling the software on the offending system.

In some cases, the process of isolating the source of a problem includes resolving the problem. For example, if you end up replacing network patch cables until a faulty one is found, replacing the bad cable resolves the problem. In other cases, however, the resolution might be more involved, such as one that requires reinstalling a server application or an operating system. Because other users might need to access that server, you might have to wait to resolve the problem until a later time, when the network is not in use and after the data stored on the server has been backed up. In some cases, it might even be necessary to bring in outside help, such as a contractor to pull new cables. Arranging for an outside technician can require careful scheduling to avoid having the contractor's work conflict with the activities of the network users. Sometimes, you can use an interim solution, such as a substitute workstation or server, until the problem can be definitively resolved.

Testing the Results

After implementing a resolution to the problem, you should return to the very beginning of the process and repeat the task that originally caused the problem. If the problem no longer occurs, you should test any other functions related to the changes you made, to ensure that fixing one problem has not created another. At this point, the time you spend documenting the troubleshooting process becomes worthwhile. Repeat the procedures used to duplicate the problem exactly to ensure that the trouble the user originally experienced has been completely eliminated, and not just temporarily masked. If the problem was intermittent to begin with, it might take some time to ascertain whether the solution has been effective. It might be necessary to check with the user several times to make sure that the problem is not recurring.

Recognizing the Potential Effects of the Solution

It is important, throughout the troubleshooting process, to keep an eye on the big network picture and not become too involved in the problems experienced by one user (or application or LAN). While resolving one problem, you could inadvertently create another that is more severe or that affects more users. For example, if users on one LAN are experiencing high traffic levels that diminish their workstation performance, you might be able to remedy the problem by connecting some of their computers to a different LAN. However, although this solution might help the users who originally experienced the problem, it might overload another LAN in the process, causing another problem that is more severe than the first one. It might be better to consider a more far-reaching solution instead, such as creating an entirely new LAN and moving some of the affected users over to it.

Documenting the Solution

Although it is presented here as a separate step, the process of documenting all of the actions you perform should begin as soon as the user calls for help. A well-organized network support organization should have a system in place in which each problem call is registered as a trouble ticket that eventually contains a complete record of the problem and the steps taken to isolate and resolve it. In many cases, a technical support organization operates using *tiers*, which are groups of technicians of different skill levels. Calls come in to the first tier, and if the problem is sufficiently complex or the first-tier technician cannot resolve it, the call is escalated to the second tier, which is composed of senior technicians. As long as all who are involved in the process document their activities, there should be no problem when one technician hands off the trouble ticket to another. In addition, keeping careful notes prevents people from duplicating one another's efforts.

The final phase of the troubleshooting process is to explain to the user what happened and why. Of course, the average network user is probably not interested in hearing all the technical details, but it is a good idea to let users know whether their actions caused the problem, exacerbated it, or made it more difficult to resolve. Educating users can lead to a quicker resolution next time or can even prevent a problem from occurring altogether.

> **NOTE   Exam Objectives**   Objective 4.2 for the Network+ exam requires students, "given a troubleshooting scenario involving a small office/home office network failure (e.g., xDSL, cable, home satellite, wireless, POTS), [to be able to] identify the cause of the failure."

NETWORK TROUBLESHOOTING SCENARIO: "I CAN'T ACCESS A WEB SITE"

A network user named Alice calls you and reports that she has been trying to access a particular Web site for several hours and is consistently receiving an error message.

This is a common occurrence for all Internet users because all Internet resources have occasional and sometimes frequent outages. However, this might also indicate a problem with Alice's computer or with the internal network. Based on the information provided in the scenario, and knowing nothing about Alice's level of expertise, you have no way of knowing whether the problem is caused by user error, a computer configuration problem, a faulty network connection, or a malfunction of the router providing the Internet access. The problem could even be caused by the Internet or the specific Web site itself—either of which is beyond your sphere of influence.

Incident Administration

The first step for any technical support call is to begin to document the incident. Many help desks use software that enables technicians to document calls and store them in a database. Using help desk software, the technician taking the call can assign a priority to each call; escalate calls to senior technicians, if necessary; list all of the information obtained from the caller; and document the steps taken to solve the problem.

Prioritizing Calls

Because you have only the most rudimentary information about Alice's problem at this point, you cannot accurately assign a priority to this call. If the problem turns out to be with the router or the network itself and a large number of users are affected, it could be very serious, especially if the organization relies on its Internet access for vital business communications. For example, if the organization is a company that sells products over the Web and the Web servers are located onsite, an Internet connection failure means that the Web site is down and no orders are coming in. In a case like this, the call might be assigned the highest possible priority. If, on the other hand, revenue-producing work can go on without Internet access, the priority of the call can be somewhat lower. If the problem lies in Alice's computer or in her procedures, the priority of the call can be much lower, unless of course Alice is the company president.

Escalating Calls

Many technical support operations separate their technicians into two or more tiers, depending on their expertise and experience. First-tier technicians typically take help desk calls, and if they determine the problem is too serious or complex for them to deal with, they escalate the call to the second tier. In a well-organized technical support team, the criteria for escalating calls are explicitly documented. For example, problems involving user error and individual workstations might remain in the first tier, while network outages and problems affecting multiple users might be immediately escalated. Escalation should also occur when a technician in the first tier makes several earnest attempts to resolve the problem and cannot do so. Of course, political concerns are likely to affect the escalation process, just like the assignment of priorities. The purpose of this hierarchical arrangement is to prevent the organization's more experienced (and presumably more highly paid) technicians from spending their time fielding calls about elementary problems.

Gathering Information

In this scenario, and in most others as well, the next step in the troubleshooting process is to ask the user about the exact circumstances under which the problem occurred. Until you have more information, it is impossible to assign a priority to the call or determine whether it should be escalated.

Let's say that when you ask Alice to describe what she was doing when the error occurred, she says that she has been trying to open a Web site in Microsoft Internet Explorer and after a few seconds received an error message. Since she had always been able to connect to the Web site before, she tried again several times over the course of an hour but received the same error message every time. Alice did not write down the error message at the time, but she was able to re-create the error by trying again to access the site. The error message was the familiar "This Page Cannot Be Displayed" screen, shown in Figure 12-1, which also says "Cannot Find Server or DNS Error."

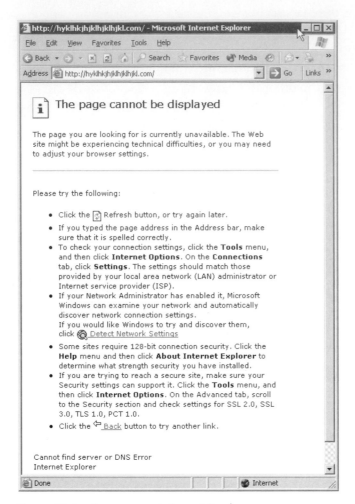

Figure 12-1   A common Internet Explorer error message

This error message is a common one, familiar to every user of Internet Explorer. This message can appear for many reasons: because the Web server the browser is trying to contact is down, because the client computer's Internet connection is broken, or because the client's Domain Name System (DNS) server fails to resolve the DNS name in the requested Uniform Resource Locator (URL). To determine the cause of the problem, you need to isolate the components that are malfunctioning, which you do by eliminating all of the properly functioning components until you are left with only the problematic ones.

Possible Cause: Internet Router Problem

Difficulty in accessing the Internet is one of the most common problems handled by the help desk in almost any organization with a network that provides routed access to the Internet. For an organization with more than a handful of users, setting up a router that connects to an Internet service provider (ISP) is the easiest and most economical way of providing users with Internet access. Depending on the size of the organization and the needs of the users, the router could be a stand-alone unit connected to an ISP using a leased telephone line, such as a T-1; a computer with a modem that connects to the ISP using a standard dial-up connection and is configured to share that connection with network users; or any one of many solutions falling between these two extremes. A network using a router to connect to the Internet is shown in Figure 12-2.

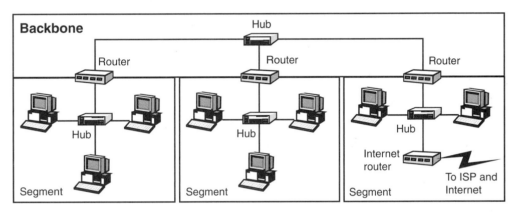

Figure 12-2   Most networks provide users with Internet access by sharing a router's connection to an ISP.

Many things can go wrong with this type of routed Internet access solution, including the following:

- **The router's connection to the ISP or the ISP's connection to the Internet is malfunctioning.**   A service outage can occur whether the router's connection to the ISP uses a standard dial-up modem, a T-1, or another service such as Integrated Services Digital Network (ISDN). In addition, the ISP providing Internet access is just as likely to suffer from network problems as your organization is. These problems can affect all of the service's or ISP's customers, and there is nothing that you can do about them, except report them to the service's or ISP's own technical support staff.

- **The router device or computer is experiencing a hardware or power failure.**   If the router connecting the network to the ISP is not functioning, the Internet access requests generated by the client applications running on the users' computers have nowhere to go. When the requested Internet resource does not respond, the client application eventually times out and displays an error message. This condition affects all of the users who access the Internet through that router.

- **There is a problem with the network that prevents access to the router.**   A broken network cable, a faulty cable connector, or a malfunctioning hub or other network connection device can all prevent a user's Internet access requests from reaching the router, even if the router is functioning properly and is connected to the ISP. The number of users affected by this type of problem depends on the location of the fault and the function of the component that has malfunctioned. For example, if the cable connecting the user's computer to the hub has been severed, only that one computer is affected. If the hub itself is malfunctioning, all of the computers connected to it are affected. If a central component, such as a backbone cable or switch, is faulty, the problem could extend to a large number of users, or even all of them.

- **The client computer is misconfigured and is not sending Internet access requests to the router.**   The computer running the Web browser or other client application could be experiencing a problem in its networking hardware, its software, or its network configuration. Client configuration problems affect only that client computer, and they are a common cause of error messages like the one Alice received.

Generally speaking, a router problem is one of the least likely causes of the problem Alice is experiencing. In addition, if the Internet access router were malfunctioning, you would probably be receiving calls from many different users with the same problem. However, a router problem is one of the easiest causes to check for, and its potential seriousness makes it a high priority. Therefore, it does no harm to eliminate the router as a possible source of the problem as one of the first steps of the troubleshooting process.

The easiest way to test the router is to try to access a Web site using a computer that shares the same routed Internet connection as Alice's computer. In Alice's organization, all of the users share a single Internet connection, so you can simply launch a Web browser and connect to a Web site to determine whether the connection and the router are functioning properly. If they are, the source of the problem is likely Alice's procedures, her computer, or her computer's connection to the router.

If your computer also fails to access the Internet, the problem could lie in any one of three areas of the network:

- **In a component that both you and the user use to access the router, such as a hub, a switch, a LAN router, or a backbone network** The next step would be to see exactly which other users on the network have the same problem. You should then be able to isolate the problem to a particular hub, cable, or other piece of equipment, depending on how widespread the problem is.

- **In the router itself** To provide the network with Internet access, the router must perform two basic tasks: access the Internet itself (through an ISP) and forward packets back and forth between the internal network and the ISP's Internet-connected network. If either one of these two functions fails, users cannot access Internet services. If the router is a computer, testing the connection to the ISP is simply a matter of running a Web browser on that computer and trying to connect to a Web site. If that succeeds, check the router configuration to see whether it is communicating with both networks properly and forwarding packets. If the router itself cannot connect to the Internet, the problem might lie in the technology used to connect the router to the ISP.

- **In the connection between the router and the ISP** All of the wide area network (WAN) technologies used to connect networks to ISPs require hardware at both sides of the connection and a service that provides the communications link between the hardware devices. If the router uses a simple dial-up connection to the ISP, the problem could lie in either one of the two modems involved or in the telephone line that provides the connection between them. You can test your line and modem by replacing them with others that you know work properly. With other technologies, the principles are the same, but testing is likely to be more difficult. It is unlikely that even a large organization has an extra T-1 line sitting around idle.

> **NOTE** *Proxy Server Connections* In some cases, network users access Web sites through a proxy server or another device that functions as an intermediary between the client and the Web server. This type of connection introduces another possible source of the problem. However, if you or other users can access the Internet through the same server, you know that it, along with the router and the ISP connection, is functioning properly.

If none of these is the cause of the problem, the difficulty lies in the ISP's network or in the Internet itself. The problem might clear up by itself in a few minutes or hours, but if Internet access is essential to the business, the ISP should be contacted immediately. Dealing with the ISP might be the responsibility of a senior technical support representative, so you might want to escalate the call if the ISP is the problem.

In Alice's case, you determine that the router is functioning normally because you can connect to a Web site using your own browser.

Possible Cause: Internet Communication Problem

The next step in narrowing down the cause of Alice's problem is to determine exactly what kinds of network communications are affected. During this procedure, you should methodically test the entire data connection from Alice's computer to the Internet. When a failure occurs, you should trace backward, component by component, until you isolate the source of the problem.

As a help desk technician, you should begin this process while you are still on the telephone with the user. First, ask the user to try connecting to a different Web site. Using one of the default links supplied with the browser is a good idea because these sites are nearly always in operation, and you minimize the possibility of user error. If you must have the user type in a Web site address, dictate the exact URL to the user, and keep it simple, such as *www.microsoft.com*. If the browser can connect to other Web sites, you know that the network, the router, and the Internet connection are functioning properly. In this case, the problem can nearly always be traced to either a Web site that is down or to user error. If the user's Web browser cannot connect to any other Web sites, you should then determine whether any other network communications are possible.

Next, ask the user to open a different client application and try to connect to the Internet. It does not matter which application you select, as long as it connects directly to a Web site. For example, an e-mail client or a newsreader is a good choice, as long as the user will not connect to a mail or news server on the local network. As a last resort, you can always have the user launch the File Transfer Protocol (FTP) client from the command line. Virtually every operating system that supports Transmission Control Protocol/Internet Protocol (TCP/IP) includes an FTP client, but you might have to walk the user carefully through the process of connecting to an FTP server.

If the user cannot access Web sites with a Web browser but can connect to the Internet using a different client application, you know that the problem lies in the browser software running on the user's computer. If the user cannot connect to the Internet using any client application (and other users can), the next step is to determine which part of the computer's Internet access architecture is failing.

Possible Cause: DNS Failure

One of the most common causes of Internet access problems (and of the error message that Alice received) is the failure of the user's computer to resolve DNS names into the Internet Protocol (IP) addresses that client applications need to communicate with Internet servers. DNS servers are a vital part of any Internet communication that uses a name to refer to an Internet server. IP communications are based solely on IP addresses, not names, so the first thing that a client application does when given a name of a computer, such as *www.microsoft.com,* is send the name to a DNS server for resolution. When you type the name of a server into your Web browser, part of the brief delay that you experience before the Web page starts loading is the result of the time it takes for the client application to generate a DNS Request message containing the server name, send it to a DNS server, and wait for a reply from the DNS server containing the IP addresses associated with the name. Only then can the client transmit its first Hypertext Transfer Protocol (HTTP) message to the Web server.

Checking the TCP/IP Client's DNS Configuration

The address of the DNS server that a computer uses to resolve names is supplied as part of the system's TCP/IP client configuration. On a computer running Microsoft Windows XP, for example, the DNS server address is found in the Internet Protocol (TCP/IP) Properties dialog box, shown in Figure 12-3.

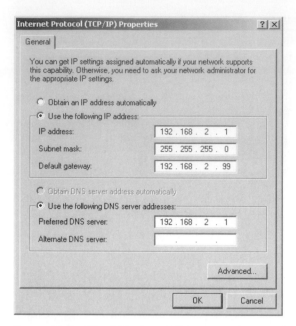

Figure 12-3   The Windows XP Internet Protocol (TCP/IP) Properties dialog box

If the addresses in the Preferred DNS Server and Alternate DNS Server fields in this dialog box do not point to DNS servers that are up and running, the name resolution process will fail when the user attempts to connect to a Web server, resulting in an error message.

The easiest way to test for a DNS name resolution problem is to use an IP address instead of a server name in the Web browser's URL field. For example, when the user's browser fails to connect to a Web server using its name but other computers can access the Internet, use the Ping program on another computer to resolve the name of the desired server into an IP address, using a command like the following:

```
ping servername
```

This command first displays the server's name followed by the server's IP address and then displays the results of the attempt to communicate with that server. If the attempt is successful, the program lists each of the replies received from the server, with information such as the number of data bytes included in the message, the time elapsed between the transmission of the request and the receipt of the reply, and the Time To Live (TTL) value for the transmission. On a computer running Windows XP, the Ping output appears as follows:

```
Pinging www.microsoft.com [38.144.95.172] with 32 bytes of data:

Reply from 38.144.95.172: bytes=32 time=320ms TTL=238
Reply from 38.144.95.172: bytes=32 time=280ms TTL=238
```

```
Reply from 38.144.95.172: bytes=32 time=381ms TTL=238
Reply from 38.144.95.172: bytes=32 time=280ms TTL=238
Ping statistics for 38.144.95.172:
    Packets: Sent = 4, Received = 4, Lost = 0 (0% loss),
Approximate round trip times in milli-seconds:
    Minimum = 280ms, Maximum =  381ms, Average =  315ms
```

> **NOTE   Ping Failures**   A failure of the Ping program to contact a Web
> server does not necessarily indicate a problem. Many Web servers today
> are located behind firewalls that block the Internet Control Message
> Protocol (ICMP) messages that Ping uses, to protect servers from ICMP-
> based denial-of-service (DoS) attacks. However, Ping should be able to
> resolve the DNS name, even if the Web server is not available.

If the Ping command fails to resolve the name (perhaps because one of the
network's DNS servers is not available), you can use the Nslookup command
to send a name resolution request to a particular DNS server that you know is
operational, on the local network or the Internet, as demonstrated in Chapter 11,
"Network Troubleshooting Tools."

If the Ping program successfully resolves the name, have the user replace the
server name in the browser's URL with the IP address you have discovered.
If the browser connects to the server with an IP address when using a server
name failed, there is definitely a problem with the DNS name resolution process.

DNS name resolution problems have two major causes: either the computer's
TCP/IP client is configured with incorrect DNS server addresses, or the DNS
servers themselves are not functioning properly. An easy way to check the
addresses of the DNS servers on a computer running Microsoft Windows is
to display the TCP/IP configuration by using the Ipconfig.exe program (for
computers running Microsoft Windows NT) or the Winipcfg.exe program
(for computers running Microsoft Windows Me, Microsoft Windows 95, and
Microsoft Windows 98). For more information about using these programs,
see Chapter 11, "Network Troubleshooting Tools." If the addresses are incorrect,
they must be changed, using the Internet Protocol (TCP/IP) Properties dialog box
shown in Figure 12-3.

> **NOTE   Troubleshooting in Person**   The user can conceivably perform
> all of the tests described thus far with instruction from a help desk
> technician over the telephone. However, you might want to modify the
> computer's TCP/IP configuration personally. Depending on the user's
> location and computing skills and the organization's technical support
> policies, you might decide to travel to the user's site and personally
> perform the tests on the computer or use a remote access tool such
> as Windows Remote Desktop.

If the computer was previously functioning properly, the way in which the DNS server addresses were changed might remain a mystery. When users are asked if they have changed anything in their computer's configuration recently, those who have been changing settings they do not understand usually answer "No." However, if your network uses Dynamic Host Configuration Protocol (DHCP) servers to configure its TCP/IP clients automatically, you should definitely check the DHCP server configuration to see if it is supplying incorrect addresses to the network clients. If it is, do not manually change the DNS server configuration in the user's computer, but correct the DHCP server's configuration instead. Also, if you are using DHCP, you should check the client DNS settings to make sure it does not have a manually configured DNS server address when it is supposed to get one from the server. After you have corrected either of these problems, you can repair the user's computer by renewing the DHCP lease with the Ipconfig.exe or Winipcfg.exe program.

Checking the DNS Server

If the DNS server addresses in the user's TCP/IP client configuration are correct, the problem might lie in the DNS servers themselves or in the computer's network connection to the DNS servers. The DNS servers that a network uses for Internet name resolution might be supplied by the organization's ISP, or they might be located onsite. If the DNS servers are at fault, multiple users should be experiencing problems.

If the DNS servers belong to the ISP, all you can do is test to see if they are available. If you can contact the DNS servers using the Ping command with an IP address, you know that they are up and running. However, this does not necessarily mean that they can process DNS Request messages. Nonetheless, if you can execute a Ping command using a server name successfully, you have proven that the DNS server can resolve the server's name into its IP address.

If the DNS servers belong to your organization, you can check them more thoroughly. However, this is another area in which the first-tier technician might escalate the call to a senior technician. A Ping test can determine that the DNS server is functioning, but checking the status of the DNS server software itself depends on the operating system and the application software running on the computer. For example, on a computer running Microsoft Windows Server 2003 and the DNS Server service, you can start by opening the Services console from the Start menu's Administrative Tools program group and checking to see that the DNS Server service is running, as shown in Figure 12-4.

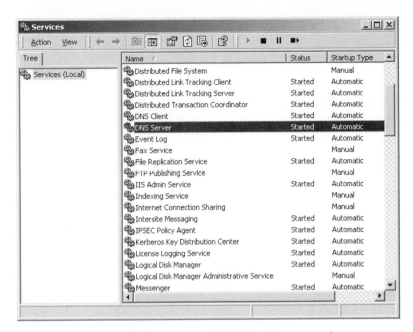

Figure 12-4   The Windows Server 2003 Services console

If the service is not running, you must find out why. The Startup Type field for the DNS Server service should be set to Automatic, indicating that the service loads when the computer starts. If the Startup Type field is set to Manual or Disabled, this is the reason the service is not running. However, before you manually start the service or change the Startup Type setting to Automatic, check with your colleagues to see whether someone has configured it this way for a good reason. If the Startup Type is set to Automatic but the service is not running, one of following three things has occurred:

■   Someone manually stopped the service.

■   The service failed to start.

■   The service shut itself down.

Check the computer's Event Viewer console (also accessible from the Administrative Tools group) for log entries that might explain why the service is not running. If the service failed to start during boot time, there should be a log entry indicating the reason. Various types of environmental problems could cause the service to shut down, including a memory shortage or a configuration problem. Troubleshooting issues like these require knowledge of the operating system and the DNS Server software.

If the DNS Server service is running but names are still not being resolved, you need to look at the server software and the DNS communications process in more detail. Examining the DNS server's configuration files is a good place to start. For example, if the server's list containing the names and addresses of the DNS root name servers has somehow been modified or erased, this would prevent names from being resolved, even if everything else is functioning correctly. The DNS server's own network connection and Internet access are also vital to the name resolution process. The server itself might be functioning properly, but if network conditions prevent it from receiving DNS Request messages from the client or if it cannot access the Internet to relay the requests to other DNS servers, the name resolution process stops.

If the DNS server's configuration files show no obvious problems, you might need to use a protocol analyzer to determine whether the DNS server is communicating with the network and the Internet properly. A protocol analyzer is a software program that captures network traffic and displays it for study, as described in Chapter 11, "Network Troubleshooting Tools." Using the protocol analyzer, you can see the DNS Request packets arriving at the server, and the server's own DNS Requests being transmitted to other DNS servers on the Internet, as shown in Figure 12-5.

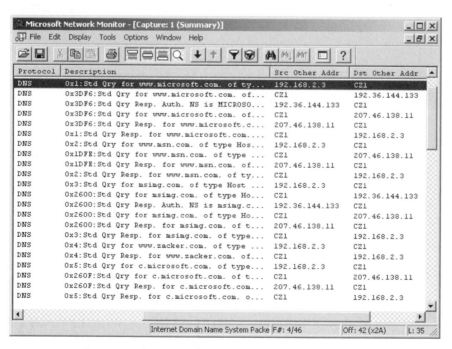

Figure 12-5   A captured DNS traffic exchange, as displayed in a protocol analyzer

To analyze network traffic in this way, you must be familiar with what is known as a *baseline*. In other words, you have to know what the network traffic pattern is supposed to look like before you can determine what's wrong. By analyzing the traffic traveling to and from the server, you might be able to isolate the problem as being in the server's communications with the local network or in its communications with the Internet.

> **NOTE** **Troubleshooting WINS Name Resolution** The procedures for diagnosing and repairing DNS name resolution problems described here are also useful in other scenarios. For example, computers running Windows might use the Windows Internet Name Service (WINS) to resolve Network Basic Input/Output System (NetBIOS) names into IP addresses, just as they use DNS servers to resolve DNS names. The same type of client and server configuration problems affecting DNS name resolution can also affect the WINS name resolution process. You can check the addresses of the WINS servers in the client computer's TCP/IP configuration and the functionality of the WINS servers in much the same way you check the equivalent DNS resources.

Possible Cause: LAN Communications Problem

If the user's problem is not being caused by an Internet communications problem or a DNS name resolution problem, it is time to start examining the computer's general network communication capabilities. You should begin by having the user try to access resources on the local network. Local network resources can include shared server drives, internal network applications (such as e-mail or database servers), and tools like Windows Explorer. The best way to start is by having the user try to access nearby resources.

Testing the Local Hub

The first test might be for the user to open My Network Places in Windows Explorer and see if computers belonging to other nearby users are visible. The assumption here is that other computers nearby are connected to the same network hub as the user experiencing the problem. If there is an internal network communications difficulty, the object is to narrow down where it might be.

You should have information about which computers are connected to specific hubs and LANs, preferably in the form of a map or diagram that shows the cables and connection devices that make up the network. This resource should be developed during the initial planning stages of the network and should be maintained consistently throughout its life. Relying on someone's memory of the network installation makes the technical support process far more difficult, especially as people leave the company or move on to other positions. You should also remember that users probably do not have access to this type of network information and would not know what to do with it if they did.

Windows Explorer displays the computers on the network in terms of domains and workgroups, which probably do not correspond to the hubs and LANs that form the network's physical configuration. If you and the user are still working together over the telephone at this point, the user might not understand many of your instructions, so it is important for you to explain carefully what must be done, without introducing unnecessary technical details. In this case, you might consider traveling to the user's site, if that is practical.

Testing the Computer Connection

If the user cannot see other computers connected to the same hub in My Network Places, the problem is likely to be in the user's connection to the hub, in the computer hardware or software, or in the user's procedures. In some cases, testing the computer's connection to the hub can be quite easy. If the computer is connected to the hub using a prefabricated network cable, you can try replacing the cable with one that you know is functioning properly. If the computer is connected to the hub using an internal cable run, begin by switching the network cable plugged into the user's computer with a cable from a nearby computer that is working properly. If the user's computer can now access the network, you know that the problem is somewhere in the original cable run, and you can start trying to determine exactly where the problem is.

> **NOTE   Internal Cabling**   Internal cable installations use three lengths of cable per connection: a patch cable connecting the computer to the wall plate, the cable inside the walls or ceilings running from the wall plate to the patch panel, and another patch cable connecting the patch panel port to a hub port. Because the patch cables are exposed, it is easy to test them first by replacing them. For more information about internal cable installations, see Chapter 2, "Network Cabling."

Begin by swapping out the patch cables at both ends of the connection with replacements that you know are working properly. If the patch cables are not the cause of the problem, you can proceed to test the internal cable run. If you have the proper cable testing equipment, you can test the cable run that way. You can use a multifunction cable tester, a wire map tester, or even an inexpensive tone generator and locator to determine whether the cable is wired properly and signals are getting through.

If there is a break in the cable, the multifunction tester can also tell you where it is in relation to the end you are testing from. If you do not have cable testing equipment, you can plug the patch cables at both ends into a different cable run that you know is working properly. Swapping out equipment wherever possible is one of the most basic and most effective troubleshooting techniques.

> **NOTE   Testing Cables**   For more information about cable testing equipment, see Chapter 11, "Network Troubleshooting Tools."

Problems with internal cable runs do not usually happen by themselves. Usually they result when someone working in the spaces where the cables are located accidentally damages one of the cables. In fact, just moving a cable inside a drop ceiling closer to a fluorescent light fixture can be enough to create communication problems on that connection. Therefore, it is strongly recommended that all cables be well secured during installation, even when they are running through relatively inaccessible areas, such as walls and ceilings.

Testing Hub Connections

If the user's computer can see and access other computers connected to the same hub, the next step is to try to access other computers on the same LAN that are connected to different hubs. If the user can access computers attached to the same hub but cannot access the other computers on the LAN connected to different hubs, the problem might be in the connection between the user's hub and the rest of the network. What you check next depends on the physical configuration of the network. For example, if the user's hub is connected to another hub, that connection might not be functioning properly for several reasons, such as the following:

- **The cable run connecting the two hubs is faulty.** As with any network communications problem, the network medium itself could be at fault. If the hubs are connected by a prefabricated cable, it could have a damaged connector or a kink that caused a break in one or more of the wires. If the hubs are connected by an internally installed cable run, the cable connectors could be wired incorrectly or one of the path cables could be damaged. Use the cable testing procedures described earlier to check the connection.

- **The connection between the hubs does not have a crossover circuit in it.** When you connect one Ethernet hub to another hub, you must plug one end of the cable into the uplink port on one (and only one) of the hubs. This reverses the crossover circuit in the connection, so that the crossovers in the two connected hubs do not cancel each other out. The problem could be that neither end of the cable is plugged into an uplink port or that both ends are plugged into an uplink port. Some hubs have a switch that you use to specify whether one of the ports functions as an uplink port. If this switch is set incorrectly, the result is the same as plugging the cable into the wrong port.

■ **One or both of the hub ports is damaged.**   The hub unit itself might not be functioning properly because of a damaged connector in one of the ports, or for other reasons. Check the link pulse light-emitting diodes (LEDs) for the ports used to connect the two hubs together. If both LEDs are not lit when the hubs are connected, the two hubs are not communicating properly.

All of the three preceding problems can also affect a switch.

> **NOTE** **Exam Objectives**   Objective 4.12 for the Network+ exam requires students, "given a network troubleshooting scenario involving a wiring/infrastructure problem, [to be able to] identify the cause of the problem (e.g., bad media, interference, network hardware)."

Testing Router Connections

If the user can access computers on other segments of the same LAN, you need to test connections to other LANs. This assumes that the organization's network is really an internetwork that consists of multiple LANs connected by routers. Once again, you can test the computer's connectivity simply by using Windows Explorer to access computers that are located on other networks. If the user's computer can access resources in all of the LANs that make up the organization's internetwork, the problem is not one of network connectivity, and you need to look at the computer itself.

If the user's computer can access resources in some LANs but not others, the problem might be in one of the routers that connect the networks together. The difficulty of locating the malfunction depends on how complicated the internetwork configuration is. If the network consists of 30 LANs interconnected by dozens of routers with redundant access paths, finding one malfunctioning router can be a complicated process, one that almost certainly has to be attended to by the technicians at the top of the organization's technical support hierarchy.

One method for isolating the router causing the user's problem is to use the Traceroute utility to see exactly where the packets generated by the computer are going. Traceroute is a TCP/IP command-line utility that transmits packets to a given destination and displays a list of the routers that the packets pass through on the way to that destination. Run Traceroute with the name of the Web server the user is trying to reach, and a display similar to the one shown below will indicate exactly how far the packets are going through the local internetwork:

```
Tracing route to www.fineartschool.com [206.73.118.1]
over a maximum of 30 hops:
1 <10   ms   1   ms  <10   ms     192.168.6.1
2  1    ms   1   ms  <10   ms     192.168.10.1
3  1    ms  <10  ms  <10   ms     192.168.17.1
```

When the packets reach a router that is malfunctioning, Traceroute should stop displaying information. In other words, the last router listed in the Traceroute display should be that of the last properly functioning router in the path to the destination. With knowledge of your network's configuration, you should be able to figure out which router the packets are trying to go to next. This is the router that either is not receiving the packets or is not forwarding them properly, causing the user's communication failure.

For example, suppose that your network consists of a number of LANs containing user computers, all of which are connected to a single backbone LAN, as shown in Figure 12-6.

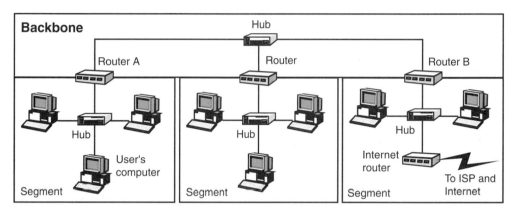

Figure 12-6   Routers provide communications between LANs; a router failure can be inconvenient or catastrophic.

> **NOTE   Exam Objectives**   Objective 4.10 for the Network+ exam requires students, "given a troubleshooting scenario involving a network with a particular physical topology (i.e., bus, star/hierarchical, mesh, ring, and wireless) and including a network diagram, [to be able to] identify the network area affected and the cause of the problem."

One of the user LANs also contains the router that connects the network to the Internet. Any of the following scenarios could cause the problem that Alice is experiencing. All of these scenarios are likely to cause more than one call to the help desk, with the last scenario probably causing a flood of complaints:

- If the router connecting Alice's LAN to the backbone (Router A) fails, Alice's computer would be able to communicate with the computers on her own LAN, but traffic could not reach the backbone or be forwarded to any of the other LANs, including the LAN containing the router that is connected to the Internet. This problem would also affect all of the other computers on Alice's LAN.

■ If the router connecting the backbone to the LAN containing the Internet router (Router B) fails, all of the users on the LANs other than the one containing the Internet router would be able to communicate among themselves, but not with users on the Internet router LAN. Also, no one would be able to access the Internet except for the users on the LAN containing the Internet router.

■ If a hub on the backbone LAN fails, the result would be the same for the user but would also affect all of the traffic between LANs on the entire internetwork. In this case, the internetwork would be reduced to a collection of unconnected LANs because the backbone is unavailable to carry traffic between them. A cable break on the backbone LAN isolates the LAN served by that cable from the rest of the network.

Sometimes router failure is a less likely cause of communication problems because of the configuration of the internetwork. The internetwork in this example has only one path between each pair of LANs. To guard against the outages caused by router failures, many internetworks are designed with redundant routers and backbones so that two major failures would have to occur at the same time to cause any of the three preceding problem scenarios.

Test your knowledge of the effects of various network faults by completing Exercise 12-2, "Network Hardware Problems," now.

Router failure usually does not result in just one help call. Alice's problem is far more likely to be caused by a procedural error, a configuration error in her computer, or possibly a minor network problem. A router failure would probably result in a general network failure that would cause a large number of simultaneous complaints, which would immediately be brought to the attention of the network's senior support staff and not left to the help desk. When the network administrators are aware of the problem, the role of the first-tier technician is to inform users that they know of the problem and that a fix is forthcoming. There is no need to troubleshoot each call individually when all the calls have the same cause.

Possible Cause: Computer Configuration Problem

If the user's computer cannot access the network in any way and you have determined that neither the network nor the cable connecting the computer to the network is at fault, it is time to look at the computer itself. Although it might seem that it has been a long journey to this point, if a user experiences a problem that prevents any network access, you can omit the hub and router troubleshooting processes described in the previous sections. You might even proceed to this point as soon as you determine that no network communication is possible.

If you determine that the problem is in the computer, the difficulty can exist at almost any level, and it is a good idea to use the Open Systems Interconnection (OSI) reference model to list the various possible causes, as explained in the following sections.

Physical Layer Problems

If you have determined that the cable used to connect the computer to the network is functioning properly, the problem could be in the computer's network interface adapter itself. One common cause of communication problems is a network interface card (NIC) that is loose in its bus slot. If the NIC is not installed firmly into the slot and secured in place with a screw or another device, a tug on the network cable can loosen the card and break the connection between the NIC and the computer. If the NIC is completely disconnected, most operating systems report that the device is not functioning. However, if the NIC is only slightly loosened and not pulled completely out of the slot, the problem could be intermittent and especially difficult to detect. The Device Manager application in Windows NT can report when a device is or is not functioning properly, as shown in Figure 12-7.

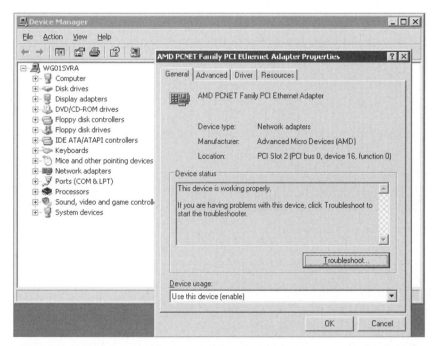

Figure 12-7   The Windows XP Device Manager displays information about the network interface adapter and other hardware devices.

NOTE   Exam Objectives   Objective 4.3 for the Network+ exam requires students, "given a troubleshooting scenario involving a remote connectivity problem (e.g., authentication failure, protocol configuration, physical connectivity), [to be able to] identify the cause of the problem."

The network interface adapter could also be physically damaged by a power surge, static electricity, or a manufacturing defect. If the adapter's cable connector is damaged, the contacts in the cable plug might not connect properly to the contacts in the adapter's jack. Such problems are difficult to detect, and you usually check the network interface adapter only when you have ruled out all other possible causes of the problem. The solution is nearly always to replace the network interface adapter, but technicians rarely do this until they have checked the configuration of the computer's networking software. If the network interface adapter comes with a diagnostic program, however, and a loopback connector is available, you can test the adapter without having to open up the computer.

> **NOTE** **Loopback Testing**   *For more information about network adapter loopback testing, see Chapter 11, "Network Troubleshooting Tools."*

Data-Link Layer Problems

Along with the network interface adapter itself, the network interface adapter device driver implements the data-link layer protocol in the computer. The driver must be configured with the same hardware settings as the network interface adapter so that the two can communicate. Incorrect configuration settings can prevent a computer from communicating with the network, but this generally does not occur in a computer that has been functioning properly, unless someone manually changes the configuration settings or a device installation affects them.

When something used to work but now does not, you should ask the user what has changed on the computer. Has the user installed any new hardware or software? Has the user changed any configuration settings? The answer from the user is usually "No," even when it becomes increasingly obvious that something has changed.

In most cases, the hardware settings of both the network interface adapter and the network interface adapter driver are configurable. You generally configure the adapter driver using an interface provided by the operating system, like that shown in Figure 12-8.

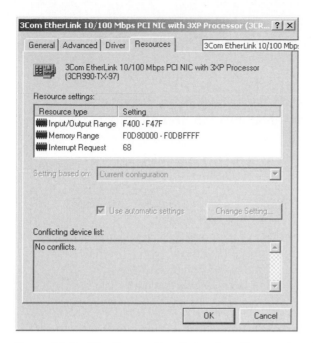

Figure 12-8 The Properties dialog box for a network interface adapter driver

Today, most network interface adapters are installed using plug and play (PnP), which automatically configures both the adapter and its driver to use the same settings. The settings chosen are based on an evaluation of the hardware requirements for all of the devices in the computer, so installing a new piece of hardware into the computer can cause PnP to alter the settings of existing devices. Although not common, it is possible for PnP to select hardware settings that cause either the adapter or its driver to malfunction. If you determine that some new hardware device has been installed, you might have to disable or remove it to determine whether it is the cause of the network interface adapter's configuration problem. If it is, you might have to manually configure the new device to use it in the computer.

If the network interface adapter configuration or driver parameters have been manually changed (presumably by accident), you should delete the device from the system configuration (again using Device Manager), restart the computer, and let PnP detect the adapter and reinstall it, reconfiguring both the adapter and the driver in the process.

Network and Transport Layer Problems

Although they span other layers as well, the primary functions of the TCP/IP protocols are at the network and transport layers, and the TCP/IP client configuration is one of the chief causes of network communication problems. Improperly configured DNS server addresses can prevent the computer from resolving server names into addresses and, as a result, prevent the user from accessing the Internet. WINS servers perform the same type of name resolution process for NetBIOS names, and incorrect WINS server addresses can prevent the computer from accessing some of the other computers on the network. A computer running Windows that is not configured with WINS server addresses can still resolve the name of other computers on its own LAN by using broadcast messages. However, broadcasts cannot reach the computers on other LANs, so WINS is needed to resolve these names.

> **NOTE   Using NetBIOS**   WINS support is included in Microsoft Windows 2000, Windows XP, and Windows Server 2003 only to enable the computer to communicate with other computers running older operating systems that use NetBIOS names, such as Windows NT and Windows 98. The current versions of Windows use the Active Directory directory service, which relies on DNS servers to resolve names.

Incorrect DNS and WINS server addresses can prevent a computer from accessing other computers by name, but other TCP/IP configuration parameters can have an even greater effect on network communications. An incorrect IP address or subnet mask can completely prevent all network communications, and—even worse—an IP address duplicated on a second computer can prevent both computers from accessing the network. Therefore, network communications can be interrupted if the IP address on the user's computer has been changed or if a computer somewhere else on the network has been configured to use the same IP address as the user's computer.

To test for a duplicate IP address, shut down the user's computer and use another workstation to ping the IP address of the user's computer. If you receive a response to the Ping command, another computer is using that same IP address.

An incorrect or missing default gateway parameter can also cause the user's problem. A workstation that is not configured with a correct default gateway address can access the other computers on its own LAN, but it cannot access any of the other LANs on the internetwork. Without a default gateway address, the computer does not know where to send packets that are destined for other networks. This prevents the user's Web browser from connecting to any sites on the Internet. In Windows NT, to modify any of the TCP/IP configuration parameters listed here, use the Internet Protocol (TCP/IP) Properties dialog box as described earlier in this chapter.

If the network has DHCP servers that configure the network's TCP/IP clients, none of the fields in the workstation's Internet Protocol (TCP/IP) Properties dialog box should have values in them. Manually configured TCP/IP parameters take precedence over those supplied by DHCP. If someone has been "experimenting" by supplying his own TCP/IP values, remove them before reactivating the DHCP client.

You also need to know what allocation mode the DHCP servers are using. If they are using automatic allocation, which assigns the IP address to clients permanently, moving the computer to a different subnet requires that you manually release the assigned IP address and renew it so that the DHCP server can assign one from the proper subnet. This is another way for the computer to have an incorrect IP address. If you move computers around on the network frequently, consider using dynamic allocation, which leases addresses to computers for a short period of time and renews them each time the computer starts.

Application Layer Problems

Application layer networking protocols are generally not configurable, but problems at the application level can affect network communications. Virus infections, for example, can affect network communications, and new viruses that can have unpredictable effects on a computer are constantly being invented. If you do not already have antivirus software installed on the computer, you should install it, make sure the virus signatures are updated, and run a complete system scan, just to be safe.

Although it does not affect Internet access directly, having the incorrect network client installed on a computer can also cause network communications problems. For computers running Windows, the Client for Microsoft Networks module provides the redirector that enables the computer to send resource access requests to other computers running Windows. If this component is removed, a break in the protocol stack occurs and network communication ceases.

Applications themselves can be damaged or improperly configured as well, interfering with network communications. For example, if Alice were to modify the configuration of her browser, causing it to access the Internet by dialing out to an ISP instead of using the LAN, she would be unable to access any Web sites if a modem was not installed or a dial-up account was not properly configured. This problem would be specific to the browser, however, and would be caught when you had Alice try to use another application to access the Internet.

> **NOTE**   **Exam Objectives**   Objective 4.11 for the Network+ exam requires students, "given a network troubleshooting scenario involving a client connectivity problem (e.g., incorrect protocol/client software/authentication configuration, or insufficient rights/permission), [to be able to] identify the cause of the problem."

Possible Cause: User Error

User error is one of the most common causes of help desk calls. Listing this possible cause last does not imply that you should go through all of the testing procedures described thus far before addressing the possibility of user error. In fact, you can often quickly determine that the user's equipment and the network are functioning properly and that the problem must be in something the user did. However, in the interests of diplomacy, it is often a good idea to be certain that a procedural error is the problem before you broach the subject with the user. Some people are perfectly willing to admit that they might be at fault, while others can be very sensitive about it. Part of your job is to resolve callers' problems without making them feel foolish, a skill that is becoming increasingly rare in the technical support field.

User error can easily be the reason for a failure to access a Web site, and it can sometimes be difficult to detect when working with the user over the telephone. Many common Internet access problems are caused by entering incorrect URLs into the browser. For this reason, when you are having the user test the system by trying to access other sites, it is best to use existing bookmarks or favorites whenever possible. It might seem as though the user is experiencing a severe Internet connectivity problem, and you might be tempted to perform all sorts of network and hardware tests like those described earlier. Before engaging in such tests, however, make sure that the user is not making beginners' errors such as typing URLs with backslashes instead of forward slashes or inserting three forward slashes after the *http:* prefix instead of two.

In fact, user error is the cause of Alice's problem. She had somehow gotten the impression that three forward slashes were correct and was using them even when you were working with her over the telephone dictating the URLs of other sites she should try to test her Internet connectivity. You started your dictation with *www*, knowing that typing the *http://* prefix is not necessary in most cases, but Alice added it to each URL on her own, assuming that it had to be there, using three forward slashes instead of two. You could have solved this particular problem almost immediately if you had gone to Alice's location and watched her type the URLs. This is not to say that every call to the help desk should be immediately followed by a trip to the user's location. In many cases, that would be impractical. However, this particular case demonstrates how important the communication between the technician and the user can be.

Many other common procedural errors can interfere with a user's network connectivity, and many of these can be very difficult to catch over the telephone. Sometimes there is no substitute for watching what the user is doing. User logons, for example, are a common source of difficulties. Users often call the help desk because they cannot log on to the network. If they have been trying to log on repeatedly and are failing every time, you should first check to see if the user has been locked out of the account. Many networks are configured to disable accounts after a certain number of failed logon attempts, in an effort to prevent brute-force attacks by intruders. (A *brute-force attack*, in this case, is an attempt to penetrate an authentication protocol by trying every possible password.) If the account is not locked, password policies might also be to blame. Users might ignore a message telling them that a periodic password change is required or might attempt to reuse an old password when policy dictates against it. Two other common occurrences among Windows users are trying to log on to the wrong domain or using the wrong account to log on to the local system. The Domain setting in the Logon dialog box might have been changed somehow, which is something that you are not likely to realize without actually watching the user try to log on.

SUMMARY

- The process of troubleshooting a network involves several steps, including identifying, duplicating, isolating, resolving, and documenting the problem.

- Isolating a network problem is a matter of eliminating hardware and software components that are not possible causes.

- Maintaining a carefully documented and methodically applied troubleshooting process is an essential part of maintaining a network.

- Administrative tasks such as record keeping, call prioritizing, and call escalation are essential activities in a professional technical support organization.

- The first step in troubleshooting any networking problem is to gather information from the user experiencing the problem.

- For an Internet access problem, checking the router that connects the network to the Internet service provider (ISP) is fast and easy, and is always a good idea.

- Domain Name System (DNS) name resolution problems are a common cause of Internet access failures.

- Solving a network communications problem is a matter of isolating the component that is malfunctioning.

- If the network is functioning properly, you should look at the user's computer for the problem.

- User error is also a common cause of Internet access difficulties, but you should approach this subject delicately with the user.

EXERCISES

Exercise 12-1: Network Troubleshooting

1. Place the following steps of the problem isolation process in the proper order:
    a. Reproduce the problem using a different computer.
    b. Reproduce the problem yourself.
    c. Have the user reproduce the problem.
    d. Reproduce the problem using a different user account.

Exercise 12-2: Network Hardware Problems

On an internetwork consisting of several user segments connected by a backbone, with an Internet router connected directly to the backbone, specify whether the following network conditions would normally cause Internet access problems for one user only, for all of the users connected to one hub, for all of the users on one LAN, or for the entire internetwork.

1. Both ends of a cable connecting two hubs are plugged into uplink ports.

2. The router connecting the network to the ISP is down.

3. The cable connecting a user's computer to the hub is cut.

4. The ISP's connection to the Internet fails.

5. The router connecting a user LAN to the backbone malfunctions.

REVIEW QUESTIONS

1. To which of the following problems would you assign the highest priority for your network support team? Explain why.

   a. The printer in the Order Entry department is not working.

   b. The corporate e-mail server is down.

   c. A hub is malfunctioning in the Sales department.

   d. The CEO's workstation is locked up.

2. In a two-tiered network support system, what do the tiers refer to?

   a. File servers storing network documentation

   b. Priorities for trouble tickets

   c. Problem call databases

   d. Technicians of different skill levels

3. Without a DNS server, a user can still access the Internet using which of the following techniques?

   a. By using links saved as favorites or bookmarks instead of typing URLs

   b. By using NetBIOS names instead of DNS names

   c. By using hardware addresses instead of DNS names

   d. By using IP addresses instead of DNS names

4. A user cannot access the shared server drive that he uses every day, where his working files are stored. Which of the following questions would you ask the user first? State your reason.

   a. Can you access any other network resources?

   b. Did you have any problems logging on to the network?

   c. Can you access the Internet?

   d. Is your network cable connected to the computer?

5. Which of the following is *not* a possible cause of Internet access failure?

   a. A missing WINS server address

   b. A DNS server failure

   c. An ISP connection failure

   d. A mistyped URL

6. Which of the following network and transport layer problems can be caused by another computer on the network?

   a. A missing DNS server address

   b. An incorrect subnet mask

   c. A duplicate IP address

   d. An incorrect default gateway address

7. A computer running Windows without a WINS server address cannot access which of the following resources?

   a. Internet Web sites

   b. Computers running Windows that are connected to the same hub

   c. Computers that are not running Windows and that are connected to the same LAN

   d. Computers running Windows that are connected to other LANs

8. Which of the following should you do if a user has changed the network interface adapter configuration and can no longer access the network?

    a. Replace the adapter with a new one.

    b. Delete the adapter driver and let PnP reinstall it.

    c. Modify the adapter's configuration parameters by using the utility supplied by the manufacturer.

    d. Modify the adapter driver's configuration parameters by using the operating system interface.

9. Which of the following is the easiest way to test a patch cable for a fault?

    a. Replace it with one that you know is working properly.

    b. Connect it to a multifunction cable tester.

    c. Plug the computer end of the cable into the wall plate and the wall plate end into the computer.

    d. Connect it to a computer that you know is functioning properly.

10. When a computer lacks a correct default gateway address, how far do packets destined for other networks travel?

    a. As far as the Internet access router

    b. As far as the backbone

    c. As far as the hub

    d. As far as the local network

11. Which of the following network problems generally affects services other than Internet access on a Windows-based network?

    a. An ISP connection failure

    b. A backbone failure

    c. A DNS failure

    d. A T-1 failure

CASE SCENARIOS

Case Scenario 12-1: Identifying the Affected Area

A user experiencing a network communications problem calls the help desk, and you are sent over to help him. The user can re-create the problem on his computer. You have him log on by using another computer connected to the same LAN hub as his computer and try to reproduce the problem there. On the other computer, the problem does not occur. Based on this information, which of the following can you assume to be true?

    a. The problem must be internal to the user's computer.

    b. The hub is not the source of the user's problem.

    c. The cable connecting the user's computer to the hub must be faulty.

    d. None of the above.

Case Scenario 12-2: Assigning Priorities

During a busy shift at the network help desk at Wingtip Toys, a call comes in at 9:05 A.M. from an angry user whose mouse is not working. At 9:07 A.M., the vice president of the Marketing department calls to report that the hard drive in the file server where the company's ad campaigns are stored has failed. At 9:15 A.M., the manager of the Order Entry department calls to report that the e-mail server that delivers the product orders generated through the company's Web site is down. Between 9:25 and 9:45 A.M., four users on the LAN in the Sales department cannot access the company intranet server containing insurance forms. As the help desk manager, which of these problems should you address first, and why?

    a. Fix the user's mouse because her call came in first.

    b. Fix the Marketing department's file server because a vice president outranks the other users.

    c. Fix the Order Entry e-mail server because it is needed to receive incoming orders.

    d. Fix the Sales department's intranet server access because this problem has generated the most complaints.

Case Scenario 12-3: Locating a Problem's Source

You are working at the network help desk for a large corporation when several calls come in over the course of a few minutes, all from users reporting failures to access Internet resources. Some of the users cannot access Web sites, while others cannot use FTP or retrieve their Internet e-mail. All of the calls come from users scattered around the third floor of the building, which has four hubs joined together to form a single LAN. The LAN is connected to the building's backbone network with a router. Which of the following would you check first as the possible source of the problem?

    a. The router connecting the third-floor LAN to the building's backbone network

    b. The hubs connecting the computers on the third floor to the network

    c. The router connecting the corporate network to the Internet

    d. The users' TCP/IP configuration parameters

GLOSSARY

2B + D An alternative name for the Basic Rate Interface (BRI) service provided by the Integrated Services Digital Network (ISDN).

5-4-3 rule An Ethernet cabling guideline stating that an Ethernet local area network (LAN) can consist of up to five cable segments, connected by four repeaters. Up to three of those cable segments can be mixing segments.

1Base5 An early Ethernet twisted pair specification that was designed to coexist with telephone signals on the other two cable pairs. 1Base5 never achieved wide acceptance, due in part to its slow 1 Mbps transmission speed.

10Base2 Another name for the Ethernet physical layer specification (also known as thin Ethernet, ThinNet, or Cheapernet) that uses RG-58 coaxial cable in a bus topology. The "10" refers to the network's speed of 10 Mbps, the "base" refers to the network's baseband transmissions, and the "2" refers to the network's maximum segment length of approximately 200 meters (actually 185 meters).

10Base5 Another name for the Ethernet physical layer specification that is also known as thick Ethernet or ThickNet, which uses RG-8 coaxial cable in a bus topology. The "10" refers to the network's speed of 10 Mbps, the "base" refers to the network's baseband transmissions, and the "5" refers to the network's maximum segment length of 500 meters.

10Base-F A collective term for the three 10-Mbps Ethernet physical layer specifications that use fiber optic cable, as defined in Institute of Electrical and Electronics Engineers (IEEE) 802.3, including 10Base-FB, 10Base-FL, and 10Base-FP. The use of fiber optic cable for Ethernet networks was relatively rare until the advent of Fast Ethernet because the 10-Mbps speed limitation of the 10Base-F networks made them impractical.

10Base-FB Another name for one of three 10-Mbps Ethernet physical layer standards defined in the Institute of Electrical and Electronics Engineers (IEEE) 802.3 document that use 62.5/125 multimode fiber optic cable in a star topology. 10Base-FB has a maximum segment length of 2000 meters and was intended for use as a backbone solution to connect hubs over long distances using synchronous signaling. Like the other 10Base-F specifications, it was rarely used.

10Base-FL Another name for one of three 10-Mbps Ethernet physical layer standards defined in the Institute of Electrical and Electronics Engineers (IEEE) 802.3 document that use 62.5/125 multimode fiber optic cable in a star topology. 10Base-FL has a maximum segment length of 2000 meters and can connect two repeaters, two computers, or a computer to a repeater. Like the other 10Base-F specifications, it was rarely used.

10Base-FP Another name for one of three 10-Mbps Ethernet physical layer standards defined in the Institute of Electrical and Electronics Engineers (IEEE) 802.3 document that use 62.5/125 multimode fiber optic cable in a star topology. 10Base-FP has a maximum segment length of 500 meters and uses a passive star coupler to connect up to 33 computers. It was designed to be the desktop fiber optic solution of the 10Base-F specifications, but, like the other 10Base-F specifications, it was rarely used.

10Base-T Another name for an Ethernet physical layer specification that uses unshielded twisted pair (UTP) cables in a star topology. The "10" refers to the network's speed of 10 Mbps, the "base" refers to the network's baseband transmissions, and the "T" refers to the use of twisted pair cable. The maximum cable segment length for a 10Base-T network is 100 meters.

100Base-FX Another name for a 100-Mbps Fast Ethernet physical layer specification defined in the Institute of Electrical and Electronics Engineers (IEEE) 802.3u document that uses 62.5/125 multimode fiber optic cable in a star topology with a maximum segment length of 412 meters and runs at 100 Mbps.

100Base-T A collective term for the three 100-Mbps Ethernet physical layer specifications defined in the Institute of Electrical and Electronics Engineers (IEEE) 802.3u document and commonly known as Fast Ethernet. The three physical layer options for Fast Ethernet are 100Base-TX, 100Base-T4, and 100Base-FX.

100Base-T2 An unimplemented Fast Ethernet physical layer specification that called for the use of two of the wire pairs in a Category 3 unshielded twisted pair (UTP) cable.

100Base-T4 Another name for a 100-Mbps Fast Ethernet physical layer specification defined in the Institute of Electrical and Electronics Engineers (IEEE) 802.3u document that uses Category 3 (CAT3) unshielded twisted pair (UTP) cable in a star topology, with a maximum segment length of 100 meters. 100Base-T4 can achieve its high speed using a lesser grade of cable because it uses all four pairs of wires in the cable, whereas other Ethernet UTP specifications, such as 100Base-TX and 10Base-T, use only two pairs. Because nearly all of the UTP cable installed today is at least Category 5 (CAT5), 100Base-T4 is seldom used, but it remains a viable alternative for sites with older cable installations.

100Base-TX Another name for a 100-Mbps Fast Ethernet physical layer specification defined in the Institute of Electrical and Electronics Engineers (IEEE) 802.3u document that uses Category 5 (CAT5) or better unshielded twisted pair (UTP) cable in a star topology, with a maximum segment length of 100 meters. 100Base-TX achieves its high speed using only two pairs of the wires in the cable because the specification insists on the use of high-quality cable. 100Base-TX is the most popular of the Fast Ethernet specifications.

100Base-X A collective term for the 100Base-FX and 100Base-TX Fast Ethernet specifications, both of which use the 4B/5B signal encoding method.

1000Base-CX Another name for a 1000-Mbps Gigabit Ethernet physical layer specification defined in the Institute of Electrical and Electronics Engineers (IEEE) 802.3z document, which runs over 150-ohm shielded copper cable with a maximum segment length of 25 meters.

1000Base-FX Another name for a 1000-Mbps Gigabit Ethernet physical layer specification defined in the Institute of Electrical and Electronics Engineers (IEEE) 802.3z document, which runs over 62.5/125 multimode fiber optic cable with a maximum segment length of 412 meters.

1000Base-LH Another name for a 1000-Mbps Gigabit Ethernet physical layer specification defined in the Institute of Electrical and Electronics Engineers (IEEE) 802.3z document, which runs over 9/125 singlemode fiber optic cable with a maximum segment length of 10,000 meters.

1000Base-LX   Another name for a 1000-Mbps Gigabit Ethernet physical layer specification defined in the Institute of Electrical and Electronics Engineers (IEEE) 802.3z document, which runs over either 9/125 singlemode fiber optic cable, with a maximum segment length of 5000 meters, or 50/125 or 62.5/125 multimode fiber optic cable with a maximum segment length of 550 meters.

1000Base-SX   Another name for a 1000-Mbps Gigabit Ethernet physical layer specification defined in the Institute of Electrical and Electronics Engineers (IEEE) 802.3z document, which runs over 50/125 multimode fiber optic cable with a maximum segment length of 550 meters or 62.5/125 multimode fiber optic cable with a maximum segment length of 275 meters.

1000Base-T   Another name for a 1000-Mbps Gigabit Ethernet network defined in the Institute of Electrical and Electronics Engineers (IEEE) 802.3ab document, which uses Category 5 (CAT5) or Category 5e (CAT5e) unshielded twisted pair (UTP) cable in a star topology, with a maximum segment length of 100 meters.

1000Base-X   A collective term referring to all of the physical layer specifications for Gigabit Ethernet that use the 8B/10B signal encoding scheme, originally used on Fibre Channel networks. 1000Base-X includes all of the Gigabit Ethernet specifications except for 1000Base-T.

1000Base-ZX   Another name for a 1000-Mbps Gigabit Ethernet physical layer specification defined in the Institute of Electrical and Electronics Engineers (IEEE) 802.3z document, which runs over 9/125 singlemode fiber optic cable with a maximum segment length of 100,000 meters.

10Broad36   A seldom-used Ethernet physical layer specification that calls for broadband transmissions over 75-ohm coaxial cable.

abstract syntax   The native format used by a computer to encode information generated by an application or process. The presentation layer of the Open Systems Interconnection (OSI) reference model receives data from the application in the system's abstract syntax and is responsible for converting it to a common transfer syntax understood by both communicating systems. *See also* transfer syntax.

Active Directory directory service   The enterprise directory service included with the Microsoft Windows Server 2003 and Microsoft Windows 2000 Server operating systems. Active Directory is a hierarchical directory service that consists of objects that represent users, computers, groups, and other network resources. The objects are arranged in a tree display that consists of hierarchical layers ranging upward from organizational units, to domains, to trees, and to forests. Objects are composed of attributes that contain information about the resource the object represents. When users log on to the network, their user names and passwords are authenticated against the Active Directory database by a computer that has been designated as a domain controller. This one single logon can grant users access to resources anywhere on the network. *See also* directory service.

Address Resolution Protocol (ARP)   A Transmission Control Procotol/Internet Protocol (TCP/IP) protocol used to resolve the Internet Protocol (IP) addresses of computers on a local area network (LAN) into the hardware (or MAC) addresses needed to transmit data-link layer frames to them. Before transmitting an IP datagram, TCP/IP clients broadcast an ARP request message containing the IP address of the destination computer to the local network. The computer using that IP address must then respond with an ARP reply message containing its hardware address. With the information in the reply message, the computer can encapsulate the IP datagram in the appropriate data-link layer frame and transmit it to the destination system.

ad hoc   A type of communication used on wireless LANs (WLANs) in which devices equipped with wireless network interface adapters communicate with each other at will. *See also* infrastructure topology.

ADSL   *See* Asymmetrical Digital Subscriber Line (ADSL).

ADSL Termination Unit-Remote (ATU-R)   The hardware device located at the client side of an ADSL connection. Also called a *DSL transceiver* or (incorrectly) a *DSL modem*. The ATU-R connects to the computer using either a universal serial bus (USB) port or a standard Ethernet network interface adapter. *See also* Asymmetrical Digital Subscriber Line (ADSL), Digital Subscriber Line Access Multiplexer (DSLAM).

American National Standards Institute (ANSI)   A private, non-profit organization that administers and coordinates the U.S. voluntary standardization and conformity assessment system. ANSI is the official U.S. representative to the International Organization for Standardization (ISO), as well as several other international bodies.

ANSI   *See* American National Standards Institute (ANSI).

AppleTalk   A proprietary suite of networking protocols developed by Apple for use by its Macintosh computers. AppleTalk includes AppleShare, a file and printer-sharing solution that enables a Macintosh computer to function as a network server. AppleTalk is rarely used today because Macintosh computers now communicate using the industry-standard Transmission Control Protocol/Internet Protocol (TCP/IP) protocols.

application layer   The top layer of the Open Systems Interconnection (OSI) reference model. The application layer provides the entrance point used by applications to access the networking protocol stack. Some of the protocols operating at the application layer include the Hypertext Transfer Protocol (HTTP), the Simple Mail Transfer Protocol (SMTP), the Dynamic Host Configuration Protocol (DHCP), the File Transfer Protocol (FTP), and the Simple Network Management Protocol (SNMP).

archive bit   A one-bit flag included with all file systems that backup software programs use to determine whether a file has been modified. When a file is backed up, the backup software program typically resets (or strips away) its archive bit. The next time the file is modified, the archive bit is activated. The backup software can then run a job that backs up only the files with active archive bits, which reduces the time and media needed to perform the backup.

ARP   *See* Address Resolution Protocol (ARP).

Arp.exe   A command-line utility provided by the Microsoft TCP/IP client that is included with the Windows operating systems. Arp.exe enables you to display and manipulate the information stored in the cache created by the Address Resolution Protocol (ARP). By preloading the ARP cache, you can save time and network traffic by eliminating the

ARP transaction that the TCP/IP client uses to resolve the IP address of each system it transmits to into a hardware address. *See also* Address Resolution Protocol (ARP).

Asymmetrical Digital Subscriber Line (ADSL)   A point-to-point, digital wide area network (WAN) technology that uses standard telephone lines to provide consumers with high-speed Internet access, remote local area network (LAN) access, and other services. The term "asymmetric" refers to the fact that the service provides a higher transmission rate for downstream than for upstream traffic. Downstream transmission rates can be up to 8.448 Mbps, whereas upstream rates range up to 640 Kbps. *See also* Digital Subscriber Line (DSL).

Asynchronous Transfer Mode (ATM)   A network communications technology based on 53-byte cells, designed to carry voice, data, and video traffic over local area networks (LANs) and wide area networks (WANs) at speeds ranging from 25.6 Mbps to 2.46 Gbps.

ATM   *See* Asynchronous Transfer Mode (ATM).

attachment unit interface (AUI)   An interface that provides the connection between a computer and the RG-8 coaxial cable used by thick Ethernet networks. A thick Ethernet network interface adapter has a 15-pin AUI port, which is used to connect an AUI cable that runs to the RG-8 cable. The other end of the AUI cable is connected to a device called a *vampire tap,* which clamps onto the RG-8 cable and has teeth that pierce its protective insulation to make an electrical connection with the conductor inside. The term "attachment unit interface" is used by the Institute of Electrical and Electronics Engineers (IEEE) 802.3 standard; the DIX Ethernet standards refer to the

same components as the transceiver port and the transceiver cable.

attenuation   The progressive weakening of a signal as it travels over a cable or other medium. The longer the distance a signal travels, the weaker the signal gets, until it becomes unreadable by the receiving system. On a data network, attenuation is one of the prime factors limiting the length of network cable segments. Different types of cables have different rates of attenuation. As a rule, copper cables are more prone to attenuation than fiber optic cables, and thinner copper cables are more prone to attenuation than thicker ones.

ATU-R   *See* ADSL Termination Unit-Remote (ATU-R).

AUI   *See* Attachment Unit Interface (AUI).

authoritative server   A Domain Name System (DNS) server that has been designated as the definitive source of information about the computers in a particular domain. When resolving a computer's DNS name into its Internet Protocol (IP) address, DNS servers consult the authoritative server for the domain in which that computer is located. Whatever information the authoritative server provides about that domain is understood by all DNS servers to be correct. *See also* Domain Name System (DNS).

autochanger   A hardware device consisting of one or more backup drives, a media array, and a robotic mechanism that inserts media into and removes it from the drives. An autochanger is used to perform automated backups of large amounts of data.

automatic allocation   An operational mode of Dynamic Host Configuration Protocol (DHCP) servers in which the server permanently assigns an Internet Protocol (IP) address and other Transmission Control Protocol/Internet Protocol (TCP/IP) configuration settings to a client from a pool of addresses.

See also dynamic allocation, which assigns addresses in the same way, but reclaims them when a lease of a given duration expires, and manual allocation, which permanently assigns specific addresses to clients. *See also* Dynamic Host Configuration Protocol (DHCP).

backbone network   A network used to connect a series of other networks together, forming an internetwork. Typically, a backbone is a high-speed local area network (LAN) used to route traffic from one horizontal LAN to another. Client workstations are typically not connected to the backbone, although servers sometimes are.

baseband network   A network that uses a medium that can carry only one signal at a particular time. Most LANs are baseband networks; your local cable television (CATV) system is an example of a broadband network. *See also* broadband network.

Basic Rate Interface (BRI)   An Integrated Services Digital Network (ISDN) service that consists of two 64-Kbps B channels plus one 16-Kbps D channel, enabling users to combine the B channels for a single 128-Kbps data pipe, or use them separately. Also called *2B+D*, BRI is the primary consumer ISDN service used for Internet access and remote networking. *See also* B channel, D channel, Primary Rate Interface (PRI), Integrated Services Digital Network (ISDN).

B channel   A 64-Kbps digital communications channel that is one of the fundamental units of service provided by the Integrated Services Digital Network (ISDN). B channels carry the actual data generated by the user's applications. The Basic Rate Interface (BRI) ISDN service consists of two B channels plus one 16-Kbps D channel; the Primary Rate Interface (PRI) service consists of 23 B channels and one 64-Kbps D channel. *See also* Integrated Services Digital Network (ISDN).

bindery   The server-based, flat file directory service used in Novell NetWare versions 3.2 and earlier. The bindery is a simple directory of user and group accounts used by NetWare to authenticate user access to server resources. Unlike more advanced directory services, which provide services for the entire enterprise, the NetWare bindery is specific to a single server. If a network has multiple NetWare servers, each has its own separate bindery, and users must have bindery accounts on each server they want to access.

bmp   A file format commonly used to store graphic images in bitmap form.

BNC   Short for bayonet-Neill-Concelman, a type of cable connector used on thin Ethernet networks.

BOOTP   *See* Bootstrap Protocol (BOOTP).

Bootstrap Protocol (BOOTP)   A server application that can supply client computers with Internet Protocol (IP) addresses, other Transmission Control Protocol/Internet Protocol (TCP/IP) configuration parameters, and executable boot files. As the progenitor to the Dynamic Host Configuration Protocol (DHCP), BOOTP provides the same basic functions, except that it does not allocate IP addresses from a pool and reclaim them after a specified length of time. Administrators must supply the IP address and other settings for each computer to be configured by the BOOTP server. *See also* Dynamic Host Configuration Protocol (DHCP), Reverse Address Resolution Protocol (RARP).

branching tree   *See* hierarchical star.

BRI   *See* Basic Rate Interface (BRI).

bridge   A network connectivity device that operates at the data-link layer of the Open Systems Interconnection (OSI) reference model and filters network traffic based on packets' destination addresses. When you connect two network segments with a bridge, packets generated by the computers on one segment are only propagated to the other segment if they are addressed to a computer on that segment. The bridge learns which computers are connected to each segment by reading the source addresses in the packets it processes and storing the information in a table; this learning process is called *transparent bridging*. Other types of bridges can connect networks running different media or data-link layer protocols or connect two network segments at different locations using a wide area network (WAN) link.

broadband network   A network that uses a medium that can carry multiple signals simultaneously, using a technique called *multiplexing*. The most common example of broadband communications is the typical cable television (CATV) network, which transmits the signals corresponding to dozens of TV channels over one cable. *See also* baseband network.

broadcast   A message transmitted to all of the other computers on the local network. Data-link layer protocols have special addresses designated as broadcast addresses, which means that every computer that receives the message will read it into memory and process it. Local area networks (LANs) use broadcasts for a variety of tasks, such as to discover information about other computers on the network.

broadcast domain   A collection of computers that will all receive a broadcast message transmitted by any one of the other computers. All of the computers on a local area network (LAN), for example, are in the same broadcast domain, as are the computers on two network segments connected by a bridge, because bridges always propagate broadcast transmissions. Two networks connected by a router, however, are in different broadcast domains, because routers do not propagate broadcasts. *See also* collision domain.

bus   A network cabling topology in which each device is connected to the next device, forming a daisy chain with two ends, each of which must be terminated. *See also* topology.

cable television (CATV) network   A private metropolitan area network (MAN) constructed and owned by a cable television company for the purpose of delivering TV signals to customers in a given region. Because the network technology they use is compatible with data networking, many CATV companies are now also in the business of providing Internet access to consumers using the same network that delivers the television service. The downstream transmission rates for a CATV Internet connection far exceed those of standard dial-ups and most other consumer Internet solutions, and the cost is usually very competitive.

Carrier Sense Multiple Access with Collision Avoidance (CSMA/CA)   A variation on the Carrier Sense Multiple Access with Collision Detection (CSMA/CD) Media Access Control (MAC) method, which substitutes a system of verifications and acknowledgments for the collision detection mechanism. *See also* Carrier Sense Multiple Access with Collision Detection (CSMA/CD).

Carrier Sense Multiple Access with Collision Detection (CSMA/CD)　The Media Access Control (MAC) mechanism used by Ethernet networks to regulate access to the network. Before they can transmit data, CSMA/CD systems listen to the network to determine if it is in use. If the network is free, the system transmits its data. However, sometimes another computer transmits at precisely the same time, causing a signal quality error or collision. Collisions are normal occurrences on Ethernet networks, and network interface adapters can detect them and compensate for them by discarding the collided packets and retransmitting them in a controlled manner.

CAT3　The Category 3 grade of unshielded twisted pair (UTP) cable that was at one time the most common medium used for telephone and data networks. New installations now use Category 5 (CAT5) cable, because it supports higher transmission speeds, although there are still some protocols that are designed specifically for use on older CAT3 networks, such as 100Base-T4 and 100VG-AnyLAN.

CAT5　The Category 5 grade of unshielded twisted pair (UTP) cable that is the current industry standard for telephone and data networking.

CAT5e　Also called *Category 5e* or *Enhanced Category 5*, a relatively new grade of unshielded twisted pair (UTP) cable designed for use on data networks running at very high speeds, such as Gigabit Ethernet.

CAT6　Ratified in 2002, a grade of unshielded twisted pair (UTP) cable that provides higher performance levels than Category 5e (CAT5e) and more stringent specifications for resistance to crosstalk and system noise. CAT6 cables are rated at a frequency of 250 MHz. CAT6 is also called *Category 6*.

Category *n*　A term used to specify a grade of unshielded twisted pair (UTP) cable, using standards developed by the Telecommunications Industry Association/Electronic Industries Alliance (TIA/EIA).

CATV　*See* cable television (CATV) network.

CCITT　*See* Comité Consultatif International Téléphonique et Télégraphique (CCITT).

CD-R　A write-once/read-many (WORM) storage medium that can hold approximately 670 MB of data on a compact disc.

CD-ROM　A read-only storage medium that can hold approximately 670 MB of data on a compact disc.

CD-RW　A rewritable storage medium that can hold approximately 670 MB of data on a compact disc.

cell switching　A type of network communications similar to packet switching. In cell switching, messages are broken up into discrete units of uniform size and transmitted to the destination.

channel service unit/data service unit (CSU/DSU)　A hardware device that terminates the end of a leased line connection and provides testing and diagnostic capabilities. *See also* leased line.

cheapernet　A slang term for a thin Ethernet (10Base2) network. At the time of its greatest popularity, cheapernet was significantly less expensive than its primary competitor, thick Ethernet (10Base5).

circuit switching　A type of network communications in which two communicating systems establish a connection that remains open throughout the life of the transaction. The telephone network is an example of a circuit-switched network. After placing a call, the telephone system establishes a path through the network connecting the two telephones, and all communications follow that path until it is broken by one of the callers disconnecting. *See also* packet switching.

client   A program designed to communicate with a server program on another computer, usually to request and receive information. The client provides the interface with which the user can view and manipulate the server data. A client can be a module in an operating system, such as the Client for Microsoft Networks in Microsoft Windows, which enables the user to access resources on the network's other computers, or a separate application, such as a Web browser or e-mail reader.

client/server networking   A computing model in which data processing tasks are distributed between clients, which request, display, and manipulate information, and servers, which supply and store information. Since each individual client is responsible for displaying and manipulating its own data, the server is relieved of a large part of the processing burden. The alternative is a mainframe or minicomputer system in which one computer performs all of the processing for all of the users, who work with terminals that do not have processors (dumb terminals).

cluster   A group of two or more server computers connected together so that they function as a single unified resource, for purposes of fault tolerance, load balancing, and parallel processing. Clustering enables the server array to survive the failure of one or more computers and makes it possible to upgrade the system simply by adding additional computers to the cluster.

coaxial cable   A type of cable used in various types of networking. A coaxial cable consists of two conductors, one wrapped around the other and separated by an insulating layer, enclosed in a protective sheath. The data signals are transmitted over the inner conductor that forms the solid core of the cable. The outer conductor, made of a wire mesh, functions as a ground. The two types of coaxial cable used in local area networking are called *RG-8* and *RG-58,* also known as thick Ethernet and thin Ethernet, respectively.

collision   In local area networking, a condition in which two computers transmit data at precisely the same time, and their signals both occupy the same cable, causing data loss. On some types of networks, such as Ethernet, collisions are a normal occurrence, whereas on Token Ring networks, they indicate a serious problem. Also called a *signal quality error.*

collision domain   A group of computers in which any two that transmit at exactly the same time will cause a collision. All of the computers on a local area network (LAN) are in the same collision domain, for example, whereas the computers on two network segments connected by a bridge or a router are in two different collision domains. This is because the processing performed by routers and bridges introduces a slight delay between the generation of a packet on one segment and the propagation of the packet to the other segment.

Comité Consultatif International Téléphonique et Télégraphique (CCITT)   An organization (in English, the International Telegraph and Telephone Consultative Committee) that, until 1992, developed and published international communications standards, such as those that govern modem signaling, compression, and error correction protocols. The organization is now known as the Telecommunications Standardization Sector of the International Telecommunications Union (ITU-T). The CCITT also published the document that defined the Open Systems Interconnection (OSI) reference model, called "The Basic Reference Model for Open Systems Interconnection."

compression ratio   The degree to which data can be compressed for storage on another medium, such as a backup medium. Compression ratios can range from 1:1 (no compression possible) to 8:1 or higher, depending on the format of the data stored in the individual files.

connectionless protocol   A type of protocol that transmits messages to a destination without first establishing a connection with the destination system. Connectionless protocols have very little overhead and are used primarily for transactions that consist of a single request and reply. The Internet Protocol (IP) and the User Datagram Protocol (UDP) are both connectionless protocols.

connection-oriented protocol   A type of protocol that transmits a series of messages to a destination to establish a connection before sending any application data. Establishing the connection ensures that the destination system is active and ready to receive data. Connection-oriented protocols are typically used to send large amounts of data, such as entire files, which must be split into multiple packets and which are useless unless every packet arrives at the destination without error. The Transmission Control Protocol (TCP) is a connection-oriented protocol.

convergence   The process by which dynamic routers update their routing tables to reflect the current state of the internetwork. The primary advantage of dynamic routing is that it enables routers to modify their routing information automatically as the configuration of the network changes. For example, if a router malfunctions, the other nearby routers, after failing to receive regular updates from it, will eventually remove it from their routing tables, thus preventing computers on the network from using that router. The elapsed time between the failure of the router and its removal from the routing tables of the other routers is the convergence period.

counters   The individual system attributes or processes monitored by the Performance console in Microsoft Windows 2000 and the Performance Monitor application in Microsoft Windows NT.

CRC   *See* cyclical redundancy check.

crossover cable   An unshielded twisted pair (UTP) cable in which the transmit contacts in each connector are wired to the receive contacts in the other connector. Using a crossover cable on a UTP Ethernet network eliminates the need for a hub. Crossover cables are used on small two-node networks and as a troubleshooting tool on larger networks.

crossover connection   A twisted-pair network connection in which the transmit contacts at each end of a cable are wired to the receive contacts at the other end of that cable, without the use of a hub. Normally, a hub is required for a twisted-pair network, because the hub crosses the transmit and receive signals, enabling computers to communicate with each other. Standard twisted-pair cables are wired straight through, meaning that the transmit contacts at one end of a cable are connected to the transmit contacts at the other end of that cable and the receive contacts to the receive contacts. To connect two computers directly using a twisted-pair cable and no hub, you must use a crossover cable in which the crossover is implemented in the cable wiring.

crosstalk A type of signal interference caused by signals transmitted on one pair of wires bleeding over into the other pairs. Crosstalk can cause network signals to degrade, eventually rendering them unusable. The individual wire pairs inside a twisted-pair cable are twisted at different rates because this helps to suppress the effects of crosstalk. Crosstalk is also the main reason you should not run other signals over the two unused wire pairs in a UTP Ethernet cable.

CSMA/CA *See* Carrier Sense Multiple Access with Collision Avoidance (CSMA/CA)

CSMA/CD *See* Carrier Sense Multiple Access with Collision Detection (CSMA/CD).

cyclical redundancy check (CRC) An error detection mechanism in which a computer performs a calculation on a data sample with a specific algorithm and then transmits the data and the results of the calculation to another computer. The receiving computer then performs the same calculation and compares its results to those supplied by the sender. If the results match, the data has been transmitted successfully. If the results do not match, the data has been damaged in transit.

daemon The UNIX term for a computer program or process that runs continuously in the background and performs tasks at predetermined intervals or in response to specific events. Daemons typically perform server tasks, such as spooling print jobs, handling e-mail, and transmitting Web files. A daemon is called a *service* by Microsoft Windows operating systems.

DAT *See* digital audio tape (DAT).

data encapsulation The process by which information generated by an application is packaged for transmission over a network by successive protocols operating at the various layers of the Open Systems Interconnection (OSI) reference model. A protocol packages the data it receives from the layer above by adding a header (and sometimes a footer) containing protocol-specific information used to ensure that the data arrives at its destination intact.

datagram A term for the unit of data used by the Internet Protocol (IP) and other network layer protocols. Network layer protocols accept data from transport layer protocols and package it into datagrams by adding their own protocol headers. The protocol then passes the datagrams down to a data-link layer protocol for further packaging before they are transmitted over the network.

Datagram Delivery Protocol (DDP) The network layer protocol used by the AppleTalk protocol suite to carry end-to-end data across a network. *See also* AppleTalk.

data-link layer The second layer from the bottom of the Open Systems Interconnection (OSI) reference model. Protocols operating at the data-link layer are responsible for packaging network layer data, addressing it to its next destination, and transmitting it over the network. Some of the local area network (LAN) protocols operating at the data-link layer are Ethernet, Token Ring, and the Fiber Distributed Data Interface (FDDI). Wide area network (WAN) protocols operating at the data-link layer include the Point-to-Point Protocol (PPP) and the Serial Line Internet Protocol (SLIP).

D channel   A digital communications channel running at 16 or 64 Kbps that is one of the fundamental units of service provided by the Integrated Services Digital Network (ISDN). D channels carry control traffic only, and are not factored into the user bandwidth provided by the service. The Basic Rate Interface (BRI) ISDN service consists of two B channels plus one 16-Kbps D channel; the Primary Rate Interface (PRI) service consists of 23 B channels and one 64-Kbps D channel. *See also* Integrated Services Digital Network (ISDN).

default gateway   The router on the local network used by a TCP/IP client computer to transmit messages to computers on other networks. To communicate with other networks, TCP/IP computers consult their routing tables for the address of the destination network. If they locate the address, they send their packets to the router specified in the table entry, which relays them to the desired network. If no specific entry for the network exists, the computer sends the packets to the router specified in the default gateway entry, which the user (or a DHCP server) supplies as one of the basic configuration parameters of the TCP/IP client.

Destination Address   A 48-bit field in data-link layer protocol headers that contains a hexadecimal sequence used to identify the network interface to which a frame will be transmitted.

Destination IP Address   A 32-bit field in the Internet Protocol (IP) header that contains a value used to identify the network interface to which a packet will be transmitted.

DHCP   *See* Dynamic Host Configuration Protocol (DHCP).

differential backup   A type of backup job that uses a filter that causes it to back up only the files that have changed since the last full backup job. The filter evaluates the state of each file's Archive bit, which a full backup job clears. Creating or modifying a file sets its Archive bit, and the differential job backs up only the files that have their Archive bit set. The differential job does not modify the state of the bits, so the next differential job will also back up all of the files that have changed since the last full backup. Differential jobs use more tape or other media than incremental jobs, because they repeatedly back up the same files, but they're easier to restore in the event of a disaster. You only have to restore the last full backup and the most recent differential to completely restore a drive. *See also* incremental backup.

Differential Manchester encoding   A physical layer encoding scheme, used on Token Ring networks, that is a variation on Manchester encoding.

digital audio tape (DAT)   A data storage medium that uses cartridges containing 4-mm wide magnetic tape, most commonly for system backups.

digital linear tape (DLT)   A data storage medium that uses cartridges containing one-half inch magnetic tape, most commonly used for system backups.

Digital Subscriber Line (DSL)   A type of point-to-point, digital WAN connection that uses standard telephone lines to provide high-speed communications. DSL is available in many different forms, including Asymmetrical Digital Subscriber Line (ADSL) and High-bit-rate Digital Subscriber Line (HDSL). The various DSL technologies differ greatly in their speeds and in the maximum possible distance between the installation site and the telephone company's nearest central office. DSL connections are used for many applications, ranging from LAN and PBX interconnections to consumer Internet access. *See also* Asymmetrical Digital Subscriber Line (ADSL).

Digital Subscriber Line Access Multiplexer (DSLAM)   The hardware device located at the server side of an ADSL connection. *See also* ADSL Termination Unit-Remote (ATU-R), Asymmetrical Digital Subscriber Line (ADSL).

directory service   A database containing information about network entities and resources, used as a guide to the network and an authentication resource by multiple users. Early network operating systems included basic flat file directory services, such as Microsoft Windows NT domains and the Novell NetWare bindery. Today's directory services, such as Microsoft Active Directory directory service and Novell Directory Services (NDS) tend to be hierarchical and designed to support large enterprise networks. *See also* Active Directory directory service, Novell Directory Services (NDS).

direct route   An Internet Protocol (IP) transmission to a destination on the local network, in which the Destination IP Address and the data-link layer protocol's Destination Address identify the same computer. *See also* indirect route, in which the IP destination is on another network and the data-link layer Destination Address identifies a router on the local network used to access the destination network.

distance vector protocol   A dynamic routing protocol that rates the relative efficiency of network routes by the number of hops to the destination. This is not necessarily an efficient method, because having networks of different speeds can cause a route with fewer hops to take longer to transmit

data than one requiring more hops. The most common of the distance vector routing protocols is the Routing Information Protocol (RIP). *See also* link state protocol *and* Routing Information Protocol (RIP).

DIX Ethernet   An acronym for Digital Equipment Corporation (DEC), Intel, and Xerox, the three corporations responsible for developing and publishing the original Ethernet standard.

DLT   *See* digital linear tape (DLT).

DNS   *See* Domain Name System (DNS).

domain   A group of computers and other devices on a network that are administered as a single unit. On the Internet, domain names are hierarchical constructions (such as microsoft.com) that form the basis for the Domain Name System (DNS). On a Microsoft Windows network, a domain is a group of users, computers, and other resources for which information is stored in a directory service, on a server called a *domain controller.*

domain controller   A computer running Microsoft Windows that has been designated for storing and processing directory service information. Microsoft Windows NT domains and the Active Directory directory service store their directory service databases on domain controllers, which also authenticate users accessing network resources.

Domain Name System (DNS)   A distributed, hierarchical namespace designed to provide Transmission Control Protocol/Internet Protocol (TCP/IP) networks (such as the Internet) with friendly names for computers and users. Although TCP/IP computers use Internet Protocol (IP) addresses to identify each other, people work better with names. Domain Name System (DNS) provides a naming system for network resources and a service for resolving those names into IP addresses. TCP/IP computers frequently access DNS servers to send them the names of the computers they want to access. The DNS server communicates with other DNS servers on the network to find out the IP address associated with the requested name and then sends it back to the client computer, which initiates communications with the destination system using its IP address.

double ring   A network cabling topology that consists of two separate rings with traffic running in opposite directions, used primarily by the Fiber Distributed Data Interface (FDDI) protocol. Devices are connected to both rings, providing a measure of fault tolerance in the event of a cable failure that causes a break in one of the rings. Unlike the standard ring topology, the double ring is usually implemented physically, not logically. *See also* ring, topology, Fiber Distributed Data Interface (FDDI).

driver   A software component that enables an application or operating system to use a particular hardware device. Also called a *device driver*.

drive spanning   A process by which a computer creates a single logical storage unit called a *volume* by combining the disk space of two or more drives. The volume appears to users as a single logical entity, but data is actually being stored on multiple drives. The primary drawback of this arrangement is that if one of the drives fails, the entire volume is lost.

DSL   *See* Digital Subscriber Line (DSL).

DSLAM   *See* Digital Subscriber Line Access Multiplexer (DSLAM).

DSL modem   Inaccurate terminology for the hardware unit that provides ADSL client connectivity, which is correctly called an *ADSL Termination Unit-Remote (ATU-R)*.

duplexing   A data availability technique that involves storing identical copies of data on two different drives connected to different host adapters. The drives appear as a single volume to users, and all files written to the volume are copied to both drives automatically. If one of the drives or adapters fails, the other continues to make the data available until the failed component is repaired or replaced. *See also* mirroring.

dynamic allocation   An operational mode of Dynamic Host Configuration Protocol (DHCP) servers in which the server assigns an Internet Protocol (IP) address and other TCP/IP configuration settings to a client from a pool of addresses, and then reclaims them when a lease of a given duration expires. This enables you to move computers to different subnets without having to manually release the previously allocated IP addresses from the other subnets. *See also* automatic allocation, manual allocation, Dynamic Host Configuration Protocol (DHCP).

Dynamic Host Configuration Protocol (DHCP)   A service that automatically configures the Transmission Control Protocol/Internet Protocol (TCP/IP) client computers on a network by assigning them unique Internet Protocol (IP) addresses and other configuration parameters. DHCP servers can assign IP addresses to clients from a pool and reclaim them when a lease of a set duration expires. Virtually all operating systems include a DHCP client, and most of the major server operating systems—such as Microsoft Windows 2000 Server, Microsoft Windows NT Server, Novell NetWare, and many forms of UNIX—include DHCP server software. DHCP is a cross-platform service that can support various operating systems with a single server. *See also* automatic allocation, dynamic allocation, manual allocation.

dynamic routing   A system in which routers automatically build their own routing tables using specialized protocols to communicate with other nearby routers. By sharing information in this way, a router builds up a composite picture of the internetwork on which it resides, enabling it to route traffic more efficiently. The two basic types of routing protocols are distance vector routing protocols, like the Routing Information Protocol (RIP), and link state routing protocols, like the Open Shortest Path First (OSPF) protocol. *See also* Routing Information Protocol (RIP).

E-1   A dedicated telephone connection, also called a *leased line,* running at 2.048 Mbps. An E-1 is the European equivalent of a T-1. *See also* T-1, leased line.

E-3   A dedicated telephone connection, also called a *leased line,* running at 34.368 Mbps. An E-3 is the European equivalent of a T-3. *See also* T-3, leased line.

EIA/TIA   *See* Telecommunications Industry Association/Electronic Industries Alliance (TIA/EIA)

electromagnetic interference (EMI)   In data networking, any electromagnetic disturbance that interrupts or degrades the transmission of signals over a network medium.

e-mail   A service that transmits messages in electronic form to specific users on a network.

EMI   *See* electromagnetic interference.

encryption   The process of making information indecipherable in order to protect it from unauthorized viewing or use, especially during transmission or when the data is stored on a transportable magnetic medium. A key is required to decode the information.

end system   On a Transmission Control Protocol/Internet Protocol (TCP/IP) network, a computer or other device that is the original sender or ultimate recipient of a transmission. The end systems in a TCP/IP transmission are identified by the Source IP Address and Destination IP Address fields in the Internet Protocol (IP) header. All of the other systems (that is, routers) involved in the transmission are known as *intermediate systems.*

ephemeral port number   A Transmission Control Protocol (TCP) or User Datagram Protocol (UDP) port number of 1024 or higher, chosen at random by a Transmission Control Protocol/Internet Protocol (TCP/IP) client computer during the initiation of a transaction with a server. Because the client initiates the communication with the server, it can use any port number beyond the range of the well-known port numbers (which run up to 1023). The server reads the ephemeral port number from the transport layer protocol header's Source Port field and uses it to address its replies to the client. *See also* well-known port.

Ethernet   A common term used to describe Institute of Electrical and Electronics Engineers (IEEE) 802.3, a data-link layer local area network (LAN) protocol developed in the 1970s, which is now the most popular protocol of its kind in the world. Ethernet runs at 10 Mbps, is based on the Carrier Sense Multiple Access with Collision Detection (CSMA/CD) Media Access Control (MAC) mechanism, and supports a variety of physical layer options, including coaxial, unshielded twisted pair (UTP), and fiber optic cables. More recent revisions of the protocol support speeds of 100 Mbps (Fast Ethernet) and 1000 Mbps (Gigabit Ethernet). *See also* Carrier Sense Multiple Access with Collision Detection (CSMA/CD).

Fast Ethernet   The updated version of the Ethernet local area network (LAN) protocol that increases transmission speed from 10 to 100 Mbps, preserving nearly all of Ethernet's defining elements, such as its frame format, its physical layer options, and the Carrier Sense Multiple Access with Collision Detection (CSMA/CD) Media Access Control (MAC) mechanism. Fast Ethernet is defined in a new document, Institute of Electrical and Electronics Engineers (IEEE) 802.3u, published in 1995. Fast Ethernet supports three primary physical layer options: 100Base-TX for Category 5 (CAT5) unshielded twisted pair (UTP) cable, 100Base-T4 for Category 3 (CAT3) UTP cable, and 100Base-FX for multimode fiber optic cable.

fast link pulse (FLP)   The signal generated by Fast Ethernet network interface adapters and hubs, which the devices use to signal that they have been cabled together properly and to automatically negotiate the fastest transmission speed they have in common. When an adapter or hub receives the FLP signal from the device to which it is connected, it activates a light-emitting diode (LED), which indicates that communication is taking place. FLP signals are completely compatible with the normal link pulse (NLP) signals used by 10Base-T Ethernet devices, differing only in that they include a link code word that specifies the transmission speeds they support.

FAT   *See* file allocation table (FAT).

FDDI   *See* Fiber Distributed Data Interface (FDDI).

Fiber Distributed Data Interface (FDDI)   A data-link layer local area network (LAN) protocol running at 100 Mbps, designed for use with fiber optic cable. Typically used for backbone networks, FDDI uses the token passing Media Access Control (MAC) mechanism and supports a double ring topology that provides fault tolerance in the event of a system disconnection or cable failure. Originally the principal 100-Mbps LAN protocol, FDDI has since largely been replaced by the Fast Ethernet and Gigabit Ethernet fiber optic options.

fiber optic   A network cable technology that uses signals consisting of pulses of light rather than the electrical charges used by copper cables. Fiber optic cable is completely resistant to electromagnetic interference (EMI) and is also able to span far longer distances than copper cables, indoors or outdoors. The core conductors in a fiber optic cable are made of glass or plastic and are surrounded by a cladding that reflects the light back on itself, keeping it in the core of the cable. The light source is a light-emitting diode (LED) or a laser, depending on the type of cable. Fiber optic cable is generally more efficient than copper-based cable in almost every way, but it's more expensive than copper and more difficult to install, requiring specialized tools and skills. *See also* multimode fiber, singlemode fiber.

Fiber Optic Inter-Repeater Link (FOIRL)   The earliest Ethernet physical layer specification to use fiber optic cable. FOIRL was defined in the DIX Ethernet II document. FOIRL uses 62.5/125 multimode fiber optic cable in a star topology, with a maximum segment length of 1000 meters. FOIRL was rarely used, and was replaced in the Institute of Electrical and Electronics Engineers (IEEE) 802.3 standard by the 10Base-F specification (10Base-FL, 10Base-FB, and 10Base-FP).

file allocation table (FAT)   The file system used by the DOS operating system, which is based on a table that specifies which disk clusters contain the files stored on a disk. The Microsoft Windows 95, Microsoft Windows 98,

Microsoft Windows Me, Microsoft Windows NT, and Microsoft Windows 2000 operating systems currently support the 16-bit version of the FAT file system. Windows 95 OSR2, Windows 98, Windows Me, and Windows 2000 also support FAT-32, a newer version that uses 32-bit FAT entries, enabling the file system to support much larger disk drives. The FAT file system is sufficient for a standard workstation but lacks the security capabilities required by server drives. For this reason, the Microsoft operating systems designed for heavier network use—Microsoft Windows 2000 and Microsoft Windows NT—also include the NT file system (NTFS), which has greater security capabilities.

File Transfer Protocol (FTP) An application layer Transmission Control Protocol/Internet Protocol (TCP/IP) protocol designed to perform file transfers and basic file management tasks on remote computers. FTP is a mainstay of Internet communications. FTP client support is integrated into most Web browsers, and FTP server support is integrated into many Web server products. FTP is also an important UNIX tool—all UNIX systems support both FTP client and server functions. FTP is unique among TCP/IP protocols because it uses two simultaneous Transmission Control Protocol (TCP) connections. One, a control connection, remains open during the entire life of the session between the FTP client and the FTP server. When the client initiates a file transfer, a second connection is opened between the two computers to carry the transferred data. This connection closes at the conclusion of the data transfer.

firewall A hardware or software product designed to isolate part of an internetwork to protect it against intrusion by outside processes. Typically used to protect a private network from intrusion from the Internet, firewalls use a number of techniques to provide this protection, while still allowing certain types of traffic through. Some of these techniques include packet filtering and Network Address Translation (NAT). Firewalls were once intended only for large network installations, but there are now smaller firewall products designed to protect small networks and individual computers from Internet intruders.

fish tape A tool used by cable installers to push or pull cables up or down inside walls. It consists of a flexible metal tape with a hook on the end wound onto a reel (much like a plumber's snake). Cable installers connect the end of a cable to the hook and draw it through a wall by unwinding a length of tape and extending it through the cavity inside the wall.

flow control A function of certain data transfer protocols that enables a system receiving data to transmit signals to the sender instructing it to slow down or speed up its transmissions. This prevents the receiving system from overflowing its buffers and being forced to discard incoming data. For example, the Transmission Control Protocol (TCP) implements its flow control mechanism by using a Windows field to specify the number of bytes that it can receive from the sender.

FLP *See* fast link pulse (FLP).

FOIRL *See* Fiber Optic Inter-Repeater Link (FOIRL).

fox and hound wire tester The colloquial name for a simple type of cable tester, also called a *tone generator and locator.*

frame A unit of data that is constructed, transmitted, and received by data-link layer protocols such as Ethernet and Token Ring. Data-link layer protocols create frames by packaging the data they receive from network layer protocols inside a header and footer. Frames can be different sizes, depending on the protocol used to create them.

frame relay   A wide area networking technology in which two systems are each connected to a frame relay network called a *cloud,* and a virtual circuit is established between them through the cloud. The advantages of frame relay over a leased line are that the amount of bandwidth provided by the connection is flexible and that one site can be connected to numerous other sites using multiple virtual circuits. *See also* leased line.

FTP   See File Transfer Protocol (FTP).

full-duplex   A form of communications in which two connected systems can send signals to the other system simultaneously. For example, a telephone call (in which both parties can talk at once at any time) is an example of full-duplex communication, while a citizen's band (CB) radio (on which you must press a key to transmit signals and release the key to receive them) is an example of a half-duplex communication device.

gateway   On a Transmission Control Protocol/Internet Protocol (TCP/IP) network, the term "gateway" is often used synonymously with the term "router," referring to a network layer device that connects two networks together and relays traffic between them as needed, such as the default gateway specified in a TCP/IP client configuration. However, the term "gateway" is also used to refer to an application layer device that relays data between two different services, such as an e-mail gateway that enables two separate e-mail services to communicate with each other.

GB   Gigabyte, equal to 1000 megabytes (MB) or 1,000,000 kilobytes (KB) or 1,000,000,000 bytes.

GBps   *See* gigabytes per second.

Gbps   *See* gigabits per second.

gif   A compressed file format commonly used to store graphic images in bitmap form.

Gigabit Ethernet   The latest version of the Ethernet data-link layer protocol, defined in the Institute of Electrical and Electronics Engineers (IEEE) 802.3z and IEEE 802.3ab documents and running at 1000 Mbps. Gigabit Ethernet is designed for backbone networks and server connections and supports a variety of unshielded twisted pair (UTP) and fiber optic cabling options. The UTP option uses all four of the wire pairs in the cable to carry signals, instead of the two pairs used by most of the other Ethernet types. As with the other Ethernet varieties, Gigabit Ethernet uses the Carrier Sense Multiple Access with Collision Detection (CSMA/CD) Media Access Control (MAC) mechanism.

gigabits per second (Gbps)   A unit of measurement typically used to measure network transmission speed.

gigabytes per second (GBps)   A unit of measurement typically used to measure the speed of data storage devices.

grandfather-father-son   A media rotation scheme used by many backup software programs. "Grandfather" refers to monthly backup jobs, "father" to weekly jobs, and "son" to daily jobs.

graphical user interface (GUI)   An element of a program or operating system that takes advantage of the computer's graphical capabilities, enabling the user to manipulate software components represented by objects on the display.

half-duplex   A form of communications in which two connected systems can only send signals in one direction at a time. For example, a citizen's band (CB) radio (on which you must press a key to transmit signals and release the key to receive them) is an example of a half-duplex communications device, whereas a telephone call (in which both parties can talk at once at any time) is an example of full-duplex communication. Most local area network (LAN) protocols operate in half-duplex mode, although there is a full-duplex version of Ethernet.

HDSL   *See* High-bit-rate Digital Subscriber Line (HDSL).

hierarchical star   A network cabling topology in which a standard star network is augmented by the addition of one or more hubs, connected to the original ones. Also called *a branching tree network. See also* topology.

High-bit-rate Digital Subscriber Line (HDSL)   A point-to-point, digital wide area network (WAN) technology used by telephone companies and other large corporations to transmit data at T-1 speeds.

hop   A unit of measurement used to quantify the length of a route between two computers on an internetwork, as indicated by the number of routers that packets must pass through to reach the destination end system. For example, if packets must be forwarded by four routers in the course of their journey from end system to end system, the destination is said to be four hops away from the source. Distance vector routing protocols like the Routing Information Protocol (RIP) use the number of hops as a means to compare the relative efficiency of routes.

Hosts   An American Standard Code for Information Interchange (ASCII) text file used by Transmission Control Protocol/Internet Protocol (TCP/IP) computers to resolve host names into Internet Protocol (IP) addresses. The Hosts file is a simple list of the host names used by TCP/IP computers and their equivalent IP addresses. When a user or an application refers to a

computer using a host name, the TCP/IP client looks it up in the Hosts file to determine its IP address. The Hosts file was the original name resolution method for what later became the Internet, until the number of computers on the network grew too large to manage using this technique. Eventually, the Domain Name System (DNS) was created to perform the same function in a more efficient and manageable way. TCP/IP computers can still use a Hosts file for name resolution, but because the names and addresses of each computer must be added manually, this method is rarely used today.

HTTP   *See* Hypertext Transfer Protocol (HTTP).

hub   A hardware component to which cables running from computers and other devices are connected, joining all of the devices into a network. In most cases, the term "hub" refers to an Ethernet multiport repeater, a device that amplifies the signals received from each connected device and forwards them to all of the other devices simultaneously. *See also* multiport repeater.

Hypertext Transfer Protocol (HTTP)   An application layer protocol that is the basis for World Wide Web communications. Web browsers generate HTTP Get request messages containing Uniform Resource Locators (URLs) and transmit them to Web servers, which reply with one or more HTTP Response messages containing the requested files. HTTP traffic is encapsulated using the Transmission Control Protocol (TCP) at the transport layer and the Internet Protocol (IP) at the network layer. Each HTTP transaction requires a separate TCP connection.

IANA   *See* Internet Assigned Numbers Authority (IANA).

IBM data connector (IDC)   A proprietary connector used to attach Token Ring systems to multistation access units (MAUs) using Type 1 cables and to connect MAUs together. On today's Token Ring networks, Type 1 cables and IDC connectors have largely been replaced by RJ-45 connectors and unshielded twisted pair (UTP) cables.

ICMP   *See* Internet Control Message Protocol (ICMP).

IDC   *See* IBM data connector (IDC).

IEEE   *See* Institute of Electrical and Electronic Engineers (IEEE).

IEEE 802.2   A standards document published by the Institute of Electrical and Electronic Engineers (IEEE) defining the Logical Link Control (LLC) sublayer used by the IEEE 802.3, IEEE 802.5, and other protocols.

IEEE 802.3   A standards document published by the Institute of Electrical and Electronic Engineers (IEEE) defining what is commonly referred to as the Ethernet protocol. Although there are slight differences from the original DIX Ethernet standards, such as the omission of the Ethertype field and the separation of the data-link layer into two sublayers—the Media Access Control (MAC) sublayer and the Logical Link Control (LLC) sublayer—IEEE 802.3 retains the defining characteristics of Ethernet, including the Carrier Sense Multiple Access with Collision Detection (CSMA/CD) MAC mechanism. IEEE 802.3 also adds to the physical layer options defined in the DIX Ethernet standards by including support for unshielded twisted pair (UTP) cable.

IEEE 802.3ab   A standards document published by the Institute of Electrical and Electronic Engineers (IEEE) defining an implementation of the 1000-Mbps Gigabit Ethernet protocol using Category 5 (CAT5) unshielded twisted pair (UTP) cable and a 100-meter maximum segment length. Released after the original Gigabit Ethernet protocol standard (IEEE 802.3z), this specification is intended to be an upgrade path to Gigabit Ethernet for existing UTP regular or Fast Ethernet networks. To achieve a transmission speed of 1000 Mbps, this standard calls for the use of all four pairs of wires in the cable, plus a signaling scheme called *Pulse Amplitude Modulation-5 (PAM-5)*.

IEEE 802.3d   A standards document published by the Institute of Electrical and Electronic Engineers (IEEE) defining the Fiber Optic Inter-Repeater Link (FOIRL) specification.

IEEE 802.3i   A standards document published by the Institute of Electrical and Electronic Engineers (IEEE) defining the 10Base-T specification.

IEEE 802.3j   A standards document published by the Institute of Electrical and Electronic Engineers (IEEE) defining the 10Base-FP, 10Base-FB, and 10Base-FL specifications.

IEEE 802.3u   A standards document published by the Institute of Electrical and Electronic Engineers (IEEE) defining the Fast Ethernet data-link layer local area network (LAN) protocol. Running at 100 Mbps, Fast Ethernet uses the same frame format and the Carrier Sense Multiple Access with Collision Detection (CSMA/CD) Media Access Control (MAC) mechanism as standard Ethernet, and supports three physical layer options: 100Base-TX, 100Base-T4, and 100Base-FX. Many Fast Ethernet hardware products support both 10 Mbps and 100 Mbps speeds and use an enhanced link pulse signal called *fast link pulse (FLP)* to negotiate the fastest possible transmission speed with the connected device.

IEEE 802.3z   A standards document published by the Institute of Electrical and Electronic Engineers (IEEE) defining the 1000-Mbps Gigabit Ethernet data-link layer protocol. Designed primarily for use on backbone networks and server connections that require high speeds, IEEE 802.3z was the first Gigabit Ethernet standard published, and includes a variety of physical layer options, most of which call for various types of fiber optic cable. Like the other varieties of Ethernet, Gigabit Ethernet uses the Carrier Sense Multiple Access with Collision Detection (CSMA/CD) Media Access Control (MAC) mechanism.

IEEE 802.5   A standards document published by the Institute of Electrical and Electronic Engineers (IEEE) defining a Token Ring-like data-link layer protocol. *See also* Token Ring.

IEEE 802.11   A standards document published by the Institute of Electrical and Electronic Engineers (IEEE) defining a wireless local area network (LAN) running at speeds of up to 11 Mbps using any one of three physical layer technologies: direct sequence spread spectrum (DSSS), frequency hopping spread spectrum (FHSS), and infrared.

IETF   *See* Internet Engineering Task Force (IETF).

ifconfig   A UNIX utility program used to configure a network interface and display the network interface's configuration parameters. The similar Ipconfig.exe is a program available in Microsoft Windows that performs the display functions only.

IMAP   *See* Internet Mail Access Protocol (IMAP).

incremental backup   A type of backup job that uses a filter that causes it to back up only the files that have changed since the last backup job. The filter evaluates the state of each file's Archive bit, which a full backup job or an incremental backup job clears. Creating or modifying a file sets its Archive bit, and the incremental job backs up only the files with an Archive bit that is set. It then resets the Archive bits (unlike a differential job, which does not reset the bits). Incremental jobs use the least amount of tape or other medium, but they are more difficult to restore in the event of a disaster. You must restore the last full backup job and all of the incremental jobs performed since that last full backup, in the correct chronological order, to fully restore a drive. *See also* differential backup.

Independent Computing Architecture (ICA)   A protocol developed by Cyrix Systems that provides communication between thin clients and network servers. Thin clients are terminals that exchange keystrokes, mouse actions, and display data with servers that run the user operating system and applications.

indirect route   An Internet Protocol (IP) transmission to a destination on a different network, in which the Destination IP Address and the data-link layer protocol's Destination Address identify different computers. *See also* direct route, in which the IP destination is on the same network and the data-link layer Destination Address identifies the same computer as the Destination IP Address.

infrastructure topology   A type of communication used on wireless LANs (WLANs) in which devices equipped with wireless network interface adapters communicate with a standard cabled network using a network access point. *See also* ad hoc topology, network access point.

Institute of Electrical and Electronics Engineers (IEEE)   An organization, founded in 1984, dedicated to the development and publication of standards for the computer and electronics industries. IEEE is best known in computer networking for the IEEE 802 series of documents defining the data-link layer local area network (LAN) protocols commonly known as Ethernet and Token Ring.

Integrated Services Digital Network (ISDN)   A dial-up communications service that uses standard telephone lines to provide high-speed digital communications. Originally conceived as a replacement for the existing analog telephone service, it never achieved its anticipated popularity. Today, ISDN is used in the United States primarily as an Internet access technology, although it is more commonly used for wide area network (WAN) connections in Europe and Japan. The two most common ISDN services are the Basic Rate Interface (BRI), which provides two 64-Kbps B channels and one 16-Kbps D (control) channel, and the Primary Rate Interface (PRI), which provides 23 64-Kbps B channels and one 64-Kbps D channel.

intelligent hub   Also called a *smart hub,* a local area network (LAN) cabling nexus that not only functions at the physical layer by propagating traffic to all of the other computers on the network, but can buffer data and retransmit it out through specific ports as needed, and in some cases monitor the activity on all of its ports and transmit information about its status to a network management console.

intermediate system   On a Transmission Control Protocol/ Internet Protocol (TCP/IP) network, a router that relays traffic generated by an end system from one network to another. The end systems in a TCP/IP transmission are identified by the Source IP Address and Destination IP Address fields in the Internet Protocol (IP) header. All of the other systems (that is, routers) involved in the transmission are known as intermediate systems.

International Organization for Standardization (ISO)   An organization, founded in 1946, that consists of standards bodies from over 75 countries, such as the American National Standards Institute (ANSI) from the United States. The ISO is responsible for the publication of many computer-related standards, the most well-known of which is "The Basic Reference Model for Open Systems Interconnection," commonly known as the Open Systems Interconnection (OSI) reference model. (ISO is not merely an acronym; it's a name derived from the Greek word isos, meaning "equal.")

International Telecommunications Union (ITU)   An organization, founded in 1865, devoted to the development of treaties, regulations, and standards governing telecommunications. Since 1992, it has included the standards development organization formerly known as the Comité Consultatif International Téléphonique et Télégraphique (CCITT), which was responsible for the creation of modem communication, compression, and error correction standards.

Internet   A packet-switching internetwork that consists of thousands of individual networks and millions of computers located around the world. The Internet is not owned or administered by any central managing body; all administration chores are distributed among users all over the network.

internet   *See* internetwork.

Internet Assigned Numbers Authority (IANA)   The organization responsible for assigning unique parameter values for the Transmission Control Protocol/Internet Protocol (TCP/IP) protocols, including Internet Protocol (IP) address assignments for networks and protocol number assignments. The "Assigned Numbers" Requests for Comments (RFC) document (currently RFC 1700) lists all of the protocol number assignments and many other unique parameters regulated by the IANA.

Internet Control Message Protocol (ICMP)   A network layer Transmission Control Protocol/Internet Protocol (TCP/IP) protocol that carries administrative messages, particularly error messages and informational queries. ICMP error messages are primarily generated by intermediate systems that have no other means of signaling errors to the end system that transmitted the packet because the packets they route travel no higher than the network layer. Typical ICMP error messages inform the sender that the network or host to which a packet is addressed could not be found, or that the Time To Live value for a packet has expired. ICMP query messages request information (or simply a response) from other computers, and are the basis for TCP/IP utilities like Ping, which is used to test the ability of one computer on a network to communicate with another.

Internet Engineering Task Force (IETF)   The primary standards ratification body for the Transmission Control Protocol/Internet Protocol (TCP/IP) protocol and the Internet. The IETF publishes Requests for Comments (RFCs), which are the working documents for what eventually become Internet standards. The IETF is an international body of network designers, operators, software programmers, and other technicians, all of whom devote part of their time to the development of Internet protocols and technologies.

Internet Mail Access Protocol (IMAP)   An application layer Transmission Control Protocol/Internet Protocol (TCP/IP) protocol used by e-mail clients to download mail messages from a server. E-mail traffic between servers and outgoing e-mail traffic from clients to servers uses the Simple Mail Transfer Protocol (SMTP). *See also* Post Office Protocol 3 (POP3).

Internet Protocol (IP)   The primary network layer protocol in the Transmission Control Protocol/Internet Protocol (TCP/IP) suite. IP is the protocol that is ultimately responsible for end-to-end communications on a TCP/IP internetwork, and includes functions such as addressing, routing, and fragmentation. IP packages data that it receives from transport layer protocols into data units called *datagrams* by applying a header containing the information needed to transmit the data to its destination. The IP addressing system uses 32-bit addresses to uniquely identify the computers on a network, and specifies the address of the destination system as part of the IP header. IP is also responsible for routing packets to their destinations on other networks by forwarding them to other routers on the network. When a datagram is too large to be transmitted over a particular network, IP breaks it into fragments and transmits each in a separate packet.

Internet service provider (ISP)   A type of company whose business is supplying consumers or businesses with Internet access. At the consumer level, an ISP provides users with dial-up access to the ISP's networks, which are connected to the Internet, as well as other end-user services, such as access to Domain Name System (DNS), e-mail, and news servers. At the business level, ISPs provide high-bandwidth Internet connections using leased telephone lines or other technologies, and sometimes also provide other services, such as registered Internet Protocol (IP) addresses, Web site hosting, and DNS domain hosting.

internetwork   A group of interconnected local area networks (LANs) and/or wide area networks (WANs) that are connected so that any computer can transmit data to any other computer. The networks are connected by routers, which are responsible for relaying packets from one network to another. The largest example of an internetwork is the Internet, which is composed of thousands of networks located around the world. Private internetworks consist of a smaller number of LANs, often at various locations and connected by WAN links.

Internetwork Packet Exchange (IPX)   A network layer protocol used by Novell NetWare networks. IPX performs many of the same functions as the Internet Protocol (IP), but instead of being a self-contained addressing system like IP, IPX is designed for use on local area networks (LANs) only and uses a network identifier assigned by the network administrator plus the network interface adapter's hardware address to identify the individual computers on the network. Unlike IP, IPX is not based on an open standard. Novell owns all rights to the protocols of the IPX protocol suite, although Microsoft has developed its own IPX-compatible protocol for inclusion in the Windows operating systems.

intranet   A Transmission Control Protocol/Internet Protocol (TCP/IP) network owned by a private organization that provides services such as Web sites only to that organization's users.

IP   See Internet Protocol (IP).

IP address   A 32-bit address assigned to Transmission Control Protocol/Internet Protocol (TCP/IP) client computers and other network equipment that uniquely identifies that device on the network. The Internet Protocol (IP) uses IP addresses to transmit packets to the destinations. Expressed as four 8-bit decimal values separated by periods (for example, 192.168.71.19), the IP address consists of a network identifier (which specifies the network that the device is located on) and a host identifier (which identifies the particular device on that network). The sizes of the network and host identifiers can vary depending on the address class. For a computer to be accessible from the Internet, it must have an IP address containing a network identifier registered with the Internet Assigned Numbers Authority (IANA).

IP Authentication Header (AH)   An IPSec protocol that provides data integrity and anti-replay functions, but not encryption.

Ipconfig.exe   A Microsoft Windows 2000 and Microsoft Windows NT command-line utility used to view the Transmission Control Protocol/Internet Protocol (TCP/IP) configuration parameters for a particular computer. A graphical version of the tool, Winipcfg.exe, is included with Microsoft Windows 95, Microsoft Windows 98, and Microsoft Windows Me. Ipconfig.exe is most useful on computers with TCP/IP clients configured automatically by a Dynamic Host Configuration (DHCP) server because it is the easiest way to view the assigned settings for the client system. You can also use Ipconfig.exe to release and renew DHCP-assigned TCP/IP configuration parameters.

IP Encapsulating Security Payload (ESP)   An IPSec protocol that provides encryption, data integrity, and anti-replay functions.

IPSec   *See* IP Security protocol (IPSec).

IP Security protocol (IPSec)   A set of Transmission Control Protocol/Internet Protocol (TCP/IP) protocols designed to provide encrypted network layer communications. For computers to communicate using IPSec, they must share a public key.

IPv6   A new version of the Internet Protocol (IP) that expands the IP address space from 32 to 128 bits. *See also* Internet Protocol (IP).

IPX   *See* Internetwork Packet Exchange (IPX).

ISDN   *See* Integrated Services Digital Network (ISDN).

ISO   *See* International Organization for Standardization (ISO).

ISP   *See* Internet service provider (ISP).

ITU   *See* International Telecommunications Union (ITU).

Jaz   The proprietary name for a magnetic cartridge drive holding 1 or 2 gigabytes (GB) of data.

jpg   A compressed file format commonly used to store graphic images in bitmap form.

Kbps   *See* kilobits per second.

Kerberos   An authentication protocol that uses public key technology to provide users with secured access to network resources.

kilobits per second (Kbps)   A unit of measurement typically used to measure network transmission speed.

LAN   *See* local area network (LAN).

late collision   On an Ethernet network, a data collision between two transmitted packets that occurs after one or both packets has completely left the transmitting system. The physical layer specifications of the Ethernet protocols are designed to ensure that the first bit transmitted by a computer reaches its destination before the last bit leaves that computer. This allows the transmitting system to detect collisions when they occur. Collisions are normal on an Ethernet network, but if a cable segment is too long, or if there are too many hubs on the path to the destination, late collisions can occur after packets have left the transmitting system, which makes it impossible for the Ethernet adapter in the transmitting system to detect them. Unlike the normal type of collision, late collisions are a serious problem on an Ethernet network and should be addressed immediately. *See also* collision, Ethernet.

Layer 2 Tunneling Protocol (L2TP)   A protocol used to establish virtual private network (VPN) connections across the Internet. *See also* virtual private network (VPN).

leased line   A permanent telephone connection between two points that provides a predetermined amount of bandwidth at all times. *See also* T-1, T-3.

lease identification cookie   A string that consists of a computer's Internet Protocol (IP) address and its hardware address, which a Dynamic Host Configuration Protocol (DHCP) server uses to uniquely identify a client in its database. *See also* Dynamic Host Configuration Protocol (DHCP).

linear tape-open (LTO)   A data storage medium that uses cartridges containing one-half-inch wide magnetic tape, most commonly used for system backups.

link code word   A 16-bit data packet included in the fast link pulse (FLP) signals generated by Fast Ethernet devices that contains the speeds at which the device can transmit data and whether or not the device supports full-duplex transmissions.

link pulse   A signal transmitted by Ethernet devices that indicates when the devices are communicating properly. Ethernet unshielded twisted pair (UTP) network interface adapters and hubs typically have light-emitting diodes (LEDs) that light up when the device receives a link pulse signal from a device to which it is connected. 10Base-T devices use a normal link pulse (NLP) signal, which is used only for link integrity testing. Fast Ethernet devices use a fast link pulse (FLP) signal, which also includes a link code word that enables the devices to negotiate the fastest possible transmission speed they have in common. *See also* fast link pulse (FLP), normal link pulse (NLP).

link segment   A network segment that connects only two computers together, such as a cable that connects a computer to a hub. *See also* mixing segment, which consists of cables that run from computer to computer in daisy-chain fashion. The Ethernet protocol distinguishes between mixing segments and link segments in the physical layer configuration guidelines that specify how many repeaters are permitted on a network.

link-state protocol   A dynamic routing protocol that rates the relative efficiency of network routes by the properties of the connections providing access to the destination. *See also* distance vector protocols, which use the number of hops to rate the efficiency of a network. The most common of the link state protocols is the Open Shortest Path First (OSPF) protocol. *See also* Open Shortest Path First (OSPF).

LLC   *See* Logical Link Control (LLC) sublayer.

Lmhosts   An American Standard Code for Information Interchange (ASCII) text file used by Windows Transmission Control Protocol/Internet Protocol (TCP/IP) computers to resolve Network Basic Input/Output System (NetBIOS) names into Internet Protocol (IP) addresses. Like the Hosts file used to resolve host names into IP addresses, an Lmhosts file is a list of the NetBIOS names assigned to computers on the network and their corresponding IP addresses. Lmhosts files can also contain special entries used to preload the computer's NetBIOS name cache or to identify the domain controllers on the network. Windows systems can use individual Lmhosts files for NetBIOS name resolution, but they more commonly use either network broadcast transmissions or the Windows Internet Naming Service (WINS).

local area network (LAN)   A collection of computers that are connected to each other using a shared medium. The computers communicate with each other using a common set of protocols. *See also* wide area network (WAN), metropolitan area network (MAN).

Logical Link Control (LLC) sublayer   One of the two sublayers of the data-link layer defined by the Institute of Electrical and Electronic Engineers (IEEE) 802 standards. The LLC standard (IEEE 802.2) defines additional fields carried within the data field of data-link layer protocol headers. *See also* Media Access Control (MAC) sublayer.

loopback connector   A hardware tool used to test a network interface adapter by redirecting outgoing signals back into the device.

LTO   *See* linear tape-open (LTO).

MAC   *See* Media Access Control (MAC).

MAN   *See* metropolitan area network (MAN).

management information base (MIB)   An object-oriented database in which a network management agent stores the information that it will eventually transmit to a network management console using a protocol like the Simple Network Management Protocol (SNMP). Agents are built into network hardware and software products to enable them to report the status of the product to a central console monitored by a network administrator.

Manchester encoding   A self-timing physical layer encoding scheme used on Ethernet networks.

manual allocation   An operational mode of Dynamic Host Configuration Protocol (DHCP) servers in which the server assigns clients Internet Protocol (IP) addresses and other TCP/IP configuration settings specified by the server administrator for each computer. The IP addresses are not assigned randomly from a pool, as in the automatic and dynamic allocation modes. The end result is no different than configuring the TCP/IP clients by hand, but using the manual allocation mode of a DHCP server prevents the administrator from having to travel to the client computer and prevents other computers on the network from being assigned duplicate addresses. Manual allocation is typically used for clients that must have a specific IP address, such as a Web server that must be accessible from the Internet using a DNS name. *See also* Dynamic Host Configuration Protocol (DHCP).

MAU   *See* multistation access unit.

maximum transmission unit (MTU)   The largest physical packet size that a system can transmit over a network. As packets are routed through an internetwork, they might have to pass through individual networks with different MTUs. When a packet exceeds the MTU for a particular network, the network layer protocol (Internet Protocol, or IP, in most cases) divides the packet into fragments smaller than the MTU for the outgoing network. The protocol then repackages each fragment into a separate packet and transmits them. If necessary, fragments can be split into still smaller fragments by other routers along the way to the destination. Packets remain fragmented for the rest of their journey and are not reassembled until they reach the end system that is the packet's ultimate destination.

MB   Megabyte, equal to 1000 kilobytes (MB) or 1,000,000 bytes.

MBps   Megabytes per second, a unit of measurement typically used to measure the speed of data storage devices.

Mbps   *See* megabits per second.

media   In networking, a term used to describe the data-carrying hardware mechanism that computers and other network devices use to send information to each other. In computers, a term used to describe a means of storing data in a permanent fashion, such as a hard or floppy disk.

Media Access Control (MAC)   A method by which computers determine when they can transmit data over a shared network medium. When multiple computers are connected to a single network segment, two computers transmitting data at the same time cause a collision, which destroys the data. The MAC mechanism implemented in the data-link layer protocol prevents these collisions from occurring or permits them to occur in a controlled manner. The MAC mechanism is the defining characteristic of a data-link layer local area network (LAN) protocol. The two most common MAC mechanisms in use today are Carrier Sense Multiple Access with Collision Detection (CSMA/CD), which is used by Ethernet networks, and token passing, which is used by Token Ring and Fiber Distributed Data Interface (FDDI) networks, among others.

Media Access Control (MAC) sublayer   One of the two sublayers of the data-link layer defined by the Institute of Electrical and Electronic Engineers (IEEE) 802 standards. The MAC sublayer defines the mechanism used to regulate access to the network medium. *See also* Logical Link Control (LLC) sublayer.

megabytes per second (MBps)   A unit of measurement typically used to measure the speed of data storage devices.

mesh   In local area networking, a cable topology in which each device is connected to every other device with a separate length of cable. In this respect, the mesh network is purely theoretical, because it would be impractical to implement or impossible with more than a handful of devices. In internetworking, the term "mesh" refers to a fabric of connected networks that provides more than one route to a particular destination. *See also* topology.

metric   A field in a Transmission Control Protocol/Internet Protocol (TCP/IP) computer's routing table that contains a value rating the relative efficiency of a particular route. When routing packets, a router scans its routing table for the desired destination, and if there are two possible routes to that destination listed in the table, the router chooses the one with the lowest metric value. Depending on how the routing information is inserted into the table, the metric can represent the number of hops needed to reach the destination network, or it can contain a value that reflects the actual time needed to reach the destination.

metropolitan area network (MAN)   A data network that services an area larger than a local area network (LAN) and smaller than a wide area network (WAN). Most MANs today service communities, towns, or cities and are operated by cable television (CATV) companies using fiber optic cable.

MIB   *See* management information base (MIB).

minimal routing   The process of routing Internet Protocol (IP) using only the default routing table entries created by the operating system. *See also* static routing, dynamic routing.

mirroring   A data availability technique that involves storing identical copies of data on two different drives connected to a single host adapter. The drives appear as a single volume to users, and all files written to the volume are automatically copied to both drives. If one of the drives fails, the other continues to make the data available until the failed drive is repaired or replaced. *See also* duplexing.

mixing segment   A network segment that connects more than two computers, such as a thin Ethernet segment, which consists of cables that run from computer to computer in daisy-chain fashion. The Ethernet protocol distinguishes between mixing segments and link segments in the physical layer configuration guidelines that specify how many repeaters are permitted on a network. *See also* link segment.

modem   Short for modulator/demodulator, a hardware device that converts the digital signals generated by computers into analog signals suitable for transmission over a telephone line, and back again. A dial-up connection between two computers requires a modem at each end, both of which support the same communication protocols. Modems take the form of internal devices that plug into one of a computer's expansion slots, or external devices that connect to one of the computer's serial ports. The term "modem" is also used incorrectly, in many cases, to describe any device that provides a connection to a wide area communications service, such as a cable television (CATV) or Digital Subscriber Line (DSL) connection. These devices are not actually modems, because the service is digital, and no analog/digital conversion takes place.

MSAU   *See* multistation access unit.

MTU   *See* maximum transmission unit (MTU).

multicast   A network transmission with a destination address that represents a group of computers on the network. Transmission Control Protocol/Internet Protocol (TCP/IP) multicast addresses are defined by the Internet Assigned Numbers Authority (IANA) and represent groups of computers with similar functions, such as all of the routers on a network. *See also* broadcast, unicast.

multifunction cable tester   An electronic device that automatically tests a variety of network cable properties, compares the results to established standards, and specifies whether the cable is functioning within the defined parameters for those properties.

multihomed   A computer with two or more network interfaces, whether they take the form of network interface adapters, dial-up connections using modems, or other technologies. On a Transmission Control Protocol/Internet Protocol (TCP/IP) network, each of the network interfaces in a multihomed computer must have its own Internet Protocol (IP) address.

multimode fiber   A type of fiber optic cable typically used on local area networks (LANs) and supported by a number of data-link layer protocols, including standard Ethernet, Fast Ethernet, Gigabit Ethernet, and Fiber Distributed Data Interface (FDDI). Multimode fiber optic uses a light-emitting diode (LED) as a light source, unlike singlemode fiber optic, which uses a laser. Multimode fiber has a smaller bend radius, enabling it to bend around corners more easily than singlemode. As a result, multimode is better suited for relatively short distance connections than is singlemode. However, even multimode fiber can span much longer distances than most copper-based cables. *See also* singlemode fiber.

multiple master replication   A technique usually associated with a directory service, in which identical copies of a database are maintained on various computers scattered throughout a network. In multiple master replication, users can make changes to any copy of the database, and the changes to that copy are replicated to all of the other copies. This is a complex technique, because it is possible for different users to make changes to the same record on different masters. The system must therefore have a mechanism for reconciling data conflicts in the various masters, such as using time stamps or version numbers to assign priorities to data modifications. Microsoft's Active Directory directory service uses multiple master replication. *See also* single master replication.

multiplexing   Any one of several techniques used to transmit multiple signals over a single cable or other network medium simultaneously. Multiplexing works by separating the available bandwidth of the network medium into separate bands, by frequency, wavelength, time, or other criteria, and transmitting a different signal in each band. Local area network (LAN) media carry only one signal, and therefore do not use multiplexing, but some networks, such as cable television (CATV) and telephone networks, do.

multiport repeater   Another name for an Ethernet hub. A repeater is a physical layer device that amplifies incoming signals and retransmits them, enabling network segments to span longer distances without suffering from the effects of attenuation. A multiport repeater is a device that accepts multiple network connections. Signals arriving through any of the device's ports are amplified and retransmitted out through all of the other ports simultaneously. All of the hubs used on Ethernet networks are multiport repeaters.

multistation access unit (MAU or MSAU)   The hub used on a Token Ring network. Token Ring hubs are more complicated than Ethernet hubs because instead of repeating incoming signals out through all ports simultaneously, a MAU sends incoming signals out through each port in turn and waits for the signal to be returned by the connected computer. This forms the logical ring from which Token Ring networks get their name. To prevent breaks in the network, MAUs also perform an initialization process to insert each active computer into the ring.

multitasking   The technique by which a computer with one processor executes multiple tasks simultaneously. By splitting the software processing into separate processes called *threads*, the processor in the computer can switch rapidly from one thread to another, devoting some of its clock cycles to each. There are two types of multitasking: cooperative and preemptive. In cooperative multitasking, the operating system passes control of the processor to

each application in turn, and it is up to the application to return control to the operating system. A badly written application can fail to return control, causing the entire system to run inefficiently, or even crash. In preemptive multitasking, the operating system has complete control over the allocation of processor time to each application. Even if an application crashes, the rest of the processes continue to run normally.

name resolution   The process of converting a computer or other device's name into an address. Computers communicate using numeric addresses, but humans work better with names. To be able to send data to a particular destination identified by name in the user interface, the computer must first resolve that name into an address. On Transmission Control Protocol/Internet Protocol (TCP/IP) networks, for example, Domain Name System (DNS) names and Network Basic Input/Output System (NetBIOS) names must be resolved into Internet Protocol (IP) addresses. There are several name resolution methods that computers can use, depending on the type of name and type of address involved, including table lookups using text files such as Hosts and Lmhosts; independent processes, such as broadcast message generation; and network services, such as DNS and the Windows Internet Naming Service (WINS). *See also* Address Resolution Protocol (ARP).

NAT   *See* Network Address Translation (NAT).

Nbtstat.exe   A Microsoft Windows command-line utility that displays information about the NetBIOS Over TCP/IP (NetBT) connections that the system uses when communicating with other computers running Windows on a Transmission Control Protocol/ Internet Protocol (TCP/IP) network.

NCP   *See* NetWare Core Protocol (NCP).

NDIS *See* Network Driver Interface Specification (NDIS).

NDS *See* Novell Directory Services (NDS).

NetBEUI *See* NetBIOS Extended User Interface (NetBEUI).

NetBIOS *See* Network Basic Input/Output System (NetBIOS)

NetBIOS Extended User Interface (NetBEUI) A transport protocol sometimes used by the Microsoft Windows operating systems for local area networking. NetBEUI was the default protocol in the first version of Microsoft Windows NT and in Microsoft Windows for Workgroups; it has since been replaced as the default Windows protocol by Transmission Control Protocol/Internet Protocol (TCP/IP). NetBEUI is a simplified networking protocol that requires no configuration and is self-adjusting. However, the protocol is suitable only for small networks, because it is not routable. NetBEUI identifies computers by the Network Basic Input/Output System (NetBIOS) names (or computer names) assigned during the Windows installation. Because NetBIOS uses no network identifier, there is no way for the protocol to route traffic to systems on another network.

netstat A command-line utility supplied with UNIX and Microsoft Windows operating systems. The netstat utility displays information about a Transmission Control Protocol/ Internet Protocol (TCP/IP) computer's current network connections and about the traffic generated by the various TCP/IP protocols.

NetWare Core Protocol (NCP) A protocol in Novell NetWare's Internetwork Packet Exchange (IPX) protocol suite that is responsible for all of the file-sharing traffic generated by Novell NetWare clients and servers.

NetWare Link Services Protocol (NLSP) A dynamic routing protocol created by Novell for its NetWare operating system. NLSP enables NetWare routers to exchange routing information with less overhead than protocols that rely on repeated broadcast transmissions, such as the Routing Information Protocol (RIP).

network access point A hardware device used on wireless local area networks (LANs) employing the infrastructure topology to provide an interface between a cabled network and wireless devices. The access point is connected to a standard network using a cable and also has a transceiver enabling it to communicate with wireless computers and other devices. *See also* infrastructure topology.

Network Address Translation (NAT) A firewall technique that enables Transmission Control Protocol/Internet Protocol (TCP/IP) client computers using unregistered Internet Protocol (IP) addresses to access the Internet. Client computers send their Internet service requests to a Network Address Translation- (NAT-) equipped router, which substitutes its own registered IP address for the client's unregistered address, and forwards the request on to the specified server. The server sends its reply to the NAT router, which then relays it back to the original client. This renders the unregistered clients invisible to the Internet, preventing direct access to them. *See also* firewall.

network attached storage (NAS) A network data storage technology that uses a dedicated hardware device with a drive array and an embedded operating system.

Network Basic Input/Output System (NetBIOS) An application programming interface (API) that provides computers with a namespace and other local area networking functions.

Network Driver Interface Specification (NDIS) A multiprotocol device driver interface used by the Windows operating system for its network interface adapter drivers. The NDIS driver enables a single adapter and its data-link layer protocol to support traffic generated by the Transmission Control Protocol/Internet Protocol (TCP/IP), Internetwork Packet Exchange (IPX), and NetBIOS Extended User Interface (NetBEUI) protocols, in any combination.

Network File System (NFS) A standardized file sharing application used primarily by UNIX and Linux operating systems that enables one computer to mount the drives of another computer on the network into its own file system. File sharing interoperability with UNIX and Linux computers is frequently implemented in the form of an NFS product for another operating system, such as Microsoft Services for UNIX.

Network Information System (NIS) A directory service designed for UNIX and Linux computers that stores frequently-replicated configuration files in a central location, where they can be accessed by any system that needs them.

network interface adapter A hardware device that provides a computer with access to a local area network (LAN). Network interface adapters can be integrated into a computer's motherboard or take the form of an expansion card, in which case they are called *network interface cards (NICs)*. The adapter, along with its driver, implements the data-link layer protocol on the computer. The adapter has one or more connectors for network cables, or some other interface to the network medium. The network interface adapter and its driver are responsible for functions such as the encapsulation of network layer protocol data into data-link layer protocol frames, the encoding and decoding of data into the signals used by the network medium, and the implementation of the protocol's Media Access Control (MAC) mechanism.

network layer The third layer from the bottom of the Open Systems Interconnection (OSI) reference model. Protocols operating at the network layer are responsible for packaging transport layer data into datagrams, addressing them to its final destination, routing them across the internetwork, and fragmenting the datagrams as needed. The Internet Protocol (IP) is the most common protocol operating at the network layer, although Novell NetWare networks formerly used a proprietary network layer protocol called *Internetwork Packet Exchange (IPX)*.

Network News Transfer Protocol (NNTP) A Transmission Control Protocol/Internet Protocol (TCP/IP) protocol used to post, distribute, and retrieve Usenet messages to and from news servers throughout the Internet.

Network Terminator 1 (NT-1) Short for network terminator, the hardware device on the client side of an Integrated Services Digital Network (ISDN) installation that provides the straight tip (S/T) interface used to connect equipment to the service, such as ISDN telephones, fax machines, and the terminal adapter that connects to a computer. In some cases, the NT-1 is a separate piece of equipment, but it can also be integrated into a single unit along with a terminal adapter for installations in which only a single computer is to be connected to the service.

Network Time Protocol (NTP) An application layer Transmission Control Protocol/Internet Protocol (TCP/IP) protocol used to synchronize the clocks in network computers.

NIC *See* network interface adapter.

NIS *See* Network Information System (NIS).

NLP *See* normal link pulse (NLP).

NLSP *See* NetWare Link Services Protocol (NLSP).

NNTP *See* Network News Transfer Protocol (NNTP).

node Any uniquely addressable device on a network, such as a computer, router, or printer.

nominal velocity of propagation (NVP) The speed at which signals travel through a particular length of cable. Cable testing devices such as time domain reflectometers (TDRs) use the NVP to compute the length of a particular cable segment by dividing it into the measured time needed for a generated test signal to travel to the other end of the cable and back. The manufacturer supplies the NVP for a particular cable.

normal link pulse (NLP) The signal generated by standard Ethernet network interface adapters and hubs, which the devices use to signal that they have been cabled together properly. When an adapter or hub receives the NLP signal from the device to which it is connected, it lights up a light-emitting diode (LED), which indicates that communication is taking place. *See also* fast link pulse (FLP).

Novell Directory Services (NDS) Formerly known as NetWare Directory Services, now known as eDirectory, the first hierarchical, object-oriented directory service to achieve commercial success. NDS was first released as part of NetWare 4.0 in

1993 and has matured into a robust product that now supports other platforms in addition to NetWare, such as UNIX and Microsoft Windows. NDS provides networks with single logon capabilities and the ability to support third-party applications through the use of schema extensions. *See also* directory service, schema.

NT-1 *See* Network Terminator 1 (NT-1)

NTFS Short for NT file system; one of the file systems included with the Microsoft Windows 2000 and Microsoft Windows NT operating systems. NTFS supports larger volumes than the file allocation table (FAT) file system supported by Microsoft Windows, includes transaction logs to aid in recovery from disk failures, and enables network administrators to control access to specific directories and files. The main drawback to NTFS is that the drives are not accessible by any operating systems other than Windows 2000 and Windows NT. If you boot the computer with an MS-DOS disk, for example, the NTFS drives are invisible.

NVP *See* nominal velocity of propagation (NVP).

open circuit A type of cable fault in which one or more wires is not properly connected to the proper contact at the other end of the connection. Cable testing equipment typically detects open circuits by transmitting a test signal from one end of the cable and then failing to detect it at the other end. *See also* short circuit.

Open Shortest Path First (OSPF) A dynamic routing protocol that exchanges information with other routers on the network to update the system's routing table with current information about the configuration of the internetwork. OSPF is a link state protocol that evaluates routes based on their actual performance, rather than using a less accurate measurement like the number of hops needed to reach a particular destination. *See also* distance vector protocols, Routing Information Protocol (RIP).

Open Systems Interconnection (OSI) reference model   A theoretical model defined in documents published by the International Organization for Standardization (ISO) and the Telecommunication Standards Section of the International Telecommunications Union (ITU-T). The OSI model is used for reference and teaching purposes and divides the computer networking functions into seven layers: application, presentation, session, transport, network, data-link, and physical (from top to bottom). However, the layers do not correspond exactly to any of the currently used networking protocol stacks.

operating system   The primary program running on a computer, which processes input and output, runs other programs, and provides access to the computer's hardware.

organizationally unique identifier (OUI)   The three-byte hexadecimal value assigned by the Institute of Electrical and Electronic Engineers (IEEE) identifying the manufacturer of a network interface adapter. The OUI is used as the first three bytes of the adapter's hardware address.

OSI   *See* Open Systems Interconnection (OSI) reference model.

OSPF   *See* Open Shortest Path First (OSPF).

OUI   *See* organizationally unique identifier (OUI).

packet   The largest unit of data that can be transmitted over a data network at any one time. Messages generated by applications are split into pieces and packaged into individual packets for transmission over the network. Each

packet is transmitted separately and can take a different route to the destination. When all of the packets arrive at the destination, the receiving computer reassembles them into the original message. This is the basic functionality of a packet-switching network.

packet filter   Packet filtering is a firewall technique in which a router is configured to prevent certain packets from entering a network. Packet filters can be created based on hardware addresses, Internet Protocol (IP) addresses, port numbers, or other criteria. For example, you can configure a router to allow only certain computers to access the network from the Internet, or allow your network users access to Internet e-mail but deny them access to Internet Web servers. Although typically used to prevent intrusion into a private network from the Internet, packet filtering can also be used to limit access to one of the local area networks (LANs) on a private internetwork.

packet switching   A type of network communications in which messages are broken up into discrete units and transmitted to the destination. These units, called *packets*, can take different routes to the destination and might arrive there in a different order than that in which they were sent, but the receiving system can reassemble them in the proper order. Packet switching is what makes it possible for the computers on a local area network (LAN) to share a single network medium. If the computers transmitted entire messages at once, they could monopolize the network for long periods of time, preventing other computers from transmitting.

PAM-5   *See* Pulse Amplitude Modulation-5 (PAM-5).

PBX   *See* private branch exchange.

PC Card   A peripheral device standard designed for laptops and other portable computers, which enables manufacturers to create network interface cards (NICs), modems, and other devices packaged in a form approximately the size of a credit card.

PDU   *See* protocol data unit (PDU).

peer-to-peer networking   A networking system in which each computer can function both as a client and a server. Each computer also maintains its own security settings, which enables it to control access to its own resources. Peer-to-peer networking is useful on small networks, because no centralized administration is needed and users can easily maintain their own security settings. On larger networks, peer-to-peer networking is inefficient because users need a separate account for every computer they want to access, and because the access control capabilities are usually less flexible and less robust than those of a centrally administered client/server network.

phantom collision   A phenomenon that occurs when excessive crosstalk on a twisted-pair cable causes a computer to detect signals on both the transmit and receive wire pairs at the same time. To the network interface adapter, these simultaneous signals indicate the existence of a packet collision, and the adapter takes the appropriate steps to clear the network of data and retransmit the supposedly damaged packet. In fact, no real collision has occurred, but the end result is the same as if one had.

physical layer   The bottom layer of the Open Systems Interconnection (OSI) reference model. The physical layer defines the nature of the network medium itself, how it should be installed, and what types of signals it should carry. In the case of local area networking, the physical layer is closely related to the data-link layer immediately above it, because the data-link layer protocol includes the physical layer specifications.

Ping   A Transmission Control Protocol/Internet Protocol (TCP/IP) command-line utility used to test whether a computer can communicate with another computer on the network. Ping generates Internet Control Message Protocol (ICMP) Echo Request messages and transmits them to the computer specified on the command line. The target computer, on receiving the messages, transmits them back to the sender as ICMP Echo Replies. The system running Ping then displays the elapsed times between the transmission of the requests and the receipt of the replies. Virtually every TCP/IP client implementation includes a version of Ping.

Plain Old Telephone Service (POTS)   A common phrase referring to the Public Switched Telephone Network (PSTN), the standard copper-cable telephone network used for analog voice communications around the world.

Point-to-Point Protocol (PPP)   A data-link layer Transmission Control Protocol/Internet Protocol (TCP/IP) protocol used for wide area network (WAN) connections, especially dial-up connections to the Internet and other service providers. Unlike its progenitor, the Serial Line Internet Protocol (SLIP), PPP includes support for multiple network layer protocols, link quality monitoring protocols, and authentication protocols. PPP is used for connections between two computers only and therefore does not need many of the features found in local area network (LAN) protocols, such as address fields for each packet and a Media Access Control (MAC) mechanism.

Point-to-Point Protocol over Ethernet (PPPoE)   A Transmission Control Protocol/Internet Protocol (TCP/IP) standard that defines a method for establishing individually negotiated Point-to-Point Protocol (PPP) connections between computers on an Ethernet network and services on other networks, accessible through a Digital Subscriber Line (DSL) or cable television (CATV) connection. *See also* Point-to-Point Protocol (PPP).

Point-to-Point Tunneling Protocol (PPTP)   A data-link layer protocol used to provide secured communications for virtual private network (VPN) connections. VPNs are private network connections that use the Internet as a network medium. To secure the data as it is transmitted across the Internet, the computers use a process called *tunneling,* in which the entire data-link layer frame generated by an application process is encapsulated within an Internet Protocol (IP) datagram. This arrangement violates the rules of the Open Systems Interconnection (OSI) reference model, but it enables the entire Point-to-Point Protocol (PPP) frame generated by the user application to be encrypted inside an IP datagram.

POP3   *See* Post Office Protocol 3 (POP3).

port   A code number identifying a process running on a Transmission Control Protocol/Internet Protocol (TCP/IP) computer. Transport layer protocols, such as the Transmission Control Protocol (TCP) and the User Datagram Protocol (UDP), specify the port number of the source and destination application processes in the header of each message they create. The combination of an Internet Protocol (IP) address and a port number (which is called a *socket*) identify a specific application on a specific computer on a specific network. Port numbers lower than 1024 are called *well-known port numbers,* which are assigned by the Internet Assigned Numbers Authority (IANA) to common applications. The TCP port number 80, for example, is the well-known port number for Web servers. Port numbers 1024 and above are ephemeral port numbers, which are selected at random by clients for each transaction they initiate with a server. Alternatively, a port is a hardware connector in a computer or other network device that is used to attach cables that run to other devices.

Post Office Protocol 3 (POP3)   An application layer Transmission Control Protocol/Internet Protocol (TCP/IP) protocol used by e-mail clients to download messages from an e-mail server. E-mail traffic between servers and outgoing e-mail traffic from clients to servers uses the Simple Mail Transfer Protocol (SMTP). *See also* Internet Mail Access Protocol (IMAP).

POTS   *See* Plain Old Telephone Service (POTS).

PPP   *See* Point-to-Point Protocol (PPP).

PPTP   *See* Point-to-Point Tunneling Protocol (PPTP).

presentation layer   The second layer from the top of the Open Systems Interconnection (OSI) reference model. The presentation layer is responsible for translating the syntaxes used by different types of computers on a network. A computer translates the data generated by its applications from its own abstract syntax to a common transport syntax suitable for transmission over the network. When the data arrives at its destination, the presentation layer on the receiving system translates the transfer syntax into the computer's own native abstract syntax.

PRI   *See* Primary Rate Interface (PRI).

Primary Rate Interface (PRI) An Integrated Services Digital Network (ISDN) service that consists of 23 64-Kbps B channels plus one 64-Kbps D channel, providing an aggregate bandwidth equal to that of a T-1 line. The B channels can be combined into a single data pipe, used individually, or in any combination. The PRI service is rarely used in the United States but is a popular business service in Europe and Japan. *See also* B channel, D channel, Integrated Services Digital Network (ISDN).

Private branch exchange (PBX) A private telephone network used within an organization that shares a number of outside telephone lines among its users.

promiscuous mode An operational mode available in some network interface adapters that causes the adapter to read and process all of the packets transmitted over the local area network (LAN), not just the packets addressed to it. Protocol analyzers use promiscuous mode to capture comprehensive samples of network traffic for later analysis.

protocol A documented format for the transmission of data between two networked devices. A protocol is essentially a language that a computer uses to communicate, and the other computer to which it is connected must use the same language for communication to take place. In most cases, network communication protocols are defined by open standards created by bipartisan committees. However, there are still a few proprietary protocols in use. Computers use many different protocols to communicate, which has given rise to the Open Systems Interconnection (OSI) reference model, which defines the layers at which different protocols operate.

Protocol An American Standard Code for Information Interchange (ASCII) text file found on Transmission Control Protocol/Internet Protocol (TCP/IP) systems that lists the codes used in the Protocol field of the Internet Protocol (IP) header. This field identifies the transport layer protocol that generated the data carried within the datagram, ensuring that the data reaches the appropriate process on the receiving computer. The protocol numbers are registered by the Internet Assigned Numbers Authority (IANA) and are derived from the "Assigned Numbers" Request for Comments (RFC) document.

protocol data unit (PDU) A generic term for the data constructions created by the protocols operating at the various layers of the Open Systems Interconnection (OSI) reference model. For example, the PDU created by data-link layer protocols are called *frames,* and network layer PDUs are called *datagrams.*

protocol stack The multilayered arrangement of communications protocols that provides a data path ranging from the user application to the network medium. Although based on the Open Systems Interconnection (OSI) reference model, not every layer in the model is represented by a separate protocol. On a computer connected to a local area network (LAN), for example, the protocol stack generally consists of protocols at the application, transport, network, and data-link layers, the latter of which includes a physical layer specification.

proxy server An application layer firewall technique that enables Transmission Control Protocol/ Internet Protocol (TCP/IP) client systems to access Internet resources without being susceptible to intrusion from outside the network. A proxy server is an application that runs on a computer with a registered Internet Protocol (IP) address, whereas the clients use unregistered IP addresses, causing them to remain invisible from the Internet. Client applications are configured to send their Internet service requests to the proxy server instead of directly to the Internet, and the proxy server relays the requests to the appropriate Internet server, using its own registered address. On receiving a response from the Internet server, the proxy server relays it back to the original client. Proxy servers are designed for specific applications, and the client must be configured with the address of the proxy server. Administrators can also configure the proxy server to cache Internet information for later use and to restrict access to particular Internet sites. *See also* firewall, Network Address Translation (NAT).

PSTN   *See* Public Switched Telephone Network (PSTN).

Public Switched Telephone Network (PSTN)   The standard copper-cable telephone network used for analog voice communications around the world. Also known as Plain Old Telephone Service (POTS).

Pulse Amplitude Modulation-5 (PAM-5)   A signaling scheme used in the 1000Base-T Gigabit Ethernet variant. PAM-5 is one of the elements that makes it possible for 1000Base-T to run using standard Category 5 (CAT5) unshielded twisted pair (UTP) cable.

QIC   *See* quarter-inch cartridge (QIC).

quarter-inch cartridge (QIC)   A data-storage medium that uses cartridges containing quarter-inch-wide magnetic tape, most commonly used for system backups.

RARP   *See* Reverse Address Resolution Protocol (RARP).

redirector   A network client component that determines whether a resource requested by an application is located on the network or on the local system and sends the request either to the local I/O system or to the networking protocol stack. A computer can have multiple redirectors to support different networks, such as a Microsoft Windows network and a Novell NetWare network.

remote bridge   A device operating at the data-link layer of the Open Systems Interconnection (OSI) reference model. A remote bridge is used to connect two local area networks (LANs) at different locations with a wide area network (WAN) link, such as a dial-up modem connection or a leased telephone line. By bridging the two network segments, the amount of traffic passing over the WAN is limited, which compensates for its relative slow speed and high cost. *See also* bridge.

Remote Monitoring (RMON) protocol   A network management protocol that enables hardware and software devices to transmit status information to a central network management console.

repeater   A physical layer device that amplifies network signals, enabling them to travel longer distances without suffering from the effects of attenuation. Repeaters for Ethernet networks using coaxial cable have two ports, one for incoming traffic and one for outgoing traffic. However, most of the repeaters used today have multiple ports to support networks using a star topology. The hubs used for unshielded twisted pair (UTP) Ethernet networks today are all multiport repeaters, which amplify signals as they transmit them out through all of the device's ports simultaneously. *See also* attenuation, hub, multiport repeater.

Request for Comments (RFC)   A document published by the Internet Engineering Task Force (IETF) that contains information about a topic related to the Internet or to the Transmission Control Protocol/Internet Protocol (TCP/IP) suite. For example, all of the TCP/IP protocols have been documented and published as RFCs and eventually might be ratified as Internet standards. Some RFCs are only informational or historical, however, and are not submitted for ratification as standards. After they are published and assigned numbers, RFCs are never changed. If a new version of an RFC document is published, it is assigned a new number and cross-indexed to indicate that it renders the old version obsolete.

resolver   Another name for the Domain Name System (DNS) client found on every Transmission Control Protocol/Internet Protocol (TCP/IP) computer. Whenever the computer attempts to access a TCP/IP system using a DNS name, the resolver generates a DNS Request message and sends it to the DNS server specified in the computer's TCP/IP client configuration. The DNS server then takes the necessary steps to resolve the requested name into an Internet Protocol (IP) address and returns the address to the resolver in the client computer. The resolver can then give the IP address to the TCP/IP client, which uses it to transmit a message to the desired destination. *See also* Domain Name System (DNS).

resource record   The unit in which a Domain Name System (DNS) server stores information about a particular computer. The information stored in a resource record depends on the type of record it is, but typically a resource record includes the host name of a computer and its equivalent Internet Protocol (IP) address. In most cases, administrators must manually create the resource records on a DNS server, but recent additions to the DNS standards define a method for dynamically updating the information in resource records as needed. This capability is central to the DNS functionality required by the Active Directory directory service. *See also* Domain Name System (DNS).

Reverse Address Resolution Protocol (RARP)   An alternative mode of the Address Resolution Protocol (ARP) that enables a computer to retrieve an Internet Protocol (IP) address from an RARP server by broadcasting its hardware address. Designed for use on diskless workstations, RARP is limited in that it can receive only an IP address from the server, and not other Transmission Control Protocol/Internet Protocol (TCP/IP) configuration parameters, and also in that an administrator must manually configure the RARP server with a specific IP address for every RARP client. RARP is the progenitor of the Bootstrap Protocol (BOOTP) and the Dynamic Host Configuration Protocol (DHCP).

reverse name resolution   The process of resolving an Internet Protocol (IP) address into a Domain Name System (DNS) name, which is the opposite of the normal name-to-address resolution performed by DNS servers. Reverse DNS name resolution is accomplished using an extension to the DNS namespace consisting of a domain called *in-addr.arpa,* which contains four levels of subdomains named using the numbers 0 through 255. These subdomains contain resource records called *pointers;* each pointer contains an IP address and its equivalent DNS name. A DNS server looks up an IP address by locating the domain name equivalent to the address. For example, the IP address 192.168.1.15 becomes the domain name 15.1.168.192.in-addr-arpa.

RFC   *See* Request for Comments (RFC).

RG-8   A type of coaxial cable, also known as thick Ethernet, which is specified by the original DIX Ethernet specification as well as the later Institute of Electrical and Electronics Engineers (IEEE) 802.3 standard. RG-8 cable is 0.405 inches thick and relatively inflexible, and is installed using a bus topology. *See also* coaxial cable, thick Ethernet.

RG-58   A type of coaxial cable, also known as thin Ethernet, which is specified by the original DIX Ethernet specification as well as the later Institute of Electrical and Electronics Engineers (IEEE) 802.3 standard. RG-58 cable is 0.195 inches thick and relatively flexible, uses bayonet-Neill-Concelman (BNC) connectors to join the ends, and is installed using a bus topology. *See also* coaxial cable, thin Ethernet.

ring   A network cabling topology in which each device is connected to the next device, forming a loop with no ends. In most cases, the ring is implemented logically by the internal wiring of a hub, and the physical network takes the form of a star. *See also* star, topology.

RIP   *See* Routing Information Protocol (RIP).

RJ-11   Short for Registered Jack-11, a four-pin or six-pin modular connector that is used in telephone networking. *See also* RJ-45.

RJ-45   Short for Registered Jack-45, an eight-pin modular connector that is used in telephone and data networking. The majority of local area networks (LANs) today use RJ-45 connectors with unshielded twisted pair (UTP) cables. *See also* RJ-11.

RMON   *See* Remote Monitoring protocol (RMON).

root name server   One of a handful of servers that represent the top of the Domain Name System (DNS) namespace by supplying other DNS servers with the Internet Protocol (IP) addresses of the authoritative servers for all of the top-level domains in the DNS. When resolving a DNS name into an IP address, a DNS server that cannot resolve the name itself sends a DNS Request to one of the root name servers identified in the server's configuration. The root name server reads the top-level domain (that is, the last word, such as com in www.microsoft.com) from the requested name and supplies the requesting server with the IP address for that top-level domain. The requesting server then transmits the same request to the top-level domain server that the root name server supplied. The root name servers are also the authoritative servers for some of the top-level domains, so they can eliminate a step from the process and supply the address of the second-level domain's authoritative server. *See also* Domain Name System (DNS), authoritative server.

routed   A UNIX daemon, pronounced "route-dee," that was the original implementation of the Routing Information Protocol (RIP), the most popular of the distance vector routing protocols. *See also* distance vector protocol, dynamic routing.

router   A network layer hardware or software device that connects two networks together and relays traffic between them as needed. A router uses a table containing information about the other routers on the network to examine the destination address of each packet it receives, select the most efficient route to that destination, and forward the packet to the router or computer that is the next step in its path. Routers can connect two local area networks (LANs) together or provide access to remote resources by connecting a LAN to a distant network using a wide area network (WAN) link. One of the most common scenarios involves using routers to connect a LAN to the network of an Internet service provider (ISP), thus providing Internet access to all of the LAN's users.

Routing Information Protocol (RIP)   A dynamic routing protocol that enables Internet Protocol (IP) and Internetwork Packet Exchange (IPX) routers to receive information about the other routers on the network, which enables them to keep their routing tables updated with the latest information. RIP works by generating broadcast messages at frequent intervals, which contain the contents of the router's routing table. Other routers use this information to update their own tables, thus spreading the routing information all over the network. Routers also interpret the absence of RIP messages from a particular router as a sign that it is not functioning and then remove that router from their tables after a given interval. RIP is frequently criticized for the large amount of broadcast traffic that it generates on the network, and for the limitations of its distance vector routing method, which evaluates routes based solely on the number of hops between the source and the destination. *See also* distance vector protocol, dynamic routing.

routing table   A list maintained in every Transmission Control Protocol/Internet Protocol (TCP/IP) computer of network destinations and the routers and interfaces that the computer should use to transmit to them. In a computer that is not a router, the routing table contains only a few entries, the most frequently used of which is the default gateway entry. On a router, the routing table can contain many entries that are either manually added by a network administrator or automatically created by a dynamic routing protocol. When there is more than one routing table entry for a specific destination, the computer selects the best route based on a metric, which is a rating of the route's relative efficiency.

SAN   *See* Storage Area Network.

SC   *See* subscriber connector (SC).

schema   The structure of a database system. In a hierarchical directory service, such as Microsoft's Active Directory directory service or NetWare's Novell Directory Services (NDS), the schema contains object classes, which specify what objects can be created in the directory, the relationships between the object classes in the directory tree, and the attributes that make up each object class. Third-party applications can expand the schema for these directory services, enabling the creation of new object classes or the addition of new attributes to existing object classes. In Active Directory, it's also possible to modify the schema manually using the Active Directory Schema console.

scope   The pool of Internet Protocol (IP) addresses on a given subnet that a Dynamic Host Configuration Protocol (DHCP) server is configured to assign to clients when using the automatic or dynamic allocation method. *See also* Dynamic Host Configuration Protocol (DHCP), automatic allocation, dynamic allocation.

SCSI   *See* Small Computer System Interface (SCSI).

Secure Hypertext Transfer Protocol (S-HTTP or HTTPS)   A security protocol that provides authentication and encryption services to Web client/server transactions. *See also* Hypertext Transfer Protocol (HTTP).

Secure Sockets Layer (SSL)   A security protocol that provides authentication and encryption services to Web client/server transactions. *See also* Hypertext Transfer Protocol (HTTP).

segment   A section of a network that is bounded by hubs, bridges, routers, or switches. Depending on the data-link layer protocol and type of cable being used, a segment can consist of more than one length of cable. For example, a thin Ethernet network uses separate pieces of coaxial cable to connect each computer to the next one on the bus, but all of those pieces of cable together are called a *segment.*

Sequenced Packet Exchange (SPX)   A connection-oriented, transport-layer protocol in the Novell NetWare Internetwork Packet Exchange (IPX) protocol suite.

Serial Line Internet Protocol (SLIP)   A data-link layer Transmission Control Protocol/Internet Protocol (TCP/IP) protocol used for wide area network (WAN) connections, especially dial-up connections to the Internet and other service providers. Because it is used for connections between two computers only, SLIP does not need many of the features found in local area network (LAN) protocols, such as address fields for each packet and a Media Access Control (MAC) mechanism. SLIP is the simplest of protocols, consisting only of a single End Delimiter byte that is transmitted after each Internet Protocol (IP) datagram. Unlike its successor, the Point-to-Point Protocol (PPP), SLIP has no inherent security capabilities or any other additional services. For this reason, it is rarely used today.

service   The Microsoft Windows term for a computer program or process that runs continuously in the background and performs tasks at predetermined intervals or in response to specific events. Called a *daemon* by UNIX

operating systems, services typically perform server tasks, such as sharing files and printers, handling e-mail, and transmitting Web files.

service-dependent filtering   A type of packet filtering used in firewalls that limits access to a network based on the port numbers specified in packets' transport layer protocol headers. The port number identifies the application that generated the packet or that is destined to receive it. With this technique, network administrators can limit access to a network to specific applications or prevent users from accessing specific applications outside the network. *See also* firewall, port, packet filtering.

service pack (SP)   A software update package provided by Microsoft for one of its products. A service pack contains a collection of fixes and enhancements packaged into a single self-installing archive file.

Services   An American Standard Code for Information Interchange (ASCII) text file found on Transmission Control Protocol/Internet Protocol (TCP/IP) systems that lists the codes used in the Source Port and Destination Port fields of the Transmission Control Protocol (TCP) and User Datagram Protocol (UDP) headers. These fields identify the application process that generated the data carried within the packet, or for which it is destined. The port numbers are registered by the Internet Assigned Numbers Authority (IANA).

session layer   The third layer from the top of the Open Systems Interconnection (OSI) reference model. There are no specific session layer protocols, but there are 22 services that the session layer performs, which are incorporated into various application layer protocols. The most important of these functions are dialog control and dialog separation. Dialog control provides two modes for communicating systems: two-way alternate (TWA) mode or two-way simultaneous (TWS) mode. Dialog separation controls the process of inserting checkpoints in the data stream to synchronize functions on the two computers.

shielded twisted pair (STP)   A type of cable used for local area networking in environments where additional shielding against electromagnetic interference (EMI) is needed. The cable consists of eight copper wires twisted into four pairs, with different twist rates and foil or mesh shielding around each pair. The four pairs are then encased in an insulating sheath that provides even more protection.

short circuit   A type of cable fault in which two or more of the conductors inside the cable are in contact with each other. Shorts can be caused by a faulty cable installation, in which connectors are improperly attached, or a break in the insulation surrounding the cable's conductors, due either to mishandling or a manufacturing defect. Even the most basic cable testers can easily detect shorts.

signal quality error   The technical term used in the Institute of Electrical and Electronics Engineers (IEEE) 802.3 standard for a packet collision, which occurs when two computers on a shared network medium transmit data at precisely the same time. *See also* collision.

signaled error   A transmission error that has already been detected by a protocol operating at a lower layer of the networking stack.

Simple Mail Transfer Protocol (SMTP)   An application layer TCP/IP protocol used to carry e-mail messages between servers and from clients to servers. To retrieve e-mail from mail servers, clients typically use the Post Office Protocol (POP3) or the Internet Mail Access Protocol (IMAP).

Simple Network Management Protocol (SNMP)   An application layer Transmission Control Protocol/Internet Protocol (TCP/IP) protocol and query language used to transmit information about the status of network components to a central network management console. Components embedded into network hardware and software products called *agents* are responsible for collecting data about the activities of the products they service, storing the data in a management information base (MIB), and transmitting that data to the console at regular intervals using SNMP messages.

single master replication   A technique usually associated with a directory service in which identical copies of a database are maintained on various computers scattered throughout a network. In single master replication, users can make changes on only one copy of the database (the master), and the master replicates those changes to all of the other copies. This is a relatively simple technique compared to multiple master replication, because data only travels in one direction. However, the system is limited in that users might have to connect to a master located at another site to make changes to the database.

singlemode fiber   A type of fiber optic cable typically used for long-distance connections between networks, supported by a relatively small number of data-link layer protocols, such as Gigabit Ethernet. Singlemode fiber optic uses a laser as its light source, unlike multimode fiber optic, which uses a light-emitting diode (LED). Singlemode fiber has a larger bend radius than multimode fiber, which makes singlemode more difficult to bend around corners. As a result, singlemode is better suited than multimode for long-distance connections.

sliding window   A technique used to implement flow control in a network communications protocol. By acknowledging the number of bytes that have been successfully transmitted and specifying the number of bytes that it is capable of receiving, a computer on the receiving end of a data connection creates a "window" that consists of the bytes the sender is authorized to transmit. As the transmission progresses, the window slides along the byte stream, and might change its size, until all data has been transmitted and received successfully.

SLIP   *See* Serial Line Internet Protocol (SLIP).

Small Computer System Interface (SCSI)   A peripheral device interface that enables you to connect internal and external devices (especially storage devices) to a computer. SCSI is the preferred interface for network servers.

SMTP   *See* Simple Mail Transfer Protocol (SMTP).

SNMP   *See* Simple Network Management Protocol (SNMP).

SNMP agent   A software component integrated into a network hardware or software product, which is designed to gather ongoing status information about the product, store it in a management information base (MIB), and transmit it to a central network management console at regular intervals, using Simple Network Management Protocol (SNMP) messages.

socket   On a Transmission Control Protocol/Internet Protocol (TCP/IP) network, the combination of an Internet Protocol (IP) address and a port number, which together identify a specific application process running on a specific computer. The Uniform Resource Locators (URLs) used in Internet client applications express a socket as the IP address followed by the

port number, separated by a colon, as in 192.168.1.17:80.

Source IP Address   A 32-bit field in the Internet Protocol (IP) header that contains a value used to identify the particular network interface from which a packet originated.

SP   *See* service pack (SP).

spanning tree algorithm (STA)   A protocol used by network bridges in cases where a network contains redundant bridges for fault-tolerance purposes. The presence of multiple bridges on the same network, performing the same tasks, can result in data loss when each bridge lists a computer as being part of a different network segment, or can even result in a bridge loop, in which packets are forwarded endlessly from bridge to bridge. Using the STA, the redundant bridges communicate among themselves and select one of the bridges to process packets, while the others remain idle until the active bridge fails.

split pair   A type of twisted-pair cable fault in which two or more wires are connected to the wrong contacts in the same way at both ends of the cable. The cable appears to be wired correctly, because each contact in one connector is connected to the equivalent contact in the other connector, but the wires are not twisted into the appropriate pairs. If two signal-carrying wires are twisted together (instead of the normal configuration, in which each signal-carrying wire is twisted together with a ground wire), the cable generates excessive amounts of crosstalk, which can result in phantom collisions or other communication problems. Because the wiring appears to be correct, split pairs are not detectable by standard cable testing devices that transmit a signal at one end of the wire and receive it at the other end. To detect split pairs, you must measure the crosstalk produced by the cable, which requires a high-end multifunction cable tester.

ST *See* straight tip (ST) connector.

STA *See* spanning tree algorithm.

star A network cabling topology in which each device is connected to a central nexus called a *hub*. *See also* topology.

stateful packet inspection A generic term for a firewall process that examines connection information and traffic patterns, as well as packet contents, to determine whether packets should be permitted to pass through the firewall.

static routing A method for creating a Transmission Control Protocol/Internet Protocol (TCP/IP) router's routing table, in which the table entries are manually created by a network administrator. *See also* dynamic routing, in which routing table entries are automatically created by specialized routing protocols that exchange information with the other routers on the network.

S/T interface On an Integrated Services Digital Network (ISDN) installation, the interface provided by a Network Terminator 1 (NT-1), to which you can connect ISDN devices (like ISDN telephones or faxes) or a terminal adapter (to which you can connect standard analog communications devices). In some cases, the NT-1 and the terminal adapter are integrated into a single unit, eliminating the need for straight tip (S/T) interface connectors.

storage area network (SAN) A dedicated local area network (LAN) that connects servers with storage devices, often using the Fibre Channel protocol, reducing the storage-related traffic on the user network.

STP *See* shielded twisted pair (STP).

straight-through connection A twisted-pair cable wiring scheme in which each of the eight wires is connected to the same contact in the connectors on both ends of the cable. This type of cable, by itself, does not permit communications between computers to take place, because the transmit signals generated by each computer are wired to the transmit contacts in the other computer. For communication to be possible, the transmit contacts in one computer must be wired to the receive contacts in the other computer, resulting in what is called a *crossover circuit*. Twisted-pair Ethernet networks rely on hubs to provide the crossover circuit, which enables all of the cables to be wired straight through. To connect two computers directly, without a hub, you must use a crossover cable, which provides the crossover circuit in the cable's wiring. *See also* crossover connection, crossover cable.

straight tip (ST) A connector used with fiber optic cables.

striping A data availability technique in which data is written to clusters on multiple drives in an alternating pattern (that is, one cluster is written to one drive, then the next cluster to a different drive, and so on). The drives appear as a single volume to users, but because the computer is reading data from two or more physical drives, it is possible for the heads in one drive to be moving to the next cluster while the heads in the other drive are actually reading a cluster. This speeds up the disk read process, because one of the drives is always reading data; if only a single drive were used, it would have to stop reading after every cluster so the heads could move to their next location. The drawback of the striping method is that the failure of one drive causes the loss of the entire volume.

subnet   A group of computers on a Transmission Control Protocol/Internet Protocol (TCP/IP) network that share a common network identifier. In some cases, a TCP/IP network is divided into multiple subnets by modifying the subnet mask and designating some of the host identifier bits as subnet identifier bits. This enables the administrator to divide a network address of a particular class into multiple subnets, each of which contains a group of the hosts supported by the class.

subnet mask   A Transmission Control Protocol/Internet Protocol (TCP/IP) configuration parameter that specifies which bits of the Internet Protocol (IP) address identify the host and which bits identify the network on which the host resides. When the subnet mask is viewed in binary form, the bits with a value of 1 are the network identifier and the bits with a value of 0 are the host identifier.

subscriber connector (SC)   A connector used with fiber optic cables.

switch   A data-link layer network connection device that looks like a hub, but forwards incoming packets only to the computers for which they are destined. Switches essentially eliminate the medium sharing from Ethernet networks by providing each computer with a dedicated connection to its destination. Using switches, you can build larger network segments, because there is no contention for the network medium and no increase in collisions as the number of computers connected to the network rises. *See also* hub, which forwards incoming packets out through all of its ports.

Synchronous Optical Network (SONET)   A physical layer standard that defines a method for building a synchronous telecommunications network based on fiber optic cables.

SONET provides connections at various optical carrier (OC) levels running at different speeds, ranging from 51.84 Mbps (OC-1) to 9953.280 Mbps (OC-192).

T-1   A dedicated telephone connection, also called a *leased line,* running at 1.544 Mbps. A T-1 line consists of 24 64-Kbps channels, which can be used separately, in combinations, or as a single data pipe. Large companies use T-1 lines for both voice and data traffic; smaller companies can lease part of a T-1, which is called a *fractional T-1 service.* Although it uses the telephone network, a T-1 used for data networking does not use a dial-up connection; it is permanently connected to a specific location. *See also* leased line.

T-3   A dedicated telephone connection, also called a *leased line,* running at 44.736 Mbps. *See also* leased line.

TCP   *See* Transmission Control Protocol (TCP).

TCP/IP   *See* Transmission Control Protocol/Internet Protocol.

TDR   *See* time domain reflectometer (TDR).

TE-1   A device designed to connect directly to the straight tip (S/T) interface provided by an Integrated Services Digital Network (ISDN) installation.

TE2   A device that cannot connect directly to the straight tip (S/T) interface provided by an Integrated Services Digital Network (ISDN) installation and requires an intervening terminal adapter.

Telecommunications Industry Association/Electronic Industries Alliance   A cooperative trade association responsible for the "Commercial Building Telecommunication Cabling Standard," also known as TIA/EIA 568, which specifies how network cables should be installed in a commercial site.

Telecommunications Network Protocol (Telnet)   An application layer Transmission Control Protocol/Internet Protocol (TCP/IP) client/server protocol used to remotely control a computer at another location. A mainstay of UNIX networking, Telnet is a true remote control application. When you access another computer and run a program, it is the processor in the remote computer that executes that program. The Telnet service is command-line based, making it relatively useless on computers running Microsoft Windows, which rely on a graphical interface. However, all versions of Windows include a Telnet client. Microsoft Windows 2000 also includes a Telnet server, but compared with a UNIX Telnet implementation, there are relatively few things that you can do with it.

telepole   A cable installation tool that consists of a telescoping pole with a hook on the end, used for pushing cables through ceiling and wall spaces.

Telnet   *See* Telecommunications Network Protocol (Telnet).

terminal adapter   A hardware component used to connect a TE2 device to an Integrated Systems Digital Network (ISDN) connection. The terminal adapter plugs into the straight tip (S/T) interface provided by the NT-1. In some cases, a terminal adapter and an NT-1 are integrated into a single unit, which is specifically designed for installations in which a computer will be the only device using the ISDN connection. *See also* Integrated Services Digital Network (ISDN), NT-1, TE2, S/T interface.

termination   The connection of a resistor pack to the ends of a bus network to prevent signals reaching the end of the

cable from reflecting back in the other direction. All bus networks, including thick and thin Ethernet and the Small Computer System Interface (SCSI) bus used for storage arrays in computers, must be terminated at both ends, or communications will not be reliable.

thick Ethernet   Also called *10Base5,* an Ethernet physical layer specification that uses RG-8 coaxial cable in a bus topology, with network segments up to 500 meters long and running at 10 Mbps. Thick Ethernet was the original Ethernet physical layer option introduced in the DIX Ethernet standard and was maintained in the Institute of Electrical and Electronics Engineers (IEEE) 802.3 standard. However, because of its difficult installation, it was quickly replaced by thin Ethernet, which has now been replaced by unshielded twisted pair (UTP) cable.

thin Ethernet   Also called *10Base2,* an Ethernet physical layer specification that uses RG-58 coaxial cable in a bus topology, with network segments up to 185 meters long and running at 10 Mbps. Thin Ethernet was the dominant Ethernet physical layer option for several years, but it has since been replaced by unshielded twisted pair (UTP) cable, which is easier to install and maintain and can run at faster speeds.

tif   A file format commonly used to store graphic images in bitmap form.

time domain reflectometer (TDR)   A cable testing device that measures the length of a cable by transmitting a test signal and measuring the time it takes for the signal to travel to the other end and back. By supplying the cable's nominal velocity of propagation (the speed at which signals travel through the cable), the TDR can compute the length of the cable. In most cases, the time domain reflectometry function is incorporated into a multifunction cable tester, but it is sometimes a separate unit. *See also* nominal velocity of propagation (NVP).

token passing   A Media Access Control (MAC) mechanism used on ring topology networks that uses a separate frame type called a *token,* which circulates around the network from computer to computer. Only the computer in possession of the token is permitted to transmit its data, which prevents computers from transmitting at the same time, causing collisions. On receipt of the token, a computer transmits a packet and either regenerates a new token immediately or waits for the packet to circulate around the network and return to its source, at which time the computer removes the packet and transmits the token frame. Unlike the Carrier Sense Multiple Access with Collision Detection (CSMA/CD) MAC mechanism, no collisions occur on a properly functioning token passing network. Token passing is used by several different data-link layer protocols, including Token Ring and Fiber Distributed Data Interface (FDDI).

Token Ring   A data-link layer protocol originally developed by IBM, used on local area networks (LANs) with a ring topology. Running at 4 Mbps or 16 Mbps, Token Ring networks use the token passing Media Access Control (MAC) mechanism. Although they use a logical ring topology, Token Ring networks are physically cabled like a star, using a hub called a *multistation access unit (MAU)* that transmits incoming packets out through each successive port in turn. Early Token Ring networks used a shielded twisted pair (STP) cable known as IBM Type 1, but today, most Token Ring networks use unshielded twisted pair (UTP) cable.

Token Ring media filter   A hardware adapter device that enables you to connect a computer with a Type 1 Token Ring network interface adapter to an unshielded twisted pair (UTP) network.

tone generator and locator   An inexpensive cable testing tool that consists of a transmitter device, which you connect to a cable or a wire, which generates a test signal, and a probe that can detect the signal when you touch it to the cable or the cable sheath. You can use a tone generator to test entire cables or individual wires, but because you must test each wire individually, this is not a practical tool for the cable installer seeking to test a large number of cable runs. A tone generator and locator is also known as a "fox and hound."

top-level domain   The highest level in the Domain Name System (DNS) namespace, and the right-most word in a DNS name. For example, in the DNS name www.microsoft.com, com is the top-level domain.

topology   The method used to install network cabling and connect the network computers to the cable. The topology is determined by the data- link layer protocol and cable type you choose. The three basic network topologies are the bus, in which one computer is connected to the next in daisy-chain fashion; the star, in which all of the computers are connected to a central hub; and the ring, in which the computers are logically connected to each other with the ends joined together.

traceroute   A TCP/IP command-line utility that displays the path that packets are taking to a specific destination. Traceroute uses Internet Control Message Protocol (ICMP) Echo Request and Echo Reply messages with varying Time To Live (TTL) values in the IP header. This causes packets to time out at each successive router on the way to the destination, and the error messages generated by the timeouts enable the Traceroute program to display a list of the routers forming the path to the destination.

transfer syntax   A format used to encode application information for transmission over a network. The presentation layer of the Open Systems Interconnection (OSI) reference model is responsible for converting application data from its native abstract syntax to a common transfer syntax understood by both communicating systems. *See also* abstract syntax.

translation bridge   A data-link layer network connection device that connects networks using different media (such as two different types of Ethernet) or different data-link layer protocols (such as Ethernet and Token Ring). In addition to selectively propagating packets to the other network segment, this type of bridge also strips off the data-link layer protocol header and rebuilds a new one using the other protocol. *See also* bridge, router, transparent bridge.

Transmission Control Protocol (TCP)   A Transmission Control Protocol/Internet Protocol (TCP/IP) transport layer protocol used to transmit data generated by applications, such as entire files. TCP is a connection- oriented protocol that provides guaranteed delivery service, packet acknowledgment, flow control, and error detection. The two computers involved in the TCP transaction must exchange a specific series of messages called a *three-way handshake* to establish a connection before any application is transmitted. The receiving computer also transmits periodic acknowledgment messages to verify the receipt of the data packets. After the data is transmitted, the two computers also perform a connection termination procedure. These additional messages, plus the large 20-byte TCP header in every packet, greatly increase the protocol's control overhead.

Transmission Control Protocol/Internet Protocol   A set of networking protocols used on the Internet that provides communications across interconnected networks that consist of computers with diverse hardware architectures and various operating systems. TCP/IP includes standards for how computers communicate and conventions for connecting networks and routing traffic.

transparent bridging   A data-link layer network connection device that connects two network segments and filters packets based on their hardware addresses, which it learns automatically, only forwarding packets that are addressed to the other network segment. A transparent bridge records the address of every packet it processes to build a list of the computers on each of the network segments it connects. This prevents the network administrator from having to manually identify the computers on each network segment. *See also* bridge, router, translation bridge.

transport layer   The middle (fourth) layer of the Open Systems Interconnection (OSI) reference model. The transport layer contains protocols providing services that are complementary to the network layer protocol. A protocol suite typically has both connection-oriented and connectionless protocols at the transport layer, providing different types of service to suit the needs of different applications. In the Transmission Control Protocol/Internet Protocol (TCP/IP) suite, the transport layer protocols are the Transmission Control Protocol (TCP) and the User Datagram Protocol (UDP).

trap   A message generated by a Simple Network Management Protocol (SNMP) agent and transmitted immediately to the network management console, indicating that an event requiring immediate attention has taken place.

Trivial File Transfer Protocol (TFTP)   A connectionless, application layer Transmission Control Protocol/Internet Protocol (TCP/IP) protocol that transmits data files in User Datagram Protocol (UDP) packets with no authentication and no interactive interface.

tunneling   A technique for transmitting data over a network by encapsulating it within another protocol. For example, Novell NetWare networks at one time supported Transmission Control Protocol/Internet Protocol (TCP/IP) only by encapsulating Internet Protocol (IP) datagrams within NetWare's native Internetwork Packet Exchange (IPX) protocol. The Point-to-Point Tunneling Protocol (PPTP) also uses tunneling to carry Point-to-Point Protocol (PPP) frames inside IP datagrams.

Type 1 cable   A type of shielded twisted pair (STP) cable used for longer cable runs on Token Ring networks.

Type 6 cable   A type of shielded twisted pair (STP) cable used for patch cable connections on Token Ring networks.

UART   *See* universal asynchronous receiver-transmitter (UART).

UDP   *See* User Datagram Protocol (UDP).

U interface   The connection provided by the telephone company in an Integrated Services Digital Network (ISDN) installation, to which you attach an NT-1. *See also* Integrated Services Digital Network (ISDN), NT-1.

unicast   A network transmission addressed to a single computer only. *See also* broadcast, multicast.

universal asynchronous receiver-transmitter (UART)   A component found in internal modems and computers' serial ports that is responsible for handling the systems' asynchronous serial communications. High-speed external modems should always use a serial port having a 16550 UART chip. Current-production internal modems all have integrated 16550 UARTs.

universal serial bus (USB)   An external peripheral bus standard that is rapidly replacing many of the other device ports commonly used on computers.

unqualified name   An incomplete Domain Name System (DNS) name that identifies only the host, not the domain in which the host resides. Some Transmission Control Protocol/Internet Protocol (TCP/IP) clients can handle unqualified names by automatically appending to them the name of the domain in which the computer is located or by appending user-specified domain names.

unshielded twisted pair (UTP)   A type of cable used for data and telephone networking that consists of eight copper wires twisted into four pairs with different twist rates, encased in a protective sheath. The twisting of the wire pairs reduces the crosstalk generated by signals traveling over the wires and minimizes their susceptibility to electromagnetic interference (EMI). UTP cables are graded by the Telecommunications Industry Association/Electronic Industries Association (TIA/EIA) using a series of categories. Most UTP cable installed today is Category 5 (CAT5), although Enhanced Category 5 (Category 5e, or CAT5e) cable is also available.

unsignaled error   A transmission error that has not been detected by a protocol operating at a lower layer of the networking stack.

USB   *See* universal serial bus (USB).

Usenet   An Internet bulletin board system consisting of tens of thousands of conferences, called *newsgroups,* covering a wide range of technical, recreational, and informational topics. Users access Usenet conferences by using newsreader software to connect to a news server. This access is usually provided by Internet service providers (ISPs).

User Datagram Protocol (UDP)   A connectionless Transmission Control Protocol/Internet Protocol (TCP/IP) transport layer protocol used for short transactions, usually consisting of a single request and reply. UDP keeps overhead low by supplying almost none of the services provided by its connection-oriented transport layer counterpart, the Transmission Control Protocol (TCP), such as packet acknowledgment and flow control. UDP does offer an error detection service, however. Because it is connectionless, UDP generates no additional handshake messages, and its header is only 8 bytes long.

UTP   *See* unshielded twisted pair (UTP).

V.90   The current standard for 56-Kbps dial-up modem communications, ratified by the International Telecommunications Union (ITU) in 1998 to reconcile the competing X2 and K56 flex standards. Virtually all modems manufactured today support the V.90 standard.

virtual LAN (VLAN)   A technique often used on switched networks to make a group of computers behave as though they are connected to the same local area network (LAN), even though they are physically connected to different network segments. Computers can remain in the same VLAN even when they are physically moved to a different segment.

virtual private network (VPN)   A technique for connecting to a network at a remote location using the Internet as a network medium. A user can dial into a local Internet service provider (ISP) and connect through the Internet to a private network at a distant location, using a protocol like the Point-to-Point Tunneling Protocol (PPTP) to secure the private traffic.

virus   A deliberately created, potentially damaging program or routine that infects a computer from an outside source (such as a file download or a floppy disk) and then replicates itself, enabling it to infect other computers.

VLAN   *See* virtual LAN (VLAN).

VPN   *See* virtual private network (VPN).

WAN   *See* wide area network (WAN).

well-known port   Transmission Control Protocol/Internet Protocol (TCP/IP) port numbers that have been permanently assigned to specific applications and services by the Internet Assigned Numbers Authority (IANA). Well-known ports make it possible for client programs to access services without having to specify a port number. For example, when you type a Uniform Resource Locator (URL) into a Web browser, the port number 80 is assumed, because this is the port associated with Web servers. *See also* ephemeral port.

wide area network (WAN)   A network that spans a large geographical area using long-distance point-to-point connections, rather than shared network media as with a local area network (LAN). WANs can use a variety of communication technologies for their connections, such as leased telephone lines, dial-up telephone lines, and Integrated Services Digital

Network (ISDN) or Digital Subscriber Line (DSL) connections. The Internet is the ultimate example of a WAN. *See also* local area network (LAN).

Windows Internet Name Service (WINS)   A service supplied with the Microsoft Windows NT and Microsoft Windows 2000 operating systems that registers the Network Basic Input/Output System (NetBIOS) names and Internet Protocol (IP) addresses of the computers on a local area network (LAN) and resolves NetBIOS names into IP addresses for its clients as needed. WINS is the most efficient name resolution method for NetBIOS-based networks because it uses only unicast transmissions. Other methods rely on the repeated transmission of broadcast messages, which can generate large amounts of network traffic.

Winipcfg.exe   A graphical utility included with Microsoft Windows 95, Microsoft Windows 98, and Microsoft Windows Me that you can use to view the Transmission Control Protocol/Internet Protocol (TCP/IP) configuration parameters for a particular computer. A command-line version of the tool (Ipconfig.exe) is included with Microsoft Windows 2000 and Microsoft Windows NT. Winipcfg.exe is most useful on computers with TCP/IP clients configured automatically by a Dynamic Host Configuration Protocol (DHCP) server, because it is the easiest way to view the assigned settings for the client system. You can also use Winipcfg.exe to release and renew DHCP-assigned TCP/IP configuration parameters.

WINS   *See* Windows Internet Naming Service (WINS).

wire map tester   A relatively inexpensive cable testing device used to detect open circuits, short circuits, and transposed wires in twisted-pair cable installations. The tester consists of two units that connect to the ends of the cable. One unit transmits test signals and the other unit detects them. The wire map tester is faster and more convenient than a tone generator and locator because it tests all eight wires in a twisted-pair cable run at the same time.

X.500   A standard published by the International Telecommunications Union (ITU) and the International Organization for Standardization (ISO) defining the structure of a global directory service. Microsoft's Active Directory directory service and NetWare's Novell Directory Services (NDS) are both based on the X.500 design.

zip   A file format that is typically used to package multiple files into a single compressed file (called an *archive*) for transmission over a network.

Zip   The proprietary name for a magnetic cartridge drive holding 100 MB or 250 MB.

BIBLIOGRAPHY

Cisco Systems. "Overview of Routing Between Virtual LANs." This document is available at the Cisco Systems Web site at *http://www.cisco.com/univercd/cc/td/doc/product/software/ios113ed/113ed_cr/switch_c/xcvlan.htm.*

Institute of Electrical and Electronics Engineers. "Use of the IEEE Assigned Organizationally Unique Identifier with ANSI/IEEE Std 802-1990 Local and Metropolitan Area Networks." This document is available at the IEEE Web site at *http://standards.ieee.org/regauth/oui/tutorials/lanman.html.*

Internet Engineering Task Force. RFC 768: "User Datagram Protocol." Official standard for the protocol. This document is in the public domain and is available as a free download at *http://www.rfc-editor.org/rfc.html.*

Internet Engineering Task Force. RFC 783: "TFTP Protocol (Revision 2)." Official standard for the protocol. This document is in the public domain and is available as a free download at *http://www.rfc-editor.org/rfc.html.*

Internet Engineering Task Force. RFC 791: "Internet Protocol." Official standard for the protocol. This document is in the public domain and is available as a free download at *http://www.rfc-editor.org/rfc.html.*

Internet Engineering Task Force. RFC 792: "Internet Control Message Protocol." Official standard for the protocol. This document is in the public domain and is available as a free download at *http://www.rfc-editor.org/rfc.html.*

Internet Engineering Task Force. RFC 793: "Transmission Control Protocol." Official standard for the protocol. This document is in the public domain and is available as a free download at *http://www.rfc-editor.org/rfc.html.*

Internet Engineering Task Force. RFC 826: "Ethernet Address Resolution Protocol: Or Converting Network Protocol Addresses to 48-Bit Ethernet Address for Transmission on Ethernet Hardware." Official standard for the protocol. This document is in the public domain and is available as a free download at *http://www.rfc-editor.org/rfc.html.*

Internet Engineering Task Force. RFC 854: "Telnet Protocol Specification." Official standard for the protocol. This document is in the public domain and is available as a free download at *http://www.rfc-editor.org/rfc.html.*

Internet Engineering Task Force. RFC 959: "File Transfer Protocol." Official standard for the protocol. This document is in the public domain and is available as a free download at *http://www.rfc-editor.org/rfc.html.*

Internet Engineering Task Force. RFC 1001: "Protocol Standard for a NetBIOS Service on a TCP/UDP Transport: Concepts and Methods" and RFC 1002: "Protocol Standard for a NetBIOS Service on a TCP/UDP Transport: Detailed Specifications." Official standards for the protocol. These documents are in the public domain and are available as a free download at *http://www.rfc-editor.org/rfc.html.*

Internet Engineering Task Force. RFC 1034: "Domain Names–Concepts and Facilities" and RFC 1035: "Domain Names–Implementation and Specification." Official standards for the protocol. These documents are in the public domain and are available as free downloads at *http://www.rfc-editor.org/rfc.html*.

Internet Engineering Task Force. RFC 1157: "Simple Network Management Protocol (SNMP)." Official standard for the protocol. This document is in the public domain and is available as a free download at *http://www.rfc-editor.org/rfc.html*.

Internet Engineering Task Force. RFC 1661: "The Point-to-Point Protocol (PPP)." Official standard for the protocol. This document is in the public domain and is available as a free download at *http://www.rfc-editor.org/rfc.html*.

Internet Engineering Task Force. RFC 1918: "Address Allocation for Private Internets." Official standard for the protocol. This document is in the public domain and is available as a free download at *http://www.rfc-editor.org/rfc.html*.

Internet Engineering Task Force. RFC 1939: "Post Office Protocol–Version 3." Official standard for the protocol. This document is in the public domain and is available as a free download at *http://www.rfc-editor.org/rfc.html*.

Internet Engineering Task Force. RFC 2060: "Internet Message Access Protocol–Version 4, Rev 1." Official standard for the protocol. This document is in the public domain and is available as a free download at *http://www.rfc-editor.org/rfc.html*.

Internet Engineering Task Force. RFC 2131: "Dynamic Host Configuration Protocol." Official standard for the protocol. This document is in the public domain and is available as a free download at *http://www.rfc-editor.org/rfc.html*.

Internet Engineering Task Force. RFC 2411: "IP Security Document Roadmap." Official standard for the protocol. This document is in the public domain and is available as a free download at *http://www.rfc-editor.org/rfc.html*.

Internet Engineering Task Force. RFC 2460: "Internet Protocol, Version 6 (IPv6) Specification." Official standard for the protocol. This document is in the public domain and is available as a free download at *http://www.rfc-editor.org/rfc.html*.

Internet Engineering Task Force. RFC 2616: "Hypertext Transfer Protocol–HTTP/1.1." Official standard for the protocol. This document is in the public domain and is available as a free download at *http://www.rfc-editor.org/rfc.html*.

Internet Engineering Task Force. RFC 2821: "Simple Mail Transfer Protocol." Official standard for the protocol. This document is in the public domain and is available as a free download at *http://www.rfc-editor.org/rfc.html*.

Microsoft Corporation. "Introduction to Interoperability: Using Windows 2000 in a Mixed Environment." This document is available at the Microsoft Web site at *http://www.microsoft.com/windows2000/server/evaluation/business/interopsol.asp*.

Microsoft Corporation. Microsoft Encyclopedia of Networking. Redmond, Washington: Microsoft Press, 2000. Contains information on a vast number of networking topics.

Microsoft Corporation. "Security Administration Operations Guide." This white paper is available at the Microsoft Web site at *http://www.microsoft.com/technet/prodtechnol/windows2000serv/maintain/opsguide/secadmog.mspx*.

Microsoft Corporation. "Storage Management Operations Guide." February, 2001. This white paper is available at the Microsoft Web site at *http://www.microsoft.com/technet/prodtechnol/windows2000serv/maintain/opsguide/stormgog.mspx.*

Microsoft Corporation. "Windows 2000 Interoperability Features." This document is available at the Microsoft Web site at *http://www.microsoft.com/windows2000/server/evaluation/features/interop.asp.*

Microsoft Corporation. Windows 2000 Server Resource Kit. Volume: Internetworking Guide. Redmond, Washington: Microsoft Press, 2000.

Microsoft Corporation. Windows 2000 Server Resource Kit. Volume: TCP/IP Core Networking Guide. Redmond, Washington: Microsoft Press, 2000.

Spurgeon, Charles. "Quick Reference Guides to 10 Mbps Ethernet" and "Quick Reference Guides to 100 Mbps Ethernet." These documents are available at Charles Spurgeon's Web site at *http://www.ethermanage.com/ethernet/ethernet-home.html.*

Spurgeon, Charles. "Quick Reference Guide to Auto-Negotiation." This document is available at Charles Spurgeon's Web site at *http://www.ethermanage.com/ethernet/100quickref/ch13qr_1.html.*

Zacker, Craig. *Networking: The Complete Reference.* Emeryville, California: McGraw-Hill Osborne Media, 2001.

Zacker, Craig. *TCP/IP Administration.* Indianapolis, Indiana: Hungry Minds, 1998.

Zacker, Craig. *Upgrading and Troubleshooting Networks: The Complete Reference.* Emeryville, California: McGraw-Hill Osborne Media, 2000.

Zacker, Craig and Microsoft Corporation. MCSE Self-Paced Training Kit (Exam 70-293): "Planning and Maintaining a Microsoft Windows Server 2003 Network Infrastructure." Redmond, Washington: Microsoft Press, 2003.

INDEX

Numerics

1000Base-CX, 175
1000Base-LH, 175
1000Base-LX, 174
1000Base-SX, 174
1000Base-T, 172–173
1000Base-X, 174
1000Base-ZX, 175
100Base-FX, 174
100Base-T, 172
100Base-T4, 84
10Base 2, 157
10Base 5, 157
10Base-F, 173
10Base-FB, 173
10Base-FL, 173
10Base-FP, 174
10Base-T, 60, 157, 170–171
10Base-T hubs, 529
1ºDHCPDISCOVER value, 407
2B+D. *See* Basic Rate Interface (BRI) service
2ºDHCPOFFER value, 407
3ºDHCPREQUEST value, 407
4ºDHCPDECLINE value, 407
5-4-3 rule, 176
5ºDHCPACK value, 407
6ºDHCPNAK value, 407
7ºDHCPRELEASE value, 407
802.11a standard, 189
802.11b standard, 189
802.11g standard, 189
802.3. *See* IEEE 802.3 revisions
8ºDHCPINFORM value, 407

A

A (Acknowledge) indicator, 188
AARP. *See* AppleTalk Address Resolution Protocol (AARP)
Abort Delimiter frames, 184
abstract syntax, 34
Access Control field, 183
access point, 51, 190
ACK flag bit, 254, 258
Acknowledgment Number
   message field, 254, 271
   value, 261
acknowledgments
   delayed, 261
   negative, 262
   positive, with retransmission, 261
   selective, 262
Active Directory
   directory service, 370, 399–400, 461
   domain, 332
ad hoc topology, 50–51, 190
adaptive proxy, 452

Add Counters dialog box, 539–540
address, 406
Address (A) resource record, 415
Address Expression dialog box, 545
Address Family Identifier field, 324
Address Resolution Protocol (ARP), 211, 293–296, 562–563
   caching, 296
   communications, 295–296
   message format, 293–295
addresses
   anycast, 226
   Class A, 218, 219, 225
   Class B, 218, 219, 225
   Class C, 218, 219, 225
   Class D, 218
   Class E, 218
   hardware, 20
   I/O port, 116
   Internet Protocol (IP), 494
   Media Access Control (MAC), 20, 443
   memory, 116
   multicast, 218
   network, 217, 220–221
   registered, 224–225
   static, 562
   unregistered, 224–225
addressing, Ethernet, 20, 23
ADSP. *See* AppleTalk Data Stream Protocol
AFP. *See* Apple Filing Protocol (AFP)
agents, 111, 305
Alerter service, 369
All Rings Broadcast (ARB) frames, 132
Allocation Number message field, 271
American National Standards Institute (ANSI), 8
ANSI. *See* American National Standards Institute
ANSI/TIA/EIA-T568-B, 52–54
anti-replay, 456
anycast addresses, 226
API. *See* application programming interface
Apple EtherTalk, 238
Apple Filing Protocol (AFP), 381
Apple LocalTalk, 238
Apple Macintosh, 381–382
AppleShare, 381
AppleShare IP, 381
AppleTalk, 238–241, 381
AppleTalk Address Resolution Protocol (AARP), 239
AppleTalk Data Stream Protocol (ADSP), 31
application layer, 34–35, 292
   communications, 304
   protocol functions, 304–306
   protocol identification, 30
   protocols, 35, 303–306
   troubleshooting, 607–608

application programming interfaces (APIs), 284
application support
    in Linux, 380
    in Microsoft Windows, 369–370
    in NetWare, 375–376
    in UNIX, 380
archive bit, 477
ARP Reply message, 296
ARP Reply value, 294
ARP Request packet, 295
ARP Request value, 294
ARP. *See* Address Resolution Protocol (ARP)
Arp.exe utility, 563
ARPANET, 282
AS. *See* autonomous system (AS)
asymmetrical services, 500
Asynchronous Transfer Mode (ATM), 9, 19,
        507–508
ATM. *See* Asynchronous Transfer Mode (ATM)
attachment unit interface (AUI) cables, 45, 170
attacks
    brute-force, 609
    denial of service (DoS), 442
    detecting, 444
    filtering, 442
    teardrop, 445
    Trojan horse, 449
attenuation, 62, 175, 554
attributes, 395
ATU-R. *See* ADSL Termination Unit-Remote (ATU-R)
AUI connectors, 56
AUI. *See* attachment unit interface (AUI)
authentication, 370, 394, 460
    phase, 513
    server, 461
autochangers, 473–474
Autoexec.ncf file, 119, 343
automatic allocation, 404
autonegotiation, 111
autonomous system (AS), 322

B

B channels, 497
backbone cabling, 53
backbone networks, 136
backoff period, 166
Backup Domain Controller (BDC), 397
backups
    cataloguing, 481–482
    choosing hardware for, 470–475
    choosing software for, 475–484
    database storage, 482
    defined, 469
    differential, 477–479
    drive manipulation, 479
    filters, using, 475–477
    full, 477, 478
    incremental, 477–479
    log files, 481
    logging, 481–482

media rotation, 482
network functions, 484
performing, 469–484
restoring data from, 482–483
scheduling, 480
target selection, 475–477
bandwidth sharing, 502
baseband communications, 8–10
baseband LANs, 108
baseline, 596
Basic Rate Interface (BRI) service, 497
basic service area (BSA), 50
basic service set (BSS), 50, 190
bayonet-Neill-Concelman (BNC) connectors, 56
BDC. *See* Backup Domain Controller (BDC)
Berkeley Software Distribution (BSD) UNIX, 376
binaries, converting, 222–223
Bind command, 343
bipolar digital signals, 504
BNC. *See* bayonet-Neill-Concelman (BNC)
BOOTP. *See* Bootstrap Protocol (BOOTP)
Bootstrap Protocol (BOOTP), 295, 403
bound state, 409
branching tree network. *See* hierarchical star
        topology
BRI service. *See* Basic Rate Interface (BRI) service
bridge loop, 132
bridges, 129
    collisions on, 132–133
    connecting LANs with, 130–134
    local, 134
    network layer protocols, 130
    overview, 134–135
    remote, 135
    translation, 134
    transparent, 131–132
bridging
    source route, 132
    transparent, 131
broadband communications, 8–10
broadband transmissions, 501
broadcast domains, 133–134, 143
broadcast messages, 133–134
broadcasts, 283, 408
BSA. *See* basic service area (BSA)
BSD UNIX. *See* Berkeley Software Distribution
        (BSD) UNIX
BSS. *See* basic service set (BSS)
buffers, 107
    receive, 107
    transmit, 107
bulk cables, 71, 75
bursts, 505
bus
    expansion, 106
    Industry Standard Architecture (ISA), 106
    mastering, 110
    Peripheral Component Interconnect (PCI), 106
    topology, 3, 45–46

C

C (Copy) indicator, 188
cable length, 554
cable modem, 501
cable runs
  installing, 78–79
  troubleshooting, 599
cable television (CATV) networks
  bandwidth sharing, 502
  disadvantages, 502
  overview, 501–503
  security concerns, 502
cable testers
  fox and hound, 551
  multifunction, 555–556, 600
cable testing
  fiber optic, 556
cable ties, 69
cable topologies, 44–52
cables, 48
  attachment unit interface (AUI), 45, 170
  bulk, 71, 75
  casing, 55
  CAT5 UTP, 180
  Category 3 (CAT3), 60
  Category 5 (CAT5), 60
  Category 5e (CAT5e), 60
  Category 6 (CAT6), 60
  coaxial, 55–58
  coaxial, RG-58, 55
  coaxial, RG-8, 55
  crossover, 83, 126, 528, 550–551
  external, installing, 66–68
  fiber optic, 62–65
    connecting, 95–96
    testing, 556
  grades, selecting, 59
  IBM Type 1, 179–180
  installing on Ethernet networks, 175–178
  internal, dropping, 80–81
  length standards, 76
  length, estimating, 72
  lobe, 179
  multimode fiber optic, 63
  patch, 74–75, 179, 598
  plenum, 55
  protecting, 70
  pulling, 65
  shielded twisted-pair (STP), 175
  silver satin, 95
  singlemode fiber optic, 63
  STP, Type 1A, 61
  STP, Type 2A, 61
  STP, Type 6A, 61
  STP, Type 9A, 61
  straight-through, 528
  testing, 95
  troubleshooting, 598–599
  twisted-pair, 58–61, 175
  Type 3, 180
  types, 54–65
  UTP, 58, 75
  UTP grades, 59–60
cables, connecting
  external, 86–87
  internal, 87–96
  punching down, 89–91
cables, installing
  cable runs, 78–79
  external, 65–74
    around doorways, 71–72
    between floors, 73–74
    drilling through walls, 73
    securing, 68–70
    to other rooms, 72–73
  internal, 74–82
  loose cables, 67
  patch cables, 74–75, 94, 180, 598
  problems to avoid, 77
cables, securing internal, 80
cables, STP grades, 61
cables, troubleshooting external, 67
cabling guidelines
  Fast Ethernet, 177
  Gigabit Ethernet, 178
  standard Ethernet, 176–177
cabling standards, 52–54
  ANSI/TIA/EIA-T568-B, 52–54
  J-STD-607-A, 54
  TIA/EIA STP, 61
  TIA/EIA-606, 54
caching, 420
CAL. *See* Client Access License (CAL)
Canonical Name (CNAME) resource record, 415
capture filters, 545
Capture Summary window, 546–547
  Detail pane, 548
  Hex pane, 548
  Summary pane, 548
CardBus, 113
Carrier Sense Multiple Access with Collision
    Avoidance (CSMA/CA), 191–192
Carrier Sense Multiple Access with Collision
    Detection (CSMA/CD), 108, 165–167
carrier sense phase, 165
cartridge drives, 473
CAT5 UTP cables, 180
Category 3 (CAT3) cables, 60
Category 5 (CAT5) cables, 60
Category 5e (CAT5e) cables, 60
Category 6 (CAT6) cables, 60
CATV networks. *See* cable television (CATV)
    networks
CBIR. *See* committed burst information rate (CBIR)
CDDI. *See* Copper Distributed Data Interface
    (CDDI)
CD-ROM drives, 472
cell switching, 9
certifiers, 554
chaddr field, 406
channel service unit/data service unit (CSU/DSU),
    504

channels
  B, 497
  D, 497
  DMA, 116
Checksum field, 229, 240
Checksum message field, 254, 267
Checksum message format, 298
checksum processing, 110
chipping code, 191
ciaddr field, 406
CIFS. *See* Common Internet File System (CIFS)
CIR. *See* committed information rate (CIR)
circuits, 10
  crossover, 84–85, 126
circuit-switching network, 10
CKK. *See* complementary code keying (CKK)
claim token, 184
Class A addresses, 218, 219, 225
  subnet mask, 220
Class B addresses, 218, 219, 225
  subnet mask, 220
Class C addresses, 218, 219, 225
  subnet mask, 220
Class D addresses, 218
Class E addresses, 218
Class I hubs, 177
Class II hubs, 177
Client Access License (CAL), 363, 364
client configuration, troubleshooting, 588
Client for Microsoft Networks, 385
client networking stack, 384
client/server networks, 358
clients, 358, 382–383, 384
clustering, 466, 467
coaxial cables, 55–58
  RG-58, 55
  RG-8, 55
coaxial Ethernet, 169–170
Code message format, 297
Code subfield, 407
coil and throw technique, 79
collision case, 32
collision detection phase, 165
collision domain, 132
collision LEDs, 530
collisions, 165
  late, 166
  on bridges, 132–133
  phantom, 528
combination adapters, 113
Comité Consultatif International Téléphonique et
    Télégraphique (CCITT) *See*
    Telecommunication Standardization Sector of
    the International Telecommunication Union
    (ITU-T)
Command field, 235
command frames, 184
committed burst information rate (CBIR), 505
committed information rate (CIR), 505
Common Internet File System (CIFS), 389

communications
  baseband, 8–10
  broadband, 8–10
  full-duplex, 529
complementary code keying (CKK), 191
Completion Code message field, 273
compression, 472
Computer Browser service, 369
computer configuration, troubleshooting, 603–608
computer connections, troubleshooting, 598–599
concentrator, 46, 123
Connection Control message field, 270
Connection Number High message field, 272, 273
Connection Number Low message field, 272, 273
Connection Status message field, 273
connectionless protocols, 27–28, 252
connection-oriented protocols, 27
connections
  crossover, 85
  E-1, 503
  E-3, 503
  end-to-end, 508
  half close, 265
  physical layer, 494
  terminating, 265
  WAN, 495–508
connectors
  attaching, 94–95
  AUI, 56
  bayonet-Neill-Concelman (BNC), 56
  components, 88–89
  hardware loopback, 551
  IBM data connector (IDC), 61
  N-connector, 56
  network cable, 113
  RJ-11, 58
  RJ-45, 58, 94
  straight tip (ST), 63
  subscriber (SC), 63
  T-connector, 56
contact ports, 267
container objects, 395, 399
Control Bits message field, 254
control bits, SYN, 256
convergence, 325
Copied Flag subfield, 208
Copper Distributed Data Interface (CDDI), 185
CRC calculation, 110
CRC value, 25
CRC. *See* cyclical redundancy check (CRC)
crimper, 95
crossbar switches, 144
crossover cables, 83, 126, 528, 550–551
crossover circuits, 84–85, 126
crossover circuits, troubleshooting, 599
crossover connections, 85
crosstalk, 58, 175, 500, 528, 553
  equal level far end crosstalk (ELFEXT), 555
  near end crosstalk (NEXT), 554
CSMA/CA. *See* Carrier Sense Multiple Access with
    Collision Avoidance (CSMA/CA)

CSMA/CD. *See* Carrier Sense Multiple Access with Collision Detection (CSMA/CD)
CSU/DSU. *See* channel service unit/data service unit (CSU/DSU)
cut-through switches, 144
cyclical redundancy check (CRC), 21, 107, 229, 254

D

D channel, 497
DAC. *See* dual attachment concentrator (DAC)
daemons, 380
DAS. *See* dual attachment station (DAS)
data
  ensuring availability, 462–466
  integrity, 460
  restoring, 482–483
Data (variable) field, 188
Data And Pad field, 162
data buffering, 107
data compression, 7
data encapsulation, 13–16, 107, 204–205, 228
data encryption, 7
Data field, 207, 230, 240
data frames, 182–183
Data message field, 255, 267, 271–273
Data message format, 298
Data Offset message field, 254
data reception, 109
data segmentation, 28
data structures, naming, 20
Data subfield, 407
data transfer, 107
data transmission, 109, 259
Data1 field, 236
Data2 field, 236
databases
  flat file, 394
  hierarchical, 394
datagram envelope, 212
Datagram Length field, 240
datagrams, 22, 204
datagrams, IP, 516
data-link communications, 20
data-link layer, 3, 18–22, 107, 494
  defined, 19
  encryption, 455
  frames, 107, 137
  protocols, 17, 112, 137, 211
  troubleshooting, 605–606
data-link layer protocols, 17, 112, 137, 211
Datastream Type message field, 270
DDP Type field, 239–240
decimals, converting, 222–223
decoding, signal, 108
default gateway, 332
  addresses, configuring, 341
  parameter, 325
delay skew, 555
delayed acknowledgments, 261
Delimiter field, 235
delta files, 484

denial of service (DoS) attack, 442
Destination Address field, 161, 183, 188, 240
Destination Connection ID message field, 270
Destination IP Address field, 207
Destination Name field, 236
Destination Network Address field, 229
Destination Node Address field, 229
Destination Number field, 236
Destination Port message field, 253, 266
Destination Port number, 264
destination service access point (DSAP), 164
Destination Socket field, 229
Destination Socket Number field, 240
Destination Unreachable error message, 300
device drivers, 117
Device Manager, 118
devices
  advanced network connection, 129–145
  physical-layer, 125
DFS. *See* distributed file system (DFS)
DHCP. *See* Dynamic Host Configuration Protocol (DHCP)
Diagnostic and Monitoring Protocol (DMP), 238
dialog, 32
dialog boxes
  Add Counters, 539–540
  Address Expression, 545
  Event Properties, 534
  Internet Protocol (TCP/IP) Properties, 607
  Network Monitor Capture Filter SAPs And ETYPEs, 544
  Properties, 118–119
dialog control, 32
dialog separation, 33
differential backups, 477–479
Differential Manchester, 18
Differential Manchester encoding, 108
dig tool, 569
digital modems, 504
Digital Subscriber Line (DSL), 499–501
Digital Subscriber Line Access Multiplexer (DSLAM), 500
DIP switches. *See* dual inline package (DIP) switches
direct memory access (DMA), 107
direct route, 308
Direct Sequence Spread Spectrum (DSSS), 191
Direct Subscriber Line (DSL)
  modems, 500
  services and properties, 499–500
  speeds, 500
  transceivers, 500
directory
  schema, 396
  tree, 395
directory services, 364
  overview, 394–401
  X.500 standard, 396
disaster recovery, 483
disk duplexing, 464
disk mirroring, 463
disk striping, 463

distance limitations, 83
distance vector protocol, 323
distributed file system (DFS), 370
distribution system (DS), 190
DIX Ethernet, 156–157
    contrasted with IEEE 802.3, 157–159
DLT drives, 471
DMA channels, 116
DMA. *See* direct memory access (DMA)
DMP. *See* Diagnostic and Monitoring Protocol
    (DMP)
DNS server addresses parameter, 325
DNS tab, 334–336
DNS. *See* Domain Name System (DNS)
domain controllers, 397–398
Domain Name System (DNS), 266, 304
    controls, 335
    name resolution, 418–419
    name structure, 415–416
    names, 415
    namespace, 413, 416
    overview, 412–422
    performance object, 540
    primary suffix, 335
    server addresses, configuring, 340–341
    server addresses, improper configuration of, 606
    servers, 417
    servers, combined, 420
    speeding up, 419–420
    troubleshooting, 591–597
        configuration files, 595
        DNS servers, 594–597
        name resolution problems, 593
        TCP/IP client configuration, 591–594
Domain Name System (DNS) Server, 370
domain names, 415
domains, 397
    defined, 414
    hierarchy levels, 416–418
    Internet, 397
    second-level, 417
    top-level, 416–417
Don't Fragment bit, 215
Don't Fragment Was Set error message, 215
DoS attack. *See* denial of service (DoS) attack.
DOS kernel, 359
dotted decimal notation, 216
double ring, 185
downstream speeds, DSL, 500
drive interfaces, selecting, 474–475
drive spanning, 463
drives
    cartridge, 473
    CD-ROM, 472
    DLT, 471
    DVD-ROM, 472
    Jaz, 473
    LTO, 471
    magnetic tape, 471–473
    manipulating, 479
    QIC, 471
    Zip, 473

DS. *See* distribution system (DS)
DSAP. *See* destination service access point (DSAP)
DSL. *See* digital subscriber line (DSL)
DSLAM. *See* Digital Subscriber Line Access
    Multiplexer (DSLAM)
DSSS. *See* Direct Sequence Spread Spectrum (DSSS)
dual attachment concentrator (DAC), 185
dual attachment station (DAS), 185
dual inline package (DIP) switches, 117
dual ring of trees, 186
DVD-ROM drives, 472
dynamic allocation, 404
Dynamic Host Configuration Protocol (DHCP), 217,
    266, 304
    architecture, 403–404
    client, 404
    communications, 408–409
    components, 403
    leasing, 409–410
    message format, 405–407
    origins, 402–403
    server configuration, troubleshooting, 594
    servers, 140, 404
    using, 402–410
Dynamic Host Configuration Protocol (DHCP)
    Server, 370
dynamic NAT, 448
dynamic proxy, 452
dynamic routing, 314–315, 321–325

E

E (Error) indicator, 188
E-1 connection, 503
E-3 connection, 503
early token release, 181
E-carrier services, 503
Echo Reply messages, 302, 558, 559
Echo Request messages, 302, 442, 558, 559
eDirectory
    properties, 395
    tree, 396
EFS. *See* Encrypting File System (EFS)
EGP. *See* Exterior Gateway Protocol (EGP)
electromagnetic interference (EMI), 17
electrostatic discharge, 114
ELFEXT. *See* equal level far end crosstalk (ELFEXT)
EMI. *See* electromagnetic interference (EMI)
encoding
    Differential Manchester, 108
    Manchester, 108
    signal, 108
Encrypting File System (EFS), 365
encryption, 455, 460
End Delimiter byte, 509
End Delimiter field, 183
End of Frame Sequence field, 188
End Of Options List (EOOL) option, 209, 214, 256
end systems, 24, 212
Ending Delimiter field, 188
end-to-end connections, 508
ephemeral port numbers, 269

equal level far end crosstalk (ELFEXT), 555
equipment room, 53
error correction, 7
error detection, 7, 21, 262–263
error displays, 530–531
error messages, 530–531
   Destination Unreachable, 300
   Don't Fragment Was Set, 215
   Fragmentation Needed, 215
   ICMP, 298–301
   Redirect, 300–301
   saving, 530
   Source Quench, 300
   Time Exceeded, 301
Ethernet, 3, 19
   addressing, 162
   coaxial, 169–170
   components, 160
   DIX, 156–157
   Fast, 60
   fiber optic, 173–175
   field interpretation, 163
   frame field functions, 160–162
   hub configuration rules, 178
   hubs, 124–127, 527
   IEEE 802.3, 157
   network interface adapter, 501
   networks, 156
   physical layer specifications, 157, 160, 167–178
   standards, 156–160
   UTP, 83, 170–173
Ethertype, 158, 163–164
Ethertype/Length field, 162
event classifications, in log entries, 533–534
event logs, 531–535
Event Properties dialog box, 534
expansion bus, 106
extended network, 239
extension point, 190
Exterior Gateway Protocol (EGP), 322
Exterior Gateway Protocol (EGP) value, 215
external installation, defined, 65
external transceivers, 171

F

Fast Ethernet, 60
fast link pulse (FLP) signals, 111, 529
FAT file system, 367
fault tolerance, 462–468
FDDI frames, 187–188
FDDI. *See* Fiber Distributed Data Interface (FDDI)
FDDITalk, 238
FHSS. *See* Frequency Hopping Spread Spectrum (FHSS)
Fiber Distributed Data Interface (FDDI), 19, 49, 185–188
fiber optic cables, 62–65
   connecting, 95–96
   multimode, 63
   testing, 556
fiber optic Ethernet, 173–175

Fiber Optic Inter-Repeater Link (FOIRL), 173
Fibre Channel, 106
fields
   Access Control, 183
   Address Family Identifier, 324
   chaddr, 406
   Checksum, 229, 240
   ciaddr, 406
   Command, 235
   Data, 207, 230, 240
   Data (variable), 188
   Data And Pad, 162
   Data1, 236
   Data2, 236
   Datagram Length, 240
   DDP Type, 240
   Delimiter, 235
   Destination Address, 161, 183, 188, 240
   Destination IP Address, 207
   Destination Name, 236
   Destination Network Address, 229
   Destination Node Address, 229
   Destination Number, 236
   Destination Socket, 229
   Destination Socket Number, 240
   End Delimiter, 183
   End of Frame Sequence, 188
   Ethertype/Length, 162
   file, 406
   Flag, 512
   Flags, 207, 214
   flags, 406
   Fragment Offset, 207, 214
   Frame Check Sequence, 162, 183, 188
   Frame Control, 183, 188
   Frame Status, 183
   giaddr, 406
   Header Checksum, 207, 214
   hlen, 405
   Hop Count, 240
   hops, 406
   htype, 405
   Identification, 206
   Information, 183
   Internet Header Length (IHL), 206, 214
   IP Address, 324
   Length, 229, 235
   Metric, 324
   Next Hop IP Address, 324
   op, 405
   Open Shortest Path First (OSPF), 325
   Option Data, 208, 255
   Option Kind, 255
   Option Length, 208, 255
   Option Type, 208
   Optional, 236
   Options, 207, 214
   options, 406
   Packet Type, 229
   Preamble, 161, 187
   Protocol, 207, 512
   Response Correlator, 236

fields, (continued)
  Route Tag, 324
  secs, 406
  siaddr, 406
  sname, 406
  Source Address, 161, 183, 188, 240
  Source IP Address, 207
  Source Name, 236
  Source Network Address, 230
  Source Node Address, 230
  Source Number, 236
  Source Socket, 230
  Source Socket Number, 240
  Start Of Frame Delimiter, 161
  Starting Delimiter, 187
  Subnet Mask, 324
  Time To Live (TTL), 207, 558
  Total Length, 206, 214
  Transmit Correlator, 236
  Transport Control, 229
  Type Of Service, 206
  Version, 206
  xid, 406
  yiaddr, 406
File and Printer Sharing for Microsoft Networks, 385
file attributes, 477
file field, 406
file servers, 358
file services, 364, 378
file services, NetWare, 374–375
file sharing, 367–368
file systems
  FAT, 367
  NTFS, 367
File Transfer Protocol (FTP), 304, 378–379, 442
Filtcfg.nlm utility, 440
filtering
  by hardware address, 443
  by IP address, 443
  by port number, 443
  service-dependent, 442
  TCP/IP client, 439
filters
  applying, 548
  capture, 545
  firewall-based, advantages of, 440
FIN flag bit, 254, 265
firewalls
  defined, 436
  internal, 436
  overview, 436–445
  packet filtering, 437–444
  packet inspection, stateful, 445
  stateful, 439
  stateless, 439
fish tape, 81
flag bits
  ACK, 254, 258
  FIN, 254, 265
  PSH, 254
  RST, 254
  SYN, 254, 258
  URG, 254

Flags field, 207, 214, 512
flags field, 406
Flags subfield, 210
flat file databases, 394
flow control, 7, 29, 264
FLP signals. See fast link pulse (FLP) signals
FOIRL. See Fiber Optic Inter-Repeater Link (FOIRL)
format prefix, 226
forwarder, 421
fox and hound cable tester, 551
FQDN. See fully qualified domain name (FQDN)
fractional T-1 service, 503
FRAD. See frame relay assembler/disassembler (FRAD)
Fragment Offset field, 207, 214
fragmentation, 24, 204, 213–215
Fragmentation Needed error message, 215
Frame Check Sequence field, 162, 183, 188
Frame Control field, 183, 188
frame format, 20, 160
frame relay, 139
  cloud, 506
  connection, 505
  overview, 505–506
frame relay assembler/disassembler (FRAD), 506
Frame Status field, 183
frames, 20, 160
  Abort Delimiter, 184
  command, 184
  data, 182–183
  data-link layer, 107, 137
  FDDI, 187–188
  PPP, 511–513, 516
  token, 183, 188
  Token Ring, 182–184
Frequency Hopping Spread Spectrum (FHSS), 191
FTP. See File Transfer Protocol (FTP)
full backups, 477, 478
full-duplex communications, 529
full-duplex mode, 109–110
full-duplex protocol, 258
fully connected topology, 49–50
fully qualified domain name (FQDN), 415
Function message field, 272
functions
  Gateway, 310
  Interface, 310
  Metric, 310
  Netmask, 310
  Network Destination, 309

G

Gateway function, 310
Gateway Service for NetWare, 388
gateways, 144–145, 212
  incorrect parameters, 607
  missing default addresses, 607
Gateway-to-Gateway Protocol (GGP) value, 215
GET Request packet, 548
giaddr field, 406
Gigabit Ethernet standard, 60
graphical user interface (GUI), 359
grounding, 114
GUI. See graphical user interface (GUI)

H

half close connection, 265
half-duplex mode, 109
hardware address filtering, 443
hardware addresses, 20
hardware loopback connectors, 551
Hardware Size message field, 294
Hardware Type message field, 294
hash message authentication code (HMAC),
    456–457
Hdetect.nlm, 120
Header Checksum field, 207, 214
headers, 13–16
  TCP, 253–255
hierarchical databases, 394
hierarchical star topology, 47
hlen field, 405
HMAC. *See* hash message authentication code
    (HMAC)
hop, 25
Hop Count field, 240
hops field, 406
horizontal cabling, 53
horizontal segments, 136
host files, 410–412
host identifiers, 216, 219
host software, 494
host tables
   disadvantages, 411–412
   functions, 411
host tool, 569
host, defined, 211
Hot Add Memory, 366
HTTP. *See* Hypertext Transfer Protocol (HTTP)
HTTPS. *See* Secure Hypertext Transfer Protocol
    (S-HTTP or HTTPS)
htype field, 405
hubs, 3, 46, 123, 527
   10Base-T, 529
   backbone failure, 602
   Class I, 177
   Class II, 177
   connecting, 125–127
   damaged ports, 600
   Ethernet, 124–127, 527
   network, 123–128
   smart, 125
   speed, 124–125
   stackable, 127
   switching, 141
   troubleshooting
     connections, 599–600
     local, 597–598
Hypertext Transfer Protocol (HTTP), 305

I

I/O port addresses, 116
IAB. *See* Internet Architecture Board (IAB)
IANA. *See* Internet Assigned Numbers Authority
    (IANA), 215

IAS. *See* Internet Authentication Service (IAS)
IBM data connector (IDC), 61, 180
IBM Type 1 cables, 179–180
ICA. *See* Independent Computing Architecture (ICA)
ICF. *See* Internet Connection Firewall (ICF)
ICMP. *See* Internet Control Message Protocol (ICMP)
ICS. *See* Internet Connection Sharing (ICS)
IDC. *See* IBM data connector (IDC)
IDE devices, 474
Identification field, 206
IEEE 802.11
  MAC layer, 191–192
  physical layer specifications, 190–191
IEEE 802.2 standard, 158
IEEE 802.3 Ethernet, 157
IEEE 802.3 revisions, 159–160
IEEE. *See* Institute of Electrical and Electronics
    Engineers (IEEE)
IESG. *See* Internet Engineering Steering Group
    (IESG)
IETF. *See* Internet Engineering Task Force (IETF),
    287
ifcfg-eth0 file, 338–340
ifconfig utility, 121, 340, 560–562
IGMP. *See* Internet Group Management Protocol
    (IGMP)
IIS. *See* Microsoft Internet Information Services (IIS)
IMAP4. *See* Internet Mail Access Protocol 4 (IMAP4)
incremental backups, 477–479
Independent Computing Architecture (ICA), 516
indirect route, 308
Industry Standard Architecture (ISA) bus, 106
Inetcfg.nlm, 120
  file, 343
  tool, 320
Information field, 183
infrared signals, 191
infrastructure services, 364
infrastructure topology, 51–52
initial sequence number (ISN), 257
Install.nlm, 119
Institute of Electrical and Electronics Engineers
    (IEEE), 157
Integrated Services Digital Network (ISDN),
    497–498
Interface function, 310
interface ID, 226
interface variable, 563
Interior Gateway Protocols (IGPs), 322
intermediate systems, 24, 212
internal address tables, 131
International Organization for Standardization
    (ISO), 7
Internet
  domains, 397
  Web servers, 442
Internet Architecture Board (IAB), 286
Internet Assigned Numbers Authority (IANA), 215,
    217, 286, 446
Internet Authentication Service (IAS), 364
Internet Connection Firewall (ICF), 363

Internet Connection Sharing (ICS), 140, 307, 363, 450
Internet Control Message Protocol (ICMP), 213, 291, 297–303
  error message, 298–301
  message field, 297–298
  messages, 442
  query message, 302–303
Internet Control Message Protocol (ICMP) value, 215
Internet Engineering Steering Group (IESG), 286
Internet Engineering Task Force (IETF), 8, 202, 286–287
  membership and activities, 287
Internet Group Management Protocol (IGMP), 291
Internet Group Management Protocol (IGMP) value, 215
Internet Header Length (IHL) field, 206, 214
internet layer, 291
Internet Mail Access Protocol 4 (IMAP4), 305
Internet Protocol (IP), 23, 202, 297
  address allocation, 404
  addresses, 415, 443, 494
    filtering limitations, 443
  addresses, registered, 446
  addresses, releasing, 410
  addresses, troubleshooting, 592, 607
  datagram, 411
  datagram format, 205–207
  datagrams, 442, 516
  functions, 203–216
  options, 208–210
  protocol upgrades, 203
  router, 308
  routers, 213
  routing, 204, 212–213, 306–325
  spoofing, 445
  standards, 202–203, 215
  subnet calculators, 222
Internet Protocol (TCP/IP), 385
Internet Protocol (TCP/IP) Properties dialog box, 607
Internet Protocol Control Protocol (IPCP), 511
Internet Research Task Force (IRTF), 287
Internet service provider (ISP), 2
Internet Timestamp (TS) option, 209–210
internetwork, 3–4
Internetwork Packet Exchange (IPX), 23, 210, 227–231, 460
  addressing, 228, 230
  data encapsulation, 228–230
  functions, 227–231
  routing, 228, 231
Internetwork Packet Exchange Control Protocol (IPXCP), 511
interrupt request (IRQ) line, 113, 116
intraNetWare, 375
IP Address field, 324
IP address parameter, 325

IP addresses, obtaining, 225
IP Addresses/Timestamps subfield, 210
IP addressing, 204, 210–211
  assignments, 217
  calculating with subtraction method, 224
  classes, 217–219
  converting binaries and decimals, 222–223
  overview, 216–226
IP Authentication Header (AH), 456
IP Encapsulating Security Payload (ESP), 457
IP in IP value, 215
IP Security (IPSec), 365, 371, 454–459
  acceleration, 455
  encryption, 454
  implementations, 459
  integrity, 456–457
  processing, 110–111
  protocols, 456–457
  standards, 455
IP Settings tab, 333–334
IP v6 addressing, 225–226
IP. See Internet Protocol (IP)
ipaddress variable, 563
Ipconfig.exe, 560–562, 593
IPCP. See Internet Protocol Control Protocol (IPCP)
ipfw tool, 440
iPrint, 375
IPSec. See IP Security (IPSec)
IPSecurity (IPSec), 365, 371
iptables tool, 440, 451
IPX. See Internetwork Packet Exchange (IPX)
IPXCP. See Internetwork Packet Exchange Control Protocol (IPXCP)
IRQ line. See interrupt request (IRQ) line
IRQs, 116
IRTF. See Internet Research Task Force (IRTF)
ISA bus. See Industry Standard Architecture (ISA) bus
iSCSI, 374
ISDN. See Integrated Services Digital Network (ISDN), 498
ISN. See initial sequence number (ISN)
ISO. See International Organization for Standardization (ISO)
ISP. See Internet service provider (ISP)
iterative query, 421

J

jam pattern, 166
Jaz drives, 473
J-STD-607-A, 54
jukeboxes, 473
jumper blocks, 117

K

KDC. See Key Distribution Center (KDC)
Kerberos protocol, 370, 461–462
Key Distribution Center (KDC), 461

L

L2F. *See* Layer Two Forwarding (L2F)
L2TP. *See* Layer Two Tunneling Protocol (L2TP)
LAN. *See* local area network (LAN)
late collisions, 166
latency, 144
Layer 3 switching, 143
Layer Two Forwarding (L2F) protocol, 459
Layer Two Tunneling Protocol (L2TP), 459–460
LCP. *See* Link Control Protocol (LCP)
leaf objects, 395, 399
lease identification cookie, 408
leased lines, 496
   E-1, 503
   E-3, 503
   overview, 503–505
   T-1, 503
   T-3, 503
LED. *See* light-emitting diode (LED)
Length field, 229, 235
Length message field, 267
Length subfield, 407
light-emitting diode (LED), 63, 111, 526
   and system power, 527
   collision, 530
   link pulse, 526–528
   speed indicator, 529
line of sight technology, 191
Line Printer Daemon (LPD), 380
Line Printer Remote (LPR), 380
link code word, 529
Link Control Protocol (LCP), 510
Link Dead phase, 513
Link Establishment phase, 513
link layer protocols, 291–292
Link Open phase, 514
link pulse LEDs, 526–528
link pulse signal, 111
link quality monitoring phase, 514
Link Quality Report Protocol, 514
link segments, 170, 177
link termination phase, 514
link-state protocol, 325
Linux, 376
   application support, 380
   client capabilities, 391–392
   deploying, 377
   interfaces, 378
   netfilter module, 445
   overview, 376–381
   performance monitoring, 540–541
   servers, connecting to, 390–391, 394
LLC Frame, 188
LLC. *See* Logical Link Control (LLC)
Lmhosts file, 336
lobe cables, 179
local area network (LAN), 3–4
   attributes, 3
   baseband, 108
   bridging, 130–134
   speeds, 503
   topology, 3
   troubleshooting, 599–604
   virtual, 143
local bridges, 134
LocalTalk adapter, 381
log entries, 533
   event classifications, 533–534
log files, 481
   specifying size, 531–532
logging options, 531–532
Logical Link Control (LLC), 158
logs, 526–549
loopback connectors, 551
loopback state, 128
Loose Source Routing (LSR) option, 209, 214
low power mode, 112
LPD. *See* Line Printer Daemon (LPD)
LPR. *See* Line Printer Remote (LPR)
LTO drives, 471

M

MAC Frame, 188
MAC layer, IEEE 802.11, 191–192
Mac OS X, 381
MAC. *See* Media Access Control (MAC)
Macintosh
   client capabilities, 392–394
   servers, connecting to, 391–392
magnetic tape
   capacities, 472
   drives, 471–473
Mail Exchange (MX) resource record, 415
MAN. *See* metropolitan area network (MAN)
management information base (MIB), 536
Manchester encoding, 18, 108
manual allocation, 404
masquerading, 448
matrix switches, 144
MAU. *See* multistation access unit (MAU)
maximum segment size (MSS), 258–259
Maximum Segment Size (MSS) option, 256
maximum transmission unit (MTU), 213
Media Access Control (MAC), 21, 107, 127–128,
      158, 160, 293, 443
   addresses, 20, 443
   Type 3, 180
Media Access Control (MAC) mechanism, 160
media rotation, 482
media specifications, 158
media testers, 554
memory
   addresses, 116
   shared, 107
mesh LAN, calculating connections, 50
mesh topology, 49–50
message fields
   Acknowledgment Number, 254, 271
   Allocation Number, 271
   Checksum, 254, 267
   Completion Code, 273
   Connection Control, 270

message fields, (continued)
   Connection Number High, 272, 273
   Connection Number Low, 272, 273
   Connection Status, 273
   Control Bits, 254
   Data, 255, 267, 271–273
   Data Offset, 254
   Datastream Type, 270
   Destination Connection ID, 270
   Destination Port, 253, 266
   Function, 272
   Hardware Size, 294
   Hardware Type, 294
   ICMP, 297–298
   Length, 267
   NCP Reply, 273
   NCP Request, 272
   Opcode, 294
   Option, 255
   Protocol Size, 294
   Protocol Type, 294
   Request Type, 272
   Reserved, 254
   Sender Hardware Address, 295
   Sender Protocol Address, 295
   Sequence Number, 253, 270, 272, 273
   Source Connection ID, 270
   Source Port, 253, 266
   SPX, 270–271
   Subfunction, 272
   Subfunction Length, 272
   Target Hardware Address, 295
   Target Protocol Address, 295
   Task Number, 272, 273
   TCP, 253–255
   UDP, 266–267
   Urgent Pointer, 254
   Window, 254
message formats
   Checksum, 298
   Code, 297
   Data, 298
   Type, 297
messages
   ARP Reply, 296
   broadcast, 133–134
   Echo Reply, 302, 558–559
   Echo Request, 302, 442, 558–559
   ICMP query, 302–303
   multicast, 133
   Router Advertisement, 303
   Router Solicitation, 303
   Status Query, 238
   Status Response, 238
   SYN, 258
   unicast, 133, 408
Messenger service, 369
metadirectory, 365
Metric field, 324
Metric function, 310

metropolitan area network (MAN), 5, 502
MIB. *See* management information base (MIB)
Microsoft ASP.NET, 363
Microsoft Clients for NetWare, 386–388
Microsoft Internet Information Services (IIS) 6, 363,
   370
Microsoft Internet Security and Acceleration (ISA)
   Server 2000, 453
Microsoft Metadirectory Services (MMS), 365
Microsoft Network Monitor, 543
Microsoft Windows, 359–371
   application support, 369–370
   client capabilities, 383–391
   history, 359–361
   servers, connecting to, 391, 393
Microsoft Windows Event Viewer console, 532–534
Microsoft Windows for Workgroups, 385
Microsoft Windows NT, 359
   domains, 397–399
Microsoft Windows Server 2003, 361–367, 371, 439
Microsoft Windows Server 2003 System Monitor,
   537–540
Microsoft Windows servers, connecting to, 385–386
Microsoft Windows XP, 361
minimal routing, 314
mixing segments, 169, 176
MMS. *See* Microsoft Metadirectory Services (MMS)
modems
   cable, 501
   digital, 504
   DSL, 500
   identifying, 504
   overview, 495–496
monitor setting bit, 181
Monitor.nlm utility, 541–542
More Fragments bit, 214
MSS. *See* maximum segment size (MSS)
MTU. *See* maximum transmission unit (MTU)
multicast addresses, 218
multicast identifiers, 218
multicast messages, 133
multicasts, 283
multifunction, 598
multifunction cable testers, 554–556, 598
multihomed system, 307
multimode fiber optic cable, 63
multiple access phase, 165
multiple master replication, 399
multiplexing, 10
multiport repeaters, 124
multistation access unit (MAU), 127, 179
   Token Ring, overview, 127–128
   Type 3, 180
mutual authentication, 456

N

name caching, 420
Name Management Protocol (NMP), 236–237
name resolution, 237, 411
name resolution, reverse, 421–422

Name Server (NS) resource record, 414
name servers, 413
NAS. *See* network attached storage (NAS)
NAT. *See* Network Address Translation (NAT)
Native File Access, 374
Nbtstat.exe program, 566–568
N-connectors, 56
NCP functions, 272
NCP Reply message field, 273
NCP Request message field, 272
NCP. *See* NetWare Core Protocol (NCP)
NCPB. *See* Novell NetWare Core Packet Burst (NCPB)
NDPS. *See* Novell Distributed Print Services (NDPS)
near end crosstalk (NEXT), 554
negative acknowledgments, 262
negative receive data (RD-) contacts, 85
negative transmit data (TD-) contacts, 85
NetBDSD, 376
NetBEUI Frame, 234–238
NetBEUI. *See* NetBIOS Extended User Interface (NetBEUI)
NetBIOS
   information, transporting, 232
   names, 423
   naming, 233–234
NetBIOS Enhanced User Interface (NetBEUI), 23
NetBIOS Extended User Interface (NetBEUI), 210, 232–238, 423, 460
   standards, 233
   troubleshooting, 233
NetBIOS/host name parameter, 326
netfilter, 451
Netlogon service, 369
Netmask function, 310
Netstat program, 563–568
   using on UNIX and Linux, 565–566
Netstat.exe
   default network connection listing, 564
   interface statistics, 564
   routing table display, 565
   syntax, 564
   using on Windows, 564–565
NetWare
   application support, 375–376
   bindery, 394–395
   defaults, 227
   file services, 374–375
   print services, 374–375
   protocols, 373–374
   servers, 358
   servers, connecting to, 386–389, 392, 393
NetWare Client for Mac OS, 393
NetWare Core Packet Burst (NCPB) protocol, 271
NetWare Core Protocol (NCP), 27, 271–273
NetWare FTP Server, 375
NetWare Link Services Protocol (NLSP), 231
NetWare Remote Manager (NRM), 344
NetWare SFT III, 467
NetWare Web Search Server 3.0, 375
network adapter configuration tools, 118–122
network adapter drivers, 19

Network Address Translation (NAT), 364
   communications, 446–447
   dynamic, 448
   implementations, 450–451
   routers, 439, 446
   security, 449
   static, 447
   types, 447–448
   using, 446–451
Network Address Translation (NAT) servers, 140
network addresses
   obtaining, 217
   subnetting, 220–221
   subnetting between bytes, 221–222
network attached storage (NAS), 466
Network Basic Input/Output System (NetBIOS), 31, 232
network busy token, 181
network cable connectors, 113
network communications, overview, 2
network connection devices, advanced, 129–145
network control protocols, 511
Network Destination function, 309
Network File System (NFS), 379–380
network hubs, 19, 123–128
network identifiers, 216, 219, 295
Network Information Center (NIC), 412
Network Information System (NIS), 400–401
network interface adapters, 19
   configuring, 116–117
   configuring with Microsoft Windows, 118–119
   defined, 106
   device driver configuration, troubleshooting, 605
   drivers, 113, 384
   Ethernet, 501
   functions, 107–112
   hardware requirements, 113
   installing, 114–115
   overview, 106
   physical damage, 604
   selecting, 112–114
   testing, 116
   troubleshooting, 122–123
   UTP, 527
network interface card (NIC), 106
   improper installation, 605
network interface type, 113
network layer, 22–26, 204
   bridging, 130
   error detection, 25–26
   protocol identification, 21
   protocols, 23, 210
   routing, 25
   troubleshooting, 606–607
network layer protocols, 210
   configuring, 314
   Internet Protocol (IP), 23
   Internetwork Packet Exchange (IPX), 23
   NetBIOS Extended User Interface (NetBEUI), 23
   Transmission Control Protocol/Internet Protocol (TCP/IP), 23

Network Load Balancing (NLB), 363
network management systems, 111
network medium, 2–3
Network Monitor Capture Filter SAPs And ETYPEs
    dialog box, 544
network performance logs and indicators, 526–549
network switches, 19
Network Terminator (NT-1), 497
Network Time Protocol (NTP), 305
network traffic
    capturing, 544–546
    displaying captured, 546–549
    troubleshooting, 602
networks
    backbone, 136
    backup functions, 484
    cable television (CATV), overview of, 501–503
    circuit-switching, 10
    client/server, 358
    Ethernet, 156
    management products, 535–536
    peer-to-peer, 358–359
    redundancy, 468
    remote, 493
    testing and monitoring tools, 550–556
    token passing, 108
    unshielded twisted pair (UTP), 109
Next Hop IP Address field, 324
NEXT. *See* near end crosstalk (NEXT)
NFS client, 390
NFS gateway, 391
NFS server, 390
NFS. *See* Network File System (NFS)
NIAS. *See* Novell Internet Access Server (NIAS)
NIC. *See* network interface card (NIC)
NIS
    client, 401
    server, 401
    slave, 401
NIS. *See* Network Information System (NIS)
NLP. *See* normal link pulse (NLP)
NLSP. *See* Novell NetWare Link Services Protocol
    (NLSP)
NMP. *See* Name Management Protocol (NMP)
No Operation (NOP) option, 209, 214
No Operation option, 256
nodes, 3, 365
nominal velocity of propagation (NVP), 554
nonextended network, 239
normal link pulse (NLP), 111
normal link pulse (NLP) signals, 529
Novell BorderManager, 440
Novell Clients for NetWare, 388
Novell Distributed Print Services (NDPS), 375
Novell DNS/DHCP services, 376
Novell eDirectory, 395–397
Novell Internet Access Server (NIAS), 451
Novell Native File Access, 389
Novell NetWare, 269–273, 371–376
    network adapters, configuring, 119–120
Novell Storage Services (NSS), 374

NRM. *See* Novell NetWare Remote Manager (NRM)
nslookup utility, 568–569, 593
NT-1. *See* Network Terminator 1 (NT-1)
NTFS file system (NTFS), 367
NTP. *See* Network Time Protocol (NTP)
NVP. *See* nominal velocity of propagation (NVP)
Nwconfig.nlm, 119

O

octets, 216
offered window, 264
OLTS. *See* optical loss test set (OLTS)
op field, 405
Opcode message field, 294
open circuit, 552
Open Shortest Path First (OSPF) field, 325
Open Shortest Path First (OSPF) routing protocol,
    364
Open Systems Interconnection (OSI) reference
    model, 10–35
OpenBSD, 376
OpenView, 535
optical loss test set (OLTS), 556
optical time domain reflectometer (OTDR), 556
Option Class subfield, 208
Option Data field, 208, 255
Option Kind field, 255
Option Length field, 208, 255
Option message field, 255
Option Number subfield, 208
Option subheader, 255
Option Type field, 208
Optional field, 236
options
    End Of Options List (EOOL), 209, 214, 256
    Internet Timestamp (TS), 209–210
    IP, 208–210
    logging, 531–532
    Loose Source Routing (LSR), 209, 214
    Maximum Segment Size (MSS), 256
    No Operation, 256
    No Operation (NOP), 209, 214
    Record Route (RR), 210, 214
    SACK, 256
    SACK Permitted, 256
    Selective Acknowledgment, 256
    Strict Source Routing (SSR), 210, 214
    TCP, 255–256
    TS, 214
    TSOPT – Timestamp, 256
    WSOPT Window Scale, 256
Options field, 207, 214
options field, 406
Options tab, 337
organizationally unique identifier (OUI), 162, 217
OSI reference model. *See* Open Systems
    Interconnection (OSI) reference model
OSPF routing protocol. *See* Open Shortest Path First
    (OSPF) routing protocol
OTDR. *See* optical time domain reflectometer (OTDR)
Overflow subfield, 209

P

packet acknowledgment, 7, 29
packet captures, 544
packet collision, 21
packet filtering, 129, 130
  bidirectional, 441
  drawbacks of, 444
  inclusive, 441
  overview, 437–438
  processing overhead, 438
  RRAS, capabilities of, 439
packet filters
  configuring, 441
  creating, 441–444
  dynamic, 439
  exclusive, 441
  implementing, 438–441
packet routing, 137–138
packet switching, potential problems, 9
Packet Type field, 229
packets, 7, 15, 138
  acknowledging, 259–262
  GET Request, 548
packet-switching network, 9
PAM-5. *See* Pulse Amplitude Modulation-5 (PAM-5)
PAP. *See* Printer Access Protocol (PAP)
parallel conversion, 108
parameters
  default gateway, 325
  DNS server addresses, 325
  IP address, 325
  NetBIOS/host name, 326
  Route.exe, 317
  subnet mask, 325
  WINS server addresses, 326
partitions, 397
password variable, 304
patch cables, 74–75, 179, 598
  installing, 94
patch panel, 88–89
path maximum transmission unit (MTU), 259
payload data, 107
PBX, 503
PC Card, 106
PCI bus, 113
PCI. *See* Peripheral Component Interconnect (PCI)
PDU. *See* protocol data unit (PDU)
peer-to-peer networks, 358–359
Performance console, 537–540
performance counters, 537
performance indicators, 526–549
Performance Logs And Alerts, 537
performance monitoring, 536–542
Peripheral Component Interconnect (PCI) bus, 106, 113
permanent virtual circuit (PVC), 503
persistent route, 316
phantom collisions, 528

physical layer, 17
  connections, 494
  Ethernet specifications, 157, 160, 167–178
  FDDI specifications, 185–186
  IEEE 802.11 specifications, 190–191
  LAN specifications, 17
  signaling, 18
  specifications, 21
  Token Ring specifications, 179–180
  troubleshooting, 603–604
  WAN specifications, 18
physical signaling, 158
physical-layer devices, 125
pigtail, 96
Ping utility, 302, 557–558
  syntax, 558
  troubleshooting DNS, 592–593
PKI. *See* Public Key Infrastructure (PKI)
Plain Old Telephone Service (POTS), 495
plenum cable, 55
plug and play (PnP) standard, 113
plug and play (PnP), troubleshooting, 605
PnP. *See* plug and play (PnP)
Pointer (PTR) resource record, 415
Pointer subfield, 209
Point-to-Point Protocol (PPP), 18, 291, 508, 510–514
  authentication protocols, 510
  communications, 510–511
  connection establishment phases, 513–514
  frame, 511–513, 516
Point-to-Point Protocol over Ethernet (PPPoE), 514–515
Point-to-Point Tunneling Protocol (PPTP), 515
POP3. *See* Post Office Protocol 3 (POP3)
port address translation (PAT). *See* masquerading
port forwarding, 449–450
port numbers, 259
  ephemeral, 269
  filtering by, 442
  well-known, 268, 437
ports, 267–269
  Ring In, 128
  Ring Out, 128
  switched uplink, 125
  uplink, 125–126, 599
ports, well-known, 267
positive acknowledgement with retransmission, 261
positive receive data (RD+) contacts, 85
positive transmit data (TD+) contacts, 85
Post Office Protocol 3 (POP3), 305, 437
POTS. *See* Plain Old Telephone Service (POTS)
power sum ELFEXT (PSELFEXT), 555
power sum NEXT (PSNEXT), 555
PPP. *See* Point-to-Point Protocol (PPP)
PPPoE. *See* Point-to-Point Protocol over Ethernet (PPPoE)
PPTP. *See* Point-to-Point Tunneling Protocol (PPTP)
Preamble field, 161, 187
presentation layer, 33–34

Primary Domain Controller (PDC), 397
Primary Rate Interface (PRI) service, 497
print servers, 358
print services, 364, 374, 378
Printer Access Protocol (PAP), 31
printer sharing, 367–368
processing
   checksum, 110
   TCP segmentation, 110
processor offloading, 110–111
promiscuous mode, 130, 543
propagation delay, 555
Properties dialog box, 118–119
protocol analyzers, 542–549
   malicious use, 542
   troubleshooting with, 596
protocol data unit (PDU), 14, 205, 252
protocol drivers, 384
Protocol field, 207, 215, 512
Protocol file, 216
protocol identification, 204, 215–216
protocol identifiers, 442
Protocol Size message field, 294
protocol stack, 5
Protocol Type message field, 294
protocols
   Address Resolution Protocol (ARP), 211,
      293–296, 562–563
   Apple EtherTalk, 238
   Apple Filing Protocol (AFP), 381
   Apple LocalTalk, 238
   AppleTalk, 238–241
   AppleTalk Address Resolution Protocol (AARP),
      239
   AppleTalk Data Stream Protocol (ADSP), 31
   application layer, 34–35, 292, 303–306
   Asynchronous Transfer Mode (ATM), 507–508
   Bootstrap Protocol (BOOTP), 295, 403
   connectionless, 27–28, 252
   connection-oriented, 27
   data-link layer, 17, 112, 137, 211
   DDP, 239
   defined, 6
   Diagnostic and Monitoring Protocol (DMP), 238
   Domain Name System (DNS), 266, 304
   Dynamic Host Configuration Protocol (DHCP),
      217, 266, 304
   Exterior Gateway Protocol (EGP), 322
   FDDITalk, 238
   File Transfer Protocol (FTP), 304
   full-duplex, 258
   Hypertext Transfer Protocol (HTTP), 305
   identification, 163–165
   interaction, 12–13
   Interior Gateway Protocol (IGP), 322
   Internet Control Message Protocol (ICMP), 213,
      297–303
   Internet Mail Access Protocol 4 (IMAP4), 305
   Internet Protocol (IP), 23, 202, 203, 297
   Internet Protocol Control Protocol (IPCP), 511

   Internetwork Packet Exchange Control Protocol
      (IPXCP), 511
   IPSecurity (IPSec), 365, 371, 456–457
   Kerberos, 370, 461–462
   Layer Two Forwarding (L2F), 459
   Layer Two Tunneling Protocol (L2TP), 459–460
   Link Control Protocol (LCP), 510
   link layer, 292
   Link Quality Report Protocol, 514
   link-state, 325
   method of documenting, 285
   mutability, 285
   Name Management Protocol (NMP), 236–237
   NetBEUI Frame, 234–238
   NetWare, 373–374
   NetWare Core Packet Burst (NCPB), 271
   NetWare Core Protocol (NCP), 27, 271–273
   network control, 511
   network layer, 23, 210
      configuration of, 514
   Network Time Protocol (NTP), 305
   overview, 5–8
   Point-to-Point Protocol (PPP), 18, 291, 508
      authentication, 510
      overview of, 510–514
   Point-to-Point Protocol over Ethernet (PPPoE),
      overview of, 514–515
   Point-to-Point Tunneling Protocol (PPTP), 515
   Post Office Protocol 3 (POP3), 305, 437
   Printer Access Protocol (PAP), 31
   quality of service, 285
   reliable, 252
   Remote Monitoring (RMON), 535
   remote networking, overview of, 508–517
   Reverse Address Resolution Protocol (RARP), 295,
      402
   Routing Information Protocol (RIP), 231,
      322–325, 364
   scalability, 285
   Secure Hypertext Transfer Protocol (S-HTTP or
      HTTPS), 305
   Secure Sockets Layer (SSL), 460–461
   security, overview of, 454–462
   Sequenced Packet Exchange (SPX), 27, 227,
      269–271
   Serial Line Internet Protocol (SLIP), 22, 291,
      508–510
   Server Message Blocks (SMB), 367
   Service Advertising Protocol (SAP), 231
   Session Management Protocol (SMP), 237–238
   Simple Mail Transfer Protocol (SMTP), 34, 305,
      437
   Simple Network Management Protocol (SNMP),
      111, 305, 535–536
   simultaneous development, 285
   support, 292
   task delegation, 285
   Telnet, 306
   Token Ring, 178
   TokenTalk, 238

protocols, (continued)
  Transmission Control Protocol (TCP), 202,
      252–265, 442
  Transmission Control Protocol/Internet Protocol
      (TCP/IP), 282, 292–306
  Transmission Control Protocol/Internet Protocol
      (TCP/IP) transport layer, 303
  transport layer, 26, 216
  Trivial File Transfer Protocol (TFTP), 306, 403
  unreliable, 252
  user, 292
  User Datagram Protocol (UDP), 27, 238, 252,
      266–267, 442
provider ID, 226
proxy
  adaptive, 452
  packet inspection, 452
proxy servers
  implementing, 453
  troubleshooting, 589
  using, 451–453
PSELFEXT. See power sum ELFEXT (PSELFEXT)
pseudo-header, 263
PSH flag bit, 254
PSNEXT. See power sum NEXT (PSNEXT)
PSTN. See Public Switched Telephone Network
      (PSTN)
Public Key Infrastructure (PKI), 365
Public Switched Telephone Network (PSTN), 10,
      495–496
Pulse Amplitude Modulation-5 (PAM-5), 173
punchdown block, 88
punchdown block tool, 90
PVC. See permanent virtual circuit (PVC)

Q

QIC drives, 471
quads. See octet
queries, 421
  iterative, 421
  recursive, 421

R

raceway, 70
RAID. See redundant array of independent disks
      (RAID)
RARP Reply value, 294
RARP Request value, 294
RARP. See Reverse Address Resolution Protocol
      (RARP)
RAS. See Remote Access Service (RAS)
rc file, 562
rebinding time value, 410
receive buffers, 107
Record Route (RR) option, 210, 214
recursive query, 421
Redirect error message, 300–301
redirector, 384
redundant array of independent disks (RAID), 106,
      464–466
  levels and functions, 465–466

referrals, 421
registered addresses, 224–225
registry ID, 226
reliable protocols, 252
Remote Access Service (RAS), 494
remote bridges, 135
Remote Monitoring (RMON) protocol, 535
remote networking protocols, 508–517
remote networks, 493
  connection requirements, 494
Remote Wake on LAN, 527
renewal time value, 409
repeat mode, 180
repeaters
  defined, 124
  multiport, 124
Reply/Response Type message field, 273
Request for Comments (RFC), 202, 287–288
  index, 288
  status indicators, 288
Request for Comments (RFC) 1034, 412
Request for Comments (RFC) 1035, 412
Request for Comments (RFC) 1042, 203
Request for Comments (RFC) 1055, 509
Request for Comments (RFC) 1122, 290
Request for Comments (RFC) 1332, 511
Request for Comments (RFC) 1510, 461
Request for Comments (RFC) 1552, 511
Request for Comments (RFC) 1661, 511
Request for Comments (RFC) 1662, 511
Request for Comments (RFC) 1663, 511
Request for Comments (RFC) 1812, 203
Request for Comments (RFC) 1813, 379
Request for Comments (RFC) 1881, 203
Request for Comments (RFC) 1887, 203
Request for Comments (RFC) 1989, 511
Request for Comments (RFC) 1994, 511
Request for Comments (RFC) 2131, 403
Request for Comments (RFC) 2132, 403
Request for Comments (RFC) 2328, 325
Request for Comments (RFC) 2401, 455
Request for Comments (RFC) 2402, 455
Request for Comments (RFC) 2406, 455
Request for Comments (RFC) 2409, 455
Request for Comments (RFC) 2411, 455
Request for Comments (RFC) 2460, 203
Request for Comments (RFC) 2474, 206
Request for Comments (RFC) 2516, 514
Request for Comments (RFC) 2661, 459
Request for Comments (RFC) 3513, 203
Request for Comments (RFC) 3585, 455
Request for Comments (RFC) 3586, 455
Request for Comments (RFC) 3596, 203
Request for Comments (RFC) 791, 202, 218
Request for Comments (RFC) 792, 297
Request for Comments (RFC) 793, 252
Request for Comments (RFC) 826, 291, 293
Request for Comments (RFC) 894, 203, 291
Request for Comments (RFC) 950, 203
Request Type message field, 272
Reserved message field, 254

resolv.conf file, 340–341
resolvers, 413, 421
resource records, 414–415
    Address (A), 415
    Canonical Name (CNAME), 415
    Mail Exchange (MX), 415
    Name Server (NS), 414
    Pointer (PTR), 415
    Start of Authority (SOA), 414
Response Correlator field, 236
return loss, 555
Reverse Address Resolution Protocol (RARP), 295,
    402
reverse lookup domains, 423
reverse name resolution, 421–422
RFC. *See* Request for Comments (RFC)
RG-58 coaxial cables, 55
RG-8 coaxial cables, 55
Ring In port, 128
Ring Out port, 128
ring purge, 184
ring topology, 3, 47–49
RIP. *See* Routing Information Protocol (RIP)
RJ-11 connectors, 58
RJ-11 jacks, 495
RJ-45 connectors, 58, 94
RJ-45 jacks, 495
RMON. *See* Remote Monitoring (RMON)
root
    domains, 417
    name servers, 416
round trip delay times, 166, 178
Route Tag field, 324
route tool, 318–319
Route.exe
    parameters, 317
    syntax, 315–316
Routecon.nlm, 319–320
routed daemon, 318
Router Advertisement message, 303
Router Solicitation message, 303
routers, 3, 24–25, 135–140, 144, 212, 306, 310
    backbone to LAN failure, 602
    connections, malfunctioning, 587–588
    connections, troubleshooting, 600–602
    hardware or power failure, 588
    IP, 308
    NAT, 439
    network access problems, 588
    products, 307–308
    stand-alone, 308
    types, 140
    WAN, 139
routing, 24–25, 212, 308
    dynamic, 314–315, 321–325
    IP, 306–325
    minimal, 314
    overview, 135–140, 306–307
    packet, 137–138
    static, 314–315
    WAN, 139–140

Routing And Remote Access Service (RRAS), 364,
    370, 494
Routing Information Protocol (RIP), 231, 322–325,
    364
routing tables, 137, 332
    building, 314–325
    default entries, 310–312
    entries, 25, 312–314
    format, 309–310
    overview, 308–314
RRAS. *See* Routing And Remote Access Service
    (RRAS)
RST flag bit, 254

S

S/T interface, 497
SACK option, 256
SACK Permitted option, 256
SAN. *See* storage area network (SAN)
SAP. *See* service access point (SAP)
SAP. *See* Service Advertising Protocol (SAP)
SC. *See* subscriber connector (SC)
scalability, 285
scanners, 554
SCSI devices, 474
SDH. *See* Synchronous Digital Hierarchy (SDH)
second-level domains, 417
secs field, 406
Secure Hypertext Transfer Protocol (S-HTTP or
    HTTPS), 305
Secure Sockets Layer (SSL), 460–461
security protocols, 454–462
security services, 365
segmentation, 7
segments, 136
    defined, 253
    horizontal, 136
    link, 177
    mixing, 176
Selective Acknowledgment option, 256
selective acknowledgments, 262
Sender Hardware Address message field, 295
Sender Protocol Address message field, 295
sequence number, 259
Sequence Number message field, 253, 270, 272–273
Sequence Number value, 445
sequence numbering, 260
Sequenced Packet Exchange (SPX), 27, 227,
    269–271
sequences, 253
serial conversion, 108
Serial Line Internet Protocol (SLIP), 22, 291,
    509–510
server cluster, 365
Server Message Block (SMB)
    connections, 363
    protocol, 367
server operating systems, 359–382
Server service, 369

servers, 358
  Dynamic Host Configuration Protocol (DHCP),
    140
  ensuring availability, 467–468
  file, 358
  NetWare, 358
  network address translation (NAT), 140
  print, 358
service access point (SAP), 164
Service Advertising Protocol (SAP), 231
session layer, 30–33
  functions, 32
  redundancy, 31
  tokens, 32
Session Management Protocol (SMP), 237–238
shielded twisted pair (STP) cable, 61, 175
shielded twisted-pair (STP), 175
shoeshining, 475
short circuit, 552
S-HTTP. *See* Secure Hypertext Transfer Protocol
    (S-HTTP or HTTPS)
siaddr field, 406
signal decoding, 108
signal encoding, 108
signal quality error (SQE), 165
signaled error, 29
signals
  bipolar digital, 504
  Direct Sequence Spread Spectrum (DSSS), 191
  fast link pulse (FLP), 111, 529
  Frequency Hopping Spread Spectrum (FHSS),
    191
  infrared, 191
  link pulse, 111
  normal link pulse (NLP), 529
  overview, 5
silver satin cable, 95
Simple Mail Transfer Protocol (SMTP), 34, 305, 437
Simple Network Management Protocol (SNMP),
    111, 305, 535–536
single attachment station (SAS), 185
single master replication, 397
singlemode fiber optic cable, 63
sliding window, 264
SLIP. *See* Serial Line Internet Protocol (SLIP)
smart hubs, 125
SMB. *See* Server Message Block (SMB)
SMP. *See* Session Management Protocol (SMP)
SMTP. *See* Simple Mail Transfer Protocol (SMTP)
sname field, 406
SNAP. *See* Subnetwork Access Protocol (SNAP)
SNMP. *See* Simple Network Management Protocol
    (SNMP)
sockets, 267–269
SONET. *See* Synchronous Optical Network (SONET)
Source Address field, 161, 183, 188, 240
Source Connection ID message field, 270
Source IP Address field, 207
Source Name field, 236
Source Network Address field, 230
Source Node Address field, 230

Source Number field, 236
Source Port message field, 253, 266
Source Quench error message, 300
source route bridging, 132
Source Socket field, 230
Source Socket Number field, 240
spanning tree algorithm (STA), 132
speed indicator LEDs, 529
split pair, 553
spoofing, 443
SPX message field, 270–271
SPX. *See* Sequenced Packet Exchange (SPX)
SQE. *See* signal quality error (SQE)
SRI. *See* Stanford Research Institute (SRI)
SSL. *See* Secure Sockets Layer (SSL)
ST connector. *See* straight tip (ST) connector
STA. *See* spanning tree algorithm (STA)
stackable hubs, 127
standardization process, 289–290
standards
  802.11a, 189
  802.11b, 189
  802.11g, 189
  DIX Ethernet and IEEE 802.3, contrasting,
    157–159
  Ethernet, 156–160
  Gigabit Ethernet, 60
  IEEE 802.2, 158
  IEEE 802.3, 159–160
  IEEE 802.3 Ethernet, 157
  IEEE 802.3 revisions, 159–160
  IP, 202–203
  TIA/EIA STP, 61
  wiring, 92–94
standards, cabling
  ANSI/TIA/EIA-T568-B, 52–54
  J-STD-607-A, 54
  TIA/EIA-606, 54
Stanford Research Institute (SRI), 412
star topology, 3, 46–47, 177
Start Delimiter field, 183
Start of Authority (SOA) resource record, 414
Start Of Frame Delimiter field, 161
Starting Delimiter field, 187
stateful packet inspection, 445
static addresses, 562
static NAT, 447
static routes, 314
  managing, 315–320
    in NetWare, 319–320
    in UNIX/Linux, 318–319
    in Windows, 315–318
Station Management (SMT) Frame, 188
Status Query message, 238
Status Response message, 238
storage area network (SAN), 106, 366, 466
store and forward, 125
store and forward switches, 144
STP. *See* shielded twisted pair (STP) cable
straight tip (ST) connector, 63
straight-through cables, 528

straight-through connections, 84
Strict Source Routing (SSR) option, 210, 214
stripping mode, 181
subdomains, 417, 422
subfields
    Code, 407
    Copied Flag, 208
    Data, 407
    Flags, 210
    IP Addresses/Timestamps, 210
    Length, 407
    Option Class, 208
    Option Number, 208
    Overflow, 209
    Pointer, 209
Subfunction Length message field, 272
Subfunction message field, 272
subnet ID, 220, 226
Subnet Mask field, 324
subnet mask parameter, 325
subnet masking, 219–224, 331
subnet masks, incorrect, 606
subnet notation, 221
subnets, 143, 219
subnetting, network addresses, 220–221
Subnetwork Access Protocol (SNAP), 164
subscriber connector (SC), 63
subscriber ID, 226
Sun Solaris, 376
support protocols, 292
switched uplink ports, 125
switches, 3, 46, 143
    crossbar, 144
    cut-through, 144
    defined, 141
    dual inline package (DIP), 117
    installing, 142–143
    matrix, 144
    store and forward, 144
    types, 144
switching
    Layer 3, 143
    overview, 141–144
switching hub, 141
SYN control bit, 256
SYN flag bit, 254, 258
SYN floods, 445
SYN message, 258
Synchronous Digital Hierarchy (SDH), 507
Synchronous Optical Network (SONET), 507
Synchronous Optical Network (SONET) optical
        carrier levels, 507
syntax
    abstract, 34
    transfer, 34
syslogd tool, 535
system bus type, 113
System Monitor, 537
    histogram view, 538
    report view, 538

T

T-1 connection, 503
T-1 service, fractional, 503
T2 value, 410
T-3 connection, 503
tables
    address, sizes of, 131
    internal address, 131
    routing, 137
tape libraries, 473
target, 475
Target Hardware Address message field, 295
Target Protocol Address message field, 295
Task Number message field, 272–273
T-carrier services, 503
T-connectors, 56
TCP segmentation processing, 110
TCP value, 215
TCP. See Transmission Control Protocol (TCP)
TCP/IP. See Transmission Control Protocol/Internet
        Protocol (TCP/IP)
TDR. See time domain reflectometer (TDR)
TE1 devices, 498
TE2 devices, 498
teardrop attacks, 445
Telecommunication Standardization Sector of the
        International Telecommunication Union
        (ITU-T), 8
telecommunications closet, 53
Telecommunications Industry
        Association/Electronic Industries Alliance
        (TIA/EIA), 8
telepole, 79
Telnet, 306, 378–379
terminal adapters, 498
terminal connections, 516–517
terminal equipment (TE), 497
Terminal Server, 364
termination, 45
testers, wire map, 553
TFTP. See Trivial File Transfer Protocol (TFTP)
TGS. See Ticket-Granting Server (TGS)
TGT. See ticket-granting ticket (TGT)
Thick Ethernet, 45
thin client computing, 516
Thin Ethernet, 45
three-way handshake, 257, 547
TIA/EIA STP standards, 61
TIA/EIA UTP cable categories, 59
TIA/EIA. See Telecommunications Industry
        Association/Electronic Industries Alliance
        (TIA/EIA)
TIA/EIA-606, 54
Ticket-Granting Server (TGS), 461
ticket-granting ticket (TGT), 461
time domain reflectometer (TDR), 554
Time Exceeded error message, 301
Time To Live (TTL) field, 207, 558
timestamp, 256
token frames, 183, 188
token passing, 108, 180–181

Token Ring, 3, 19, 178
  frames, 182–184
  MAUs, overview, 127–128
  networks, 178
TokenTalk, 238
tone generators and locators, 551–553, 598
top utility, 541
top-level domains, 416–417
topologies
  ad hoc, 50–51, 190
  bus, 3, 45–46
  cable, 44–52
  defined, 3
  hierarchical star, 47
  infrastructure, 51–52
  mesh, 49–50
  ring, 3, 47–49
  star, 3, 46–47, 177
  wireless, 50–52
Total Length field, 206, 214
Traceroute utility, 213, 301, 559–560, 600
  disadvantages, 560
transceiver, 55
transceiver cables. *See* attachment unit interface
    (AUI) cables
transfer syntax, 34
translation bridges, 134
Transmission Control Protocol (TCP), 202,
    252–265, 442
  communications, 256–265
  connections, 257
  connections, establishing, 257–259
  headers, 253–255
  message fields, 253–255
  options, 255–256
  packet captures, 544
Transmission Control Protocol/Internet Protocol
    (TCP/IP), 23
  addressing, 283–284
  client filtering, 439
  configuration, 494
  configuring, 325–344
    advanced properties, 333–337
    client settings, 328–333
    essential properties, 328
    in NetWare, 342–344
    in UNIX/Linux, 338–341
    in Windows, 326–337
    parameters, 338–340
    with DHCP, 327
  conflicts, avoiding, 328
  filtering, 337
  graphical configuration tools, 341
  modularity of, 284–285
  platform independence of, 282–283
  protocol development, 282–285
  protocol stack, 290–292
  protocols, 282, 292–306
  routing, 313, 364
  services, overview, 401–424
  specifications, 202

standards, 285–290
transport layer protocols, 303
utilities, 557–569
transmission speed, 112, 176
transmit buffers, 107
transmit contacts, 84
Transmit Correlator field, 236
transmit mode, 181
transparent bridges, 131–132
Transport Control field, 229, 231
transport layer, 26–30, 203, 292
  and Novell NetWare, 269–273
  and TCP/IP, 252, 265
  error detection and correction, 29–30
  functions, 28–30
  protocol identification, 26
  troubleshooting, 606–607
transport layer protocols, 26, 216
  NetWare Core Protocol (NCP), 27
  Sequenced Packet Exchange (SPX), 27
  User Datagram Protocol (UDP), 27
transport mode, 458–459
traps, 111, 536
Trivial File Transfer Protocol (TFTP), 306, 403
Trojan horse attacks, 449
troubleshooting
  application layer problems, 607–608
  assigning priorities to problems, 579
  cable runs, 599
  cables, 598–599
  cables, external, 67
  client configuration, 588
  computer configuration, 603–608
  computer connections, 598–599
  crossover circuits, 599
  data-link layer problems, 605–606
  DHCP server configuration, 594
  DNS, 591–597
    configuration files, 595
    name resolution problems, 593
  documenting solution, 583–584
  escalating calls, 585
  establishing symptoms, 578–580
  establishing what has changed, 581–582
  gateways, 607
  gathering information, 585–586
  hub connections, 599–600
  identifying affected area, 580–581
  implementing solution, 582
  incident administration, 584–585
  Internet router problems, 587
  local hubs, 597–598
  network clients, 607
  network interface adapters, 122–123, 604
  network layer problems, 606–607
  network traffic, 602
  NIC installation, 603
  physical layer problems, 603–604
  plug and play (PnP), 605
  prioritizing calls, 585
  procedure, overview of, 578

troubleshooting, (continued)
  proxy server connections, 589
  recognizing potential effects of solution, 583
  router connections, 587–588, 600–602
  selecting most probable cause, 582
  TCP/IP client configuration, 591–594
  testing results, 583
  Traceroute utility, 600
  transport layer problems, 606–607
  viruses, 607
  WINS name resolution, 597
troubleshooting scenarios
  computer configuration, 603–608
  DNS failure, 591–597
  Internet communication problems, 590–591
  LAN communications, 597–602
  user error, 608–609
  Web site inaccessibility, 584
troubleshooting tools
  cables, 598–599
  multifunction cable testers, 598
  protocol analyzers, 596
  tone generators and locators, 598
  wire map testers, 598
truncated binary exponential backoff, 166
TS option, 214
TSOPT – Timestamp option, 256
tunnel mode, 458–459
tunneling, 515
TWA. *See* two-way alternate (TWA)
twisted-pair cables, 58–61, 175
two-computer networking, 82–85
two-way alternate mode (TWA), 32
two-way simultaneous mode (TWS), 32
TWS. *See* two-way simultaneous (TWS)
Type 3 cables, 180
Type 3 MAUs, 180
Type 3 networks, 180
Type message format, 297
Type Of Service field, 206

U

U interface, 497
UDP datagrams, 405
UDP message field, 266–267
UDP. *See* User Datagram Protocol (UDP)
unbounded media, 50
unicast messages, 133, 283, 408
Uniform Resource Locator (URL), 460
universal serial bus (USB), 108
UNIX
  application support, 380
  Berkeley Software Distribution (BSD), 376
  client capabilities, 391–392
  deploying, 377
  interfaces, 378
  network adapters, configuring, 121–122
  overview, 376–381
  performance monitoring, 540–541
  processor support, 377
  servers, connecting to, 390–391, 394
  variants, hardware-specific, 376

UNIX System V, 376
UNIX/Linux, network adapters, configuring,
  121–122
unqualified name, 335
unregistered addresses, 224–225
unreliable protocols, 252
unshielded twisted pair (UTP), 3, 83
  cables, 46, 58, 60, 75
  network interface adapters, 527
  networks, 109
  wire pairs, 60
unsignaled error, 30
uplink ports, 47, 85, 125–126, 599
upstream speeds, DSL, 500
URG flag bit, 254
Urgent Pointer message field, 254
URL. *See* Uniform Resource Locator (URL)
USB. *See* universal serial bus (USB)
User Datagram Protocol (UDP), 27, 238, 252,
  266–267, 442
  value, 215
user error, troubleshooting, 608–609
User Manager For Domains utility, 398
user protocols, 292
username variable, 304
utilities
  Arp.exe, 563
  Filtcfg.nlm, 440
  Hdetect.nlm, 120
  ifconfig, 560–562
  Ipconfig.exe, 560–562
  Monitor.nlm, 541–542
  nslookup, 568–569
  Ping, 557–558
  TCP/IP, 557–569
  top, 541
  Traceroute, 559–560
  Winipcfg.exe, 560–562
UTP cables
  Category 6 (CAT6), 60
  grades, 59–60
UTP Ethernet, 83, 170–173
UTP. *See* unshielded twisted pair (UTP)

V

values
  1ºDHCPDISCOVER, 407
  2ºDHCPOFFER, 407
  3ºDHCPREQUEST, 407
  4ºDHCPDECLINE, 407
  5ºDHCPACK, 407
  6ºDHCPNAK, 407
  7ºDHCPRELEASE, 407
  8ºDHCPINFORM, 407
  Acknowledgment Number, 261
  ARP Reply, 294
  ARP Request, 294
  Exterior Gateway Protocol (EGP), 215
  Gateway-to-Gateway Protocol (GGP), 215
  Internet Control Message Protocol (ICMP), 215
  Internet Group Management Protocol
    (IGMP), 215

values, (continued)
  IP in IP, 215
  RARP Reply, 294
  RARP Request, 294
  Sequence Number, 445
vampire tap, 56
variables
  interface, 563
  ipaddress, 563
  password, 304
  username, 304
vector ID, 184
Version field, 206
virtual LAN (VLAN), 143
virtual private network (VPN), 503, 515–516
viruses, troubleshooting, 607
VLAN. *See* virtual LAN (VLAN)
voltage spike, 166
VPN. *See* virtual private network (VPN)

W

Wake on LAN, 112
wall plates, 88
WAN. *See* wide area network (WAN)
well-known port numbers, 268, 437
well-known ports, 267
wide area network (WAN), 4
  connections, 495–508
  routing, 139–140
  speeds, 503
Window message field, 254
window scale extension, 256
Windows Internet Name Service (WINS), 370,
      423–424

Windows Services for UNIX, 391
Windows System Resource Manager (WSRM), 366
Winipcfg.exe, 560–562
  troubleshooting DNS, 593
WINS client, 424
  incorrect server addresses, 606
  name resolution, troubleshooting, 597
  server addresses parameter, 326
  tab, 336–337
WINS. *See* Windows Internet Name Service (WINS)
wire map testers, 553, 598
wire pairs, unused, 171
wireless networking, 189–192
wireless topologies, 50–52
wiring standards, 92–94
Workstation service, 369
wrapped ring, 185
WSOPT Window Scale option, 256
WSRM. *See* Windows System Resource Manager
      (WSRM)

X

X.500 directory service standard, 396
xDSL, 499
xid field, 406

Y

yiaddr field, 406

Z

Zip drives, 473
zones, 239, 381

SYSTEM REQUIREMENTS

To complete the exercises in this textbook, you need a computer that meets the following minimum system requirements.

SOFTWARE REQUIREMENTS

- Microsoft Windows Server 2003, Enterprise Edition. (A 180-day evaluation edition of Windows Server 2003, Enterprise Edition, is included on the CD-ROM.)

- Microsoft PowerPoint or Microsoft PowerPoint Viewer. (PowerPoint Viewer is included on the Supplemental Materials CD-ROM included with the textbook.).

- Microsoft Word or Microsoft Word Viewer. (Word Viewer is included on the Supplemental Materials CD-ROM included with the textbook.)

- Microsoft Internet Explorer 5.01 or later.

HARDWARE REQUIREMENTS

- Minimum CPU: 133 MHz for x86-based computers and 733 MHz for Itanium-based computers (733 MHz is recommended).

- Minimum RAM: 128 MB (256 MB is recommended).

- Disk space for setup: 1.5 GB for x86-based computers and 2.0 GB for Itanium-based computers.

- Display monitor capable of 800 x 600 resolution or higher.

- CD-ROM drive.

- Microsoft mouse or compatible pointing device.

UNINSTALL INSTRUCTIONS

The time-limited release of Microsoft Windows Server 2003, Enterprise Edition, will expire 180 days after installation. If you decide to discontinue use of this software, you will need to reinstall your original operating system. You might need to reformat your drive.